Introduction to Data Base Management in Business

JAMES BRADLEY
University of Calgary

HOLT, RINEHART AND WINSTON
New York   Chicago   San Francisco   Philadelphia
Montreal   Toronto   London   Sydney
Tokyo   Mexico City   Rio de Janeiro   Madrid

Library of Congress Cataloging in Publication Data

Bradley, James, 1942–
    Introduction to data base management in business.

    Bibliography: p.
    Includes index.
    1. Business—Data processing. 2. Data base management.
I. Title.
HF5548.2.B678 1983   658'.054   82–23302

ISBN 0-03-061693-X

3 4 5 039 9 8 7 6 5 4 3 2 1

CBS COLLEGE PUBLISHING
Holt, Rinehart & Winston
The Dryden Press
Saunders College Publishing

Preface

Information has always been important in business decisions. With advancing technology however, and with the resulting increase in the complexity of business organizations, the quality and variety of information needed for business and management decisions is steadily increasing. Since technology will undoubtedly continue to advance, the need for information at all levels in business organizations can only grow. We have thus entered an age where it is the superior use of information that will determine the success of corporations and the wealth of nations. This information is increasingly to be found in data bases. Data base management is thus important, and is becoming the foundation for all data processing and a great deal more. It is also exciting, and every business student graduating in the 1980s should take a course in it. This book is written for just such a course.

Inevitably a wide variety of business students will be required to study data base management, and so the book begins at an elementary level and makes few assumptions about the computer skills of the students. In later sections, however, there is some material that may well challenge the most gifted honors student.

The book is also designed for self-study, and so minimizes the burden on the instructor. It covers the full spectrum of the subject nevertheless, and its design permits it to be used both with short introductory courses and with more intensive two-semester courses. Thus the book is suitable both for those who are aiming only at a sound working knowledge of the subject, as well as for those aiming at developing considerable expertise in data base management.

Many years of experience with data base management have convinced me that the subject is more difficult to teach than most. Some reasons for this are the wide scope of the subject, the existence of different approaches to data base management, and a lack of any standard terminology. Indeed, it often appears that no vendor of a data base management system is satisfied unless his or her terminology is distinctly unique. Another problem for an instructor is the common lack of a good selection of data base systems on the campus or departmental computer.

Every effort has been made to remove these difficulties. Throughout the book I have used a terminology that is both consistent and as near to common usage as possible. However, the special terms used with specific data base systems are also introduced and explained. In addition, a common diagrammatic method is used with all approaches to data base management. Finally, in order to help students concentrate on the differences among the major approaches to data base management, I have restricted the number of data bases used to just two. One data base is about components used in manufacturing, while the other is about the banking business. Included as well are some minor variations on the theme of these two data bases. Examples of additional data bases can be found in the instructor manual.

The problem of availability of data base systems is difficult both for author and instructor. For obvious reasons the book is restricted to only the most commonly used systems, and I have tried to facilitate the instructor who has access to some of them. With each data base example in either the text or the instructor manual, I have therefore included sufficient detail to enable instructors or students to implement the data base on their computer with a minimum of effort. To give complete data base definitions would not be possible given the wide variety of operating systems and machines on which data base systems can be installed. Note that since IBM operating systems dominate in the commercial world, with many examples I have tacitly assumed an IBM operating system environment—although I have kept the accompanying details to a minimum.

Even if no data base system is available for student use, an effective course can still be given using this book. For each system described, the organization of the material and the examples of data base manipulation are carefully designed to permit students to learn in the absence of access to a working system. If access is possible, so much the better.

Most of the later chapters have an accompanying supplement or additional perspective. These additional perspectives contain supplementary material that is less important, more advanced, or simply just emerging. They can all be skipped without loss of continuity. They are included to widen the perspectives of both student and teacher, and to be used in more advanced courses. Note that in most cases the material in these additional perspectives is not more difficult than in other parts of the book, and should be used by instructors when it suits their purposes.

The accompanying instructor manual contains useful suggestions on how to design a course in data base management, and how to tackle specific topics. In addition it contains a test bank of some 500 questions with answers, together with answers to selected questions in the text. Furthermore, the manual contains most of the diagrams and tables used in the text, but in a form suitable for making transparencies. Additional data bases and data base definitions are also to be found in the manual.

I am grateful to the many people who helped in the preparation of this book. In particular, Ken Howard at the University of Victoria's Computer Center must be thanked for the long hours spent at a terminal helping me with the intricacies of ADABAS. I must also thank Professors David W. Chilson, F. Paul Fuhs, Patrick Lamont, and Daniel R. Rota for their painstaking reviews of the manuscript and their many excellent suggestions that were incorporated in the text. An acknowledgment is also warranted to MIT's Paul A. Samuelson, from whom I borrowed the idea of placing the additional perspectives at the ends of many of the chapters.

James Bradley

For the sake of persons of different types, scientific truth should be presented in different forms, and should be regarded as equally scientific, whether it appears in the robust form and the vivid coloring of a physical illustration, or in the tenuity and paleness of a symbolic expression.

James Clerk Maxwell
Address to the British Association for the Advancement of Science, 1870.

Contents

Foundations

This book is about the management of data in large enterprises, mostly by means of a fairly new tool called a *data base management system*. As such the book is about a fairly specialized branch of management, but one that nevertheless is crucial for the overall management of business and public organizations.

Although management methods exhibit wide variation in practice, it is easy to define what management is. Management may be defined as *the creation and maintenance of useful and productive order.* At the risk of oversimplification, we can conveniently separate the management activities related to the *creation* of useful and productive order from those related to the *maintenance* of that order once created. Thus it is one task of management to create a new factory, and a different task to maintain that factory as a useful and productive enterprise in the community.

As with the management of factories and other forms of human endeavor, the management of business data depends on an initial creation of useful and productive structures. Prior to the invention of the electronic computer, management of business data was largely restricted to the manual maintenance of accounting data. With the computer came the organization of data into *computer files* containing thousands and often hundreds of thousands of *records*. Here indeed was a useful and productive order, or so it appeared in the beginning. The maintenance of this orderly arrangement of data became the task of the data processing department in a large enterprise. The data in the computer files had to be updated at regular intervals to ensure currency; and because of the need for information by all kinds of people in a large organization, there was a continual increase in the number and kinds of computer files that had to be maintained. This method of managing data by means of computer files worked well in the beginning, but as the number of computer files increased, it became apparent that such *collections* of computer files no longer constituted a useful and productive arrangement of the enterprise's data. In fact, with many enterprises, it would be safe to state that a destructive degree of disorder had crept into the once orderly collections of files. The detailed reasons for this phenomenon are described in Chapter 4, but for the moment it is sufficient to state that by the late 1960s there was a need for a new arrangement of data.

Data bases

The new arrangement of data was called a *data base*. It is probably true to state that modern data bases are among the most highly ordered collections of data ever conceived by man. Complex software products known as data base management systems are used to create and maintain these data bases. But what is unique about these highly ordered collections of data is that the inherent order is flexible, that is, by means of the sophisticated data base management system, the data base can be relatively easily reordered to meet the needs of an enterprise. The needs of an enterprise are constantly changing, and we must never forget that a data base, while fascinating, is not an end in itself. It exists to help an enterprise to be productive and useful, and in practice this ultimately means to help the enterprise to sell a product or service.

Multiple data bases

The old files of conventional data processing were supposed to be independent of each other, but in reality they contained an increasing amount of duplicate data that was often inconsistent. They were also highly inflexible. *A data base is a highly integrated but flexible collection of computer files that cross-reference each other, with little or no duplication of data.*

When the data base systems necessary for managing data bases first appeared, it was thought that the ultimate goal was the creation of one large central data base for the enterprise that would replace all the inflexible computer files.

It was not long before it was painfully experienced that such a grandiose concept had little chance of success in practice, since an attempt to construct such a central data base is likely to bankrupt the enterprise. That expenditures are for acquiring the benefits of advanced technology is no guarantee that they are not also extravagant. A single all-embracing central data base to replace all the conventional files of an enterprise requires expenditures that are all too often an extravagance.

Instead of the large super data base, many different data bases are nowadays used within an enterprise along with many different conventional computer files. These data bases are sometimes called *subject data bases*, since a subject data base contains all the data relevant to a certain type of entity or subject that is important for the enterprise (see Ref. 4). Examples are electronic components, customers, finished products, and so on. But independent conventional computer files are still very much in evidence. Many of them are specialized files that are used in association with data bases. However, many are simply files that contain important data that could well be aggregated into data bases, if and when the cost can be justified. In many cases, for reasons of low return on investment, this will never happen, so that for most enterprises the management of data will include the creation and maintenance of both conventional files and data bases, at least for the foreseeable future.

Managing the data base environment

There is more to the management of data than just having computers for creation and manipulation of data bases. The data in a data base is normally shared between users in many parts of an organization and at many different organizational levels. This gives rise to benefits in the form of increased opportunity for the managers of the enterprise to improve the quality of their decisions. This is of fundamental importance, for in today's highly automated but complex business environment, it is more the quality of decisions that counts than how hard a manager works. But the sharing of data among different departments and even divisions in an enterprise has its administrative costs, partly incurred by the need to hire *data base administration personnel*. Thus the use of the data base tool has a marked effect on the way an enterprise is managed.

The design of this book is based on the premise that a manager can fully appreciate the opportunities and problems inherent in the data base environment only if he or she has a basic grasp of the underlying technology and its historical development. We therefore begin with a study of the technology and defer discussion of the data base environment and data base administration until Chapter 13.

The technology

Data base management has its roots in the technology of processing business data in conventional computer files. There are many different ways of organizing computer files depending on the application. When computer files are integrated under the control of a software system called a data base management system, we have a data base. Thus in order to fully appreciate data bases, we need to have an understanding of conventional computer files as they are used in business. As mentioned earlier, despite the trend to data bases, it is certain that nondata base files are going to be with us for a long time to come. For these reasons it is necessary to begin a study of data bases with a review of computer files, and this is the purpose of the first two chapters of this book. In the present chapter we begin right at the beginning and look at computer facilities for reading in and writing out data, and at data storage facilities. These topics are the very foundation for data base technology.

Most of the book is therefore devoted to giving the reader a basic grasp of data base technology. It is inevitable that it does contain some technical material. Our aim, however, is to impart an understanding of the basic ideas and methods and not to develop technical expertise. For this reason, only absolutely essential technical material is included. In addition, the subject is developed in a step-by-step fashion, starting with the most elementary concepts.

1.1 THE MANAGEMENT OF INPUT/OUTPUT

The *input/output facilities* of a computer are fundamental for business data processing. Data to be processed must be input from some external *storage medium*, and following processing, data must be output and stored. In most of this book we shall be dealing with large quantities of business data that are stored on magnetic disks and occasionally on magnetic tapes. It is therefore important that the reader acquire an elementary understanding of how input/output with these disks and tapes is managed. As we shall see, input/output is managed by both hardware and software facilities. Although these facilities are quite complex, the basic ideas involved are easily grasped by students with only an elementary knowledge of computing. Indeed, it turns out that input/output managment methods have a lot in common with methods used in business logistics.

It is computer programs that initiate the input and output of data, and so we begin our study with a careful examination of what goes on when a computer program is executed.

What does what in a computer

In Figure 1.1 we have a diagram showing the *central processing unit* (CPU) and *internal memory* of a computer. The CPU is the calculating device of a computer and the place where all arithmetic and other operations are carried out. The internal or *main memory* is made up of many storage cells, each of which can hold either an instruction or an item of data. The CPU can connect to any memory cell, but only to one at a time (color connection in the diagram).

In the diagram the memory contains some instructions from a program excerpt and some data items being manipulated by the program instructions. The instructions refer to the memory cells or locations containing the data items, and this collection of memory cells is called the *program data area*. The instructions of a program are carried out by the CPU in a regular sequence, in the order of ascending memory-cell address value, until either a STOP instruction is executed or a GOTO instruction is executed. A GOTO instruction causes a break in the regular execution sequence, a new execution sequence starting from the address specified in the GOTO instruction (see third instruction in diagram).

To actually execute or carry out an instruction, the CPU becomes directly connected to the memory location containing that instruction, and a copy of the instruction is transferred to the CPU. The CPU then accesses the memory locations referred to in the instruction and carries out the arithmetic or other operation specified in the instruction. In the diagram we have used symbolic

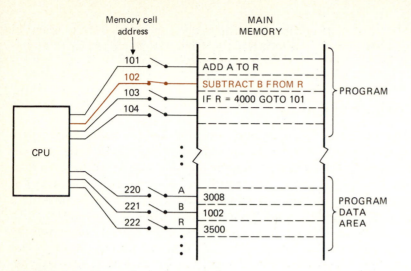

FIGURE 1.1 Shows how the central processing unit (CPU) executes a simple program excerpt residing in the main memory. When a program instruction is carried out, the memory location containing it is directly connected to the CPU, to which the instruction is transferred.

names such as B and R for the memory locations containing data to be manipulated. In an actual executing program the instruction

SUBTRACT B FROM R

would be replaced by the equivalent of

SUBTRACT CONTENTS OF LOCATION 221 FROM CONTENTS OF LOCATION 222

In a program written in FORTRAN or COBOL, we use symbolic names for the memory locations that contain data to be manipulated, it being the job of the FORTRAN or COBOL compiler to translate these symbolic names to memory addresses in its preparation of the program for execution.[1]

At this point the reader may well have checked back to the title to confirm that it concerned data bases and not computer machine language. However, our purpose in beginning this way is to make sure that the reader is quite clear about what does what in a computer. From the discussion above we see that it is the CPU that does all that is done, that is, it is the CPU that carries out or executes an instruction in a program by manipulating the data in the program's data area. An analogy may help. In the baking of a cake, we can regard the cook as corresponding to the CPU, the recipe to the program, and the program's data to the ingredients. Thus the cook bakes a cake by manipulating the ingredients according to

---

[1]The compiler does not complete the job however. It is completed by a loader program that places or loads the user program in main memory for execution.

the instructions in the recipe. Similarly, the CPU processes data by manipulating the data in the program data area in accordance with the instructions in the program. However, in common computer parlance we often say that a program carries out some processing function. For example, we might say that program X computes an employee's net pay, which is equivalent to saying that a certain recipe bakes a cake. Of course it is the CPU under the control of program X that computes the net pay, just as it is a cook guided by a recipe who bakes a cake. Thus stating that a program carries out a processing function is quite clearly a misuse of the English language, but this misuse is well established, and no great harm results from it provided we have only one processor that is executing programs. In a computer system, however, there are typically several processors, most of them involved in input/output, as we shall soon see, and we need to be careful about stating what does what in order to avoid misunderstandings.

We shall not make any further use of diagrams of the type shown in Figure 1.1, relying instead on the type shown in Figure 1.2, which essentially describes the same thing. Here we depict a CPU and a main memory containing a program accompanied by data in a program data area. We use the two-headed arrow to indicate that the CPU may connect to any memory location occupied by a program instruction or data in order to execute the program. A black arrow indicates that a program may be executed by the CPU, while a color arrow indicates that a program actually is being executed.

Input/output and external storage media

Our next consideration has to do with how data gets in and out of a program data area. Suppose the data to be processed is on a magnetic tape or disk. Since the CPU under program control manipulates only data in a program data area in main memory, there has to be a way to move data to be processed from the tape or disk to the program data area, and vice versa. The solution to this problem leads us to the *multiprogramming operating system*, a basic software component of every larger computer system and a component to which a data base management system must interface. A brief review of multiprogramming systems will therefore be relevant.

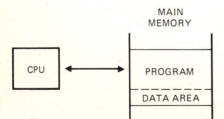

FIGURE 1.2 Simple representation of a program on main memory that may be executed by a CPU. The two-headed arrow indicates that the CPU may connect to a memory location, permitting transfer of data or an instruction to the CPU, or transfer of data from the CPU to the main memory.

Multiprogramming operating systems

In a primitive computer system it is the CPU that connects directly to an external device such as a tape drive or card-reader; in such a primitive system the CPU accesses data in the external medium and places it in main memory, doing this under the control of some input/output subprogram in main memory. Unfortunately, accessing external storage is a very slow process compared with accessing main memory; for example, a modern CPU could make about 1 million main memory accesses in the time it takes to make about 10 disk accesses. Put another way, the CPU can process a very large amount of data in a main memory program data area in the time taken to get additional data in from an external storage device. (The reason for this is that the external devices are electromechanical, while main memory is electronic.) Thus input/output is a bottleneck for computer systems, no matter whether the input/output is with a simple tape file, or with a complex data base.

The common solution to the problem is to use a multiprogramming operating system along with simple subsidiary or assistant processors called *input/output processors,* or *channels.* When the CPU can no longer continue execution of a program because additional data must be obtained from an external device, the job of procuring this data is handed over to an I/O processor, while the CPU executes some other program with sufficient data in its program data area. The situation as far as programs in main memory is concerned is depicted in Figure 1.3. Main memory can be regarded as divided into *partitions,* or *regions.* A typical partition holds a program that carries out some data processing function (an *application program*), together with the program's data area and some additional subprograms and data areas which we will come back to shortly. One

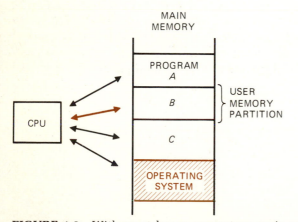

FIGURE 1.3 With most larger computers, main memory contains several user programs in different stages of execution, but at any instant only one program is being executed (colored arrow). Each program (plus certain subsidiary programs and data areas) can be taken as occupying a memory partition. At least one memory partition is reserved for the operating system, a system program that determines (among other things) which program will execute next.

or more of these memory partitions are also allocated to the multiprogramming operating system, which is a large systems program that controls the execution of the application programs and the input/output processors (not shown in Figure 1.3). At any instant, the program in only one partition is being executed by the CPU. When the CPU executes an instruction requiring access to an external device (typically a READ or WRITE instruction), control passes to the operating system; i.e., operating system routines are executed, and the operating system then starts one or more I/O processors. Control then passes back to some other application program. Thus at any given instant, the programs in the various partitions of memory are all in various stages of execution, but only one partition is actually executing. At the same time one or more I/O processors are transmitting data.

Role of I/O processors

In Figure 1.4, we show in more detail the contents of a typical main memory partition containing an application program, and we also show a single I/O processor or channel connected to a *disk controller* which is in turn connected to one or more disk units. To understand exactly the role of the memory partition, I/O processor, and disk controller, let us suppose that user program A is executing, and that the program contains a READ instruction requiring that data be obtained from a disk. When the CPU executes the READ instruction, the CPU switches execution to the *access method*. The access method is really a large subprogram of the operating system, but it resides in the partition belonging to our user program A. The access method checks in an area of program A's

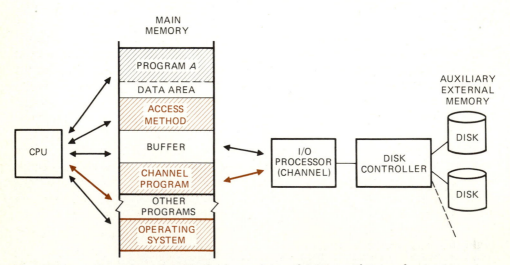

FIGURE 1.4 Shows how data (in the form of records) is input from and output to external memory (shown here as disk units). The heavy black lines in the main memory show the boundaries of memory partitions. The top partition contains a user program with its data area, plus a buffer area (which can hold one or more blocks of records), plus two subsidiary programs which are really part of the operating system, namely, an access method and a channel program.

partition known as a *buffer* to see if the required data is in it; if it is, the data is moved to program *A*'s data area, and program *A* resumes execution. If the required data is not in the buffer, a relatively complex sequence of events take place, which we shall merely outline here.

First the access method constructs a message which it places in a queue in a *message buffer* in the operating system partition and passes control to the operating system. The operating system now executes, and examines the message received from program *A*'s access method (messages from other partitions are also queued in the operating system message buffer, all requiring attention, but we ignore this here). The message is a request for data to be taken from a specified disk and placed in the buffer in program *A*'s partition. Under operating system control, the CPU then starts execution of an idle I/O processor or channel. This channel then executes a special program called a *channel program*, which also resides in program *A*'s partition. The channel executes the channel program by connecting directly to the memory locations containing the channel program instructions. It can also connect directly to the disk controller. When channel program instructions are executed by the channel, the channel activates the disk controller, which positions a selected read/write arm on the required track and transmits data to the buffer. The buffer thus serves as a loading/unloading ramp for data transmitted between external storage and main memory.

Meanwhile, as soon as execution of the channel program by the channel has begun, the operating system passes control to some other applications program in a different partition, and execution of that program resumes. Thus, during the time the I/O processor is executing a channel program in program *A*'s partition, the CPU is executing an application program in some other partition (color arrows in diagram). As we have seen, obtaining data from external devices is a slow process, so that the CPU can execute a great many application program instructions in the time it takes a channel to fill a buffer. In practice, several channels will be in operation at any instant, each inputting or outputting data for an application program. When the buffer in program *A*'s partition is finally filled, the I/O processor sends the equivalent of a message to the operating system, which eventually returns execution control to program *A*'s partition. However, it is the access method that first resumes execution and delivers a portion of the data in the buffer to program *A*'s data area, control only then being returned to program *A*. A similar, but opposite, sequence of events takes place when the CPU executes a WRITE instruction, requiring that data be moved from the program data area to an external storage device. For additional details see Refs. 2 and 3.

Bakery management analogy

The role of the multiprogramming operating system and I/O processors may also be fairly accurately illustrated by considering a bakery management analogy. Suppose that the bakery's only cook (the CPU) is baking many different cakes at the same time, each cake having its distinct recipe (program) and ingredients (program data). Let us suppose further that bulk stores of ingredients for each cake are stored in cellars with steep and long staircases down to them, and that assistants are used to transport bulk stores to small storage rooms right beside the kitchen. Now suppose that the cook runs short of a certain ingredient while baking cake A (using recipe A). Following an administrative procedure (the access method), the cook will check in the correct storage room (the buffer); if the required ingredient is there, the cook moves a portion to the pile of ingredients (program data for cake A) in the kitchen. If the ingredient is not in the store, using another administrative routine (the operating system), the cook calls for an assistant to fetch the required ingredient from the appropriate cellar. The assistant (I/O processor) laboriously fetches the required ingredient from the cellar (external storage) according to a procedure for that type of ingredient (the channel program) and places it in the storage room (buffer) near the kitchen. Because of the steep and long staircase down to the cellar, an assistant fetches ingredients very slowly, and meanwhile the cook is busy following the recipe for some other cake. Eventually, the cook moves a portion of the retrieved ingredient from the storage room (buffer) to the pile of ingredients in the kitchen (program data) and resumes baking according to recipe A.

Blocks of records

We have so far tacitly neglected to say much about exacly what kind of data is transmitted between external storage and program data area, except that the transmission takes place in two stages, namely, bulk data transmission under channel program control from external storage to main memory buffer, and smaller quantities from buffer to program data area. The bulk quantity is known as a *data block,* or *transmitted data block,* and the smaller quantity is called a *record.*

The transmitted data block is the *unit of transmission* between external memory and main memory. It is also the *unit of storage* in external memory, although particularly with disk storage, the block as stored may not be quite the same as the one transmitted. The transmission process is illustrated in Figure 1.5. The external memory (in this case disk memory) contains a sequence of physical storage blocks each consisting of the data block originally transmitted to the disk, plus some *system data* to more easily facilitate location and identification of the block. As we have seen, when a channel transmits a data block to main memory, it places it in a buffer. Thus a buffer must be large enough to hold the block. In practice, the operating system assigns at least one buffer to every file manipulated by a program, and *the transmitted block size equals the buffer size.*

A transmitted data block contains *records* (Figure 1.5), and the number of records in a block is known as the *blocking factor.* A record is a collection of *data items,* or *fields,* that usually contain information about a single entity, such as a customer, a purchase item, or a project. (Thus a customer record might contain a *primary key field* such as customer-number to uniquely identify the record, as well as other fields such as credit-status that contain information about the customer.) Following transmission of a data block to the buffer, the access method may use the primary key field to select a record from the data block in the buffer for further transmission to the program data area for processing. (Processing that involves physical transmission of records between buffer and program

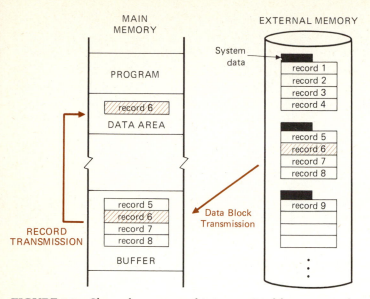

FIGURE 1.5 Shows how a record is transmitted from external memory to the data area of a program in main memory.

data area is called *move mode processing*, and is the most common. PL/1 and COBOL also provide for processing of records in the buffer. This is called *locate mode processing* and most operating systems allow it because it is more efficient. With a few operating systems all processing is in the buffer. For details of locate mode processing, see Ref. 2.)

Logical and physical storage files

If we know the number of *bytes* (characters) in each field of a record, then by simple addition we can arrive at the number of bytes in the record. Multiplication by the blocking factor then gives us the number of bytes of record data in the transmitted data block (assuming all records are the same length, which they usually are). Now the *physical storage file* is made up of *physical storage blocks*, which are transmitted data blocks to each of which some system data has been added (Figure 1.6a). However, it is more convenient to think of a *logical storage file*, simply made up of the records grouped into *logical storage blocks* as shown in Figure 1.6a. Here the logical storage block is the same as the transmitted data block. Note that the physical storage file physically exists (on a disk), as does a transmitted data block (in some buffer), but the logical storage file is simply an imaginary collection of the records processed by a program and does not physically exist as a collection.

[Sometimes files have records of varying length. Here again the logical storage file is just the imaginary collection of records. However, the transmitted data block has extra system fields added on to contain the lengths of the records and the logical storage block (Figure 1.6b). A physical storage block is created by adding additional systems data to the transmitted block. The physical storage

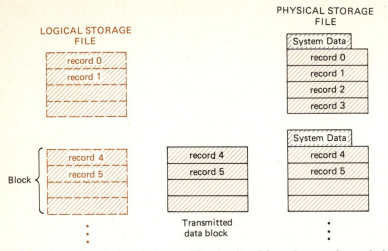

(a) Logical and physical storage files for fixed length records on disk. (The structure of a physical storage block on disk storage is given in Figures 1.13 and 1.14.)

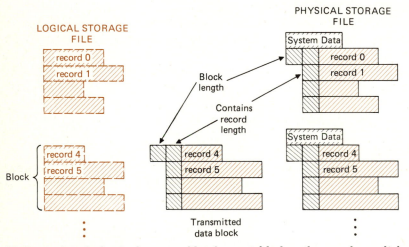

(b) Logical and physical storage files for variable length records on disk storage.

FIGURE 1.6

file in this case is thus quite complex, and complete details are beyond the scope of this book (see Ref. 1). However it is normally sufficient to deal only with the simple logical storage file.]

It is logical storage files that programmers manipulate when they write COBOL (and other higher language programs), thus escaping having to deal with the complexities of the physical storage file. The physical storage file must be considered in detail, however, whenever calculations of the amount of *storage space* taken up by the file are being made. With IBM systems the physical storage file is often called a *dataset*. We now examine the physical storage media in some detail.

1.2 TAPE AND DISK STORAGE MEDIA

Large quantities of computer-readable data are most commonly stored on tapes and disks. Tapes are compact, inexpensive, fast to mount (on a tape drive), and convenient for archiving infrequently used files. Unfortunately the records can only be read *sequentially*, that is, one after another. Disk packs on the other hand permit direct access to the data but are less compact, much more expensive, much slower to mount, and relatively heavy. Because of their direct access capability, disks are the medium for storing the physical storage files of data bases. However, we cannot ignore tapes, since these are also used with data bases, although only in a limited way.

Tapes and tape drives

A schematic of a *tape drive* is shown in Figure 1.7. Unlike the drive of an ordinary tape recorder, the tape does not move continuously while a tape file is being processed. Rather it moves in fits and starts. Between each block of data on a tape there is a gap, called the *interblock gap*, or the *start/stop gap* (Figure 1.7). As we have seen, data is read one block at a time, and while a block is being processed the tape is stopped, and the *read/write head* of the tape drive is over an interblock gap. To allow for the tape to accelerate and decelerate quickly, "buffers" of loose tape are maintained (by a photocell arrangement) between the read/write head and the reels (at *A* and *B* in the diagram).

Tape data storage

Tape reels are typically 2400 feet in length (when new; older tapes sometimes have lengths chopped off). They also come with different *data densities* and interblock gap sizes, as shown on the next page.

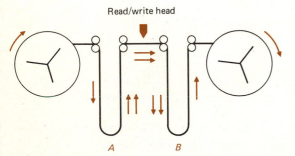

FIGURE 1.7 Tape drive schematic. The tape moves only when a block is being read or written. The loose tape at *A* and *B* enables the tape to accelerate and decelerate quickly; the heavier reels catch up later.

DENSITY (bits per inch)	GAP (inches)	GAP (bytes)
800	0.6	480
1600	0.6	960
6250	0.3	1875

The 1600 bits per inch (bpi) tape density is probably the most widely used. [Watch out for the density being quoted as bits per inch. Because a byte of data is stored transverse to the length of the tape (Figure 1.9), there can be 1600 bytes of data to an inch of 1600-bpi tape. Thus an interblock gap of 0.6 inch could have held 0.6*1600 bytes or 960 bytes.]

We see that the interblock gap is quite large with tapes. Thus if we are storing records each of length 104 bytes with a blocking factor of 10 on a 1600-bpi tape, the physical storage block length will be 1040 bytes; but taking the gap into account, there has to be allocated 1040 + 960 bytes of tape, or 2000 bytes. Thus the tape would be able to hold only

$$\frac{2400*12*1600}{2000} \quad \text{blocks}$$

that is, 23,040 blocks, or 230,400 records. Had no interblock gaps been necessary, the tape could have theoretically held

$$\frac{2400*12*1600}{1040} \quad \text{blocks}$$

that is, 44,307 blocks, or 443,070 records, which is almost twice as many. But interblock gaps cannot be done without, and it should be clear that they can

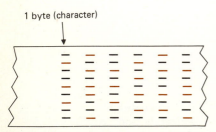

FIGURE 1.8 Blocks of records on tape. The interblock gaps provide a stopping place for the read/write heads. With fixed length records, the logical storage block, transmitted data block, and physical storage block are all identical.

1 byte (character)

FIGURE 1.9 A character of data is stored transverse to the length of the tape by magnetic recording.

drastically reduce the amount of data that can be placed on a tape. The only remedy is to use physical storage blocks as large as possible compared with the gap size in bytes. However, large blocks mean correspondingly large buffers in main memory, and large amounts of main memory for large buffers are rarely available. Commonly, block sizes are between 2000 and 3000 bytes.

Tape data transmission

The time to read a block of data has two components:

1. The time to start the tape
2. The time to transmit the data

The tape accelerates while the head is over the gap, but by the time it has reached the data, the tape is moving at its normal speed and data is being transmitted at the *nominal data transmission rate*. Widely used IBM tape drives can read or write 1600-bpi tapes at a speed of 100 inches per second (about 5 miles per hour), which gives a nominal data transmission rate of 1600*100, or 160,000 bytes per second.

The time to transmit a 2000-byte block will therefore be 2000/160,000 seconds, or 12.5 milliseconds. The time to start the tape is about 4 milliseconds, so that the total time is about 12.5 + 4, or 16.5, milliseconds.

It is important to grasp that this is a very long time indeed by computer standards. The CPU can access data in main memory in a fraction of a microsecond by comparison. As we will also see, the time taken to transfer a 2000-byte block from a disk is also very long.

Disk packs and disk drives

A *disk pack* consists of a set of metal disks mounted on a single spindle, which rotates continuously when the *disk drive* is turned on (contrast with tapes, which move only when a block is being transmitted). Except for the top surface, which is used for control purposes, there is a set of concentric (like the rings of the planet Saturn) recording surfaces on each disk surface. As shown in Figure

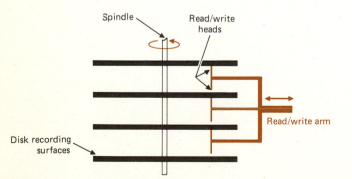

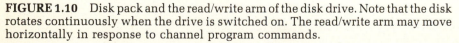

FIGURE 1.10 Disk pack and the read/write arm of the disk drive. Note that the disk rotates continuously when the drive is switched on. The read/write arm may move horizontally in response to channel program commands.

Cylinder

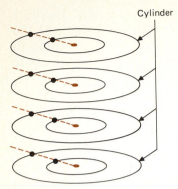

FIGURE 1.11 Tracks of the same radius form a cylinder, all the data on which may be read without motion of the read/write arm.

1.10, a set of read/write heads, arranged like the teeth of a comb, can move as a group so that the read/write heads at the end of an arm can be positioned above (or below) all those tracks with the same radius. The set of tracks from all the surfaces with the same radius is referred to as a *cylinder of tracks,* and in any given position of the "comb" of read/write heads, heads will be above or below all the tracks of a cylinder, enabling all these tracks to be written or read without further movement of the arms. Movement of the arm to a new cylinder is known as a *seek* and is relatively slow, the average seek time for the widely used IBM 3350 disk being 25 milliseconds. In storage terms, a disk pack is said to be made up of cylinders, with each cylinder made up of tracks (Figure 1.11).

An I/O processor has direct access to a track of a disk pack, by initiating a seek operation to select the correct cylinder and then enabling a read/write head to select the correct track within a cylinder. Of course the tracks on a disk pack may be read sequentially just like a tape, in which case all the tracks of the first cylinder are read, then the tracks of the next cylinder, and so on in cylinder sequence (Figure 1.12). Note that each track has a well-defined start point,

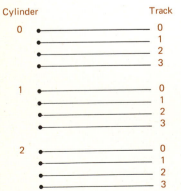

Cylinder   Track

0 ●——————————— 0
  ●——————————— 1
  ●——————————— 2
  ●——————————— 3

1 ●——————————— 0
  ●——————————— 1
  ●——————————— 2
  ●——————————— 3

2 ●——————————— 0
  ●——————————— 1
  ●——————————— 2
  ●——————————— 3

FIGURE 1.12 Data is processed cylinder by cylinder during sequential processing.

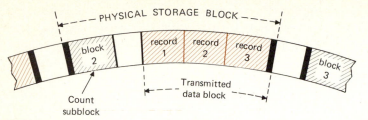

FIGURE 1.13 IBM's count-data architecture. The physical storage block contains the number of the block on the track. This permits the controller to retrieve a block without having to count from the start of a track. With variable length records, tags are attached to the records to give their lengths (see Figure 1.6*b*). IBM sequential disk files and relative (usually hash) files are stored in count-data format and are described in Chapter 2.

denoted by black circles in Figures 1.11 and 1.12, and by a physical mark on the disk pack that can be detected electronically.

Data storage on disks

With IBM systems, data blocks are stored on disk tracks in either *count-data* or *count-key data architecture* as shown in Figures 1.13 and 1.14. With count-data architecture an additional *count subblock* is stored along with a data block. This subblock basically contains the number of a block on a track, which may be checked by the disk controller under channel program control. Thus the count subblock gives a block a unique address, and we may refer to block 3 of track 4 of cylinder 15. Thus, as we saw earlier, the physical storage block on a track requires more bytes of storage medium than the corresponding transmitted data block in a main memory buffer. With the widely used IBM 3350 disk, the additional space per block is 185 bytes, so that a 2000-byte transmitted data block takes up 2185 bytes (including gaps) on an IBM 3350 disk track. A track of an IBM 3350 disk can nominally hold 19,254 bytes, and since such a track must

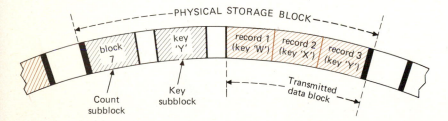

FIGURE 1.14 IBM's count-key data architecture. In addition to the count subblock for the block number, the key of the last record in the block is recorded in the key subblock of the physical storage block. With variable length records, tags are attached to the records to give their lengths (Figure 1.6*b*). IBM indexed-sequential files (see Chapter 2) are stored in count-key data format. That part of the count-key data block containing the transmitted data block is called the data subblock. The data subblock is actually more complex than shown above. For details see the last section of Appendix 1.

have only complete storage blocks, the number of 2000-byte data blocks such a track can hold is the nearest integer below 19,254/2185 blocks, or 8 blocks. (An IBM 3350 disk drive has 555 cylinders and 30 tracks per cylinder, so that it could hold 555*30*8, or 133,200, 2000-byte blocks, or about 9 times as many as a 2400-foot 1600-bpi tape.)

With count-key data architecture (Figure 1.7*b*), there is an additional *key subblock*, which contains the key of the last record in the data block. This is used for further identification of a data block with direct access file organizations. It complicates storage utilization calculations quite a bit. Storage of a 2000-byte transmitted data block on a track of an IBM 3350 now requires an additional 267 bytes plus twice the bytes in the record key. If we suppose that the key field or data item in each record of the 2000-byte block is 10 bytes long, then the physical storage block would be 2010 + 267 + 10 bytes, or 2287 bytes. Dividing this quantity into the number of bytes on a track gives us the number of such blocks a track can hold. For further details, see Appendix 1.

The other way of storing data on a track is to divide the disk track up into equal *sectors*. This is done by having physical markers on the surface of a disk that can be detected by the disk control mechanism. A sector is usually small in size, about equal to the size of the smallest conceivable data block, a typical sector size being 512 bytes. Since a typical data block will be larger than a sector, several sectors will normally be required for a data block (Figure 1.15). A data block on a track is uniquely addressable by means of the cylinder number, the track number, and the sector number of the sector on which it begins.

Note that with both the IBM and sector approach, the amount of data that can be placed on a track is the same for all tracks regardless of radius. Thus data is more compressed on the inner tracks (Figure 1.16). Note also, that unlike the case of tape storage, a byte or character of data is stored along a track (Figure 1.17). IBM sequential disk files and *relative* (usually *hash*) files are stored in count-data format, while IBM indexed-sequential files are stored in count-key data format (see Chapter 2).

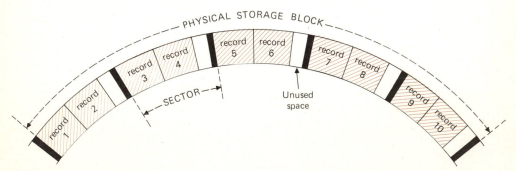

FIGURE 1.15 Shows how a data block consisting of 10 records is stored on a disk track divided into sectors just slightly larger than 2 records. The physical storage block takes up five sectors, and there is some unused storage space in each sector. Each sector is directly accessible, but the contents of the five sectors will be transmitted as a result of a single access.

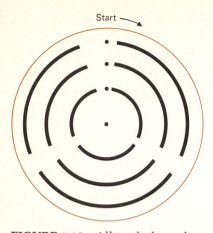

Start →

FIGURE 1.16 All tracks have the same capacity, so that data is more compressed on an inner track. With IBM storage architectures, only integer numbers of blocks can be stored, so that unused space may occur at the end of a track. Were a block just larger than half a track, almost half the space on the track would be wasted.

Sequential transmission of disk data

Let us suppose that we have a file of records stored on a disk, where the logical storage block is 2000 bytes long. Now this file could in theory be processed either *sequentially* or *directly*. When it is processed sequentially (see Figure 1.2), all the blocks on one cylinder are read in sequence, then all the blocks on the next cylinder are read, and so on. Thus, within a given cylinder, reading the next consecutive block does not require any movement of the read/write arm, that is, a seek. However since the blocks on a cylinder are read one by one, and since there can be an arbitrary time interval between the reading of two consecutive blocks, then to read any block, the read/write head will have to wait until the track involved rotates sufficiently for the block to be read. Thus there will be a *rotational delay* before actual transmission can commence, and on average this delay will be equal to half the time for the disk to make one revolution.

This means that the time required to read (or write) the next block in a sequential file is the sum of:

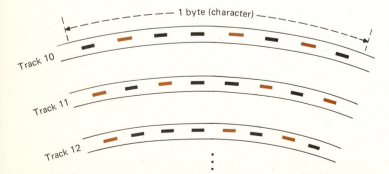

1 byte (character)

Track 10

Track 11

Track 12

FIGURE 1.17 Data is magnetically stored bit by bit along a disk track.

1. The rotational delay
2. The time to directly transmit the data

With the widely used IBM 3350 disk (and its recently released successor, the IBM 3380 disk), the disk rotates once every 16.7 milliseconds, so that the average rotational delay is about 8.3 milliseconds. The nominal transmission rate for disks is usually much higher than for tapes, and in the case of the IBM 3350 disk it is 1.2 million bytes per second. Hence the time to transmit a 2000-byte block will be 2000/1200 milliseconds, which is nearly 2 milliseconds. Thus the time to read or write the 2000-byte block will be about 8.3 + 2, or about 10, milliseconds. We recall that with the 1600-bpi tape it was about 16 milliseconds.

Direct transmission of disk data

A disk file may often be processed directly, so that blocks may be read in any order. Thus between two consecutive block reading operations, a seek operation will usually be necessary. As we have seen, with an IBM 3350 disk the average seek time is about 25 milliseconds. We must use an average since the seek time will be at a maximum when the arms have to move from an outer cylinder to an inner cylinder, and at a minimum when they move from one cylinder to an adjacent cylinder. Whenever the arms have moved to the correct cylinder, the rotational delay is now experienced while the block rotates to a position under the read/write head. And then we have the time to directly transmit the data block. The time to read or write a block is therefore the sum of:

1. The seek time
2. The rotational delay
3. The time to directly transmit the data

Thus the total time to read or write a 2000-byte block will be 25 + 8.3 + 2, or about 35, milliseconds on average (since the sum of rotational delay and transmission time is the same as in the sequential transmission case). This is a very long time by computer standards; it is responsible for much of the poor performance of file and data base systems. However, the dominant seek time can be eliminated by using very expensive disks with a read/write head over every (or nearly every) track. Such special system disks are used only with systems where speed of access is critical, such as with virtual operating systems (see Section 1.3).

For further details of IBM 3350 and 3380 disks, see Appendix 1. Additional information can be obtained from Refs. 1 and 2.

1.3 VIRTUAL OPERATING SYSTEMS

There remains a need to clarify an important aspect of multiprogramming operating systems that for expositional purposes has so far been ignored. There are two basic types of multiprogramming operating systems, the conventional type, which is what we have described so far, and what are generally known as *virtual operating systems*. Virtual operating systems began to replace the conventional systems in the early 1970s and are now the most common. Essentially, virtual operating systems function in much the same way as the conventional systems except for the incorporation of a *demand-paging facility* which permits the execution of programs which are too big to reside in main memory.

Only a small portion of a user program run under a virtual operating system resides in main memory at any given instant. The complete user program plus all the usual buffers, access methods, and channel programs (that is, the contents of a partition of the conventional operating system) now reside in a special auxiliary memory. This auxiliary memory is called *external page storage* and is usually a fast system disk. These application programs and accompanying routines and data areas are also divided into pages (each about 4000 bytes long). Thus the contents of external page storage with a virtual system are the same as the contents of the main memory of a conventional system (Figures 1.3 and 1.4), except that the external page storage is now divided into pages. It is also useful to continue to regard the external page storage as divided into partitions, one for each user program.

System operation

At any instant (Figure 1.18), only a few pages from each partition are in main memory, and an instruction from only one page is being executed. When all the instructions in a page have been executed, and if the next page of the program is

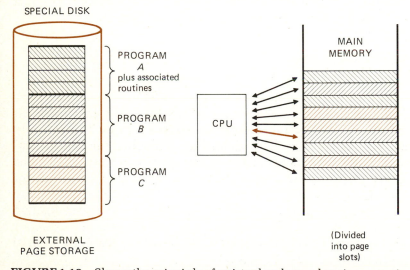

SPECIAL DISK

PROGRAM
A
plus associated
routines

PROGRAM
B

PROGRAM
C

CPU

MAIN
MEMORY

EXTERNAL
PAGE STORAGE

(Divided
into page
slots)

FIGURE 1.18   Shows the principle of a virtual or demand paging operating system. Complete user programs, and associated routines and data areas, do not reside in main memory. Instead they reside on a special system disk and are divided up into short lengths of about 4K bytes, called pages. Thus the programs are kept in a special external memory, usually called external page storage, which is normally much larger than the main memory. At any given instant, only a few pages of a program are in main memory, so that only those pages of the program may be executed by the CPU. When the CPU needs a page of a program (or associated data area) not in main memory, the operating system causes it to be read into main memory. While the new page is being read in, the operating system will cause the CPU to execute a page of some other program.

not in main memory, then the required page is read into—or *paged into*—main memory by a component of the operating system called the *paging supervisor*; meanwhile the CPU has switched execution to the page of some other application, switching back to execute the page just paged in at some later point in time.

Thus the essential difference between the virtual operating system and a conventional system is the continual paging in and out of main memory of the pages of the different partitions. This demand paging facility improves the efficiency of the computer system by permitting the execution of programs which are too large to fit into either main memory or a vacant main memory partition (in a conventional operating system). Unfortunately, taking the demand paging facility into account needlessly complicates the human perception of the operation of a computer system and makes effective diagrammatic techniques extremely difficult, if not impossible. Thus the facility effectively enfogs the whole subject right at the foundation. In order to simplify future discussions and to make the drawing of diagrams possible, we will therefore adopt the convention that an application program, along with accompanying routines and data areas, occupies an arbitrarily large partition of main memory. It is to be understood that in practice such a partition would reside in external page storage and be paged in and out of main memory. An excellent early discussion of virtual operating systems is found in Ref. 3.

1.4 BATCH AND ON-LINE PROCESSING

There are two major overall methods of processing business data, and these methods are applicable not only with conventional files but also with data bases. They are the *batch* method and the *on-line* method of processing.

Batch processing

Business data processing in the beginning of the data processing era was almost always batch processing. The programs for batch processing of conventional files was placed in a queue of similar jobs on some input device. In the beginning this was typically a card-reader, but later tapes and disks were also used. When space became available in a partition of the memory of the computer, the next job was loaded into memory for execution. As the program for the job was executed, typically records from some files were read in and used to update the records of some other file; similarly with other jobs.

The typical job would be repeated at regular intervals, daily, weekly, or monthly, and so on, but with new data. Typically a job involved updating a main or *master* file from a smaller *transaction* file; for example, a file containing employee records was updated from a file containing records for employees hired during the preceding week. Thus the records in the transaction file were typically accumulated or batched over a period of time before being used to update a master file. This method of processing business data is probably still the dominant one, as evidenced by the daily, weekly, and monthly schedules of most data processing centers. It is very efficient.

On-line processing

A much more expensive alternative to batch processing is on-line processing. Here a program can be made to execute simply by issuing a command at a terminal. When the program executes, it can communicate with the user via the terminal. Typically an on-line program originates a *message* or request for data to update master files and the user responds by entering the required data. Thus if the master file were a file of employee records, whenever a new employee arrived or an old one left, the on-line updating program could be activated via the terminal, the operator would enter the data about the latest required change to the employee file, and the program would carry out the update. With this technique, the master files or data bases are always current. In contrast, with the batch technique, if the files are updated overnight following batching of the previous day's transactions, the file is out of date by the end of the following business day.

Operating systems for batch and on-line processing

The original multiprogramming operating systems of the 1960s were exclusively batch-oriented, as are the virtual operating systems that evolved from them, such as IBM's OS/MVS or Honeywell's GCOS. Typically, batch jobs are queued on a disk and allocated to a memory partition (paged in, in the case of a virtual operating system) as space becomes available when an earlier job finishes. A batch job usually consists of an updating program, and master files are updated by this program from data on transaction files. All this takes place with little or no human intervention, often in the middle of the night.

However, on-line processing is typically carried out with batch operating systems as well. This is accomplished by reserving a special partition called an *on-line partition*, in which an on-line updating and information retrieval program can execute as requested from a terminal. The user at a terminal does not actually interact directly with an on-line program but rather with a special on-line management system called a *teleprocessing monitor*. A teleprocessing monitor, which executes within the on-line partition, can interact with many terminals concurrently and responds to an individual request or message for update of a master file by executing the required updating program. At any given moment there will be many requests from many users, and many on-line programs in various stages of execution—all within the on-line partition. It is the function of the teleprocessing monitor or equivalent system to coordinate communications with the terminals and the execution of the different on-line programs. Customer Information Control System (CICS) from IBM is one of the most widely used teleprocessing monitors, and we return to it in Chapter 12 on data base teleprocessing. There is also some further preliminary coverage in Chapter 4.

Time-sharing or interactive operating systems

On-line systems are widely used in commerce with both conventional files and data bases. However, they are frequently confused with *time-sharing* or *interac-*

tive operating systems, examples of which are IBM's VM/CMS and Honeywell's MULTICS. These systems use large numbers of small partitions so that many user programs can execute concurrently; that is, each user program is allowed a brief time slice in which to execute. At the same time the programs can accept input data from a user terminal and display output data at a user terminal. Often each user has his or her own private data files, which is one reason why such systems are widely used in academic and research environments. These systems are unfortunately not as efficient in handling large quantities of business data as batch operating systems. Nevertheless, many commercial users at different terminals can easily use a time-sharing operating system to access a common collection of conventional master files or even a data base, and in many of the examples in the earlier part of this book we assume that a time-sharing or interactive operating system is being used. It is such operating systems that most students at universities and colleges typically have access to. We return to this subject in Chapter 12.(See also Ref. 3.)

Future developments

Operating systems and systems for managing data bases are heavily intertwined, although in this book we make every effort to keep the subjects separate. The major development period for operating systems was in the 1960s, while for data base systems it was the 1970s. It now appears that the 1980s will be a new period of development for operating systems, and there are signs that the result will be operating systems that combine the advantages of batch processing, interactive processing, and perhaps on-line processing.

SUMMARY

1. Data bases evolved from conventional files, which tend to become disorderly very easily. In an enterprise there are typically several data bases as well as many conventional files. One single data base for an enterprise has proved illusory. It is easier to manage data in a data base than in conventional files, but an understanding of computer files is necessary for an understanding of data bases. A data base is a collection of files that cross-reference one another.

2. Computer files are stored as collections of blocked records on tape and disk. The CPU manipulates data in a data area in main memory according to instructions in a program, which is also in main memory. Access methods and input/output processors are used to transfer data between program data area and computer files. Because this is a slow process, execution of many different programs is interleaved and managed by the operating system. The file as processed by a program is called a logical storage file, which is simpler in general than the physical storage file, which is the file that is actually stored in the storage medium. Logical and physical storage files are composed of logical and physical storage blocks, respectively, which contain records.

3. On tape physical storage blocks are separated by large gaps, to enable the tape to start and stop. Significant space may be wasted in these gaps, unless the blocks are considerably larger than the gaps. The time to read a block includes

the time for the tape to accelerate to normal speed. With IBM and related systems, physical storage blocks on a disk track are formatted in count data or count-key data format. These formats allow for the addition of system data to the logical storage blocks to permit easier retrieval. When computing how much space on a disk is needed for a file, these formats must be taken into account. Additional details are in Appendix 1. The tracks of the same radius on a disk pack constitute a cylinder, and all the tracks of a cylinder may be accessed with only a single movement of the read/write head, that is, with a single seek. Even if no seek is required to read a block, there is a rotational delay while the required block moves under the read/write head with the track rotation. The time to access a typical block directly on disk is very high, and is of the order of 0.035 second on average (35 milliseconds), which is about twice as long as the time to read a typical block with commonly used tape systems.

4. Virtual operating systems have evolved from conventional operating systems. With conventional systems, which are now rarely used, to permit many programs to execute concurrently, each program is allocated a portion of main memory or an operating system partition, and control is switched between the partitions by the operating system to keep the CPU busy in the face of delays caused by partitions waiting for input/output of data. To enable more and very large programs to execute, in a virtual system a partition is divided into pages and resides on disk as external page storage, and only a few pages at a time are brought into main memory for execution. Virtual systems are otherwise the same as conventional systems, and for many purposes it is convenient to forget about the underlying paging.

5. Files and data bases may be processed in either batch or on-line mode; with batch processing, updates are regularly accumulated over a daily, weekly, or other period before being applied to a file or data base as a batch. With on-line processing any of a large number of persons at different terminals enter updates as they become available. In commerce a virtual (batch) operating system is used for both batch and on-line processing; however, with on-line processing, a single operating system partition (an on-line partition) is often used together with a teleprocessing monitor to manage the terminals and on-line updating and re-trieval programs. Time-sharing or interactive operating systems use large numbers of partitions to permit large numbers of users at terminals to execute their programs concurrently and interactively.

QUESTIONS

1. A general definition of management is: *The creation and maintenance of useful and productive order.* Make use of this definition and the key words creation, maintenance, useful (or utility), productive (or productivity), and order, to discuss the management of the following:
   (a) A nuclear power plant
   (b) Police records
   (c) A commercial forest

     (d) Hospital records

     (e) A small manufacturer of bicycles

     (f) A small bank (with a single branch)

     (g) A city transit system

     (h) The accounts of a medium-sized manufacturer

     (i) A local airline

2. In a large organization an education department keeps a computer file on all employees for purposes of education. The personnel department also keeps a computer file in which the skills of employees are recorded. Suggest some ways in which the files could become increasingly disorderly in the course of time.

3. Contrast a computer file with a file on paper.

4. If a computer data base is a collection of computer files that cross-reference one another to avoid duplication of data, discuss the management of a data base constructed from files on paper.

5. Use the discussion from Question 4 to explain what a data base is to a hypothetical manager of a business enterprise who does not understand computers.

6. When data in a computer file on disk or tape is being manipulated by a program run on a large computer, discuss the role of the CPU, the processing program, the program data area, and the input/output processors.

7. Explain how a multiprogramming operating system enables many different file processing programs to execute concurrently.

8. Explain to a hypothetical manager who does not understand computers just what is meant by the statement: Program X computes a 5 percent salary increase for every employee described in file A.

9. Explain the difference between an access method and an input/output processor or channel program.

10. Describe an assembly plant operation that is analogous to a multiprogramming operating system. The plant should have several assembly lines, a loading/unloading ramp that can handle container traffic, and it should be served by distant warehouses, both for components used in the assembly lines and for finished products.

11. Explain the relationship between a (transmitted) data block and a buffer. Give also an analogy in terms of a container and a loading/unloading ramp.

12. Explain the following terms:

     (a) Physical storage block

     (b) Logical storage block

     (c) Logical storage file

     (d) Physical storage file

     (Note that texts not dealing with data bases omit the term *storage*, and refer only to logical and physical files. When we bring data bases into the picture, we must include the term storage, because, as will be explained in Chapter 4, we must also deal with other kinds of files.)

13. In a logical storage file the records are each 80 bytes or characters long. If the blocking factor is 25, what is the length of a logical storage block?

14. Are logical and physical storage block lengths the same when a magnetic tape is the storage medium?
15. Define an IBM dataset.
16. Why is a large interblock gap needed with tapes?
17. A 1600-bpi tape contains 80-byte fixed length records with a blocking factor of 10. If we include the interblock gap, how much space in bytes is taken up by each block on the tape? 17.60
18. If there were no interblock gaps, in theory how many bytes of data could a standard 1600-bpi tape hold? (This is sometimes called the *nominal tape capacity*.) The correct answer is 46,080,000.
19. If a logical storage block is 3040 bytes long, how many can be stored on a standard 1600-bpi tape?
20. On a 1600-bpi tape the records are fixed length and 154 bytes long. If the blocking factor is 10, how many records can be stored on the tape? 184.3
21. A standard 2400-foot reel of 1600-bpi tape contains storage blocks that are 2040 bytes long, and the tape is full. If the blocking factor is 10, what must it be changed to in order for the data to just fill a previously damaged reel of 1600-bpi tape that is now only 2000 feet long?
22. On a 1600-bpi tape we have 20,000 records, each 152 bytes long and blocked with a blocking factor of 20. What percentage of the 2400-foot reel is still available for use?
23. If a tape contains 5000 blocks, and the time required to read a block is 0.02 second (20 milliseconds), and a block is read on average every quarter second, how long will it take to read the 5000 blocks?
24. If a 1600-bpi tape is read at a rate of 100 inches per second, how long will it take to read a block 4000 bytes long? (Remember to include the time to start the tape; see page 15.)
25. Explain the cylinder concept as used with disk storage media.
26. If we include the space taken up by gaps and system data (see Figures 1.6a and 1.13), how much space in bytes is required to hold a 3000-byte logical storage block in count-data format on a track of an IBM 3350 disk? 3185
27. If there were no gaps or system data, how many bytes could a track of an IBM 3350 disk hold? (This quantity is the nominal track capacity.) 19,254
28. What is the largest logical storage block (see Figure 1.6a) in bytes that can be stored on a track of an IBM 3350 disk in count-data format? (This quantity is the maximum track capacity.) 19269
29. If logical storage blocks, each equal in size to the maximum track capacity, are stored in count-data format and fill a cylinder of an IBM 3350 disk, how much data in bytes is stored? (This quantity is the maximum cylinder capacity.) 577,070
30. If a logical storage block is 2500 bytes, how many can be stored in count-data format on a single track of an IBM 3350 disk? How many on a cylinder?
31. What is the size of the smallest logical storage block, which, when stored in count-data format, will require the allocation of a complete track? 9443
32. If we include the space taken up by gaps and system data (see Figures 1.6a and 1.14), how much space in bytes is required to hold a 3000-byte logical 3,297

storage block in count-key data format on an IBM 3350 disk track, assuming that the records have a key that is 15 bytes long?

33. What is the largest logical storage block (see Figure 1.6a) in bytes that can be stored in count-key data format on an IBM 3350 disk track, if the records have a key length of 12 bytes?

34. What is the size of the smallest logical storage block with 15-byte record keys, which, when the block is stored in count-key data format on an IBM 3350 disk track, will require the allocation of a complete track?

35. It is proposed to store 100-byte records, each with a 10-byte key on an IBM 3350 disk, using a blocking factor of 30. How many records can a cylinder hold if:
(a) The data is stored in count-data format.
(b) The data is stored in count-key data format.

36. Explain the concepts of seek time, rotational delay, and the time to directly transmit data as they apply to disk storage media.

37. Suppose a file of blocked records on a disk is being processed sequentially. Why is it that there is a rotational delay before each block can be transmitted?

38. A sequential file (in count-data format) on an IBM 3350 disk has 2000-byte logical storage records. How much time is required to read a block?

39. A direct access file in count-key data format contains 3000-byte storage blocks, and 8-byte keys, and is stored on an IBM 3350 disk. What is the time required to directly access a record?

40. Repeat Questions 26 to 36 and 38 and 39 for the case of an IBM 3380 disk. (There is an increased degree of complexity with calculations for this disk, and readers should not attempt the questions without a thorough study of Appendix 1. These questions are included for the sake of completeness only, as it is expected that the IBM 3380 disk will become widely used. No new principles are involved, however.)

41. Explain the concepts of (a) demand paging, (b) external page storage.

42. Explain the benefits of a virtual operating system.

43. What is the essential difference between a virtual and conventional multiprogramming operating system?

44. Explain the concept of a memory partition as it applies to:
(a) A conventional multiprogramming operating system
(b) A virtual operating system

45. Explain the following concepts: (a) batch processing, (b) batch operating system, (c) on-line processing, (d) on-line partition, (e) time-sharing or interactive operating system, (f) teleprocessing monitor.

REFERENCES

1. Bohl, M., 1981. *Introduction to IBM Direct Access Storage Devices*. SRA, Palo Alto, Calif.

2. Bradley, J., 1982. *File and Data Base Techniques*. Holt, Rinehart & Winston, New York.

3. Madnick, S. E., and J. J. Donovan, 1974. *Operating Systems*. McGraw-Hill, New York.

4. Martin, J., 1981. *An End-User's Guide to Data Base*. Prentice-Hall, Englewood Cliffs, N.J.

5. Weldon, J., 1981. *Data Base Administration*. Plenum Press, New York.

2

Conventional Storage Files

Business data for computer processing is stored either in conventional storage files or in data bases. There has been a marked trend toward the use of data bases in the past 15 years, but it is probably true to say that most business data is still stored in conventional storage files, so that such files are worth studying in their own right. However, a *storage data base* is a collection of *storage files* that cross-reference one another, so that a knowledge of conventional *storage files* is essential for an understanding of data bases. Furthermore, conventional storage files are used as auxiliary storage files alongside data bases, for such purposes as data base loading, unloading, backup, and log-files.

It should therefore be clear that a review of the essentials of conventional storage file processing is a prerequisite for a study of data bases. There are three main types of conventional storage files, namely, sequential files, hash files, and indexed-sequential files, and we begin with a brief summary of each file type.

Sequential files. Records of a *sequential* file are physically stored in ascending or descending *primary key* order. (A *primary key field* contains a value that uniquely identifies a record.) Records can be retrieved only in sequential order. Thus if the file had 20,000 records, retrieving the 10,000th record would require the reading of 10,000 records. A sequential file may be on tape or disk.

Hash files. Records are not stored in ascending or descending primary key order. Each record is assigned to disk storage at a *disk address* that is obtained from applying a standard calculating procedure (called a *hashing routine*) to the primary key. When a hash file has been loaded, a record may be retrieved by applying the hashing routine to the primary key and obtaining the disk address; records may thus be retrieved directly, without significant retrieval of other records. Because the hashing routine scatters the records over the disk storage space in a disorganized manner, records in a hash file cannot easily be retrieved in ascending or descending primary key order.

Indexed-sequential files. Records are stored on disk in ascending primary key order. Records are written out cylinder by cylinder, and as the records are written out, the access method creates an index using the primary keys of the records. The index relates primary key values to record disk addresses, so that a record may be directly retrieved by presenting its primary key. Because the records are stored in ascending primary key order, they may be processed in sequential order as well, as if they formed a disk sequential file. Because of the time required to access and search the index, direct access to an indexed-sequential file is much slower than with a hash file.

Beginning with sequential files, we now describe these file types in more detail.

2.1 SEQUENTIAL FILES

Sequential files, or more precisely, sequential storage files, are probably the most common type of storage file; they were the first type of computer file to be used in the early days of computing. In those days, in the late 1950s, sequential files were stored almost exclusively on tape. Today they are also commonly stored on disk.

A sequential file consists of blocked records, where a record is composed of data items or *fields* that describe some entity of the real world, such as a customer, an account, or an inventory item. As mentioned in the previous chapter, a field (or group of fields) is used to uniquely identify a record, and thus the entity described, and is called the primary key field.

In a sequential tape file the records are blocked as described in Chapter 1 and are usually stored in ascending (or descending) primary key sequence. With a sequential disk file, records are written out cylinder by cylinder in ascending or descending primary key sequence. With IBM sequential disk files the data is stored on a track in count-data format.

Creation of sequential storage files

Large files are almost always created by batch processing. Typically, the source data is keyed onto cards, tape, or disk using an off-line facility, that is, a work-station not under the control of the CPU of the computer. The resulting source file is then placed on a card-reader, tape drive, or disk drive for computer processing. Source records are then read in one by one, processed, and then written out on tape or disk. The processing can be minimal, or it can be quite complex, involving editing or the checking of the validity of the data against data stored in other files. The newly created file can be a *master file,* in which case it contains data of lasting importance and likely to be frequently updated. Examples are files containing personnel records, accounts receivable records, stock trading records, and so on. The newly created file may also be a smaller *transaction file,* which will be used to update a master file. Examples are files containing new employee records, cash receipts, latest stock trading records, and so on.

Computer programs for processing business data are usually written in either COBOL or PL/1. COBOL is most commonly used, but the use of PL/1 is increasing. In this book we use COBOL, but our coverage will be in the form of an overview aimed at placing file and data base processing in perspective. Readers interested in complete programming details are advised to consult a text on COBOL programming.

Logical and physical storage files in COBOL

As is well known, a COBOL program has four *divisions,* namely, the IDENTIFICATION, ENVIRONMENT, DATA, and PROCEDURE divisions; in addition certain *command language* specifications usually accompany the program when it is submitted for execution. Generally speaking, the logical storage files and records are specified in the ENVIRONMENT and DATA divisions, while the physical storage file is specified in the operating system command language specifications. The command language specifications enable the operating system to construct the access methods and channel programs for processing the files. Such command language specifications can be complex, especially with operating systems that are batch processing-oriented, such as IBM's OS/MVS. Under OS/MVS the command language is called *job control language* (JCL), and for every file used in a COBOL program there has to be JCL specification. Under IBM, a physical storage file is called a *dataset,* and the JCL specification of a dataset is called a *dataset definition (DD) statement.* However, under VM/CMS, a virtual IBM operating system designed for interactive processing, the command language (known as Cambridge Monitor System or CMS) is much easier to use. Because of their complexity, we largely avoid command languages in this book, but readers must be aware of their existence and how they fit into the overall scheme of things.

Master file

We will suppose for the sake of example that an investment firm is setting up a sequential master file in which each record contains the weekly trading for the stock of a corporation listed on a leading stock exchange. Some records (for Allied Chemical, American Memories, Consolidated Computer, and Diverse Industries) are shown in Figure 2.1. There are 100 records for each stock, giving trading data for week 0, week 1, week 2, and so on, until week 99. A record for week 0 gives the trading data for the week just ended, and that for week 99 gives the trading data for 99 weeks ago. Thus the file contains about a 2-year trading history for each stock.

From left to right in the table, the fields give the name of the stock, the

CO-WEEK					
CO	WEEK	PE	VOL	PRICE	CHGE
ALLDCHEM	00	13.30	560	66.50	-0.50
ALLDCHEM	01	13.40	1200	67.00	+0.25
.	.		.	.	
.	.		.	.	
ALLDCHEM	98	13.81	3200	55.25	0.00
ALLDCHEM	99	13.81	480	55.25	-0.125
AMMEM	00	15.00	2500	15.00	-0.75
AMMEM	01	15.75	1550	15.75	-0.25
.	.		.	.	
.	.		.	.	
AMMEM	98	12.33	1400	18.50	+0.25
AMMEM	99	12.17	890	18.25	+0.25
CONCOMP	00	14.41	3100	86.50	+0.25
CONCOMP	01	14.37	2900	86.25	+0.25
.	.		.	.	
.	.		.	.	
CONCOMP	98	15.55	2950	77.75	-0.25
CONCOMP	99	15.65	2840	78.25	+0.125
DIVIND	00	15.00	930	22.50	-0.50
.	.		.	.	
.	.		.	.	
.	.		.	.	

FIGURE 2.1 The contents of the logical storage file STOCK. Each record gives a summary of the trading in a given stock for a given week. VOL gives the volume of shares traded in hundreds. PE gives the price/earnings ratio for the stock in dollars per share. Week 00 is the current week, week 01 is the previous week, and so on for the past 100 weeks.

number of the week, the price of the stock per dollar of corporate earnings (price/earnings ratio), the volume of weekly trading (in 100s of shares), and the price per share in dollars at the weekly close of trading. As we will see later, each record will take up 30 *characters* or *bytes* of storage. If we assume 1000 corporations listed on the exchange, the file will contain 1000*100 records, that is, 100,000 records at 30 bytes per record. Thus the total size of the file would be about 3 million bytes; this amount of data is far too large to fit into main memory of a computer and must be stored on tape or disk. We will use the logical file name **STOCK** for the file. (There is an alternative design for **STOCK** that would save space: The 100 weeks of trading data for each company could form a single storage record.)

Loading procedure

The logical file **STOCK** is to be stored on disk and loaded from data on a tape file with the logical file name **SOURCE** (see Figure 2.2). We can imagine that the weekly stock trading records have first been punched onto cards and then copied

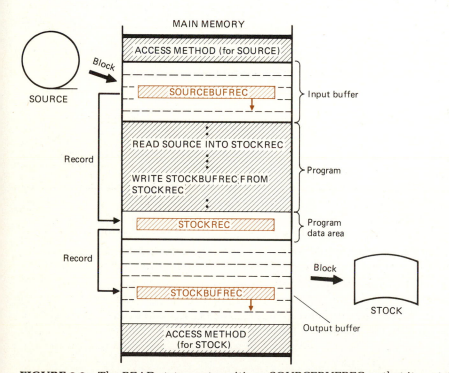

FIGURE 2.2 The READ statement positions SOURCEBUFREC so that it contains the next (logical) record in the buffer and delivers that record to STOCKREC; had no unprocessed records been left in the buffer, the access method would first have caused a new block to have been delivered from SOURCE to the buffer. The WRITE statement moves the record in STOCKREC to the next empty position in the output buffer, which will be the buffer record variable STOCKBUFREC. When the output buffer is full, the access method moves it to the file STOCK.

onto tape, or entered directly onto tape using off-line equipment. Either way, we assume that all necessary validation checking of the data has been carried out and that the data in SOURCE is valid. It now remains to copy the contents of SOURCE into STOCK. In general, loading a sequential file is merely a copying operation, although the necessary program can become quite complex if extensive validation checking must be carried out during the loading process.

Data is read from SOURCE into a main memory buffer, a block at a time. A structure variable SOURCEBUFREC has a mobile location in the buffer and always contains the record being processed. Execution of a COBOL READ statement causes SOURCEBUFREC to move to the next record location in the input buffer and the new contents of SOURCEBUFREC to be copied into the program data area structure variable STOCKREC. A further structure variable STOCKBUFREC has a mobile location in the output buffer. When a WRITE command is executed in the COBOL program, the record in STOCKREC is copied into STOCKBUFREC, which has just moved to the next empty record location in the output buffer. When the output buffer is full, the contents are transmitted to the file STOCK by the access method as described in Chapter 1. SOURCE, STOCK, SOURCEBUFREC, STOCKBUFREC, and STOCKREC must be declared in the COBOL program for the processing. The file names SOURCE and STOCK are the file names used in the program and are therefore logical storage file names. Each file also has a physical name recorded physically at the beginning of the physical storage file, but this is used only in the JCL.

Double buffers

In Figure 2.2 we show a single input buffer for blocks from SOURCE and a single output buffer for the file STOCK. In practice at least two input and two output buffers would be used with sequential files (also with indexed-sequential files that are processed sequentially). Such double buffers are assigned automatically by the operating system. Double buffers reduce the time during which an application program is not eligible to execute because it is waiting either for input of a block or output of a block. For example, suppose that two input buffers were being used with SOURCE in Figure 2.2. Execution of the first READ statement would cause the access method to deliver two blocks to the two buffers. Subsequent READ statement executions will cause all the records in one buffer to be moved to the program data area for processing, at which point the access method will pass a request to the operating system for an additional block from SOURCE. However, the application program does not have to wait for this block to be delivered before it can run, because there is a second block in the second buffer. The converse is true with double output buffers. In this way double buffers improve performance.

COBOL specification of the files and records

COBOL file and record specifications are scattered over the INPUT-OUTPUT section of the ENVIRONMENT division, as well as the FILE section of the DATA division, the WORKING-STORAGE section of the DATA division, and the accompanying JCL, assuming an IBM operating system. Figure 2.3 gives an

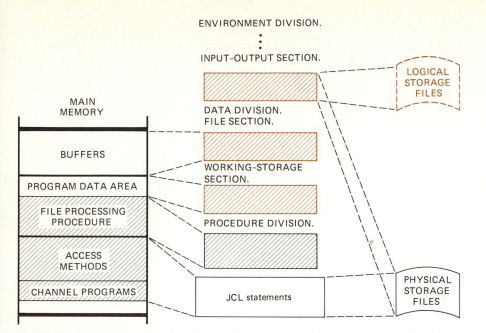

FIGURE 2.3 The specification of logical and physical (storage) files in the different parts of a COBOL program.

overview of file and record specifications in a COBOL program. The logical files are declared and named in the INPUT-OUTPUT section, but there is also a reference to where the physical file is specified. To a large extent the buffer and therefore the transmitted data block are specified in the FILE section; in addition, the buffer record structures (such as SOURCEBUFREC in Figure 2.2) are specified here. In the WORKING-STORAGE section we have specifications for the record structures of the program data area (such as STOCKREC in Figure 2.2). The actual procedure or programming routine is of course in the PROCEDURE division.

In the JCL we have complete specifications of all physical files, and it is largely from these specifications that the operating system builds up the associated data structures that are used to construct the necessary access methods and channel programs. Details of the JCL specifications required may be found in Ref. 2.

The actual method of specifying the logical and physical storage files is shown in Figure 2.4. Here an arbitrary logical file LODGEK is being declared as a sequential file. The ASSIGN TO clause states that LODGEK corresponds to a physical storage file specified in a dataset definition or DD-statement called ANYNAME. In this DD-statement ANYNAME the physical storage file (or *dataset*) called FIZZEK is specified; if no physical storage file called FIZZEK actually exists at the start of processing, a new one is created and FIZZEK is the physical name recorded in the physical storage file. The rest of the DD-statement specifies such details as the disk unit, the disk space required, the blocking factor, and so on.

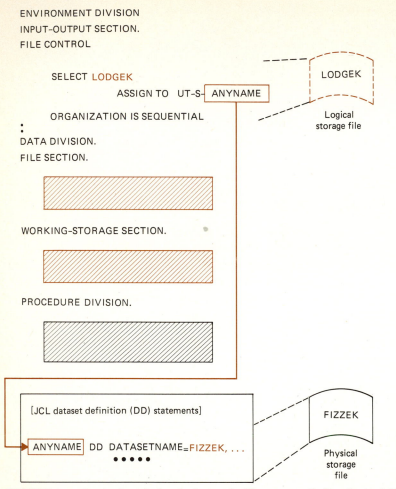

ENVIRONMENT DIVISION

INPUT-OUTPUT SECTION.

FILE CONTROL

    SELECT LODGEK

        ASSIGN TO   UT-S- ANYNAME   LODGEK

      ORGANIZATION IS SEQUENTIAL   Logical
                                   storage file

DATA DIVISION.

FILE SECTION.

WORKING-STORAGE SECTION.

PROCEDURE DIVISION.

[JCL dataset definition (DD) statements]   FIZZEK

ANYNAME DD DATASETNAME=FIZZEK, ...
            • • • • •   Physical
                                  storage
                                  file

FIGURE 2.4 Logical and physical storage file names. Only a logical file name is used in a program and is declared in the FILE-CONTROL section, as with the logical file LODGEK above. The corresponding physical storage file **FIZZEK** is specified in a DD statement that we have arbitrarily named ANYNAME.

Thus in COBOL under IBM we have three names associated with a file: the name the program uses or the logical (storage) file name, the dataset name, and the name of the DD-statement or *ddname*. All this is very confusing; in PL/1 at least, there are only two names, for PL/1 uses the *ddname* as the logical file name. For further details see Ref. 3.

Specifications for the files SOURCE and STOCK

In Figure 2.5 we have COBOL specifications for the structure **SOURCEBUFREC** associated with the logical file **SOURCE** (Figure 2.2). We also have specifications for the structure **STOCKBUFREC** associated with **STOCK**, as well as for the structure **STOCKREC** in the program data area (Figure 2.2). No fields need normally be specified for a buffer structure, just the length of the record it is to hold.

```
DATA DIVISION.
FILE SECTION.
FD SOURCE
  .
  .
  .
01   SOURCEBUFREC PIC X(30).       (Holds record of file SOURCE)
FD STOCK
  .
  .
  .
01   STOCKBUFREC PIC X(30).        (Holds record of file STOCK)


WORKING-STORAGE SECTION.
01   STOCKREC.                     (Holds a record of the file STOCK or SOURCE)
     02   CO-WEEK.
          03 CO PIC X(10).         (Holds up to 10 characters of any kind)
          03 WEEK PIC 99.          (Holds numbers as big as 99)
     02 PE PIC S999V99.            (Holds numbers as big as +999.99)
     02 VOL PIC S99999.            (Holds numbers as big as +99999)
     02 PRICE PIC S999V99.         (Holds numbers as big as +999.99)
```

FIGURE 2.5 Specification of the buffer record variables SOURCEBUFREC and STOCKBUFREC in the FILE section of the DATA division. The program data area (working-storage) record variable STOCKREC is specified in the WORKING-STORAGE section of the DATA division. Adding up the total character capacity of each of the fields of STOCKREC gives 30 characters. STOCKBUFREC and SOURCE-BUFREC are also specified as having space for 30 characters. (Decimal points are not actually stored; otherwise we would need 32 characters.)

The specification of **STOCKREC** includes all the fields of a record from **STOCK**. Fields are specified as numeric or alphanumeric as required. **CO** is clearly alphanumeric, while **VOL** is clearly numeric. The total number of characters (or bytes) specified adds up to 30, and this is the length of a logical storage record from **STOCK**. **STOCKBUFREC** and **SOURCEBUFREC** are also specified as 30-byte records.

COBOL loading procedure for the stock trading file STOCK
The loading procedure is trivially simple and is shown in Figure 2.6a.[1] The file must first be "opened" for input and output of records, respectively; this causes

---

[1]Note that this is not a programming text, and we do not hestitate to use **GOTO** where it will enable a program to be more easily understood. Naturally we structure the brief programming excerpts in this book as clearly as possible given the aims of the book, but readers who are interested in structured COBOL programming and extensive use of the **PERFORM** verb should consult one of the many texts on the subject.

```
PROCEDURE DIVISION.
STARTUP.
      OPEN INPUT SOURCE.
      OPEN OUTPUT STOCK.
*Access method and channel program for inputting SOURCE records now ready.
*Access method and channel program for outputting STOCK records now ready.
MAINLOOP.
      READ SOURCE INTO STOCKREC
                AT END CLOSE SOURCE
                        CLOSE STOCK
                           STOP RUN.
      WRITE STOCKBUFREC FROM STOCKREC.
      GO TO MAINLOOP.
```

(a) Routine for loading the file STOCK from the file SOURCE. The loading is merely a copying operation.

```
Disk and tape files
      READ filename INTO program data-area structure.
      WRITE buffer structure FROM program data-area structure.
Disk files
      REWRITE buffer structure FROM program data-area structure.
```

(b) Summary of file manipulation commands with sequential files.

FIGURE 2.6

the operating system to ready the necessary access methods and channel programs. Then a record from **SOURCE** is read into **STOCKREC** and written back out onto **STOCK** via **STOCKBUFREC**. This process is continued until there are no **SOURCE** records left, when the files are closed and the program stops. Refer also to Figure 2.2.

We note that a **READ** statement moves a record from the buffer record structure variable to the program data area variable. Conversely a **WRITE** statement moves a record from the program data area variable to the output buffer structure variable. Nevertheless, we code (Figure 2.6b):

```
READ SOURCE . . .
```

and not

```
READ SOURCEBUFREC . . .
```

This is one of the central quirks of COBOL. (Note also that the **READ** statement can be used with records on punched cards, and that a **WRITE** statement can be used to have a record printed as a line on a line-printer.)

Sequential file updating

Master sequential files are invariably updated from one or more transaction files using batch processing. Transactions are saved up over a period of time and used for periodic updates. The transaction file is typically a tape file of modest size, but the master file may be either on tape or disk. Updating procedures are usually straightforward, but the exact procedure used depends on whether the master file is on tape or disk.

The updating process

Each transaction record is used to update a group of master records, where the number in the group commonly consists of one record. For each record in the transaction file there must be a record in the master file with the same primary key. If the transaction file is sorted in ascending primary key sequence, then both files may be read in sequentially; a transaction record is first read and then a succession of master records until a key match is encountered. The data in the transaction record is then used to update the corresponding master record. This record is then output, and the next transaction is read in and dealt with in the same way.

Updating on tape

If the master file is on tape, it is not usually possible to make any change to a record on that tape. It is technically possible only to read in records from the tape (and to add on records at the end of the file if there is room). This is caused by the motion of a tape in one direction only during processing, so that once a block of records has been transmitted to the buffer, the tape read/write head is positioned at the start of the next block (in the interblock gap), from which position it can only move forward. Thus as each tape master record is read in by an updating program, it must be written out again onto a new tape master file, whether or not the old master record read in needed to be updated. This is the classical method of master file updating, first introduced in the 1950s. The old master is usually referrred to as the father file, and the new master as the son file. The method is also illustrated in Figure 2.7a. A decided advantage of this method of updating is that it facilitates inexpensive archival storage of earlier generations of master files, a minimum in practice being retention of the grandfather and father files, along with the transaction files. There is thus backup data to help maintain the *integrity* of the data in a current master file. The integrity of the data in a master file (or data base) has to do with ensuring its accuracy and freedom from inconsistency. The disadvantage of this method is that it usually requires three tape drives, which is expensive. Note that a tape file may be opened either for reading forward or backward, although it may only be written forward.

Updating a disk master

Figure 2.7b illustrates the updating of the disk master file **MASTER** by means of the transaction file **TRANS**. During the updating process, all the records of **MASTER** are read sequentially in cylinder/track order (see Figure 1.12), but only

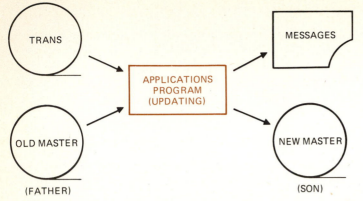

(a) Updating a master file (father) on tape from a transaction file (TRANS). A new tape master file (son) is created in the process.

(b)   Updating a master file on disk (MASTER) from a transaction file (TRANS). All records of the master file are read by the updating program, and records that are altered are rewritten back onto the master file.

FIGURE 2.7

blocks containing updated records are written out. Such a new updated block is overwritten on the original block on a disk track. This is possible because a block on a track continues to rotate under the read/write head while one or more records from a copy of that block are being updated in main memory by the updating program (see Figure 2.8).

The advantages of this method are speed (we avoid a lot of unnecessary output) and the need for only one disk drive. The disadvantage is that the original master is destroyed in the process. However there is a solution to the obvious problem of restoring the master if it is accidently updated incorrectly: We provide for a *backup file*. The records from the master are periodically *dumped* onto a tape file that serves as a *backup file*, and all updates to the master file since a dump are kept on a *log file*. Data bases are almost always kept on disk, and since a data base ultimately consists of storage files, backup and log files are also needed with data bases.

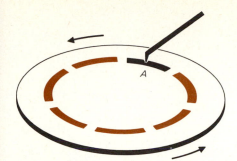

FIGURE 2.8 Illustrates how a record of a disk file may be updated during sequential processing. Each block is read in turn, and in between the reading of blocks the disk may rotate many times. If a record of a block that has been read (block A) is updated, then a REWRITE statement issued by the updating program will cause the new updated block to be rewritten on top of the old block A. In order to carry out the rewriting, the disk controller simply waits until block A is once more under the read/write head. This is not possible with tape storage.

It is only possible to update a disk sequential file without creating a new sequential file, if no insertions are involved. With insertions we have the same difficulty as with the tape file, and a new master must be written out. However, with current large-capacity disks, it is often possible to have the father and son file on the same disk, as well as the transaction file. Thus it is possible to do a great deal of sequential file processing with one disk drive, while with tape processing we need a minimum configuration of three tape drives.

Updating the stock trading file STOCK
The stock trading file **STOCK** in Figure 2.1 would have to be updated weekly from a file such as **TRANS** shown in Figure 2.9. A **TRANS** record contains the latest weekly trading summary for a stock listed in **STOCK**. The updating is simple in principle but is probably more complex than is the case with many business files. This minor complexity is caused by having to maintain in **STOCK** the latest 100 weekly summaries of trading in each stock.

If we examine the updating shown in Figure 2.9 for a typical stock such as American Memories, the American Memories **TRANS** record becomes the American Memories **STOCK** record for week 0, while the American Memories **STOCK** record for week 99 is eliminated. The week number for the other 99 original American Memories records is also increased by 1. Thus if there are 1000 records in **TRANS** (the number of listings on the exchange), there should be 100,000 in **STOCK**; during the updating, 1000 **STOCK** records will be deleted, 99,000 records will be updated, and 1000 new records will be inserted into **STOCK**. Hence all records in **STOCK** are affected by the updating.

Updating routine for STOCK
The COBOL updating routine is shown in Figure 2.10b, while the record structures used in the program are listed in Figure 2.10a; it may be assumed that **MAINSTOCKREC** and **AUXSTOCKREC** have the field declarations shown ear-

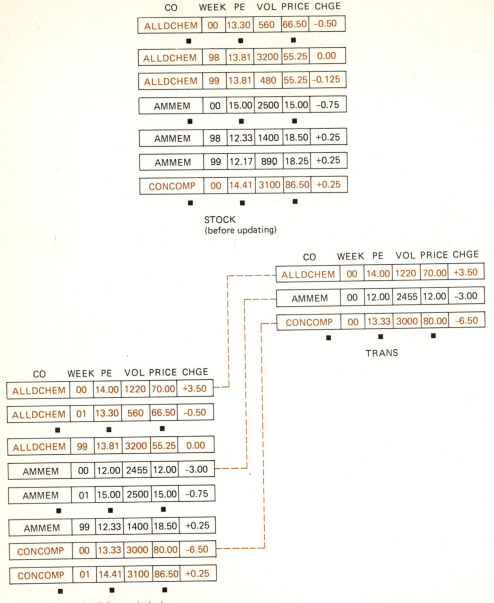

FIGURE 2.9 Updating the master file STOCK with the latest weekly trades in the transaction file TRANS.

lier for **STOCKREC** in Figure 2.5. We need the two program data area structures **MAINSTOCKREC** and **AUXSTOCKREC**, since the updating consists of removing a record from **STOCK** and replacing it with another; the record removed is not discarded, however, except in the case of a record for week 99, and a removed record is used to replace the next record removed. Thus we first read a **TRANS**

Logical file	Buffer record	Program data-area record or records
TRANS	TRANSBUFREC (not needed)	MAINSTOCKREC
STOCK	STOCKBUFREC	MAINSTOCKREC, AUXSTOCKREC

(a) File and record names.

```
PROCEDURE DIVISION.
STARTUP.
     OPEN INPUT TRANS.
     OPEN I-O STOCK.
MAINLOOP.
*In each execution of this loop a TRANS record is placed in STOCK.
     READ TRANS INTO MAINSTOCKREC
              AT END CLOSE TRANS, CLOSE STOCK, STOP RUN.
     READ STOCK INTO AUXSTOCKREC.
     REWRITE STOCKBUFREC FROM MAINSTOCKREC.
     COMPUTE COUNTER = 1.
     PERFORM UNTIL COUNTER = 100
              MOVE AUXSTOCKREC TO MAINSTOCKREC
              COMPUTE WEEK = COUNTER.
              READ STOCK INTO AUXSTOCKREC
              REWRITE STOCKBUFREC FROM MAINSTOCKREC
              COMPUTE COUNTER = COUNTER + 1
     END-PERFORM.
     GO TO MAINLOOP.
```

(b) Updating procedure; every record in STOCK is affected.

FIGURE 2.10 Updating of STOCK from the file TRANS (see Figure 2.9 as well).

record into MAINSTOCKREC, and then a STOCK record (old week 0) into AUXSTOCKREC. We then use a REWRITE statement to move the TRANS record in MAINSTOCKREC to the place in STOCK left vacant by the STOCK record (old week 0) now in AUXSTOCKREC. The record in AUXSTOCKREC is then moved to MAINSTOCKREC and its WEEK field value changed to 1. A further REWRITE statement moves this record (old week 0, new week 1) into the position in STOCK occupied by the record for old week 1, but not before this record for old week 1 has been safely moved to AUXSTOCKREC by another READ statement. The new record in AUXSTOCKREC is then moved to MAINSTOCKREC and becomes the record for new week 2, and so on.

We should note that before processing can begin, the file **TRANS** should be opened for input of records, while **STOCK** is opened for input/output (I/O) of records. Only a file on a disk can be opened for input/output. We should also note that the updating routine in Figure 2.10*b* is the essential core only; the routine does not take care of such eventualities as no trading in a stock, a stock split, or even a change of corporate name. Inclusion of such extensions would be at odds with the purpose of this book, which is the illustration (in concrete terms) of the utility of using data bases and associated files in business. We will in all cases be satisfied with the essential core.

Impact of sequential file processing on management

Batch processing of sequential files is a relatively efficient process, even though it usually means that every record must be read. From the point of view of middle and top management this means that sequential files are suitable for generating a wide variety of reports on a regular basis. Programs for the generation of these reports usually take some time to develop so that, for example, a manager in our investment firm could not phone the data processing department with a request for regular reports giving 3-week extrapolations of stock prices based on the data in the file **STOCK** and expect to have the first report in time for the start of trading the following Monday.

Nevertheless, managers can obtain many very useful reports on a regular basis if they are clear on what they require, are willing to invest a little time to document their requirements, and work closely with the data processing department while the required report program package is being developed. The initiative should not be left to the data processing department; the result may well be the all too common voluminous computer printouts that nobody has the time to decipher. Even worse, higher level management all too often "arranges" for the generation of reports for the "benefit" of their subordinates; the subordinates, not wishing to offend their superiors, quietly consign the reports to the wastebasket.

Reports generated from the file STOCK

Many useful reports could be generated from the sequential file **STOCK** on a regular basis. A few examples are:

1. Names of companies whose price has increased or decreased by more than 25 percent in the past 3 weeks
2. Calculation of a weighted moving average for each stock (a *weighted* moving average places greater emphasis on the most recent price; see Ref. 4)
3. Extrapolations of the prices of selected stocks such as those in item 1
4. Selection of companies for which the trading volume V times the price change P, that is, $V \times P$, is greater than $500,000 (indicating strong buying) or less than $500,000 (indicating strong selling)

The file **STOCK** is typical of many used in business that involve a time series of either prices or sales volumes or both. For example, most production and

```
PROCEDURE DIVISION.
STARTUP.
     OPEN INPUT STOCK.
MAINLOOP.
*In each execution of MAINLOOP, the 100 records for each stock are read in.
     READ STOCK INTO STOCKREC, AT END CLOSE STOCK, STOP RUN.
     MOVE PRICE IN STOCKREC TO LATESTPRICE
     READ STOCK INTO STOCKREC.
     READ STOCK INTO STOCKREC.
*STOCKREC now holds PRICE value for week 02.
     COMPUTE CHANGE = (LATESTPRICE - PRICE) * 100.0 / PRICE.
     IF CHANGE > 25.0 THEN
               DISPLAY CO, "INCREASED", CHANGE, "PERCENT".
     IF CHANGE < -25.0 THEN
          DISPLAY CO, "DECREASED", CHANGE, "PERCENT".
*Now we cruise past the remaining 97 records for that stock.
     PERFORM UNTIL WEEK = 99
               READ STOCK INTO STOCKREC
     END-PERFORM.
     GO TO MAINLOOP.
```

FIGURE 2.11 Core COBOL excerpt for generating the names of companies whose stock price has increased or decreased by more than 25 percent in the past 3 weeks. STOCKREC is the program data area structure variable; CHANGE and LATEST-PRICE are numeric variables declared in the WORKING-STORAGE section.

marketing managers need a monthly or quarterly prediction of sales volumes for each product being marketed. For products that are price sensitive to market forces, for example, precious metals, oil, or other commodities, price predictions will also be needed.

A COBOL procedure excerpt for generating the report in item 1 above is illustrated in Figure 2.11; it is of course merely the core of the procedure. In practice such a procedure would have to be able to handle odd situations, such as stocks not traded and stock splits. Armed with such a report every Monday morning, our investment manager would be better able to select stocks for further analysis.

2.2 INDEXED-SEQUENTIAL FILES

The outstanding problem with sequential files is that the records always have to be accessed sequentially. Thus, to access a record with a given key value, all the preceding records in the file have to be accessed first. In an extreme case, if a sequential file had 100,000 records and we needed to update 10 of them, then we would have to read an average of 10,000 records for each record being updated. The solution to the problem is direct access to a record on presentation of a primary key value, and this is possible with certain disk file organizations.

With both count-data and count-key data formatted storage files in IBM systems (Chapter 1), there is a unique number associated with each block on a track. This number is in the count subblock of the block (see Figure 1.13) and may be read by the disk controller under channel program control. This permits the system to directly retrieve a block of data from a disk and place it in a buffer. The mechanism is straightforward. The disk controller first moves the read/write arms of the disk to the correct cylinder and then selects the correct read/write arm—and thus the correct track. Next it examines the contents of each count subblock on the track until the desired block is reached and finally transmits the data subblock of this storage block to the buffer. Thus the *physical address* of a block on a disk is made up of a cylinder number, a track number, and a block number, and given such an address the computer system can access the block.

However, users normally wish to retrieve a record on the basis of the value of the primary key field of the record, and certainly not on the basis of a disk address. Thus when the access method is requested to deliver a record with a given key value, there has to be a way for it to obtain the address of the block containing the record from the value of the record key. There are two main ways in which this may be done. One of them involves the creation of an index for the file. Sequential files with such an index are called *indexed-sequential files*; they will be examined in this section. The other method of direct access involves the use of a hashing routine, and we shall study it later.

Basic ideas

Indexed-sequential files are simple in principle and easy to manipulate in COBOL or PL/1 by means of **READ**, **WRITE**, and **REWRITE** commands. Essentially an indexed-sequential *logical* storage file is the same as a sequential *logical* storage file on disk, but with an associated index. (We recall from Chapter 1 that a *logical* storage file is the simplified file as viewed by a programmer and manipulated by PL/1 or COBOL commands, while the *physical* storage file is the physical file as it is formatted on disk or tape.) Because an indexed-sequential file has its records stored in ascending primary key order, it may be processed sequentially, like a normal sequential file; but because it also has an index, a record can be directly accessed by means of a COBOL **READ** command when the record's primary key is made available to the system. (Note that an IBM disk sequential file is physically stored in count-data format, as we saw in Section 2.1, whereas an IBM indexed-sequential file is stored in count-key data format; the reason for count-key data format will become apparent shortly.)

Not everything about indexed-sequential files is simple however. Unfortunately, the operating system command language statements (such as IBM JCL statements) needed to specify the physical storage file (or dataset) can be quite complex, so that such files are often set up with the aid of systems programmers who have mastered the necessary details. Often there are several datasets to be set up for a single logical storage file (one for the index, one for the sequential file, and one for overflow records that cannot be inserted into the sequential file because of lack of space). Each of these three datasets with IBM indexed-sequential files must have a JCL DD-statement; such JCL specifications are beyond the scope of this book. Further information on this topic can be found in Refs. 2 and 3.

Part of the simplicity of manipulating indexed-sequential files is due to the fact that the index of an indexed-sequential file does not have to be manipulated by the application program. From a programming viewpoint, the file is created as if it were a sequential file, and the index is created automatically by the underlying access method.

The simple one-level index

We can get a good idea about indexes as used in indexed-sequential files by looking at the simplest possible index, namely, a one-level index. Such an index for the indexed-sequential version of the file **STOCK** from the previous section is shown in Figure 2.12*a*.

As far as the actual records of the file **STOCK** are concerned, we have shown them as though they formed a sequential file ordered in ascending primary key order. However, we show several tracks of a cylinder of the file. Each track contains the trading history of five stocks. Since we have 100 records for each stock, that means 500 records per track. We have arbitrarily decided a blocking factor of 100, so that a block contains all the records for the trading history of a single stock. Actually, with this blocking factor, the 500 records will fill an IBM 3350 disk track.

Each track of the file is shown as forming an *indexed group*, that is, a group of records for which there is an entry in the index. An entry in the index consists of the *key of the last record* in an indexed group, together with the *disk address of the first record* in the same indexed group of records. Thus if we take the first indexed group, that is, the records of track 0, the key of the last record is 'DUNCORP 99', and the address of the first record, that is, the record with key 'ALLDCHEM 00', is cylinder 0, track 0, block 0. This data is placed in the index as the first entry (Figure 2.12*a*). A disk track does not have to form an indexed group, and literally any number of records would do. But a track is fairly convenient and is commonly used.

Now suppose that we wish to retrieve the record describing trading in the stock 'FOODCORP' 78 weeks ago, that is , the record with key 'FOODCORP 78'. The file could be opened for sequential input and each record read in sequence until the record with key 'FOODCORP 78' is encountered. Alternatively, we could open the file for direct input and issue a COBOL READ statement using 'FOODCORP 78' as the key of the required record. In order to obtain this record directly, the access method must first obtain its disk address. It cannot do this exactly by means of the index, but it can come close. First the access method sequentially searches the index, until it comes to an entry with a key value *greater* than the key of the record sought. Referring to Figure 2.12*a*, we see that this entry is for the key 'GENPROD 99'. This means that the required record must be one of those in the indexed group (or track in this case) whose highest key is 'GENPROD 99'. From the index entry the address of the first record of this group is cylinder 0, track 1, block 0. This is as near as the access method can come to the

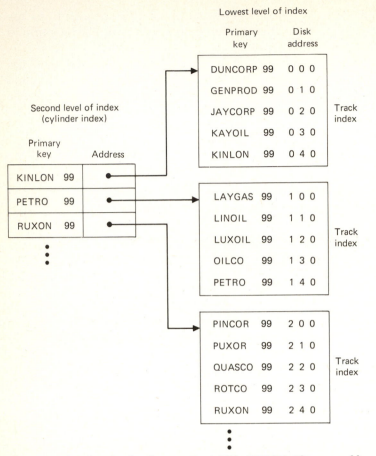

(b) A two-level index for the sequential file STOCK. The second level is an index to the index in Figure 2.12a, shown extended above.

location of the required record using the index—it can locate the indexed group or track containing it. Now it has to search the indexed group (track 1 in this case) for the record.

Via the channel, the access method now causes the controller to search track 1 for the required record. This is where IBM's count-key data format comes in. IBM indexed-sequential files are stored in count-key data format; that is, for every data block on the track there is an associated key subblock that holds the key of the last record in the block (see Figure 1.14). The controller scans track 1, starting with block 0, examining the key subblock of each block in turn. When it encounters the first block whose key subblock holds a value greater than the target key value of 'FOODCORP 78', it transmits that block to the buffer, since it must contain the target record. The access method then extracts the target record from the buffer and transfers it to the program data area.

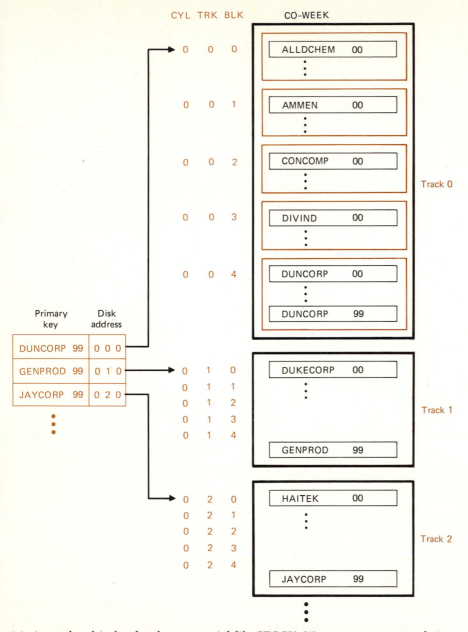

(a) A one-level index for the sequential file STOCK. We assume 100 records in a data block and five blocks on a disk track. There is an index entry for each track. The data in the file is the same as that in Figure 2.1.

FIGURE 2.12

Size of a one-level index

In practice, the number of entries in a one-level index can be quite large, so that it can take a long time to search it sequentially. The time can be significantly reduced if the index has multiple levels. Up to five levels are usually possible, but we will limit ourselves to an examination of a two-level index, as this is suffcient to illustrate the principle. Note that the disk address in an index entry "points" to data located elsewhere, and for this reason such a field containing an address is called a *pointer*. In diagrams the field value is often replaced by an arrow (Figure 2.12*b*).

A two-level index

A two-level index for our file **STOCK** is shown in Figure 2.12*b*. The first level of the index is the same as that shown in Figure 2.12*a*, except that we have grouped together all the entries from tracks on the same cylinder. Each such group of entries is often called a track index. For each track index there is an entry in the second level of the index, and this second level of the index is really an index to the first level. The second level of the index is often called a cylinder index since each entry contains the highest key in a cylinder.

The index is used as follows. Suppose we need the record with key 'REV-CORP 60'. We issue the **READ** statement with key 'REVCORP 60'. The access method sequentially searches the cylinder index until it comes to the entry with key 'RUXON 99'; it then uses the address in this entry to locate the track index whose first entry contains the key 'PINCOR 99'. This track index is then searched until the entry with key 'ROTCO 99' is reached; since the disk address in this entry is cylinder 2, track 3, the contents of track 3 of cylinder 3 are then scanned by the disk controller, and the data block containing 'REVCORP 60' transmitted to the buffer. A three-level index would be searched in a similar manner.

We note that this searching and maintenance of the index is carried out by the file access method and is completely transparent to the program, except for one effect. The lower levels of a large index reside on disk, as well as the sequentially ordered records. Thus to retrieve a record by direct access, two or three accesses must first be made to the index before the required block of records can be accessed. Thus the average number of disk accesses required to retrieve a record by direct access is high, typically between two and four accesses; we recall that a single direct access on a disk takes about 35 milliseconds. Direct access with indexed-sequential files is thus very slow. In contrast, as we shall see later, with hash files, between one and two accesses per record retrieved is easily possible.

It should be clear to the reader that the index of an indexed-sequential file is only slightly more involved than the book index common in most libraries.

Types of indexed-sequential files

There are two main types of indexed-sequential files, and these are distinguished by the way in which insertion of records is handled. A careful study of the file in Figure 2.12*a* shows that there can easily be a severe problem inserting records into the file. As the file stands in Figure 2.12*a* there is simply no room.

Remember an indexed-sequential file is first of all a sequential file, and that means that the records must be maintained in ascending primary key sequence. Thus if we wanted to insert the record with key 'DATACORP 00', we would have to do it between the records 'CONCOMP 99' and 'DIVIND 00' (see Figure 2.12a), where there is plainly no room.

We could perhaps make room by pushing all the records past 'CONCORP 99' down, but if the file is big, and indexed-sequential files usually are, we shall have to move a lot of records, so that we must look for some other method. A solution might be to leave space, that is, empty blocks, at regular intervals, but that method will fail if we have to insert a large clump of records with keys that are close in value, and this does happen in practice.

There are two methods of handling the insertion problem that are widely used:

1. *Separate overflow area technique.* With this technique, the insertion of records in sequential order gives rise to overflow records for which there is no room in the main body of the file. All the records overflowing from a given indexed group are placed in a separate overflow area but are chained together in such a way that the sequential order of the records in the file is preserved.
2. *Splitting the indexed group technique.* With this method, when a record is to be inserted into an indexed group in which there is no room, the indexed group is split in two, and the two indexed groups are chained together to preserve the sequential order of the records in the file.

The separate overflow technique was the first to be introduced and is that used in ISAM (Indexed Sequential Access Method) files, while the splitting technique is that used with VSAM (Virtual Storage Access Method) files. Both ISAM and VSAM files are widely used with the major multiprogramming operating systems from IBM. We will therefore examine ISAM and VSAM in turn. (Note that ISAM is pronounced "eye-sam" and VSAM is pronounced "vee-sam.")

ISAM and the separate overflow area technique

In an ISAM file, a track of records is an indexed group. However, on each cylinder, the first track (track 0) is used for an index (called a track index) to the records of the cylinder (Figure 2.13). For each indexed group or track there is an entry in the track index, and this entry contains the number of the track (the address of the indexed group) and the key of the last record on the track. The last few tracks of each cylinder are normally reserved for records that overflow from the indexed groups of records on what are called the *prime tracks* of the cylinder. When a record cannot be inserted into a prime track, the access method makes room by pushing the last record of the track into the overflow area (see Figure 2.13).

The overflow records from a given track are chained together in the overflow area in ascending record key order so that sequential order is maintained, that is, to each record in the overflow area is attached an address or pointer giving the

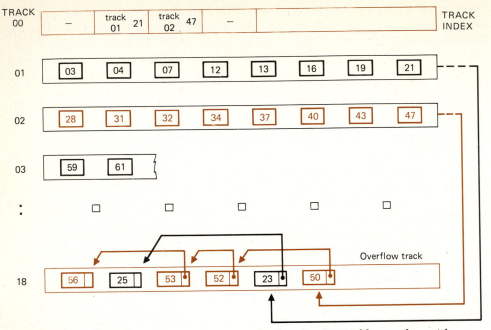

FIGURE 2.13 Some prime data tracks on a cylinder of an ISAM file together with an overflow track. Records inserted on a track may cause records at the end of the track to be placed on the overflow track (track 18), but sequential order is preserved by means of a pointer chain.

exact location in the overflow area of the next record in the file in ascending record key order. Thus the records on the prime data tracks, that is, the records in the indexed groups, are maintained in ascending record key order by virtue of their position, while the records belonging to that track but in the overflow area are maintained in ascending record key order by means of the pointer chain. If a new record with key 20 were inserted into the file in Figure 2.13, the situation would be:

```
TRACK 01:          .....     16              19      20
OVERFLOW TRACK                        25 ←──────────── 23 ←── 21
TRACK 02            28        31              32      ......
```

since the record with key 21 at the end of track 01 is removed and placed at the start of the overflow chain, but after the last record on the overflow track.

In Figure 2.13 there is a pointer from each prime data track to the start of its overflow chain in the overflow area. In reality the pointer is not in the prime data track but in the track index entry for that track (don't forget that a track is an indexed group in an ISAM file) in the index. But this detail does not affect the overall logic of the way the overflow records are maintained, and it is simpler to imagine the pointer as emanating from the prime data track as shown in the diagram.

The disadvantage of this method of handling insertions is the number of accesses required to retrieve an overflow record. Indexed-sequential files are generally slow because of the need to use the index with direct access of a record. But if many of the records are in overflow chains, then each preceding record on the chain must first be accessed, which significantly increases the number of accesses required to retrieve the average record. Thus the performance of an ISAM file needs to be continually monitored, and when too many records have overflowed, it has to read out as a sequential file and reload as a new indexed-sequential file. Just after loading there will not be any records in the overflow area. The frequency of such reorganizations of an ISAM file may be significantly reduced if, on loading, empty space is left at the end of each prime data track. Such empty space permits the access method to move records "up" or "to the right" to accommodate an inserted record. Only when there is no space at the end of a track does the access method relegate the last record on the track to the overflow area following an insertion.

With ISAM we should also note that deleted records are not normally removed from a prime data track. Instead they are marked as deleted by placing the COBOL **HIGH-VALUE** constant in the first character of the record. If a deleted or *dummy record* is the last record on a track, then an insertion does not cause the dummy to be placed in the overflow area, although records are moved to the right. Furthermore, if a dummy record is occupying the space that would otherwise suit a record to be inserted, then that dummy record will be replaced by the inserted record, without any records having to be moved up. Thus the existence of a certain percentage of dummy records or *empty space* on a prime data track will help to keep down the number of records in the overflow area, and the insertion of dummy records when an ISAM file is being loaded is common practice. It is clear that these dummy records are most effective in reducing overflow when placed at the end of a track. Loading programs for achieving this are quite detailed however and beyond the scope of this book (see Ref. 1). Figure 2.14 gives an overview of an ISAM file.

VSAM and the splitting technique

The idea of using empty space to avoid the need for an overflow area is further refined in the VSAM indexed-sequential file organization. But before we look at this powerful method of looking after inserted records, we should point out that even though the "VS" in the acronym VSAM stands for virtual storage, the techniques used have nothing whatever to do with virtual storage or memory as described briefly in Section 1.3. The "VS" is more intended to convey the fact that the access method for maintaining a VSAM file is so large a program that it is to be run under a demand paged or virtual operating system.

We saw that with an ISAM file the basic indexed group of records was the collection of records on a disk track, so that the size of the indexed group depended quite literally on the type of disk being used, since different disk types have different track lengths. With a VSAM file the indexed group may be chosen by the file designer, so that it does not have to be equal to the number of records a track can hold. However, in practice it may well be the same as the track capacity, and it is convenient to think of it in that way. In VSAM jargon, an

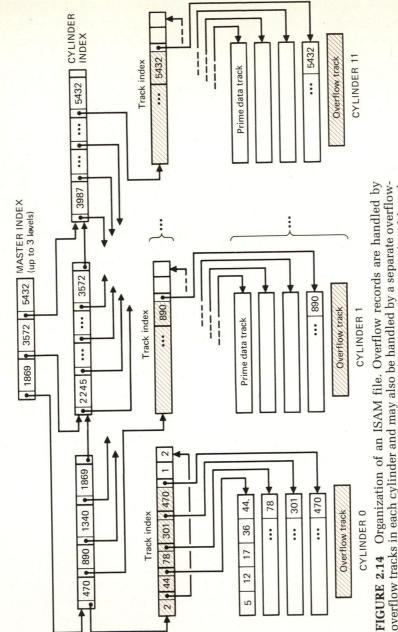

FIGURE 2.14 Organization of an ISAM file. Overflow records are handled by overflow tracks in each cylinder and may also be handled by a separate overflow-record cylinder (not shown). The diagram assumes no overflow records. Although not shown, the track index has an additional component to deal with overflow records. (Reprinted from the author's *File & Data Base Techniques*, Holt, Rinehart & Winston, 1982.)

indexed group is called a *control interval*, or sometimes a *logical track*. In addition, just as tracks on a disk are grouped into cylinders, the control intervals or logical tracks of a VSAM file are grouped into *logical cylinders* or *control areas*.

In Figure 2.15, on the left, we have some control intervals from a control area. When a file is loaded, the record keys are maintained in ascending sequential order as with ISAM, but space for later insertion of records is formatted automatically at the end of each control interval. Furthermore, some of the control intervals in a control area are left empty. Both the amount of empty space per control interval and the number of empty control intervals in a control area must be specified in the Job Control Language statements for the file creation program.

When a record is inserted into the file, if the appropriate control interval is not full, then the records are simply moved up by the access method to make space for the inserted record. Thus, in Figure 2.15, if we insert the record with key 26 into control interval 02 (on the left), the situation following the insertion is in the corresponding control interval on the right. But suppose that we wish to insert a record with key 13 into the file. It clearly should be placed in control interval 01 between the records with keys 11 and 15. However, control interval

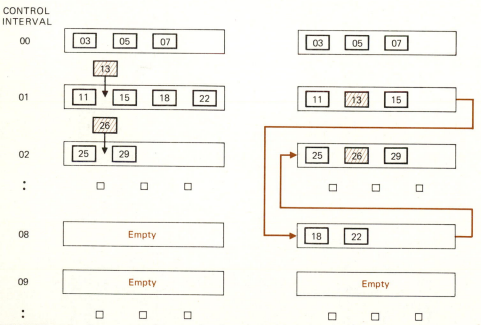

FIGURE 2.15 Some control intervals of a VSAM file before (left) and after (right) insertion of the records with keys 13 and 26. There is space in control interval 02 for record 26, but control interval 01 is split in two in order that record 13 may be inserted. A pointer chain is used to maintain sequential order. Initially empty control intervals are used to facilitate splitting.

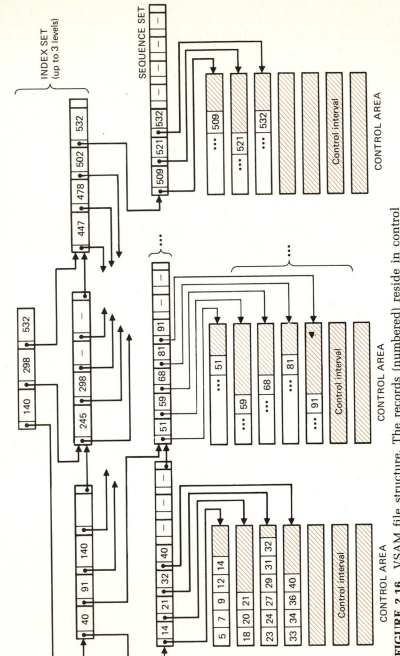

FIGURE 2.16 VSAM file structure. The records (numbered) reside in control intervals, and a group of control intervals constitutes a control area. Shaded parts of control intervals are empty. (Reprinted from the author's *File & Data Base Techniques, Holt, Rinehart & Winston, 1982.*)

01 is full, and in order to accommodate this insertion, the access method undertakes a control interval split. Half the records from control interval 01 are placed in one of the empty control intervals, in the diagram control interval 08, thus leaving room for the record with key 13 to be inserted into control interval 01, as is shown in Figure 2.15 (on the right). Control intervals are chained together to maintain sequential order where necessary. Following the insertion of the record with key 13, the control intervals would be processed sequentially in the order 00, 01, 08, 02, ... Thus the splitting of control intervals where necessary to accommodate insertions is the essential feature of VSAM. Control areas may also be split in a similar manner, if a control area does not have a vacant control area to allow for the splitting of a control interval. Thus a number of empty control areas are usually specified as well when the file is created.

In theory a VSAM file can grow indefinitely by means of the splitting process, not unlike a colony of biological microorganisms. Of course the creation of new control intervals and control areas requires new index entries. In ISAM files, placement of records in an overflow area also requires alterations to the index. However, apart from such detailed differences, the index structures are basically the same with both ISAM and VSAM. An overview of a VSAM file is shown in Figure 2.16.

Disk track and control interval formats with ISAM and VSAM

We recall that a track in an ISAM dataset contains a sequence of storage blocks. Similarly, a VSAM control interval or logical track is made up of a sequence or "train" of physical storage blocks. With ISAM files however, the programmer must specify a block size, either in the program or in the accompanying DD-statement. This is not necessary with VSAM files, for VSAM automatically formats the control intervals into storage blocks of an appropriate size. Furthermore, VSAM keeps control information at the end of each control interval. This control information contains the position and length of each record within the control interval, as well as the amount of free space. Both ISAM and VSAM can handle variable length records. Finally, while we stated in Chapter 1 that the unit of transmission is a data block, VSAM transfers only complete control intervals between buffer and disk storage, although it does so a block at a time.

Creation and batch processing of indexed-sequential files

We have seen that the creation and maintenance of indexes and the handling of insertions are carried on automatically by the underlying access method. In consequence the ANS COBOL statements connected with indexed-sequential files are quite independent of the type of indexed-sequential file being manipulated, that is, they do not reflect whether the file allows insertions by means of an overflow area or by means of a splitting technique. However, under IBM, there are some minor differences between the COBOL used with ISAM files and that used with VSAM files. It must be stressed that these differences are minor, although it is nevertheless unlikely that a program that could manipulate a VSAM file would be able to correctly manipulate the same file of records reloaded as an ISAM file. Here it is worth repeating that this text is not meant as a programming text, and readers who are interested in the details of the difference between ISAM and VSAM COBOL statements should consult Ref. 2. In this book we will outline the creation and manipulation of VSAM files, since the necessary COBOL is closer to the ANS COBOL than is the case with ISAM files. For purposes of illustration and comparison, we will deal with the stock trading file from Figure 2.1.

VSAM file specification in COBOL

As with a sequential file, a VSAM indexed-sequential file is specified in three parts of a COBOL program, namely, in the **INPUT-OUTPUT** section of the **EN-VIRONMENT** division, and in the **FILE** and **WORKING-STORAGE** sections of the **DATA** division (see Figures 2.3 and 2.4). Except for the specification of the logical storage file in the **INPUT-OUTPUT** section (see Figure 2.17), the necessary COBOL specifications are not all that different from the case of sequential files. Referring to Figure 2.17 (and comparing with Figure 2.4), the new features are that we must specify that the file is indexed and that the field **CO-WEEK** will be used as the record key for **STOCK** records. **CO-WEEK** must also be declared as a field of the buffer record structure as shown in Figure 2.18.

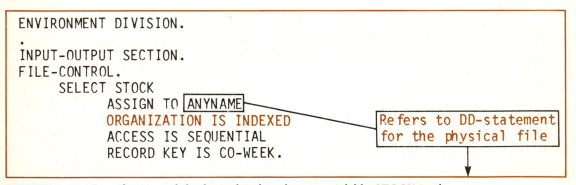

FIGURE 2.17 Specification of the logical indexed sequential file STOCK in the INPUT-OUTPUT section of the ENVIRONMENT division. Compare with the speci-fication for the sequential file STOCK in Figure 2.4. Apart from the specification that the file is INDEXED, we have specified that CO-WEEK is to be used by the access method in the construction of the index. CO-WEEK is therefore the primary key field for the file STOCK and must be fully specified in the FILE SECTION specification of the buffer structure STOCKBUFREC (see Figure 2.18). Note also that the above specification is for sequential access, such as when the file is being created. In a program requiring direct access to STOCK (such as the updating program in Figure 2.19), ACCESS IS RANDOM must replace ACCESS IS SEQUEN-TIAL above.

```
DATA DIVISION.
FILE SECTION.
FD SOURCE
 .
 .
 .
01   SOURCEBUFREC PIC X(30).        (Holds record of file SOURCE)
FD STOCK
 .
 .
 .
01   STOCKBUFREC PIC X(30).         (Holds record of file STOCK)
     02 CO-WEEK.                    (The key)
        03 CO PIC X(10).            (Holds up to 10 characters of any kind)
        03 WEEK PIC 99.             (Holds numbers as big as 99)
     02 PE PIC S999V99.             (Holds numbers as big as +999.99)
     02 VOL PIC S99999.             (Holds numbers as big as +99999)
     02 PRICE PIC S999V99.          (Holds numbers as big as +999.99)

WORKING-STORAGE SECTION.
01   STOCKREC LIKE STOCKBUFREC.     (Holds a record of the file STOCK or SOURCE)
```

FIGURE 2.18 Specification of the buffer records for SOURCE and STOCK, as well as the program data area record structure STOCKREC. CO-WEEK must be specified as a field of the buffer record (STOCKBUFREC) for the file STOCK, since it has been specified as the key in the specification of the logical file (Figure 2.17). The program for loading STOCK from SOURCE is the same as that given in Figure 2.6.

Loading STOCK as an indexed-sequential file

The configuration for loading STOCK as a indexed-sequential file is the same as that used for loading STOCK as a sequential file (see Figure 2.2), and the file is loaded from the sequential tape file SOURCE containing the data shown in Figure 2.1. The procedure core for the loading is also the same as in the sequential file case (see Figure 2.6a); a READ statement transfers a record to STOCK-REC, and a WRITE statement transfers it to the indexed-sequential file STOCK. What is different is that the access method uses the CO-WEEK value in each record transferred to STOCK to construct the index. The COBOL READ and WRITE statements used are therefore those in Figure 2.6b.

Batch updating of the indexed-sequential file STOCK

As with the sequential file version of STOCK, the latest weekly trading data will have to be entered into STOCK every week, an activity most easily carried out by the data processing department as a batch job using sequential processing. The updating routine core will be exactly the same as that used with the sequential version of STOCK (see Figure 2.10). See Figure 2.6b for the READ, WRITE, and REWRITE statements.

Regular report generation from the indexed-sequential file STOCK

By processing the indexed-sequential version of STOCK sequentially, a large variety of reports on the present, past, and possible future behavior of stocks can be generated on a weekly or monthly basis. The file would be processed in much the same way as in the sequential file case; the processing would typically be batch processing carried out by the data processing department. An example is the processing carried out by the program excerpt in Figure 2.11.

Interactive processing of indexed-sequential files

Interactive updating

While major updating of an indexed-sequential file is frequently carried out by conventional batch processing, there is commonly also a need for minor updating that must be carried out at once. As an example, suppose a corporation listed in the file STOCK changes its name. This kind of change does not occur very often, but when it does happen, the file STOCK would need to be updated at once if the file is to remain current. This type of nuisance updating is not something that the data processing department is organized for, and responsibility for it is often best left with the user department. To handle the case of a name change to a stock, the data processing department could provide the user department with a user-friendly interactive program for carrying out the updating.

An example of the core of an interactive program for changing the names of stocks in the indexed-sequential file STOCK is shown in Figure 2.19. The ENVIRONMENT and DATA division specifications in Figures 2.17 and 2.18 apply, except that the FILE CONTROL specification ACCESS IS SEQUENTIAL in Figure 2.17 must be changed to ACCESS IS RANDOM to permit direct (or "random") updating. To prevent unauthorized use, the program is equipped with a password ('BLUE CHIP'). To directly read the record for the trading in 'TEXOIL' 2 weeks ago (for example), we first place the values 'TEXOIL' and 2 in the key field CO-WEEK and then issue a conventional READ statement:

```
MOVE 2 TO WEEK IN STOCKBUFREC, MOVE "TEXOIL" TO CO IN STOCKBUFFREC
READ STOCK INTO STOCKREC
```

If we wanted to delete this record, we would place the key value in CO-WEEK and issue DELETE STOCK, and if we wanted to write out a new record already in the program data area structure STOCKREC, we would simply issue

```
WRITE STOCKBUFREC FROM STOCKREC
```

In the process of executing this instruction, the CO-WEEK value in STOCKREC would be moved to the buffer structure STOCKBUFREC (along with the other field values), so that the system would be able to extract the key in order to place the record in the existing file in sequential order and, if necessary, update the index.

In the program in Figure 2.19 we must use READ, DELETE, and WRITE commands to change a stock name, as requested by a user. Normally to update a field value, it is sufficient to issue a REWRITE command following a READ. However CO is part of the key, and a field that is part of a key cannot be updated,

```
PROCEDURE DIVISION.
STARTUP.
    OPEN I-O STOCK
    DISPLAY "GIVE AUTHORIZATION FOR UPDATE"
    ACCEPT PASSWORD
    IF PASSWORD NOT = "BLUE CHIP"
    THEN DISPLAY "ACCESS DENIED: INCORRECT AUTHORIZATION"
    STOP RUN.
MAINLOOP.
    DISPLAY "GIVE OLD NAME".
    ACCEPT OLDNAME.
    DISPLAY "GIVE NEW NAME".
    ACCEPT NEWNAME.
    COMPUTE COUNT = 0, WRONG-KEY = "FALSE".
    MOVE OLDNAME TO CO IN STOCKBUFREC, MOVE COUNT TO WEEK IN
    STOCKBUFREC.
            READ STOCK INTO STOCKREC
                    INVALID KEY MOVE "TRUE" TO WRONG-KEY.
            IF WRONG-KEY = "TRUE"
                    THEN DISPLAY "OLD STOCK NOT IN FILE. UPDATE NOT
                    CARRIED OUT"
                        COMPUTE COUNT = 100
                    ELSE MOVE NEWNAME TO CO IN STOCKREC, DELETE STOCK
                        WRITE STOCKBUFREC FROM STOCKREC
                        COMPUTE COUNT = COUNT + 1.
    PERFORM UNTIL COUNT = 100
        MOVE OLDNAME TO CO IN STOCKBUFREC, MOVE COUNT TO WEEK IN
        STOCKBUFREC
        READ STOCK INTO STOCKREC
        MOVE NEWNAME TO CO IN STOCKREC, DELETE STOCK
        WRITE STOCKBUFREC FROM STOCKREC
        COMPUTE COUNT = COUNT + 1
    END PERFORM.
    IF WRONG-KEY = "FALSE"
        THEN DISPLAY OLDNAME, "CHANGED TO", NEWNAME, "IN FILE STOCK".
    DISPLAY "FURTHER NAME CHANGES? RESPOND YES OR NO".
    ACCEPT RESPONSE.
    IF RESPONSE = "YES" THEN GO TO MAINLOOP
            ELSE DISPLAY "PROGRAMMED UPDATING OF FILE STOCK TERMINATES"
                STOP RUN.
```

FIGURE 2.19 Interactive program excerpt for changing the names of companies in the file STOCK. This is the core of the updating routine and does not take into account everything that could go wrong. For example, if the trading record for week 4 were missing from a stock whose name was being changed, the program would terminate abruptly leaving the file STOCK in an inconsistent state. For a given name change, 100 records must be deleted and another 100 inserted. For ENVIRONMENT and DATA DIVISION specifications for this procedure, see Figures 2.17 and 2.18. A typical dialogue resulting from this program is shown in Figure 2.20.

```
GIVE AUTHORIZATION FOR UPDATE
BLUE CHIP
GIVE OLD NAME
TEXGAS
GIVE NEW NAME
AMGAS
OLD STOCK NOT IN FILE. UPDATE NOT CARRIED OUT
FURTHER NAME CHANGES? RESPOND YES OR NO.
YES.
GIVE OLD NAME
TEXOIL
GIVE NEW NAME
AMGAS
TEXOIL CHANGED TO AMGAS IN FILE STOCK
FURTHER NAME CHANGES? RESPOND YES OR NO.
NO
PROGRAMMED UPDATING OF FILE STOCK TERMINATES
```

FIGURE 2.20 The dialogue between the computer (color) and the user (black) when the updating program excerpt in Figure 2.19 is executed. The user wishes to change the name of Texas Oil Company ('TEXOIL') to American Gas Company ('AMGAS'), but initially incorrectly enters 'TEXOIL' as 'TEXGAS'. Note that 100 records are deleted and a further 100 inserted as a result of the dialogue.

since this would destroy the sequential order in the file and possibly also the index. If it has to be done, we must read the record, delete it, update the key in the retrieved record, and then write it out as a new record with a **WRITE** statement. This is the procedure followed in the program in Figure 2.19. The procedure is merely an essential core and does not allow for everything that could go wrong. A typical dialogue that ensues when the program is run is shown in Figure 2.20.

Interactive updating in on-line systems

On-line systems are designed to eliminate the batch updating function. In such systems data is entered as it is captured, and the necessary direct access files are updated by direct access. A common example is an on-line order-entry system. On receipt of an order for a company's product, a salesclerk enters an order at a terminal as requested by the order processing system (a large program), which then updates such master files as the finished products inventory file, the accounts receivable file, the sales summary file, and the general ledger. We return to systems of this kind in Chapter 11. But the reader should note that on-line updating is not necessarily always superior to batch updating. For example, it is clear that the most effective method of adding the latest weekly stock trading data to the file **STOCK** is by batch updating. However, with on-line updating, the files are always current.

Interactive report generation from the indexed-sequential file

When small quantities of data are needed from large files at irregular intervals, interactive programs that access a file directly and which are run by the user of

```
PROCEDURE DIVISION.
STARTUP.
    OPEN INPUT STOCK.
    DISPLAY "STOCK TRADING INFORMATION SERVICE IN SESSION".
MAINLOOP.
    DISPLAY "GIVE STOCK NAME".
    ACCEPT CO IN STOCKBUFREC
    DISPLAY "GIVE NUMBER OF PREVIOUS WEEKS TRADING REQUIRED".
    ACCEPT N-OF-WEEKS.
    COMPUTE COUNT = 0, WRONG-KEY = "FALSE".
    MOVE COUNT TO WEEK IN STOCKBUFREC.
    READ STOCK INTO STOCKREC
      INVALID KEY MOVE "TRUE" TO WRONG-KEY.
      IF WRONG-KEY = "TRUE" THEN DISPLAY CO IN STOCKBUFREC,
       "NOT IN FILE STOCK"
      COMPUTE COUNT = N-OF-WEEKS
    ELSE DISPLAY "WEEK      VOLUME      PRICE"
         MOVE PRICE IN STOCKREC TO DOLLAR-PRICE
         DISPLAY WEEK IN STOCKREC, "    ", VOL IN STOCKREC, "  ",
         DOLLAR-PRICE
         COMPUTE COUNT = COUNT + 1.
    PERFORM UNTIL COUNT = N-OF-WEEKS
         MOVE COUNT TO WEEK IN STOCKBUFREC
         READ STOCK INTO STOCKREC
         MOVE PRICE IN STOCKREC TO DOLLAR-PRICE
         DISPLAY WEEK IN STOCKREC, "     ", VOL IN STOCKREC, "  ",
         DOLLAR-PRICE.
         COMPUTE COUNT = COUNT + 1
    END-PERFORM.
    DISPLAY "FURTHER TRADING INFORMATION NEEDED? RESPOND YES OR NO"
    ACCEPT RESPONSE.
    IF RESPONSE = "YES" THEN GO TO MAINLOOP
        ELSE DISPLAY "INFORMATION RETRIEVAL SESSION ENDED"
             STOP RUN.
```

FIGURE 2.21 Interactive program excerpt for retrieving trading records from the indexed-sequential file STOCK. The program will display the trading records for one or more stocks. The number of weeks of trading required and the name of the stock are entered by the user at the terminal. The numeric variable DOLLAR-PRICE is much the same as PRICE except that it will contain a $ symbol and a decimal point, which would not be displayed by DISPLAY PRICE.

the data are a common solution. For example, as a result of study of weekly reports or other data, an investment manager might decide that she should look at the trading history of one or more stocks, such as the stock **KENTECH**. Since retrieving the trading history of stocks would be a common activity among investment managers, an interactive program for this purpose could be made available by the data processing department. An example of the core of such a

```
STOCK TRADING INFORMATION SERVICE IN SESSION
GIVE STOCK NAME
KENTECH
GIVE NUMBER OF PREVIOUS WEEKS TRADING REQUIRED
20
WEEK      VOLUME      PRICE
00        0790        $54.25
01        1256        $54.00
  .         .           .
  .         .           .
  .         .           .
19        0300        $44.75
FURTHER TRADING INFORMATION NEEDED? RESPOND YES OR NO
YES
GIVE STOCK NAME
KENTEK
GIVE NUMBER OF PREVIOUS WEEKS TRADING REQUIRED
30
KENTEK NOT IN FILE STOCK
FURTHER TRADING INFORMATION NEEDED? RESPOND YES OR NO.
YES
GIVE STOCK NAME
KENTECH
GIVE NUMBER OF PREVIOUS WEEKS TRADING REQUIRED
30
WEEK      VOLUME      PRICE
00        0680        $54.25
  .         .           .
  .         .           .
  .         .           .
29        1500        $48.75
FURTHER TRADING INFORMATION NEEDED? RESPOND YES OR NO.
NO
INFORMATION RETRIEVAL SESSION ENDED
```

FIGURE 2.22 A typical dialogue between the computer (color) and the user (black) when the program excerpt in Figure 2.20 is executed. The user is interested in the trading history of the stock KENTECH, which at one point is mistakenly entered as KENTEK. If a graphics package is available, the retrieved data could be displayed graphically on a graphics terminal (Figure 2.23).

program is shown in Figure 2.21. The program requires that both the name of the stock and the number of previous weeks trading history required be entered by the user. If the stock is in the file, the program responds with a table of trading records. This is illustrated by the sample dialogue in Figure 2.22. Were a graphics package and graphics terminal available, the table of trading records could be further processed and displayed as a graph as shown in Figure 2.23.

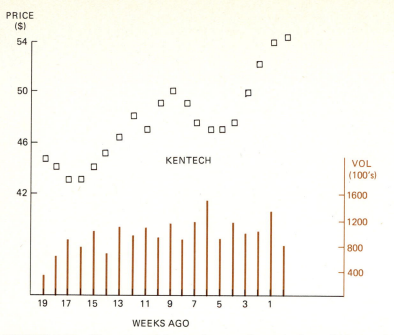

FIGURE 2.23 Were a graphics package and terminal available, a table of stock trading records output by the program in Figure 2.21 could be displayed as shown here.

However, a description of the hardware and software techniques required to make this possible are beyond the scope of this book. For further information on graphics display techniques the reader is referred to Ref. 6.

2.3 HASH FILES

We saw that the main disadvantage of indexed-sequential files is the need to access the index during processing by direct access, with the result that about three disk accesses are typically needed for each record retrieved. This means that an indexed-sequential file that is part of a nationwide on-line system may prove to be a bottleneck; a stream of requests for an average of 15 records per second would result in about 45 disk accesses per second, while typical disk access times of about 35 milliseconds mean that there can be a maximum of about 33 accesses per second (assuming that the file resides on a single disk with a single read/write actuator). Examples of such on-line systems are airline reservation systems and order-entry systems for large corporations. For this type of application hash files are widely used, since a hash file may be designed with an *average search length* quite close to unity, that is, on average it will take about one disk access to retrieve a record from the file. The great disadvantage of hash files is that they are not convenient for sequential batch processing (although it can be done). However, for the type of on-line application for which they are commonly used, this is not an important consideration. Hash files are also commonly used as data base storage files.

Hashing principles

Programs usually retrieve a record on the basis of its primary key, while the underlying retrieval software (the access method) retrieves a record on the basis of the disk address containing that record. We saw in Section 2.2 that the purpose of an index was to relate each primary key in a file to the corresponding disk address. Instead of an index we may use a *hashing routine* for this purpose, where a hashing routine is a user-generated procedure for generating a disk address from a primary key by means of a fixed calculation method. An example of this process is shown in Figure 2.24.

Figure 2.24 depicts the creation of a hash file for accounts receivable (AR) records. The hashing routine uses the primary key of each record (the account number field) to calculate the disk address. As a result of this process the records will be scattered all over the available disk addresses (often called *buckets*) of the file. They will certainly not be in ascending primary key order as in sequential and indexed-sequential files, and it is for this reason that sequential processing of hash files is difficult. To retrieve a record from the file given the primary key value, the hashing routine is again used to calculate the disk address and an appropriate **READ** command issued for the record in this disk address.

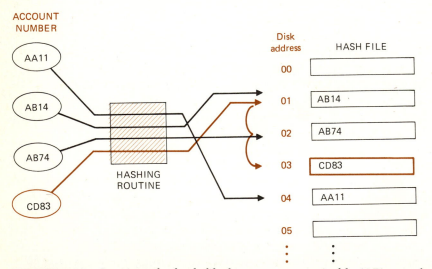

FIGURE 2.24 Creation of a hash file for accounts receivable (AR) records. The hashing routine uses the primary key of a record (the account number field) to calculate the disk address into which the record will be placed. Thus the record with key 'AB14' is placed in address 01. Sometimes two or more records are assigned the same address by the hashing routine, which can cause the disk address to overflow. If each address in the diagram can hold only one record, then the record with key 'CD83' is an overflow record. A common method of dealing with an overflow record is to place it in an empty address further along (as shown). This method of dealing with overflow records is called the progressive overflow technique.

COBOL READ/WRITE commands for hash files

To be able to work with a hash file, we need a WRITE command that will place a record in a specified disk address and a READ command that will read the contents of a specified disk address. Such commands are available in COBOL. The READ/WRITE commands look the same as before except that the READ command uses the value in a special variable as the disk address to be accessed; the WRITE command functions the same way.

Suppose that the special variable is named DISK-ADDRESS; in a program reading records of the hash file AR-HASH in Figure 2.24, we could have:

```
COMPUTE DISK-ADDRESS = 02
READ AR-HASH INTO AR-REC
```

As a result of this, the access method ensures that the record in address 02, that is, the record with primary key 'AB74', is placed in the program data area record AR-REC for the accounts receivable hash file AR-HASH. Similarly, a WRITE command would place a record into the address whose value was in the variable DISK-ADDRESS. In COBOL, DISK-ADDRESS is known as the *relative key variable* and must be specified in the INPUT-OUTPUT section of the ENVIRONMENT division (see page 83).

At this point the reader will be relieved to discover that the disk addresses used in practice, for example, with COBOL relative files, are not actually the physical disk addresses but relative addresses that indicate a storage block's position relative to the start of the file. Thus the first address in the file will be address 0, the second address 1, the third address 2, and so on, even though the physical value of address 0 might well be something like block 0, track 10, cylinder 6. This is why the COBOL file organization suitable for use with hash files is usually called *relative file organization*. The access method for a relative file is provided with the physical address of the start of the file, so that given a relative address it can easily deduce the physical address. With IBM systems, count-data format is used.

Overflow records

The snag with hash files is that the hashing routine seldom assigns each record to an empty disk space when the file is created. An example of this is included in Figure 2.24. Here the record with key 'AB14' is first assigned to address 01, and then the record with key 'CD83' is assigned to the same address. It is possible for a hashing routine to assign many records to the same address.

With the example in Figure 2.24, if each address can hold two records, that is, if the address capacity is 2, then no harm is done by this duplicate assignment or *collision*. But if the address capacity is only one, as is most commonly the case, then the disk address is said to overflow, and the record with key 'CD83' is an overflow record.

Progressive overflow

Overflow records are most commonly dealt with by the *progressive overflow* technique (sometimes called *open addressing*). The address a record is originally assigned to by the hashing routine is called its *home address*. With progressive overflow, an overflow record is placed in the first empty address greater than the home address. Thus in Figure 2.24 the record with key 'CD83' cannot be placed in its home address 01, and so it is placed in the empty address 03 as an overflow record.

This process is more fully described in Figure 2.25. Here a record is depicted as a ball and each disk address as a bucket, where in the diagram a bucket can hold only one ball without overflowing. In Figure 2.25a we show the assignment of 10 records (balls) to 10 disk addresses (buckets) by a hashing routine that distributes the records in a fairly random fashion. We see that buckets 2, 4, and 9 are overflowing as a result of the assignment. In Figure 2.25b, the overflow records are placed in empty buckets by progressive overflow. Each overflow record is given an address higher than its home address, except for some overflow records with home address near the end of the file. If there is no empty space near the end, the search for an empty bucket is continued from the start of the file. Thus the record with key 'G' is finally placed in address 0.

Average search length

The most important single parameter for the efficiency of a hash file is the *average search length*, which is the average number of disk accesses required to

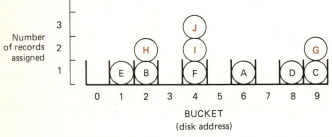

(a) Ten records (circles) assigned (fairly randomly) to 10 disk addresses (buckets). Each disk address can hold only one record; excess records assigned are overflow records.

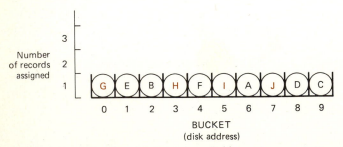

(b) The principle of progressive overflow management. Overflow records from (a) are placed in empty disk addresses with higher address values.

FIGURE 2.25 Progressive overflow management in hash files.

retrieve a record. For example, with the records in Figure 2.25, it will require 1 disk access to retrieve the record with key 'E', because it is in its home address, which can be obtained directly from the hashing routine. On the other hand, it will take four disk accesses to obtain the record with key 'J', since the home address 4 must first be accessed, followed by addresses 5, 6, and finally 7. Thus there has to be a search for an overflow record starting at the home address.

The reader should be able to see that it will take six accesses to retrieve all six home address records in the file in Figure 2.25b, while it will take 2 + 2 + 4 +2 accesses to retrieve the overflow records with keys 'H', 'I', 'J', and 'G', respectively. Thus it will take 16 accesses to retrieve all the records directly or an average of 1.6 accesses per record, the average search length for the file. This figure would probably be too high for many hash files used in on-line systems. The major aim of the hash file designer is to get the average search length as close to unity as possible.

Chained progressive overflow and linked lists

It is clear that *it is the additional disk accesses required to retrieve overflow records that causes the average search length to exceed unity*. One method of reducing the number of accesses, given the overflow records, is to use a pointer chain to connect all the progressive overflow records to their home address. Thus, referring to Figure 2.25b, record 'F' would have a pointer field containing address 5 (the address of overflow record 'I'), and record 'I' would have a pointer field containing address 7 (the address of overflow record 'J'). With such a pointer chain, it would require only three disk accesses to retrieve record 'J'. This method of handling progressive overflow is known as *chained progressive overflow*; it gives a significantly lower average search length than straight progressive overflow but makes all application programs that use the file significantly more complex, since the chains have to be maintained in the face of insertions and deletions of records.

Each chain of overflow records is an example of a linked list. In a linked list of records, the records are connected serially by pointers. An overflow chain for records overflowing from an ISAM track (Figure 2.13) is another example of a linked list. A linked list can have either one-way or two-way pointers. With one-way pointers each records contains a pointer to the next record in the chain. With two-way pointers each record contains a pointer to the next record in the chain, and a pointer to the previous or prior record in the chain. Two-way pointers make it easier to insert a record into a chain, as we shall see in Chapter 3, where linked lists are discussed more fully.

The other methods of reducing the average search length involve having fewer overflow records, as we will now see.

Methods of reducing the number of overflow records

There are three main ways of reducing the number of overflow records in a hash file:

1. Development of a hashing routine that spreads the records evenly over the available disk addresses
2. Use of a low *load factor*, that is, use of considerably more disk space than is needed
3. Use of a large *address capacity*, that is, each disk address should be able to hold much more than one record

We examine these three methods in turn.

Hashing routine development

To reduce or even totally eliminate hashing collisions, we need a hashing routine which will spread or distribute the records over as many disk addresses as possible. Such is clearly not the case with the hashing routine that gave rise to the distribution of records in Figure 2.25a. There are some addresses that have been assigned two or three records, while many disk addresses have been assigned none at all. We can use a histogram to more conveniently describe a distribution of records arising from a hashing routine, and we give one in Figure 2.26 for distribution in Figure 2.25a. The histogram is also better suited for illustrating the nature of a distribution since it is not any more difficult to draw when the number of records involved is large. Imagine trying to redraw Figure 2.25a if we were dealing with thousands of records. From the histogram in Figure 2.26, we can see at a glance that four addresses were assigned no records, three addresses were assigned one record, two addresses were assigned two records, and one address was assigned three records.

A distribution of records over as many disk addresses as possible, that is, a *uniform* or *ideal distribution*, is an obvious design aim when constructing a hashing routine, but such a routine is rarely available in practice, so that we are forced to make the best of distributions which are less than ideal. This leaves us no choice but to look at the range of distributions that could occur, and the range goes all the way from the ideal to simply terrible. This is illustrated in Figure 2.27. Here we consider the case of 1000 records being assigned to 1000 addresses

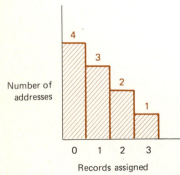

FIGURE 2.26 How records are assigned to disk addresses may be displayed as a histogram. The histogram above is for the file in Figure 2.25a. We see that four disk addresses got zero records, three addresses got one record, and so on.

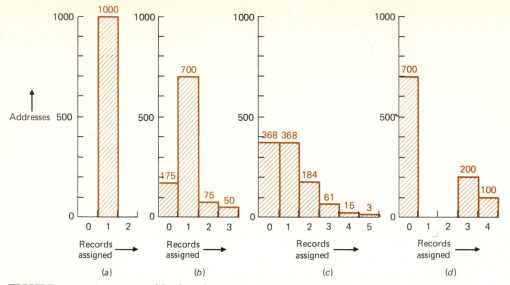

FIGURE 2.27 Some possible distributions resulting from the assignment of 1000 records to 1000 disk addresses by a hashing routine. The distributions range from excellent (a) to terrible (d). It is convenient to assume that each address can hold one record.
(a) Uniform or ideal distribution;
(b) better than random but worse than ideal distribution;
(c) random distribution;
(d) worse than random distribution.

by different hashing routines (where for convenience the reader may assume that a single disk address can hold only one record). We have illustrated four important types of distribution in Figure 2.27, and we will discuss them one by one.

Ideal distribution. It is easy to see why the distribution in Figure 2.27a is ideal. Exactly one record has been assigned to each of the 1000 addresses, there being no addresses with no records assigned and no addresses with more than one record assigned. Thus with this distribution there are no collisions and hence no overflow records to worry about.

Random distribution. A random distribution is shown in Figure 2.27c. Here the hashing routine always assigns a record to a disk address in a completely random manner; by random manner we mean that when a new record is being assigned to a disk address, it is as if a 1000-face dice were being tossed in the air, that is, every disk address is equally likely [we could also consider the distribution in Figure 2.27c as being the result of 1000 hailstones falling (randomly) into 1000 buckets]. The distribution in Figure 2.27c is but one example of a large number of possible distributions. Thus if we assign 700 records to 1000 addresses (in a random fashion), we will get a different but still random distribution. (In general the random distribution can be obtained from the formula:

$$F = R \left(\frac{r}{R} \right)^x \frac{1}{x!} \exp \left(-\frac{r}{R} \right)$$

where F is the number of disk addresses assigned x records, when r records are assigned to R disk addresses. When $r = 1000$ and $R = 1000$, the formula reduces to

$$F = \frac{R}{x!} \exp(-1) = \frac{1000}{x!} \frac{1}{2.7183} = \frac{368}{x!}$$

which gives the distribution shown in Figure 2.27c. See also Ref. 1.)

Looking closely at Figure 2.27c, we see that when each disk address can hold only one record, 184 disk addresses each have one overflow record, 61 disk addresses each have two overflow records, and so on. Thus we get 184 + 61*2 + 15*3 + 3*4, or 363, overflow records altogether. Thus 36.3 percent of the records overflow, which is quite bad, and we try to do better if at all possible. However, there are simple methods of constructing hashing routines that will give a random distribution.

Better than random but less than ideal distributions. It is distributions of this kind that we generally hope to obtain from a hashing routine. In Figure 2.27b, majority of addresses (700) have been assigned one record, and 75 addresses have been assigned two records, and so on. This means that there are only 75 + 50*2, or 175, overflow records which is much better than the case where the distribution is random.

Worse than random distributions. A distribution that is worse than random is shown in Figure 2.27d. Here the majority of addresses have no records assigned. There are 200 addresses with three records assigned and 100 with four records assigned. This means we will get 200*2 + 100*3, or 700, overflow records, which is 70 percent of the records assigned. This is very bad, but as we shall see, there is no excuse for using a hashing routine that gives a distribution that is worse than random, since it is always possible to construct a routine that gives a random distribution.

From the above examples, one thing becomes clear. When a hashing routine is developed, it must be tested to determine if the distribution it produces is acceptable. Since we can always produce a random distribution using established methods, any hashing routine producing a distribution that is significantly worse than a random distribution should be rejected. Thus the random distribution is important as a measure of acceptability of hashing routines and may thus be used as a quality control tool.

There are two main types of hashing routines: those which are practically guaranteed to give a random distribution and those which probably will not. However, all routines have in common that they first convert any nonnumeric characters in the key to numeric quantities. A simple way of doing this would be to substitute 01 for 'A', 02 for 'B', and so on. Thus the key 'AM77' would first be converted to 011377. Other more sophisticated ways are available as well, these rely mostly on the fact that characters are stored in main memory as numeric quantities anyway.

The division method.   This is one of the most commonly used methods of producing a hashing routine that gives a distribution that is better than random. It consists of dividing the numeric version of the key by a prime or odd number and using the remainder as the key. The divisor should be just less than the number of disk addresses available.

The radix transformation method.   This method almost always results in a random distribution. It should be used only when other methods have produced distributions that are worse than random. The method consists of changing the radix of a numeric key, usually from 10 to 11, and using a rightmost group of digits as the key. For example, the key 1234 can be written

$$1*10^3 + 2*10^2 + 3*10^1 + 4*10^0$$

where the radix is 10. Changing the radix from 10 to 11 gives

$$1*11^3 + 2*11^2 + 3*11^1 + 4*11^0$$

which gives 1610 on evaluation. We might then use 610 as the disk address.

The two methods outlined above are the most important, but there are many possible variations in practice.

Implications of a low load factor

It is possible to reduce the number of overflow records by using much more disk space than is necessary to hold all the records, that is, by employing a *low load factor*. The load factor is the percentage of the space taken up by all the records in the file. For example, the load factor for the file in Figure 2.25a, shown again as Figure 2.28a, is 100 percent.

Consider now the file in Figure 2.28a. The distribution is fairly close to random, and let us therefore assume that it is the result of using a radix transformation in the hashing routine. Suppose now that we increase the amount of disk space by 50 percent as shown in Figure 2.28b, but still assign 10 records, and still employ a hashing routine based on a radix transformation, that is, a randomizing routine. If we do this, the 10 records will be scattered randomly over 15 addresses instead of 10, so that there is a smaller chance that a collision will occur. Hence we can expect fewer overflow records, as shown in Figure 2.28b.

Since we need to leave some space in a hash file for insertions anyway, having a load factor of less than 100 percent is a convenient method of reducing the number of overflow records and hence reducing the average search length. Load factors of between 60 and 80 percent are commonly employed.

Implications of a large address capacity

Referring to Figure 2.28a again, suppose that we keep the amount of disk space the same (capable of holding 10 records) but increase the capacity of each address to two records, so that we have only five disk addresses. Suppose now that the distribution in Figure 2.28a was the result of a hailstorm dropping 10

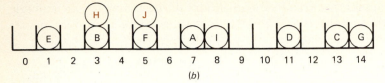

(b)

(b) Effect of increasing the buckets from 10 to 15. Records are more spread out giving less overflow. Note that the load factor is now only 66 percent; we thus waste disk space.

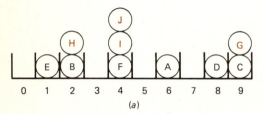

(a)

(a) Ten records assigned to 10 buckets in a fairly random manner (same as Figure 2.25a). The load factor is 100 percent.

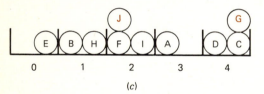

(c)

(c) Effect of increasing the address capacity while keeping the total disk space (and thus the load factor) unaltered. Records that in (a) would have been assigned to two different addresses are now assigned to one address, so that the averaging effect reduces the number of overflow records.

FIGURE 2.28   Effect on overflow of (b) decreasing the load factor and (c) increasing the address capacity while holding the load factor constant.

hailstones into 10 buckets; had the buckets been made bigger as shown in Figure 2.28c, then the hailstones that fell into two buckets in Figure 2.28a would now fall into one bucket in Figure 2.28c. For example, stones H and B that came to buckets 2 and 3 in Figure 2.28a would now fall into bucket 1 in Figure 2.28c. But since H and B both fell into bucket 2 in Figure 2.28a, this causes one overflow record, whereas in the case of Figure 2.28c there will be no overflow record.

From this simple analysis we arrive at the most important single conclusion about the way to design hash files. *Increasing the disk address capacity while keeping the load factor constant will reduce the number of overflow records and hence the average search length.* (Note that the load factor is 100 percent in both Figure 2.28a and c.) Unfortunately it can be technically difficult to construct a hash file with address capacity greater than one, especially when we use COBOL with common operating systems such as OS/MVS. The COBOL facilities are designed for an address capacity of 1. In practice, at an address there is a block with blocking factor equal to one, and if we want a greater address capacity, all user application programs must incorporate their own blocking and deblocking facilities. This makes the writing of such programs much more expensive. However, where a low average search length is necessary at all costs, it is probably best to use a large address capacity.

Peterson's experimental curves in Figure 2.29a show how the average search length is affected by both address capacity and the load factor (Ref. 5). Note that even if an address capacity greater than 1 is used, the load factor is always kept

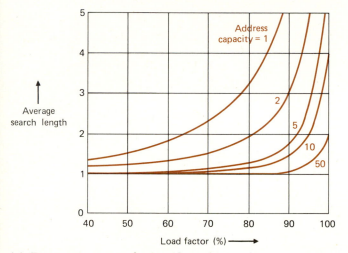

(a) Peterson's curves showing how the average search length falls with decreasing load factor and increasing disk address capacity. The curves assume that the hashing routines are generating random distributions and that progressive overflow is being used. The curves were derived experimentally. (Copyright 1957 by International Business Machines Corporation; reprinted by permission.)

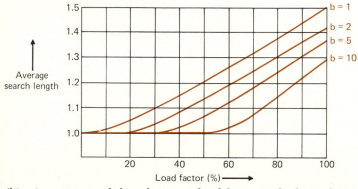

(b) Average search length versus load factor with chained progressive overflow management, that is, records overflowing from a home address are placed in empty addresses and linked by a chain of pointers. The curves assume a random distribution of the records in the file. The curve for address capacity 1 is exact. The other curves are worst case, and in practice average search lengths greater than 1.1 will be up to about 5% lower. The curves are reprinted from the author's *File & Data Base Techniques*, Holt, Rinehart and Winston, 1982.

FIGURE 2.29

less than 100 percent to allow for insertions. The curves in Figure 2.29a are for randomizing hashing routines using progressive overflow and show the situation immediately after initial loading of the file. The average search length tends to increase somewhat following deletions and insertions.

The effect of increasing the address capacity when chained progressive overflow is used is illustrated in Figure 2.29b. The curves also assume a randomizing hashing routine. For a given load factor, the average search length clearly falls with increased address capacity. The curve for $b = 1$ is exact; for higher b values the curves are worst case, and average search lengths should be slightly lower in practice. If we use a hashing routine that gives a distribution that is better than random, then the average search lengths will be lower than those given in Figure 2.29a and Figure 2.29b.

Summary of hash file design steps

A great deal of preliminary design work is needed to produce a hash file with a low average search length. From the principles outlined above, we can give an approximation of the necessary steps:

1. Determine the required average search length for the application.
2. If the average search length needed is very low, use chained progressive overflow, otherwise progressive overflow. Note that it is more expensive to program with chained progressive overflow.
3. Determine how many net insertions of records will be made during the life of the file, and thus place an upper limit on the file load factor. For example, if the file initially will have 75,000 records and we expect to insert 25,000, then it might be advisable to begin with a load factor less than 75%.
4. We now determine the required address capacity (blocking factor). We try to use address capacity equal to one if we can. Using our target average search length value and approximate idea of load factor we select a point on one of the curves in either Figure 2.29a or, depending on the type of overflow management decided on earlier.
6. The point on the curve selected will determine the initial load factor and blocking factor. From a knowledge of exactly how many records will be in the file initially, we can determine the number of disk addresses (R) required. If r is the number of records to be loaded initially and f is the load factor in percent, then the file should be able to hold $100r/f$ records when full. If b is the blocking factor, then we need an R value equal to $100r/fb$.
7. Using the value for R we can now construct a hashing routine. Initially we use the division method and variations on this theme. A test program should be written to determine the distributions produced by different hashing routines. If a distribution very close to ideal is produced (an unlikely event), then it may be necessary to repeat steps 2 to 6 with a less pessimistic design. Remember Figures 2.29a and b assume a random

distribution. If only distributions that are worse than random can be generated, use a radix transformation and variations on this theme to generate a random distribution, the distribution of last resort.

Creation of a hash file for accounts receivable records

We shall now examine the steps for loading a hash file called **AR-HASH** for accounts receivable (AR) records. For this purpose we shall use the records in a sequential file called **AR-SOURCE** (Figure 2.30), the records of which are much simplified compared with what would be used in practice. To be able to illustrate the loading process by means of diagrams, we shall use only the eight records shown in Figure 2.30.

Essential steps

The essential steps in the loading process are:

1. Develop and test a hashing routine. This has been discussed already.
2. Prepare the file from which the hash file will be loaded. As we shall see, this file will be called **AR-ADDR**, and it will contain **AR-SOURCE** records, to each of which has been attached an extra field containing the disk address obtained by applying the hashing routine to the primary key field **ACC-NUMB** (see Figure 2.30, and for a preview see also Figure 2.33).
3. Load the home address records of the hash file, and place any overflow records in a temporary file called **AR-OVFLO**. The loading process is by sequential access. We assume an address capacity of unity.
4. Load the overflow records of the hash file by direct access, obtaining the overflow records from **AR-OVFLO**. We shall assume that they are loaded using the progressive overflow technique.

We now examine steps 2 to 4 in more detail.

ACC-NUMB (customer account number)	CRED-LIM [credit limit ($)]	BALANCE [balance owed ($)]
AA11	9,000	5,654.75
AB14	79,000	14,345.90
AB74	4,900	1,784.00
CD83	99,000	35,987.00
EF93	9,990	7,281.55
JK23	49,000	17,800.00
JY45	29,000	20,450.60
PT65	89,000	44,879.75

FIGURE 2.30 Some records of a sequential accounts receivable file (AR-SOURCE) arranged in ascending account number order. The primary key field ACC-NUMB is underlined.

(a) Each record of AR-SOURCE is read in and the hashing routine applied to the key field ACC-NUMB (see Figure 2.30). The resulting relative disk address formed is added to the record as a new field ADDR and used to construct the new file AR-AUXIL (see Figure 2.31b).

ACC-NUMB	CRED-LIM	BALANCE	ADDR (relative disk address)
AA11	9,000	5,654.75	06
AB14	79,000	14,345.90	03
AB74	4,900	1,784.00	11
CD83	99,000	35,987.00	04
EF93	9,900	7,281.55	03
JK23	49,000	17,800.00	08
JY45	29,000	20,450.60	11
PT65	89,000	44,879.75	06

AR-AUXIL

(b) The contents of AR-AUXIL produced by applying the hashing routine to the key field of the file AR-SOURCE. The resulting relative disk addresses are in the ADDR fields.

FIGURE 2.31

Preparing the source records for the hash file

We start with the source records in **AR-SOURCE** (Figure 2.30). First this file is processed to produce a new version **AR-AUXIL**, to each of the records of which has been attached a field **ADDR** containing a relative disk address, which is the result of applying the hashing routine to the record's **ACC-NUMB** value. Thus the records of the file **AR-AUXIL** are the same as those of **AR-SOURCE** except for the additional field. Like the records of **AR-SOURCE**, those of **AR-AUXIL** are sorted in ascending **ACC-NUMB** order. The processing is illustrated in Figure 2.31a and b.

At this point we may consider the hash file **AR-HASH** to be simply a collection of empty record slots (see Figure 2.32) numbered 0, 1, 2, ... in relative disk address sequence. Now the initial home address records will be loaded into **AR-HASH** in this relative disk address sequence. We therefore need to sort **AR-AUXIL** records in disk address sequence, that is, we sort on the **ADDR** field (see Figure 2.31b). As a result of this sort (depicted in Figure 2.33a), we get the file **AR-ADDR** shown in Figure 2.33b and mentioned earlier in connection with step 2 of the loading process.

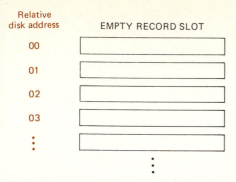

FIGURE 2.32 Before a hash file is loaded with records, it may be imagined to consist of a collection of empty record slots numbered in ascending relative disk address sequence. Normally the home address records are loaded sequentially in this disk address sequence. With IBM relative files, the record slot is the data subblock of a count-data block (see Figure 1.13).

(a) The records of AR-AUXIL from Figure 2.31b are now sorted on the field ADDR to give the file AR-ADDR from which the hash file AR-HASH can be loaded.

ACC-NUMB	CRED-LIM	BALANCE	ADDR
EF93	9,900	7,281.55	03
AB14	79,000	14,345.90	03
CD83	99,000	35,987.00	04
PT65	89,000	44,879.75	06
AA11	9,000	5,654.75	06
JK23	49,000	17,800.00	08
AB74	4,900	1,784.00	11
JY45	29,000	20,450.60	11

AR-ADDR

(b) Showing the contents of AR-ADDR, in which the accounts receivable records are sorted on the relative disk address field ADDR. We can see that more than one record has the same disk address. For each group of records assigned the same address, only the first record of the group (the home address record) will be placed in the address assigned—the remaining records of the group (shown in color) are overflow records.

FIGURE 2.33

We see that some **AR-ADDR** records (Figure 2.33b) have been assigned to the same disk address by the hashing routine, since groups of records have the same **ADDR** value. Only the first record of such a group (the home address record) will be placed in the disk address assigned to it by the hashing routine (the home address); the remaining records of such a group (the overflow records) will be assigned other addresses during the loading process.

Loading the home address records

The home address records from **AR-ADDR** (in black in Figure 2.33b) are sequentially loaded into the hash file during this stage of the loading. Of course all the records from **AR-ADDR** are read in sequentially, but if a record read in has an **ADDR** field value the same as that of the previous record read in, it is not placed in the hash file **AR-HASH**; instead it is placed in the temporary overflow sequential file **AR-OVFLO**, since such a record is an overflow record and cannot be placed in its home address (color records in Figure 2.33b). The overall loading process is illustrated in Figure 2.34a.

As mentioned in an earlier section, the manipulation of COBOL hash files requires the use of a *relative key variable* with **READ** and **WRITE** statements. The

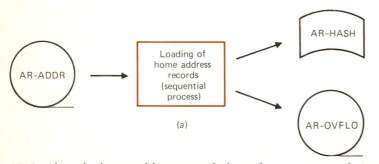

(a)

(a) Loading the home address records from the source records in AR-ADDR (see Figure 2.33b). Home address records are placed in AR-HASH, while overflow records are placed in the temporary overflow file AR-OVFLO. During the process, all of the slots in the hash file receive records (see Figure 2.35); those slots receiving records from AR-ADDR get the additional character 'blank' as the first character of the record. The other records are dummy records and have a '9' as the first character.

(b) Loading the overflow records from the overflow file AR-OVFLO. For each record from AR-OVFLO a search of AR-HASH must be made for an empty slot (dummy record). First the home address is examined, then the next higher address, and so on until a dummy record is encountered. The result of the processing is shown in Figure 2.35 (colored records).

FIGURE 2.34

relative key variable can hold a relative disk address. If we suppose that in this case we use the variable DISK-ADDRESS as the relative key variable, then we would declare it in the ENVIRONMENT division (see Figure 2.4 as well) along with a declaration of the relative or hash file AR-HASH:

```
ENVIRONMENT DIVISION.

        .
        .
        .

INPUT-OUTPUT SECTION.
FILE-CONTROL
        SELECT AR-HASH
                ASSIGN TO DA-R-ARHASHED
        ORGANIZATION IS RELATIVE
        ACCESS IS SEQUENTIAL
                RELATIVE KEY IS DISK-ADDRESS.
```

We also specify that the file be processed sequentially (during the loading of the home address records). (In the ASSIGN clause, DA means direct access file, R means relative file, and the arbitrary name ARHASHED is the ddname (see Figure 2.4) for the DD-statement describing the physical storage file, which does not concern us in this overview.)

During the loading, the hash file AR-HASH will be open for SEQUENTIAL OUTPUT. In order to be able to write out a record in AR-HASH in its correct home address, the home address value must first be placed in the relative key variable DISK-ADDRESS:

```
MOVE ADDR TO DISK-ADDRESS.
WRITE AR-HASH-BUFREC FROM AR-HASH-REC.
```

The access method takes the record in the program data area variable AR-HASH-REC and places it first in the buffer record variable AR-HASH-BUFREC and then in the disk file in the record slot whose address is in the variable DISK-ADDRESS.

The home address records from AR-ADDR are placed in AR-HASH in ascending relative disk address order. Thus we first write out a record in address 03, then in 04, then 06, and so on (see Figures 2.33b and 2.35). However, the records we write out have an additional one-character field DELETE-TAG (Figure 2.35) containing a blank character. At the same time the access method automatically writes dummy records in the slots not used, such as slots 00, 01, 02, and 05. A dummy record has a '9' in the field DELETE-TAG.

Thus at the end of this stage of the loading process, the file AR-HASH contains home address records (black records in Figure 3.35) and dummy records (empty slots) whose first character is a '9'. The overflow records from AR-ADDR are now in the file AR-OVFLO.

Relative disk address	DELETE-TAG	ACC-NUMB	CRED-LIM	BALANCE	ADDR
00	b	JY45	29,000	20,450.60	11
01	9	–	–	–	–
02	9	–	–	–	–
03	b	EF93	9,990	7,281.55	03
04	b	CD83	99,000	35,987.00	04
05	b	AB14	79,000	14,345.90	03
06	b	PT65	89,000	44,879.75	06
07	b	AA11	9,000	5,654.75	06
08	b	JK23	49,000	17,800.00	08
09	9	–	–	–	–
10	9	–	–	–	–
11	b	AB74	4,900	1,784.00	11

FIGURE 2.35 The contents of the hash file AR-HASH when loading is complete. The disk addresses on the leftmost column are not stored with the records. Overflow records not in their home address are in color. The first character of a record (DELETE-TAG) indicates whether the record is valid or a dummy (empty).

Loading the overflow records

Loading the overflow records is the most complicated part of the loading process. We read in each record from **AR-OVFLO** (see Figure 2.34b) and write it out in the first empty address space or slot with an address greater than the home address of the record. To find this empty slot, the records in **AR-HASH** must be searched starting at the home address of the overflow record. The record in the home address plus 1 is read, then that in home address plus 2, and so on. Thus the hash file has to be processed by direct access, and we specify **ACCESS IS RANDOM** in the **INPUT-OUTPUT** section of the **ENVIRONMENT** division.

While searching for an empty slot, we increment the value in the relative key variable **DISK-ADDRESS** and then read the record in that address:

```
COMPUTE DISK-ADDRESS = DISK-ADDRESS + 1.
READ AR-HASH INTO AR-HASH-REC.
```

where **AR-HASH-REC** is the program data area variable for **AR-HASH** records. We then check the value in **DELETE-TAG**. If the record is a dummy, then there is space, and the overflow record from **AR-OVFLO** is written out in that slot; otherwise we increment the value in **DISK-ADDRESS** and continue the search. If the search goes past the last address in the file, it is continued from address 0. Thus the record with key 'JY45' (see Figure 2.35) has its home address in slot 11 which is full. The search then starts at address 0, which happens to be empty, and the record is placed here.

Note that use of **AR-OVFLO** to hold the overflow records could be avoided. To get the overflow records, we could simply read **AR-ADDR** (see Figure 2.33b) sequentially and extract all those records whose **ADDR** value occurs in the preceding record.

Statistics

During both stages of loading, statistics are collected for quality control purposes, and the most important statistic is the average search length, which can easily be computed by counting the number of accesses required to place an overflow record in an empty slot. The average search length for the file will be affected by updating.

Maximum search length

The maximum search length is the largest possible number of accesses required to retrieve a record from the file. This is usually printed out when the hash file is created. It is needed for retrieving records from the file. When attempting to retrieve a record, if a retrieval program carries out a number of accesses equal to the maximum search length for the file, the requested record cannot be in the file. In addition to printing the maximum search length out, it is good file management practice to reserve the last (or additional) slot of the file for statistical information about the file, and the maximum search length and perhaps also the average search length can be stored here.

Like the average search length, the maximum search length will be affected by updating, so that this parameter needs to be continually monitored.

Updating of hash files

Hash files may be updated by either batch or on-line processing, although batch processing is awkward, since the records are not stored in ascending key order.

Batch processing

With a hash file, batch processing is frequently direct access processing. The transaction records are often batched together for the daily, weekly, or monthly update, whatever the case may be. However, these transactions are not sorted on the primary key. Instead we process the hash file by direct access (**ACCESS IS RANDOM** is specified), and for each transaction record in turn, a direct access is made to the home address of the corresponding hash file record. If the record is not in its home address, it is probably an overflow record and several accesses may have to be made for it. Deleting a record will consist of placing a '9' in the first byte.

Another much less common method requires that additional pointers be incorporated into the records of the hash file, so that the records also form a chain of records in ascending primary key order. This is another example of a *linked list*, and we shall return to the concept in Chapter 3. The transaction records may now be sorted in ascending key order. Subsequently both the transaction records and the hash file records may be read in by the updating program in ascending key sequence. Nevertheless, the hash file would still be processed by direct access in order that the pointer chain could be followed by the updating program.

On-line updating
As with batch processing, the file is opened for direct access and is different from common batch updating methods in that only small quantities of hash file records are updated at one time, that is, the transactions are not batched and are dealt with as they occur.

Information retrieval from hash files

Regular report generation
As with updating, regular and batch-oriented report generation is for the most part awkward with hash files and often requires an intervening sort. For example, suppose we need a management report from the file **AR-HASH** giving the records from those customers whose balance exceeds $100,000. It is clear that we could process **AR-HASH** sequentially, first retrieving the record in address 00, then the one in address 01, and so on. Each record that was not a dummy and had a **BALANCE** value in excess of $100,000 would be retrieved. However, it would be desirable to present the report to a user with the account numbers ordered alphabetically, so that a sort of the retrieved records would be necessary.

Interactive information retrieval
Hash files are widely used for interactive information retrieval. The simplest kind of information retrieval depends on presentation of the required record key, so that the retrieval program and access method can obtain the record by accessing the appropriate disk address directly (or nearly directly, for if the required record is an overflow record, a search will have to be made for it). Such retrieval programs can be run from a terminal in a user's office without the involvement of the data processing department. As an example, let us suppose that a financial manager requires information about the outstanding balances of two of the firm's customers. If the customer account numbers involved were 'JK23' and 'AB14', the terminal dialogue could be as in Figure 2.36. The dialogue assumes that the manager makes a mistake (as would often be the case) in

```
ACCOUNTS RECEIVABLE INFORMATION RETRIEVAL SERVICE
GIVE ACCOUNT NUMBER
JK23
CREDIT LIMIT: 49000
BALANCE     : 17800.00
HAVE YOU ANOTHER QUERY?
YES
GIVE ACCOUNT NUMBER
AD14
ACCOUNT NUMBER ENTERED IS NOT IN MASTER
HAVE YOU ANOTHER QUERY?
YES
GIVE ACCOUNT NUMBER
AB14
CREDIT LIMIT: 79000
BALANCE     : 14345.90
HAVE YOU ANOTHER QUERY?
NO
SESSION TERMINATED
```

FIGURE 2.36   Terminal dialogue used to obtain information from the accounts receivable file AR-HASH which was created as a hash file in the preceding section. The records in the file are assumed to be those displayed in Figure 2.35. The dialogue results from executing the program excerpt in Figure 2.37.

entering one of the keys. The hash file involved could be **AR-HASH** with the data shown in Figure 2.35.

For the sake of completeness, we will include the core of the information retrieval program (see Figure 2.37). **AR-HASH-REC** holds an **AR-HASH** record and has the fields shown in Figure 2.35. An important variable is **SEARCHES**, which keeps track of the number of disk accesses made in the search for an overflow record. The search is stopped when the value of **SEARCHES** is greater than the maximum search length for the file. We also use the variable **TARGET**, which holds the account number being sought. Finally we use the variable **RESPONSE**, an alphabetic variable to hold the values 'YES' or 'NO'. As can be seen, the excerpt is complicated only by the need to carry out a progressive search for an overflow record in the loop **SEARCHLOOP**.

The final paragraph of the procedure contains the same hashing routine that was used in the creation of the file **AR-HASH**. We omit the technical details of this routine, since they are of little importance for our exposition.

Growth of hash files

During updating, a preponderance of record insertions over deletions will cause the file to grow. Such growth can be a severe problem with a hash file, since it will increase the loading factor and thus increase the average search

```
PROCEDURE DIVISION.
STARTUP.
      OPEN INPUT AR-HASH.
      DISPLAY "ACCOUNTS RECEIVABLE INFORMATION RETRIEVAL SERVICE".
MAINLOOP.
      MOVE ZEROES TO SEARCHES.
      DISPLAY "GIVE ACCOUNT NUMBER".
      ACCEPT TARGET.
      PERFORM HASH-PARAGRAPH
*     This causes TARGET to be hashed and the calculated address placed in the
*     relative key variable DISK-ADDRESS.
SEARCHLOOP.
         COMPUTE SEARCHES = SEARCHES + 1.
         IF SEARCHES > MAX-SEARCH-LENGTH
         THEN DISPLAY "ACCOUNT NUMBER ENTERED IS NOT IN MASTER"
         ELSE
             READ AR-HASH INTO AR-HASH-REC
             IF TARGET = ACC-NUMB IN AR-HASH-REC AND TAG = LOW-VALUE
             THEN DISPLAY "CREDIT LIMIT: ", CRED-LIM IN AR-HASH-REC
                   DISPLAY "BALANCE    : ", BALANCE IN AR-HASH-REC
             ELSE
                   COMPUTE DISK-ADDRESS + DISK-ADDRESS + 1
                   GO TO SEARCHLOOP.
      DISPLAY "HAVE YOU ANOTHER QUERY?"
      ACCEPT RESPONSE.
      IF RESPONSE = "YES" THEN GO TO MAINLOOP.
      ELSE DISPLAY "SESSION TERMINATED"
          STOP RUN.
 HASH-PARAGRAPH.
         .
         .
         .
```

FIGURE 2.37 Interactive program for retrieval of information from the hash file
AR-HASH in Figure 2.35. Only the core of the program is shown. A sample dialogue
is shown in Figure 2.36.

length of the file (see Figure 2.29), so that expected growth of the file must be
taken into account when the file is designed. An even worse problem arises
when the growth causes the load factor to hit 100 percent, so that there is no more
room in the file for inserted records. There are two main solutions when this
happens. One is to increase the number of disk addresses, but since the number
of disk addresses is an important parameter in the hashing routine, it is likely
that the hashing routine will have to be tested again, so that essentially the file
has to be redesigned. The other solution is to increase the address capacity and
keep the number of disk addresses the same. This merely requires that the file be
dumped and reloaded into the expanded disk space. Of course the loading and

updating procedures for such a hash file must be written initially so that the change of address capacity can be incorporated simply by changing one or two parameters used by the programs.

SUMMARY

1. Sequential files are commonly stored on tape and disk. Updating usually requires the generation of an additional sequential file, except for updating a disk file without insertion of new records. Double buffers are normally used when sequential files are processed. COBOL **READ** and **WRITE** commands are used for reading and writing records. The logical storage file is mostly specified within the COBOL program, while the physical storage file is mostly specified in the accompanying command language (JCL, with IBM systems) specification. A file of fairly permanent data is called a master file, and a file of data used for updating is called a transaction file. Tape files are widely used for inexpensive archiving of data. Sequential files are widely used in batch processing.

2. There are two main types of indexed-sequential file organization, depending on how inserted records are handled. Records of an indexed-sequential file are maintained in ascending primary key order. When records are inserted, they can be placed in an overflow area of the disk (reserved tracks) and chained together to maintain sequential order; alternatively, the (logical) track affected by the insertion may be split into two logical tracks in order to make room. ISAM files use the overflow area method, while VSAM uses the logical track splitting method. All indexed-sequential files have an index (possibly a multiple-level index) to permit direct (or random) access to disk addresses containing the records of the file. Because the index has to be accessed before the records of the file can be accessed, direct processing the files is slow. Sequential processing of ISAM files with many overflow chains is also slow.

Because the records are maintained in ascending primary key order, indexed-sequential files are ideal for applications where a great deal of batched sequential processing is needed, but where some direct access processing is also required. The same COBOL **READ** and **WRITE** statements that are used with sequential files may be used with indexed-sequential files. However, with direct access, the primary record key involved must be placed in the primary key variable, which must be declared in the **INPUT-OUTPUT** section of the **ENVIRONMENT** division.

3. With hash files, a hashing routine is used to generate a relative disk address for a record by means of a calculation procedure applied to the record's primary key. When the same address is generated for two different records, we have a collision; in general, if a hashing routine assigns more records to an address than it can hold, the surplus records are called overflow records. An overflow management procedure is used to assign overflow records to vacant addresses; progressive and chained progressive overflow management are commonly used. The percentage of overflow records may be reduced by a good hashing routine, a low loading factor, or a high address capacity. The ultimate measure of the efficiency of a hash file is the number of disk accesses required to

retrieve a record on average, or the average search length, and should be printed out by a hash file loading program. Hash files are best loaded in two stages. First home address records are loaded, and then overflow records are loaded. Because a hashing routine scatters the records over the disk space, the records cannot easily be processed in ascending primary key order. With a well-designed hash file, an average search length close to unity is possible, so that direct access can be much faster with hash files than with indexed-sequential files. Hash files are widely used for on-line applications because of their speed.

The same COBOL **READ** and **WRITE** statements that are used with sequential files many be used with COBOL hash or relative files. However, the relative disk address involved must be placed in a relative key variable, which must be declared in the **INPUT-OUTPUT** section of the **ENVIRONMENT** division.

QUESTIONS AND PROJECTS

Questions on sequential files

1. In what order are records of a sequential file stored on a disk that is organized into cylinders?
2. With IBM systems, what block format is used on disk with sequential files?
3. Explain where the definitions of the logical storage file and the physical storage file are placed in a COBOL program and associated operating system command language specifications.
4. What is IBM JCL? What is a DD-statement?
5. Using sequential files, a COBOL input buffer record, a COBOL output buffer area, and a program data area, describe the physical movement of a record as it is read from a file and written out onto a file.
6. Explain why an IBM dataset and a physical storage file are essentially the same.
7. Explain how a COBOL file has three names with IBM systems.
8. Explain why we must create a new file to update a tape file, and why we do not need a new file to update a disk sequential file if no insertions are involved.
9. Explain the precise effect of the COBOL **READ**, **WRITE**, and **REWRITE** statements.
10. Compare and contrast the relative timing and integrity aspects of updating on disk as opposed to updating on tape.
11. Explain why it is better to have two input and two output buffers rather than just a single input and output buffer.
12. Who should be involved in an organization in making arrangements for the generation of reports from sequential files?

Projects with sequential files

13. Create a simpler version of the file **STOCK** in Figure 2.1. Use only about 10 companies, and trading data for about 5 weeks, so that your file will have about 50 records. (This simplification is to eliminate the chore of data

entry—you can use more records if you like.) The data should be either punched on cards or entered at a terminal, depending on what facilities you have available.

14. Write two versions of a batch program to carry out the weekly updating of the file **STOCK**, one for the case where the master is a disk file and the other for the case where it is a tape file.

15. Assume that two stocks in **STOCK** have just been delisted from the exchange and that two new stocks have just been listed. Write a program to update **STOCK**. The program should take into account the fact that there will be just 1 week's trading data for the newly listed stocks (that is, price, volume, price change, and price/earnings data should be entered as zero for earlier weeks).

16. Write a report program to generate a 3-week moving average for the price of each stock. (If p_1, p_2, and p_3 are the prices of a stock for week-1, week-2, and week-3, then $(p_1 + p_2 + p_3)/3$ is the 3-week moving average price for week-2.) This moving average data should be placed in a sequential file **MOVE-AVE**.

17. Using the data in **STOCK** and **MOVE-AVE**, write a program to extrapolate the stock price for 2 weeks, for stocks that have climbed 15 percent or more in the previous 2 weeks. Use any extrapolation stategy that seems reasonable. [Note, that while computers are excellent tools for managing data, using them as crystal balls to predict the course of financial markets is probably a futile (but enticing) exercise. Nevertheless, it is one that is commonly carried on in investment firms and other financial institutions.]

Questions on indexed-sequential files

18. What do indexed-sequential and sequential files have in common? What additional features do indexed-sequential files have as far as retrieval, updating, and new record insertions are concerned?

19. Explain the concept of an indexed group of blocks and the concept of a one-level index.

20. Why is a multiple-level index better with a large file?

21. Why is insertion of new records a problem in theory with indexed-sequential files?

22. Give explanations of the two ways in which the record insertion problem is overcome.

23. Redraw the ISAM file in Figure 2.13 to show what would happen if records with keys 15 and 35 are inserted.

24. Redraw the ISAM file in Figure 2.13 to show the situation after the record with keys 19 and 47 are deleted, and the records with keys 10 and 33 inserted.

25. Why is it possible to write the COBOL **PROCEDURE DIVISION** of a program to load an indexed-sequential file as if the file were a sequential file?

26. Why must a primary or record key be specified in a COBOL program to load an indexed-sequential file? Precisely how is this key specified?

27. Why does an ISAM file have to be reorganized fairly often, and what exactly is meant by this?

28. Why would you expect that fewer accesses to the disk are necessary with retrievals from a VSAM file as compared with an ISAM file?
29. Account approximately for the number of disk accesses that must be made to retrieve a single record from (a) an ISAM file and (b) a VSAM file.
30. Explain the essential differences between ISAM and VSAM files.
31. Assuming that there is room for just two more records in the control interval, show the control area and sequence set changes to the VSAM file in Figure 2.16 after the records with keys 25, 25, and 30 have been inserted.
32. Why is it convenient to use an indexed-sequential file for updating both in a batch environment, and in an on-line environment?

Projects with indexed-sequential files

33. Repeat Project 13 using an indexed-sequential version of STOCK.
34. Assume that five new stocks have been listed on the exchange, for which 1 week's trading data is currently available (that is, price, volume, price change, and price/earnings data should be entered as zero for earlier weeks). These new stocks all have names that place them in sequential order between the second and third stock in the file STOCK before update. Write a batch program for STOCK that will insert any batch of new stocks that are kept in a transaction file in ascending key order. Write also a report program that can print the entire file. Use the batch insertion program for STOCK to insert the records for the five newly listed stocks, and use the report program to print out the file afterwards. You should see that ascending sequential order has been preserved.
35. Repeat Project 34, this time using an insertion program that accepts the newly listed stocks interactively and one by one.
36. For the file STOCK, write an interactive report generation program that will print out price and volume data for a given stock for the period between two given week numbers.
37. Write an interactive program for STOCK to generate an n-week moving average (where n is an odd number accepted interactively by the program) for a given stock for the period between a given week and the current week.
38. Assuming STOCK is an indexed-sequential file, (a) do Project 14 (naturally for the disk case only), (b) do Project 16, and (c) do Project 17.

Questions on hash files

39. Explain the concept of a relative address in a hash file?
40. Why must a hashing routine always produce the same address from a given record key?
41. Explain the concepts of a hashing collision and hashing overflow record.
42. In the PROCEDURE division of a COBOL program that is reading a hash file, the value 777 is placed in the relative key variable RKV. A READ statement is then executed, and the record at address 777 is read into the program data area. How does the access method know to use the value in RKV and not the value in some other variable?

43. Using only the histogram in Figure 2.26, determine the number of addresses and the number of records in the file. What is the loading factor for this file?

44. If the file described in Figure 2.26 can hold only one record in an address, how many overflow records must there be?

45. For the file described in Figure 2.27*b*, what percentage of the records will overflow (a) if each address can hold only one record (address capacity is 1), and (b) if each address can hold up to two records (address capacity is 2)?

46. Use the random distribution formula to generate the histogram for the followings cases: (a) 500 records assigned to 1000 addresses; (b) 700 records assigned to 1000 addresses; (c) 2000 records assigned to 1000 addresses (For this to make any sense, an address would have to be able to hold at least two records, but this does not affect the random distribution formula, which merely shows how records will be assigned to addresses without regard to how many records an address can hold.)

47. If each address can hold up to three records, what is the loading factor for cases (a), (b), and (c) in the previous question? In order to be able to answer this question, it is *not* necessary to answer Question 45.

48. The division method is used to construct a hashing routine for a small file whose addresses go from 0 to 24. Using a reasonable prime or odd number as the divisor, what addresses would be generated for records with keys 572 and 436?

49. This problem demonstrates that increasing the load factor reduces the number of overflow records. For the case of 1000 records randomly assigned to 1000 addresses (distribution given in Figure 2.27*c*) compute the load factor and the percentage of records overflowing, if the address capacity is 1. Now increase the number of addresses to 2000, halving the loading factor. Use the random distribution formula to generate the new histogram from which the overflow record percentage may be calculated.

50. This problem demonstrates in a simple manner that increasing the address capacity reduces the number of overflow records. For the case of 1000 records assigned randomly to 1000 addresses (Figure 2.27*c*), compute the percentage of overflow records, assuming an address capacity of 1. Now use the random distribution formula to generate the histogram for 1000 records randomly assigned to 500 addresses, from which the percentage of overflow records should be calculated, assuming an address capacity of 2. Note that the load factor is 100 percent in both cases.

51. Explain the concept of progressive overflow or open addressing.

52. Explain the concept of average search length.

53. If progressive overflow is used with the file in Figure 2.28*c*, what will the average search length be?

54. Use Peterson's curves in Figure 2.29 to determine the average search length in the following cases where a randomizing hashing routine is used: (a) 750 records to 1000 addresses with an address capacity of 1. (b) 75,000 records to 100,000 addresses with an address capacity of 2. (c) 25,000 records to 40,000 addresses with an address capacity of 1.

55. When loading a hash file, why is it a good idea to load the home address records first and the overflow records last?

56. Explain the concept of chained progressive overflow. (See also the description of the data base system TOTAL in Chapter 11.)

57. With current COBOL facilities why is it difficult to construct a hash file with address capacity greater than 1?

58. What is the maximum search length for the file in Figure 2.25?

Hash file projects

59. Apply a selection of hashing routines to the record keys in Figure 2.30, and display the results as a histogram. Additional records can be invented to give a better statistical result.

60. Using an address capacity of unity, use COBOL to load the hash file AR-HASH using the source data in Figure 2.30, and two-stage loading. The program should print the maximum and average search lengths.

61. Write a batch program for updating the balances of selected customers in AR-HASH, as a result of accumulated transactions in a sequential file.

62. Repeat Project 60 using an interactive program, where the update data is entered at the terminal as requested by the program.

63. A hash file can be processed sequentially, but not in ascending primary key order. Write a COBOL program that prints out details of accounts where the balance exceeds $15,000 in AR-HASH.

64. Write an interactive COBOL program (similar to the one in Figure 5.36) to retrieve information about accounts entered at the terminal.

REFERENCES

1. Bradley, J., 1982. *File and Data Base Techniques.* Holt, Rinehart & Winston, New York.

2. Brown, G. D., 1977. *Advanced ANS COBOL.* Wiley-Interscience, New York.

3. Brown, G. D., 1977. *System 370 Job Control Language.* Wiley-Interscience, New York.

4. Coutie, G. A., and others, 1964. *Short Term Forecasting.* Published for Imperial Chemical Industries Ltd. by Oliver & Boyd, Edinburgh.

5. Peterson, W. W., 1957. "Addressing for Random Access Storage." *IBM J. R&D*, 1(2): 130–146. A classic paper.

6. Newman W. M., and R. F. Sproull, 1979. *Principles of Interactive Computer Graphics.* McGraw-Hill, New York.

3

Secondary Keys and Primitive Data Bases

With the sequential, hash, and indexed-sequential file organizations described in Chapter 2, we have dealt only with one type of key, namely, the primary key. We saw that the value in a primary key field uniquely identifies a record and that the key may be a single field such as ACC-NUMB in the accounts receivable file AR-HASH (Section 2.3) or a composite field such as CO-WEEK in the indexed-sequential file STOCK (Section 2.2). We have also seen that a hashing routine or an index enables a primary key to be used to obtain the disk address of the record containing that key value, thus permitting direct access to the record. So far, therefore, direct access has been based on the use of a primary key value. Put more plainly, without the primary or record key, direct access to straightforward hash and indexed-sequential files is impossible; and what is worse, sequential access may well be impossible too. A short anecdote may drive this point home.

The Traveler's Dilemma
Once, while trying to make a plane connection in foreign parts, and at one of the world's busiest airports, a certain traveler discovered that he had lost his plane ticket. He at once approached the airline reservations counter, and exhibiting all kinds of identification, he carefully explained his dilemma. The ticket clerk was sympathetic but firm and explained that a passenger record could be displayed on his terminal only if the ticket number were entered; the clerk also affirmed

CUST-AREA	POINTER1	POINTER2	POINTER3
AIRCRAFT	AB14	EF93	
COMPUTERS	AA11	AB74	PT65
INSTRUMENTS	JK23	JY45	
TELEPHONES	CD83		

Inversion CUST-AREA-INVERSION

CUST-STATE	POINTER1	POINTER2	POINTER3 ...
CALIFORNIA	AA11	CD83	
OREGON	PT65		
TEXAS	AB74	EF93	JY45
WASH.	AB14	JK23	

Inversion CUST-STATE-INVERSION

(a)

ACC-NUMB	CUST-AREA	CUST-STATE	CRED-LIM	BALANCE
AA11	COMPUTERS	CALIFORNIA	9,000	5,654.75
AB14	AIRCRAFT	WASH.	79,000	14,345.90
AB74	COMPUTERS	TEXAS	4,900	1,784.00
CD83	TELEPHONES	CALIFORNIA	99,000	35,987.00
EF93	AIRCRAFT	TEXAS	9,990	7,281.55
JK23	INSTRUMENTS	WASH.	49,000	17,800.00
JY45	INSTRUMENTS	TEXAS	29,000	20,450.60
PT65	COMPUTERS	OREGON	89,000	44,879.75

Accounts receivable file

(b)

FIGURE 3.1 At the bottom (b) is an accounts receivable file organized as an indexed-sequential file. At the top (a) are two inversions of the accounts receivable file. CUST-AREA-INVERSION and CUST-STATE-INVERSION are inversions on the fields CUST-AREA and CUST-STATE, respectively.

that he didn't know how to conduct a sequential search of the file (for the traveler knew something about computer files), that he was sure it couldn't be done anyway, and that the only way to make the plane connection was to buy another ticket (for a 3000-mile leg). (The story had a happy ending, however; our traveler did not have the funds to get another ticket, but following a sequential search of his previous locations that day, the lost ticket was finally uncovered. On the flight home he resolved to keep his ticket number separate from his ticket from then on, a resolution he has since consistently failed to keep.)

It is clear that, apart from his absentmindedness, the traveler's dilemma was due to the passenger records file having the ticket number as the primary key, and the only key. Had direct access been possible by means of *secondary key fields* that could contain values that were not necessarily unique, such as passenger surname, the traveler's dilemma might well have been avoided.

In this chapter we look at how secondary key facilities may be incorporated into direct access files and at how these keys are used. We also see how the use of certain fields as secondary keys lead us directly to the concept of a (storage) data base.

3.1 AUXILIARY DATA STRUCTURES FOR SECONDARY KEYS

We saw in Section 2.3 that to access a sequential file directly by means of a primary key, an auxiliary data structure called an index is required. Similarly, we need an auxiliary data structure to access a file directly by means of a secondary key. There are two types of structure that can be used, namely, the *inverted file,* or *file inversion*, structure and the *multiple linked-list* structure. We examine them in turn.

File inversions

Let us take the accounts receivable file from the previous chapter and expand it so that it contains two new fields, CUST-AREA and CUST-STATE. These fields respectively give the area of business in which a customer is chiefly engaged and the state (or province) in which the customer has his or her corporate headquarters (as shown in the file excerpt in Figure 3.1*b*). For convenience we will also suppose that the file has been created as an indexed-sequential file. The index is not shown, but we assume that it exists. Note that we are choosing the accounts receivable file as an indexed-sequential file purely for expositional convenience. A hash file could also be used.

Constructing an inversion

Let us now construct an inversion of the accounts receivable file on the field CUST-AREA. To do this, we could sort the accounts receivable file in ascending CUST-AREA order, at the same time removing all the fields except ACC-NUMB and CUST-AREA. This gives us the file:

ACC-NUMB	*CUST-AREA*
AB14	AIRCRAFT
EF93	AIRCRAFT
AA11	COMPUTERS
AB74	COMPUTERS
PT65	COMPUTERS

From each group of records with the same **CUST-AREA** value, for example, 'AIRCRAFT', a single record in the inversion file on **CUST-AREA** is constructed. We will call this file **CUST-AREA-INVERSION**; its contents are shown in Figure 3.1*a*. The primary key of **CUST-AREA-INVERSION** is the field **CUST-AREA**, and a record of the file contains a **CUST-AREA** value, followed by the primary key values of all the records in the accounts receivable file that have that **CUST-AREA** value. Note that since the number of accounts receivable records in which a given **CUST-AREA** value will occur varies a lot, the number of fields in **CUST-AREA-INVERSION** will also vary, so that the inverted file has variable length records. Note also that the primary key field of **CUST-AREA-INVERSION** will be a secondary key field in the accounts receivable file. Furthermore, since we would like direct access to a record of the inversion on the basis of a **CUST-AREA** value, **CUST-AREA-INVERSION** will have to be a direct access file with **CUST-AREA** as the primary key. It is usual to build an inverted file as an indexed-sequential file, since hash files with variable length records are very difficult to construct. Thus **CUST-AREA-INVERSION** in Figure 3.1*a* may be taken as an indexed-sequential file, although neither the indexed group of **CUST-AREA-INVERSION** records nor the associated index are shown.

In Figure 3.1*a*, an inversion on the accounts receivable field **CUST-STATE** is also shown, with primary key **CUST-STATE**. We shall call this file **CUST-STATE-INVERSION**. It is constructed in the same way **CUST-AREA-INVERSION** was constructed, that is, by sorting the accounts receivable file on the field **CUST-STATE**. We must now examine how inversions are used, but before doing so, a note on terminology is appropriate.

Note on terminology

Some authorities prefer to use the term "inverted file" for the set of individual inversions of all the nonprimary key fields of a file. In this view, the inverted file for the accounts receivable file would contain the inversions for the fields **CUST-AREA**, **CUST-STATE**, **CRED-LIM**, and **BALANCE**. This terminology is rather academic, since in practice a complete set of inversions is unheard of and since each inversion on a field is implemented as a separate file (it has to be, since the primary key of an inversion will have a format that depends on the inversion). In this book we shall usually refer to a structure like **CUST-AREA-INVERSION** in Figure 3.1*a* as either an *inverted file* or a *file inversion* on the field **CUST-AREA**. It is also sometimes called a *secondary index*.

Use of inverted files for access on secondary keys

To illustrate how an inverted file may be used to permit access on the basis of a secondary key, let us suppose that a manager in an accounting department has the following request:

Request-1.   What are the outstanding balances of all California customers?

The data processing department could have prepared an interactive program for requests of this type, and the manager would merely have to enter the name of the state at the terminal. The program would then carry out the following steps to complete the retrieval:

1. By direct access, read the record in the inverted file **CUST-STATE-INVERSION** with primary key value 'CALIFORNIA'. Referring to Figure 3.1a, the record retrieved would have the **ACC-NUMB** values 'AA12' and 'CD83'.
2. Use the **ACC-NUMB** values 'AA12' and 'CD83' to directly access records of the (indexed-sequential) accounts receivable file in Figure 3.1b. From these records the **BALANCE** field values are retrieved and displayed (the results displayed will be $5,654.75 and $35,987.00).

The required information is thus retrieved in very few accesses, and it is because of these few accesses that the inverted file opens up a whole new range of information retrieval possibilities. To see this, consider Request-1 again, assuming that no inverted file or equivalent structure were available and that the accounts receivable file in Figure 3.1a was very large, as could well be the case if it contained the accounts receivable of a large manufacturing organization. In such circumstances the only way the request could be complied with would be by sequential processing of the complete file, selecting 'CALIFORNIA' records as they are encountered. Such a process could take hours on a multiprogrammed computer and although the program would not be all that difficult to write, the manager of the DP department, knowing the strain that its execution could repeatedly put on their often overloaded computer, might well refuse the application for such a program, much to the annoyance of the financial manager submitting the application. This is just another one of those examples of important but otherwise trivial data "in the computer" that cannot be extracted to assist in the decision-making process. Indeed, as a result, the financial manager's dilemma could well be as serious as that of the air traveler mentioned earlier. An inverted file facility would remove the source of the difficulty.

As another example of the power of the inverted file technique, suppose that we have the following request for information for the (indexed-sequential) accounts receivable file in Figure 3.1a (we continue to imagine that the accounts receivable file is very large):

Request-2. What are the outstanding balances of all California customers in the computer business?

Again an interactive program could be prepared by the data processing department for retrievals of this type; the user at a terminal would then have to enter the name of the state and the area of business. Essentially the program would find the account numbers for customers in California and also the account numbers for customers in the computer business; account numbers common to the two groups would be for customers in California and in the aircraft business. In more detail the steps are:

1. Retrieve the **CUST-AREA-INVERSION** record with 'COMPUTERS' as the primary key. The contained **ACC-NUMB** values are shown in Figure 3.2.

2. Retrieve the CUST-STATE-INVERSION record with 'CALIFORNIA' as the primary key. The contained ACC-NUMB records are shown in Figure 3.2.
3. Take the ACC-NUMB values common to both records in Figure 3.2. (In the specific case of Figure 3.1, the account number 'AA11' is the only one common.)
4. Use each of these common fields as the primary key for direct access to the accounts receivable file, and display the value of the balance field for each record so retrieved. (In the case of the file in Figure 3.1b, the result would be $5,654.75.)

In a similar manner interactive programs could be constructed by the data processing department for a wide variety of retrieval conditions, a few of which could be:

Customers in a given state with credit limit less than a given value
Customers in a given business with balance outstanding greater than a given value
Customers in either of two given states and in a given business

Note that for each retrieval condition, a separate program is needed. A possibility is a facility that would permit the user to enter any *retrieval condition* at the terminal, thus requiring that the computer then carry out an analysis to determine what retrieval routine and what input data are required. Powerful facilities of this kind are available only with the most sophisticated data base systems, as we shall see later in the book.

Maintenance of inverted files

As presented so far, the benefits of inverted files are probably too good to be true. As might be expected there is a snag. Suppose that the accounts receivable file in Figure 3.1a is used mostly for updating. To be specific we could imagine that for every retrieval operation, there are 10 updates on average, a figure that could well be valid for the accounts receivable file of a large corporation with many active customers. The basic problem is that for a single update to the accounts receivable file, two or more updates will be necessary for each inversion. To see this clearly, consider the following cases, assuming only the inversion CUST-STATE-INVERSION and the data in Figure 3.1:

COMPUTERS	AA11	AB74	PT65

CALIFORNIA	AA11	CD83

FIGURE 3.2 Use of the inversions of the accounts receivable file in Figure 3.1a to obtain the account numbers of customers in California that are involved in computers. The required account numbers are those pointer values that are both in the inversion record with primary key 'COMPUTERS' and in the inversion record with primary key 'CALIFORNIA'. In the case above, the required account number is 'AA11'.

Record insertion in the accounts receivable file. We have two possibilities: (1) The **STATE** value in the inserted record already occurs in the accounts receivable file, or (2) it does not. We take each case in turn.

1. Suppose the record inserted was

```
KK12 MOTORS TEXAS ...
```

Then the record with primary key 'TEXAS' in CUST-STATE-INVERSION must have the pointer 'KK12' added to its list. To do this, the inversion record with key 'TEXAS' must first be read and then rewritten. Thus two file accesses are needed.

2. Suppose the record inserted was:

```
DD35 PACKAGING MICHIGAN ...
```

Then a new record must be inserted in **CUST-STATE-INVERSION** with primary key 'MICHIGAN' and pointer value 'DD35'. To do this, the inversion must first be accessed to determine whether there is a record with primary key 'MICHIGAN' in the file. Another file access is then needed to insert the new record, giving two file accesses in all.

Alteration of the **STATE** *field in the accounts receivable file.* Suppose we alter the record:

```
EF93 AIRCRAFT TEXAS ...
```

to

```
EF93 AIRCRAFT OREGON ...
```

The record in **CUST-STATE-INVERSION** with primary key 'TEXAS' will have to have the pointer 'EF93' removed (if it were the only pointer field, the record would have to be deleted). This will take two accesses, one to read the record and one to write (or delete) it.

In addition, the record in **CUST-STATE-INVERSION** with primary key 'OREGON' has to have the pointer 'EF93' added (or if no such record exists, it will have to be created). Either way we need two accesses.

Thus we need four accesses in all, just to update the inversion file following update of the accounts receivable file.

It is therefore clear that if we have 10 times as much updating of the accounts receivable file as there are retrievals from it, then even with only one inverted file, there will be a heavy burden of inverted file updates. If there are two inverted files, the situation will be twice as bad. Accordingly, inversions are always restricted to as few fields as possible, and usually we try to select those fields that are most frequently involved in retrieval requests, but infrequently involved in updates. For more details about inverted files, see Refs. 2 and 4.

Symbolic and physical pointers

The fields of a record of an inverted file are generally referred to as *pointer* fields (apart from the primary key field). We may have two types of pointers, namely, *symbolic* and *physical* pointers. Those used in Figure 3.1b are symbolic point-ers. Pointers are common in (storage) data bases, so that it is important to be clear about the difference between the two types.

Symbolic pointers. A symbolic pointer field contains the primary key value of some record of a direct access file and thus functions as a cross-reference. The record referred to by means of the symbolic pointer may be retrieved from the file that contains it (1) by a search of the index for the record's disk address if the file is indexed-sequential, or (2) by the generation of its disk (home) address by means of the proper hashing routine if the file is a hash file.

Physical pointers. A physical pointer contains the disk address of some record of a direct access file. As with a symbolic pointer a physical pointer functions as a cross-reference. The record referenced by the physical pointer may be retrieved from the file that contains it simply by directly accessing the disk address contained in the physical pointer field. The inversion **CUST-AREA-INVERSION** from Figure 3.1b is shown again in Figure 3.3 with physical pointers. We have arbitrarily structured the accounts receivable file as a hash file; notice that the pointers contain the actual addresses of the records and not just the home addresses.

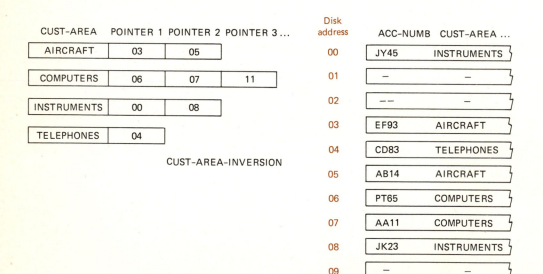

FIGURE 3.3 CUST-AREA-INVERSION

Accounts receivable file

FIGURE 3.3 CUST-AREA-INVERSION is an inversion on the field CUST-AREA of the accounts receivable file. The pointers used in the inversion are physical, that is, they refer to the disk address of records in the accounts receivable file. The accounts receivable file is shown as if it were a hash file.

Since pointers function as cross-references, they may be used to link a record in one file to one or more records in another file. Thus pointers are used to construct a collection of computer files that cross-reference each other. Such a collection of cross-referenced files is called a data base. But more about that later.

Implementing an inverted file

Inverted files are awkward to implement, mainly because of the variable length inversion records. In practice, one inversion record may contain a few pointer fields while another may contain hundreds. An inverted file may be implemented as a direct access file using either ISAM or VSAM. However, if VSAM is available there is little point in going to the expense of constructing an inverted file, for VSAM has facilities that automatically construct an inverted file when a secondary key is specified, as we shall see shortly.

Although ISAM can handle variable length records, many COBOL compilers cannot, so that a COBOL inverted file with variable length records may not be possible. An example of how to construct an inverted file with ISAM and PL/1 using variable length records is given in Ref. 2.

It is possible to use ISAM with COBOL to circumvent the difficulty of the variable length inversion records. The method involves subdividing each inversion record into fixed length portions. For example the inversion record with the key 'COMPUTERS' in Figure 3.1 could be split into two fixed-length records, each of which can hold at most two pointers:

CUST-AREA PORTION-NUMB	MORE	POINTER1	POINTER2
COMPUTERS 1	YES	AA11	AB74
COMPUTERS 2	NO	PT65	-

As many portions as necessary to accommodate the inversion record would be used. The primary key to this modified inversion file would be a composite of **CUST-AREA** and **PORTION-NUMB**. With any portion the field **MORE** would indicate if there was a subsequent portion. If insertions gave rise to the need for two new pointers for the secondary key value 'COMPUTERS', then a third portion would be inserted into the modified inversion file, and the field **MORE** in the second portion updated to 'YES'. Another advantage of this type of modified inverted file is that it can be implemented as a hash file. Facilities for hash files with variable length records are rare. The disadvantage is the increased number of disk accesses required to retrieve all the pointers for a given secondary key value. Normally the size of a portion would be quite large, so that not more than two or three portions would be needed for an inversion record.

Use of multiple linked lists

Instead of using an inverted file to permit access by means of a secondary key, it is possible to use a *multiple linked list* together with a special index. Probably the main advantage of the technique is that it avoids the need to manipulate variable length records, as is the case with inverted files. We briefly examine the concept of a linked list first.

The linked-list concept

Suppose we have a file of records on a disk, where the records are arranged in *ascending primary key sequence* in a series of disk addresses going from (say) 00 to 05 as shown (on the left) in Figure 3.4. It is clear that the records may easily be processed in ascending key order by incrementing the address used with each READ statement (done automatically if the file is a sequential file and by the program if the file is a relative file). But suppose we wish to insert a record with primary key value 720. To do this, we would have to read the records sequentially and write them out on a new file (as we saw in Chapter 2), which is not very appealing if only a few records have to be inserted and the file is large.

An alternative is to construct a relative file (the file organization used for hash files in Chapter 2) in which each record contains a physical pointer to the next record in the file in ascending primary key order as is shown in Figure 3.4 (on the right). A special record is also included to give the address of the first record of the file in ascending primary key order. As shown in Figure 3.4, the records of the file are not stored physically in ascending primary key order, although they may be processed in that way by means of the pointer system. Such a file is said to be organized as a *linked list,* and the insertion of a new record simply involves placing the record in any vacant space (usually at the end) and modifying the pointer chain accordingly.

Linked-list hash file. A large file that incorporates a single linked list is uncommon, since reading the records sequentially by following the linked list requires (slow) direct accesses. In Chapter 1, we saw that a direct access involves motion of the read/write arm (a seek) that takes about 25 mil-

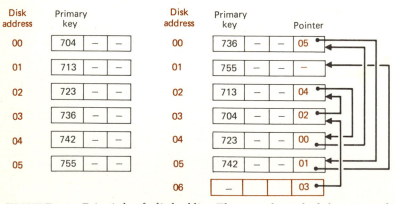

FIGURE 3.4 Principle of a linked list. The records on the left are stored on a disk in ascending primary key order and may thus be processed in that order. The records on the right are not stored in ascending primary key order, but they may be read in that order, by using the pointer field, if we start with the record in address 06. If the file on the right were a hash file, then the linked-list organization would enable it to be read in ascending key order.

liseconds, while a genuine sequential access does not. Nevertheless, the records of a large hash file are sometimes organized as a large linked list to permit processing of the file in ascending primary key order. Thus we could imagine that the primary key order of the records on the right in Figure 3.4 was due to the action of a hashing routine; records could then be accessed directly by means of the hashing routine, and sequentially by means of pointer chain. But because of the slowness of a linked list when used for sequential processing, such processing would have to be needed only infrequently to justify the file design.

A far more common application of the linked-list structure is *multiple linked lists*. With this technique, instead of one large linked list, a large number of short linked lists are used for specialized but infrequent tasks. We have already had an example with the overflow chains in ISAM files (Figure 2.13). Here most of the records of the file are in physical sequential order, permitting relatively fast sequential processing. But where a number of records have to be inserted where there is no space, these are placed in a short linked list (using physical pointers) in an overflow area, so that the complete file can still be processed in sequential order. The chains with chained progressive overflow in hash files are also linked lists. The other important example is the use of multiple linked lists for implementing secondary keys in direct access files.

Secondary keys and multiple linked lists

An example of multiple linked lists to implement the secondary keys CUST-AREA and CUST-STATE in the accounts receivable file is shown in Figure 3.5. Consider the secondary key CUST-AREA first. For each value of this secondary key in the accounts receivable file there is a linked list, and such a linked list links together all those records with the same CUST-AREA value, for example, 'AIRCRAFT'. The actual linkage is accomplished by means of the pointer A-POINTER. The pointer in a linked list can be either symbolic or physical, and in Figure 3.5 it is shown as symbolic. (Note, however, that in order for the pointer in a linked list to be symbolic, there must be direct access to the records on the basis of the primary key, which will be the case if the file is organized as either an indexed-sequential or hash file.) In Figure 3.5, arrows have been included to enable the reader to easily follow the linked lists for the different CUST-AREA values in the accounts receivable file. However, in addition to the multiple linked lists, we also need a *linked-list index* to permit direct access to each of the many linked lists.

Linked-list index.   It is a property of a linked list that there must be a special record somewhere to indicate the start of the list. Thus if we have a collection of linked lists as in Figure 3.5, we will also have a collection of these special records, one for each linked list. These special records are collected into a separate linked-list index shown in Figure 3.5 (left side) for the lists for the secondary key CUST-AREA. Each entry in the linked-list index contains a CUST-AREA value and a pointer to the first record (in ascending primary key order) in which that value occurs.

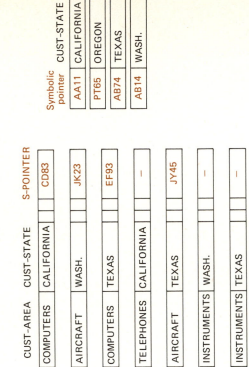

FIGURE 3.5 Shows how multiple linked lists can be used to permit secondary key access to the accounts receivable file via the secondary keys CUST-AREA and CUST-STATE. For each secondary key there is a linked-list index (extreme left and right). Each entry in the index for CUST-AREA contains the key of the first record in a linked list of records with the same CUST-AREA value; the pointer field A-POINTER points to the next record in such a list. Readers should draw the pointer system for the secondary key CUST-STATE.

In Figure 3.5 we have also included a linked-list index for the secondary key **CUST-STATE** (right). The corresponding linked lists in the accounts receivable file are implemented by means of the pointer field **S-POINTER**. We have not illustrated the linked lists by means of arrows in this case.

The main advantage of using multiple linked lists to implement secondary keys is that variable length records are avoided. As can be seen from Figure 3.5, the linked-list indexes (which in practice will be fairly large direct access files) have fixed length records. The disadvantage of the approach is that both retrieval and updating operations generally require more accesses than with inversions, as we shall see.

Use of a multiple linked list for access on a secondary key

To illustrate how a multiple linked list may be used to permit access on the basis of a secondary key, suppose that we have the files in Figure 3.5, and that a manager in the accounting department has the following request:

Request-3.   What are the outstanding balances of all California customers?

To make comparison easy, we have made Request-3 identical to Request-1 with inverted files. As before we may assume that the data processing department has made available an interactive program for requests of this type, so that the manager would merely have to enter the name of the state involved at his terminal. The program would then carry out the following steps to complete the retrieval:

1. By direct access, read the record (or entry) in the linked-list index (Figure 3.5, bottom right) with primary key value 'CALIFORNIA'. The record retrieved will contain the pointer 'AA11'.
2. Place this pointer value in the variable **NEXT-RECORD-KEY**.
3. Retrieve from the accounts receivable file the record whose key is in **NEXT-RECORD-KEY**, and move the **S-POINTER** value in this record to **NEXT-RECORD-KEY**.
4. Display the **BALANCE** value for the record retrieved in step 3.
5. If **NEXT-RECORD-KEY** contains a null value (end of linked list), then stop processing; otherwise return to step 3.

The essential difference between the above procedure and that for Request-1 is that we must program for traversal of the linked list for the secondary key 'CALIFORNIA', and as we can see this is not at all difficult. In the above retrieval, we display two **BALANCE** values (see Figure 3.5), and altogether we had three fields accesses, one to the linked-list index and two to the accounts receivable file. Thus in this case we have the same number of file accesses as with Request-1 (one to the inversion and two to the accounts receivable file).

But now let us look at a retrieval involving two secondary keys:

Request-4.   What are the outstanding balances of all California customers in the computer business?

For comparison purposes the above retrieval request is the same as that in Request-2. As before the retrieval program could accept the state and area of business when entered at a terminal. The program to carry out the request will have to traverse either the linked list for the secondary key value 'CALIFORNIA' selecting records with CUST-AREA value 'COMPUTERS', or it will have to traverse the linked list for the secondary key value 'COMPUTERS' selecting records with CUST-STATE value 'CALIFORNIA'. We arbitrarily assume that the second type of traversal is the one used by the program. The basic steps are:

1. Read the record in the linked-list index with primary key value 'COMPU-TERS'. The record retrieved will contain the pointer 'AA11', and this pointer value is placed in the variable NEXT-RECORD-KEY.
2. Retrieve from the accounts receivable file the record whose key is in NEXT-RECORD-KEY, and move the A-POINTER value in this record to NEXT-RECORD-KEY.
3. If the record retrieved in step 2 has a CUST-STATE field value 'CALIFOR-NIA', display the BALANCE value.
4. If NEXT-RECORD-KEY contains a null value, then stop processing; other-wise return to step 2.

Examining the method carefully, we see that four file accesses are required, one to the linked-list index and three to the accounts receivable file (to the records with keys 'AA11', 'AB74', and 'PT65'). However with Request-2, using the inversions in Figure 3.1, only three file accesses were needed (two to the inversions and only one to the accounts receivable file). Nevertheless, had we in the above retrieval traversed the linked list for the secondary key value 'CALI-FORNIA', then the reader should be able to see that only three file accesses would have been needed.

It would thus appear that while sometimes the number of file accesses for retrievals with multiple linked lists is the same as with inversions, the number can also be higher with multiple linked lists. In fact, it is not difficult to show that the number of accesses can be very much higher with multiple linked lists (just consider the case where we have many accounts receivable records with CUST-STATE value 'CALIFORNIA', many with CUST-AREA value 'COMPUTERS', but very few records with both values 'CALIFORNIA' and 'COMPUTERS'). We thus conclude that for purposes of information retrieval, fewer file accesses are required in general when inversions are used instead of multiple linked lists. We will see that the same is true for updating.

Maintenance of multiple linked lists

Updating a file with multiple linked lists can require many more accesses than would be the case if inversions were involved. And we can see this easily without any detailed analysis. We may use the accounts receivable file in Figure 3.5 again.

Suppose that the customer with account number 'CD83' moves the corporate headquarters from California to Delaware. Let us further suppose that the linked lists for both 'DELAWARE' and 'CALIFORNIA' are very long (hundreds of records

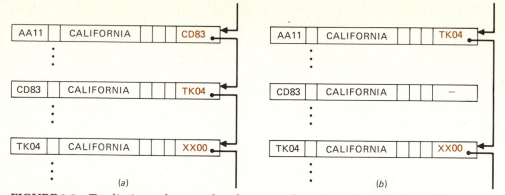

FIGURE 3.6 To eliminate the record with primary key 'CD83' from the linked list in (*a*), the pointer in the prior record of the list must be altered to point to the next record in the list as in (*b*).

each). When the **CUST-STATE** field in the record with key 'CD83' is changed from 'CALIFORNIA' to 'DELAWARE', the record with key 'CD83' must be removed from the linked list for 'CALIFORNIA' and inserted in the linked list for 'DELAWARE'. To do this, the updating program has to traverse both chains (which are long) and thus carries out many accesses.

Two-way pointer systems. We can reduce the number of accesses needed to "repair" the linked lists following an insertion or an update. The core of the problem with, for example, removal of a record from a linked list (Figure 3.6) is that we need to know both the prior and the next records in the chain.

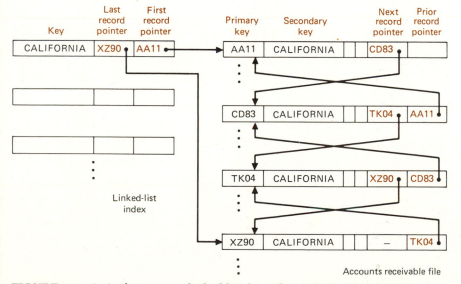

FIGURE 3.7 A single two-way linked list from the multiple linked-list version of the accounts receivable file. For each linked list there is an index entry with a pointer to the first record of the list and a pointer to the last record of the list.

The key to the next record is in the pointer field of the records being removed, but to get the key of the prior record (to change its pointer), we must start at the beginning of the chain and traverse it. The problem can be avoided by using two-way pointers (Figure 3.7); here the pointers in the index entry point to the first and last records of the list, and in each record there is a prior-pointer that points to the previous record in the chain, as well as a next-pointer that points to the next record in the chain. Clearly it will not be necessary to traverse a complete chain when two-way pointers are used; nevertheless we now have more pointers to maintain, and this results in more accesses than would be the case with inversions, although considerably less than if we had just one-way pointers. Complex pointer systems often occur in the storage records of data bases. For a detailed coverage of secondary keys and multiple linked lists, see Ref. 3.

3.2 COBOL SECONDARY KEY FACILITIES

American National Standard (ANS) COBOL allows for the use of secondary keys. However, as we have seen, for it to be possible to access a record by means of a secondary key, the underlying access method must be equipped to handle either an inversion or a multiple linked list. One such access method is VSAM from IBM, which was partly described in Chapter 2 in connection with indexed-sequential files. When a VSAM indexed-sequential file is created with COBOL, it is possible to have an inverted file (or *alternative index* in VSAM terminology) for one or more secondary keys. The inverted file is created automatically by the access method, without the user being aware of it, in much the same way as the primary key index is produced when the file is loaded. As with the primary key index, the access method also looks after all updating of the inverted files. We will now examine how secondary keys are provided for in COBOL and how they are used; we assume that we are using COBOL with VSAM as the underlying access method.

COBOL creation of a VSAM file with secondary keys

We shall create the expanded version of the accounts receivable file from Figure 3.1b as an indexed-sequential file with primary key ACC-NUMB and secondary keys CUST-AREA and CUST-STATE. First we consider the logical storage file specification and then the file creation procedure.

Logical storage file specification

As we saw in Chapter 2, the logical storage file is specified in the INPUT-OUTPUT section of the ENVIRONMENT division. But this time the INPUT-OUTPUT section declaration of the indexed-sequential file must include a specification of the secondary keys or *alternative* keys in the file. Thus in Figure 3.8, the file specification in the COBOL INPUT-OUTPUT section specifies that ACC-NUMB is the record (or primary) key and that CUST-AREA and CUST-STATE are alternative (or secondary) keys. The clause WITH DUPLICATES specifies that more than one record in the file can have the same secondary key value.

```
ENVIRONMENT.
.
INPUT-OUTPUT SECTION.
FILE-CONTROL.
     SELECT RECEIVABLES
          ASSIGN TO ARPHYS
ORGANIZATION IS INDEXED
          {SEQUENTIAL}  (When creating the file RECEIVABLES)
ACCESS IS {RANDOM    }  (When randomly accessing the file RECEIVABLES)
     RECORD KEY IS ACC-NUMB
     ALTERNATIVE RECORD KEY IS CUST-AREA WITH DUPLICATES
     ALTERNATIVE RECORD KEY IS CUST-STATE WITH DUPLICATES.
```

FIGURE 3.8 COBOL INPUT-OUTPUT specification of the indexed-sequential file RECEIVABLES (accounts receivable) with primary key ACC-NUMB, and secondary or alternative keys CUST-AREA and CUST-STATE. Since a given CUST-AREA or CUST-STATE value can occur in many records of the file RECEIVABLES, they are declared as having duplicate values (WITH DUPLICATES). ARPHYS refers to a dataset definition (DD) statement that specifies the physical storage file.

The other entries in Figure 3.8 specify an indexed-sequential file called **RECEIVABLES** (the logical storage file name) with the corresponding physical storage file to be specified in a dataset definition statement called **ARPHYS** (but not shown; see Figures 2.3 and 2.4); **ACCESS IS SEQUENTIAL** is specified when the file is being processed sequentially, and **RANDOM** when the file is being processed by direct access.

We shall omit the details of the subsequent **DATA** division specifications for the buffer area and the program data area (see Figure 2.3). However, we shall assume a buffer record structure called **RECEIVABLES-BUFREC**, and a program data area structure called **RECEIVABLES-REC**. The field **ACC-NUMB**, **CUST-AREA**, and **CUST-STATE**, which are specified as key fields in Figure 3.8, must be specified as part of the structure **RECEIVABLES-BUFREC** in the **DATA** division.

Creation of a COBOL indexed-sequential file with secondary keys
The file **RECEIVABLES** is created without regard to the existence of the secondary key fields declared in the **INPUT-OUTPUT** section. In the case of VSAM the necessary inversions are constructed as each **RECEIVABLES** record is stored; of course, since **RECEIVABLES** is an indexed-sequential file, the records for **RECEIVABLES** must be presented in ascending **ACC-NUMB** sequential order. If we assume the source records are in the sequential file **SOURCE**, the essential steps of the creation procedure are:

1. Read next **SOURCE** record into **RECEIVABLES-REC**; if no records left, then stop.
2. Write this record in the file **RECEIVABLES** using the COBOL statement:
   ```
   WRITE RECEIVABLES-BUFREC FROM RECEIVABLES-REC
   ```
3. Go to step 1.

File creation is thus quite straightforward. However, as far as retrieval on the basis of a secondary key is concerned, the records with a given secondary key value (for example, 'CALIFORNIA') are "maintained" in the order in which they were originally stored.

Order of duplicates. When the file RECEIVABLES is created, an inversion is created at the same time. Consider the inversion for CUST-STATE, which we can call CUST-STATE-INVERSION as in Figure 3.1b. In particular, let us consider the CUST-STATE-INVERSION records with primary key value 'CALIFORNIA' (refer to Figure 3.1). Since SOURCE records are added to RECEIVABLES in ascending ACC-NUMB order, records with CUST-STATE value 'CALIFORNIA' are also added to RECEIVABLES in ascending ACC-NUMB order, so that the ACC-NUMB values will be added to the CUST-STATE-INVERSION record (with primary key value 'CALIFORNIA') in ascending symbolic pointer-value order as well. (With VSAM the inverted file pointers are in fact physical, but we can ignore this to better explain the order of duplicates concept.) Thus if we retrieve the records with secondary key value 'CALIFORNIA' just after the file is created, they are available in the order in which they were originally inserted into RECEIVABLES (that is, in *chronological order*), which is the same as ascending ACC-NUMB order.

However, if we later update the RECEIVABLES file by insertion of a record with a record with ACC-NUMB value equal to (for example) 'BD56' and CUST-STATE value 'CALIFORNIA', the pointer 'BD56' is placed at the end of the list of pointers in the CUST-STATE-INVERSION record with key 'CALIFORNIA' (Figure 3.9). If we now wish to retrieve the RECEIVABLES records with secondary key 'CALIFORNIA', they are still available in chronological order but no longer in ascending ACC-NUMB order.

We thus say that VSAM records with duplicate secondary key values are *maintained* in chronological order, although this really means that such records are *available* in chronological order although they are stored in the indexed-

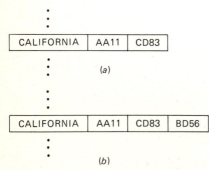

FIGURE 3.9   Shows what happens to the linked-list entry for 'CALIFORNIA' in (a) (see the multiple linked-list file in Figure 3.5) when a record with primary key 'BD56' and secondary key 'CALIFORNIA' is inserted into the accounts receivable file. The pointer 'BD56' is inserted at the end of the list of pointers (b), so that ascending (pointer) order is not preserved. The order is thus chronological.

sequential file in ascending primary key order. With some data base systems, records with the same secondary key value may be maintained in an order other than chronological.

Retrievals with COBOL secondary keys

A COBOL READ statement may be used to retrieve a record from the file RECEIVABLES on the basis of a secondary key value, provided we place the required secondary key value in the correct alternative key field (see Figure 3.8); a key clause is also required:

```
MOVE 'CALIFORNIA' TO CUST-STATE IN RECEIVABLES-BUFREC
READ RECEIVABLES INTO RECEIVABLES-REC
                   KEY IS CUST-STATE IN RECEIVABLES-BUFREC
```

When the READ statement is executed for the first time, the first record in RECEIVABLES (in chronological insertion order) with CUST-STATE value 'CALIFORNIA' is retrieved. If the READ statement is executed again (using the same value in CUST-STATE), the next RECEIVABLES record with CUST-STATE value 'CALIFORNIA' is retrieved, and so on. The records may in this way be retrieved in chronological order.

A retrieval based on a single secondary key value

As an illustration of the use of COBOL for a retrieval with one secondary key, we give the program for carrying out Request-1 from Section 3.1, which was:

Request-1.   What are the outstanding balances of all California customers?

The core excerpt is shown in Figure 3.10. It should be understood that while RECEIVABLES is being processed sequentially, only the RECEIVABLES records

```
PROCEDURE DIVISION.
STARTUP.
     OPEN INPUT RECEIVABLES.
     ACCEPT TARGET.
*The value 'CALIFORNIA' is read in and placed in the character variable TARGET.
     MOVE TARGET TO CUST-STATE IN RECEIVABLES-BUFREC.
*The declared alternative key variable now contains the target value.
SEARCHLOOP.
     READ RECEIVABLES INTO RECEIVABLES-REC,
     KEY IS CUST-STATE IN RECEIVABLES-BUFREC
                         INVALID KEY STOP RUN.
*If record with a 'CALIFORNIA' value is not found, execution stops.
     DISPLAY "CUSTOMER ACCOUNT: ",   ACC-NUMB IN RECEIVABLES-REC,
                "BALANCE: ", BALANCE IN RECEIVABLES-REC.
     GO TO SEARCHLOOP.
```

FIGURE 3.10   Core of the COBOL procedure for carrying out Request-1.

with **CUST-STATE** value 'CALIFORNIA' are accessed, since the access method uses the associated inversion (or alternate index) to locate the primary key of the next record to be retrieved.

A retrieval based on two secondary key values

To carry out Request-2 from Section 3.1, the COBOL program is not very different. The request involves the specification of two secondary key values, and is:

> *Request-2.* What are the outstanding balances of all California customers in the computer business?

The core of the retrieval program is shown in Figure 3.11. With COBOL we are forced to use a method that is much slower than that given in Section 3.1. Repeated execution of the **READ** statement causes all the accounts receivable records with **CUST-AREA** value equal to be 'COMPUTERS' to be accessed in turn. Each retrieved record then has to be examined to see if it has a **CUST-STATE** value equal to 'CALIFORNIA'. In contrast, in Section 3.1 we used the intersection of the inversion records to find the primary keys of accounts receivable records that had the correct **CUST-AREA** and **CUST-STATE** values, so that only the target accounts receivable records needed to be accessed.

Still, the method in Figure 3.11 is much faster than sequential processing of the complete accounts receivable file. To permit direct access to target records that must have specified values for two secondary keys, we would need a COBOL read statement (and an appropriate access method) that permitted **READ** statements of the type:

```
READ file-name INTO record-name
                KEY IS first alternative key-name
                KEY IS second alternative key-name
                INVALID KEY ....
```

```
PROCEDURE DIVISION.
STARTUP.
     OPEN INPUT RECEIVABLES.
     ACCEPT TARGET-S
     ACCEPT TARGET-A
     MOVE TARGET-A TO CUST-AREA IN RECEIVABLES-BUFREC.
SEARCHLOOP.
     READ RECEIVABLES INTO RECEIVABLES-REC,
     KEY IS CUST-AREA IN RECEIVABLES-BUFREC
                      INVALID KEY STOP RUN.
     IF TARGET-S = CUST-STATE IN RECEIVABLES-REC THEN
        DISPLAY "CUSTOMER ACCOUNT: ", ACC-NUMB IN RECEIVABLES-REC,
               "BALANCE: ", BALANCE IN RECEIVABLES-REC.
     GO TO SEARCHLOOP.
```

FIGURE 3.11 Core of the retrieval program for carrying out Request-2. TARGET-S will hold a CUST-STATE value, and TARGET-A a CUST-AREA value.

Such a facility does not exist in the latest version of COBOL, but it is available with many data base systems. Additional details of secondary keys with COBOL and VSAM can be found in Refs. 1 and 3.

3.3 PRIMITIVE (STORAGE) DATA BASES

By using either inversions or multiple linked lists to implement certain secondary keys, it is possible to construct, maintain, and interrogate primitive (storage) data bases; and furthermore, this can be done without the need for a special software system (called a data base management system) to manage the data base. We will look at this type of primitive data base first, since data base management had its origins in such primitive data bases in the 1960s, and since it will help the reader to gain an initial understanding of the data base concept using only the file management tools we have described so far.

Related storage files

Let us suppose that the accounts receivable file we have used with many examples so far has been set up by a manufacturer of electronic components (such as resistors, transistors, memory integrated circuits, and so on). The accounts receivable records will then apply to businesses that have purchased these electronic parts, there being an accounts receivable record for each customer of the manufacturer. In addition, for every order of components placed by the customer, there is a record in the file **ORDER**. The accounts receivable records are kept in a file called **ACC-RECEIVABLE**.

This is illustrated in Figure 3.12, showing examples of the records in the files **ACC-RECEIVABLE** and **ORDER**. Looking at the file **ORDER**, we can see that

ACC-NUMB	CRED-LIM	BALANCE
AA11	9,000	5,654.75
AB14	79,000	14,345.90
AB74	4,900	1,784.00

⋮

ACC-RECEIVABLE file

ACC-NUMB	ORDERNUMB	PART-TYPE-NUMB	QUANTITY
AB74	ON1	P9	200
AA11	ON2	P7	600
AB14	ON3	P9	800
AB74	ON4	P3	500
AB14	ON6	P7	100
AA11	ON7	P3	700
AB14	ON9	P9	600

⋮

FIGURE 3.12 The two storage files ACC-RECEIVABLE and ORDER. ACC-RECEIVABLE records describe accounts receivable records for different customers. Each ORDER record holds an order by a customer for a type of part. The order number (ORDERNUMB) is the key field, PART-TYPE-NUMB gives the number or code for the type of part ordered, and QUANTITY gives the quantity of parts ordered.

ACC-NUMB	CRED-LIM	BALANCE	ORDERNUMB	PART-TYPE-NUMB	QUANTITY
AB74	4,900	1,784.00	ON1	P9	200
AA11	9,000	5,654.75	ON2	P7	600
AB14	79,000	14,345.90	ON3	P9	800
AB74	4,900	1,784.00	ON4	P3	500
AB14	79,000	14,345.90	ON5	P7	100
AA11	9,000	5,654.75	ON6	P3	700
AB14	79,000	14,345.90	ON7	P9	600

CUST-ORDER

FIGURE 3.13 The file CUST-ORDER is formed by combining the two files in Figure 3.12. Each record of CUST-ORDER still describes an order for a quantity of parts. However, the field ACC-NUMB in the ORDER file in Figure 3.12 is now accompanied by the CRED-LIM and BALANCE fields from ACC-RECEIVABLE. Every time the account number 'AB14' occurs in a record of CUST-ORDER, the same CRED-LIM and BALANCE values have to accompany it. This duplication of data is avoided by the files in Figure 3.12.

order number 'ON3' was placed by customer 'AB14' for 800 parts of type 'P9'. From the record in ACC-RECEIVABLE with key 'AB14', we can determine that this customer has a credit limit of $79,000.

The storage files in Figure 3.12 are related. Any customer can place many orders. Thus, for the record with key 'AB14' in ACC-RECEIVABLE there are three records in ORDER, describing the orders placed by customer 'AB14'. However, for a given order described by a record in ORDER, there can only be one customer described in ACC-RECEIVABLE. Thus there is a one-to-many (1:n) relationship between the two files. Such relationships are common between files, and a collection of related files is a data base.

Elimination of redundant data

Instead of having two related files as in Figure 3.12, we have the option of combining them as in the file CUST-ORDER in Figure 3.13. A record of this file still describes an order from a customer. However, all the information about a customer that was contained in an ACC-RECEIVABLE record in Figure 3.12 is now contained in a CUST-ORDER record. Referring to Figure 3.13, since orders 'ON3', 'ON6', and 'ON9' were placed by the same customer 'AB14', the CRED-LIM and BALANCE field values must be repeated in the three CUST-ORDER records describing these orders. It is this duplication of data that is avoided by splitting CUST-ORDER into the two related files in Figure 3.12. A well-designed data base has little duplication of data, but it has many relationships between files as a result. This elimination of duplicate data is one of the great advantages of a data base.

Linking of data base files

Since there is a relationship between the records of ACC-RECEIVABLE and ORDER in Figure 3.12, in order for an applications program to make use of the relationship, there has to be a way of linking an **ACC-RECEIVABLE** record to **ORDER** records and, to a lesser extent, of linking an **ORDER** record to an **ACC-RECEIVABLE** record.

We can get a clearer idea of the nature of the relationship between **ACC-RECEIVABLE** and **ORDER** if we sort the **ORDER** file on the **ACC-NUMB** field, as is shown in Figure 3.14. For each **ACC-NUMB** value there is one **ACC-RECEIVABLE** record and many **ORDER** records. Any **ACC-RECEIVABLE** record can be called the parent record, and the group of **ORDER** records with the same **ACC-NUMB** value are called the child records. For one parent there are many children.

Returning now to the unsorted version of **ORDER** in Figure 3.12, suppose that we wish to find the outstanding balance for the customer that issued order number 'ON6', where **ACC-RECEIVABLE** is an indexed-sequential file with primary key field **ACC-NUMB** and **ORDER** is an indexed-sequential file with primary key **ORDERNUMB**. The procedure involves accessing ORDER first and then **ACC-RECEIVABLE**:

1. Access the **ORDER** record with key 'ON6'.
2. Retrieve the **ACC-NUMB** field value in this record (it's '**AB14**', see Figure 3.12).
3. Access **ACC-RECEIVABLE** directly using this **ACC-NUMB** as the primary key value.
4. Display the **BALANCE** value from the record retrieved ($14,345.90).

We thus see that it is possible to go from the **ORDER** file to the **ACC-RECEIVABLE** file merely by using the primary keys in **ORDER** and **ACC-RECEIVABLE** as well as the field **ACC-NUMB** in **ORDER**.

ACC-NUMB	CRED-LIM	BALANCE
AA11	9,000	5,654.75
AB14	79,000	14,345.90
AB74	4,900	1,784.00

ACC-RECEIVABLE

ACC-NUMB	ORDERNUMB	PART-TYPE-NUMB	QUANTITY
AA11	ON2	P7	600
AA11	ON7	P3	500
AB14	ON3	P9	800
AB14	ON6	P7	100
AB14	ON9	P9	600
AB74	ON1	P9	200
AB74	ON4	P3	500

ORDER

FIGURE 3.14 The ORDER records from Figure 3.12 have been sorted on the secondary key ACC-NUMB (which also happens to be the primary key of ACC-RECEIVABLE). The sorted version of ORDER clearly displays the relationship between ACC-RECEIVABLE and ORDER. For each ACC-RECEIVABLE record there is a group of records in ORDER. In other words, each customer has issued several orders for parts.

Let us now try to go from the **ACC-RECEIVABLE** file to the **ORDER** file. Suppose we need the outstanding balance and total number of parts of type 'P9' ordered for the account 'AB14'. We need to access all the records in **ORDER** that have the **ACC-NUMB** value 'AB14' and check each in turn for **PART-TYPE-NAME** value 'P9'. But this can be done by direct access only if the field **ACC-NUMB** in **ORDER** is a secondary key (with an associated inversion or multiple linked list), as is the case in Figure 3.15. Assuming that **ORDER** is a VSAM indexed-sequential file for which **ACC-NUMB** is a secondary key, the retrieval steps are:

1. Place zero in the auxiliary variable **TOTAL**.
2. Access **ACC-RECEIVABLE** with key 'AB14' and display **BALANCE** value.
3. Retrieve first **ORDER** record with secondary key (ACC-NUMB) value 'AB14'.
4. If **PART-TYPE-NAME** = 'P9', add **QUANTITY** value to **TOTAL**.
5. Retrieve next **ORDER** duplicate with secondary key value 'AB14'; if no next record, display **TOTAL** value and stop.
6. Go to step 4.

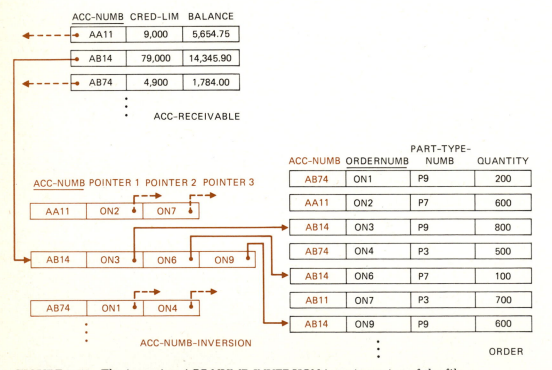

FIGURE 3.15 The inversion ACC-NUMB-INVERSION is an inversion of the file ORDER on the secondary key field ACC-NUMB, and thus permits direct access to the group of orders for a given account (see Figure 3.14). However since ACC-NUMB is the primary key of ACC-RECEIVABLE, the inversion serves to link an ACC-RECEIVABLE record for a given account (for example 'AB14') to the orders for that account (for example 'ON3','ON6' 'ON9'), all of which records are available by direct access.

Thus we can go from an **ACC-RECEIVABLE** record to related **ORDER** records by means of the secondary key **ACC-NUMB** in **ORDER** and the associated inversion (**ACC-NUMB-INVERSION** in Figure 3.15).

The reader should be clear about the implications of this. Given a record in **ORDER**, it is possible for a program to access the related record in **ACC-RECEIVABLE**, and given a record in **ACC-RECEIVABLE**, it is possible for a program to access the related records in the file **ORDER**. Thus we can state that in general, given direct access parent and child files, and a secondary key in the child file that is the primary key in the parent file, it is possible for a program to retrieve a parent record directly given a child record, and to retrieve all the child records directly given the parent record.

However, use of secondary key implementations is not the only way of connecting parent and child records in related storage files. Other pointer systems can be used, as we shall see in later chapters. Nevertheless it is fair to state that these other pointer systems are all variations on the theme of secondary key implementations.

Updating the primitive data base

Since we have a secondary key in our primitive data base, unless we use an access method like VSAM, updating the file **ORDER** will require maintenance of the pointer system. As we have seen, this is a tedious chore at best. What is worse, since we have no special management system to help us, all the details of updating the pointer system would have to be built into the updating applications program. The problem may be manageable when we have only a few files in the data base, as in Figure 3.15. But imagine the amount of programming required to maintain the pointer systems if we had a data base involving large numbers of files that were all related. And remember, with a large data base there will not be just one program manipulating the data base, but very large numbers of programs; and all these programs would have to include large quantities of code for manipulating the pointer systems. Clearly there is room for some rationalization, since the kind of pointer manipulation needed will be much the same for all applications programs.

Need for a data base management

The rationalization appeared in the form of *data base management systems* in the late 1960s, before the appearance of access methods like VSAM for handling secondary keys. As data base management systems developed, however they came to provide facilities far beyond what could be accomplished by using application programs and VSAM-like access methods to manage primitive data bases like the one shown in Figure 3.15.

Data bases of the type introduced in the preceding sections, that is, data bases constructed simply by inverting on selected fields from a collection of storage files, are not very common. Such data bases are very much in the "do-it-yourself" category, and all the techniques for managing the data base have to be incorporated into the user file processing programs. In practice, the software product known as a data base management system (DBMS) is used to carry out many of the chores associated with managing a data base. Many of the chores that have to be carried out are much the same regardless of the data base, and data base management systems are almost always *generalized*, that is, they can handle any data base, provided, as we shall see, that the data base system has access to a description of the files and other structures (inversions, and so on) making up the data base. But elimination of data base management chores is not the only benefit of using a data base management system to manage the data base. There are many others, probably the most important of which is *data independence*.

Data independence

Suppose that a corporation constructs a large data base with little duplication of data, but without using a data base management system, instead using the technique of linking storage files by means of either file inversions or multiple linked lists as described in the preceding section. Let us further suppose that there are a large number of files making up the data base and that there are a few thousand application programs looking after updating and information retrieval. Now consider what the consequences of trying to change the structure of one of the data base files would be, for example, if some new fields had to be added. Since all the application programs manipulate the data base files directly, very many programs would have to be changed, at very great expense. With most data base management systems such an alteration to data base files would not require modification of the application programs. The reason is that data base management systems provide what is called *data independence*, while the primitive data base would not. Data independence is very important and is discussed in detail in Chapter 4.

Other data base management system facilities

Data base systems also have facilities for keeping the data in the data base secure from unauthorized intruders, for keeping the data accurate, for keeping the data consistent. They also have facilities for restricting users to just certain portions of a data base. In addition, many of the latest systems provide for sophisticated information retrieval without the need to write information retrieval programs. We shall see something of how data base management systems are structured in Chapter 4.

SUMMARY

1. Standard hash and indexed-sequential files permit direct access to records on presentation of a unique primary key value. There is also a need for direct access on the basis of a nonunique secondary key value. This can be accomplished either by means of an inversion on the secondary key field, that is, an inverted file, or by means of a combination of multiple linked lists and multiple linked-list indexes. Both inverted files and multiple linked-list indexes are direct access files for which a secondary key is used as the primary key. Inverted

files are very efficient but are difficult to manage because they use variable-length records. Multiple linked-list indexes are easy to manage because they use fixed-length records, but can be very much less efficient because of the need to traverse linked lists. Both types of structure are widely used with data bases.

2. COBOL provides for the automatic management of secondary keys, where appropriate access methods such as VSAM are available. VSAM uses inverted files to provide secondary key access. A user is not aware of the underlying inverted file when writing a program with COBOL and VSAM involving a secondary key. For a VSAM file, both the primary and any secondary keys must be specified in the INPUT-OUTPUT section of a COBOL program.

3. If a facility for managing secondary keys is available, a primitive data base can easily be constructed using storage files involved in one-to-many relationships. Without a secondary key facility, it becomes prohibitively expensive to incorporate the details of managing the secondary key pointer systems in application programs. A data base management system is normally used to eliminate many of the chores of managing a data base. Data base management systems also impart additional benefits, such as the provision of data independence.

QUESTIONS

1. Why can a secondary key have duplicate values?
2. Explain the inverted file concept.
3. Using only the inversion CUST-STATE-INVERSION and the accounts receivable file in Figure 3.1, devise retrieval procedures and give the number of file (but not disk) accesses for the following requests:
   (a) What business sectors are Texas customers involved in?
   (b) What customers are either in California or Washington?
   (c) What Texas customers are in the aircraft business?
   (d) What Texas customers are not in the aircraft business?
   (e) What Texas customers are in either the aircraft or the computer business?
   (f) What customers are neither in California nor in Texas?
4. Using both the inversion CUST-AREA-INVERSION and CUST-STATE-INVERSION as well as the accounts receivable file in Figure 3.1, devise retrieval procedures and give the number of file accesses for the following requests:
   (a) What Texas customers are in the aircraft business?
   (b) What Texas customers are either in the aircraft business or the computer business?
   (c) What customers are either in California or in the computer business?
   (d) What California customers are not in the computer business?
5. For the data in Figure 3.1, devise update procedures and give the number of file accesses for the following updates:
   (a) The credit limit for customer 'AB74' is changed to $6,000.
   (b) The credit limit for all customers in the aircraft business is increased by $10,000.

(c) Customer 'AB14' moves from Washington to Texas.

(d) Customer 'AB14' moves from Washington to New York.

(e) A new customer 'AK46' in Washington in the aircraft business is entered.

(f) A new customer 'BZ42' in Texas in the food business is entered.

(g) A new customer 'BH99' in Michigan in the automotive business is entered.

(h) Customer 'PT65' is deleted.

(i) Customer 'EF93' is deleted.

6. Using the linked-list indexes and linked lists in Figure 3.5, instead of the inversions in Figure 3.1, repeat Question 4.

7. Using the linked-list indexes and linked lists in Figure 3.5, instead of the inversions in Figure 3.1, repeat Question 5.

8. Redraw the left side of Figure 3.5, so that the CUST-AREA secondary key is implemented by means of two-way linked lists. For inspiration see Figure 3.7.

9. Assuming a two-way linked list for the CUST-AREA secondary key in Figure 3.5, give procedures for the following updates:

(a) The customer 'AB74' is deleted.

(b) The customer 'AB74' switches from computers to telephones.

10. Make a drawing of a hash file containing about 15 records employing chained progressive overflow, where the chains form:

(a) Multiple one-way linked lists.

(b) Multiple two-way linked lists.

11. Assuming the primitive data base in Figure 3.15, and assuming that no VSAM-like secondary key facility is available, devise procedures to do the following:

(a) Find the order numbers for orders from customer 'AB14'.

(b) Find the order numbers for orders from customer 'AB14' for 'P7' part types.

(c) Find the customers that have not ordered 'P7' part types.

12. Repeat Question 11, assuming that the secondary key ACC-NUMB in ORDER is provided for by a VSAM-like facility, that is, the procedure can ignore the details of manipulating the inversion.

13. With the data base in Figure 3.15, assume that a VSAM-like facility is used to make secondary keys out of both ACC-NUMB in ORDER and PART-TYPE-NUMB in ORDER, and devise procedures to do the following:

(a) Find the credit limits of customers that have ordered part type 'P3'.

(b) Find the outstanding balances of customers that have ordered more than 500 of part type 'P9' in a single order.

Projects

14. Assuming that a COBOL secondary key facility is available, create an indexed-sequential version of the accounts receivable file in Figure 3.1 with CUST-AREA and CUST-STATE as secondary keys. If a secondary key facility is not available, construct the inversion using fixed length portions for each inversion record, as described in Section 3.1.

15. Use COBOL and symbolic pointers to create an indexed-sequential version of the accounts receivable file in Figure 3.5, for which the secondary key **CUST-AREA** is implemented by means of a linked-list index and associated linked lists.

16. Assuming an accounts receivable file created as in Project 14, write an interactive COBOL program to retrieve customers from the state X that are in business Y, where the values of X and Y are entered at the terminal.

17. Assuming an accounts receivable file created as in Project 14, write an interactive COBOL program to retrieve customers that are either in state X or in business Y.

18. Assuming that the accounts receivable file is created as in Project 15, write an interactive COBOL program to retrieve customers who are from the business sector X and located in the state Y.

19. Assuming the accounts receivable file as created in Project 15, write an interactive program to accept records for insertion. Note that the program should be able to handle the case where there is a **CUST-AREA** value in the new record that is not already in the linked-list index.

20. Assuming the accounts receivable file as created in Project 15, write an interactive program that will delete records whose **ACC-NUMB** values are presented.

REFERENCES

1. Bohl, M., 1981. *Introduction to IBM Direct Access Storage Devices*, SRA, Palo Alto, California.
2. Bradley, J., 1982. File and Data Base Techniques, Holt, Rinehart & Winston, New York.
3. Brown, G. D., 1977. *Advanced ANS COBOL*. Wiley-Interscience, New York.
4. Teory, T. J. and J. P. Fry, 1982. Design of Data Base Structures, Prentice-Hall, Englewood Cliffs, N. J.

3-Level Data Bases

As we saw toward the end of Chapter 3, a data base is fundamentally a collection of computer files that cross-reference each other. We shall study this cross-referencing in more detail in Chapter 5. In this chapter we develop the concept of a *three-level data base* and an associated three-level data base management system. The primitive data base introduced in the previous chapter was a one-level (namely, the storage level) data base. However, by using three-level data bases, we can have the benefit of data independence, a concept which we now introduce in some detail. It is important for an understanding of data base management principles.

4.1 DATA INDEPENDENCE

The concept of data independence has to do with the structuring of data bases and data base management software so that user application programs are unaffected by changes to many aspects of the structure (not the content) of the data base. The relevant structuring of the data base and the data base management system are intertwined, but for expositional purposes we will separate the two as far as possible. Remembering that a data base is a collection of files, we will examine the three-level structure of a data base that consists of a *single* (storage) file; this is sufficient for an explanation of the necessary principles.

Storage, conceptual, and external files

The reader will certainly have noticed that we have frequently prefixed the term "file" by the adjective "storage" throughout the preceding chapters. We used this term in anticipation of the existence of two more abstract types of files, namely, *conceptual* and *external* files. While they are certainly abstract files, these two additional types of file have great practical consequences. We will therefore begin with a revision of the storage file concept, followed by an introduction to the conceptual and external file concepts.

The storage file concept

The reader should be reasonably familiar and comfortable with the storage file concept. All the files used so far in this book were storage files. We can loosely define a storage file as a file that is manipulated by a COBOL (or other programming language such as PL/1) program using such file manipulation statements as **READ, WRITE, REWRITE**. Thus all the files of conventional data processing are storage files. In file processing it is often convenient to distinguish between two types of storage files, namely, logical storage files and physical storage files (see also Figure 1.6).

> *Logical storage file.* This is the collection of records as read into a **WORKING-STORAGE** variable by a **READ** statement. It includes any pointer fields built into the records.
> *Physical storage file.* This is the collection of records as stored on a storage medium such as a disk pack. Thus it corresponds well to an IBM dataset and is the file that is written and read by the disk controller (see Figure 1.4).

With data bases we often ignore the fine distinction between logical and physical storage files. The version of the accounts receivable file in Figure 3.5 is a good example of a typical direct access storage file. Each record contains data (accounts receivable data) that is of importance to the (corporate) enterprise; however, in addition there are pointer fields that are there to enable the records of the file to be accessed in a certain way. In Figure 3.5, they are part of a multiple linked-list pointer system that permit secondary key access with the fields **CUST-AREA** and **CUST-STATE**. As far as the user is concerned, these pointer fields are simply a necessary evil that complicate maintenance of the file. Some records of the file in Figure 3.5 are shown again in Figure 4.1c, and we shall call this file **AR-STORAGE**.

The external file concept

As mentioned, the typical user of **AR-STORAGE** is not particularly interested in the pointer fields of the file, but rather in some specific group of useful data fields. Thus one group of users may only be interested in the fields **ACC-NUMB**, **CRED-LIM**, and **BALANCE**. We could then imagine a file with only these fields, but otherwise containing the same data as **AR-STORAGE**. The file **AR-**

ACC-NUMB	CUST-AREA
AA11	COMPUTERS
AB14	AIRCRAFT

AR-EXTERNAL1

ACC-NUMB	BALANCE
AA11	5,654.75
AB14	14,345.90

AR-EXTERNAL2

ACC-NUMB	CRED-LIM	BALANCE
AA11	9,000	5,654.75
AB14	79,000	14,345.90

AR-EXTERNAL3

ACC-NUMB	CUST-AREA	CUST-STATE	CRED-LIM	BALANCE
AA11	COMPUTERS	CALIFORNIA	9,000	5,654.75
AB14	AIRCRAFT	WASH.	79,000	14,345.90

AR-CONCEPTUAL

ACC-NUMB	CUST-AREA	CUST-STATE	CRED-LIM	BALANCE	A-POINTER	S-POINTER
AA11	COMPUTERS	CALIFORNIA	9,000	5,654.75	AB74	CD83
AB14	AIRCRAFT	WASH.	79,000	14,345.90	EF93	JK23

AR-STORAGE

FIGURE 4.1 Shows how a single conceptual file and many external files may be abstracted from a storage file (or files). AR-STORAGE is the storage file and is the version of the accounts receivable (AR) file from Figure 3.5. The pointer fields (colored) are for multiple linked lists.

EXTERNAL3 in Figure 4.1*a* is such a file; it is an abstract or imaginary file and is merely abstracted from the underlying storage file. Similarly, another such file is AR-EXTERNAL2 for a group of users interested only in the fields ACC-NUMB and BALANCE, and so on. Such files are called *external files* and can be constructed with any combination of the useful data fields (but not pointer fields) from the underlying storage file. *They do not physically exist.*

The conceptual file concept

The *conceptual file* can be arrived at in two ways. In one view it is abstracted from the underlying storage file by taking only the useful data fields, so that other fields such as pointers and deletion tags are ignored. Another way of looking at it is to consider it the *common denominator file* for all the external files. Thus a field in the conceptual file is of use to some group in the enterprise; otherwise it has no business being in the file. The file AR-CONCEPTUAL in Figure 4.1b is the conceptual file abstracted from the underlying storage file AR-STORAGE. It should be clearly understood that AR-CONCEPTUAL would *never physically exist* on a disk.

Storage data independence

In this section we shall see how the concepts of concepual and storage files lead to *storage data independence*. Storage data independence is a property of user programs that can continue to execute correctly whenever changes are made to the organization of an underlying storage file; a typical change could be from indexed-sequential organization to hash file organization or from the use of an inverted file to a multiple linked list.

It is important that the reader grasp the basic principle of how storage data independence for user programs may be achieved, as it is used in many data base management systems. We shall illustrate the principle by a simple example involving the storage file AR-STORAGE and the conceptual file AR-CONCEPTUAL from Figure 4.1.

Let us suppose that a user has to manipulate the accounts receivable file AR-STORAGE (Figure 4.2), and that instead of using a single (COBOL) program containing the usual READ and WRITE statements, two programs are written, one of them a main or calling program called USER-PROGRAM and the other a subsidiary program or subprogram called STORAGE-ROUTINE. (Readers who are not familiar with the basic concept of a subprogram should consult an elementary programming text.) All the statements for processing AR-STORAGE directly, that is, READ, WRITE and REWRITE COBOL statements, are incorporated in the subprogram STORAGE-ROUTINE.

The user program is concerned only with the useful data in AR-STORAGE, that is, with the contents of the abstract conceptual file AR-CONCEPTUAL. When an AR-CONCEPTUAL record is required by USER-PROGRAM, a CALL statement is executed that transfers control parameters to the subprogram. These parameters inform the subprogram what operation is to be carried out; for example, the parameter 'FETCH' (see Figure 4.2) could imply either a direct access or sequential COBOL READ operation.

The CALL from USER-PROGRAM to STORAGE-ROUTINE will cause that subprogram to be executed and the required AR-STORAGE record read. STORAGE-ROUTINE then extracts the AR-CONCEPTUAL record from the retrieved AR-STORAGE record and passes it up to USER-PROGRAM. In this way USER-PROGRAM enjoys the illusion of reading a record from the nonexistent AR-

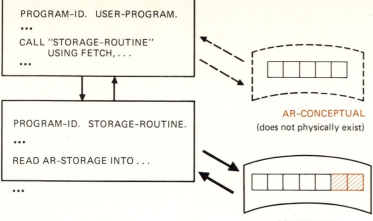

FIGURE 4.2 Shows how storage (often called physical) data independence may be achieved by using a subprogram for all storage file manipulation. If AR-STORAGE has to be changed, for example from an indexed-sequential to a hash file, or if a multiple linked list has to be replaced by an inversion, then only STORAGE-ROUTINE and AR-STORAGE has to be changed. If there are a large number of programs such as USER-PROGRAM that manipulate AR-STORAGE via STORAGE-ROUTINE, we escape having to change them, a very significant saving. Furthermore the programmer of USER-PROGRAM need not know much about the workings of STORAGE-ROUTINE, and may conveniently imagine that USER-PROGRAM manipulates AR-CONCEPTUAL.

CONCEPTUAL file. A similar sequence of events takes place when **USER-PROGRAM** inserts a record into **AR-CONCEPTUAL**; **STORAGE-ROUTINE** in fact places a record in **AR-STORAGE**.

The benefit of operating in this way should be apparent. Suppose it is necessary to make a significant change to the way in which **AR-STORAGE** is organized or stored. For example, we might want to change from indexed to hash organization. To make this change, we clearly need to load a new version of **AR-STORAGE**; and to be able to manipulate this new version, we need a new version of **STORAGE-ROUTINE**. However, we do not need a new version of **USER-PROGRAM**, which will still be able to pass over to **AR-STORAGE** a command to read or write a record from or into **AR-STORAGE**. **STORAGE-ROUTINE** will carry out the command as before, but because of the different **AR-STORAGE** file organization the actual reading or writing of the record will be done differently.

It is thus clear that this two-level arrangement imparts *storage data* (or *physical data*) *independence* to **USER-PROGRAM**, that is, it can execute correctly regardless of changes to the method of storing the storage file **AR-STORAGE**. Of course the new method of storing **AR-STORAGE** records will probably mean that the number of disk accesses to retrieve an **AR-STORAGE** record will change, that is, the *performance* or efficiency of execution of **USER-PROGRAM** will be affected. Hence by appropriate alterations to **STORAGE-ROUTINE** and **AR-STORAGE**, we can improve or *tune* the performance of **USER-PROGRAM**. Thus storage data independence and *performance tuning* are closely related; and a data-independent program can be tuned without being altered.

The great benefit of storage data independence is the very significant saving in program maintenance costs. Typically in a large organization there would be many user programs manipulating **AR-STORAGE**. If all these programs carry out their manipulation via **STORAGE-ROUTINE** and the imaginary file **AR-CONCEPTUAL**, then when a change must be made to the method of storing **AR-STORAGE**, none of these programs are affected, a very significant saving.

Performance tuning and the storage schema

In practice we would not want to write a new version of **STORAGE-ROUTINE** every time we wanted to alter the storage method for **AR-STORAGE** records. Instead **STORAGE-ROUTINE** would be originally constructed as a versatile program that could manipulate many different storage versions of **AR-STORAGE**. Which method of manipulation **STORAGE-ROUTINE** would apply would depend on the contents of a data structure used by **STORAGE-ROUTINE**. This data structure is called a *storage schema* and is either part of **STORAGE-ROUTINE** or is easily accessed by **STORAGE-ROUTINE**. With this enhanced arrangement, to alter the method by which **STORAGE-ROUTINE** manipulates **AR-STORAGE**, it is only necessary to make changes to the associated storage schema. This is the method used for tuning the storage files of data bases, as we shall soon see (the data base management system is roughly equivalent to a version of **STORAGE-ROUTINE** that could manage many storage files, exactly how any given file is to be manipulated depending on the contents of an associated storage schema).

Conceptual (or logical) data independence

Conceptual data independence is a property of a user program that can continue to execute correctly when data fields are removed from or inserted into the conceptual files manipulated by the user program (via a storage file of course). Naturally the fields removed or inserted must not actually be used by the user program. Thus if **USER-PROGRAM1** makes use of only the fields **ACC-NUMB** and **CUST-AREA** from **AR-CONCEPTUAL** (see Figure 4.1), and if **USER-PROGRAM1** is conceptual data-independent, it should make no difference to the correct execution of **USER-PROGRAM1** if, for example, the field **BALANCE** were removed entirely from the file **AR-CONCEPTUAL** (that is, if it were removed from the underlying storage file **AR-STORAGE**, since **AR-CONCEPTUAL** does not physically exist).

Conceptual data independence may be achieved by adding another subprogram level to the processing of the storage file **AR-STORAGE**, as is illustrated in

Figure 4.3. The new subprogram is **CONCEPTUAL-ROUTINE** in this case, and it passes commands to **STORAGE-ROUTINE** to manipulate the storage file **AR-STORAGE** by means of COBOL **READ, WRITE, REWRITE,** and **DELETE** commands as described in the previous section. For example, **CONCEPTUAL-ROUTINE** could retrieve an **AR-CONCEPTUAL** record using an appropriate **CALL** to **STORAGE-ROUTINE**.

If we suppose that the user program **USER-PROGRAM1** is manipulating records of the imaginary external file **AR-EXTERNAL1** as described in Figure 4.1, then to retrieve a record of **AR-EXTERNAL1**, **USER-PROGRAM1** will issue a **CALL** to **CONCEPTUAL-ROUTINE**, which will in turn issue a **CALL** to **STORAGE-ROUTINE** (Figure 4.3). **STORAGE-ROUTINE** accesses the necessary **AR-STORAGE** record, strips off the pointer fields, and delivers the corresponding **AR-CONCEPTUAL** record to **CONCEPTUAL-ROUTINE**. **CONCEPTUAL-ROUTINE** then extracts the **ACC-NUMB** and **CUST-AREA** fields necessary to form an **AR-EXTERNAL1** record and delivers this record to **USER-PROGRAM1**.

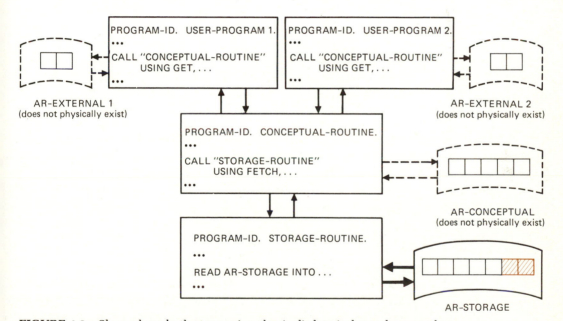

FIGURE 4.3 Shows how both storage (or physical) data independence and conceptual (or logical) data independence may be achieved by using a subprogram (CONCEPTUAL-ROUTINE) to deal with the conceptual file, while a lower level subprogram (STORAGE-ROUTINE) deals with the storage file (AR-STORAGE). A user program (such as USER-PROGRAM2) apparently manipulates an external file (such as AR-EXTERNAL2) by means of a subprogram CALL to CONCEPTUAL-ROUTINE which apparently manipulates AR-CONCEPTUAL by means of a CALL to STORAGE-ROUTINE which actually manipulates AR-STORAGE. The addition of a new field to AR-CONCEPTUAL would require changes to CONCEPTUAL-ROUTINE, STORAGE-ROUTINE, and AR-STORAGE, but not to the large number of user programs such as USER-PROGRAM1 and USER-PROGRAM2.

A similar sequence of events would take place if **USER-PROGRAM1** had to insert a new record into **AR-EXTERNAL1** (although the careful reader will note that the resulting **AR-STORAGE** record will be incomplete).

It is clear that this three-level arrangement retains the storage data independence described earlier. If we wish to alter the method of storing **AR-STORAGE** records, then only **AR-STORAGE** and **STORAGE-ROUTINE** need to be changed, and not the user program **USER-PROGRAM1** (nor the subprogram **CONCEPTUAL-ROUTINE**).

The arrangement, however, also allows for conceptual data independence. We can see from Figure 4.3 that it is possible to have many different user programs using many different external files derived from **AR-CONCEPTUAL**. Each user program manipulates its particular external file via **CONCEPT-ROUTINE** and **STORAGE-ROUTINE**. Now suppose that a new user group needs an external file with fields **ACC-NUMB** and **ASSETS**, where **ASSETS** is the corporate assets of each customer with an account in **AR-STORAGE**. It is clear that we need a new version of **AR-STORAGE** that includes the new field **ASSETS**. A new version of **STORAGE-ROUTINE** and **CONCEPTUAL** routine will also be needed to handle the longer **AR-STORAGE** and **AR-CONCEPTUAL** records. However, the existing user programs **USER-PROGRAM1**, **USER-PROGRAM2**, . . . will not be affected by this change since the external records passed between these programs and **CONCEPTUAL-ROUTINE** are unchanged. Thus these user programs possess a high degree of conceptual (or logical) data independence.

Data management implications of conceptual data independence

In practice in a large organization the need to add a new field to a widely used file is a fairly common occurrence. At the same time, in a conventional file processing environment there is little or no data independence for user programs. The users of the file that needs a new field typically object that adding the new field will require that all their programs be rewritten at great expense. The short-term and most expedient solution is always taken in such cases, and a new file is created with the new field, but the old version of the file continues to be used with all the existing programs.

Such a solution means that the two files have many common data fields. Some time later the same problem arises again when still another field is required, the result being that a third version of the file is put into use, and so on. This means that a great deal of corporate data is duplicated in many different files at computer installations. If we have three versions of an accounts receivable file with a common field, all three files will have to be updated at much the same time; otherwise they will tend to contain inconsistent data. Since the schedules of busy data processing centers rarely allow for the updating of all the files that incorporate the same field, inconsistency is unavoidable, even in the best managed installations. An obvious consequence is inconsistent and unreliable reports to management. A less obvious consequence is increased difficulty in generating reports to satisfy random but important requests for information. Fields containing data about a customer may be scattered over many different versions of the same file, where not all the versions are up to date. This means that it will be difficult, if not impossible, to write a program to tie the data in these fields together. All of this naturally leads to the common management complaint that the data processing department is unable to manage the organization's data and cannot respond in a reasonable time to straightforward requests for information in its custody.

The solution to the problem is a data base management system with a high degree of storage and conceptual data independence, and as with the idealized method of dealing with a simple file that we have been discussing in this section, the three levels of abstraction play a leading role in data base managment systems.

Conceptual and external schemas for three-level files

In a more sophisticated version of the arrangement in Figure 4.3, we would use a *storage schema* (or storage file specification) in association with STORAGE-ROUTINE to make it easier to adapt STORAGE-ROUTINE to a different version of AR-STORAGE, as explained earlier.

However, as we have seen, when a new type of field is to be added to AR-STORAGE, CONCEPTUAL-ROUTINE also has to be altered so that it can manage the new version of AR-CONCEPTUAL. In order to simplify the alteration to CONCEPTUAL-ROUTINE, the routine could be designed to operate in association with a specification of AR-CONCEPTUAL, or a *conceptual schema*. The idea is that we have only to alter this conceptual schema when AR-CONCEPTUAL is altered.

Furthermore, many different user programs can interface with CONCEPTUAL-ROUTINE. If a new user routine is created that uses an entirely new external file (but nevertheless contains a subset of the useful data fields in AR-STORAGE), then we would probably have to modify CONCEPTUAL-ROUTINE to handle this new external file as well. To simplify this task, CONCEPTUAL-ROUTINE could be designed to function in association with a specification of each external file being manipulated by a user program. Such a specification is called an *external schema*. The idea again is that the use of a new external file would require only that a new file specification be used as the external schema in association with CONCEPTUAL-ROUTINE.

The concepts of storage, conceptual, and external schemas are fundamental to data base management systems, as we shall now see.

4.2 THREE-LEVEL DATA BASE MANAGEMENT SYSTEMS

It is widely agreed that data base management systems should be able to manage three-level data bases. A three-level data base is made up of storage files on which conceptual and external files can be based. Three-level data base systems as a result provide for both storage (physical) and conceptual (logical) data independence. These three-level data base systems were formally approved in a well-known and important proposal of the Standards and Planning Committee (SPARC) of the American National Standards Institute (ANSI) in 1975 (Refs. 3

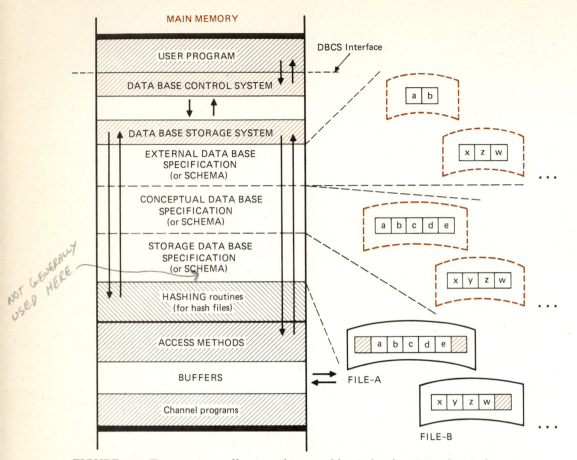

FIGURE 4.4 To manage a collection of storage files (a data base) in a data independent manner, a Data Base Control System (DBCS) replaces the CONCEPTUAL-ROUTINE from Figure 4.3. Furthermore the STORAGE-ROUTINE from Figure 4.3 is replaced by the Data Base Storage System (DBSS). For each file we have three levels of abstraction to promote data independence. Alterations to the storage file are managed by changes to the conceptual and storage schemas. A new external file is accommodated by a new external schema.

and 4). Many data base systems used in commerce conform more or less to the overall architecture set forth in the ANSI/SPARC proposal. We will first examine the architecture of a three-level or ANSI/SPARC data base system and then look at how such systems function.

The data base system

The overall architecture of a three-level data base management system is illustrated in Figure 4.4. The various parts of the system that are in main memory when a data base is being manipulated by a user program are shown. The data base is a collection of (related or integrated) storage files **FILE-A**, **FILE-B**, and so

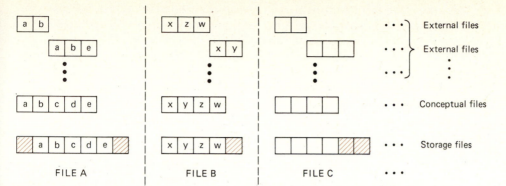

FIGURE 4.5 A data base is very simply a collection of files, such as files A, B, C, . . . above. But for every file, there will be the storage version, which actually exists on disk storage, a conceptual version, and a number of external files. Conceptual and external files do not actually physically exist. Pointer fields are shaded.

on. These files are also illustrated in Figure 4.5. For example, **FILE-A** has useful data fields a, b, c, d, and e, as well as some pointer fields. Based on **FILE-A** we can have a conceptual file with fields a, b, c, d, and e, but no pointer fields. Based on the conceptual file we can have an assortment of external files, such as one with fields a and b, another with fields a, b, and c, and so on. Similarly, for **FILE-B** we will have a conceptual file and several external files.

To manipulate the data base, the user program calls up the services of the *data base control system* (DBCS). This is often done by means of a **CALL** statement in the user program. The data base control system thus corresponds roughly to **CONCEPTUAL-ROUTINE** in the previous section, where we described the data-independent manipulation of the single storage file **AR-STORAGE**. The difference is that the DBCS can handle any number of different and related files. Strictly, the DBCS can be imagined as manipulating the conceptual files, although in reality it manipulates the underlying storage files by means of **CALL**s to the *data base storage system* (DBSS). The data base storage system manipulates the storage files by higher level (or even assembly) language statements such as **READ**, **WRITE**, **REWRITE**, and **DELETE** in COBOL and PL/1.

The storage, conceptual, and external schemas with data bases

Associated with the data base storage system is the storage data base specification or *data base storage schema*, and associated with the data base control system are the *external* and *conceptual schemas.* The external schema contains specifications of the external files being manipulated, while the conceptual schema contains specifications of the conceptual files of the data base. The schemas are included in Figure 4.4.

Storage schema. The storage schema is normally very detailed and contains a description of the fields of every file in the storage data base. Included are details of the pointer fields that are used either for implementing secondary keys or for relationships between storage files. While we have not emphasized the point so far, for every conceptual file in the data base there may in fact be several storage files, one containing the useful data and other pointer fields and others that are essentially indexes or inversions. (The converse is also possible.) The data base storage system makes use of the storage schema when accessing the storage data base. If the structure of the storage data base is altered (for example, by replacing hash files by indexed-sequential files or by replacing inversions by multiple linked lists), it is only necessary to reflect these changes in the storage schema, in order that the data base storage system be able to manipulate the new storage data base. Of course the data base storage system must be specially constructed in order for this to be possible. In this way, storage (or physical) data independence can be provided by the data base management system. Note that ANSI/SPAPC used the term *internal* instead of *storage*, in connection with the storage schema and storage data base. However, the term *storage* seems more appropriate and is probably the more widely used.

Conceptual schema.   The conceptual schema contains the specifications of all the conceptual files of the data base; in addition relationships between these conceptual files are often specified. Ideally, there should be nothing in the conceptual schema that would determine how the underlying storage files are structured. For example, a field in the conceptual schema could be specified as a secondary key without any specification of whether the implementation was by means of an inverted file or a multiple linked list.

External schema.   There can be many external schemas based on a single storage data base. The external schema contains a specification of the external files used by a particular user group; it may also contain a specification of the relationships between these external files. The specification of the files in an external schema is used both by the user program that is manipulating the data base and by the data base control system. If a new field is added to the data base storage, then it must be specified in both the storage schema and the conceptual schema. However, no change need be made to existing external schemas. Thus user programs associated with existing external schemas will not be affected by the addition of the new field to the data base. Hence the external schema concept leads to conceptual (or logical) data independence.

Examples of typical schemas

To get an idea of the structure of typical storage, conceptual, and external schemas, let us consider a simple storage data base called **STORAGE-ACCOUNTING** with two files called **ACC-RECEIVABLE** and **ORDER**, whereas in previous examples, **ACC-RECEIVABLE** contains accounts receivable records and **ORDER** contains records describing orders for electronic parts (Figure 4.6a). For each customer account there are several orders for parts, so that we have a one-to-many relationship between **ACC-RECEIVABLE** and **ORDER** records.

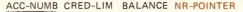

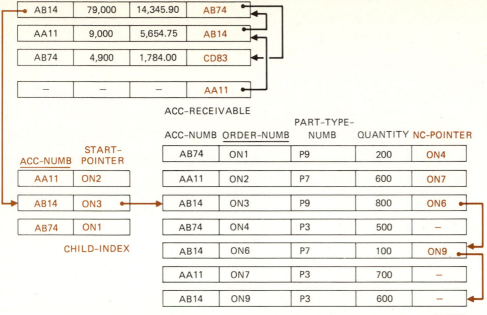

FIGURE 4.6*a* A storage data base (called STORAGE-ACCOUNTING) containing two storage files and an index (CHILD-INDEX). There are accounts receivable records in ACC-RECEIVABLE, and order records in ORDER. For each account in ACC-RECEIVABLE there are several records in ORDER, so that the two files are related by a one-to-many relationship. For a given ACC-RECEIVABLE record, the ORDER child records may be obtained by means of the secondary key ACC-NUMB in ORDER; the secondary key is implemented by means of the linked-list index CHILD-INDEX and the next-child pointer (NC-POINTER) in ORDER records. ORDER is an indexed-sequential file (index not shown) and ACC-RECEIVABLE is a hash file in which the records are available in sequential order because of the linked list formed by the next record pointer (NR-POINTER) in each record; the last record in ACC-RECEIVABLE is a dummy that contains the pointer to the first record.

Both **ACC-RECEIVABLE** and **ORDER** are direct access files, but **ORDER** is an indexed-sequential file while **ACC-RECEIVABLE** is a hash file; however, by means of a next-record pointer and a linked-list organization, **ACC-RECEIVABLE** may also be processed sequentially. Furthermore, the **ACC-NUMB** field in **ORDER** is a secondary key that is implemented by means of multiple linked lists; the next-child pointer in **ORDER** records is used for the multiple linked lists, and the entries for the start of each linked list are in the linked-list index **CHILD-INDEX**. As explained earlier, it is possible for the data base storage system (see Figure 4.4) to obtain the **ORDER** child records given a parent record in **ACC-RECEIVABLE**.

The structure of this storage data base is specified in the idealized storage schema in Figure 4.6*b*. The files must be specified, together with their organization, such as indexed-sequential or hash. Key and secondary key fields must be

```
STORAGE SCHEMA FOR STORAGE-ACCOUNTING DATA BASE.
STORAGE FILE SECTION.

        STORAGE FILE ACC-RECEIVABLE, HASH FILE
        USING HASHING ROUTINE HASHX
        DATA FIELDS.
            ACC-NUMB  PIC X(4), PRIMARY KEY FIELD
            CRED-LIM  PIC 5(9).
            BALANCE   PIC 5(9)V99.
        POINTER FIELDS.
            NR-POINTER PIC X(4), FOR SINGLE LINKED LIST
                                 USING NEXT ACC-NUMB
                                 VALUE IN ASCENDING ORDER.


        STORAGE FILE ORDER, INDEXED-SEQUENTIAL FILE
        DATA FIELDS.
            ACC-NUMB            PIC X(4), SECONDARY KEY,
                                         POINTER TO PARENT
                                         ACC-RECEIVABLE RECORD.
            ORDER-NUMB          PIC X(3), PRIMARY KEY FIELD.
            PART-TYPE-NUMB      PIC X(2).
            QUANTITY            PIC 3(9).
        POINTER FIELDS.
            NC-POINTER          PIC X(3), POINTER TO NEXT CHILD,
                                         FOR SECONDARY
                                         KEY ACC-NUMB USING
                                         ORDER-NUMB VALUE AND
                                         MULTIPLE LINKED LIST INDEX
                                         CHILD-INDEX.
INDEX SECTION.
        INDEX CHILD-INDEX,
        MULTIPLE LINKED LIST INDEX FOR SECONDARY KEY
                        ACC-NUMB IN ORDER FILE.
        FIELDS.
            ACC-NUMB FROM ORDER FILE, PRIMARY KEY.
            ORDER-NUMB FROM ORDER FILE, POINTER TO FIRST CHILD.
```

FIGURE 4.6b   Idealized but typical storage schema for the storage data base STOR-AGE-ACCOUNTING in Figure 4.6a. Files, fields, pointers, and indexes must be specified. A storage schema is computer oriented.

specified, and in the case of a hash file the name of the hashing routine. Pointer fields and their function must also be specified, together with any indexes such as **CHILD-INDEX**. While this storage schema is idealized, it is fairly typical of storage schemas in practice. In this book we will not be too concerned with the technicalities of storage schemas, concentrating instead on the specification of data bases from the corporate organizational viewpoint (that is, the conceptual schema) or from the user viewpoint (that is, the external schema). We must be aware, however, that an underlying storage schema exists.

The conceptual data base abstracted from the storage data base in Figure 4.6a is depicted in Figure 4.7a. The corresponding conceptual schema is shown on Figure 4.7b; it can be seen that this schema is much less technical than the underlying storage schema. We merely specify the organizationally useful data fields, the primary and secondary keys, and the nature of the relationship between the conceptual files. (As we shall see later, some data base management systems, notably the recently introduced relational systems, do not require an explicit specification of the interfile relationships.)

An external data base abstracted from the data in Figure 4.7a is shown in Figure 4.8a, and a corresponding (idealized) external schema is shown in Figure 4.8b. It can be seen that it is merely a subset of the conceptual schema. (With relational data base systems, and some other systems, it is possible for the external files to be made up of fields from *different* conceptual files; we will look at this possibility later.)

Schema languages

Associated with any data base management system are specific languages for specification of the schemas, as can be seen from Figures 4.6b, 4.7b, and 4.8b. These languages are often called *schema languages* or *data base description languages* (DBDL), and there is one for each type of schema. Thus we have a

ACC-NUMB	CRED-LIM	BALANCE
AA11	9,000	5,654.75
AB14	79,000	14,345.90
AB74	4,900	1,784.00

ACC-RECEIVABLE

ACC-NUMB	ORDER-NUMB	PART-TYPE-NUMB	QUANTITY
AB74	ON1	P9	200
AA11	ON2	P7	600
AB14	ON3	P9	800
AB74	ON4	P3	500
AB14	ON6	P7	100
AA11	ON7	P3	700
AB14	ON9	P3	600

ORDER

FIGURE 4.7a The conceptual data base CONCEPTUAL-ACCOUNTING abstracted from the storage data base STORAGE-ACCOUNTING in Figure 4.6a. The data base does not physically exist, but its conceptual schema does (Figure 4.7b).

```
CONCEPTUAL SCHEMA FOR CONCEPTUAL-ACCOUNTING DATA BASE.
CONCEPTUAL FILE SECTION.

        CONCEPTUAL FILE ACC-RECEIVABLE.
                ACC-NUMB, ALPHANUMERIC 4, PRIMARY KEY.
                CRED-LIM, NUMERIC 5.
                BALANCE, NUMERIC 7.

        CONCEPTUAL FILE ORDER.
                ACC-NUMB, ALPHANUMERIC 4, SECONDARY KEY.
                ORDER-NUMB, ALPHANUMERIC 3, PRIMARY KEY.
                PART-TYPE-NUMB, ALPHANUMERIC 2.
                QUANTITY, NUMERIC 3.


RELATIONSHIP SECTION.
        ACC-RECEIVABLE IS PARENT OF ORDER,
                ACC-NUMB IN ORDER DETERMINES ACC-RECEIVABLE
                PARENT RECORD.
```

FIGURE 4.7b Idealized but typical conceptual schema for the CONCEPTUAL-ACCOUNTING data base (Figure 4.7a). A conceptual schema is oriented toward the enterprise.

ACC-NUMB	BALANCE
AA11	5,654.75
AB14	14,345.90
AB74	1,784.00

EXT1-RECEIVABLES

ACC-NUMB	ORDER-NUMB	PART-TYPE-NUMB
AB74	ON1	P9
AB11	ON2	P7
AB14	ON3	P9
AB74	ON4	P3
AB14	ON6	P7
AA11	ON7	P3

EXT1-ORDER

FIGURE 4.8a The external data base EXT1-ACCOUNTING abstracted from the conceptual data base CONCEPTUAL-ACCOUNTING in Figure 4.7a. The data base does not physically exist, but its external schema does (Figure 4.8b).

```
EXTERNAL SCHEMA FOR EXT1-ACCOUNTING DATA BASE.
EXTERNAL FILE SECTION.

        EXTERNAL FILE EXT1-RECEIVABLES ABSTRACTED FROM
        ACC-RECEIVABLE.
            ACC-NUMB PIC X(4), PRIMARY KEY.
            BALANCE  PIC S(9)V99.

        EXTERNAL FILE EXT1-ORDER ABSTRACTED FROM ORDER.
            ACC-NUMB            PIC X(4), SECONDARY KEY.
            ORDER-NUMB          PIC X(3), PRIMARY KEY.
            PART-TYPE-NUMB      PIC X(2).

RELATIONSHIP SECTION.
        EXT1-RECEIVABLES IS PARENT OF EXT1-ORDER,
            ACC-NUMB IN EXT1-ORDER DETERMINES
            ACC-RECEIVABLE PARENT RECORD
```

FIGURE 4.8*b* Idealized but typical external schema for the data base EXT1-ACCOUNTING from Figure 4.8*a*. An external schema is oriented toward a user group and toward a data base manipulation program written in a host language such as COBOL or PL/1.

storage DBDL, conceptual DBDL, and external DBDL. A schema written in the corresponding DBDL is called a *source schema*; every data base management system is equipped with compilers or translaters for translating the source schemas into the machine language of the computer, and such translated schemas are called *object schemas*. The schemas in Figures 4.6*b*, 4.7*b*, and 4.8*b* are clearly source schemas.

Data dictionaries and directories

We have seen that a data base contains data about an enterprise or organization and that the external, conceptual, and storage schemas contain data about the data in the data base. Thus it is possible to consider the schemas as simple data bases in their own right. Readers should take some time to consider this concept. Referring to the conceptual schema in Figure 4.7*b*, it is clear that it is hardly structured as a collection of computer files that cross-reference each other. However, we could structure a conceptual schema as shown in Figure 4.9*a*. Each record in **DATA-BASE-FILES** describes a file in the data base, while each record in **DATA-BASE-FIELDS** describes a field in the data base. The two files in Figure 4.9*a* are related, since for one record in **DATA-BASE-FILES** there will be a number of records in **DATA-BASE-FIELDS**.

Data directory

A *data directory* contains data about a data base that can be used only by the data base system and not generally by users or management. Thus there is a need for

FILENAME	CREATOR	PARENTFILENAME
ACC-RECEIVABLE	JONES	-
ORDER	SMITH	ACC-RECEIVABLE

DATA-BASE-FILES

FILENAME	FIELDNAME	FIELDLENGTH	FIELDTYPE	STATUS
ACC-RECEIVABLE	ACC-NUMB	4	ALPHANUMERIC	PRIMARY KEY
ACC-RECEIVABLE	BALANCE	7	NUMERIC	-
ACC-RECEIVABLE	CRED-LIM	5	NUMERIC	-
ORDER	ACC-NUMB	4	ALPHANUMERIC	SECONDARY KEY
ORDER	ORDER-NUMB	3	ALPHANUMERIC	PRIMARY KEY
ORDER	PART-TYPE-NUMB	2	ALPHANUMERIC	-
ORDER	QUANTITY	3	NUMERIC	-

DATA-BASE-FIELDS

FIGURE 4.9a The conceptual schema in Figure 4.7b arranged as a data base.

facilities that permit the data base system to access it. A storage schema can be placed in a data directory, but not conceptual or external schemas.

Data dictionary

A *data dictionary* contains conceptual and external schemas, since information in the data dictionary can be of use to both the data base system and general users. For example, a user might want to know what files a certain field occurs in, and this information can be obtained from the conceptual schema in the data dictionary. Figure 4.9a is thus a simple example of a data dictionary.

Data dictionary/directory facility

A *data dictionary/directory facility* permits the schemas to be constructed as data bases and to be manipulated by the data base management system. In this arrangement (Fig. 4.9b) the data base system manages three data bases: the dictionary data base, the directory data base, and the main data base. Such a facility enables a data base system to be used for obtaining information from the data dictionary, as well as from the main data base.

With the arrangement in Figure 4.9b, we have the possibility of expanding the dictionary and the means by which it may be manipulated by the data base control system. The expanded data dictionary may include all kinds of information about the enterprise data base that is useful to users and management, but of no use to the data base control system. A list of the user groups that need the values in a given field is an example of the kind of user-oriented data that can be

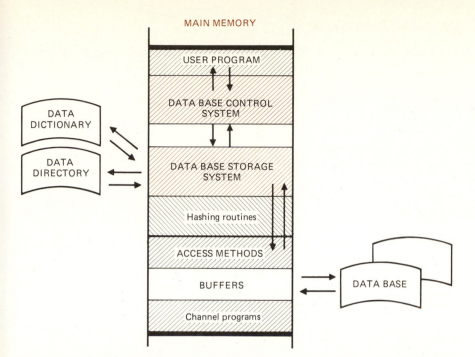

FIGURE 4.9*b* The architecture of a data base system with a data dictionary/ directory facility. External and conceptual schemas are stored in a data dictionary, which is a data base in its own right, and has a data base structure (Figure 4.9*a*). The storage schema is kept in another data base called a data directory. The data in the data dictionary is of use to users and management, and to the data base control system. The dictionary may be expanded to contain additional data of use only to users and management. With a proper data dictionary/directory facility, the data base control system permits data from this data dictionary data to be retrieved just like data from the main data base.

kept in an expanded data dictionary. Such a data dictionary facility is not incorporated in many data base systems at the time of writing. However, the trend is in the direction of the incorporation of sophisticated data dictionary/ directory facilities in data base management systems. In many cases at present, a data dictionary/data directory system is acquired separately and interfaced to the data base management system.

A data dictionary/directory facility should be regarded as an enhancement to a data base management system. It is not strictly necessary. However, the construction of at least a simple data dictionary is regarded today as essential for any organization with large quantities of data in either conventional files or data bases. A simple data dictionary can be an indexed-sequential file in which a record contains a field name, the meaning of that field, and perhaps the areas in which that field is important. This permits all data base and file designers to use standardized field names with meanings that everyone has agreed to, and can find out about merely by consulting a data dictionary. We cover data dictionaries in more detail in Chapter 13 on managing the data base environment.

4.3 USING A DATA BASE MANAGEMENT SYSTEM

We can distinguish two aspects to the use of a data base management system in an organization. There is the technical aspect, which involves the design, creation, and manipulation of data bases using the facilities provided by the data base management system. There is also the more administrative aspect, involving the supervision of all activities, including the activities of user groups, that are connected with the enterprise's data bases. The two aspects are heavily intertwined however. We begin with an overview of the more technical aspect of using a data base system.

Overview of the data base design process

The conceptual schema is designed first, using fields from the organization's data dictionary (designing a data base without a data dictionary is asking for trouble). The designers should be oriented toward the needs of the enterprise, and the initial conceptual schema is an idealized version that does not allow for the inevitable quirks of the data base system being used. The final conceptual schema is based on the idealized one. The idealized conceptual schema is frequently called the *enterprise schema*.

Then the storage schema must be designed; this is clearly a highly technical task that is dependent on the types of storage facilities that the data base management system chosen is capable of managing. Finally, initial external schemas are required for the loading process. A large data base is normally loaded in steps, testing being carried out at the end of each loading step. An external schema is required for each part of the data base being loaded and tested.

The data base manipulation language (DBML)

Consider again the data base architecture in Figure 4.4. A user program is running with the data base control system as a subprogram whose facilities are used as required by the user program by means of **CALL** statements. With a data base system a whole range of different **CALL** statements can be employed. These **CALL** statements are usually considered to be data base system *commands*, for on receipt of such a **CALL** command, the system carries out some data base operation, such as retrieving some data. The complete collection of the different data base commands available are said to constitute the *data base manipulation language* (DML), or *sublanguage*, since they are used within the higher language user program in COBOL or PL/1. (Note that the data base manipulation language together with the conceptual data base structures or *objects* that are manipulated make up what many theorists call the *interface* to the data base management system.) When data base commands are placed in or embedded in a higher language program, the higher language, such as COBOL or PL/1, is said to function as a *host* language.

User-friendly data base commands

Originally, all data base management systems required **CALL** statements in the host language; such **CALL** statements tend to have a devious syntax that is usually both forbidding and impossible to remember. Many systems today permit more user-friendly data base commands to be placed in the host language program instead of the primitive **CALL** statements. Before the host language program is compiled, it is subjected to a preprocessing or editing stage in which the syntax of the user-friendly data base commands is converted to the standard **CALL** statement syntax of the host language.

Example of a typical DBML STORE command

As a brief example of the nature of data base manipulation languages, we could consider a typical data base command for inserting a record into a data base. Suppose we are loading the conceptual data base in Figure 4.7a, and in particular we are placing records into the conceptual file **ORDER**. The records being placed in the conceptual file are of course being placed in the underlying storage file, complete with the pointer field and possible entries in **CHILD-INDEX**. The records to be placed in the conceptual data base file **ORDER** could be coming from a sequential file **SOURCE-ORDER** and are read in by a suitable COBOL **READ** statement. We consider the data base storage operation (1) using a primitive **CALL** statement and (2) using a user-friendly data base command. In both cases the host user program is in COBOL; the data base commands are shown in color, and the overall situation is depicted in Figure 4.10.

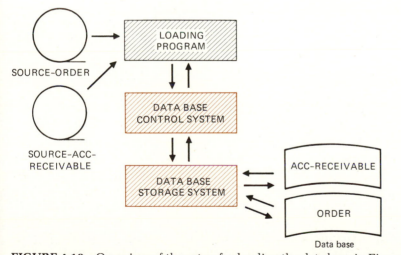

FIGURE 4.10 Overview of the setup for loading the data base in Figure 4.6a. The loading program is written in a higher language such as COBOL (or PL/1). Records from the sequential files SOURCE-ACC-RECEIVABLE and SOURCE-ORDER are read in using COBOL READ statements. A record read in is then passed to the data base control system along with a STORE command by means of a COBOL CALL statement. The contents of the source files SOURCE-ACC-RECEIVABLE and SOURCE-ORDER are the same as those of the conceptual files ACC-RECEIVABLE and ORDER in Figure 4.7a.

1. STORE *statement using* CALL

```
· · ·
READ SOURCE-ORDER INTO SOURCE-RECORD
MOVE "ORDER" TO DATA-BASE-FILE
MOVE "STORE" TO DB-OPERATION
CALL "DATA-BASE-SYSTEM"
     USING DB-OPERATION, SOURCE-RECORD, DATA-BASE-FILE,
     DB-OPERATION-STATUS
IF DB-OPERATION-STATUS NOT = "CARIED OUT OK" THEN STOP RUN.
· · ·
```

As each record is read into **SOURCE-RECORD** by the COBOL **READ** command, a **CALL** to the data base system (**DATA-BASE-SYSTEM**) is made. The contents of the **CALL** parameter **DB-OPERATION** is the value 'STORE' (in other cases it could be 'FIND' or 'DELETE', and so on), which causes the data base system to take the record in the parameter **SOURCE-RECORD** and place it in the storage file corresponding to the conceptual file whose name is in the parameter **DATA-BASE-FILE**. The record is stored as a storage record with the additional pointer field value (see Figure 4.6a) and a possible entry in **CHILD-INDEX**. If everything goes as it should (with a complex data base it often does not), the data base system places the message 'CARRIED OUT OK' in the last parameter **DB-OPERATION-STATUS**. The COBOL host program then checks for the value in **DB-OPERATION-STATUS** and takes appropriate action depending on the value detected (for simplicity we have merely coded that the program stop if all is not well). Note that the **CALL** statement in the above excerpt is idealized but is typical of **CALL** statements with many data base systems.

2. STORE *statement using user-friendly syntax*

```
· · ·
READ SOURCE-ORDER INTO SOURCE-RECORD
STORE ORDER RECORD FROM SOURCE-RECORD
IF DB-OPERATION-STATUS NOT = "OK" THEN STOP RUN.
· · ·
```

The program containing the user-friendly **STORE** command above would first be preprocessed, and this generates a source program with the **STORE** commands replaced with **CALL** commands as in the excerpt 1 above. The above program excerpt would carry out the same functions as excerpt 1. The **STORE** command above is typical but idealized for expositional purposes.

Loading the data base

Assuming that the conceptual and storage source schemas have been prepared, the next step is to have them translated to object schemas. Typically the source schemas are entered at a terminal (Figure 4.11) and are translated by a special component of the data base management system. (It may be necessary for the person entering the source schemas at the terminal to give a command in order to have the translation carried out.) The translated schemas would typically be stored on a disk for later use.

At this point hashing routines (if needed for any of the storage files) would also be entered (not shown in Figure 4.11), compiled, and the resulting object hashing routines stored as temporary disk files (Figure 4.11). The object versions of the data base control system and storage system (see also Figures 4.4 and 4.10) can be assumed to be available on disk storage (where they will have been installed when the data base system was delivered from the vendor).

The object versions of the schemas, the hashing routines, and the data base control and storage systems are now joined together (or *linked*) so that they can communicate with each other. This is normally done by an operating system component called a *linkage editor*, and the result of the linking is placed on disk storage and often called the data base system module, which will be used by all programs that access the data base for any purpose.

This first stage of the loading process is carried out by systems programmers, as it involves the basic software of both the data system and the operating system. However, with some user-friendly data base systems, the user need only enter the schemas and the data base system then automatically does the rest.

At this point we have an empty data base, and the first use of the data base is

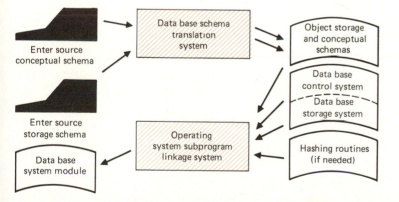

FIGURE 4.11   First stages in the loading of a typical data base. First the conceptual and storage schemas are entered at a terminal. A component of the data base system translates these source schemas into object schemas and stores them on disk for future use. Hashing routines (if required) are also prepared, compiled, and placed on disk. The data base control system and data base storage system is available from disk storage (where it will have been originally installed) as object code. The object schemas, data base control and storage system, and hashing routines are then joined together by a component of the operating system, so that they can communicate with each other (they are said to be link-edited), and stored on disk as the fundamental data base system module that will be employed by all programs that access the data base, including the loading programs. With many data base systems the linking stage is carried out automatically or nearly so.

for inserting data into it, or loading. Every user program must have an external schema, and the initial loading program is no exception. A large data base is normally loaded in steps, perhaps two or three data base files at a time. Hence an external schema being used with a loading program would cover just a portion of the conceptual data base specified in the conceptual schema.

Thus the next step is to enter an external schema at the terminal; this is then translated and the resulting object external schema placed on temporary disk storage (Figure 4.12). The source version of the loading program is then entered at the terminal, compiled, and the resulting object version placed on disk storage. The loading program, associated external schema, and the data base system module (see both Figures 4.11 and 4.12) are now linked (by an operating system component) and the result placed or "loaded" into main memory for execution. The situation now resembles that shown in Figure 4.4 (which shows the contents of main memory when a user program is being executed), an overview being shown at the bottom of Figure 4.12.

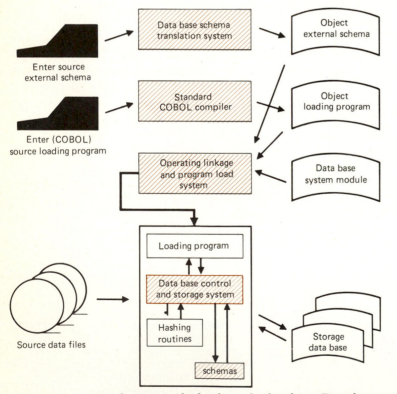

FIGURE 4.12 Final stages in the loading of a data base. First the external schema (for the portion of the data base being loaded) is entered and translated to an object schema. Then the (COBOL) loading program is entered and compiled, producing the object version. The external schema, loading program, and data base system load module (from the first stage) are then linked together and placed in main memory for execution. The records from the source data files are then read in and via the data base system stored in the proper data base storage files.

The loading program now executes. It contains **CALL** statements for requesting that the data base system store a record, and so on. The loading program now reads in records from the source files (which should have been prepared for this purpose), and the data base management system places them in their storage files accompanied by necessary pointers and indexes.

When this is completed, further user programs are run to test that the data base has been loaded properly. For example, the simplest testing program would simply read out the contents of the conceptual files in sequential order. More sophisticated testing programs could print out parent records along with their child records, and vice versa. Following testing, the next portion of the data base can be loaded (with a new external schema) and further tests carried out, and so on until the complete data base has been loaded and tested.

Note that the sequence of steps that we have just described for loading a data base is the basic sequence. With some data base systems things may appear to be simpler, since some of the basic steps, such as linkage editing, are carried out automatically without the user being aware of it.

Batch manipulation of a data base

Each user group must have an external schema for that portion of the conceptual data base that is needed for the operations of the group. As with conventional file processing there will be many updating and information retrieval tasks that need to be carried out on a regular basis. Transactions are batched to form transaction files, the records of which are read in by a batch updating program and used to update the data base (Figure 4.13). To run such a batch program, the source version and associated external schema are entered at a terminal (as was the loading program Figure 4.12).

Once the data base has been set up and the batch manipulation programs written, it is clear that routine updating and information retrieval are quite straightforward. With data base processing, in marked contrast to conventional file processing, it is easy to accommodate the addition of new fields to the data base. Because of data independence, the user programs already in existence are

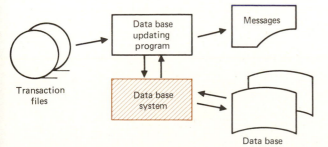

FIGURE 4.13 Batch updating a data base. Transactions are batched and used to form transaction files, typically organized sequentially. For each transaction record read in by the updating program, one or more CALLs are issued to the data base system to update one or more storage records of the data base.

not affected. However, there is one disadvantage to data base processing. Because of the overhead of a data base system, user programs employing a data base will usually run considerably more slowly than if the data base were replaced by conventional files. Thus the use of a data base management system often results in a need for either a more powerful CPU (see Chapter 1) or an additional CPU.

Interactive manipulation of a data base

Again each user group must have an external schema corresponding to the external data base it uses. The user programs are often information retrieval programs, but where user groups are in operating departments, and responsible, for example, for order entry, then interactive updating programs will be used. Typically the user programs are prewritten by programmers in the data processing department and run by the user as required. The program will ask the user for data via the terminal if it is an update program. In the case of information retrieval programs, the program will be able to undertake a certain type of retrieval, for example, finding the number of parts ordered by customers whose outstanding balances each exceed X dollars; the user would enter the value for X when the program requested it. The program would then use the value to retrieve the correct data via the data base management system and display the results at the terminal (Figure 4.14).

Data base query processors

The use of interactive information retrieval programs is not the only way to get information out of a data base interactively. Many data management systems have Data Base Query Processors for interrogation of the data base. The information that is needed from the data base is expressed by the terminal user in a query language expression; such a query language expression is not a program, but a

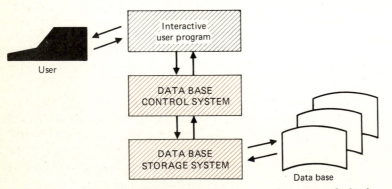

FIGURE 4.14 Use of an interactive user program for retrieval of information from a data base. The user would typically insert search parameters as needed by the program. The program would be restricted to one type of retrieval, such as finding the total parts ordered by customers whose outstanding balances each exceed X dollars (taking the data base in Figure 4.7a). The user would enter the value for X when the program was ready to read it in.

precise specification of the information required. For example, suppose we needed the account numbers for customers whose outstanding balances exceeded $10,000 (referring to the data base in Figure 4.8a); we could express this in an important query language developed at IBM and called Structured Query Language (SQL):

```
SELECT ACC-NUMB
FROM EXT1-RECEIVABLES
WHERE BALANCE > 10,000
```
Typical

We are telling the system that we want those **ACC-NUMB** values from the external **EXT1-RECEIVABLES** records for which the **BALANCE** field value is greater than 10,000. The query processor constructs a retrieval program following an analysis of this expression; this retrieval program would contain the usual **CALL** statements for communication with the data base system. The overall setup is shown in Figure 4.15. SQL is a nonprocedural language.

Concurrent use of a data base with on-line systems

So far we have somewhat tacitly assumed in our discussions that at any given time only one user program was interacting (via the data base system) with the data base. In an on-line system, however, many different user programs will be executing at the same time (concurrently) and placing **CALLs** to the data base system for retrieval update or storage of data. There may be many interactive users at remote terminals; some will be interacting with prewritten data base manipulation programs, while others will be submitting query expressions to a

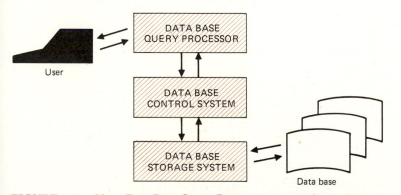

FIGURE 4.15 Use a Data Base Query Processor to permit a user to enter queries at a terminal. Such queries are in a data base query language which is nonprocedural in style, that is, the user specifies what data is needed instead of parameters for a prewritten interactive retrieval program as in Figure 4.14. The query processor generates the program necessary to retrieve the required data (not shown), which is finally displayed on the terminal. The on-line query processor would typically be part of the data base system, although it may be possible to obtain one from an independent vendor.

query processor that will construct suitable (user) programs for accessing the data base.

Teleprocessing monitors or data base/data communications systems

Sophisticated software is necessary to accommodate and supervise on-line activity. An important new software component is called a *teleprocessing monitor* (or *data base/data communications system*, sometimes abbreviated to DB/DC system). The teleprocessing monitor first of all interacts directly with all terminal users. It does this by reading from and displaying on each terminal in turn according to a built-in polling pattern. A given user is not aware that the teleprocessing monitor is concurrently dealing with other users at other terminals. The overall setup is illustrated in Figure 4.16.

A user at a terminal can instruct the teleprocessing monitor to execute a program to access the data base. The teleprocessing monitor will comply by fetching the program from its library on disk, placing (or loading) it in main memory (typically as a subprogram of the teleprocessing monitor; see Figure 4.16), and in due course allowing it to execute. However, at the same time there

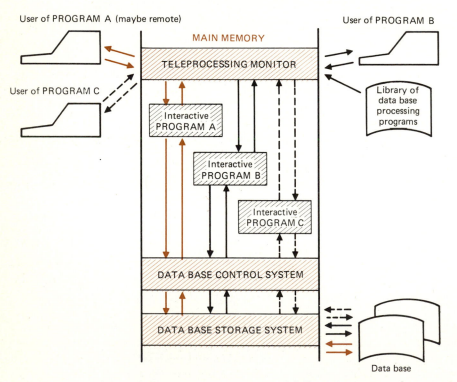

FIGURE 4.16 Shows the concurrent execution of different programs that access the data base. A complex control system called a teleprocessing monitor interacts with the (often remote) terminals, and at the same time schedules the execution of programs accessing the data base; many such programs are available (by request to the teleprocessing monitor) in a library.

will be other user programs in main memory as subprograms of the teleprocessing monitor. The teleprocessing monitor allows them to execute in turn, but one user program does not have to wait until another is completely finished executing. Each user program interacts both with the teleprocessing monitor and the data base system (see Figure 4.16). When a user program executes a **CALL** to the data base system, it will typically have to wait while the data base storage system (via the independently executing channels) has completed its access to the data base. The teleprocessing monitor is informed of this delay and initiates execution of another user program. Thus at any given time the teleprocessing monitor is in control of many programs that are accessing the data base; they are all in various stages of execution, although at any instant only the teleprocessing monitor, a user program, or the data base system is actually executing.

Thus a data base system capable of managing a data base under these circumstances is a complex and impressive piece of software. To initiate an in-house construction of such a system as a do-it-yourself project is almost certainly doomed to failure. The costs of a data base system are best shared among many installations, which in effect is the result of obtaining the data base software from a specialized software house or computer system supplier. There is additional coverage of teleprocessing monitors in Chapter 12.

Data base administration

So far we have concentrated on the more technical aspect of the use of data bases. We now look briefly at the more administrative aspect. The use of data bases affects the way in which an enterprise is managed, for the simple reason that many user groups will have pooled their data into common data bases. This pooling of data into computer data bases has many advantages for the enterprise, including:

1. Availability of more reliable reports because of elimination of data duplication and resulting inconsistency
2. Reduction in program maintenance costs because of data independence
3. Availability of query systems that provide fast responses to ad hoc requests for data from the data base
4. Reduction in the cost of new applications because of data independence and lack of data duplication, and the availability of powerful data manipulation language commands that save coding effort

It is a mistake, however, to assume that these benefits can be obtained merely by the investment in certain technical black boxes called data bases and data base management systems. The pooling of data from many different user groups in different data bases gives rise to conflicts that are often severe. It is for the prevention and resolution of such conflicts that there has to be a *data base administration group*, which is the group responsible for all activities connected with the data base, that is, with the *management of the data base environment*. Although no one person could be expected to carry out the data base administration function in an enterprise, the term *data base administrator* (DBA) is normally used in referring to the data base administration group.

While the overall function of the DBA is the prevention and resolution of conflicts, in practice the DBA has a large number of functions, both administrative and technical. The DBA also interfaces with higher data management, with user groups, with computer operations groups, with specialists in telecommunications, and deals with the data bases, data dictionary, data base systems, and data dictionary systems. Among the large number of functions of the DBA are:

1. Development of data dictionary standards, and development of the corporate data dictionary
2. Development of the enterprise schema, and construction of storage, conceptual, and external schemas
3. Setting and maintenance of standards for the use of the data base by different user groups
4. Management of data base security systems
5. Maintenance of data base system performance

A much more detailed description of the many data base administration functions is given in Chapter 13 on the management of the data base environment. We do not delve further into the activities of the DBA at this point, as readers will be in a position to appreciate the DBA contribution fully only when they have acquired a better grasp of data base management technology. In subsequent chapters we look in more detail at the structure of data bases and at the different approaches to data base management. Before leaving the subject of the DBA, however, it is worth pointing out that experience has shown conclusively that the successful management of the data base environment is impossible without a DBA (Refs. 1, 2, and 5).

SUMMARY

1. It is widely agreed that a data base system should be able to manage a three-level data base consisting of the storage data base, the conceptual data base, and various external data bases that are oriented to various user groups. The use of a three-level data base provides both storage (or physical) and conceptual (or logical) data independence. Data independence is what ensures that a program can function even if changes are made to the structure or organization of the data base.

2. A data base management system must have a complete specification of any data base that it looks after. This specification is divided into the storage schema for the storage data base, the conceptual schema for the conceptual data base, and external schemas for the external data bases. Data base design is largely concerned with the preparation of these schemas. The conceptual and external schemas can be thought of as a data base as well, usually referred to as a data dictionary.

3. Use of a data base system has technical and administrative aspects. The technical aspect involves designing, loading, and manipulating the data base. Manipulation of the data base is often by means of commands embedded in a higher language host program in COBOL or PL/1. The data base system responds to such a command by some manipulation of the data base. The data base may also be manipulated directly by entering query language expressions at a terminal. When there are many programs using a data base concurrently as well as many users at terminals, a teleprocessing monitor or data base/data communications system is used, as mentioned already in Chapter 1. The administrative aspect involves the supervision by a data base administrator of all activities connected with the data base. The overall aim of this supervision is the prevention and resolution of conflicts caused by the pooling of data by many user groups. The different groups connected with a data base and their activities constitute the data base environment.

QUESTIONS

1. Explain carefully the difference between storage and conceptual data independence.
2. Explain why conceptual files and external files do not physically exist.
3. A single file is to be constructed for use by many different groups in an organization. The outlook is for changes to the organization of the file with the course of time. If no data base management system is available, explain how you would provide for both storage and conceptual data independence.
4. What is meant by tuning a data base?
5. Explain the role of conceptual, storage, and external schemas in a system for the data independent management of a single file, such as would be used with the file in Question 3.
6. Explain the role of the conceptual, storage, and external schemas in a data base management system.
7. What is meant by an enterprise schema?
8. Why should we distinguish between a data dictionary and a data directory?
9. What is a data base description language used for?
10. Explain the difference between a source schema and an object schema.
11. What is a data base manipulation language?
12. What is a host language?
13. How does a program CALL statement serve as a command to a data base system?
14. How can the complex CALL syntax be removed from a CALL command?
15. When a CALL command has been carried out by the data base system, what should an application program do at once?
16. List the steps involved in loading a data base.
17. If the data base in Figure 3.15 had just been loaded, what tests would you recommend to ensure that it had been loaded as depicted in the diagram?
18. How can a data base be manipulated without using an applications program?

19. How can many interactive programs concurrently manipulate the same data base?
20. What is the data base environment?
21. What is the overall function of the data base administrator?

REFERENCES

1. Atre, S., 1980. *Data Base: Structured Techniques for Design, Performance, and Management.* Wiley-Interscience, New York.
2. Date, C. J., 1981. *Introduction to Database Systems.* Addison-Wesley, Reading, Mass.
3. Fry, J. P., and E. H. Sibley, 1976. "Evolution of Data Base Systems," *ACM Computer Surveys*, 8(1):7–42.
4. Jardine, D. A. (Ed.), 1977. "The ANSI/SPARC DBMS Model," *Proc. 2nd SHARE Conf. Montreal, 1976.* North-Holland, New York.
5. Weldon, J., 1981. *Data Base Administration.* Plenum Press, New York.

5

Conceptual Data Base Structures

We have seen that a data base is a collection of integrated or related files. A great deal can be learned about data bases from a study of the structure of *conceptual data bases*, which are collections of related *conceptual* files, where a conceptual file is what is left of a storage file after implementation fields such as pointers, flags, and associated indexes have been removed.

The distinction between storage and conceptual data bases is important in data base design, for it permits the conceptual data base to be designed primarily with the needs of the enterprise in mind, as opposed to the requirements of a particular computer system. In practice we sometimes distinguish between the *conceptual* and the *enterprise data base*. This permits the conceptual data base to be precisely defined as a data base (of an abstract nature) that is specific to a particular data base system, while the enterprise data base is a loosely specified data base that is not specific to any data base system, and designed first. Nevertheless the distinction is largely ignored, and we shall normally use only the term conceptual data base. How specific a particular conceptual data base is will normally be apparent from the context.

In most business organizations the conceptual data base would be designed by a team, the members of which will have expertise in both the organization and business objectives of the enterprise and the kinds of structures that may be employed in conceptual data bases. It is a general survey of these conceptual data base structures, as well as a brief look at the specific structures that may be used with specific data base management systems, that is the subject matter of this chapter.

We begin with the basic relationships that occur in data bases and the elementary data base structures they give rise to. We then proceed from these simple structures to more complex structures. A specific data base management system approach employs a given conceptual data base structure in a highly specific manner, and we end the chapter with a brief introduction to the types of conceptual schema that are supported by the major approaches to data base management systems.

5.1 THE BASIC RELATIONSHIPS IN CONCEPTUAL DATA BASES

It is the one-to-many and the many-to-many relationships that are at the foundation of conceptual data base structures. Readers should already have some idea about what a one-to-many (or 1:n) relationship is, since this type of relationship was encountered earlier with the primitive data base in Chapter 3. However, the data base in Chapter 3 involved only storage files. In our coverage of one-to-many relationships in this chapter we shall consider conceptual data bases, and we shall begin with a study of one-to-many relationships between conceptual files.

One-to-many relationships

In Figure 5.1 there is an elementary example of one-to-many relationships between conceptual files. The data base describes the inventory of different types of electronic parts at different warehouses of an electronics manufacturer. We could assume that the parts are used in the assembly of electronic equipment in different plants.

A record in WAREHOUSE describes a warehouse with the warehouse number (WHNUMB field) as the primary key field; a record in PART describes a type of part with the part-type number (PTNUMB field) as the primary key field. A record in INVENTORY gives the quantity (QTY field) of a type of part (identified by the PTNUMB field) in a warehouse (identified by the WHNUMB field). In a WAREHOUSE record, CITY gives the name of the city containing the warehouse, and WH-AREA gives the floor-area of the warehouse. In a PART record, DE-SCRIPTION gives a description of the type of part.

There are two 1:n relationships in the conceptual data base, one between WAREHOUSE and INVENTORY, and one between PART and INVENTORY. There is also a many-to-many relationship, but more about that later.

The reason for the one-to-many relationship between WAREHOUSE and INVENTORY is simple. For any warehouse there must be an inventory record for each type of part in the warehouse. Thus for each WAREHOUSE record there must be many INVENTORY records, while for each INVENTORY record there can be only one WAREHOUSE record, since an inventory record concerns only one warehouse. The 1:n relationship between the two files is clearly illustrated in Figure 5.2. Here the records of INVENTORY are displayed in warehouse-number (WHNUMB) order, and we see that for each WAREHOUSE record there is a group

WHNUMB	CITY	WH-AREA
WH1	DALLAS	37,000
WH2	NEW YORK	50,000
WH3	CHICAGO	20,000

WAREHOUSE

PTNUMB	DESCRIPTION
P2	TRANSISTOR
P4	INDUCTOR
P7	INDUCTOR
P9	CAPACITOR

PART

WHNUMB	PTNUMB	QTY
WH1	P4	675
WH1	P7	250
WH1	P9	340
WH2	P2	280
WH2	P4	200
WH2	P9	270
WH3	P2	550
WH3	P4	330
WH3	P7	170

INVENTORY

FIGURE 5.1 A simple conceptual data base about the quantity (QTY field) of different types of part in different warehouses. The conceptual file PART describes the part types, and here PTNUMB, the part type number, is the (primary) key field. The conceptual file WAREHOUSE describes the warehouses, and here WHNUMB, the warehouse number, is the key field. An INVENTORY record gives the quantity of a type of part in a warehouse, so that the primary key is a composite of the fields WHNUMB and PTNUMB. Since the fields WHNUMB and PTNUMB in INVEN-TORY connect an INVENTORY record to its (parent) WAREHOUSE and PART records, respectively, they are often called (child) connection fields.

of INVENTORY records describing the inventories of parts in the warehouse described by the WAREHOUSE record.

Similarily, there is a one-to-many relationship between the records of PART and INVENTORY, as is illustrated in Figure 5.3 in which the records of INVEN-TORY are arranged in PTNUMB order. For any part described by a PART record, there will be many inventories in different warehouses, and these inventories are described by INVENTORY records.

Parent and child records

Since for one record in WAREHOUSE there are many records in INVENTORY, we can say that the WAREHOUSE record is the *parent* record, while the INVEN-TORY records are the *child* records. Thus the records in Figure 5.2 are shown as groupings of parent and child records. So are the records in Figure 5.3. However, the groups of child records in Figure 5.2 have nothing at all to do with the groups of child records in Figure 5.3. It is just that the PART records are the child records

WHNUMB	CITY	WH-AREA
W1	DALLAS	37,000
WH2	NEW YORK	50,000
WH3	CHICAGO	20,000

WAREHOUSE

WHNUMB	PTNUMB	QTY
WH1	P4	675
WH1	P7	250
WH1	P9	340
WH2	P2	280
WH2	P4	200
WH2	P9	270
WH3	P2	550
WH3	P4	330
WH3	P7	170

INVENTORY

FIGURE 5.2 Here the records of WAREHOUSE and PART from Figure 5.1 are displayed so that we have groups of parent (WAREHOUSE) and child (INVENTORY) records. For one parent record there may be many child records. INVENTORY records are displayed in WHNUMB order.

WHNUMB	PTNUMB	QTY
WH2	P2	280
WH3	P2	550
WH1	P4	675
WH2	P4	200
WH3	P4	330
WH1	P7	250
WH3	P7	170
WH1	P9	340
WH1	P9	270

INVENTORY

PTNUMB	DESCRIPTION
P2	TRANSISTOR
P4	INDUCTOR
P7	INDUCTOR
P9	CAPACITOR

PART

FIGURE 5.3 The records of INVENTORY and PART from Figure 5.1 are displayed as groups of parent and child records. For one parent PART record there are many child INVENTORY records. Note that the child INVENTORY record groupings are quite different from those in Figure 5.2. The INVENTORY records above are displayed in PTNUMB order.

in two distinct 1:n relationships. We shall return to the implications of this in a later section.

Connection fields

We can see that the field WHNUMB in INVENTORY plays an important part as far as the relationship between WAREHOUSE and INVENTORY records is concerned. In any INVENTORY record, the WHNUMB field contains the primary key of the parent WAREHOUSE record. Thus this field WHNUMB in INVENTORY as well as the WHNUMB field in WAREHOUSE *supports* or *enables* the 1:n relationship between the two files. We therefore single these fields out for special attention and call them *connection fields* since they serve to connect the records of the two files in a one-to-many relationship. However, readers must remember that we are dealing with conceptual records and files, so that these fields must not be considered as pointer fields. (It is indeed likely that at the storage level, the two files would be connected together by some additional pointer system perhaps along the lines described in Chapter 3.)

Similarly, the relationship between PART and INVENTORY records is supported by the *child* connection field PTNUMB in INVENTORY and the *parent* connection field PTNUMB in PART (see Figures 5.1 and 5.3).

Extended Bachman diagrams

While diagrams of the type shown in Figure 5.1 are instructive, they take up a lot of space, and it is often necessary to be briefer. We can use data structure diagrams for this purpose. There are many similar diagram types in common use, and we shall use expressive diagrams called extended Bachman diagrams (see Refs. 1 and 2).[1]

An extended Bachman diagram for the files WAREHOUSE and INVENTORY from Figure 5.1 and the relationship between them is shown in Figure 5.4a. A conceptual file is represented by a rectangular box containing the names of the fields, where the primary key field, or combination of fields that can be used as a primary key, is underlined. Furthermore the child connection field is shown in color to distinguish it clearly. Finally the arrow that begins at the parent connection field and ends at the child connection field indicates the existence of a 1:n relationship and pinpoints the fields that support it. Thus an extended Bachman diagram reveals a great deal of the semantics or meaning incorporated in a data base. (Note that for reader convenience, a parent file is always drawn above a child file.)

For the relationship between PART and INVENTORY in Figure 5.1, we can also draw an extended Bachman diagram (see Figure 5.4b). We can also combine the two diagrams in Figure 5.4a and b in an extended Bachman diagram for the complete data base in Figure 5.1. This is illustrated in Figure 5.4c. In Figure 5.1 and in the extended Bachman diagrams in Figure 5.4, a child connection field

---

[1]Alternatively, entity-relationship diagrams can be used, as described in Chapter 9. Unfortunately these diagrams are more complex than extended Bachman diagrams.

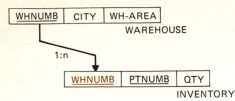

(a) Extended Bachman diagram for the relationship between the files WAREHOUSE and INVENTORY from Figure 5.1. See also Figure 5.2. Note that the relationship arrow begins on the parent connection field and ends on the child connection field.

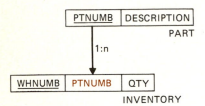

(b) Extended Bachman diagram for the relationship between PART and WARE-HOUSE from Figure 5.1. See also Figure 5.3.

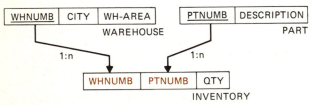

(c) Both relationships in the data base in Figure 5.1 may be depicted in an extended Bachman diagram. Each arrow denotes a distinct 1:n relationship.

FIGURE 5.4

has the same name as the parent connection field. There is no theoretical or practical requirement that this should be so. We have chosen the same names merely for the convenience of the reader.

With a larger data base containing a lot of conceptual files, diagrams of the type shown in Figure 5.1 become impractical, and we use extended Bachman diagrams or the equivalent for communicating a picture of the overall data base.

Redundancy elimination
In practice, we use a collection of *related* conceptual files in a data base to eliminate redundancy or duplication of data. In many cases a group of related conceptual files could be replaced by a single conceptual file, thus apparently simplifying the data base. However, such a single file will inevitably contain a great deal of data duplication.

As an example, suppose we replace the three files in Figure 5.1 (or Figure

CITY	WH-AREA	WHNUMB	PTNUMB	DESCRIPTION	QTY
DALLAS	37,000	WH1	P4	INDUCTOR	675
DALLAS	37,000	WH1	P7	INDUCTOR	250
DALLAS	37,000	WH1	P9	CAPACITOR	340
NEW YORK	50,000	WH2	P2	TRANSISTOR	280
NEW YORK	50,000	WH2	P4	INDUCTOR	200
NEW YORK	50,000	WH2	P9	CAPACITOR	270
CHICAGO	20,000	WH3	P2	TRANSISTOR	550
CHICAGO	20,000	WH3	P4	INDUCTOR	330
CHICAGO	20,0001	WH3	P7	INDUCTOR	170

PART-WAREHOUSE

FIGURE 5.5 The conceptual file PART-WAREHOUSE contains information about the quantity of electronic components in warehouses belonging to a corporation. The file contains the same information as the files WAREHOUSE, INVENTORY, and PART from Figure 5.1. There is heavy duplication of data in the file, caused by the need to repeat CITY and WH-AREA values in all records that contain the same WHNUMB value and the need to repeat the DESCRIPTION value in all records that contain the same PTNUMB value.

5.4c) by the single conceptual file **PART-WAREHOUSE**, an instance of which is displayed in Figure 5.5. All the information that is in the files **WAREHOUSE**, **INVENTORY**, and **PART** from Figure 5.1 is obtainable from **PART-WAREHOUSE**. A **PART-WAREHOUSE** record basically describes the quantity of a type of part in a warehouse as is the case with the file **INVENTORY** in Figure 5.1. However, a **PART-WAREHOUSE** record also contains fields that contain information about the warehouse (the **CITY** and **WH-AREA** fields), as well as a field that informs about the part (the **DESCRIPTION** field). It is these additional fields that give rise to the duplication of data.

Since a given part type may be stored in many different warehouses, a warehouse number will occur many times in **PART-INVENTORY**, for example, the warehouse number 'WH2'. But every time we have a record with **WHNUMB** value 'WH2', we must have the **CITY** value NEW YORK and the **WH-AREA** value 50,000. Hence the **CITY** and **WH-AREA** field values for a given warehouse are heavily duplicated.

Similarily, a given warehouse can have many different part types, so that a **PTNUMB** value occurs many times. Again, every time we have an occurrence of a given **PTNUMB** value, we have a duplication of the associated **DESCRIPTION** value. Thus every time we have a 'P4' value for **PTNUMB** in Figure 5.5, we must have the associated 'INDUCTOR' value for the **DESCRIPTION** field.

Primary keys in conceptual files
We shall deal with the principles of good conceptual file design later, in Chapter 9. For now we shall merely touch on the choice of primary keys. In the file **WAREHOUSE** in Figure 5.1 we chose WHNUMB, which contains the number of

the warehouse. Because the warehouse number uniquely identifies a warehouse, the choice was the obvious one, but in some cases the choice is not so obvious, so that it is useful to consider the basis for the choice of a primary key.

The records of the file WAREHOUSE each describe a warehouse, and a warehouse is thus said to be the *primary entity* described by a record. Any field in a file that uniquely identifies a primary entity may be selected as the primary key. It frequently happens that more than one field may independently serve as primary key; when this happens, the different candidate fields are known as *candidate keys*, for obvious reasons. An example is a conceptual file where the primary entity is an automobile, and we have a field L holding the license plate number, and a field E holding the engine number. L and E could be candidate key fields, since either one normally uniquely identifies the primary entity.

In the file PART in Figure 5.1 the primary entity is an electronic part type, so that the part type number uniquely identifies the primary entity and hence a record. In INVENTORY the situation is not so clear, and we should first attempt to identify the primary entity. It is clear that a record describes a property (the quantity) of a part type in a warehouse. Thus the primary entity must be a part type in a warehouse, and this is uniquely identified by the pair of fields WHNUMB and PTNUMB, so that the primary key is a composite.

A glance at the extended Bachman diagram in Figure 5.4c reveals that WHNUMB and PTNUMB in INVENTORY not only form a composite primary key but are also child connection fields. Some readers will probably wonder whether child connection fields are always part of a composite primary key, as is the case with the data base in Figure 5.4c. The answer is negative. Sometimes a child connection field is a subfield of a composite primary key and sometimes it is not. For example, in Figure 5.6 we have a data base containing the conceptual file WAREHOUSE from Figure 5.1 and a file EMPLOYEE, each of whose records describes an employee who works at a single warehouse listed in WAREHOUSE. The employee number EMPNUMB is the key field, and WHNUMB gives the number of the warehouse at which the employee works. A warehouse has many employees and an employee works at just one warehouse, so that there is a 1:n relationship between records of WAREHOUSE and EMPLOYEE.

The child connection field in the data base in Figure 5.6 is clearly WHNUMB. However, the primary key of an EMPLOYEE record is the EMPNUMB field, so that the connection field is not a subfield of the primary key in this case.

Many-to-many relationships

We have seen that in the data base in Figure 5.1 there is a 1:n relationship between WAREHOUSE and INVENTORY and a 1:n relationship between PART and INVENTORY. However, there is an additional relationship in the data base. In each warehouse there are many different part types, and each part type is to be found in many different warehouses. More specifically, for each WAREHOUSE record there are many PART records, and for each PART record there are many

WHNUMB	CITY	WH-AREA
WH1	DALLAS	37,000
WH2	NEW YORK	50,000
WH3	CHICAGO	20,000

WAREHOUSE

WHNUMB	EMPNUMB	SALARY
WH2	E1	22,000
WH1	E3	21,000
WH2	E4	25,000
WH3	E6	23,000
WH1	E7	25,000

EMPLOYEE

(a) The WAREHOUSE file is the same as the one in Figure 5.1. The EMPLOYEE record describes an employee that works in a warehouse. EMPNUMB gives an employee number and is the primary key in the EMPLOYEE file. There is a 1:n relationship between WAREHOUSE and EMPLOYEE supported by the child connection field WHNUMB [see (b)].

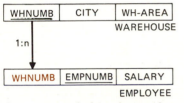

(b) An extended Bachman diagram for the data base in (a). Note that the child connection field WHNUMB and the primary key EMPNUMB are distinct.

FIGURE 5.6 A single 1:n relationship between two conceptual files.

WAREHOUSE records. We say that there is a many-to-many (n:m) relationship between the two files.[1]

The nature of this n:m relationship may be more clearly grasped if we display the data in the data base in Figure 5.1 in the form of a matrix, as in Figure 5.7. We use WAREHOUSE records to identify the rows and PART records to identify the columns, and the data at the intersection of a row and a column contains information about a given part type in a given warehouse, namely, the quantity of parts. Thus the data in the INVENTORY records from Figure 5.1 is also contained within the matrix.

It is clear from the diagram that for any given row, that is, a warehouse, there are many columns describing many part types; at the intersection of this row and a column is information about a part type in a warehouse, in this case the quantity of parts. Similarly, for any given column, that is, a type of part, there are many rows, that is, warehouses. It should thus be clear that not only is the n:m relationship between the files WAREHOUSE and PART displayed by the matrix

---

[1] We say the relationship is n:m because for any one WAREHOUSE record there can be m PART records, and for any one PART record n WAREHOUSE records, with n in general not equal to m.

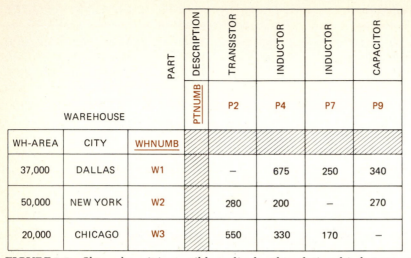

FIGURE 5.7 Shows how it is possible to display the relationship between the files WAREHOUSE and PART from Figure 5.1 as a matrix. Thus the many-to-many relationship between the two files may be referred to as a matrix relationship. Within the matrix we have intersection data, in this case the quantity (QTY value) of a type of part at a warehouse.

representation, but the two 1:n relationships between **WAREHOUSE** and **INVENTORY** and between **PART** and **INVENTORY** are also displayed. The data at the intersection of a row and column, or *intersection data*, describes a primary entity in the **INVENTORY** file, that is, it contains the properties of a given type of part in a given warehouse.

Reduction of *n:m* to 1:*n* relationships

As should be clear from the matrix in Figure 5.7, we would be justified in referring to a many-to-many relationship as a matrix relationship. Such relationships are common. Another example would be where an engineer works on many projects, where a project involves many engineers. Another one would be where a part type is supplied by many suppliers, where a supplier supplies many parts, and we shall make use of this example later in an expansion of the data base in Figure 5.1.

Now suppose that we are not interested in the inventory of parts in a given warehouse and that we have a data base where the conceptual files are simply

WHNUMB	CITY	WH-AREA	n:m	PTNUMB	DESCRIPTION

WAREHOUSE   PART

FIGURE 5.8 A data base consisting only of the two files WAREHOUSE and PART from Figure 5.1. The pair of arrows denotes the many-to-many relationship.

the files **WAREHOUSE** and **PART** from Figure 5.1 as shown in Figure 5.8. We assume that the many-to-many relationship between **WAREHOUSE** and **PART** is still in force, but from the files in Figure 5.8 we cannot tell which part type is in what warehouse and which warehouse contains what part types. Elimination of the **INVENTORY** file appears to have resulted in a loss of information. Of course at the storage level each storage **WAREHOUSE** record could be connected in a pointer system to its storage **PART** records, and vice versa, so that with a suitable storage data base the information concerning the n:m relationship need not be lost.

Nevertheless, the reader will probably feel somewhat uneasy about this. After all, when there is a 1:n relationship between two conceptual files, such as the files **WAREHOUSE** and **EMPLOYEE** in Figure 5.6, even though a parent record will most likely be connected to its child records by a pointer system at the storage level, by means of the connection fields we can also determine the groupings of parent and child records at the conceptual level. And this is very convenient for the user (and the designer of the data base). However, with the data base in Figure 5.8 we cannot tell at the conceptual level which part types are in a given warehouse. This is more than an inconvenience, it is poor design, for it is widely agreed that it should be possible to independently extract all information in a data base from the conceptual data base, even if extensive processing is required.

A common solution to the problem is the addition of an auxiliary *conceptual* file which is used merely to provide sufficient information for the n:m relationship to be determined at the conceptual level. We call this auxiliary conceptual file **HELPFILE**, and it is shown in Figure 5.9. A record of **HELPFILE** contains

WHNUMB	CITY	WH-AREA
WH1	DALLAS	37,000
WH2	NEW YORK	50,000
WH3	CHICAGO	20,000

WAREHOUSE

WHNUMB	PTNUMB
WH1	P4
WH1	P7
WH1	P9
WH2	P2
WH2	P4
WH2	P9
WH3	P2
WH3	P4
WH3	P7

PTNUMB	DESCRIPTION
P2	TRANSISTOR
P4	INDUCTOR
P7	INDUCTOR
P9	CAPACITOR

PART

HELPFILE

FIGURE 5.9 The many-to-many relationship between the two files WAREHOUSE and PART in Figure 5.8 may be determined at the conceptual level by the use of an auxiliary file HELPFILE whose fields are the keys of the files WAREHOUSE and PART.

only two fields, **WHNUMB** and **PTNUMB**. We see that there is a 1:n relationship between **WAREHOUSE** and **HELPFILE** supported by the connection filed **WHNUMB** and a 1:n relationship between **PART** and **HELPFILE** supported by the connection field **PTNUMB**.

Obtaining a description of the part types in a given warehouse is now possible using only the data in the conceptual files. For a given warehouse such as 'WH2', the child **HELPFILE** records can be determined by matching the connection field (**WHNUMB**) values. These child records contain the **PTNUMB** values ('P2', 'P4', 'P9') of the required part types. The required part type descriptions may then be found in the **PART** records with **PTNUMB** key values, 'P2', 'P4', and 'P9'. Conversely, we can obtain the warehouses that contain a given part type.

Thus if **AFILE** and **BFILE** are conceptual files with primary key fields A and B respectively, then a many-to-many relationship between the files can be decomposed into:

1. A 1:n relationship between **AFILE** and **HELPFILE** where the child connection field is **A**.
2. A 1:n relationship between **BFILE** and **HELPFILE**, where the child connection field is **B**.

This is illustrated in Figure 5.10, and decompositions of this type are common in data base design.

(a)

(a) A many-to-many relationship between two arbitrary conceptual files, AFILE (key field A) and BFILE (key field B).

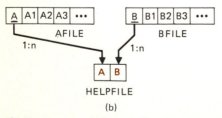

(b)

(b) By means of the auxiliary conceptual file HELPFILE, the many-to-many relationship between AFILE and BFILE in (a) may be replaced by 1:n relationships between AFILE and HELPFILE and between BFILE and HELPFILE. A record of HELPFILE contains the key fields from AFILE and BFILE, and these serve as connection fields.

FIGURE 5.10 Decomposing a many-to-many relationship into two one-to-many relationships.

5.2 DATA BASE STRUCTURES

We have seen that distinct conceptual files may be related by either 1:*n* or *n*:*m* relationships, and that two files related by an *n*:*m* relationship may be reduced to three files with just 1:*n* relationships. Thus it is convenient to deal only with 1:*n* relationships between files in a larger data base made up of many conceptual files. In this section we shall investigate more elaborate data base structures that are built up from pairs of conceptual files related by 1:*n* relationships.

Network and hierarchical data base organizations

We can distinguish easily between two types of data base organization, namely, the *network* organization and the *hierarchical* organization. A data base has a network organization when the relationships between the conceptual files give rise to a network of relationships; it has a hierarchical organization when the relationships between the files gives rise to a hierarchy. We can be more specific about this:

> *Network data base definition.* A data base is organized as a network if a record can be found with more than one parent record.
> *Hierarchical data base organization.* A data base is organized as a hierarchy if each and every record in the data base has at most one parent.

We can apply these definitions immediately to the data bases we have encountered so far. The data base in Figure 5.1 is clearly a network, since an INVENTORY record has a parent in WAREHOUSE and a parent in PART. We might also note that the data base in Figure 5.2 forms what is probably the simplest and certainly one of the most common networks. In contrast, the data base in Figure 5.6 forms a simple hierarchy, since each EMPLOYEE child record has only one WAREHOUSE parent record.

The definitions can also be applied to more complex data bases, as we shall see.

Data bases with larger numbers of conceptual files

We now extend the basic data base in Figure 5.1 by the stepwise addition of extra conceptual files. We begin by employing the conceptual file PART from the data base in Figure 5.1 in an entirely new conceptual data base illustrated in Figure 5.11*a*. As before, we consider a PART record as describing a type of part that is used by a manufacturer of electronic equipment. In order to ensure security of supply, it is common business practice to have at least two qualified[1] suppliers for any given type of part, and a record of the file SUPPLIER describes a qualified supplier of at least one type of part.

---

[1]It is common business practice to subject a supplier's product to a strict initial test before qualification is granted. Qualification is usually for a specific period of time, and further tests are necessary to obtain a renewal of the qualification.

PTNUMB	DESCRIPTION
P2	TRANSISTOR
P4	INDUCTOR
P7	INDUCTOR
P9	CAPACITOR

PART

SNUMB	SNAME	LOC
S3	TRONOTON	CALIFORNIA
S4	ROBOTEK	TEXAS
S6	MIKREL	ONTARIO
S7	RAYTEX	TEXAS

SUPPLIER

PTNUMB	SNUMB	ORDERNUMB	QTY
P4	S7	OR13	100
P2	S4	OR14	150
P4	S3	OR16	300
P7	S6	OR20	250
P7	S3	OR24	150
P2	S4	OR25	100
P4	S6	OR29	250
P9	S7	OR34	370

ORDER

(a) A data base that contains the conceptual file PART (from Figure 5.0), the conceptual file SUPPLIER that lists suppliers that supply the parts listed in PART, and the outstanding orders for parts from the suppliers, as listed in the conceptual file ORDER.

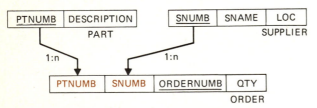

(b) An extended Bachman diagram for the files in (a). There is a one-to-many relationship between PART and ORDER records and between SUPPLIER and ORDER records.

FIGURE 5.11

At any given time our manufacturer of electronic equipment will have outstanding orders for different types of part, and a record in **ORDER** gives the type of part ordered (**PTNUMB**), the number of the supplier (**SNUMB**) from which it was ordered, the quantity (**QTY**) of that part type ordered, and the order number (**ORDERNUMB**), the primary key field.

In **SUPPLIER**, the field **SNUMB** is the supplier number, **SNAME** is the supplier name, and **LOC** gives the state or province containing the headquarters of the supplier. **SNUMB** is the primary key field.

We see that there is a 1:n relationship between **PART** and **ORDER**, since for any type of part there may be several orders outstanding, while each order is for one type of part only.[2] Similarly there is a 1:n relationship between **SUPPLIER** and **ORDER**, since a supplier has many orders to fulfill, while a single order is to be fulfilled by just one supplier. The child connection field for the relationship between **PART** and **ORDER** is the field **PTNUMB** in **ORDER**, while the child connection field for the relationship between **SUPPLIER** and **ORDER** is **SNUMB** in **ORDER**. The situation is summed up in the extended Bachman diagram in Figure 5.11*b*.

A data base for warehouses, part types, and suppliers

Since the data bases in Figures 5.1 and 5.11 both contain the file **PART**, it is possible to combine the two data bases. The new combined data base is shown in Figure 5.12 as an extended Bachman diagram. For convenience, the contents of **INVENTORY** and **ORDER** are repeated in Figure 5.13; for the other files see Figures 5.1 and 5.11.

We see that the data base has five conceptual files and four 1:n relationships. The data base essentially contains:

1. The quantity of a given type of part in a given warehouse (**INVENTORY** records)
2. The quantity of a given type of part on order from a given supplier (**ORDER** records)
3. A description of each warehouse (**WAREHOUSE** records)
4. A description of each type of part (**PART** records)
5. A description of each supplier (**SUPPLIER** records)

It would thus appear that we have considerable information in our data base about the supply of parts to the production processes of our electronics equipment manufacturer. To understand exactly how much information is in the data

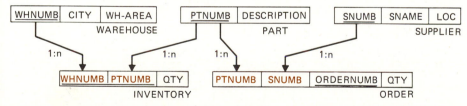

FIGURE 5.12 The data bases shown in Figures 5.1 and 5.11 may be combined, since the file PART is common to both. The data base contains information about inventories of parts in warehouses and about how many parts are on order from different suppliers. (The connection trap is evident in the above data base. We cannot infer the warehouse to which an outstanding order will be delivered. The structure must be altered in order for this to be possible. See Figure 5.15.)

---

[2]In practice an order can be for many types of part, but this introduces additional relationships that for expositional purposes it is better to avoid at this stage.

WHNUMB	PTNUMB	QTY
WH1	P4	675
WH1	P7	250
WH1	P9	340
WH2	P2	280
WH2	P4	200
WH2	P9	270
WH3	P2	550
WH3	P4	330
WH3	P7	170

INVENTORY

PTNUMB	SNUMB	ORDERNUMB	QTY
P4	S7	OR13	100
P2	S4	OR14	150
P4	S3	OR16	300
P7	S6	OR20	250
P7	S3	OR24	150
P2	S4	OR25	100
P4	S6	OR29	250
P9	S7	OR34	370

ORDER

FIGURE 5.13   The INVENTORY and ORDER files from Figure 5.12. The contents
are the same as those in the data bases in Figures 5.1 and 5.11.

base, with reference to the contents of **INVENTORY** in Figure 5.13, let us suppose
that a production process located near warehouse 'WH3' becomes unexpectedly
busy. The production manager at once asks the manager of 'WH3' to deliver 300
of part type 'P7'. The warehouse manager obtains a display of the **INVENTORY**
record with key 'WH3 P7' on a terminal, and this shows (see the **INVENTORY** file
in Figure 5.13) that there are only 170 of 'P7' left in the warehouse, which is not
enough. He first updates the **QTY** field to 0 and starts the warehouse process for
delivery of the 170 parts to the production manager.

The next task of the warehouse manager is to find out where the remaining
130 'P7' inductors are to be obtained. He asks the data base system for a display of
all the **INVENTORY** child records for the **PART** record with key 'P7'. On his
terminal appears:

```
WAREHOUSE#   PART-NUMBER   QUANTITY
   WH1           P7          250
   WH3           P7           0
```

indicating that there are some 'P7' inductors in warehouse 'WH1'. To determine
where the warehouse 'WH1' is located, the manager then asks for a display of the
record in **WAREHOUSE** with key 'WH1'. On his terminal appears:

```
WAREHOUSE#   CITY      FLOOR-AREA
   WH1       DALLAS      37,000
```

Now it will most likely be the case that the manager of the warehouse 'WH3' in
Chicago has no power to update the inventory records of a warehouse in Dallas.
Updating authority is usually restricted to only a few data base users, and each of
those users usually can update only a few conceptual files. The Chicago manager
must therefore send a requisition to Dallas (possibly via the terminal and corporate telecommunications system) for the needed 130 'P7' inductors. But before
doing so, he decides to check the **INVENTORY** child records for the **PART**
records with key 'P7' again. There appears:

```
WAREHOUSE#   PART-NUMBER   QUANTITY
    WH1          P7            0
    WH3          P7            0
```

indicating that the demand for 'P7' inductors has gone through the roof.

The connection trap

Our manager continues the hunt for the 'P7' inductors and now decides to see if there are any outstanding orders for them. He next asks the data base system for a display of the child ORDER records for the parent PART record with key 'P7'. On his terminal appears:

```
PART-NUMBER   SUPPLIER-NUMBER   ORDER-NUMBER   QUANTITY
    P7              S6              OR20          250
    P7              S3              OR24          150
```

so that there are outstanding orders for 'P7' inductors.

But which warehouses issued those orders? There is no indication in the ORDER records. However, a user might think it reasonable to assume that the ORDER records for a given part had something to do with the INVENTORY records for a given part, and come to the conclusion that the order 'OR20' (the first child ORDER record for the PART record with key 'P7') was issued by warehouse 'WH1' (the first child INVENTORY record for the PART record with key 'P7'). However, a user who makes this assumption will have fallen into what has come to be known as the *connection trap*. There is in fact no way we can determine from the data base in Figure 5.12 which order has been issued by a warehouse, and if this information is needed then the data base is poorly designed.

We can more clearly perceive the nature of the difficulty by concentrating on just the PART, INVENTORY, and ORDER files from the data base in Figure 5.12. These three files form a hierarchical data base, as shown in Figure 5.14*a*. Each INVENTORY record has just one parent PART record, as does each ORDER record. Again, for each PART parent record there are many child INVENTORY records and many child ORDER records. The 1:*n* relationships can be more clearly seen if we display the contents of the three files with the INVENTORY and ORDER records sorted on the PTNUMB connection field value. In each file we have a PTNUMB field, but there are only two relationships, namely, between PART and INVENTORY and between PART and ORDER. Even though there is a PTNUMB field in both INVENTORY and ORDER, *there is no relationship between* INVENTORY *and* ORDER. Thus we cannot say that just because warehouse 'WH1' contains 'P7' inductors, that order 'OR20' for 'P7' inductors must have been issued by warehouse 'WH1', and vice versa. If we assume a relationship between INVENTORY and ORDER, we fall into the connection trap.

Connection traps are common in data bases. They occur wherever we have three conceptual files in the form of a hierarchy as in Figure 5.14*a*. If the information apparently offered by the trap, such as the warehouse issuing an order in the case of the data base in Figure 5.14*a*, is actually needed, then a redesign of the data base is necessary.

(a) A hierarchical data base. The records of INVENTORY and ORDER are not related. A user who assumes that they are may fall into the connection trap.

ORDER

PTNUMB	SNUMB	ORDERNUMB	QTY
P2	S4	OR14	150
P2	S4	OR25	100
P4	S7	OR13	100
P4	S3	OR16	300
P4	S6	OR29	250
P7	S6	OR20	250
P7	S3	OR24	150
P9	S7	OR34	370

PART

PTNUMB	DESCRIPTION
P2	TRANSISTOR
P4	INDUCTOR
P7	INDUCTOR
P9	CAPACITOR

INVENTORY

WHNUMB	PTNUMB	QTY
WH2	P2	280
WH3	P2	550
WH1	P4	675
WH2	P4	200
WH3	P4	330
WH1	P7	250
WH3	P7	170
WH1	P9	340
WH1	P9	270

(b) The records from INVENTORY and ORDER in (a) are arranged in ascending PTNUMB order to illustrate the two separate 1:n relationships between PART and INVENTORY and between PART and ORDER.

FIGURE 5.14

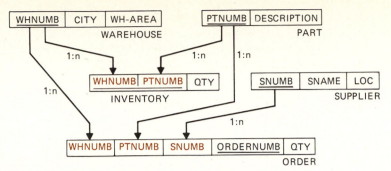

FIGURE 5.15 This data base is the same as the one in Figure 5.12 except for the addition of a single field WHNUMB to the ORDER file. This additional field gives the warehouse that has issued an outstanding order for a type of part from a supplier, thus eliminating the connection trap in the data base in Figure 5.12.

Elimination of the connection trap

To eliminate a connection trap, we have to remove the offending hierarchical structure; for example, we would have to remove the structure in Figure 5.14a from the data base in Figure 5.12. We also need to supply additional information, that is, we add more data to the data base to provide the information that the unwary would assume was available via the trap.

All this has been done with the new version of the data base from Figure 5.12 and shown in Figure 5.15. Essentially the only difference in the files is that there is a new version of the ORDER file. The new ORDER file contains a WHNUMB field. Thus an ORDER record contains the number of the warehouse issuing the order described in the record. This new version of the ORDER file is shown in Figure 5.16.

From Figure 5.15 we see that there is now an additional 1:n relationship in the data base as a result of the new field WHNUMB in the ORDER file. For any warehouse there are many outstanding orders, and for a WAREHOUSE parent record there are many ORDER records, with WHNUMB as the child connection

WHNUMB	PTNUMB	SNUMB	ORDERNUMB	QTY
WH2	P4	S7	OR13	100
WH3	P2	S4	OR14	150
WH2	P4	S3	OR16	300
WH3	P7	S6	OR20	250
WH2	P7	S3	OR24	150
WH2	P2	S4	OR25	100
WH1	P4	S6	OR29	250
WH1	P9	S7	OR34	370

ORDER

FIGURE 5.16 The new version of ORDER as used in the data base in Figure 5.15.

field for the new relationship. Thus the warehouse manager could easily find out what part types were on order for his warehouse, in his hunt for additional 'P7' inductors as described earlier. He would merely have to ask the data base system for the child records of the **WAREHOUSE** record with key 'WH3' (the manager's warehouse in the example). There would appear on the screen (see Figure 5.16):

```
WAREHOUSE   PART-NUMBER   SUPPLIER-NUMBER   ORDER-NUMBER   QUANTITY
   WH3          P2              S4              OR14          150
   WH3          P7              S6              OR20          250
```

indicating that 250 'P7' inductors were on order for his warehouse.

Three-dimensional many-to-many relationships

We notice that the **ORDER** file in the data base in Figure 5.15 is a child file in three distinct 1:n relationships. The four files involved in these relationships are shown with their relationships in Figure 5.17. This data base is not unlike the one in Figure 5.4a or Figure 5.7, except that we have three pairs of 1:n relationships instead of just one. Now we have seen that a pair of 1:n relationships with a common child file implies a many-to-many relationship between the parent files, so that the relationships in the data base in Figure 5.17 imply:

1. For each warehouse many part types, and for each part type many warehouses
2. For each warehouse many suppliers, and for each supplier many warehouses
3. For each supplier many part types, and for each part type many suppliers

We can also state the above relationships as:

1. For each warehouse many parts types and many suppliers
2. For each part type many suppliers and many warehouses
3. For each supplier many warehouses and many part types

We saw earlier that with three conceptual files, two 1:n relationships and a common child file, the relationships can be displayed as a matrix relationship

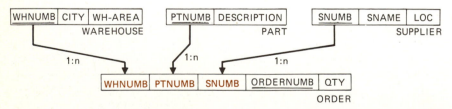

FIGURE 5.17 If we just consider a data base consisting of the conceptual files ORDER, WAREHOUSE, PART, and SUPPLIER from the data base in Figure 5.15, then we have three explicit 1:n relationships as well as an implicit three-dimensional many-to-many relationship among the files WAREHOUSE, PART, and SUPPLIER. The many-to-many relationship is further illustrated in Figure 5.18. For any warehouse there can be many different part types and many different suppliers; for any supplier there can be many warehouses and many different part types; and for any part type, there can be many warehouses and many suppliers. For the contents of ORDER, see also Figure 5.16.

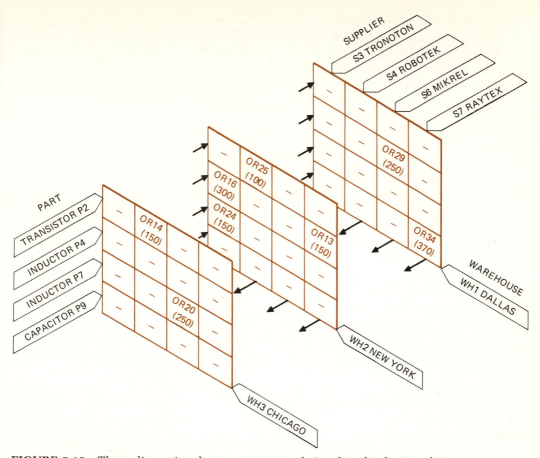

FIGURE 5.18 Three-dimensional many-to-many relationship display involving the data base in Figure 5.17.

between the parent files, with the data in the child file appearing in the cells of the matrix (see Figure 5.7). In a similar manner we can display the relationships in the data base in Figure 5.17 as a three-dimensional relationship, where **ORDER** data appears in the cells of a three-dimensional matrix (Figure 5.18).

In Figure 5.18, it must be understood that for any **PART** record, such as the one for key 'P4', there is a horizontal "plane" of **ORDER** entries, namely, 'OR16', 'OR13', and 'OR29'. For any **WAREHOUSE** record, such as the one for key value 'WH3' there is a vertical "plane" of **ORDER** entries, namely, 'OR14' and 'OR20'; and for any supplier there is also a vertical "plane" of **ORDER** entries, namely, 'OR34' and 'OR13' for the **SUPPLIER** record with key 'S7'. The **ORDER** record (or records) at the intersection of **SUPPLIER**, **PART**, and **WAREHOUSE** planes are the **ORDER** records from a given warehouse, to a given supplier, for a given type of part.

We can also have structures where a four-dimensional many-to-many relationship is implied, and so on. The four-dimensional case occurs where we have four parent files with a common child file. They occur fairly commonly.

The ORDER file in practice

We mentioned earlier that a purchase order to a given supplier rarely is for one type of item. In practice the document consists of lines, on each of which there is an order for a quantity of items of a given type. Thus for each purchase order issued by our electronics equipment manufacturer, there will be many lines, each line describing an order for a type of part. We therefore should have a PUR-ORDER file, a record of which describes a purchase order, and an ORDER-LINE file, a record of which describes a line of a purchase order; there will clearly be a 1:n relationship between the PUR-ORDER file and the ORDER-LINE file.

To see how the data base from Figure 5.15 would look if we modified it to allow for the PUR-ORDER and ORDER-LINE files, refer to Figure 5.19. In addition to the PUR-ORDER and ORDER-LINE files we have also included the EMPLOYEE file from Figure 5.6b. We recall that each EMPLOYEE record describes an employee at a warehouse, so that there is a 1:n relationship between WAREHOUSE and EMPLOYEE. In addition since it is often a person at a warehouse that initiates a purchase order for replenishment of stock, there is an EMPNUMB field in a PUR-ORDER record to contain the employee number of the initiator of the purchase order.

In Figure 5.20 we give some records from PUR-ORDER and ORDER-LINE. The field ORDERNUMB in ORDER-LINE is the child connection field for the 1:n relationship between PUR-ORDER and ORDER-LINE. A LINENUMB field contains a line number of a purchase order, and since every purchase order can have a line number 1, line number 2, and so on, a record of ORDER-LINE can be identified only by means of the two fields ORDERNUMB and LINENUMB, which therefore serve as a composite key.

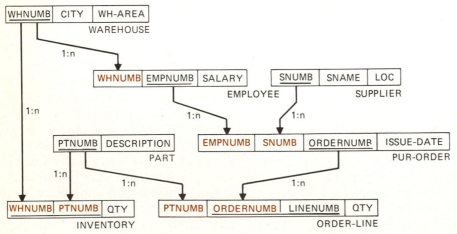

FIGURE 5.19 Extension of the data base in Figure 5.15 to allow for the employees at a given warehouse (in the EMPLOYEE file), and to allow for an order (described by a PUR-ORDER record) to consist of several lines (as in a typical purchase order in practice), each line giving the quantity of a type of part on order. A line of an order is a record in ORDER-LINE, and LINENUMB holds a line number for an order, such as 1, 2, 3, ...

EMPNUMB	SNUMB	ORDERNUMB	ISSUE-DATE
E3	S7	OR67	84/06/23
E1	S4	OR73	84/07/28
E7	S3	OR76	84/05/25
E6	S6	OR77	84/06/19
E3	S4	OR79	84/06/22
E1	S6	OR80	84/07/29

PUR-ORDER

PTNUMB	ORDERNUMB	LINENUMB	QTY
P4	OR67	1	250
P7	OR67	2	200
P9	OR73	1	160
P2	OR73	2	100
P4	OR73	3	200
P9	OR76	1	260
P2	OR77	1	140
P7	OR77	2	170
P3	OR79	1	150
P9	OR79	2	200
P2	OR80	1	160

ORDER-LINE

FIGURE 5.20 The contents of the conceptual files PUR-ORDER and ORDER-LINE from Figure 5.19. The remaining files from Figure 5.19 are displayed in Figures 5.1, 5.6a, and 5.11a.

Elementary data base design process

The data base in Figure 5.19 is a typical example of a more complex data base involving many files and relationships. This one contains information about the inventory of types of parts in warehouses, about the employees of warehouses, and about purchase orders initiated by warehouse employees for types of parts supplied by different suppliers. In general the process of designing such data bases requires starting with a simple data base, as we have done, and adding additional files step by step checking for connection traps and the existence of required information, reorganizing and adding or removing files, and so on. Finally a design is obtained that contains all the information that is needed by the enterprise about the *subject* modeled by the data base. In the data base in Figure 5.19, the subject of the data base is types of electronic parts used in manufacturing processes. The data base is still not without flaws, however, and the reader is invited to search for them.

We have covered the essentials of the more elementary structures that can occur in conceptual data bases. More advanced structures are also possible and in many cases cannot be avoided. These more advanced structures involve *recursive relationships.* (A recursive relationship occurs when there are 1:n or n:m relationships between different groups of records of the same file.) There are also design techniques for simplifying the conceptual files used in a conceptual data base, and these methods are known as *normalization techniques.* These more advanced topics will be dealt with in Chapter 9. However, our next topic will be an outline of the main approaches to data base management systems in practice, since the type of data base system being used will determine what kind of conceptual data base structures can be designed.

5.3   DATA BASE STRUCTURES WITH THE MAIN APPROACHES TO DATA BASE SYSTEMS

There are hundreds of commercial data base management packages on the market, although only a few of these are in common use. There are four distinct approaches to the design of data base systems, in accordance with the kinds of conceptual data base structures that may be managed by the system. The four approaches are:

1. *The hierarchical approach.* Here the data base structures are in the form of hierarchies.
2. *The CODASYL approach.* Here the data base structures are in the form of either networks or hierarchies. One-to-many relationships are dealt with by means of simple parent/child hierarchies called *owner-coupled sets.*[1]
3. *The relational network approach.* Again the data base structures are in the form of either networks or hierarchies. One-to-many relationships are handled by means of the connection fields. The types of conceptual file allowed are more restricted than in either (1) or (2).
4. *Hybrid approaches.* These approaches do not fit neatly into any of the above categories. Typically they contain features from the first three approaches.

In the following pages we give an overview of the first three approaches. A more detailed treatment is to be found in Chapters 6, 7, 8, 9, and 10.

The hierarchical approach

Information Management System (IMS) from IBM is the most widely used hierarchical data base system, and although current versions follow the ANSI/SPARC recommendations to a considerable degree, the conceptual and storage data base definitions are specified in a single schema. The two definitions are fairly distinct, however.

The conceptual records of an IMS conceptual data base are grouped or organized in two distinct ways:

1. Into groups of conceptual records of the same type, that is, into distinct conceptual files.

---

[1]In many texts this category is expanded to include all network-oriented data base systems. However, relational systems are also network systems, since relational data bases can form networks. We are thus forced to narrow our classification scheme.

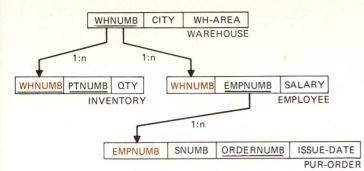

FIGURE 5.21 The conceptual files WAREHOUSE, INVENTORY, EMPLOYEE, and PUR-ORDER from the data base in Figure 5.19 form a hierarchical data base. WAREHOUSE is said to be the root conceptual file of the conceptual data base.

2. Into groups of conceptual records called *hierarchy types*. The data base in Figure 5.21, which is otherwise just a data base with a hierarchical structure, contains a single hierarchy type.

To get a better grasp of the concept of a hierarchy type, the hierarchy type depicted by the extended Bachman diagram in Figure 5.21 is displayed in full in Figure 5.22. The file **WAREHOUSE** is the *root file* of the hierarchy type, that is, the file that does not have a parent. Now for each **WAREHOUSE** record there are many **INVENTORY** records and many **EMPLOYEE** records, and for each of these **EMPLOYEE** records there are many **PUR-ORDER** records. This is displayed in Figure 5.22. That group of conceptual records made up of a root **WAREHOUSE**

WHNUMB	PTNUMB	QTY	WHNUMB	CITY	WH-AREA	WHNUMB	EMPNUMB	SALARY	EMPNUMB	SNUMB	ORDERNUMB	ISSUE-DATE
WH1	P4	675	W1	DALLAS	37,000	WH1	E3	21,000	E3	S7	OR67	84/06/23
WH1	P7	250							E3	S4	OR79	84/06/22
WH1	P9	340				WH1	E7	25,000	E7	S3	OR76	84/05/25
WH2	P2	280	W2	NEW YORK	50,000	WH2	E1	22,000	E1	S4	OR73	84/07/28
WH2	P4	200							E1	S6	OR80	84/07/27
WH2	P9	270				WH2	E4	25,000				
WH3	P2	550	W3	CHICAGO	20,000	W3	E6	23,000	E6	S6	OR77	84/06/19
WH3	P4	330										
WH3	P7	170										

INVENTORY · WAREHOUSE · EMPLOYEE · PUR-ORDER

FIGURE 5.22 The hierarchy occurrences from the data base in Figure 5.21. Each WAREHOUSE record is the root record of a tree of records, and such a tree of records is a hierarchy occurrence, shown surrounded by a rectangle. The number of hierarchy occurrences is equal to the number of records in WAREHOUSE, the root conceptual file. The hierarchy occurrences above are also displayed in Figure 5.23. The complete collection of hierarchy occurrences in a hierarchical data base is called a hierarchy type.

record, with its **INVENTORY** child records and its **EMPLOYEE** child records, together with the **PUR-ORDER** child records of these **EMPLOYEE** records, is called a *hierarchy occurrence*. Thus each hierarchy type is made up of a collection of hierarchy occurrences, and there are as many hierarchy occurrences in a hierarchy type as there are records in the root file. A hierarchy type is sometimes also called a *tree type*, and a hierarchy occurrence a *tree occurrence*.

The hierarchy occurrences underlying the hierarchy type in Figure 5.21 are displayed again in Figure 5.23. As before, the children and grandchildren of a root **WAREHOUSE** record form a distinct hierarchy occurrence. However this time the records are arranged in *hierarchical order*. Thus, going from left to right and top to bottom, a child record always follows either its parent or another record with the same parent, that is, a *twin*. In the storage data base, records are frequently stored in hierarchical order.

The manipulation commands available to a programmer typically allow for manipulation of the records within a hierarchy occurrence. For example, given a

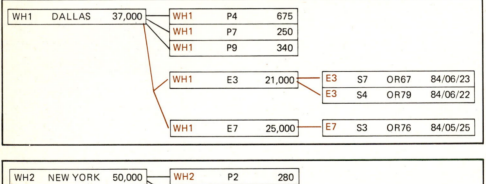
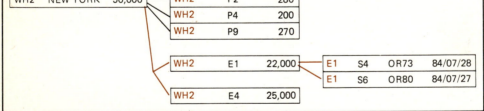
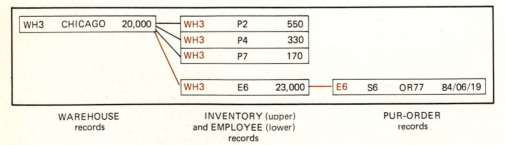

WAREHOUSE records	INVENTORY (upper) and EMPLOYEE (lower) records	PUR-ORDER records

FIGURE 5.23 Another display of the hierarchy occurrences from the data base in Figure 5.21. A rectangle surrounds each hierarchy occurrence. In this display, the records are said to be in hierarchical order.

parent record, a child could be retrieved, or a child and its children, or given a child record, the next child in hierarchical order. We cover IMS in detail in Chapter 10.

The hierarchy type used in hierarchical data bases may be looked at in another way. A structure variable in PL/1 or COBOL has a hierarchical structure and essentially forms a data tree. A collection of such structure variables of the same type then becomes a hierarchy type. Indeed from a close inspection of the storage records used in IMS it appears that it was from just such PL/1 and COBOL structure variables that IMS evolved. Another widely used hierarchical data base system is System 2000 from MRI Systems Corp. (Ref. 3), and with this system a hierarchy occurrence is specified in the conceptual schema almost as if it were a COBOL or PL/1 structure variable.

The CODASYL network approach

The CODASYL[1] approach is embodied in standards recommendations from the COSASYL organization, a voluntary body that was originally responsible for the development of the COBOL programming language. The current COSASYL recommendations have evolved from earlier recommendations developed over the past 15 years, and the latest recommendations closely follow the overall three-level architecture of the ANSI/SPARC data base system proposals; that is, we have a conceptual schema, an internal or storage schema, and various external schemas.

As with the hierarchical approach, the conceptual records of a CODASYL data base are grouped in two distinct ways:

1. Into groups of conceptual records of the same type, that is, into distinct conceptual files.

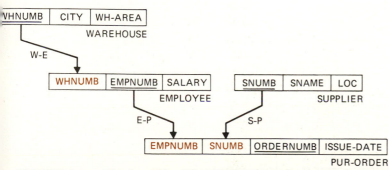

FIGURE 5.24 The four files WAREHOUSE, EMPLOYEE, SUPPLIER, and PUR-ORDER from the data base in Figure 5.19. If the conceptual files are to be in a CODASYL data base, then there will be a CODASYL or owner-coupled set (type) for each of the three 1:n relationships. Each owner-coupled set has to be given a name in the CODASYL conceptual schema. In the modified extended Bachman diagram above, the owner-coupled set for the 1:n relationship between WAREHOUSE and EMPLOYEE has been called W-E. An owner-coupled set is a grouping of records and is made up of owner-coupled set occurrences (see Figure 5.25).

---

[1]A widely used acronym for *Conference on Data System Languages.*

2. Into groups of records called *owner-coupled set types* or CODASYL *sets*. An owner-coupled set grouping of conceptual records embodies a 1:n relationship between conceptual files.

It is worthwhile gaining a grasp of the owner-coupled set concept even at this stage. In Figure 5.24 we have shown four of the files from the data base in Figure 5.19. As can be seen from the diagram, these conceptual files are related by 1:n relationships. For each 1:n relationship there can be an owner-coupled set type (we shall normally omit the word "type"), and such an owner-coupled set must be specified in the conceptual schema and given a name. In the extended Bachman diagram in Figure 5.24, we have placed the name of each owner-coupled set beside the arrow for the 1:n relationship embodied in the set. The names chosen for the sets are arbitrary.

The important point about an owner-coupled set is that it embodies a 1:n relationship between conceptual files. To see how, consider the owner-coupled set W-E in Figure 5.24 for the relationship between the WAREHOUSE and EMPLOYEE conceptual files. The complete owner-coupled set is illustrated in Figure 5.25a and consists of a collection of *owner-coupled set occurrences*. An owner-coupled set occurrence consists of a parent record from the parent file, in this case the WAREHOUSE file, and the corresponding child records from the child file, in this case the EMPLOYEE file. In CODASYL terminology, a parent record is called an *owner* record and a child record a *member* record.

The CODASYL data base manipulation language heavily involves the use of owner-coupled sets. For example, given an owner record, the system will retrieve the nth member record of the set occurrence, or it can deliver the member record of the set occurrence with a certain field value; or given a child record, it can deliver the owner record.

The owner-coupled set concept is a quite natural one. For example, when we are considering warehouse X's employees, we are considering the owner and member records of an owner-coupled set occurrence. Thus an owner-coupled set occurrence deals with the types of entities involved when we deal with the genitive case of singular nouns in ordinary English: the students (members) of the professor (owner), the products (members) of the company (owner), the parts (members) of the machine (owner), and so on. In addition, the fact that the owner-coupled set concept has a counterpart in natural language is important in the development of query languages (see Chapter 4) for the interrogation of data bases.

Figure 5.25b and c show the contents of the two owner-coupled sets E-P and S-P from Figure 5.24. We note first that some of the set occurrences have a parent without members. This is quite normal. In an owner-coupled set occurrence a parent may have zero or more member records. However, each member must have exactly one parent record in an owner-coupled set occurrence.

We note that in Figures 5.24 and 5.25 the conceptual file PUR-ORDER is a member file in two owner-coupled sets, namely, E-P and S-P. Thus the records of the file PUR-ORDER are grouped in three ways, first into the conceptual file PUR-ORDER, then into groupings of members for the owner-coupled set E-P,

(a) W-E

WHNUMB	CITY	WH-AREA
WH1	DALLAS	37,000

WHNUMB	EMPNUMB	SALARY
WH1	E3	21,000
WH1	E7	25,000

WHNUMB	CITY	WH-AREA
WH2	NEW YORK	50,000

WHNUMB	EMPNUMB	SALARY
WH2	E1	22,000
WH2	E4	25,000

WHNUMB	CITY	WH-AREA
WH3	CHICAGO	20,000

WHNUMB	EMPNUMB	SALARY
WH3	E6	23,000

(a)   WAREHOUSE records   EMPLOYEE records

(b) E-P

WHNUMB	EMPNUMB	SALARY
WH2	E1	22,000

EMPNUMB	SNUMB	ORDERNUMB	ISSUE-DATE
E1	S4	OR73	84/07/28
E1	S6	OR80	84/07/29

WHNUMB	EMPNUMB	SALARY
WH1	E3	21,000

EMPNUMB	SNUMB	ORDERNUMB	ISSUE-DATE
E3	S7	OR67	84/06/23
E3	S4	OR79	84/06/23

WHNUMB	EMPNUMB	SALARY
WH2	E4	25,000

WHNUMB	EMPNUMB	SALARY
WH3	E6	23,000

EMPNUMB	SNUMB	ORDERNUMB	ISSUE-DATE
E6	S6	OR77	84/06/19

WHNUMB	EMPNUMB	SALARY
WH1	E7	25,000

EMPNUMB	SNUMB	ORDERNUMB	ISSUE-DATE
E7	S4	OR76	84/05/25

(b)   EMPLOYEE records

(c) S-P

EMPNUMB	SNUMB	ORDERNUMB	ISSUE-DATE

SNUMB	SNAME	LOC
S3	TRONOTON	CALIFORNIA

EMPNUMB	SNUMB	ORDERNUMB	ISSUE-DATE
E1	S4	OR73	84/07/28
E7	S4	OR76	84/05/25
E3	S4	OR79	84/06/23

SNUMB	SNAME	LOC
S4	ROBOTEK	TEXAS

EMPNUMB	SNUMB	ORDERNUMB	ISSUE-DATE
E6	S6	OR77	84/06/19
E1	S6	OR80	84/07/29

SNUMB	SNAME	LOC
S6	MIKREL	ONTARIO

EMPNUMB	SNUMB	ORDERNUMB	ISSUE-DATE
E3	S7	OR67	84/06/23

SNUMB	SNAME	LOC
S7	RAYTEX	TEXAS

(c)   PUR-ORDER records   SUPPLIER records

FIGURE 5.25 Occurrences of the sets W-E (*a*), E-P (*b*), and S-P (*c*) from the data base in Figure 5.24. A set occurrence is shown within a large rectangle.

and then into different groupings of member records for the owner-coupled set S-P, as shown in Figure 5.25*b* and *c*. Note that this means that a typical **PUR-ORDER** record is a member record in two entirely different set occurrences. For example, the **PUR-ORDER** record for order number 80 is a member record of the E-P set occurrence whose owner **WAREHOUSE** record has the key 'E1', and also a member record in the S-P owner-coupled set occurrence whose owner **SUPPLIER** key is 'S6'.

The reader should be clear that the grouping of records making up an owner-coupled set is a grouping of conceptual records. No matter how many different owner-coupled sets a record is a member of, there will of course be only one underlying storage version of the record. An example of possible storage files for the files **EMPLOYEE**, **PUR-ORDER** and **SUPPLIER** from Figures 5.24 and 5.25 is illustrated in Figure 5.26. The data base system is able to deliver a member record in an owner-coupled set given the owner record, because of a suitable pointer system at the storage level. In Figure 5.26 we have used *first-member* and *next-member* pointers. In any owner-coupled set occurrence, the storage parent record contains a first-member pointer (the **FM** field) which points to the storage record corresponding to the first-member record. For an owner-coupled set occurrence of **E-P**, a storage **PUR-ORDER** record will have a next-member pointer field (**NM1** field in Figure 5.26), which points to the storage record corresponding to the next member of the **E-P** set occurrence. Many different pointer systems may be used with the storage files to implement the conceptual-level owner-coupled sets. However, in this book we will be little concerned with the technicalities of the storage level. It is sufficient to be aware that there has to be a pointer system of some kind at the storage level in order to have an owner-coupled set at the conceptual level.

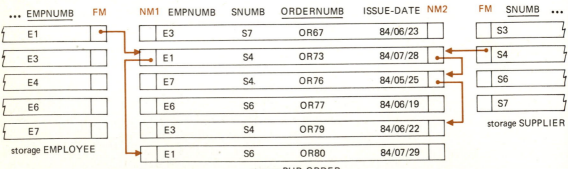

FIGURE 5.26 Storage versions of the files EMPLOYEE, PUR-ORDER, and SUPPLIER from Figure 5.25. To form the groupings of EMPLOYEE and PUR-ORDER records necessary for the set E-P, each storage EMPLOYEE record has a First Member (FM) pointer field, and each storage PUR-ORDER record has a Next Member (NM1) pointer field. Similarly, for the set S-P there is a Next Member (NM2) pointer in each storage PUR-ORDER record, and a First Member pointer in each storage SUPPLIER record. Many different pointer systems can be used to connect together the records of owner-coupled sets.

The relational approach to data base management

The relational approach to data base management resulted from research on the application of the mathematical theory of relations to data base management. Thus it has its roots in mathematics, while the hierarchical and CODASYL approaches have their roots in conventional data processing. For this reason a great deal of the terminology used originally with the relational approach was derived from mathematics and contributed to making the subject unnecessarily difficult for those not trained in mathematics. Today we tend to replace the mathematical terminology with terminology more in the tradition of data processing.

To the user, the relational approach appears quite simple. However, relational data base systems are not at all simple, and the approach appears simple to a user only because many of the difficulties and complexities are relegated to the data base management system. For this reason, although conceived some 15 years ago, the development of commercially viable relational data base systems took a lot longer than anyone imagined in the first half of the 1970s, the period during which development of relational data base systems began in earnest. The most widely known comprehensive relational data base system is System R, developed by IBM during the latter half of the 1970s.

The concept of a relation

The concept of a *relation*, or *relational file*, often gives the newcomer difficulties. The difficulties are usually due to the simplicity of the concept, and the fact that a relation is a conceptual file and not a storage file. However, while a relation is a conceptual file, not all conceptual files are relations. For the present we can use the following definition of a relation:

> *Definition of a relation.* A relation is a conceptual file, in which each record is unique, and where all records have the same number and type of fields, that is, all records have the same fixed length and format.

Thus, if we now turn back and examine the three conceptual files **WAREHOUSE**, **INVENTORY**, and **PART** in Figure 5.1, we see that these three files are relations: Each record in a file is unique, and for each file all the records have fixed length and fixed format.

Indeed, all the conceptual files we have dealt with so far in this chapter have been relations, and readers may as a result feel let down and wonder what is so special about a relation. The answer is nothing really, and the other approaches to data base management and other data base systems could well be restricted to the use of relations as their conceptual files. One difference between a relational data base system and other data base systems is that other systems can usually use conceptual files that are not relations. So it will be useful for the reader to examine an example of a conceptual file that is not a relation.

A nonrelation

Figure 5.27 contains an example of a conceptual file that is not a relation, simply because the records have variable length and variable format. The records of the

WHNUMB	CITY	WH-AREA	EMPNUMB	SALARY	EMPNUMB	SALARY	...
WH1	DALLAS	37,000	E3	21,000	E7	25,000	
WH2	NEW YORK	50,000	E1	22,000	E4	25,000	
WH3	CHICAGO	20,000	E6	23,000			

FIGURE 5.27 A conceptual file that is *not* a relation. The file is formed by joining together records from the WAREHOUSE and EMPLOYEE files from Figure 5.6a or 5.24. A record in the above file describes a warehouse and the employees who work at the warehouse. The fields used to describe an employee (the EMPNUMB and SALARY fields) will be repeated as many times as there is an employee for the warehouse described by the record. Such a group of fields is called a repeating group and cannot be used in a relation.

file are made up from the data in files **WAREHOUSE** and **EMPLOYEE** from Figure 5.6a or Figure 5.24; a typical record has a group of fields that describes a warehouse, and is followed by a succession of groups of fields, where each group describes an employee of the warehouse. A group of fields describing the employee is called a *repeating group*. Such a file is not allowed at the conceptual level with the relational approach. It *would* be allowed with many data base systems. However, such conceptual files are leftovers from the time when there were only primitive data base systems manipulating storage files (see Chapter 3). The storage files that can be manipulated by COBOL and PL/1 **READ** and **WRITE** commands permit records with repeating groups.

Record groupings in a relational data base
In a relational data base the conceptual records (or *tuples* in mathematical terminology) are grouped into relations and only relations. There are no other multiple file groupings such as hierarchy types or owner-coupled sets, which are used in other approaches to handle relationships between files. In the relational approach, the relationships between relations are handled by means of connection field values.

To get an idea about how relations and connection field values are all that is required in the relational approach, consider the data base in Figure 5.1 and imagine that it has been set up as a relational data base. Now suppose that we needed to retrieve the child **INVENTORY** records of a given **WAREHOUSE** record with key value 'WH2'. We would have to request that the data base system retrieve all those **INVENTORY** records whose **WHNUMB** field value matched the 'WH2' key value in the given **WAREHOUSE** record. The terms "child" and "parent" are not part of most relational data manipulation languages. Relationships are specified in retrieval commands simply by a specification of equality or inequality of connection field values.

The method of specifying relationships in retrieval commands by means of equating connection field values has its origins in a mathematical and *non-procedural language* called *relational predicate calculus,* from which many relational data base languages are derived. We conclude by explaining the meaning of a nonprocedural language.

Procedural and nonprocedural languages

There are two extreme types of computer languages, namely, procedural and nonprocedural languages. The common programming languages, for example, COBOL, PL/1, and FORTRAN are procedural. A procedural language is used for writing a program, where each statement of the program is a fairly simple command to the computer to carry out some action. Thus when we want to retrieve data from a data base by means of a procedural language, we must first decide the necessary steps and then make up a program consisting of host and data base manipulation language corresponding to those steps. The data manipulation language statements for IMS and CODASYL systems are therefore procedural, since their statements are used simply in addition to the statements of their host languages in a program. See Chapter 6 for examples.

In contrast, most relational data base manipulation languages are nonprocedural. With these languages it is not necessary to write a program or subprogram involving a host language in order to carry out a complex retrieval request. In a nonprocedural language we simply specify what is required to be retrieved and leave it to the data base system to analyze the request and generate the retrieval steps, which is equivalent to generating the retrieval program. Very sophisticated data base control systems are necessary for this to be possible, and this explains why so long a time has been required to develop commercially viable relational data base systems with nonprocedural data manipulation languages.

It is also possible to have nonprocedural data manipulation languages with the other approaches to data base management, especially if the conceptual files are restricted to relational files as in the relational approach. The chief advantage of a properly designed nonprocedural language is ease of use. When a nonprocedural data base language is available for interactive use, a manager or casual user at a terminal can enter a complex request for retrieval of data using only a few lines of code. In contrast the procedural language program for the same retrieval could take hundreds of lines of code. When a programmer can use nonprocedural language expressions within programs to replace large program excerpts, significant increases in programmer productivity result, since a few lines in the nonprocedural language can be written much more quickly than the correspondingly large number of procedural language lines. It does indeed seem that nonprocedural languages are the way of the future, and a great deal of emphasis is placed on them in subsequent chapters.

SUMMARY

1. In a conceptual data base there are two kinds of relationships between conceptual files, namely one-to-many (1:n) and many-to-many (n:m). In a 1:n relationship between two files, one file is the parent and another is the child; for one record of a parent file there are many records in the child file, while for one record in the child file there is but one record in the parent file. A many-to-many relationship between two files A and B can always be decomposed into a 1:n relationship between A and a third file C, and a 1:n relationship between B and

C. The connection field in a child file supports a 1:n relationship by carrying the value of the primary key of the parent record. A conceptual data base can be regarded as a collection of conceptual files that participate in 1:n relationships. If we have a file A that is the parent of both the files B and C, and when C is neither a parent nor a child of B, and does not participate in a many-to-many relationship with B, then B is not related to C; to assume that B is related to C, perhaps because B and C both carry the primary key field of A as the child connection field, is to fall into the connection trap and is a common error.

2. There are four main approaches to data base management systems, namely the hierarchical approach, the CODASYL approach, the relational approach, and the hybrid approach, the last of which is any approach that differs from the first three approaches. In the hierarchical approach conceptual records are grouped into conceptual files and into hierarchy types, where a hierarchy type is a collection of hierarchy occurrences. A hierarchy occurrence has a root record, which has no parent, and is the parent record of a collection of child records not necessarily of the same type; these child records are also parents of further children, and so on. In the CODASYL approach, conceptual records are grouped into conceptual files and owner-coupled set types, where an owner-coupled set type is a collection of owner-coupled set occurrences; an owner-coupled set occurrence contains a parent record and a collection of child records. An owner-coupled set type thus embodies a 1:n relationship. In a relational conceptual data base, conceptual records of the same type (also known as tuples) are grouped into a restricted form of conceptual file known as a relation, and that is all. Relationships between these relations of the data base are determined by connection field values. There are two extreme forms of language for manipulating data bases, namely procedural and nonprocedural languages. In a procedural language a series of steps or a procedure must be specified, whereas in a nonprocedural language the desired result is specified, thus leaving it up to a powerful data base management system to determine the necessary procedure for obtaining the desired result.

QUESTIONS

1. Distinguish between enterprise and conceptual data bases.
2. Assuming that each of the conceptual files in the data base in Figure 5.1 may be sequentially accessed in ascending primary key order, and directly accessed on the basis of a primary key value, give procedures for each of the following requests for information:
   (a) What cities have inductors?
   (b) Give a description of part types kept in warehouses in New York.
   (c) How many inductors are inventoried in Dallas?
   (d) What is the floor area of warehouses that have no transistors?
   (e) What part types (PTNUMB values) are not inventoried in New York?
   (f) What are the warehouse numbers for warehouses containing part type number 'P9'?

(g) What warehouses contain all the part types listed in the data base.

(h) What part types are to be found in every warehouse listed in the data base?

3. Make up extended Bachman diagrams for the following data bases, each of which contains two parent files and one child file:

(a) A data base about engineers and projects

(b) A data base about stocks and investment firms

(d) A data base about suppliers and trucking firms

(e) A data base about skills and machines

(f) A data base about crew members and flights

(g) A data base about parks and rangers

(h) A data base about companies and product types

4. Assuming that each of the conceptual files in the data base in Figure 5.12 may be accessed sequentially in ascending primary key order, and directly accessed on the basis of a primary key value, give procedures for each of the following requests for information:

(a) What Texas suppliers have orders for more than 200 transistors in total?

(b) What part types have been ordered from Texas suppliers only?

(c) What part types in New York warehouses are on order from California suppliers? (Can this be carried out without falling into the connection trap?)

(d) What Dallas warehouses have issued orders for part types from Robotek? (Can this be carried out without falling into the connection trap?)

(e) What part types on order from Toronto are stored in warehouses with a floor area under 25,000 square feet? (Can this be carried out without falling into the connection trap?)

(f) What Texas suppliers have orders from New York warehouses? (Can this be carried out without falling into the connection trap?)

5. Repeat the requests in Question 4 for the data base in Figure 5.15, assuming that the files can be accessed sequentially in ascending primary key order, and directly on the basis of the primary key.

6. Assuming that the files of the data base in Figure 5.17 may be accessed sequentially in ascending primary key order, and directly on the basis of the primary key, give procedures for each of the following requests for information. In addition, the result of each request should be given on the basis of the data in Figure 5.18.

(a) In what cities have warehouses issued orders for inductors from California?

(b) What Texas suppliers have no orders from New York for transistors?

(c) What part types are not in warehouses that have not issued orders for them?

7. Assuming that the files of the data base in Figure 5.19 are accessible sequentially in ascending primary key order, and directly on the basis of the primary key, give procedures for each of the following requests for information:

(a) What parts have been ordered by New York warehouses?

(b) Find the salaries of employees who have issued orders for transistors to Ontario companies?

(c) What suppliers have no orders for capacitors?

(d) How many transistors are on order by Dallas warehouses?

(e) What purchase orders do not contain orders for capacitors?

8. Use the data base in Figure 5.14 to give some examples of hierarchy occurrences.

9. Use the data base in Figure 5.14 to give examples of owner-coupled set occurrences.

10. Use the data in Figure 5.14 to construct a conceptual file that is not a relation.

REFERENCES

1. Bachman, C. W., 1969. "Data Structure Diagrams." *Data Base, J. ACM SIGBDP*, 1(2):4–10.

2. Bradley, J., 1978. "An Extended Owner-Coupled Set Data Model and Predicate Calculus for Data Base Management." *ACM Trans. on Database Systems*, 3(4):385–416.

3. MRI. *System 2000 Reference Manual*, MRI Systems Corp., Austin, Texas.

The CODASYL Approach to Data Base Management

In this chapter we shall examine the essentials of the CODASYL recommendations. We shall not look at any specific CODASYL system. There are many different implementations of the CODASYL recommendations on the market. They all vary in some degree from the CODASYL recommendations, but the variations are for the most part minor ones, and a grasp of the CODASYL specifications is sufficient for an understanding of any of the current implementations. The CODASYL recommendations have developed over a period of about 15 years, and we begin with a short history.

6.1 HISTORY OF THE CODASYL DATA BASE SYSTEM PROPOSALS

CODASYL is an acronym for Conference on Data System Languages (a name few seem able to remember), which is a voluntary organization representing user groups and manufacturers of computer equipment. It was CODASYL that was originally responsible for the development of COBOL.

The work of CODASYL is largely performed in a democratic manner by means of committees and task groups. Important committees are the CODASYL Executive Committee, which supervises the work of all other committees, the Programming Language Committee (PLC), and the Data Description Language Committee (DDLC) (see Figure 6.1).

The PLC dates from the early 1960s and was originally charged with the

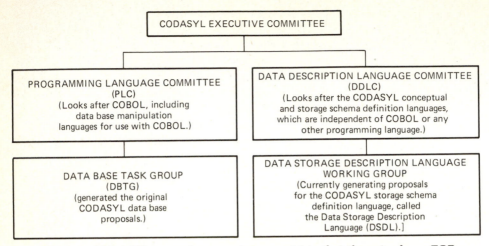

FIGURE 6.1 CODASYL committees and groups. Note that there is also a FORTRAN committee that has developed a CODASYL data base manipulation language for FORTRAN. Note that DBTG no longer exists.

approval of all changes to COBOL. During the second half of the 1960s, PLC set up a now famous task group called the Data Base Task Group (or DBTG as it is widely referred to). DBTG's task was the investigation of methodology for complex data structures on external storage devices. The complex data structures were of course data bases, and the idea was that DBTG should propose some data base management facilities for possible incorporation into COBOL.

DBTG's first report came out in 1969 and caused a heated debate. It also generated a lot of criticism, especially from researchers at IBM. As a result DBTG went back to the drawing board and essentially revised and extended their original proposals. In 1971 they issued a new report, defining a *data base manipulation language* (DML), a *schema definition language*, and a *subschema (or external schema) definition language*. The schema was essentially a combination of the ANSI/SPARC conceptual and storage schema. The lack of a clean separation between conceptual and storage data base definitions meant that the degree of data independence the system could offer would be low. For this and other reasons the 1971 report was heavily criticized, and although it was accepted by the PLC as the basis for further development, four leading computer manufacturers voted against acceptance.

A short time later the CODASYL executive committee formed a new committee called the Data Description Language Committee (DDLC, mentioned above), to take on some of the burden of developing the CODASYL data base proposals. From now on PLC would deal with the DML and the subschema definition language, since it was felt that these properly belonged in COBOL, the language for which PLC was basically responsible. At the same time the responsibility for the schema definition language was left to the new DDLC, since it was felt that the schema definition language should be independent of any programming language such as COBOL or PL/1.

As a result of the work of the two data base committees, by the midseventies CODASYL DML and subschema definition language had been incorporated into CODASYL COBOL, and recommendations for a schema definition language had been published. However, in 1975 the interim report of the ANSI/SPARC committee was released, recommending distinct storage, conceptual and external schemas. This resulted in further criticism of the CODASYL recommendations. However, in a major revision released in 1978, the old schema definition language was replaced by a language for defining conceptual schemas (also called a schema definition language), and a language for defining storage schemas, and called a Data Storage Description Language (DSDL).

Thus by the end of the decade CODASYL was recommending three-level data bases. However, CODASYL continued to revise and improve its recommendations, and another revision of the proposals appeared in 1981. This latest revision involved no major developments and merely involved a number of fairly minor improvements.

The 1978 CODASYL proposals were submitted to the American National Standards Institute for consideration as a possible American National Standard. The current ANSI working proposals vary only in minor detail from the CODASYL proposals. However, it can be expected that the ANSI proposal will be further modified in the light of the 1981 CODASYL recommendations. In this chapter we shall therefore base our discussions on the latest CODASYL proposals.

As already mentioned, the CODASYL recommendations are updated at regular intervals, and full details are to be found in the CODASYL Journals of Development (JOD). It should be noted that there are two different types of publication. First there is CODASYL COBOL JOD, which contains the proposals for the CODASYL data manipulation language, and which is issued by the PLC. Then there is the CODASYL DDLC JOD, which contains the details of the schema definition language and storage schema definition language, and which is issued by the DDLC (Refs. 3 and 4). A fairly detailed account of the CODASYL proposals is also to be found in Ref. 2.

Commercial implementations of the CODASYL recommendations

Many computer manufactures and software houses have implemented the CODASYL recommendations with varying degrees of commercial success. Sperry Univac, Honeywell, and Digital Equipment Corporation are all marketing CODASYL data base systems. A notable exception is IBM, which concentrated on the hierarchical system IMS (see Chapter 10) and the development of a relational data base system (see Chapter 7). The most successful CODASYL system is probably Cullinane Corporation's IDMS (Ref. 5), which is both widely used and is enjoying a healthy growth (at the time of writing) in the number of installations. IDMS will run under most IBM operating systems. While these commercial systems are all based on the CODASYL recommendations, they all have their own special features as well. However, the best way to gain an overall understanding of these systems is to study the essentials of the CODASYL recommendations without reference to any particular commercial implementation, which is what we propose to do in this chapter.

Technical Note: Readers familiar with CODASYL will notice that we have omitted the CODASYL concept of **AREA** (or **REALM**), since the latest CODASYL recommendations have rendered the concept obsolete.

6.2 THE CODASYL CONCEPTUAL SCHEMA

As introduced in the previous chapter, CODASYL conceptual records are grouped in two distinct ways, namely, into conceptual files and into owner-coupled sets, and this is directly reflected in the layout of a CODASYL conceptual schema, which essentially contains:

1. A definition of each of the conceptual files
2. A definition of each of the owner-coupled sets

We shall briefly examine these two types of definition, and for purposes of illustration we shall make use of the data base from Figure 5.24, shown again in Figure 6.2. The reader should be aware that our coverage will include only the essentials of the CODASYL conceptual schema definition language. We begin with the definition of the conceptual files.

Defining the CODASYL conceptual files

To define a CODASYL conceptual file, we give the file a name and specify:

1. Any *primary* or *record* key field or collection of fields
2. Any secondary key field
3. All the fields of a record of the file

We shall take these in turn using the file **WAREHOUSE** from Figure 6.2 as an example.

Primary key specification
The primary key for the **WAREHOUSE** conceptual file is **WHNUMB**, and the primary key specification would typically be:

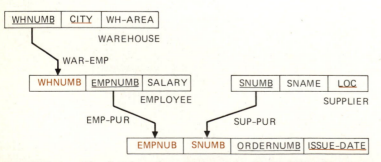

FIGURE 6.2 The data base from Figure 5.24. CODASYL primary or record keys are underlined in black, while CODASYL secondary keys are underlined in color.

```
KEY WHNUMB IS ASCENDING WHNUMB
DUPLICATES ARE NOT ALLOWED
```

If desired we may replace ASCENDING by DESCENDING. This specification ensures that if we retrieve the records of WAREHOUSE in sequential primary key order, the records will appear in ascending WHNUMB order; nevertheless in the underlying storage file the records might not be stored in ascending WHNUMB order. The storage WAREHOUSE file might well be a hash file, so that a linked list would be required to ensure that the conceptual records were available in ascending WHNUMB order (Figure 3.4). Specification of DESCEND-ING instead of ASCENDING would mean that when records were being retrieved in sequential order, the first record delivered would have the highest key value, and the last the lowest key value. Using the primary key value, a record may also be retrieved by direct access.

Secondary key specification
From Figure 6.2 we see that there is a secondary key CITY. Since it is possible and even likely that there will be several warehouses in major cities, there will be multiple records with the same CITY value. We specify:

```
KEY CITY IS ASCENDING CITY
DUPLICATES ARE LAST
```

Thus conceptual records may be read sequentially in ascending CITY order. As with the primary key specification we may replace ASCENDING by DESCEND-ING, so that the records become available in the reverse order. An underlying pointer system at the storage level will be necessary to ensure that the conceptual records are available in ascending or descending CITY order.

However, it is not enough to specify the records as being available in ascending or descending CITY order. In what order do a group of records with the same CITY value appear? This depends on whether we specify DUPLICATES ARE LAST or DUPLICATES ARE FIRST.

To see how this works, consider the file WAREHOUSE shown in Figure 6.3. In (a) we have the records as they would appear when retrieved in sequential primary key order, assuming we have specified KEY WHNUMB IS ASCENDING WHNUMB. In (b) we have the records as they would appear when retrieved in secondary (that is, CITY) key order, assuming again that we have specified KEY CITY IS ASCENDING CITY.

Now suppose that we insert a new record with primary key 'WH4' and secondary key 'DALLAS' into the file (we shall see how this is done with a STORE command later). In Figure 6.3c we have the records as they would be retrieved following the insertion, assuming we retrieve in sequential primary key order. Thus CODASYL will always keep the records available in ascending WHNUMB order despite the insertion. If we now attempt to retrieve the records in secondary key order, and had the secondary key specification in the concep-tual schema included DUPLICATES ARE LAST, the order of retrieval would be as shown in Figure 6.3d. On the other hand, DUPLICATES ARE FIRST would have resulted in the retrieval order shown in Figure 6.3e.

WHNUMB	CITY	WH-AREA
WH1	DALLAS	37,000
WH2	NEW YORK	50,000
WH3	CHICAGO	20,000

(a)Primary key WHNUMB. Records are available in ascending WHNUMB-value order.

WHNUMB	CITY	WH-AREA
WH3	CHICAGO	20,000
WH1	DALLAS	37,000
WH2	NEW YORK	50,000

(b) Secondary key CITY. Records are available in ascending CITY-value order.

WHNUMB	CITY	WH-AREA
WH1	DALLAS	37,000
WH2	NEW YORK	50,000
WH3	CHICAGO	20,000
WH4	DALLAS	15,000

(c) When a new record with key primary key 'WH4' is inserted, the records are still available in ascending WHNUMB-value order.

WHNUMB	CITY	WH-AREA
WH3	CHICAGO	20,000
WH1	DALLAS	37,000
WH4	DALLAS	15,000
WH2	NEW YORK	50,000

(d) Effect of inserting a record (color) on retrieval in CITY order, when we have DUPLICATES ARE LAST in the conceptual schema.

WHNUMB	CITY	WH-NUMB
WH3	CHICAGO	20,000
WH4	DALLAS	15,000
WH1	DALLAS	37,000
WH2	NEW YORK	50,000

(e) Effect of inserting a record (color) on retrieval in CITY order, when we have DUPLICATES ARE FIRST in the conceptual schema.

FIGURE 6.3

Essentially, specification of **LAST** ensures that a newly stored record is available only as the last of the collection of records with the same secondary key value, while **FIRST** ensures availability as the first of the group of records with the same secondary key value.

As we shall see later, we may also retrieve a record directly on the basis of a secondary key value, but since there will typically be a *group* of records with a given secondary key value, we have to retrieve all the records of this group one by one until the desired record is found. The order in which the records of the group are available by direct access is also determined by the specification of **FIRST** or **LAST** in the schema. We shall return to this when we discuss the CODASYL **FETCH** commands in the next section.

We note that specification of a secondary key in the conceptual schema will normally require the specification of a pointer system for an inverted file or multiple linked list at the storage level (see Chapter 3). We recall also that implementation of a secondary key results in a heavy updating cost because of the need to maintain the underlying pointer system. In practice, the decision to incorporate a secondary key in a file is rarely taken lightly and is ultimately a management decision.

Field specifications

The CODASYL field specifications used in the conceptual schema are similar to those used in COBOL. Thus a field can be specified as numeric or alphanumeric:

```
02   WHNUMB      PIC X(5).
02   CITY        PIC X(20).
02   WH-AREA     PIC 9(6).
```

Note that in the latest CODASYL recommendations, repeating groups of fields within the records of a conceptual file are no longer permitted. Earlier CODASYL recommendations allowed repeating groups, mainly because they were allowed in the record structures of COBOL and PL/1 storage files. This means that for most purposes we can take CODASYL conceptual files conforming to the latest recommendations as being relations; we can still construct a CODASYL conceptual file that is not a relation, however, merely having duplicate records within the file.

Complete specifications for the conceptual files

The complete specification for some of the files in Figure 6.2 is shown in Figure 6.4. The first entry in the conceptual schema specification is its name, and we have chosen the name **OUTSTANDING-ORDERS** for this subject data base. The

```
01   SCHEMA NAME IS OUTSTANDING-ORDERS
02
03   RECORD NAME IS WAREHOUSE
04   KEY WHNUMB IS ASCENDING WHNUMB
05   DUPLICATES ARE NOT ALLOWED
06   KEY CITY IS ASCENDING CITY
07   DUPLICATES ARE LAST.
08        02   WHNUMB  PIC X(5).
09        02   CITY    PIC X(20).
10        02   WH-AREA PIC 9(6).
11
12   RECORD NAME IS EMPLOYEE
13   KEY EMPNUMB IS ASCENDING EMPNUMB
14   DUPLICATES ARE NOT ALLOWED.
15        02   WHNUMB  PIC X(5).
16        02   EMPNUMB PIC X(5).
17        02   SALARY  PIC 9(6).
```

FIGURE 6.4 Part of the CODASYL conceptual schema for the data base in Figure 6.2. The schema is called OUTSTANDING-ORDERS, and the excerpt above shows the specification of the two conceptual files WAREHOUSE and EMPLOYEE.

reader is left to complete the specification for the remaining two files in Figure 6.2.

Defining the CODASYL owner-coupled sets

Specification of the owner-coupled sets in a CODASYL data base is considerably more complicated than is specification of the CODASYL conceptual files. However, before we examine in some detail how owner-coupled sets are specified, it is worth taking a second look at just what an owner-coupled set is. Before the advent of the three-level CODASYL data base at the end of the 1970s, an owner-coupled set was commonly regarded as a storage structure consisting of physical records connected by a pointer system and used as a method of access to the data base. This view is definitely outmoded, although there are still those who adhere to it.

The modern CODASYL owner-coupled set is nothing more than an additional grouping of records at the conceptual level. The most obvious grouping of conceptual records is into records of the same type, that is, conceptual files. The conceptual file grouping clearly reflects the world around us; for example, referring to the data base in Figure 6.2, we have collections of warehouses in the world, collections of warehouse employees, collections of electronics parts, suppliers, and so on. But we can also group an entity together with another type of entity, for example, a warehouse with the employees who work in it (Figure 6.5a), or an employee together with the purchase orders he or she is responsible

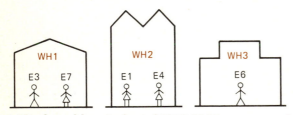

(a) Real-world equivalent of WAR-EMP owner-coupled set occurrences (see Figures 6.2 and 6.6a).

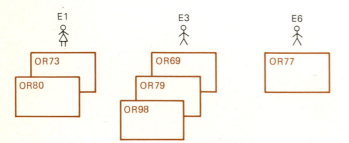

(b) Real-world equivalent of EMP-PUR owner-coupled set occurrences (see Figures 6.2 and 6.25b).

FIGURE 6.5

for (Figure 6.5b). Such a grouping of a parent and associated child records is an *owner-coupled set occurrence,* and is a grouping that reflects the business world. The collection of owner-coupled set occurrences of the same type is an *owner-coupled set* or *owner-coupled set type.* A parent record in such a set is called an *owner* record, and a child record a *member* record.

To specify a CODASYL owner-coupled set, we must state:

1. The name of the set
2. The name of the owner file
3. The way in which the member records of a set occurrence are ordered for retrieval purposes
4. The name of the member file
5. Storage and removal class—more about this later
6. Method of obtaining direct access to a set *occurrence,* or the *set occurrence,* or the *set occurrence selection mechanism*

The first four of these specifications are quite elementary, and we could begin the schema specification for the owner-coupled set **WAR-EMP** as follows:

```
SET NAME IS WAR-EMP
OWNER IS WAREHOUSE
ORDER IS PERMANENT CONNECTION IS LAST
MEMBER IS EMPLOYEE
```

Only the third line requires any explanation. **CONNECTION IS LAST** specifies in what order the conceptual member records of each **WAR-EMP** owner-coupled set occurrence are to be available to users or, in other words, how the member records are to be maintained as far as the user is concerned. When a new **EMPLOYEE** record is placed in the data base, it must be placed (1) in the **EMPLOYEE** conceptual file in the order specified in the schema for records of that file (see the previous section), and (2) in one or more owner-coupled set occurrences in the order specified in the schema specification of each of the owner-coupled sets.

The use of the word **LAST** in the specification above means that CODASYL will make an **EMPLOYEE** record, which has just been placed in (or connected to) a **WAR-EMP** owner-coupled set occurrence, the last available record of that occurrence. This is illustrated in Figure 6.6. In Figure 6.6a we have the owner-coupled set occurrences of **WAR-EMP**; however, from this diagram the method of ordering the member records of an occurrence is not at all apparent. In Figure 6.6b we place a new record (in color) in the occurrence whose **WAREHOUSE** owner record has key 'WH2'. This new record will be placed as the last of the group of member records in the occurrence.

This does not mean that the record is physically placed as the last record in the set occurrence; it merely means that if we ask CODASYL for the last record in the set occurrence owned by 'WH2', then we get the **EMPLOYEE** record 'E2'. We

---

[1]At the time of writing **INSERTION** is used instead of **CONNECTION** in the CODASYL recommendations, but the trend elsewhere in the recommendations is to replace **INSERT** with **CONNECT**.

WHNUMB	CITY	WH–AREA		WHNUMB	EMPNUMB	SALARY
WH1	DALLAS	37,000		WH1	E3	21,000
				WH1	E7	25,000
WH2	NEW YORK	50,000		WH2	E1	22,000
				WH2	E4	25,000
WH3	CHICAGO	20,000		WH3	E6	23,000

WAREHOUSE records   EMPLOYEE records

(a) The owner-coupled set WAR-EMP (see Figure 6.2) for which the order of the members of each set occurrence depends on the conceptual schema specification INSERTION IS LAST. The effect of adding a new member record to a set occurrence is shown in (b).

WHNUMB	CITY	WH–AREA		WHNUMB	EMPNUMB	SALARY
WH1	DALLAS	37,000		WH1	E3	21,000
				WH1	E7	25,000
WH2	NEW YORK	50,000		WH2	E1	22,000
				WH2	E4	25,000
				WH2	E2	19,000
WH3	CHICAGO	20,000		WH3	E6	23,000

WAREHOUSE records   EMPLOYEE records

(b) A new record (key 'E2') is added to one of the occurrences of the owner-coupled set WAR-EMP. The new record can now be retrieved as the last of the group of member records in the set occurrence.

WHNUMB	EMPNUMB	SALARY
WH2	E1	22,000
WH2	E2	19,000
WH1	E3	21,000
WH2	E4	25,000
WH3	E6	23,000
WH1	E7	25,000

EMPLOYEE

(c) If the records of EMPLOYEE are being retrieved sequentially, then it is EMPNUMB order that matters, in accordance with the conceptual schema specification for the EMPLOYEE file. Thus the new record is also inserted into EMPLOYEE in EMPNUMB order.

FIGURE 6.6 Order of members in an owner-coupled set occurrence.

must also remember that the order of the member records in an owner-coupled set occurrence will normally be distinct from the order of the records in the member file. This is illustrated in Figure 6.6c. Here the newly inserted record is also placed in the **EMPLOYEE** file in ascending **EMPNUMB** order, as specified in the previous section.

We can replace the specification **CONNECTION IS LAST** by **CONNECTION IS FIRST**. This would cause CODASYL to make a newly connected **EMPLOYEE** record available as the first record of the group of member records in the affected set occurrence. It is also possible to specify that member records be maintained in ascending or descending sort-key order, where the sort-key is some selected field from the member file. The syntax is complicated however, and we shall omit it (see Ref. 2).

We now turn to the remaining specifications for a typical owner-coupled set.

Storage and removal class

An owner-coupled set can have one of two possible storage classes and one of three possible removal classes. *Storage class* is quite distinct from *removal class*. We shall explain these two concepts separately.

STORAGE CLASS.   We may specify the storage class as **MANUAL** or **AUTOMATIC**: or

```
CONNECTION IS AUTOMATIC

CONNECTION IS MANUAL
```

The specification reflects whether, when placing a new record in the data base, we desire:

1. To be able to place the record first in its conceptual file and then later, in a separate operation, to connect the record to the appropriate owner-coupled set occurrence (manual connection)
2. Or to be able to place the record in both its file and the appropriate owner-coupled set occurrence in one operation (automatic connection)

Later in this chapter we shall examine both the **STORE** command, which is a data manipulation language command for placing records in a file, and the **CONNECT** command for connecting a record to an owner-coupled set occurrence. But we must make a limited use of them here to explain the effect of the storage class specification.

Suppose we have a record in an appropriate COBOL program structure and we wish to place this record in the data base; specifically we wish to place it in the **EMPLOYEE** file and in an occurrence of the set **WAR-EMP**. If the storage class specified in the schema were **MANUAL**, we would issue the following command within the COBOL program:

```
STORE EMPLOYEE
```

which would place the record in the **EMPLOYEE** file; later we could issue the command

```
CONNECT EMPLOYEE TO WAR-EMP
```

which would connect the record to the appropriate **WAR-EMP** set occurrence (we would also have to identify the correct set occurrence to CODASYL before issuing this **CONNECT** command, but we leave that detail until later).

On the other hand, were the storage class specification **AUTOMATIC**, we need only issue the command

```
STORE EMPLOYEE
```

which would cause CODASYL to store the record in the **EMPLOYEE** file and at the same time connect it to the appropriate set occurrence, in the simplest case the set occurrence whose owner record key was the same as the **WHNUMB** child connection field value for the record being stored.

REMOVAL CLASS. We may specify removal class as **FIXED**, **MANDATORY**, or **OPTIONAL**:

```
RETENTION IS FIXED
```
or

```
RETENTION IS MANDATORY
```
or

```
RETENTION IS OPTIONAL
```

If we specify **FIXED**, it means that a member record can never be taken out of (disconnected from) a set occurrence unless it is deleted. A specification of **MANDATORY** means that a member record can be taken out of one owner-coupled set occurrence only if it is immediately placed in another occurrence of the same owner-coupled set. Thus membership in *some* owner-coupled set occurrence is mandatory. Finally, a specification of **OPTIONAL** means that a member record can be disconnected from its set occurrence and left "dangling" in its conceptual file.

We can illustrate these possibilities using the owner-coupled set **WAR-EMP** in Figures 6.2 and 6.6. If we had a very rigid personnel policy at the corporation owning the warehouses in the **WAREHOUSE** file, so that an employee would always have to work at the warehouse to which he or she was originally assigned, then a specification of **FIXED** for the owner-coupled set would make sense (but the personnel policy probably would not). On the other hand, if a more flexible personnel policy required that a warehouse employee always be assigned to some one of the corporation's warehouses, then a specification of **MANDATORY** for the set **WAR-EMP** would be best. Finally, if a warehouse employee could go for periods of time without being assigned to any particular warehouse, then a specification of **OPTIONAL** would be appropriate.

Thus the idea of removal class places restrictions on the moving of member records among set occurrences, and these restrictions are supposed to mirror physical restrictions that are in force in the business world for the corresponding groupings of owner and member entities (see Figure 6.5).

Connection fields and set occurrence selection
Owner-coupled sets whose member records have child connection fields are sometimes called *value-based sets*. They are the simplest possible type of set and are to be recommended. However, they first appeared in the CODASYL recommendations toward the end of the 1970s. Before that CODASYL sets usually did not even have a child connection field in the member records. We may still specify sets that are not value-based; however, they are more complex to deal with, and we shall omit them (see Ref. 2) since they can now be considered obsolete.

The reader will recall that a few pages ago we made use of the **STORE** command in explaining the implications of the specification of **CONNECTION IS AUTOMATIC** in the conceptual schema. In particular, when the **STORE** command is used to place in the data base a record that is also a potential member of an **AUTOMATIC** owner-coupled set, CODASYL will place the record both in the proper file and in the appropriate occurrence of the **AUTOMATIC** owner-coupled set. The question then arises: How does **CODASYL** select the correct set occurrence? The answer is that it uses the **SET SELECTION** specification in the schema.

There are three types of **SET SELECTION** specification that may be used in specifying an owner-coupled set in the schema. Two of them are quite complicated and were originally designed for use with owner-coupled sets that are not value-based (although they can also be used with value-based sets). The third method is designed for use with value-based sets and is both elegant and simple. In the case of the set **WAR-EMP**

```
SET SELECTION IS THRU WAR-EMP OWNER IDENTIFIED BY
KEY WHNUMB EQUAL TO WHNUMB OF EMPLOYEE
```

This simply tells CODASYL to use the connection field value in a member record being connected to an owner-coupled set in order to select the parent record of the correct owner-coupled set occurrence.

It is clear that if we have no connection fields in member files, then the simple method of using the connection field value to automatically select a set occurrence for a record cannot be used, and the earlier more complex methods must be used instead. This is another reason for making all CODASYL owner-coupled sets value-based, that is, we include the connection field in a child or member file to support a 1:n relationship.

Overall set specification
We conclude this section on the specification of CODASYL owner-coupled sets by giving typical specifications for some of the sets in the data base in Figure 6.2:

```
41 SET NAME IS WAR-EMP
42 OWNER IS WAREHOUSE
43 ORDER IS PERMANENT CONNECTION IS LAST
44 MEMBER IS EMPLOYEE
45 CONNECTION IS AUTOMATIC
46 RETENTION IS MANDATORY
47 SET SELECTION IS THRU WAR-EMP OWNER IDENTIFIED BY
48        KEY WHNUMB EQUAL TO WHNUMB OF EMPLOYEE
49
50 SET NAME IS EMP-PUR
51 OWNER IS EMPLOYEE
52 ORDER IS PERMANENT CONNECTION IS LAST
53 MEMBER IS PUR-ORDER
54 CONNECTION IS MANUAL
55 RETENTION IS FIXED
56 SET SELECTION IS THRU EMP-PUR OWNER IDENTIFIED BY
57        KEY EMPNUMB EQUAL TO EMPNUMB OF EMPLOYEE
```

Readers are invited to specify the remaining owner-coupled sets in the data base in Figure 6.2 by themselves. The options used in the specification above were selected on tutorial grounds only and should not be interpreted as having any deep meaning or as the solution to a data base design problem.

This ends our discussion of the specification of the CODASYL schema. The next step in practice would be the specification of the storage schema, which is a highly technical activity. Since this book is oriented toward business and not technical data base design, we shall omit this step. However, we shall assume that a suitable storage schema has been prepared; readers who are interested in the details of the CODASYL storage schema are referred to Ref. 2. We now turn to the external schema and the manipulation of the CODASYL data base.

6.3 MANIPULATING A CODASYL DATA BASE

A lot of data base manipulation, and particularly if updating is involved, is done by means of application programs written in *host* languages such as COBOL or PL/1. Embedded in such application programs are the CODASYL data manipulation language (DML) commands that call up the services of the data base control system that in turn accesses the individual data base records. In addition to the application programs, a user group must obtain a definition of that portion of the data base it needs to use, that is, it must obtain an *external schema*.

We look at the external schema first and then at the data manipulation language.

The CODASYL external schema

To a large extent an external schema is merely a subset of the conceptual schema, reflecting the fact that an external data base is a subset of the conceptual data

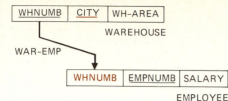

FIGURE 6.7 An external data base derived from the data base depicted in Figure 6.2.

base. Note that the CODASYL refers to an external schema as a *subschema*. Thus an external schema is usually straightforward, and as an example we give an external schema for the portion of the data base from Figure 6.2 that is shown in Figure 6.7:

```
01   TITLE DIVISION.
02   SS   PERSONNEL WITHIN OUTSTANDING-ORDERS.
03   STRUCTURE DIVISION.
04   RECORD SECTION.
05   01   WAREHOUSE.
06         02   WHNUMB    ; PIC X(5).
07         02   CITY      ; PIC X(20).
08         02   WH-AREA   ; PIC 9(6).
09   01   EMPLOYEE.
10         02   WHNUMB    ; PIC X(5).
11         02   EMPNUMB   ; PIC X(5).
12         02   SALARY    ; PIC 9(6).
13   SET SECTION.
14   SD   WAR-EMP.
```

The above subschema is for COBOL programs. As mentioned in Chapter 4, a subschema definition language depends on the programming language used with the application program. For example, if we intended to manipulate the data base by means of FORTRAN programs, we would use a subschema definition that was essentially the same but which has a syntax more like that of FORTRAN. It is quite clear that the subschema above is in the style of COBOL. (An unofficial subschema language for PL/1 is given in Ref. 2.)

The above subschema is called **PERSONNEL** and is derived from the conceptual schema **OUTSTANDING-ORDERS**, part of which was given in Section 6.2. The properties of the owner-coupled set **WAR-EMP** that are specified in the subschema will be the same as those specified in **OUTSTANDING-ORDERS**. While we have not done so in the above subschema, it would have been possible for some of the fields defined in the conceptual schema to have been omitted from **WAREHOUSE** and **EMPLOYEE** records.

In addition to defining a portion of the conceptual data base that an application program may manipulate, and thus contributing to logical or conceptual data independence (see Chapter 4), the subschema also serves to define a User

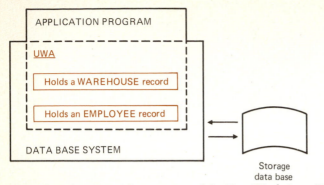

Storage
data base

FIGURE 6.8 Shows the contents of the User Work Area (UWA) for an applications program that uses the subschema for the external data base in Figure 6.7. For each external file, there is a UWA structure capable of holding any record from that file. These structures may be accessed by both the applications program and the data base system. Thus the UWA is common to both application program and data base system. The subschema also serves as a definition of the UWA.

Work Area (UWA), which can be imagined to consist of record structure variables each of which can hold a record corresponding to the external files declared in the subschema. This is illustrated in Figure 6.8.

The User Work Area (UWA)

The UWA is a kind of loading/unloading zone to be used by both the application program and the data base. If the application program needs to store a record in the data base, it first places it in the UWA structure for the file to which the record belongs. The **STORE** command is then issued, and the data base system picks up the record from the UWA structure and stores it. Similarly, if the application program needs a record from the data base, it issues a **FETCH** command, and the data base system retrieves the required record from the data base and places it in the appropriate UWA structure, whence it may be manipulated by the application program.

Note on CODASYL terminology

At this point a note on CODASYL naming methods is needed. CODASYL does not in fact make use of a conceptual file as such. Instead CODASYL deals with record types, and we notice in the conceptual schema (lines 3 and 12) that we defined the conceptual files **WAREHOUSE** and **EMPLOYEE** with statements:

```
03   RECORD NAME IS WAREHOUSE
     ...
12   RECORD NAME IS EMPLOYEE
```

Thus it is more correct with CODASYL to refer to a conceptual file of records of the type **WAREHOUSE**, instead of to the conceptual file **WAREHOUSE**. This is carried one step further in the subschema, where we in fact define a program structure variable for each external file. If we wish, we can give this structure variable the name used for the record type in the conceptual schema. Thus unlike the case in COBOL file processing (see Chapter 2) where there is a logical storage file name and a corresponding structure variable name, with a CODASYL data base we deal only with the structure variable name.

Loading the CODASYL data base

Once all the schemas have been defined and translated, the next step is to load or populate the data base. This is normally done in steps, and a few data files are loaded at a time. Following each loading step extensive testing is carried out.

In principle, loading the data base is a relatively simple operation, especially if all the owner-coupled sets are value-based and have **AUTOMATIC** storage class, in which case the only CODASYL data manipulation language command needed is the **STORE** comand.

We shall briefly illustrate by giving the essentials of loading the portion of the data base in Figure 6.2 that is defined by the subschema **PERSONNEL** (see Figure 6.7). The data to be placed in the data base has to be available from somewhere, and we shall assume that it resides on two tape files **TWAREHOUSE** and **TEMPLOYEE**. The loading operation then consists of issuing COBOL **READ** commands (as explained in Chapter 2) to read in **TWAREHOUSE** records one by one, and then placing each of these in the data base file **WAREHOUSE** by means of a **STORE** command. This is illustrated in the system diagram in Figure 6.9 and in the COBOL excerpt in Figure 6.10. Normally a parent or owner file is stored first. Then the member records are read in and stored in the child or member file, in this case **EMPLOYEE**.

Note that a COBOL **READ** command places a record from **TWAREHOUSE** or **TEMPLOYEE** in the UWA structures **WAREHOUSE** or **EMPLOYEE**. The **STORE** command execution then causes CODASYL to take the record from the UWA structure and place it in the file specified in the command. Since **WAR-EMP** is specified as an **AUTOMATIC** set, an **EMPLOYEE** record is placed both in the **EMPLOYEE** file and in a **WAR-EMP** set occurrence by the **STORE** command.

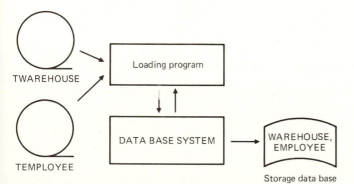

FIGURE 6.9 Method of loading the portion of the data base in Figure 6.2 that is defined by the subschema PERSONNEL. The data base files are WAREHOUSE and EMPLOYEE, and the respective records are obtained from the tape files TWARE-HOUSE and TEMPLOYEE.

```
WAREHOUSE-LOAD-LOOP.
     READ TWAREHOUSE INTO WAREHOUSE
                 AT END CLOSE TWAREHOUSE, GO TO EMPLOYEE-LOAD-LOOP.
     STORE WAREHOUSE.
*Data base system takes WAREHOUSE record from UWA WAREHOUSE structure defined
          *in subschema included in the program at the beginning.
     GO TO WAREHOUSE-LOAD-LOOP.
EMPLOYEE-LOAD-LOOP.
     READ TEMPLOYEE INTO EMPLOYEE
                 AT END CLOSE TEMPLOYEE, STOP RUN.
     STORE EMPLOYEE.
*This STORE command not only places a record in the EMPLOYEE file
*it uses the WHNUMB connection field value from the record to select
*a WAR-EMP owner-coupled set occurrence and connect the record to it.
     GO TO EMPLOYEE-LOAD-LOOP.
```

FIGURE 6.10 Essential core of the loading program for loading WAREHOUSE, EMPLOYEE, and WAR-EMP from the data base in Figure 6.2. In practice the program would contain a great deal of error checking.

Thus the command:

```
STORE EMPLOYEE
```

causes:

1. The record in the **EMPLOYEE** UWA structure to be placed in the **EMPLOYEE** file.
2. The record thus placed in the **EMPLOYEE** file to be connected to the **WAR-EMP** owner-coupled set occurrence whose parent record has a **WHNUMB** key value matching the **WHNUMB** child connection field value of the record being coupled (see Figure 6.6a and b). In connecting a record, the data base system complies with the order for **WAR-EMP** set occurrences specified in the schema (see line 43). In this case it would be connected as in Figure 6.6b, since **CONNECTION IS LAST** is specified in the schema.

Because the set **PUR-EMP** is MANUAL, we would need a **STORE** followed by a **CONNECT** command to load a **PUR-ORDER** record. Notice that the loading program excerpt in Figure 6.10 is the barest of the bare bones of a data base loading program in practice. The usual COBOL **IDENTIFICATION, ENVIRONMENT,** and **DATA** divisions (see Chapter 2) are omitted, as well as the additional divisions that comprise the subschema **PERSONNEL** (given earlier). Furthermore, a program should check a CODASYL status variable called **DB-STATUS** following each DML command; CODASYL places a code in **DB-STATUS** following execution of a DML command to signal successful completion or unsuccessful completion. There are many unsuccessful codes, and a program has to be able to take action depending on the code returned. We shall give an example of this later.

Testing the data base

Following loading of a portion of the data base, tests must be carried out to ensure that the job has been done properly. A simple test is to have the complete data base files printed out, although if the data base is very large, it may be sufficient to have sample parts of the data base files printed out instead. In the simplest test, the records of each file could be printed in the order specified in the schema. Another test is to have each owner-coupled set occurrence printed out, first an owner-record of an occurrence and then member records. The members should of course appear in the order for owner-coupled set occurrences specified in the schema. A further test could involve printing out member records (such as **EMPLOYEE** records) in primary key order accompanied by their owner records (such as **WAREHOUSE** records). Many other equally effective tests can also be devised.

Following successful testing of a portion of the data base, the next portion can be loaded, and so on.

The CODASYL currency concept

Before we show how a CODASYL data base may be manipulated, we must examine a concept that is basic for all the CODASYL DML commands (including the **STORE** command just used). This is the CODASYL currency concept, and we must distinguish between CODASYL *currency indicators* and *current records*.

Currency indicators

A CODASYL data base typically contains many different conceptual files and sets, and at any instant an application program may be in the process of dealing with many different records scattered across these many files and sets. Some method is therefore needed for the program to keep track of its processing position, and the CODASYL data base system maintains a table of currency indicators for each program (or *run-unit*) using the data base. A *currency indicator* is the disk address of a recently accessed record.

To be specific, there is a currency indicator for each file in the data base, a currency indicator for each owner-coupled set, and a currency indicator for the whole data base.

The *currency indicator for a file* F is called the current record of the type F indicator, or the current record of (file) F indicator, or more simply the current of F indicator. This indicator is the disk address (or storage record address) of the most recently accessed record of the file F. Thus for the subschema **PERSONNEL** that we had earlier, CODASYL would maintain a current record of **WAREHOUSE** indicator and a current record of **EMPLOYEE** indicator.

The *currency indicator for a set* X is called the current record of the set X indicator, or simply the current of X indicator. This indicator is the disk address of the most recently accessed record in an owner-coupled set; since an owner-coupled set consists normally of two types of record—the owner type and the member type—*the current of set indicator can be the disk address of either an owner record in the set* or a member record. Thus with the set **WAR-EMP** specified in the subschema **PERSONNEL**, the current record of **WAR-EMP** indicator could be the disk address of either an **EMPLOYEE** record or a **WARE-HOUSE** record.

The *currency indicator for the data base* is called the current of run-unit (CRU) indicator. This is the disk address of the most recently accessed record in the whole data base.

Current records

The *current records* are simply the records identified by the currency indicators. Thus the current record of the file **F** or the current of **F** is the most recently accessed record of the type or file F. Similarly, the current record of the set **X** or the current of **X** is the most recently accessed record in the set X (either a member record or an owner). Finally the current record of run-unit or current of run-unit (CRU) is the most recently accessed record in the data base.

Data base keys

The disk address of a storage record corresponding to a conceptual (or external record) is called a *data base key,* so that the currency indicators are in fact data base keys. Normally the application program is not concerned with data base keys, for it is the data base system that maintains the currency indicators. However, the applications programmer is very much concerned with the current records.

Currency tables

There are two types of currency tables, namely, *currency indicator tables* and *current record tables* (or *user currency tables*). A currency indicator table gives the currency indicator values following each execution of a CODASYL command in an application program, and as we saw earlier, such a table is maintained by the CODASYL system for each application program that is executing. The program has no access to the currency indicator values.

A current record table, or user currency table, gives the record keys (not the data base keys) of the current records following each execution of a CODASYL command in an application program. An example of a user currency table is given in Figure 6.12 for the application program whose pathway through the **PERSONNEL** data base is shown in Figure 6.11. In Figure 6.11 the circles indicate the sequence of records accessed by the application program via CODASYL DML commands. The particular sequence was arbitrarily chosen and has no hidden meaning. The CODASYL commands used would probably be **FIND** commands, as we shall see shortly. Following each access, that is, following each execution of a CODASYL command, CODASYL will update the CRU indicator, the current of **WAREHOUSE** indicator, the current of **EMPLOYEE** indicator, and the current of **WAR-EMP** indicator. Corresponding to each currency indicator is a current record, and in the table in Figure 6.12 we give the primary or record keys of these current records following each access. It is difficult for a user to construct a currency *indicator* table, since the data base key values are normally unavailable.

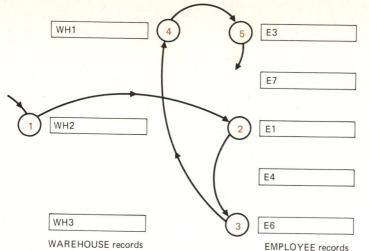

FIGURE 6.11 Shows the path taken by some applications programs through the data base specified by the subschema PERSONNEL (see also Figures 6.6a and 6.7). First (1) the record with key 'WH2' is accessed, then (2) the record with key 'E1', next (3) the record with key 'E4', and so on, in the sequence shown by the numbers (in color) in the circles. The corresponding current records are given in the current record table in Figure 6.12.

User currency tables are very useful in practice when application programs to manipulate a CODASYL data base are being written. Execution of most CODASYL commands affect the currencies; at the same time the outcome of the execution of a CODASYL command may depend on the state of the currencies prior to the execution of that command. Construction of a user currency table enables the programmer to more easily construct a program that will correctly chart a path or *navigate* through the data base.

Currencies affected by STORE command

We are now in position to examine the remaining CODASYL commands. The reader will recall that we have already introduced the **STORE** command for loading the data base. (It is also used just for storing a new record in an existing data base.) We shall not deal further with this command, except to state that

POSITION	1	2	3	4	5
CRU	WH2	E1	E6	WH1	E3
Current of WAREHOUSE	WH2	WH2	WH2	WH1	WH1
Current of EMPLOYEE	–	E1	E6	E6	E3
Current of WAR-EMP	WH1	E1	E6	WH1	E3

FIGURE 6.12 Current record table for the path through the PERSONNEL data base in Figure 6.11. The current records are denoted by their record keys (not the data base keys). If data base keys were used (normally we do not know what the values are), the table would be a current indicator table.

following successful execution of a STORE command, the record stored becomes:

1. The current record of run-unit
2. The current record of the file into which the record is inserted
3. The current record of all AUTOMATIC sets to which it was connected
4. The current record of all sets for which it becomes the owner record

We can see from this that a programmer must be aware of the currency implications of every CODASYL command used in an application program.

The CODASYL data manipulation language commands

We have no need to give a detailed description of all the CODASYL commands in order to impart to the reader the basic ideas behind manipulating a CODASYL data base via an application program. A description of the most basic commands will suffice. Readers who require a more thorough coverage are referred to Ref. 2.

We can conveniently classify the commands into those that cause records to be retrieved or selected and those that cause the data base to be updated. The retrieval commands can be further classified into those that deal with a conceptual file only and those that deal with an owner-coupled set. We briefly review the main commands in the light of this classification.

I. *Retrieval commands*
   A. *Conceptual file* FETCH *commands*
      1. There is a command that selects a record by direct access on the basis of either a primary or secondary key value.
      2. There is a command that selects the records of a file in record or secondary key order, that is, records are selected one after another in sequential order, as if they were on a tape.
   B. *Owner-coupled set* FETCH *commands*
      1. There is a command that selects the member records of an owner-coupled set occurrence one by one in the order specified in the schema for member records of that owner-coupled set.
      2. There is a command to select the owner record of a given owner-coupled set occurrence.
II. *Updating commands*
      1. There is a MODIFY command that can update one or more fields of a record in the data base.
      2. There is an ERASE command for deleting a record in the data base.
      3. There is a DISCONNECT command for disconnecting a record from an owner-coupled set occurrence of which it is a member; the record remains in the data base.
      4. There is a CONNECT command for connecting a record already in the data base to an owner-coupled set occurrence.
      5. There is the STORE command already dealt with.

We now examine these commands in more detail.

The CODASYL FETCH commands

All the **FETCH** commands have in common that the record selected becomes the current record of run unit, the current record of the file to which it belongs, and the current record of all sets in which it participates either as a member or as an owner record; the record is also placed in the UWA structure for records of that type, so that it becomes accessible to manipulation via ordinary program statements.

Record key FETCH command

This command retrieves a record of a file by direct access on presentation of the primary key of the desired record. If we wanted to retrieve the **WAREHOUSE** record with key (**WHNUMB**) value 'WH2', we would code in COBOL:

```
MOVE 'WH2' TO WHNUMB IN WAREHOUSE.
```

*Key of required record in **WHNUMB** field of UWA structure.

```
FETCH ANY WAREHOUSE USING WHNUMB.
```

*Record placed in UWA structure; it also becomes CRU, and so on.

```
DISPLAY CITY IN WAREHOUSE, WH-AREA IN WAREHOUSE.
```

*COBOL statement to print out field values from record in UWA.

The same command may be used to retrieve records on presentation of a secondary key value; however, we need to insert the word **DUPLICATE** into the command. Suppose we want to retrieve all the **WAREHOUSE** records with the value 'DALLAS' for the secondary key **CITY**. We would code in COBOL:

```
MOVE 'DALLAS' TO CITY IN WAREHOUSE.
MAINLOOP.
    FETCH DUPLICATE WAREHOUSE USING CITY.
    IF DB-STATUS = 'NONE LEFT' THEN STOP RUN.
    DISPLAY WHNUMB IN WAREHOUSE, WH-AREA IN WAREHOUSE.
    GO TO MAINLOOP.
```

First the value 'DALLAS' is placed in the secondary key field in the UWA. The first execution of the **FETCH** command places in the UWA the first (in the order specified in the schema) **WAREHOUSE** record with the secondary key value 'DALLAS'. Of course in general there will be a number of records with this **CITY** value. Going around the loop, the next time the **FETCH** command is executed, the next (in the order specified in the schema) **WAREHOUSE** record with the **CITY** value 'DALLAS' is retrieved, and so on until all of this group of records have been retrieved. Following execution of a command, CODASYL places a completion code in **DB-STATUS**, and there is a code for 'no records left'. When this code is detected, the program stops.

[The precise semantics of the duplicate version of the **FETCH** command are quite complex. Should the CRU before execution of the command match the type of record to be retrieved, then the command retrieves the next (in the order specified in the schema) record with the specified secondary key value. When the CRU does not match the type of record to be retrieved, the first record with the specified secondary key value is retrieved, where first is in the context of the order specified in the schema for records with that type of secondary key.]

Sequential FETCH command

This command permits sequential (or skip sequential) processing of a CODASYL file. The processing can be in primary or secondary key order. We could use the command to print out the contents of the **EMPLOYEE** file. We would code:

```
    FETCH FIRST EMPLOYEE.
    DISPLAY WNHUMB, EMPNUMB, SALARY.
MAINLOOP.
    FETCH NEXT EMPLOYEE.
    IF DB-STATUS = 'NONE LEFT' THEN STOP RUN.
    DISPLAY WHNUMB, EMPNUMB, SALARY.
    GO TO MAINLOOP.
```

The **FETCH NEXT** version strictly retrieves the next record following the CRU, where next is in the context of the order specified for **EMPLOYEE** records in the schema for processing with the primary key **EMPNUMB**. A secondary key can be used instead of a primary key. Sequential processing would then retrieve the records in the order specified in the schema for processing with this key.

Another version of the command enables the CODASYL file to be processed skip sequentially; that is, the records are read in primary or secondary key order, but only target records with a certain field value are selected. Suppose we wanted the employee numbers of all employees that were earning $25,000. We could code:

```
    MOVE 25000 TO SALARY IN EMPLOYEE.
```

*The field **SALARY** in **EMPLOYEE** UWA structure has target value

```
    FETCH FIRST EMPLOYEE USING SALARY.
    DISPLAY EMPNUMB
MAINLOOP.
    FETCH NEXT EMPLOYEE USING SALARY.
    DISPLAY EMPNUMB.
    GO TO MAINLOOP.
```

This time **FETCH NEXT** strictly retrieves the next *target* record following the CRU, where next is in the order for **EMPLOYEE** records that is specified in the schema, and a target record satisfies the search condition that follows **USING** in the command.

Set-scan FETCH command

The two previous commands permit access to a CODASYL conceptual file. The set-scan **FETCH** command permits the member records of an owner-coupled set occurrence to be scanned one by one in the order specified in the schema for the

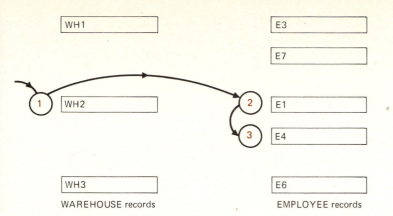

FIGURE 6.13 A scan through a WAR-EMP set occurrence using the CODASYL set scan FETCH command. The sequence of CRUs is denoted by the numbered circles.

member records of the specific owner-coupled set. Suppose we needed the salaries of employees at the warehouse 'WH2'. A simple strategy would be to access the **WAREHOUSE** record with key 'WH2', and then the member records of the **WAR-EMP** set occurrence it is the owner of, by means of the set-scan **FETCH** command. This is illustrated in Figure 6.13. We could code:

```
        MOVE 'WH2' TO WHNUMB IN WAREHOUSE.
```

*WHNUMB primary key field in **WAREHOUSE** UWA structure
*contains search parameter 'WH2'.

```
        FETCH ANY WAREHOUSE USING WHNUMB.
```

*Direct access to owner record.

```
        COMPUTE NTH = 1.
    MAINLOOP.
        FETCH NTH EMPLOYEE WITHIN WAR-EMP.
```

*Depending on value of **NTH**, the 1st, 2nd, 3rd, . . . member record is
*placed in UWA.

```
        IF DB-STATUS = 'NONE LEFT' THEN STOP RUN.
        DISPLAY SALARY IN EMPLOYEE
        COMPUTE NTH = NTH + 1.
        GO TO MAINLOOP.
```

The example of the set-scan **FETCH** command in the above excerpt:

```
        FETCH NTH EMPLOYEE WITHIN WAR-EMP
```

should be examined carefully. It is one of the most important CODASYL DML commands and is the main way in which a program navigates from one CODASYL file to a related file. The version of the command above retrieves the nth member record of a **WAR-EMP** set occurrence, and most importantly, the

POSITION	1	2	3
CRU	WH2	E1	E2
Current of WAREHOUSE	WH2	WH2	WH2
Current of EMPLOYEE	-	E1	E2
Current of WAR-EMP	WH2	E1	E2

FIGURE 6.14 The user currency table resulting from the scan of the WAR-EMP set occurrence in Figure 6.13.

WAR-EMP set occurrence selected for scanning is *the occurrence that contains the current record of the set* WAR-EMP. This is illustrated in the user currency table in Figure 6.14 for the excerpt above.

In another slightly less convenient version of the command, the numeric variable (arbitrarily chosen) NTH can be replaced by either FIRST or NEXT. FIRST means that retrieval of the first member record of the owner-coupled set occurrence that contains the current record of set. NEXT means retrieval of the record following the current record of set, within the set occurrence containing the current record of set. Both first and next are in the context of the order specification in the schema for member records of the type of set involved.

Owner FETCH command

This is a simple but commonly used command for retrieving the owner record of a set occurrence. With reference to the data base in Figures 6.6a and 6.7, suppose that we wished to find the city in which employee 'E4' worked. An obvious strategy would be to retrieve the EMPLOYEE record for employee 'E4' and then find the WAREHOUSE owner record. We could code:

```
MOVE 'E4' TO EMPNUMB IN EMPLOYEE.
FETCH ANY EMPLOYEE USING EMPNUMB.
FETCH OWNER WITHIN WAR-EMP.
```

*Thus the owner WAREHOUSE record is placed in the UWA structure for
*WAREHOUSE records.

```
DISPLAY CITY IN WAREHOUSE.
```

The FETCH OWNER command strictly retrieves the owner record of a selected occurrence of the set specified, and the selected occurrence is the one containing the current record of set. It should be noted that this command also enables a program to navigate from one file to another.

FIND and GET commands

Instead of the FETCH commands described above, we could use combinations of FIND and GET commands. For every FETCH command there is a corresponding FIND command, and the FIND command corresponding to a FETCH command is obtained simply by changing the word 'FETCH' to the word 'FIND'. The effect of executing a FIND command is exactly the same as executing a FETCH command except that the record selected is not placed in the UWA, although all the usual currency indicators are updated. To get the selected record into the UWA, we then must issue a **GET** command, which essentially places the current record of run unit in the UWA. To illustrate this, let us repeat the previous program excerpt. We recall that we needed to retrieve the city in which employee 'E4' worked. We could code instead:

```
MOVE 'E4' TO EMPNUMB IN EMPLOYEE.
FIND ANY EMPLOYEE USING EMPNUMB.
```

*The **EMPLOYEE** record with key 'E4' becomes CRU and current record of
*WAR-EMP.

```
FIND OWNER WITHIN WAR-EMP.
```

*The **WAREHOUSE** record with key 'WH2' becomes the CRU.

```
GET WAREHOUSE.
```

*The CRU is placed in the UWA **WAREHOUSE** structure.

```
DISPLAY CITY IN WAREHOUSE.
```

With the **FIND ANY** command as used above we have no need to get at the selected **EMPLOYEE** record, and so we do not have a follow-up **GET** command; the command merely makes the selected record the CRU and the current record of **WAR-EMP**, thus identifying the set occurrence whose owner record we are interested in. The **FIND OWNER** command makes the owner record of this set occurrence the CRU, which the subsequent **GET** command transfers to the **WAREHOUSE** UWA structure. The **CITY** value in this structure can then be output.

The CODASYL updating commands

The execution of a **FETCH** or **FIND** command may cause updating of the currency indicators for a given program, but it does not give rise to any change in the data base. In contrast, the updating commands make a permanent change to the data base. We take the more important updating commands in turn.

The MODIFY command

This command is quite simple, as long as we do not try to update a connection field. Suppose we wish to give employee 'E4' a raise, so that the new salary is $27,000. We would use the **MODIFY** command to modify or update the **SALARY** field of the **EMPLOYEE** record with key 'E4'. However, we must first make the record to be updated the current record of run unit and also place it in the proper UWA structure:

```
MOVE 'E4' TO EMPNUMB IN EMPLOYEE.
FETCH ANY EMPLOYEE USING EMPNUMB.
```

*Employee **E4**'s record now in UWA.

```
MOVE 27000 TO SALARY IN EMPLOYEE
```

*SALARY field for UWA record updated, but not for corresponding record in
*data base.

```
MODIFY EMPLOYEE.
```

*Record for 'E4' in data base replaced by record in UWA.

The command **MODIFY X** changes the record in the data base that is the CRU and
uses the data in the **X** UWA structure to do it, provided an **X** record is the CRU.

There are some complications if we attempt to change the connection field
value of a record in an owner-coupled set supported by the connection field.
Suppose we decide to transfer employee 'E4' to warehouse 'WH1'. If we merely
changed the connection field **WHNUMB** value in the relevant **EMPLOYEE** record
to 'WH1', that would mean that the record for employee 'E4' was a member in the
wrong occurrence of the owner-coupled set **WAR-EMP** (see Figure 6.15).

Now we should recall that **WAR-EMP** is a value-based set, that is, a set where
the connection field value determines membership, as specified in the schema at
the end of Section 6.2 (lines 47, 48). CODASYL could in theory do either of two
things in this situation: It could reject the attempt to update the connection field
on the grounds of invalidation of the current set membership, or it could permit
the update and disconnect the record from its owner-coupled set and then
connect it to the owner-coupled set occurrence that has an owner record that has
a key matching the new child connection field value. This second alternative is
the one chosen by CODASYL. Thus in Figure 6.15, when the original **WHNUMB**

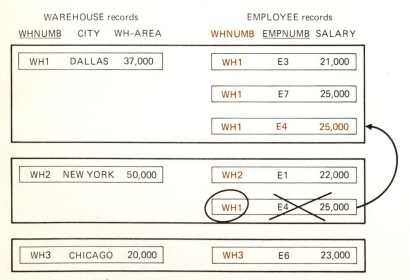

FIGURE 6.15   When a MODIFY command updates a child connection field value,
it can invalidate the set membership of the record affected. The WHNUMB value
(circled) of an EMPLOYEE record has been changed from 'WH2' to 'WH1' above.
CODASYL carries out the updating as instructed, but it also disconnects the record
from the set occurrence of WAR-EMP owned by the WAREHOUSE record with key
'WH2' and connects it to the WAR-EMP set occurrence owned by the WAREHOUSE
record with key 'WH1', as illustrated.

value ('WH2') for the EMPLOYEE record with key 'E4' is updated to 'WH1', the EMPLOYEE record is disconnected from the WAR-EMP occurrence owned by the WAREHOUSE record with key 'WH2' and then connected to the set occurrence owned by the WAREHOUSE record with key 'WH1'. In this way the new set occurrence is selected automatically by means of the schema SET SELECTION specification.

A further complication is that this switching of set occurrence membership of a record by a MODIFY command is possible only if the set retention class is not FIXED, since FIXED means that a member record cannot be taken out of a set occurrence unless of course it is deleted altogether. Thus CODASYL will reject an attempt to update the connection field of a record, if that connection field determines membership in an owner-coupled set with retention class FIXED.

There are also complexities with respect to the effect of the execution of a MODIFY command on the currencies. A record modified becomes the CRU. However, if the command changes the membership of a record of type X in a set S, and if the current record of S is the record being modified, then the current of S indicator is set to null. It is difficult to see what else could be done to the current of set indicator in such circumstances.

There are some additional complexities concerning currencies that are beyond the scope of this book. It should be clear that the MODIFY command can be quite complex and that the complexities are due to the existence of owner-coupled sets.

DISCONNECT and CONNECT commands

If a set has retention class OPTIONAL, so that a member record can be taken out of its set occurrence but still be in the data base in its proper file, then it is possible to use the DISCONNECT command with a member record of that set. The command is simple and disconnects the current record of the file specified in the command from its set occurrence in the set specified in the command. If the set WAR-EMP were OPTIONAL, we could thus issue:

```
DISCONNECT EMPLOYEE FROM WAR-EMP.
```

The CONNECT command does the opposite; it connects the current record of the file specified in the command to the set specified in the command, and the set occurrence selected is the one that contains the current record of set. Thus we might issue:

```
CONNECT EMPLOYEE TO WAR-EMP.
```

To illustrate the CONNECT and DISCONNECT commands in action, we could use them to update the data base when employee 'E4' is transferred to warehouse 'WH1'. Previously we used the MODIFY command for this purpose. This time our strategy will be to disconnect the EMPLOYEE record with key 'E4' from its WAR-EMP set occurrence. Then we shall update the connection field to 'WH1' and then connect the record to the owner-coupled set occurrence owned by the WAREHOUSE record with key value 'WH1'. For this strategy to be possible, the retention class of WAR-EMP must be OPTIONAL, in order for a member record to be disconnected, and we should make this assumption with the following COBOL excerpt (refer to Figure 6.15):

```
MOVE 'E4' TO EMPNUMB IN EMPLOYEE.
FIND ANY EMPLOYEE USING EMPNUMB.       (1)
DISCONNECT EMPLOYEE FROM WAR-EMP.      (2)
GET EMPLOYEE.
MOVE 'WH1' TO WHNUMB IN EMPLOYEE.
MOVE 'WH1' TO WHNUMB IN WAREHOUSE.
FIND ANY WAREHOUSE USING WHNUMB.       (3)
```

*The WAREHOUSE record with key 'WH1' is now the current of WAR-EMP,
*in preparation for the use of the CONNECT command. However, the
*EMPLOYEE record we wish to connect must first be made the current re-
*cord of EMPLOYEE. In addition, the EMPLOYEE record we wish to
*connect is the updated record currently in the EMPLOYEE UWA struc-
*ture. We therefore use MODIFY to update the corresponding record in
*the data base (the current record of EMPLOYEE), making the updated
*EMPLOYEE record the current record of EMPLOYEE and the CRU, ready
*for application of the CONNECT command.

```
MODIFY EMPLOYEE.                       (4)
CONNECT EMPLOYEE TO WAR-EMP.           (5)
```

The effect of this excerpt is thus the same as the earlier excerpt using MODIFY. It is clearly a lot less awkward to use MODIFY to update membership in a set occurrence. The current CONNECT command is part of the trouble, for it is not quite suited for use with value-based sets. The command connects the current of the file specified to the set occurrence containing the current record of that set occurrence. Thus great care must be taken to ensure that the currencies are correct before the command can be issued (see the user currency table for the

COMMAND	(1)	(2)	(3)	(4)	(5)
CRU	E4(old)	E4(old)	WH1	E4(new)	E4(new)
Current of WAREHOUSE	-	-	WH1	WH1	WH1
Current of EMPLOYEE	E4(old)	E4(old)	E4(old)	E4(new)	E4(new)
Current of WAR-EMP	E4(old)	-	WH1	WH1	E4(new)

FIGURE 6.16 The sequence of currency values when a connection field is changed by a DISCONNECT, MODIFY, CONNECT sequence as given in the text. The EMPLOYEE record with WHNUMB connection field 'WH2' is to be updated so that the WHNUMB value is 'WH1', which means a change in set membership. The original (old) EMPLOYEE record with key 'E4' is first selected, placed in the UWA, changed in the UWA, updated in the data base by MODIFY (to become 'new' EMPLOYEE record with key 'E4'), and then connected to the WAREHOUSE owner with key value 'WH1'. The command numbers are those placed at the right of the commands in the text. Note that when the current record of WAR-EMP is discon-nected, that currency is set to null [command (2)].

excerpt above in Figure 6.16). A simpler CONNECT command would connect the current of file to the set occurrence whose owner record has a key matching the child connection field value.

ERASE and ERASE ALL commands

The ERASE command is used to delete a record from the data base. To delete the WAREHOUSE record with key value 'WH2', we could code:

```
MOVE 'WH2' TO WHNUMB IN WAREHOUSE.
FIND ANY WAREHOUSE USING WHNUMB.
DELETE WAREHOUSE.
```

The DELETE command deletes the current record of the file specified if and only if the record to be deleted does not have member records in a MANDATORY set occurrence. Thus if the specification of MANDATORY is used in the schema for WAR-EMP, then the deletion attempt would be rejected, the reason being that a member record in a MANDATORY set could either be switched to a different set occurrence before its owner is deleted, or be deleted.

This restriction on the use of ERASE does appear to reflect practical management policy in business. Management can hardly close down or otherwise eliminate a warehouse without first either transferring its employees or terminating them.

Had WAR-EMP been an OPTIONAL set, then ERASE would have deleted the owner WAREHOUSE record, while its EMPLOYEE members would simply have been disconnected from their set occurrence. In contrast, had the set been FIXED, then not only would ERASE have deleted the WAREHOUSE record, it would also have deleted the EMPLOYEE member records of the deleted WAREHOUSE record. In addition, for each such EMPLOYEE record deleted, its member records (for example, PUR-ORDER records; see Figure 6.2) would have been treated as if the ERASE command had been applied to the EMPLOYEE records, and so on in a cascade of deletions.

It is clear that some care has to be exercised when using the CODASYL ERASE command. Misuse can easily result in a cascade of undesired deletions. An even more dangerous version of the command is ERASE ALL. If we issue:

```
ERASE ALL WAREHOUSE
```

then the current record of WAREHOUSE will be deleted regardless of the membership class of the set WAR-EMP. In addition, the EMPLOYEE members of the deleted WAREHOUSE record will be deleted, as would their members, and so on in a deletion cascade.

Selection of data base manipulation strategies

Today, because of the wide availability of relatively low-cost computing power, programmers writing conventional application programs do not go to significant lengths to wring the last ounce of inefficiency out of their programs. The high cost of programming labor relative to the cost of central processing units has largely made such endeavors uneconomical. It may therefore come as a surprise to many managers to learn that an effort must be made to prevent low performance with programs that manipulate data bases.

The problem is due to (1) the complexity of data bases and (2) the fact that storage records reside on disks. The fact that data bases are complex means that in practice there will be many different ways a program could navigate (see Figure 6.11) through the data base seeking out records to be retrieved or updated. For example, if 20 records spread over different conceptual files needed to be selected by an application program, the actual number selected (that is, the total number of CRU values) could be very much higher, even 100 times higher, if the program's selection strategy is a poor one.

An almost trivial example of this can be seen with the retrieval request:

Find the employees that work in warehouse 'WH2' and make more than $24,000 per annum.

Referring to Figures 6.6a and 6.7, we see that there are two obvious strategies:

Strategy 1. Access the **WAREHOUSE** record with key value 'WH2', and then scan through its **EMPLOYEE** member records in the **WAR-EMP** set occurrence thus selected. Print out each **EMPLOYEE** record that has a **SALARY** value greater than $24,000.

Strategy 2. Scan through the **EMPLOYEE** file sequentially in ascending **EMPNUMB** order. Print out each **EMPLOYEE** record that has a **WHNUMB** value equal to 'WH2' and a **SALARY** value greater than $24,000.

It is clear that both strategies will produce the required result, but at a great difference in cost, as measured by the number of record accesses needed. In the first case we access one **WAREHOUSE** record and a limited number of **EMPLOYEE** records, namely, the number in an owner-coupled set occurrence. In the second case we have to access all the records in the **EMPLOYEE** file, and there will generally be a great deal more records in the **EMPLOYEE** file than in a **WAR-EMP** set occurrence.

The fact that the underlying storage files are on disk storage means that access to a data base record is a very time-consuming process, typically 35 milliseconds per access, or an access rate of only 30 records per second, as we saw in Chapter 1. By comparison, a modern mainframe CPU can execute about 100 million instructions per second.

Thus if we combine the effects of slow disk access with a bad strategy that increases the number of disk accesses 100-fold, a data base program that otherwise could run in minutes if properly written could easily take hours to execute. This could be tolerated if such a low performance program were used only once in a while, but would be completely intolerable for production programs that were used regularly. For these reasons care must be taken with the strategy behind production programs that deal with a data base. This is true for all data base systems that use a procedural DML, and not just CODASYL systems.

Concurrent processing

As mentioned in Chapter 4, in a large organization there are normally many users of a data base. It frequently happens that two or more programs that manipulate a data base are executing *concurrently*, that is, at any given instant only one of the programs is actually executing, but all the programs are at some stage in their execution, and control of which program will execute next rests with the teleprocessing monitor (see Chapter 4) or equivalent control system.

Although only one program that manipulates the data base can be executing at a given instant, concurrent execution of a number of programs can cause difficulties if special precautions are not taken. Some common difficulties are that (1) two concurrent programs can interfere with each other's updating of the data base, and (2) two concurrent programs can become *deadlocked*. We shall look at these possibilities in some detail in the light of the CODASYL proposals, as much the same principles apply with other data base systems.

Interference

We can best see how two concurrent programs can interfere with one another and ruin a data base by looking at an almost trivial example. Suppose that we have two programs **PAY-INCREASE** and **TRANSFER** for the manipulation of the external data base described by the subschema **PERSONNEL** (see Figures 6.6a and 6.7). The program **TRANSFER** is used to update the data base when an employee is transferred from one warehouse to another, while the program **PAY-INCREASE** is used to update the data base when an employee gets a raise. Suppose now that employee 'E1' is given an increase in salary to $24,000 and shortly after is transferred to warehouse 'WH3' from 'WH2'; the updates to the data base will be carried out by the programs **PAY-INCREASE** and **TRANSFER**, and we shall assume that the computer operations department schedules the two programs for concurrent execution.

Let us assume that the execution of the two programs is interwoven (by the teleprocessing monitor) as follows:

1. **TRANSFER** executing. A copy of the **EMPLOYEE** record with key 'E1' is placed in **TRANSFER**'s UWA ready for updating.
2. **PAY-INCREASE** executing. A copy of the **EMPLOYEE** record with key 'E1' is placed in **PAY-INCREASE**'s UWA ready for updating.
3. **TRANSFER** executing. WHNUMB value in **TRANSFER**'s UWA record is updated to 'WH3'. A MODIFY command alters the data base **EMPLOYEE** record to match the UWA **EMPLOYEE** record.
4. **PAY-INCREASE** executing. SALARY value in **PAY-INCREASE**'s UWA record is updated to $24,000. (Note that the old WHNUMB value of 'WH2' still appears in this record.) A MODIFY command alters the data base record to match the UWA employee record.

We can see that the final execution of **PAY-INCREASE** will undo the update of WHNUMB to 'WH3', and thus only the SALARY field will have been updated as a result of the concurrent execution of the two programs.

How can such interference be prevented? There are a number of techniques, but they all more or less hinge on the concept of a *transaction*, and the prevention of updates during the period a program is completing a transaction. In the above example with TRANSFER and PAY-INCREASE we have basically two transactions:

1. Get an EMPLOYEE record into the UWA. Update the SALARY field. Alter the corresponding EMPLOYEE record in the data base to match the UWA record. End of transaction.
2. Get the EMPLOYEE record into the UWA. Update the WHNUMB field. Alter the corresponding EMPLOYEE record in the data base to match the UWA record. End of transaction.

Thus the program TRANSFER should not be allowed to update the EMPLOYEE file, that is, begin its transaction involving the EMPLOYEE file, until PAY-INCREASE is finished with its transaction involving EMPLOYEE, or vice versa.

CODASYL has facilities to permit concurrent updating of the data base. The commands involved are the READY and FINISH commands. Essentially we issue the READY command to mark the beginning of a transaction, and FINISH to mark the end of one.

An example of the READY command is

        READY EMPLOYEE USAGE MODE IS EXCLUSIVE UPDATE

and an example of the FINISH command is

        FINISH EMPLOYEE

The use of the specification EXCLUSIVE means that the command is asking CODASYL for exclusive rights over the EMPLOYEE file, that is, until a subsequent FINISH EMPLOYEE command is executed, no other concurrent program will be allowed to access the EMPLOYEE file. The file is then said to be *locked* against concurrent update and retrieval. Should there be a concurrent program currently accessing the EMPLOYEE at the time the above READY command is executed, then permission to proceed will be denied until no other concurrent program has control over the EMPLOYEE file.

Instead of an EXCLUSIVE specification we may specify PROTECTED, which permits other concurrent programs to access the file but not update it. The file is then locked against concurrent update only. A fine-grained locking of individual records is also possible by a specification of SHARED. The details of this are quite complex however and readers are referred to Ref. 2.

In the READY command we may also specify RETRIEVAL instead of UP-DATE, and this means that the program is restricted to information retrieval, instead of both updating and retrieval when UPDATE is specified.

We can show how the programs TRANSFER and PAY-INCREASE could update the data base concurrently with CODASYL when employee 'E1' is transferred to warehouse 'WH3' and given a pay increase to $24,000:

1. TRANSFER executing. READY EMPLOYEE USAGE MODE EXCLUSIVE

UPDATE command issued. EMPLOYEE record copied into UWA. WHNUMB field updated.

2. PROGRAM-X executing. This program accesses the data base but cannot get permission to access the EMPLOYEE file.

3. PAY-INCREASE executing. READY EMPLOYEE USAGE MODE EXCLUSIVE UPDATE issued. Permission to proceed denied because program TRANSFER has control of EMPLOYEE file.

4. TRANSFER executing. MODIFY command alters EMPLOYEE record in data base to match updated record in UWA. Command FINISH EMPLOYEE issued, marking the end of the transaction.

5. PAY-INCREASE executing. This program is now given EXCLUSIVE UPDATE control. The relevant EMPLOYEE record is copied into the UWA, its WHNUMB SALARY field is updated to $24,000, and the MODIFY command is issued to transfer the UWA update to the data base. Then the command FINISH EMPLOYEE is issued, thus ending this transaction.

Deadlock

Figure 6.17 shows how two trailer trucks can become deadlocked at an intersection. Truck *A* cannot move forward until truck *B* moves forward, but truck *B* cannot move forward until truck *A* moves forward.

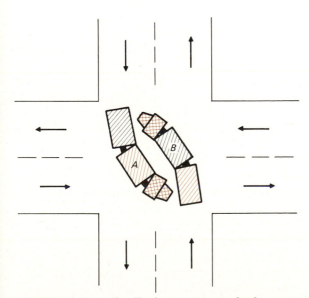

FIGURE 6.17 A deadlock situation at a highway intersection. The truck *A* cannot go forward because *B* cannot go forward, and *B* cannot go forward because *A* cannot go forward. Possible solutions are (a) the situation should not be allowed to arise, and a driver should not enter the intersection until it is clear; and (b) when deadlock does occur, one of the trucks should reverse and allow the other to proceed.

A similar situation can develop with two concurrent programs. Suppose that program A needs exclusive control over the files WAREHOUSE and EMPLOYEE (see Figure 6.7) to complete a transaction, while at the same time there is a concurrently executing program B that also needs control of EMPLOYEE and WAREHOUSE to complete a transaction. Let us now consider the following sequence of events as interwoven execution of programs A and B proceeds:

1. *A executes.* A issues READY WAREHOUSE . . . EXCLUSIVE command, and the request is granted. A needs control of EMPLOYEE before processing of its transaction can proceed, but before the proper READY command can be issued, the teleprocessing monitor switches control to program B.

2. *B executes.* B issues READY EMPLOYEE . . . EXCLUSIVE command, and the request is granted. Program B still needs control of WAREHOUSE, and then issues the command READY WAREHOUSE . . . EXCLUSIVE, but this request is denied because program A has control of WAREHOUSE. Program B is placed in a "wait" state, and meanwhile the teleprocessing monitor switches control to program A.

3. *A executes.* To get control of EMPLOYEE, program A issues the command READY EMPLOYEE . . . EXCLUSIVE, but control of EMPLOYEE is denied, and program A is placed in a "wait" state.

As a result program A has to wait for B, while B has to wait for A, so that we have a deadlock situation.

If we glance at the diagram of the two deadlocked trucks in Figure 6.17, we can get some ideas about how to solve this problem. There are two obvious approaches, namely, prevention of deadlock and cure after deadlock has occurred. In the case of the trucks, to prevent such a deadlock from occurring, we could have a rule that a driver is not to enter an intersection until it is clear of all traffic, or in other words, the driver should not enter until he can have complete control of the intersection. A similar solution is available with CODASYL; it requires that a program issue a READY command for all the files that it needs to begin processing a transaction. Going back to the case of programs A and B both needing control of the files WAREHOUSE and EMPLOYEE, deadlock could not arise if the READY commands in the two programs were issued as follows:

1. *A executes.* Program A issues the command:

   ```
   READY WAREHOUSE EMPLOYEE USAGE MODE EXCLUSIVE UPDATE
   ```

   thus requesting control over both EMPLOYEE and WAREHOUSE files. Assume that the request is granted and that the teleprocessing monitor then permits B to execute.

2. *B executes.* Program B issues the command:

   ```
   READY WAREHOUSE EMPLOYEE USAGE MODE EXCLUSIVE UPDATE
   ```

But since *A* has control of both **WAREHOUSE** and **EMPLOYEE**, program *B*'s request is denied, and *B* goes into a "wait" state.

Program *A* would then execute and complete its transaction, and only when it had released **WAREHOUSE** and **EMPLOYEE** (by means of the **FINISH** command) would it be possible for program *B* to gain control of them and complete its transaction. However, deadlock could not ensue.

Returning to the deadlocked trucks in Figure 6.17, if we accept that deadlock can occur, we are forced to consider how to undo the deadlock when it does occur. In the case of the trucks, the answer is obvious: One or both of the trucks have to back up in order that it be possible for one of them to proceed. To manage this backing up, a third party is often involved, for it is sometimes not possible for the drivers causing the problem to grasp the overall situation; typically the third party is a police officer.

In a similar manner CODASYL provides for a "backing up" or rollback when deadlock occurs. The details are beyond the scope of this book, but the essentials are as follows. When deadlock occurs, the data base control system (the police officer) places a code in the status variable **DB-STATUS**. An application program should be programmed to inspect **DB-STATUS** for the deadlock code following CODASYL commands that could lead to deadlock. If deadlock is detected, the application program issues the one-word command **ROLLBACK**. This **ROLL-BACK** command rolls back the application to what is called a *quiet point*, undoing all updates to the data base since that quiet point. The quiet points in an application are established at strategic intervals by issuing the CODASYL command **COMMIT**. In order to be able to undo all updates to the data base since the last quiet point before the **ROLLBACK** command is issued, CODASYL must keep a record of all updates to the data base. This is done in a separate file called a log file, and from the record of data base updates in the log file, CODASYL is able to undo the updates to the data base.

The log file can also be used to repair the data base, when it is incorrectly updated, or when there is an accident, such as a disk head crash. A good implementation of CODASYL would permit automatic recovery from many types of accident.

Security from unauthorized access

Data bases usually contain important and valuable information, and most CODASYL systems use a system of *locks* and *keys* to discourage access to the data base by unauthorized persons. A lock is the specification of a password in an external schema. Typically a lock is specified for a command applied to a certain type of record. An application program must then produce the password before the command in question can be applied to that type of record. Thus the password is the key. A different lock and key can be set up for every combination of command and file or set, although too many locks and keys slow down processing, just as they would in an ordinary office. The question of data base security and the data base administrator's role is discussed further in Chapter 13.[1]

6.4 HIGHER MANAGEMENT USE OF A DATA BASE

Seen from a management perspective, there are three levels of use of data bases that correspond to the three levels of management of a large enterprise. We have lower or operational-level use, middle or functional-level use, and higher or strategic-level use.

Operational-level use generally involves the storage and manipulation of information for which there is either a legal requirement (for example, salaries of employees) or a business requirement (credit limits of customers), and generally there are large numbers of standard programs that manipulate the data bases at this level. Such programs usually process the data base as the result of some transaction such as an order or a sale. With a CODASYL data base such programs would typically be written in COBOL or PL/1 and use the CODASYL DML commands described in Section 6.3.

Middle management deals with data bases at the functional level, such as element fabrication or assembly in manufacturing, or sales administration in marketing. The middle manager responsible for any of these functions rarely personally collects or organizes information to be used for updating the data base. That is done at the operations level. However, the middle manager has a great need for information about how well the particular function for which he or she is responsible is being carried out. If the operational-level use of the data base has been properly implemented, that is, if there is a good *operations system*, a lot of the information that the middle manager needs for routine control purposes will be in the data base in up-to-the-minute data base files. The problem is to get it out. Typically this information is available to middle management in the form of regular reports that are the result of executing standard report programs. Because of the inevitable delay in getting hard copy reports to middle management from the data processing department, the trend has been for middle management to have terminals from which they can execute their individual report programs and see the reports displayed in their screens. A request for a printout will be made (via the terminal) only if needed. It is not altogether certain that this proliferation of terminals at the middle management level is cost-effective at all times. Routine report generation by the data processing department is certainly cheaper, but in areas that are difficult to manage because of the need for a great deal of decision making, the benefits of providing the manager with a terminal will probably exceed the cost. An obvious example is the branch manager of a bank.

---

[1]Many years before the invention of data base systems, this type of lock and key was used by J. R. R. Tolkien in his adventure fantasy "The Lord of the Rings." When the company lead by Gandalf reaches the long abandoned Mines of Moria, they find the great door locked. But on the door is the inscription, "Speak Friend and Enter." This is the definition of the lock. After fruitless attempts to uncover the key, only just in time Gandalf realizes that the key is the word *friend*. When he voices it, the door opens, and the company passes safely through.

Higher management deals with data bases at the strategic level, such as when there is a major decision in a manufacturing enterprise about manufacturing some new product. At a major strategy meeting a vice president for marketing will say that we can sell it (the potential product) if manufacturing can make it; the manufacturing vice president says that we can make it if engineering can design it and we get financial backing for the necessary expansion of plant facilities. The vice president for engineering says that engineering can do it given the time and permission to increase the staff to take on the additional work load; the vice president for corporate finance wants some figures (preferably sober) about the market value of the new product, the cost of manufacturing it, the cost of engineering it, and the cost of additional facilities: the finance vice president also needs to begin a study of alternative methods of financing the venture, whether to recommend issue of additional common shares, or preferred shares, or corporate bonds, or short-term bank financing, or whether the whole thing can be financed from corporate cash flow. Thus nothing can be decided at the strategy session without a great deal of strategic information.

Where does higher management obtain such strategic information? In the early 1970s it was commonly thought that *management information systems* that manipulated a large corporate data base would supply most of the information in such cases. Experience since then has shown such ideas to be naive, since few have been able to construct such a large corporate data base. Today it is more modestly agreed that the corporate data bases that contain the operational information (derived from operational-level use of data bases) can make a significant contribution to the supply of information necessary for strategic decision making. The remaining information comes from all the conventional sources, such as the financial press, articles, marketing reports, the "grapevine," and so on. However, an additional source that is becoming popular is the data base service company. Such companies have specialized data bases and charge their customers a fee for using them.

Thus we see that higher management can use the data bases as well, in the never-ending quest for information relating to strategic decisions, and this is the basis of the strategic-level use of data bases. There are two main types of strategic-level use of data bases: preprogrammed use and ad hoc use. In preprogrammed use, the higher manager has a large number of programs available at a terminal, and these programs retrieve and process information in the data base. If the programs are capable of a great deal of processing of the information in the data base in response to data or parameters input at the terminal by the manager, such a collection of programs is usually referred to as a *decision support system*. Such systems are usually powerful in areas where the processing programs are available. However, such power is available at the price of inflexibility.

With ad hoc use, the manager has access to a data base via a user-friendly query or retrieval language. In theory, if the required data is in the data base, then with the ideal retrieval language, a manager should be able to formulate a request to get it out. In addition, a good retrieval language should have arithmetic functions that permit generation of the average of a column of data, the maximum or minimum, and so on.

Use of powerful retrieval languages

The use of powerful retrieval languages by higher management is still in its infancy. One good reason for this is that such retrieval languages have proved very difficult to develop and implement. The most powerful language currently under development is IBM's SQL (Structured Query Language), but that is for use with IBM's relational data base system, System R, which we will learn more about in the next chapter. While there are many retrieval languages available with CODASYL systems, no official recommendation has been developed by CODASYL, and furthermore all the available retrieval languages at the time of writing are quite primitive and can carry out only restricted retrievals.

Recent developments: SQL/N

However, in recent years significant developments have taken place. While it appears that SQL will be the standard for many years to come as far as powerful retrieval languages are concerned, SQL is not easy to use where more elaborate retrievals are involved, and in such cases requires the user to have a highly developed ability in handling mathematical sets, an ability many managers are not likely to have. There has been considerable development activity aimed at solving this problem, and the author has recently succeeded in developing an extended version of SQL called SQL/N (the N is an acronym for natural). This language is much easier for managers to use than SQL, and has the advantage of being applicable to relational data bases and to CODASYL or any other data bases in which the conceptual files are relations (as is the case with all the examples so far in this book). As we shall see in Chapter 9, there are good reasons for the current widespread agreement that all conceptual files should be designed as relations, no matter what type of data base system is being employed. A description of SQL/N is included in the chapter supplement, and readers are invited to study it either before SQL, in order to make it easier to learn SQL, or after SQL, in order to learn how the difficulties with SQL are avoided in SQL/N. Besides being easier to use than SQL, SQL/N is also much more powerful and can easily express retrieval requests that are either impossible with SQL, or can be expressed only with great contrivance. SQL/N is upward compatible with SQL; that is, any SQL expression is also a SQL/N expression, although the converse is not true. Because SQL/N can be used with CODASYL data bases, the examples in the chapter supplement can be taken as examples of ad hoc use of a CODASYL data base.

Economics of retrieval language use by higher management

This brings us to an important issue. Should higher-level management be required to learn to use a powerful retrieval language such as SQL or SQL/N? At the time of writing the answer is not at all clear. On the one hand, there is no doubt that acquisition of the skills necessary for querying the corporation's data bases via a powerful retrieval language and a terminal would significantly increase the effectiveness of an executive. However, an executive's time is valuable and instead of spending this valuable time learning the technicalities of a query language (and probably some peripheral languages as well—for example, the operating system command language), it might be cheaper to employ an assistant who could deal with the terminal as needed.

Indeed, as the economist Samuelson has pointed out (Ref. 6), it is still economic for a doctor who is the fastest typist in town to employ a typist, for an hour spent by the doctor in the practice of medicine would be far more remunerative than an hour spent as the town's fastest typist. In the same way it can be argued that an executive worth over $100,000 per annum has no business spending time querying the corporation's data bases, if there is an assistant available who can do it at a quarter of the executive's annual salary. And this would still be true even if the executive was an expert in the local query language.

On the other hand, the analogy of Samuelson's doctor and typist does not quite fit the case of a highly paid executive who is also competent to query a data base. It is a fairly simple matter to instruct a typist to carry out a typing assignment, but instructing an assistant to obtain certain data from a data base can be quite time consuming, and there is no guarantee that the assistant will understand exactly what the executive wants, obtaining instead what he or she thinks the executive wants, or worse, what he or she thinks the executive ought to want. In the final analysis it may be cheaper for the executive to do the job without the assistant, even when the executive's salary far exceeds that of the assistant. Where an assistant is employed, the executive would be well advised to develop precise written specifications for any information to be retrieved by the assistant.

SUMMARY

1. The CODASYL recommendations have been developed over the past 15 years by the voluntary organization that was responsible for the development of COBOL. Many commercial data base systems are based on these recommendations. It is expected that the CODASYL recommendations will eventually form the basis of an American National Standard for data base management systems (although not the only standard).

2. The CODASYL schemas follow the ANSI/SPARC recommendations that there be a storage schema, a conceptual schema, and external schemas. The basic structures in a CODASYL schema are the grouping of records of the same type into conceptual files, and the grouping of parent and child records into owner-coupled set types, where an owner-coupled set type is composed of owner-coupled set occurrences. These groupings must be specified in the conceptual schema. The external schema is essentially a subset of the conceptual schema, although it also specifies record structures that may be used in a COBOL program for records transmitted to and from the data base, that is, it specifies a user work area (UWA).

3. The data manipulation language provides for direct and sequential access to the conceptual files, and for scanning the member (child) records of owner-coupled set occurrences. CODASYL uses currency indicators to keep track of a program's position in the data base; for example the current of run unit indicator is the physical address of the most recently accessed record in the data base. We have current of file and current of set indicators as well. These indicators can sometimes complicate the otherwise simple CODASYL DML commands. As well as the usual commands for changing a field in a record, inserting a new record, and deleting a record, there is a command to remove a record from an owner-coupled set occurrence (**DISCONNECT**) and a command to connect a record to an owner-coupled set occurrence (**CONNECT**).

4. The CODASYL DML is procedural, like many other DMLs, and when we design a CODASYL program to manipulate a data base, we must select the strategy that gives the lowest number of disk accesses. CODASYL has facilities, which are fundamentally similar to those of other systems, for preventing concurrently executing programs from either interfering with one another or becoming deadlocked. It also has security facilities for preventing unauthorized access to data. Currently there is no official proposal for a powerful *ad hoc* query language to compete with SQL. SQL/N is an example of what is possible in this area.

5. In a large organization a data base is used at three levels, the lowest or operational level, the middle or functional level, and the higher or strategic level. At the operational level the data base is normally manipulated by prewritten programs, at the functional level it is normally used for generating routine reports, while at the strategic level, it can be used for generating answers to *ad hoc* requests for information. It is as yet unclear whether it will be economical for a higher-level manager to learn to use data base query languages, as opposed to using a skilled assistant.

QUESTIONS

1. Complete the specification in Figure 6.4 for the conceptual files in Figure 6.2.
2. Complete the specification of the owner-coupled sets in Figure 6.2.
3. CODASYL permits a conceptual data base to be implemented at the storage level by a wide variety of pointer systems, including those for linked lists and inverted files. Devise a pointer system for the storage version of the file **WAREHOUSE** specified in Figure 6.4. The pointer system should take care of the secondary key specification.
4. Distinguish between storage and removal class for records in an owner-coupled set.
5. Why would you expect that the sets **EMP-PUR** and **SUP-PUR** in Figure 6.2 would be specified with retention class **FIXED**?
6. What is a value-based set with CODASYL?
7. Devise a pointer system for the storage version of the owner-coupled sets shown in Figure 6.6a.

8. In Figure 6.6, where would the EMPLOYEE record with key value 'E2' go, had the order specification for the owner-coupled set WAR-EMP been CONNECTION IS FIRST?

9. Explain the concept of SET SELECTION with CODASYL. Give an example where it is used.

10. Why is SET SELECTION using connection field values natural and simple?

11. Explain the concept of user work area (UWA) in connection with a program that is manipulating a data base.

12. What are CODASYL DML commands, and how do these fit with the concept of a host language?

13. Extend the program in Figure 6.10, so that the complete data base in Figure 6.2 can be loaded. Assume that the sets EMP-PUR and SUP-PUR are AUTOMATIC.

14. Repeat Question 13, using the CONNECT command, and assuming that EMP-PUR and SUP-PUR are MANUAL.

15. Distinguish between the CODASYL concepts of currency indicators and current records.

16. In what way does a currency indicator table differ from a current record table?

17. In Figure 6.11, if we assume that the record with key 'WH3' becomes the CRU after the record with key 'E6' but before the record with key 'WH1', with the sequence of other CRU values remaining the same, modify the currency table in Figure 6.12.

18. In Figure 6.11, if a new program has a succession of CRUs denoted by the succession of primary key values: 'WH3', 'WH1', 'E7', 'E3', 'WH1', and 'E1', construct a user currency table for the program.

19. Suppose that the field SALARY for the file EMPLOYEE in Figure 6.2 is defined as a secondary key, use the duplicate versions of the record-key FETCH command to construct a short program excerpt to retrieve the employee numbers of employees earning $25,000.

20. Use the record key FETCH command to construct a short program excerpt to retrieve the salaries of employees 'E3' and 'E6'.

21. Use the sequential FETCH command to write a short program excerpt to retrieve the salaries of all employees in the EMPLOYEE file.

22. Use the skip-sequential facility of the sequential FETCH command to write a short program excerpt to retrieve the records for employees who make less then $24,000.

23. Use the set-scan FETCH command to write a short program excerpt to retrieve the salaries of employees who work at warehouse 'WH2'.

24. Repeat Question 23 for the case where only salaries less than $24,000 must be retrieved.

25. Use both the duplicate version of the record key FETCH command and the set-scan FETCH command to retrieve the salaries of employees in New York.

26. Use the owner FETCH command to retrieve the name of the city where employee 'E6' works.

27. Repeat Question 25 using the sequential FETCH command and the owner FETCH command.

28. Use the set-scan **FIND** command together with the **GET** command to write a short program excerpt to retrieve the salaries of employees who work at warehouse 'WH2' and earn less than $24,000.

29. Use the **MODIFY** command to change the city for warehouse 'WH2' from New York to Newark.

30. Use the **MODIFY** command to write a short program excerpt to update the **WHNUMB** value to 'WH2' for the **EMPLOYEE** record with key value 'E7'. See Figure 6.15.

31. Repeat Question 30 using **CONNECT** and **DISCONNECT**.

32. Referring to the data base in Figures 6.2 and 5.25, write a program excerpt to retrieve the warehouse number for each warehouse whose employees all earn more than $21,000.

33. Referring to the data base in Figures 6.2 and 5.25, write a program excerpt to retrieve the names of suppliers that have received orders from warehouse employees at warehouse 'WH2'.

34. Referring to the data base in Figures 6.2 and 5.25, write a program excerpt to retrieve the names of cities containing warehouses that have issued orders to California suppliers.

35. Write a program excerpt to retrieve the names of cities that contain warehouses that have at least one employee earning less than $22,000.

36. Give another example where two concurrent programs updating the **EMPLOYEE** file interfere with each other's updating.

37. Use the transaction concept and the file locking concept to rewrite the programs in Question 36 so that interference cannot occur.

38. You are the president of a large insurance company or bank. Argue the pros and cons of an edict requiring that all executives learn the query language used with the corporation's data bases.

ADDITIONAL PERSPECTIVE
THE NATURAL QUANTIFIER BASED QUERY LANGUAGE SQL/N

SQL/N (Structured Query Language/Natural) is an extended version of SQL, a language that is rapidly becoming a standard with relational data bases. SQL/N is both easier to use than SQL and more powerful. SQL is described in detail in Chapter 7. The ease of use and power of expression with SQL/N are a result of the incorporation of *natural quantifiers*, that is, the quantifiers of ordinary English. These quantifiers are applied to owner-coupled set occurrences, but in a manner that corresponds exactly to their use in English with nouns in the genitive case, for example, the English expressions "all of a department's employees," or "at least two of a company's executives." Here a department's employees and a company's executives can be regarded as owner-coupled set occurrences, if there are records describing departments, employees, companies, and executives. The phrases "all of" and "at least two of" are examples of natural quantifiers since they specify a quantity. The discovery that natural quantifiers apply to owner-coupled set occurrences is significant for future development. SQL/N was developed from both SQL and an earlier language known as the EOS predicate calculus (Refs. 1 and 2). Readers should be aware that SQL/N has not currently been implemented, and should merely be taken as an example of what is possible. SQL/N can be applied to any data base whose conceptual files are structured as relations, including CODASYL data bases.

We begin with the structure of the most elementary type of SQL/N expression and then follow up with a range of expressions for retrievals of increasing complexity. An elementary SQL/N expression has the structure:

<u>SELECT</u> *field-names*
<u>FROM</u> *quantity-of file-name* OWNER/MEMBER RECORD/RECORDS
<u>WHERE</u> *logical-condition*

Using the data base in Figure 6.6a or Figure 6.7, a simple SQL/N expression could be

```
SELECT CITY
FROM THE FIRST WAREHOUSE RECORD
WHERE (WH-AREA = 50,000)
```

The expression clearly is requesting the **CITY** value from the first record in the **WAREHOUSE** file (in ascending primary key order) for which the **WH-AREA** is 50,000 units. If we replace **THE FIRST** by:

1. **THE LAST**, then we get the **CITY** value from the last **WAREHOUSE** record satisfying the logical condition.
2. **THE NEXT**, then we get the **CITY** value from the next **WAREHOUSE** record (that is, the one following the current **WAREHOUSE** record) that satisfies the logical condition.
3. **THE FIRST** n, **THE LAST** n, **THE NEXT** n, then we get, respectively, the **CITY** value from the first n, the last n, and the next n records following the current record that each satisfy the logical condition.
4. **EACH**, then we get the list of **CITY** values (with duplicate values present) from each and every one of the **WAREHOUSE** records that satisfy the logical condition. If we want duplicate values removed, we must use **SELECT UNIQUE** instead of **SELECT**.
5. Nothing at all, the effect is as if **EACH** were used.

Note that in the general structure of an SQL/N expression above, a word not underlined, such as **RECORD**, may be omitted. Furthermore, as we shall see, the term *logical-expression* in the general structure can expand to handle conditions involving many files. A further point is that retrieval of a field from a single record makes that record the current record, which is equivalent to the current of run unit with CODASYL.

An additional convenience is a provision for scanning through the fields of records satisfying the retrieval conditions, so that if we wanted to scan through the cities for warehouses with a floor area larger than 25,000 units, referring to Figure 6.6a, we could code:

```
Manager:    SELECT    CITY
            FROM THE FIRST WAREHOUSE
            WHERE (WH-AREA > 25,000)
Response:   37,000
Manager:    SELECT NEXT
Response:   50,000
Manager:    NEXT
Response:   NONE LEFT
```

Thus if we issue a **SELECT** command that retrieves a record or a field from a record, then issuing **SELECT NEXT** immediately afterwards retrieves the next record (or field from that record) that satisfies the retrieval conditions in the original full **SELECT** command. Similar conveniences have been incorporated in some commercially available query systems. We can now examine some requests for information that are aimed at the data base in Figure 6.2 or Figure 5.24 with the file contents shown in Figure 5.25.

Retrieval-1: Single data base file

Request: With what suppliers has employee 'E3' placed orders?

```
Expression: SELECT    SNUMB
            FROM EACH   PUR-ORDER RECORD
            WHERE   (EMPNUMB = 'E3')
Response:   S7
            S4
```

The data base system scans through the **PUR-ORDER** file retrieving each record for which the **EMPNUMB** value is 'E3'.

Retrieval-2: Two data base files

Request: What cities have a warehouse with at least one employee earning exactly $25,000?

```
Expression: SELECT CITY
            FROM EACH WAREHOUSE OWNER RECORD
            WHERE (THERE IS AT LEAST 1 EMPLOYEE MEMBER RECORD
                    WHERE (SALARY = 25,000))
Response:   DALLAS
            NEW YORK
```

The data base system scans through the **WAREHOUSE** file looking for suitable **WAREHOUSE** records. For each **WAREHOUSE** record encountered it checks to see if there is at least one suitable **EMPLOYEE** member record in the **WAR-EMP** occurrence owned by that **WAREHOUSE** record; a suitable **EMPLOYEE** record has a **SALARY** field value equal to $25,000. We have tried to illustrate this in Figure 6.18.

In the above SQL/N expression the phrase **THERE IS AT LEAST 1** is a *natural quantifier* since it states what quantity of records must satisfy the condition in the **WHERE**-clause that follows. The *natural* quantifiers are those that occur in

WHNUMB	CITY	WH–AREA		WHNUMB	EMPNUMB	SALARY
WH1	DALLAS	37,000		WH1	E3	21,000
				WH1	E7	25,000
WH2	NEW YORK	50,000		WH2	E1	22,000
				WH2	E4	25,000
WH3	CHICAGO	20,000		WH3	E6	23,000

WAREHOUSE records   EMPLOYEE records

FIGURE 6.18 Shows how WAREHOUSE records are selected that satisfy the retrieval conditions for Retrieval-2. A rectangle encloses an occurrence of the owner-coupled set WAR-EMP. The data base system checks each WAREHOUSE record in turn, and for each such WAREHOUSE record the system also checks the member EMPLOYEE records to see if the group of members satisfy the logical condition following WHERE in the retrieval expression. Only when the logical condition is satisfied is the CITY value from the WAREHOUSE record involved actually retrieved.

natural languages such as English. The following is a selection of the natural quantifiers that can be used with SQL/N:

	FOR version	THERE version
1a	FOR AT LEAST n	THERE ARE AT LEAST n, THERE EXISTS AT LEAST n
1b.	FOR AT LEAST ONE	THERE IS AT LEAST ONE, THERE EXISTS AT LEAST ONE
2a.	FOR n, FOR EXACTLY n	THERE ARE n, THERE ARE EXACTLY n
2b	FOR ONE, FOR EXACTLY ONE, FOR THE ONE	THERE IS ONE, THERE IS EXACTLY ONE, THERE IS A
3	FOR AT MOST n	THERE ARE AT MOST n
4.	FOR LESS THAN n	THERE ARE MORE THAN n
5.	FOR THE MAJORITY OF	THERE IS A MAJORITY OF
6.	FOR AT LEAST x PERCENT OF	THERE ARE AT LEAST x PERCENT OF
7.	FOR AT MOST x PERCENT OF	THERE ARE AT MOST x PERCENT OF
8.	FOR EXACTLY x PERCENT OF	THERE ARE EXACTLY x PERCENT OF
9.	FOR LESS THAN x PERCENT OF	THERE ARE LESS THAN x PERCENT OF
10.	FOR MORE THAN x PERCENT OF	THERE ARE MORE THAN x PERCENT OF
11.	FOR EACH, FOR EVERY, FOR ALL, FOR EACH IF ANY, FOR ALL IF ANY	
12.	FOR NO	THERE ARE NO
13.	FOR ALL BUT n	
14.	FOR ONE AND FOR ALL,	

In SQL/N we can have two versions of most of the natural quanitifiers, namely a **FOR** version or *FOR-quantifier*, and a **THERE** version or *THERE-quantifier*. There is no difference in meaning, although they give rise to a greater variety of SQL/N constructions, as we shall see.

Note that with non CODASYL data bases we would replace **OWNER** by **PARENT** and **MEMBER** by **CHILD**.

Retrieval-3: Two data base files

Request: What cities have a warehouse where there are exactly two employees with a salary greater than $20,000?

```
Expression: SELECT CITY
            FROM EACH WAREHOUSE OWNER RECORD
            WHERE (THERE ARE EXACTLY 2 EMPLOYEE MEMBER
                    RECORDS WHERE (SALARY > 20,000))
  or:       SELECT CITY
            FROM EACH WAREHOUSE OWNER RECORD
            WHERE (FOR EXACTLY 2 EMPLOYEE MEMBER RECORDS
                    (SALARY > 20,000)
Response:   DALLAS
            NEW YORK
```

If we turn back to the general structure of an SQL/N expression, we see that we have a logical condition, or *logical-condition*, following each **WHERE** on the last line. This logical condition may be further expanded to contain an additional **WHERE** clause followed by another logical condition:

Thus *logical-condition* has either the structure:

(*THERE-quantifier file-name* **MEMBER/OWNER RECORD(S)**
WHERE *logical-condition* **AND/OR WHERE** *logical-condition* **AND/OR**
WHERE . . .)

or the structure:

(*FOR-quantifier file-name* **MEMBER/OWNER RECORD(S)**
logical-condition **AND/OR** *logical-condition* **AND/OR** . . .)

And within a logical condition expression, *logical-condition* can be further expanded with either of the structures described above; in this way *logical-condition* and thus an SQL/N expression is capable of unlimited expansion, just as unlimited expansion of an English sentence is possible, but not very practical (except perhaps in legal documents). The three versions of the following retrieval expression illustrate some of the possibilities (see also Figure 6.19).

Retrieval-4: Three data base files

Request: In what cities has an employee, who works at a warehouse over 30,000 units in floor area, placed one or more orders with supplier 'S4'?

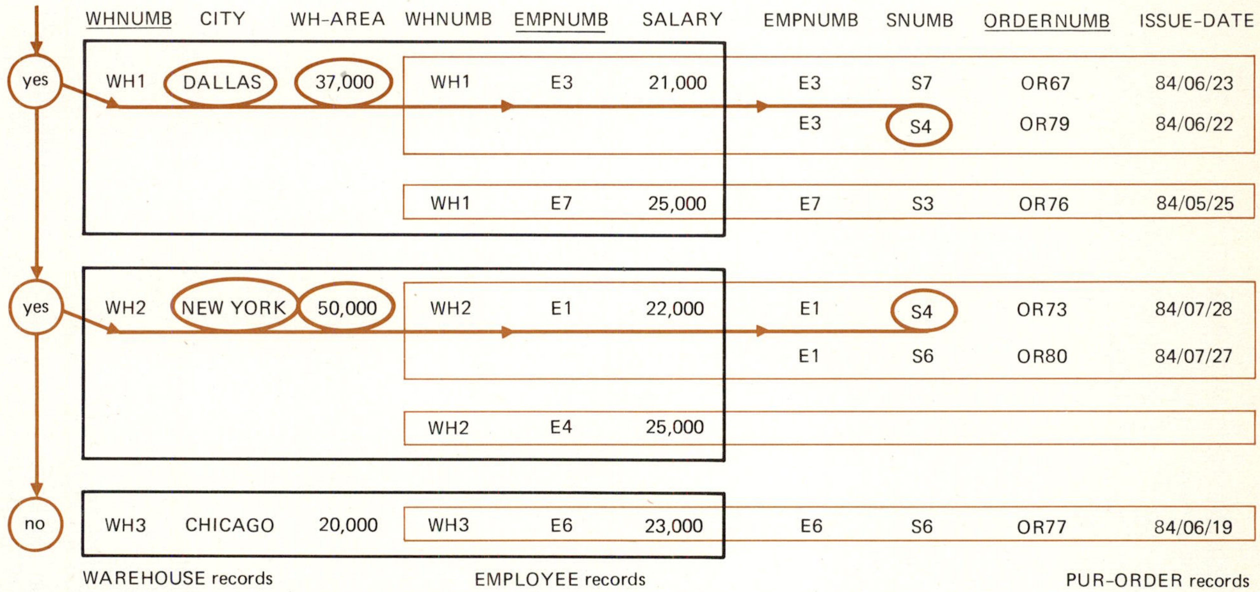

WAREHOUSE records

EMPLOYEE records

PUR-ORDER records

FIGURE 6.19 Shows how WAREHOUSE records that satisfy the conditions in Retrieval-4 are selected. A color rectangle is an occurrence of the owner-coupled set EMP-PUR, while a black rectangle is an occurrence of the owner-coupled set WAR-EMP. The system checks the WH-AREA value for each WAREHOUSE record; if a WAREHOUSE record passes this check, its member EMPLOYEE records in WAR-EMP are checked, and for each such EMPLOYEE record, its members in PUR-EMP are checked, to see if the condition in the second WHERE clause is met.

```
Expression:     SELECT CITY
                FROM EACH WAREHOUSE OWNER RECORD
                WHERE (WH-AREA > 30,000)
         AND WHERE (THERE IS AT LEAST 1 EMPLOYEE MEMBER RECORD
                      WHERE (THERE IS AT LEAST 1 PUR-ORDER MEMBER RECORD
                              WHERE (SNUMB = 'S4')))
```

```
Response:   DALLAS
            NEW YORK
```

The data base system scans through the **WAREHOUSE** file. If a **WH-AREA** field value satisfies the first **WHERE** clause, then it is selected for further study. If the selected **WAREHOUSE** record has one or more **EMPLOYEE** member records, then these **EMPLOYEE** records are selected for further study. If any one of these **EMPLOYEE** records has at least one **PUR-ORDER** member record that satisfies the third **WHERE** clause, then the originally selected **WAREHOUSE** record is retrieved and its **CITY** value extracted.

We could have a slightly different version using the **FOR**-quantifier equivalent of the **THERE**-quantifier:

```
Expression:     SELECT CITY
                FROM EACH WAREHOUSE OWNER RECORD
                WHERE (WH-AREA > 30,000)
          AND  WHERE (FOR AT LEAST 1 EMPLOYEE MEMBER RECORD
                       (THERE IS AT LEAST 1 PUR-ORDER MEMBER RECORD
                        WHERE (SNUMB = 'S4')
```

and another version would be:

```
Expression:     SELECT CITY
                FROM EACH WAREHOUSE OWNER RECORD
                WHERE (WH-AREA > 30,000)
          AND  WHERE (THERE IS AT LEAST 1 EMPLOYEE MEMBER RECORD
                       (WHERE (FOR AT LEAST 1 PUR-ORDER RECORD
                        (SNUMB = 'S4')
```

Expression involving three files are not likely to be needed very often, since such complex retrieval requests are not common.

Retrieval-5: Two data base files

Request: What are the floor areas of New York warehouses whose employees all make more than $20,000?

```
Expression:     SELECT WH-AREA
                FROM EACH WAREHOUSE OWNER RECORD
                WHERE (CITY = 'NEW YORK'
          AND  WHERE (FOR EACH EMPLOYEE MEMBER RECORD
                       (SALARY > 20,000))
```

```
Response:       50,000
```

Note that there is no **THERE**-quantifier equivalent of the quantifier **FOR EACH**.

Retrieval-6: Two data base files

Request: Find the employees making less than $23,000 that work in warehouses with a floor area larger than 30,000 units.

Expression:
```
SELECT EMPNUMB
FROM EACH EMPLOYEE MEMBER RECORD
WHERE (SALARY < 23,000)
AND    WHERE (FOR THE ONE WAREHOUSE OWNER RECORD
                    (WH-AREA > 30,000))
```

Response: E3
          E1

Note that in this case we scan through the **EMPLOYEE** file, selecting records that satisfy the condition in the first **WHERE** clause for further study. For such a selected **EMPLOYEE** record, its **WAREHOUSE** owner in the set **WAR-EMP** is then examined to see if the condition following the last **WHERE** clause is satisfied.

Retrieval-7: Three data base files

Request: Find the employees making less than $23,000 that (a) work in warehouses with a floor area larger than 30,000 units, and (b) have never issued an order to supplier 'S6'.

Expression:
```
SELECT EMPNUMB
FROM EACH EMPLOYEE RECORD
WHERE (SALARY < 23,000)
AND    WHERE (THERE IS EXACTLY 1 WAREHOUSE OWNER RECORD
                 WHERE (WH-AREA > 30,000))
AND    WHERE (THERE ARE NO PUR-ORDER MEMBER RECORDS
                 WHERE (SNUMB = 'S6'))
```

Response: E3

Note that both the **THERE**-quantifiers could be replaced with the equivalent **FOR**-quantifiers.

Retrieval-8: Required data in two files

Request: Find the employee number, salary, and city of employment for each employee making less than $23,000 in a warehouse with a floor area larger than 30,000 units.

Expression:
```
SELECT EMPNUMB, SALARY
FROM EACH EMPLOYEE MEMBER RECORD
WHERE (SALARY < 23,000)
AND    WHERE (THERE IS EXACTLY 1 WAREHOUSE OWNER RECORD
                 WHERE (WH-AREA > 30,000)
              AND WHERE (CITY IS A TARGET)
```

Response: E3   21,000   DALLAS
          E1   22,000   NEW YORK

Following the last **WHERE** we use a new logical condition:

field **IS A TARGET**

which indicates that a field value in a selected record is to be retrieved.

QUESTIONS

39. Construct SQL/N expressions for each of the following information retrieval requests, which are directed toward the data base in Figures 6.2 and 5.25. In each case show the result of the execution of the SQL/N expression:
    (a) Find the employee numbers for employees who work at warehouse 'WH2'.
    (b) Find the names of suppliers who are located in California.
    (c) Find the locations of suppliers who have received orders from employee 'E6'.
    (d) Find the locations of suppliers who have at least two orders from employee 'E7'.
    (e) Find the cities that have warehouses with no employees earning more than $24,000.
    (f) Find the warehouses for which the majority of employees make more than $22,000.
    (g) Find the warehouses in New York whose employees all make more than $21,000.
    (h) What warehouses have employees earning more than $22,000 who have placed orders with supplier 'S6'?
    (i) What warehouses in Chicago have employees earning more than $22,000 who have placed orders with a supplier called Mikrel?
    (j) Find the names of Texas suppliers who have orders from warehouses in New York.
40. Apply SQL/N to the retrieval requests in Questions 33 through 36.

REFERENCES

1. Bradley, J., 1978. "An Extended Owner-coupled Set Data Model and Predicate Calculus for Data Base Management." *ACM Trans. on Database Systems*, 3(4):385–416.
2. Bradley, J., 1982. *File and Data Base Techniques*. Holt, Rinehart and Winston, New York.
3. CODASYL, Data Description Language Committee, 1981. *DDLC Journal of Development*. Available from: Federal Dept. of Supply and Services, Hull, Quebec, Canada.
4. CODASYL, COBOL Committee, 1981. Journal of Development. Available as with Ref. 3.
5. Cullinane Corporation. *IDMS Concepts and Facilities*. Cullinane Corp., Boston.
6. Samuelson, P. A., 1979. *Economics*. McGraw-Hill, New York.

7

The Relational Approach to Data Base Management

The relational approach to data base management is of fundamental importance and is having a profound influence on the development of other approaches. Paradoxically the relational approach is not widely used at the time of writing, but that is because it has taken a very long time to bring a comprehensive relational system on the market. As mentioned in Chapter 5, while the relational approach is simple in principle, in practice it is difficult to implement well (Ref. 6). However, the difficulties are expected to disappear as time goes on, and it is expected that the relational approach will be commonly used (if not the most commonly used) in business by the second half of the 1980s. Accordingly, the student of business needs to be acquainted with the approach.

Some currently available relational systems are ORACLE from Relational Systems and MULTICS Relational Data Store from Honeywell. The most important system is probably System R from IBM; a prototype of this system has been constructed and tested, although performance problems have delayed its release. The language used for manipulating the data base with these three systems is SQL (Ref. 4), mentioned in the previous chapter. In this chapter we shall study SQL in some detail.

We begin by examining the schemas used to define a relational data base. Relational data base systems are three-level systems, as described in Chapter 4, so that we have a conceptual schema, storage schema, and external schema. Following a description of the schemas we shall see how a relational data base is manipulated using SQL.

We attempt to illustrate the basic principles of the relational approach in this chapter, avoiding peripheral implementation details where possible. However, where it is necessary to give examples of the use of a real data base management system, we shall employ IBM's System R (Refs. 2, 4, and 5), since this will probably set the standard for relational systems for many years to come. Where convenient we shall compare the relational and CODASYL approaches, and to make this as convenient as possible, we shall use the data bases from Chapter 6.

7.1 THE RELATIONAL SCHEMAS

We shall look at the conceptual schema in some detail, since an understanding of the principles behind it is crucial to an understanding of the relational approach. In contrast there is nothing special in the storage schema definition, as it involves the usual pointers, storage files, inversions, and indexes. Indeed the details of the storage schema will be quite specific to the particular implementation, so that from a business standpoint our coverage need only be minimal. In contrast again, the relational external schema can involve some additional principles found only in the relational approach at the time of writing. However, these additional principles (involving what are called *user views*) can be deferred until after we have studied SQL.

The relational conceptual schema

The great characteristic of the relational conceptual schema is its simplicity. Essentially it contains only a specification of each of the relations that occur in the data base. We gave a definition of a relation in Chapter 4, but it is worth repeating:

> *Definition of a relation.* A relation is a conceptual file in which (1) each conceptual record is unique and (2) each conceptual record has the same number and type of fields, that is, the relation contains only fixed format, fixed length conceptual records.

Thus the simple conceptual files in Figure 7.1, which we used in a CODASYL data base in the previous chapter, are in fact relations. This may well puzzle or even disappoint the reader who may well be eager to understand the new features of the relational conceptual schema. The truth is that the relational conceptual schema is distinguished not by the features it contains but by the features it does not contain. If we compare with a CODASYL conceptual schema, the essential differences are:

1. In a conceptual CODASYL data base the conceptual files may be relations, or they may not; for example, a conceptual file may contain duplicate records. Nevertheless it is good practice to use relations as CODASYL conceptual files.

2. In a CODASYL conceptual data base the 1:n relationships between conceptual files are specified in the conceptual schema by means of owner-coupled sets. In a relational data base relationships between relations are

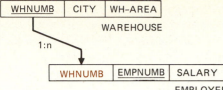

FIGURE 7.1(*a*)   Use of an extended Bachman diagram to depict the relationship between the relation WAREHOUSE and the relation EMPLOYEE.

WHNUMB	CITY	WH-AREA
WH1	DALLAS	37,000
WH2	NEW YORK	50,000
WH3	CHICAGO	20,000

WAREHOUSE

WHNUMB	EMPNUMB	SALARY
WH2	E1	22,000
WH1	E3	21,000
WH2	E4	25,000
WH3	E6	23,000
WH1	E7	25,000

EMPLOYEE

FIGURE 7.1(*b*)   Some conceptual records of the relations WAREHOUSE and EMPLOYEE. The child connection field (or foreign key) is shown in color.

not explicitly specified in the conceptual schema. They are implicitly specified, however, because of the specification of the connection fields supporting the relationships (Chapter 5).

As an example of a relational conceptual schema, we give one for the conceptual data base in Figure 7.1; the conceptual schema definition language is the one used with IBM's System R:

```
CREATE TABLE    WAREHOUSE    (WHNUMB    (CHAR(5), NONULL),
                             CITY      (CHAR(20),
                             WH-AREA   (INTEGER) )

CREATE TABLE    EMPLOYEE     (WHNUMB    (CHAR(5), NONULL),
                             EMPNUMB   (CHAR(5), NONULL),
                             SALARY    (INTEGER) )
```

System R permits the definition of a conceptual schema interactively at a terminal, by means of a **CREATE TABLE** command issued for each relation to be specified as shown above. With System R a relation at the conceptual level is often called a *base table*.

The simplicity of the schema definition above is apparent. We specify only the relations and their fields. Normally we would also specify the primary keys in the conceptual schema. However with System R we specify primary keys in the internal schema. Nevertheless we do specify that primary key and connection field values not be null (**NONULL**).

It was mentioned above that relationships are only implicitly specified by means of the connection fields (sometimes referred to as *foreign keys* in the literature). This is quite sufficient. We notice in the above conceptual schema definition that both the parent connection field **WHNUMB** in **WAREHOUSE** and the child connection field **WHNUMB** are specified as having up to five characters of data. This means that a **WHNUMB** value in **EMPLOYEE** can be tested for equality with a **WHNUMB** value in **WAREHOUSE**, and this is the principal means by which a relationship is specified in relational data manipulation languages.

For example, suppose we wish to retrieve all the child **EMPLOYEE** records of a given **WAREHOUSE** record. The necessary relational data manipulation language command would essentially request those **EMPLOYEE** records for which the **WHNUMB** value is equal to the **WHNUMB** value of the given **WARE-HOUSE**. In this way an explicit declaration of the 1:*n* relationship between **WAREHOUSE** and **EMPLOYEE** in the relational conceptual schema is avoided.

Relational terminology

The relational approach has its roots in the mathematical theory of relations. While we have explained the concept of a relation in terms of conceptual files, it may also be defined in terms of *mathematical sets,* a mathematical set being a collection of unique entities. The mathematical influence is also apparent in the absence of specifications of relationships in the conceptual schema. The specification of the supporting connection fields is all that is necessary and is quite sufficient. Again, to specify children of a parent record or vice versa in a data manipulation language statement, it is only necessary to specify equality of connection field values, this being quite sufficient and all that is necessary.

As a result of this mathematical foundation, the literature on relational data bases is full of mathematical terms. These terms are usually precisely defined but are often meaningless to readers whose background is business or data processing. Fortunately there is usually a corresponding term in data processing, and we give a list of the most important relational terms for reference purposes (see also Refs. 1 and 4). Furthermore, as relational data base techniques begin to penetrate the commercial market, the trend has been for vendors to use terminology that is either close to that used in conventional data processing or is simple and obvious.

Relation. A restricted conceptual file as explained earlier. With System R the term *base table* is often used. The term *relational conceptual file* or *relational file* is also sometimes used. A relation can also be defined as a mathematical set of tuples.

Tuple. A conceptual record of a relation. Referring to Figure 7.1:

```
WH2 NEW YORK  50,000
```

is a tuple of the relation **WAREHOUSE**. With System R the term *row* is often used.

Degree of a relation. The number of fields in a conceptual record.

Attribute of a relation. A complete column of a relation when looked upon as a table. The term is not used in conventional data processing. The nearest equivalent is field type.

Domain of a relation.   A domain is a universal list of values from which a column in a relation is derived. For example, the domain **D-CITY** could contain a list of all the cities in the world, so that the column under the field **CITY** in **WAREHOUSE** in Figure 7.1 is derived from this domain. For every field in a relational data base there is an underlying domain. In some relational systems, when a field type is specified in the conceptual schema, the name of the underlying domain must also be specified; for example, with the data base in Figure 7.1 we could have:

```
RELATION WAREHOUSE    WHNUMB CHAR(5)    DOMAIN D-WHNUMB
                      CITY CHAR(20)     DOMAIN D-CITY
                      WH-AREA INTEGER   DOMAIN D-WH-AREA

RELATION EMPLOYEE     WHNUMB CHAR(5)    DOMAIN D-WHNUMB
                      EMPNUMB CHAR(5)   DOMAIN D-EMPNUMB
                      SALARY  INTEGER   DOMAIN D-SALARY
```

The idea is that if two fields from different relations are derived from the same domain, then they can be tested for equality, as can be **WHNUMB** values from **WAREHOUSE** and **EMPLOYEE** records. In the specification above this is another implicit method of specifying that the **WHNUMB** field is a connection field supporting a one-to-many relationship. System R does not use the domain concept.

Foreign key.   Child connection field.

Use of relations with other approaches to data base management

The advantage of the concept of a relation is its simplicity. In fact the concept has an even greater inherent simplicity than has so far been explained. A full explanation of the other properties of a relation, however, is best given later (in Chapter 9). Thus if we are willing to accept that a relation is the ideal conceptual file, we might ask why other approaches do not also adopt the relation as the basic conceptual file. The answer is the historical development of these approaches. They originated before the concept of a relation was even heard of in data processing, and it was natural for these approaches to use the data base equivalent of the records that were common in data processing, and these records included variable length records. Many existing CODASYL, hierarchical, and hybrid data bases contain varying length records, so that even new three-level releases of the corresponding data base systems have to be able to handle these older data bases. As is well known, when a facility is placed in a computer language, if later developments show that the facility is no longer useful, it cannot be removed because of the existing investment in applications making use of it.

Nevertheless it is sensible to make use of relations in the design of new data bases using CODASYL, hierarchical, and other approaches. As mentioned earlier, we used relations for the conceptual files with the CODASYL material in Chapter 6. The observant reader will also have noticed that we employed only relations in the descriptions of relationships between conceptual files and elementary data base design methods in Chapter 5.

The relational storage schema

The relational storage schema is no different in principle from storage schemas with other approaches to data base management. There is at least one storage file corresponding to each conceptual file, and there are typically primary indexes for direct access on the basis of primary keys, secondary indexes for access via secondary keys, and pointer systems to connect parent records in one storage file to child records in another storage file.

These facilities exist in System R. Indexes for primary and secondary key access are provided, the word **UNIQUE** distinguishing between the two types. Thus to specify a primary key index called **WHNUMB-INDEX** for the primary key **WHNUMB** in **WAREHOUSE**, and a secondary key index **CITY-INDEX** for the secondary key **CITY** in **WAREHOUSE**, we can interactively issue the terminal commands:

```
CREATE UNIQUE INDEX WHNUMB-INDEX ON WAREHOUSE (WHNUMB)
CREATE INDEX CITY-INDEX ON WAREHOUSE (CITY)
```

The word **UNIQUE** indicates that the elements (that is, the **WHNUMB** key values) pointed to by the lowest level of the index (see Chapter 2) are unique. System R was developed under both the interactive operating system VM/CMS and the batch operating system OS/MVS, so that as the reader will probably have guessed, the System R storage schema indexes are really VSAM indexes, covered in Chapters 2 and 3.

In addition to the indexes for direct access, System R provides for pointer chains that connect a parent record with its child records. Child records belonging to a parent are connected in a linked list as described in Chapter 3. These pointer systems in System R are referred to as *links* (see Figure 4.6a).

The external relational schema

We can distinguish two types of external schemas for relational data bases, and for the purpose of this book, we shall refer to these types as elementary and advanced. The elementary type will be dealt with here, while we shall postpone a discussion of the advanced type until after we have studied SQL, the well-known relational data manipulation language.

In an elementary external relational schema, we merely define a number of relations, each of which is derived from a relation defined in the conceptual schema. In an elementary external relational schema, a derived relation is either identical to a relation of the conceptual schema, or it is a conceptual schema relation with one or more columns removed and any resulting duplicate external records removed as well.

WHNUMB	EMPNUMB	SALARY
WH15	E50	28,000
WH13	E55	27,000
WH15	E59	28,000
WH18	E62	27,000
WH13	E64	27,000

EMPLOYEE

(a)

WHNUMB	SALARY
WH15	28,000
WH13	27,000
WH15	28,000
WH18	27,000
WH13	27,000

Two columns from
EMPLOYEE

(b)

WHNUMB	SALARY
WH15	28,000
WH13	27,000
WH18	27,000

VIEW1

(c)

FIGURE 7.2 The derivation of the external relation or view VIEW1 from the conceptual schema relation EMPLOYEE. VIEW1 is to contain the fields WHNUMB and SALARY, and the first step is the removal of the WHNUMB and SALARY columns (b) from the relation EMPLOYEE (a). However, the resulting conceptual file in (b) is not a relation since it contains duplicate records. To form VIEW1 in (c), these duplicates are removed. Note that VIEW1 is not a particularly useful relation, and it is doubtful that anyone would ever want to define it. The process of extracting columns and removing duplicate records is called *projection*.

This last point about removal of duplicate records is illustrated in Figure 7.2. As explained several times, a relation does not have duplicate records by definition. However, if we remove one or more columns, the result is not necessarily a relation since there may be duplicate rows present. To make it into a relation, these duplicate rows have to be removed. Thus an external conceptual file in the relational approach is also a relation. (This process is the relational *projection* operation; see the supplement to Chapter 8.)

With System R an external conceptual file or relation is called a *view*. Thus if we issue the interactive command:

```
DEFINE VIEW  VIEW1 (EMPNUMB, SALARY)
AS SELECT EMPNUMB, SALARY FROM EMPLOYEE
```

we have defined an external relation called **VIEW1** containing the fields **EMPNUMB** and **SALARY** from the relation **EMPLOYEE** defined in the conceptual schema.

7.2 OVERVIEW OF SYSTEM R IN AN INTERACTIVE ENVIRONMENT

Before going on to examine SQL, we give an overview of System R in Figure 7.3. This overview should be compared with Figure 4.9. The User-Friendly System (UF System) is the terminal control system, which accepts the **CREATE TABLE**, **CREATE INDEX**, **DEFINE VIEW** commands for specifying the schemas; it also accepts SQL retrieval expressions and many other commands. These commands are then passed to the Relational Data (Base) System (RD System), which is roughly equivalent to the data base control system described in Chapter 4 (see Figure 4.9).

The RD System places conceptual and external schemas in the System R data

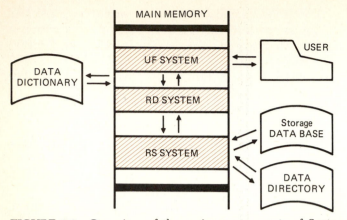

FIGURE 7.3 Overview of the major components of System R in an interactive environment. A user may issue commands both to define the data base and to manipulate the data base. The UF System is the terminal control system, the RD System is roughly equivalent to the data base control system described in Chapter 4, and the RS System is roughly the equivalent to data base storage system also described in Chapter 4. Conceptual and external schema specifications are stored in the data dictionary, while the storage schema specification is stored in the data directory.

dictionary following the relevant schema definition commands; however, execution of commands defining a storage schema causes the storage schema definition to be placed in a data directory. (As was explained in Chapter 4, the difference between a basic data dictionary and data directory is that while the data base system has access to both the data dictionary and data directory, a user has access only to the data dictionary; for example, a user could formulate an SQL request to retrieve the number of fields in relation X, which is described in the data dictionary.) The RD System also accepts SQL data base manipulation commands passed from the UF System; the RD System translates these commands into what are known as access routines that call up the services of the Research Storage System.

The Research Storage System (RS System) is responsible for arranging for each access of the storage data base. Many accesses may be required for a response to a single SQL command. The RS System does not itself access the data base, however; it issues **CALLs** to the underlying access methods that are responsible for reading and writing records on storage files (see Chapter 1).

7.3 STRUCTURED QUERY LANGUAGE (SQL)

SQL is easily the most important relational data base manipulation language at the time of writing and is provided for by practically all relational data base systems that have been developed or are currently under development. However, that does not mean that SQL is cast in stone, for it was designed some 10 years ago (Ref. 3) and contains features that could certainly be improved upon, and no doubt will be in the course of time. In Chapter 6 we saw that SQL/N is a candidate extension of SQL that permits the use of natural quantifiers

SQL with System R can be used either directly from a terminal as a query and updating language, or it can be *embedded* in a host language such as COBOL or PL/1. There are a fair number of unpleasant details involved with the use of embedded SQL, and so we concentrate on a discussion of SQL as it would be used at a terminal. Embedded SQL is essentially the same except for the additional technicalities, and is described in the chapter supplement. We shall first introduce the elementary structure of SQL, followed by some examples of SQL expressions. More advanced SQL structures and expressions then follow. Our aim is the provision of sufficient material for the reader to actually learn SQL, such as its importance. SQL is an example of a nonprocedural data base manipulation language.

Structure of SQL

An SQL expression is constructed from what are called **SELECT-FROM-WHERE** blocks. A simple SQL statement would be a single **SELECT-FROM-WHERE** block. In a more complex expression one **SELECT-FROM-WHERE** block can be nested within another such block. A **SELECT-FROM-WHERE** block has the structure:

> **SELECT** *fieldname, fieldname . . .*
> **FROM** *relation, relation . . .*
> **WHERE** *logical-expression* **AND/OR** *logical-expression* **AND/OR . . .**

At first glance the basic structure looks very close to the SQL/N structure described in the previous chapter. However, there are two important differences. First, the expression retrieves at once the fields specified from *all* the records of the relation specified (most commonly only one relation is specified), provided that the contents of the record satisfy the conditions specified in the **WHERE** clause. Thus a conceptual file of records is retrieved; we recall that with SQL/N we could retrieve one record at a time if desired. Second, no quantifiers are needed in the logical expressions (although it is possible to use one simple quantifier, as we shall see later).

We shall go deeper into the structure of a logical expression shortly. For now we illustrate the use of a single **SELECT-FROM-WHERE** block in some simple retrievals.

SQL retrievals with a single SELECT-FROM-WHERE block

The following retrievals all refer to the data base in Figure 7.1. For convenience we assume that the user's external schema is identical to the conceptual schema.

Retrieval-1: No WHERE clause
Retrieve all the **SALARY** *values from the* **EMPLOYEE** *relation.*

```
SELECT SALARY
FROM EMPLOYEE
```

The result is, referring to Figure 7.1b:

```
22,000
21,000
25,000
23,000
25,000
```

We see that the list contains duplicates, as does the **SALARY** column in the **EMPLOYEE** relation. In the relational approach to data base management all nonstorage files, that is, conceptual files, external files, and retrieved files, are supposed to be relations, at least in theory. However, with SQL that restriction is relaxed as far as retrievals are concerned, and duplicate rows are not removed unless we specifically request it.

If we wanted to retrieve a relation in response to the above request, we would specify:

```
SELECT UNIQUE SALARY
FROM EMPLOYEE
```

UNIQUE causes duplicates to be removed.

Retrieval-2: Retrieval of complete records
Retrieve all the records in **WAREHOUSE**.

```
SELECT *  - ALL
FROM WAREHOUSE
```

The response is:

```
WH1    DALLAS    37,000
WH2    NEW YORK  50,000
WH3    CHICAGO   20,000
```

The asterisk in the top line signifies that we want all the fields in the records. Of course we could replace the above expression with:

```
SELECT WHNUMB,CITY, WH-AREA
FROM WAREHOUSE
```

Retrieval-3: Simple WHERE clause
Retrieve the employee numbers of employees earning more than $23,000.

```
SELECT EMPNUMB
FROM EMPLOYEE
WHERE (SALARY > 23000)
```

The response is:

```
E4
E7
```

Retrieval-4: Elimination of duplicates

In what warehouses are there employees earning more than $21,000?

```
SELECT UNIQUE WHNUMB
FROM EMPLOYEE
WHERE (SALARY > 21000)
```

The response is:

```
WH2
WH3
WH1
```

In this case we are clearly interested in a list of unique warehouse numbers. In the case of Retrieval-1 we were clearly interested in all salaries whether duplicates or not. The decision whether or not to have duplicates eliminated is an important one in SQL and often has a significant effect on the processing of the data retrieved. Going back to Retrieval-1 again, had we been interested in the average salary of employees listed in **EMPLOYEE**, then use of the relation obtained by inserting **UNIQUE** into the retrieval expression would clearly lead to an incorrect average being calculated (by whatever further processing was used). We shall return to this point again when we come to computational retrievals.

Retrieval-5: More complex WHERE clause

Give the employee numbers of employees that work in warehouse 'WH1' or 'WH2' and make less than $25,000.

```
SELECT EMPNUMB
FROM EMPLOYEE
WHERE   (SALARY < 25000)
AND ((WHNUMB = 'WH1') OR (WHNUMB = 'WH2'))
```

The response would be:

```
E1
E2
```

Care has to be taken with more complex logical expressions. The **EMPNUM** value is selected from an **EMPLOYEE** record only if the expression (**SALARY** < **25000**) is true *and* either (**WHNUMB** = 'WH1') or (**WHNUMB** = 'WH2') is also true.

The SQL retrieval mechanism

The system (Figure 7.3) uses sophisticated procedures to carry out a retrieval request specified in an SQL expression, and for the most part the method of generating these procedures is beyond the scope of this book. However, readers can conveniently visualize the process as follows.

Assuming that there is only one relation specified after **FROM** (as has been the case so far), then the system can be imagined as checking each record of the relation in turn in ascending primary key sequence. If the record currently under investigation satisfies what is specified in the **WHERE** clause, then it is selected, and the values in the fields specified after **SELECT** are displayed.

A slight variation of this visualization may be employed by the user when fields from more than one relation are to be retrieved. We now look at such a retrieval.

Retrieval-6: Retrieval data in two relations

Find the employee numbers for employees earning more than $22,000, and the cities in which these employees work.

```
SELECT EMPNUMB, CITY
FROM EMPLOYEE, WAREHOUSE
WHERE (SALARY > 23000) AND (EMPLOYEE.WHNUMB = WAREHOUSE.WHNUMB)
```

The response is:

```
E4    NEW YORK
E7    DALLAS
```

There are two ways to look at the retrieval procedure here. In the first way of looking at it, if there are two relations following **FROM** in the retrieval expression, then these two relations have to have a relationship between them otherwise the expression would make no sense. We know that in this case there is a one-to-many relationship between the relations **WAREHOUSE** and **EMPLOYEE**. In such cases we can visualize the system checking through *each record of the child relation*, in this case the **EMPLOYEE** relation, to see if it is acceptable. Acceptability depends on whether the fields in the child record and the fields of its parent record satisfy the logical expressions following **WHERE**. (In this retrieval we specify the child-parent relationship by equating the connection fields.) If a child record is acceptable, then the specified field from this record, together with the specified field from its parent record, is displayed.[1]

The other way of looking at it is much more in the spirit of the relational approach. We imagine that a new relation (which we shall call **WAREHOUSE-EMPLOYEE** is created temporarily by the system from the two relations **WAREHOUSE** and **EMPLOYEE**. It does this by replacing the connection field value **WHNUMB** in each **EMPLOYEE** record, as illustrated in Figure 7.4. This process is called a *natural join* (as described in the supplement to Chapter 8.) Anyway, the effect of the natural join is to generate a new relation where each record describes an employee *and* the warehouse he or she works in. The system can now scan through this relation, record by record, extracting the fields from those records that satisfy the conditions that follow **WHERE**. We emphasize that this is only a way for the user to visualize the retrieval process; in practice it is unlikely that a system would do it in exactly this manner, as it would involve far two many disk accesses and thus be far too slow.

---

[1]Note that in SQL expression **WAREHOUSE.WHNUMB** means the **WHNUMB** field of the **WARE-HOUSE** record under consideration.

WHNUMB	CITY	WH–AREA	EMPNUMB	SALARY
WH2	NEW YORK	50,000	E1	22,000
WH1	DALLAS	37,000	E3	21,000
WH2	NEW YORK	50,000	E4	25,000
WH3	CHICAGO	20,000	E6	23,000
WH1	DALLAS	37,000	E7	25,000

WAREHOUSE–EMPLOYEE

FIGURE 7.4 The imaginary relation WAREHOUSE-EMPLOYEE is formed by joining together the relations EMPLOYEE and WAREHOUSE from Figure 7.1. To make the join, we use each EMPLOYEE record for which we replace the child connection field WHNUMB by the fields of the WAREHOUSE record with the same WHNUMB value. This process is called a natural join, and the fields WHNUMB in WAREHOUSE and WHNUMB in EMPLOYEE are called the join fields.

We give one further example involving retrieval of information from two relations.

Retrieval-7: Retrieval data in two relations
Find the employee numbers of employees who work in warehouses bigger than 40,000 units, and find also the cities in which these employees work.

```
SELECT EMPNUMB, CITY
FROM EMPLOYEE, WAREHOUSE
WHERE (WH-AREA > 40000) AND (EMPLOYEE.WHNUMB = WAREHOUSE.WHNUMB)
```

The response is:

```
E1
E4
```

As with the previous retrieval, we can imagine that the system scans through the **EMPLOYEE** relation examining each record in turn for compliance with the **WHERE** condition in the expression. However, to determine if the **WHERE** condition is satisfied, the system must check the parent **WAREHOUSE** record of the **EMPLOYEE** record under consideration. Alternatively, we can imagine that the system scans through the derived relation **WAREHOUSE-EMPLOYEE** in Figure 7.4. Note that either way we must equate the connection fields in the expression.

Structure of SQL expressions with nested SELECT-FROM-WHERE blocks

We shall examine first the case where we have a SELECT-FROM-WHERE block containing a second or nested SELECT-FROM-WHERE block. We saw earlier that a SELECT-FROM-WHERE block has the structure:

> SELECT *fieldname, fieldname, . . .*
> FROM *relation, relation, . . .*
> WHERE *logical-expression* AND/OR *logical-expression* AND/OR . . .

and it is clear that everything that follows WHERE is a condition that is either true or false. Indeed we have had a WHERE clause involving AND and OR in Retrieval-5. The WHERE clause in that case was

```
WHERE (SALARY 25000 ) AND ((WHNUMB = 'WH1') OR (WHNUMB = 'WH2'))
```

and each of the logical expressions so far inserted into SQL expressions involved field values from records belonging to the relations specified after FROM, that is, from the records being considered for possible retrieval.

However, when the condition for retrieval of a record in the relation X depends on the value of fields in records of a related relation Y, the records of which are not being retrieved, then we use a nested SELECT-FROM-WHERE block within a logical expression. The complete structure of an SQL expression can therefore be given as:

> SELECT *fieldname, fieldname, . . .*
> FROM *relation*
> WHERE *logical-expression-1* AND/OR *logical-expression-1* AND/OR . . .
> AND/OR *logical-expression-2* AND/OR *logical-expression-2* AND/OR . . .

Thus we have two types of logical expression, namely, *logical-expression-1*, which is what we have had in Retrieval-1 through Retrieval-7, and *logical-expression-2*, which is an expression containing a further SELECT-FROM-WHERE block.

There is more than one way to construct *logical-expression-2*, and we start with the two constructs that are the easiest to use:

1. *field* IS IN *SELECT-FROM-WHERE block*, or
   field IS NOT IN *SELECT-FROM-WHERE block*.
2. EXISTS *SELECT-FROM-WHERE block*, or
   NOT EXISTS *SELECT-FROM-WHERE block*.

We shall give an additional construct later. Note that since an SQL expression (given above) and a SELECT-FROM-WHERE block have exactly the same structure, not only can a logical expression in an SQL expression contain a nested SELECT-FROM-WHERE block, but that nested SELECT-FROM-WHERE block can in turn contain a logical expression that contains a SELECT-FROM-WHERE block, and so on. Thus, quite complex SQL expressions can be generated.

We begin with some examples involving a single-nested SELECTED-FROM-WHERE block. Refer to Figure 7.1.

Retrieval-8: Use of IS IN

In what cities is there at least one warehouse employee making $25,000?

```
SELECT CITY
FROM WAREHOUSE
WHERE  WHNUMB  IS IN  (SELECT WHNUMB
                       FROM EMPLOYEE
                       WHERE (SALARY = 25000))
```

The response is:

```
DALLAS
NEW YORK
```

We see that the expression contains two **SELECT-FROM-WHERE** blocks, namely, an outer block and an inner block. To understand the expression, it is best to start by looking at the inner block as a complete SQL expression and so evaluate what it would retrieve if it were. This would be the following list of **WHNUMB** values:

```
WH2
WH1
```

which are the warehouse numbers for warehouses with an employee earning $25,000. So the expression above is really the same as:

```
SELECT CITY
FROM WAREHOUSE
WHERE WHNUMB IS IN ('WH2','WH1')
```

Incidently this is also a valid SQL expression; it is requesting the **CITY** value from each **WAREHOUSE** record with a **WHNUMB** value in the list ('WH2', 'WH1'), that is, with a **WHNUMB** value in that list of **WHNUMB** values from warehouses with an employee earning $25,000.

The method of expressing a relationship in a retrieval expression using **IS IN** followed by a **SELECT-FROM-WHERE** block does not come naturally to most users. However, it does bring out the essence of the relational approach. Relationships are not explicitly specified in a relational conceptual schema, but instead are specified in manipulation language (for example, SQL) expressions by equating the parent and child connection field values for each one-to-many relationship used in the expression. However, it can be argued that the method is not all that awkward for the average user. For example, we could rewrite the retrieval request as:

Retrieve each city with a warehouse that is among those warehouses with at least one employee earning $25,000.

and the structure of this sentence corresponds fairly closely to the structure of the SQL expression using **IS IN**. Perhaps **IS IN** should be changed to **IS AMONG**!

Retrieval-9: Use of IS NOT IN

What is the floor area of those warehouses in which the employees all make more than $21,000?

Before trying to write the SQL expression, we should point out that the request can be rewritten:

What is the floor area of those warehouses in which there is no employee making $21,000 or less?

We can do this because of the interplay between the natural quantifier "for all," or "for each," and the natural quantifier "there is not," or "there is no" or "there does not exist," and so on. If we state that for each dollar bill the color is green, that is the same as saying that there is no dollar bill for which the color is not green.

We can further rewrite the above request to more closely mirror the structure of an SQL expression using **IS NOT IN**:

Retrieve each floor area for a warehouse that is not among those warehouses with employees making $21,000 or less.

The SQL expression is:

```
SELECT WH-AREA
FROM WAREHOUSE
WHERE  WHNUMB  IS NOT IN (SELECT WHNUMB
                          FROM EMPLOYEE
                          WHERE (SALARY > = 21000))
```

and the response is:

```
50,000
20,000
```

The inner **SELECT-FROM-WHERE** block specifies the set of **WHNUMB** values for warehouses that have an employee earning $21,000 or less, and this set contains the sole element 'WH1'. We then retrieve from **WAREHOUSE** the **WH-AREA** value from each record whose **WHNUMB** value is not in this set.

Thus the retrieval appears to be reasonably straightforward. However, there is a fundamental subtlety that shows up in this retrieval, and which is quite common in SQL expressions of this type. If the user is not aware of this subtlety, wrong information can be retrieved.

It should always be remembered that big data bases in large enterprises can contain data that is important for the welfare of individuals, organizations, and in times of national emergency, even nations. The possibility that a decision maker could easily retrieve incorrect information must therefore be investigated seriously.

To understand what could go wrong with the above retrieval, let us suppose that there has been inserted an additional record in the **WAREHOUSE** relation, as shown in Figure 7.5. The new record describes a warehouse ('WH5') in Denver. For this record there are as yet no employees (we may assume that it has just

WHNUMB	CITY	WH-AREA
WH1	DALLAS	37,000
WH2	NEW YORK	50,000
WH3	CHICAGO	37,000
WH5	DENVER	13,000

WAREHOUSE

WHNUMB	EMPNUMB	SALARY
WH2	E1	22,000
WH1	E3	21,000
WH2	E4	25,000
WH3	E6	23,000
WH1	E7	25,000

EMPLOYEE

FIGURE 7.5 Shows the relations WAREHOUSE and EMPLOYEE after a new record (with key 'WH5') has been placed in WAREHOUSE. The warehouse described by the new record has no employees listed in the EMPLOYEE relation. Unless care is taken, SQL will often retrieve fields from such a record, although such retrieval may not be intended by the user.

recently been acquired), so that there are no **EMPLOYEE** records with the child connection key value 'WH5'. If the above SQL expression is applied to the data base in Figure 7.5, the response will be:

        50,000
        20,000
        13,000

so that the floor area of our new warehouse is retrieved, even though it has no employees at all.

To see how this comes about, we must examine the logic of the SQL expression carefully. We must also remember that SQL has its roots in the theory of mathematical sets, to which the strict rules of logic apply. Looking at the inner **SELECT-FROM-WHERE** block, we see that it still specifies the set of **WHNUMB** values ('WH1'), giving the warehouses whose employees do not all make more than $21,000. Accordingly, when the SQL expression specifies retrieval of the **WH-AREA** value in each **WAREHOUSE** record whose **WHNUMB** value **IS NOT IN** this set of **WHNUMB** values, we are in effect specifying that it is acceptable to retrieve a **WH-AREA** value from a **WAREHOUSE** record, provided the warehouse does not have employees who earn $21,000 or less. Thus it is acceptable for a warehouse to have no employees at all—there simply must not be employees earning $21,000 or less.

Thus the retrieval request specified by the SQL expression is really:

What is the floor area of warehouses whose employees (if there are any employees) all earn more than $21,000?

and this will in many cases not be what was intended by the original request. What would probably have been intended is:

What is the floor area of each warehouse that (1) has one or more employees, who (2) all earn more than $21,000.

With this request we are quite clearly specifying that we are not interested in warehouses that have no employees. There is no problem about SQL's capability of expressing this more exact request. SQL is very powerful. (In fact it is said to be *relationally complete*, that is, if the data is in the data base, then an SQL expression can be constructed to get it out, provided the required data is not obtained by means of computations on the data in the data base). Unfortunately the required expression is more complex and involves two different nested **SELECT-FROM-WHERE** blocks. Referring back to the structure of an SQL expression, we need an expression with the following structure:

SELECT *field*
FROM *relation*
WHERE *logical-expression-1* **AND** *logical-expression-2*

The necessary SQL expression is:

```
SELECT WH-AREA
FROM WAREHOUSE
WHERE    WHNUMB   IS IN (SELECT WHNUMB
                              FROM EMPLOYEE)
AND   WHNUMB   IS NOT IN (SELECT WHNUMB
                          FROM EMPLOYEE
                          WHERE (SALARY   = 21000))
```

If the expression were applied to the data base in Figure 7.5, the response would be:

```
50,000
20,000
```

By means of the first inner **SELECT-FROM-WHERE** block, we are stating that a **WAREHOUSE** record is acceptable only if its **WHNUMB** value occurs in the **EMPLOYEE** relation, that is, if the warehouse described has employees listed in the **EMPLOYEE** relation. By means of the second inner **SELECT-FROM-WHERE** block, we are stating that a warehouse record is acceptable if in addition it has a **WHNUMB** value that is not in the set of **WHNUMB** values for warehouses with employees earning $21,000 or less.

It should thus be clear that SQL is not all that easy to use with more sophisticated retrievals. Readers who have studied SQL/N in Chapter 6 will probably be able to see that one of the difficulties is that SQL does not have the broad range of quantifiers available in SQL/N and English. It is these quantifiers that the writer of precise English sentences uses to avoid the logical difficulties encountered with Retrieval-9.

For readers who have studied SQL/N, we now show how Retrieval-9 would be handled in that language. Readers who have not studied SQL/N should skip to Retrieval-10.

Use of SQL/N with Retrieval-9
As we have seen, there are two ways in which the retrieval could be interpreted, and we shall give the SQL/N expression for each interpretation.

FIRST INTERPRETATION.   *What is the floor area of warehouses whose employees (if there are any employees) all earn more than $21,000?*

```
SELECT  WH-AREA
FROM WAREHOUSE
WHERE (FOR EACH IF ANY EMPLOYEE MEMBER RECORD
        (SALARY > 21000)
```

The quantifier **FOR EACH** or **FOR ALL** in SQL/N is the same as **FOR EACH IF ANY** or **FOR ALL IF ANY**, meaning the logical expression is to be tested as true only if there are any **EMPLOYEE** member records.

The response for the data base in Figure 7.5 is:

```
50,000
20,000
13,000
```

SECOND INTERPRETATION.   *What is the floor area of warehouses that each have one or more employees, all of whom earn more than $21,000?*

```
SELECT WH-AREA
FROM WAREHOUSE
WHERE (FOR ONE AND ALL EMPLOYEE MEMBER RECORDS
        (SALARY > 21000)
```

Here we are stating that we wish to retrieve a **WAREHOUSE** parent record, provided there is one **EMPLOYEE** child with **SALARY** greater than $21,000, and provided all child **EMPLOYEE** records have a **SALARY** value greater than $21,000. This can be concisely specified using the natural quantifier FOR ONE AND ALL.

The response for the data base in Figure 7.5 is

```
50,000
20,000
```

At risk of tiring the reader with the ins and outs of Retrieval-9, the SQL quantifier **EXISTS** can be used to replace **IS IN**, as indicated earlier in the structure of logical-expression-2.

Retrieval-10: Use of quantifier EXISTS with Retrieval-9
We shall make use of the quantifier **EXISTS** with the two interpretations of Retrieval-9.

FIRST INTERPRETATION.   *What is the floor area of warehouses whose employees (if there are any employees) all earn more than $21,000?*

```
SELECT WH-AREA
FROM WAREHOUSE
WHERE  NOT EXISTS (SELECT *
                   FROM EMPLOYEE
                   WHERE (SALARY < = 21,000)
                   AND (EMPLOYEE.WHNUMB = WAREHOUSE.WHNUMB)
```

Referring to the data base in Figure 7.5, the response is:

50,000
20,000
13,000

To understand the expression, refer to Figure 7.6. We scan through the WAREHOUSE relation, examining each record in turn for acceptability. For each WAREHOUSE record we may imagine that the system then examines the records specified by the inner SELECT-FROM-WHERE block. This group of EMPLOYEE records should not exist, that is, the set of records specified should be empty for the WAREHOUSE record being examined to be acceptable.

It is worth examining the inner SELECT-FROM-WHERE block more closely. It specifies those EMPLOYEE records whose child connection field matches the parent connection key for the WAREHOUSE record being examined, and whose SALARY field value is less than or equal to $21,000. In other words it is specifying the child EMPLOYEE records (of the WAREHOUSE record being examined) that have a SALARY field less than or equal to $21,000. (Thus in an indirect manner it is a specification of the members of an owner-coupled set occurrence

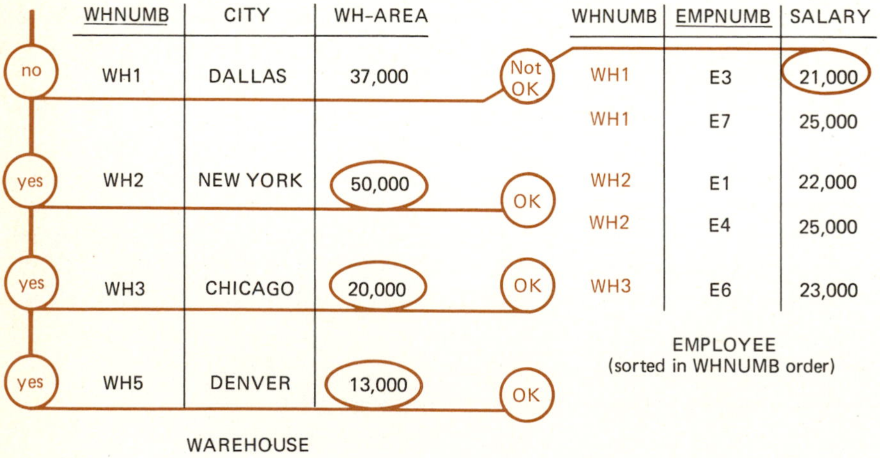

FIGURE 7.6 Shows how an SQL expression using NOT EXISTS for the first interpretation of Retrieval-9 can usefully be imagined to be executed by the relational data base system. For each WAREHOUSE record, the system checks the child EMPLOYEE records, if there are any.

that is being used, and we could use the SQL/N quantifier **THERE ARE NO** to mirror the above expression:

```
SELECT WH-AREA
FROM  WAREHOUSE
WHERE (THERE ARE NO EMPLOYEE MEMBER RECORDS
        WHERE (SALARY < = 21000))
```

Note that this is an SQL/N, not an SQL, expression.)

SECOND INTERPRETATION.   *What is the floor area of warehouses that each have one or more employees, all of whom earn more than $21,000?*

```
SELECT WH-AREA
FROM WAREHOUSE
WHERE  EXISTS (SELECT *
                FROM EMPLOYEE
                WHERE (EMPLOYEE.WHNUMB = WAREHOUSE.WHNUMB))
AND      NOT EXISTS (SELECT *
                FROM EMPLOYEE
                WHERE (SALARY < = 21000)
                    AND (EMPLOYEE.WHNUMB = WAREHOUSE.WHNUMB))[1]
```

With the data base in Figure 7.5 (or Figure 7.6) the response is:

```
50,000
20,000
```

To see how the expression is constructed, refer to Figure 7.6. We scan through the **WAREHOUSE** relation, checking each record in turn for acceptability. For each **WAREHOUSE** record, we check to see if there are child **EMPLOYEE** records, as specified in the first inner **SELECT-FROM-WHERE** block. We also check to see that there is no **EMPLOYEE** child record with the **SALARY** field value less than or equal to $21,000. If these conditions are met, then the **WH-AREA** field is selected from the **WAREHOUSE** record being examined.

Retrieval-11: Use of IS IN or EXISTS
What cities have a warehouse that is larger than 30,000 units in floor area and has at least one employee earning exactly $25,000?

```
SELECT CITY
FROM WAREHOUSE
WHERE (WH-AREA > 30,000)
    AND WHNUMB IS IN (SELECT WHNUMB
                        FROM  EMPLOYEE
                        WHERE (SALARY = 25000))
```

---

[1]In an SQL expression, EMPLOYEE.WHNUMB means a WHNUMB field value from an EMPLOYEE record.

The response is:

```
DALLAS
NEW YORK
```

Referring to Figure 7.5 (Figure 7.6 would perhaps do as well), we scan through the WAREHOUSE relation, selecting for examination those WARE-HOUSE records that have a WH-AREA field value greater than $30,000. For each of these selected WAREHOUSE records, we check to see if the WHNUMB field value is to be found in the list of WHNUMB values for EMPLOYEE records with SALARY field value equal to $25,000. The CITY value is taken from WARE-HOUSE records that pass this examination.

The structure of the above expression involves the use of logical-expression-1 and logical-expression-2 following WHERE. We recall that the general structure of the WHERE clause is:

WHERE *logical-expression-1* AND/OR *logical-expression-1* AND/OR . . .
    AND *logical-expression-2* AND/OR . . .

Logical-expression-2 involves a nested SELECT-FROM-WHERE block.

The quantifier EXISTS can always be used in place of IS IN with a minor modification to the inner SELECT-FROM-WHERE block:

```
SELECT CITY
FROM WAREHOUSE
WHERE (WH-AREA > 30000)
   AND EXISTS (SELECT *
                 FROM EMPLOYEE
WHERE (SALARY = 25,000)
   AND (EMPLOYEE.WHNUMB = WAREHOUSE.WHNUMB))
```

Use Figure 7.6 to see how the expression works. Whenever we use EXISTS, we are in effect specifying the members of owner-coupled set occurrences. Thus for each WAREHOUSE record that has the required WH-AREA value, we check the child EMPLOYEE records to see if there is one that has a SALARY value exactly equal to $25,000.

Retrieval-12: Use of EXISTS and IS IN
What employees making more than $22,000 work in Dallas?

```
SELECT EMPNUMB
FROM EMPLOYEE
WHERE (SALARY > 22000)
   AND WHNUMB IS IN (SELECT WHNUMB
                       FROM WAREHOUSE
                       WHERE (CITY = 'DALLAS'))
```

The response would be:

```
E7
```

The expression has no new features as structure is concerned. However, we are seeking child **EMPLOYEE** records depending on a property of a parent **WAREHOUSE** record. In previous examples we sought parent **WAREHOUSE** records depending on properties of child **EMPLOYEE** records. We could use **EXISTS** instead of **IS IN**:

```
SELECT EMPNUMB
  FROM EMPLOYEE
   WHERE (SALARY > 22,000)
     AND EXISTS (SELECT *
                   FROM WAREHOUSE
                   WHERE (CITY = 'DALLAS')
                     AND (WHNUMB = EMPLOYEE.WHNUMB))
```

Elementary logic and SQL expressions

By now readers will certainly have concluded that the construction of SQL expressions requires a certain minimum proficiency in the use of logic. Fortunately, in the vast majority of expressions only elementary logic is required, but for the benefit of readers who are uncertain about what a logical expression is or about how such an expression can be evaluated, we now include a review of the subject. Readers who are comfortable with the type of logical expressions presented so far might well skip this section; however, they should note that it contains a brief discussion of logical expressions that contain elementary sets, which is what is specified in a **SELECT-FROM-WHERE** block and which is rarely included in discussions on elementary logic. Such expressions are of course central to SQL.

AND, OR, NOT, and the comparison operators

It is the comparison of two quantities that give rise to the simplest logical expressions. To symbolize the comparison operation, we use the comparison operators $=, \neg=, >, <, >=,$ and $<=$.[1] Thus we can have *simple logical expressions* where we know the logical value, for example:

(4 = 4)	Value **TRUE**
(5 = 4)	Value **FALSE**
(5 > 4)	Value **TRUE**
(5 $\neg$ = 4)	Value **TRUE**

and also simple logical expressions where we do not know the logical value until we have evaluated the value of each variable involved:

(X = 4)	Value **TRUE** or **FALSE** depending on value of **X**
(CITY = 'NEW YORK')	Value **TRUE** or **FALSE** depending on value of **CITY**
(SALARY = 20,000)	Value **TRUE** or **FALSE** depending on value of **SALARY**

---

[1] The symbol "$\neg$=" means "not equal to."

Simple logical expressions may be combined using the logical operators AND, OR, and NOT. Thus we may have the *compound logical expressions:*

```
( (CITY = 'NEW YORK')  AND  (WH-AREA < 40,000) )
( (CITY = 'DALLAS') OR (WH-AREA = 30,000))
(SALARY = 20,000) AND  NOT(WHNUMB = 'WH1')
```

With compound logical expressions involving three or more simple logical expressions, the parentheses affects the value of the expression. Thus,

```
( (3=2) AND (2=2) )   OR (9 > 6) is TRUE
(3=2)  AND  ( (2=2)  OR (9 > 6) ) is FALSE
```

Truth tables are often useful for evaluating logical expressions. Thus if L1 and L2 are logical expressions (we can best think of them as simple logical expressions), then for the logical expressions (L1 AND L2), (L1 OR L2), and NOT(L1) the following truth tables are valid:

L1	L2	L1 AND L2
TRUE	TRUE	TRUE
TRUE	FALSE	FALSE
FALSE	TRUE	FALSE
FALSE	FALSE	FALSE

L1	L2	L1 OR L2
TRUE	TRUE	TRUE
TRUE	FALSE	TRUE
FALSE	TRUE	TRUE
FALSE	FALSE	FALSE

L1	NOT(L1)
TRUE	FALSE
FALSE	TRUE

Thus the rule for logical-AND is that both L1 and L2 must be TRUE for the compound expression to be true, while with logical-OR either L1 or L2 must be TRUE for the compound expression to be true.

To evaluate a complex logical expression involving three or more simple logical expressions, we first evaluate what is inside the parentheses and then treat the result as another logical expression. For example, suppose that L1 is FALSE, L2 is TRUE, and L3 is TRUE; then:

```
(L1 AND L2) OR L3
```
Evaluates to FALSE OR L3, which is TRUE

However,

```
(L1 AND (L2 OR L3)
```
Evaluates to L1 AND TRUE, which is FALSE

Imperatives and predicates

An SQL expression contains both an imperative and a predicate, as do all relational retrieval languages and many other languages as well. The imperative states what must be done to a potential list of objects, while the predicate gives conditions that place restrictions on the selection of the objects to which the command will be applied. We have this in everyday English. Thus the investment manager might issue the order:

Acquire 1000 shares of any company that has a price/earnings ratio less than 8 and has its headquarters in Frankfurt.

The imperative is clearly:

Acquire 1000 shares of any company

The object of the imperative is any company, while the predicate is:

$$(P/E < 8) \quad AND \quad (HQ = 'FRANKFURT')$$

Predicates are always logical expressions, and in SQL the predicate follows the first instance of the word **WHERE** so that SQL really has the simple structure:

<u>SELECT</u> *objects* <u>WHERE</u> *predicate*

The predicate in SQL may be a simple logical expression as in:

```
SELECT EMPNUMB
FROM EMPLOYEE
WHERE (SALARY = 25,000)
```

or it may be a complex or compound logical expression:

```
SELECT EMPNUMB
 FROM  EMPLOYEE
WHERE ((SALARY = 25,000) OR (SALARY = 22,000))
        AND (WHNUMB = 'WH1')
```

But regardless of how complex the predicate is, an **EMPNUMB** value will be selected only from **EMPLOYEE** tuples for which the predicate is **TRUE**.

But we have seen that we can have nested **SELECT-FROM-WHERE** blocks following **WHERE**, so that these nested blocks must be part of the predicate. Since we have also seen that a predicate is a logical expression constructed from simpler logical expressions, the question most students of the subject sooner or later get around to asking is: Is a **SELECT-FROM-WHERE** block itself a logical expression? The answer is most certainly not, and treating such blocks as logical expressions is a very common error among SQL beginners. Thus the expression:

```
SELECT CITY
FROM WAREHOUSE
WHERE (SELECT WHNUMB
        FROM EMPLOYEE
        WHERE (SALARY = 20000))
```

is *complete nonsense*, for what follows **WHERE** is not a logical expression. We must therefore examine more closely what constitutes a simple logical expression when a **SELECT-FROM-WHERE** block is involved.

Simple logical expressions and SELECT-FROM-WHERE blocks

We saw previously (page 267) that the well-known comparison operators are commonly used to form simple logical expressions. However, there are other ways of making up a simple logical expression. The most important of these are (1) membership in a group or set of elements, (2) existence of a certain quantity of elements, and (3) comparison of two different groups or sets of elements. We take them in turn.

1. MEMBERSHIP IN A SET OF ELEMENTS. Suppose we have a set (**A**) of elements such as persons:

```
        'SMITH', BROWN,' 'GREEN,' 'BLACK', WHITE'
```
then
```
( 'BROWN' IS IN THE  SET
  ('SMITH', 'BROWN', 'GREEN', 'BLACK', 'WHITE') )
```

is also a simple logical expression that in this case is TRUE. If we state:
```
(PERSON IS NOT IN
  ('SMITH', 'BROWN', 'GREEN', 'BLACK', 'WHITE') )
```

this is also a simple logical expression that is either TRUE or FALSE depending on the value in the variable PERSON. Also
```
(PERSON IS IN A)
```

is TRUE or FALSE depending on what is the value of the variable PERSON and the set of values in the set A. However, it is a set of values that is specified by a SELECT-FROM-WHERE block, so that the following is also a simple logical expression:
```
(WHNUMB   IS IN  (SELECT WHNUMB
                  FROM EMPLOYEE
                  WHERE (SALARY = 20000 ) )
```

and is either TRUE or FALSE. In SQL, simple logical expressions of this type can be combined with conventional logical expressions to give compound expressions such as:
```
(CITY = 'DALLAS)   AND   (WHNUMB  IS IN   (SELECT WHNUMB
                                           FROM EMPLOYEE
                                           WHERE (SALARY = 20000)))
```

Any compound logical expression of this type can be used to form the predicate in the basic SQL expression:

SELECT *object* WHERE *predicate*

2. EXISTENCE OF CERTAIN QUANTITIES OF ELEMENTS.   Suppose we have a set or group (A) of person elements as in (1) above. Then
```
(THERE EXISTS AT LEAST ONE ('SMITH', 'BROWN','GREEN',
                            'BLACK', 'WHITE') ELEMENT)
```
is a logical expression, which in this case is clearly TRUE. If we state:
```
(THERE EXISTS AT LEAST ONE A ELEMENT)
```
or just (EXISTS A) for short, then this is clearly also a simple logical expression that will be TRUE or FALSE depending on whether A contains any elements. However, as we have seen, a SELECT-FROM-WHERE block is a specification of a

set of elements, that is, a set of external records. Thus

```
(EXISTS (SELECT *
         FROM EMPLOYEE
         WHERE ((SALARY = 25,000)
         AND (WHNUMB = WAREHOUSE.WHNUMB))))
```

is another kind of simple logical expression and will have the value **TRUE** if the **SELECT-FROM-WHERE** block specifies or "retrieves" any records; otherwise it will have the value **FALSE**. As in the case of **IS IN** logical expressions, this type of simple logical expression may be used in the construction of more involved logical expressions that can serve ás SQL predicates.

3. COMPARISON OF SETS OF ELEMENTS. A simple logical expression can also be constructed by comparing the size and contents of two sets of elements. Suppose that we have the sets:

set A: ('SMITH','BROWN", 'GREEN')
set B: ('BROWN', 'GREEN', 'SMITH')
set C: ('SMITH', 'GREEN', 'JONES', 'BROWN')
set D: ('BROWN', 'GREEN')

Then the logical expression (A = B) is **TRUE**, the logical expression D ≠ B is **TRUE**, (C = D) is **FALSE**, (C CONTAINS A) is **TRUE**, (B CONTAINS D) is **TRUE**, (A DOES NOT CONTAIN C) is **TRUE**, and so on.

It will come as no surprise to the reader that SQL permits logical expressions of this type, where at least one of the sets of elements involved is a **SELECT-FROM-WHERE**-block. Many of the simple logical expressions that are possible have the syntax:

(*S-F-W-block* = *S-F-W-block*)
(*S-F-W-block* ⌐= *S-F-W-block*)
(*variable* = *S-F-W-block*) That is, there is only one element in the S-F-W block.
(*variable* ⌐= *S-F-W-block*) Again, only one element in the S-F-W-block.
(*S-F-W-block* **CONTAINS** *S-F-W-block*)
(*S-F-W-block* **DOES NOT CONTAIN** *S-F-W-block*)
(*set* **CONTAINS** *S-F-W-block*)
(*set* **DOES NOT CONTAIN** *S-F-W-block*)
(*S-F-W-block* **CONTAINS** *set*)
(*S-F-W-block* **DOES NOT CONTAIN** *set*)
(*set* = *S-F-W-block*)
(*set* ⌐= *S-F-W-block*)

It turns out that this type of simple logical expression is needed mainly in more complicated or perhaps even more subtle retrievals. We shall look at some retrievals involving them next.

SQL expressions involving comparison of sets of elements

The retrieval examples presented here are slightly more difficult than those presented earlier, and readers interested in a more cursory treatment of SQL could conveniently skip these examples.

Retrieval-13: Single-element-set comparison

Find the employees earning the same salary as employee 'E4'.

We could rephrase this as: Find each employee that has a salary equal to the salary of employee 'E4'.

```
SELECT EMPNUMB
FROM EMPLOYEE
WHERE  SALARY = (SELECT  SALARY
                   FROM EMPLOYEE
                   WHERE EMPNUMB = 'E4')
```

With the data base in Figure 7.1 the response would be:

```
E4
E7
```

For every **EMPLOYEE** record examined, the set specified in the inner S-F-W-block is always a set with one element (25,000). Thus the expression retrieves the employee numbers of each employee earning $25,000.

The difficulty with expressions of this type lies not so much in the understanding of them but rather in their formulation. The structure of the above expression is not difficult either. Following **WHERE** we have a simple logical expression, as explained earlier.

Retrieval-14: Use of CONTAINS

Find the warehouses at which salaries of $21,000 and $25,000 are paid to employees.

```
SELECT WHNUMB
FROM  WAREHOUSE
WHERE (SELECT SALARY
        FROM EMPLOYEE
        WHERE (WNHUMB = WAREHOUSE.WHNUMB))
      CONTAINS
        (21000,  25000)
```

The response is:

```
WH1
```

When the **WAREHOUSE** record being investigated has key 'WH1', the set specified by the S-F-W-block is (21000, 25000), so that the **WHNUMB** value from this record can be selected. For all other **WAREHOUSE** records, the set of salary values specified by the S-F-W-block does not contain the specified set (21000, 25000).

We could use the **IS IN** type of logical expression for this retrieval. However, the following expression, which at first glance might seem reasonable, *is incorrect:*

```
SELECT WHNUMB
FROM WAREHOUSE
WHERE WHNUMB IS IN (SELECT WHNUMB
                    FROM EMPLOYEE
                    WHERE ((SALARY = 21000)
                        OR (SALARY = 25000))
```

It would retrieve:

```
WH1
WH2
```

Readers should attempt to construct a correct SQL expression that uses **IS IN** logical expressions.

Retrieval-15: Use of CONTAINS with Retrieval-9

We recall that this retrieval had two interpretations. We take only the first interpretation:

What is the floor area of warehouses whose employees (if there are any employees) all earn more than $21,000?

```
SELECT WH-AREA
FROM WAREHOUSE
WHERE (SELECT EMPNUMB
        FROM EMPLOYEE
        WHERE (SALARY > 21000))
CONTAINS
        (SELECT EMPNUMB
        FROM EMPLOYEE
        WHERE (WHNUMB = WAREHOUSE.WHNUMB))
```

The response with the data base in Figure 7.5 is:

```
50,000
20,000
13,000
```

To understand how this expression works, consider the second nested S-F-W-block. It in effect specifies the list of **EMPNUMB** values for the child **EMPLOYEE** records of the **WAREHOUSE** record being examined. These **EMPNUMB** values must be from **EMPLOYEE** records that all have a **SALARY** value greater than $21,000. Thus they must be a subset of, or be contained in, the **EMPNUMB** values from all **EMPLOYEE** records with the **SALARY** value greater than $21,000, and it is this set of **EMPNUMB** values that is specified by the first nested S-F-W-block. The set is always:

```
('E1', 'E4', 'E6', 'E7')
```

In order for the **WAREHOUSE** record with key 'WH2' to be retrieved, the above set must contain the **EMPNUMB** values from that **WAREHOUSE** record's child **EMPLOYEE** records, that is, it must contain the set ('E1', 'E4'). We see that it does, and so the record with key 'WH2' is retrieved and the **WH-AREA** value is extracted from it. Notice that the **WH-AREA** value from the record with key 'WH5' is also retrieved. As we might expect, the reason this time will again tell us a great deal about the fundamental nature of SQL.

When the **WAREHOUSE** record being examined for possible retrieval has the key value 'WH5', that is, a record with zero child **EMPLOYEE** records, the set specified by the first S-F-W-block is still

```
('E1', 'E4', 'E6', 'E7')
```

However, the set specified by the second S-F-W-block is now empty, since the **WAREHOUSE** record involved has no child records in **EMPLOYEE**. The logical expression:

```
('E1', 'E4', 'E6', 'E7')   CONTAINS ( )
```

is **TRUE**, since any set contains a null or empty set. Thus the **WAREHOUSE** record with key 'WH5' will be retrieved.

It seems unlikely that users would prefer the use of **CONTAINS** in retrievals of this type. Use of **IS NOT IN** appears to be more convenient.

Retrieval-16: Many-to-many relationships

What are the salaries of employees who have issued purchase orders to all suppliers?

This request applies to the data base in Figures 7.7 and 7.8. For this data base we see that an employee (in the **EMPLOYEE** relation) deals with many suppliers (in the **SUPPLIER** relation), while a supplier deals with many employees. We had this in Chapter 5. The retrieval request is for those **EMPLOYEE** records for employees that deal with every supplier listed in the relation **SUPPLIER**. The SQL expression is:

```
SELECT SALARY
FROM EMPLOYEE
WHERE (SELECT SNUMB
        FROM PUR-ORDER
        WHERE (EMPNUMB = EMPLOYEE.EMPNUMB))
      =
      (SELECT SNUMB
      FROM  SUPPLIER)
```

The response is:

```
21,000
```

The second nested S-F-W-block contains the set of all the suppliers in the **SUPPLIER** relation. The first nested S-F-W-block contains the **SNUMB** values

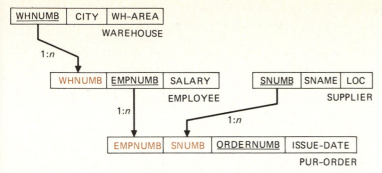

FIGURE 7.7 An external relational data base derived from the data base in Figure 5.19, which we assume has been defined as a relational conceptual data base. The data in this external data base is shown in Figure 7.8.

WHNUMB	CITY	WH-AREA
WH1	DALLAS	37,000
WH2	NEW YORK	50,000
WH3	CHICAGO	20,000
WH5	DENVER	13,000

WAREHOUSE

WHNUMB	EMPNUMB	SALARY
WH2	E1	22,000
WH1	E3	21,000
WH2	E4	25,000
WH3	E6	23,000
WH1	E7	25,000

EMPLOYEE

SNUMB	SNAME	LOC
S3	TRONOTON	CALIFORNIA
S4	ROBOTEK	TEXAS
S6	MIKREL	ONTARIO
S7	RAYTEX	TEXAS

SUPPLIER

EMPNUMB	SNUMB	ORDERNUMB	ISSUE-DATE
E3	S7	OR67	84/06/23
E1	S4	OR73	84/07/28
E7	S4	OR76	84/05/25
E6	S6	OR77	84/06/19
E3	S4	OR79	84/06/23
E1	S6	OR80	84/07/29
E3	S6	OR90	85/06/22
E3	S3	OR91	85/07/13

FIGURE 7.8 Contents of the external data base in Figure 7.7.

from the child **PUR-ORDER** records of the **EMPLOYEE** record under considera-tion, that is, the set of supplier numbers for the suppliers the employee under examination deals with. Suppose we are considering employee 'E3' for possible retrieval from the **EMPLOYEE** relation. From the child **PUR-ORDER** records we can determine that this employee deals with the suppliers ('S7', 'S4', 'S6', 'S3'). The complete list of supplier numbers taken from the **SUPPLIER** relation is ('S3', 'S4', 'S6', 'S7'). Thus the two sets are equal, so that employee 'E3' may be retrieved, giving $21,000 as the **SALARY** value.

It is possible to construct this expression using the **EXISTS** type of logical expression. However, the expression is complex and requires the nesting of a S-F-W-block within a nested S-F-W-block. It helps if we rewrite the request as:

Select the salary value for each employee for whom there is no supplier that he or she does not deal with.

```
SELECT SALARY
FROM EMPLOYEE
WHERE NOT EXISTS (SELECT *
                  FROM SUPPLIER
                  WHERE NOT EXISTS (SELECT *
                                    FROM PUR-ORDER
                                    WHERE (SNUMB = SUPPLIER.SNUMB)
                                    AND (EMPNUMB = EMPLOYEE.EMPNUMB)))
```

The expression is something of a brain-twister. Suppose we are checking an **EMPLOYEE** record for possible retrieval, and let us call this employee record X. Now let us attempt to specify or "retrieve" a **SUPPLIER** record for which no **PUR-ORDER** child record has the **EMPNUMB** value in X. Clearly, if there exists such a **SUPPLIER** record, then the employee described in X cannot possibly deal with all the suppliers described in the **SUPPLIER** relation.

Although this formulation is probably more difficult than the first one, the two expressions have in common that two nested S-F-W-blocks are needed. The observant reader should by now also have noticed the expressive power of the English language. Quite involved retrieval requests can often be simply ex-pressed in English in just one line or less, whereas corresponding expressions in SQL often require quite complex formulations. Retrieval-16 is almost a classic example of this, and similar retrievals with many-to-many relationships are frequently cited. A similar example with the data base in Figure 7.8 would be:

Find the locations of suppliers who deal with all employees.

and the reader should try it as an exercise.

More complex SQL expressions

Our remaining retrievals will involve further requests that are apparently simple but which involve quite complex SQL expressions. They could well be skipped by all except those who wish to perfect their knowledge of SQL.

Retrieval-17: Four relations

In what cities have orders been issued to California suppliers?

What we in fact wish to retrieve is each WAREHOUSE record that has at least one child EMPLOYEE record that has at least one child PUR-ORDER record that has a parent SUPPLIER record with LOC value equal to 'CALIFORNIA'. The SQL expression is:

```
SELECT CITY
FROM WAREHOUSE
WHERE WHNUMB IS IN (SELECT WHNUMB
                    FROM EMPLOYEE
                    WHERE EMPNUMB IS IN (SELECT EMPNUMB
                                         FROM PUR-ORDER
                                         WHERE SNUMB IS IN (SELECT
                                         SNUMB FROM SUPPLIER
                                         WHERE (LOC = 'CALIFORNIA'))))
```

For comparison purposes we give also the SQL/N expression:

```
SELECT CITY
FROM WAREHOUSE
WHERE (THERE IS AT LEAST ONE CHILD EMPLOYEE RECORD
WHERE (FOR AT LEAST ONE CHILD PUR-ORDER RECORD
       (THERE IS EXACTLY ONE PARENT SUPPLIER
        WHERE (LOC = 'CALIFORNIA'))))
```

Referring to Figure 7.8, the response would be:

```
DALLAS
```

Retrieval-18: Four relations

Give the names of Texas companies that have orders from Dallas warehouses.

What we are looking for here is each supplier that has at least one order from an employee from a warehouse in Dallas.

```
SELECT SNAME
FROM SUPPLIER
WHERE (LOC = 'TEXAS')
   AND SNUMB IS IN (SELECT SNUMB FROM PUR-ORDER

                    WHERE EMPNUMB IS IN
                    (SELECT EMPNUMB
                     FROM EMPLOYEE
                     WHERE WHNUMB IS IN (SELECT WHNUMB
                                         FROM WAREHOUSE
                                         WHERE (CITY = 'DALLAS'))))
```

The response is:

```
ROBOTEK
RAYTEX
```

Retrieval-19: Use of a label
Find the warehouses at which at least two different salaries are paid.

```
SELECT UNIQUE WHNUMB
FROM EMPLOYEE X-EMPLOYEE
WHERE WHNUMB IS IN (SELECT WHNUMB
                    FROM EMPLOYEE
                    WHERE (SALARY ⌐= X-EMPLOYEE.SALARY)
```

The response is:

```
WH2
WH1
```

SQL expressions that require the use of a label are among the most complex, but they do give a deeper understanding of the nature of SQL. Consider the imperative part of the expression first, and refer to Figure 7.8. We are asking SQL to scan through the records of **EMPLOYEE** and check each one for acceptability. Let us suppose that the scan has reached the first record, and that we are therefore interested in the check of the record:

```
WH2  E1  22,000
```

for acceptability. The requirements that this record must fulfill are specified in the predicate, but we have stated in the imperative part of the expression that we can refer to the record being checked as the **X-EMPLOYEE** record.

In the predicate we are stating that 'WH2' must be among the list of WHNUMB values taken from records that have a **SALARY** value different from $22,000, that is, different from the **SALARY** value in that record being checked, that is, the **X-EMPLOYEE** record. This list of WHNUMB values will be:

```
('WH1', 'WH2', 'WH3')
```

so that the predicate is **TRUE** and the first record of **EMPLOYEE** is acceptable, permitting its WHNUMB value 'WH2' to be extracted.

This whole procedure is repeated for the second record in **EMPLOYEE**, and so on. Note that there is a chance that duplicate WHNUMB values will be retrieved, so that a specification of UNIQUE is necessary.

Computational SQL retrievals

As mentioned earlier, SQL is relationally complete, that is, if the data is stored in the data base and can be specified as a relation, then it is possible to construct an SQL expression to get it out. It is important to understand that this definition of relational completeness does not include capability of retrieving:

1. Data that is not physically stored in the data base, but which can be calculated from data in the data base. An example would be the average salary of employees described in the **EMPLOYEE** relation.
2. Data for which a logical expression in the retrieval request predicate depends on data calculated from data in the data base. An example would be retrieval of the warehouse number of the warehouse with the best paid employee described in the **EMPLOYEE** relation; here the system would have to compute the maximum **SALARY** value before each **EMPLOYEE** record could be checked for compliance with the retrieval predicate.
3. Data that needs to be calculated from data in the data base as in (1), but which also depends on the result of other calculations as in (2). An example is retrieval of the average floor area of those warehouses whose employees all earn less than average.

Retrievals that require a computation in any of the ways described above are called *computational retrievals*. Where calculations are performed on the target of an SQL expression as in (1), the retrieval may be called a *target computational retrieval*. Where the target of the SQL expression depends on comparisons with the results of computations on data in the data base as in (2), the retrieval may be called a *predicate computational retrieval*. A retrieval that is both a target computational retrieval and a predicate computational retrieval, as in (3), is sometimes referred to as a *combined target and predicate computational retrieval*.

Computational retrievals are common and, as the use of data retrieval languages such as SQL becomes more widespread among management personnel, may well become more common than noncomputational retrievals. It is probably also true that the subject takes us beyond the realm of data base management and into the realm of decision support systems. We can identify two distinct methods of dealing with such retrievals:

1. *Use of computational functions in the retrieval language.* This method allows for the use of common functions in languages such as SQL. We shall give examples of the use of such functions later. The main functions are:

`COUNT(field)`	Counts the number of field values specified
`SUM(field)`	Sums the values of the fields specified
`AVG(field)`	Takes the average value of the fields specified
`MAX(field)`	Computes the maximum value in the fields specified
`MIN(field)`	Computes the minimum value in the fields specified

   It is clear that these functions are quite simple and will be of little help if the computations involved are complex.
2. *Application of independent data manipulation systems.* In the simplest case this method requires the application of a statistical package such as SPSS to the relations containing the data on which sophisticated statistical computations are required. A variation involves first narrowing down the amount of data to be fed to the statistical package; this can

be done by first applying SQL expressions to retrieve the data required for further processing.

When special calculations are involved, then programs that carry out the special calculations must be written or acquired. A collection of such programs that can carry out calculations in a special area is referred to today as a *decision support system*, especially if the programs involved can be run interactively from a terminal. Examples of decision support systems are:

(*a*) A market response system, for predicting product sales as a result of marketing efforts such as advertising. The data base would contain data about customers, past sales, competing products, and so on.

(*b*) An investment portfolio management system, for comparing portfolio performance with management goals and for predicting effects of portfolio changes.

Further analysis of the second method of dealing with computational retrievals is beyond the scope of this book. Readers are referred to Ref. 1. We now give some examples of the first method with SQL, beginning with target computational retrievals.

Retrieval-20: COUNT function
Find the number of supplier locations.

```
SELECT COUNT (UNIQUE LOC)
FROM  SUPPLIER
```

If we neglect the **COUNT** function, the expression retrieves:

```
CALIFORNIA
TEXAS
ONTARIO
```

The **COUNT** function then counts the number of these, and the result would be 3. Note that we must use **UNIQUE** with **COUNT** in current System R SQL, except when counting records.

```
SELECT COUNT (*)
FROM SUPPLIER
```

would count the number of records in **SUPPLIER** and thus give the number of suppliers.

Retrieval-21: SUM function
Find the total annual payroll.

```
SELECT SUM (SALARY)
FROM EMPLOYEE
```

This will cause all the **SALARY** values in the **EMPLOYEE** relation to be summed, whether duplicates or not. Note that in this case the expression

```
SELECT SUM (UNIQUE SALARY)
FROM EMPLOYEE
```

would be wrong, because duplicate salaries would not be included in the summation.

Retrieval-22: Sum function
Find the total annual payroll for Dallas and Chicago combined.

```
SELECT SUM (SALARY)
FROM EMPLOYEE
WHERE WHNUMB IS IN (SELECT WHNUMB
                    FROM WAREHOUSE
                    WHERE (CITY= 'DALLAS') OR (CITY = 'CHICAGO')
```

Again the **SALARY** values retrieved will contain duplicates, and all these values are summed by the **SUM** function.

Retrieval-23: AVE function
Find the average floor area of warehouses whose employees all make more than $21,000 annually (that is, none of whose employees make $21,000 or less).

```
SELECT AVE (WH-NUMB)
FROM WAREHOUSE
WHERE WNHUMB IS NOT IN (SELECT WHNUMB
                        FROM EMPLOYEE
                        WHERE (SALARY < = 21000))
```

The list of floor areas retrieved is:

```
50,000
20,000
```

and the average of this calculated. While it makes no difference with the data in **WAREHOUSE** (see Figure 7.8), insertion of **UNIQUE** before **WH-AREA** would be wrong in general. If two different warehouses have the same floor area, we would still want to include two equal areas in the computation of the average.

Retrieval-24: MAX function
Who makes the most at warehouse 'WH2'?

```
SELECT MAX (SALARY)
FROM EMPLOYEE
WHERE (WHNUMB = 'WH2')
```

The expression retrieves the **SALARY** values:

```
22,000
25,000
```

and produces the maximum value. Use of MIN instead of MAX would give the minimum value. Notice that with MAX and MIN it makes no difference whether or not UNIQUE is used. The maximum and minimum values of a list of values will be the same whether or not duplicates are present.

Retrieval-25: Computations on child records for each parent
What is the total payroll at each warehouse?

```
SELECT  WHNUMB, TOTPAY
FROM WAREHOUSE
WHERE TOTPAY = (SELECT SUM(SALARY)
                FROM EMPLOYEE
                WHERE (WHNUMB = WAREHOUSE.WHNUMB))
```

This retrieval requires close study. The first point is that we must imagine that each record in WAREHOUSE has an additional field TOTPAY (see Figure 7.9). A TOTPAY field contains no data, but it may be assigned data on the basis of a computation specified in a S-F-W-block. In the above expression we are requesting that the WHNUMB value and the TOTPAY value be retrieved for a WAREHOUSE record, provided the sum of the SALARY values in all child EMPLOYEE records are placed in or assigned to the TOTPAY field. The data retrieved is:

```
WH1    46,000
WH2    47,000
WH3    23,000
```

We could go about this retrieval differently, and begin by retrieving the WHNUMB and SALARY values from the EMPLOYEE relation alone, requesting that the retrieved data be ordered on WHNUMB value:

```
SELECT WHNUMB, SALARY
FROM EMPLOYEE
ORDER BY WHNUMB ASC
```

[This last line is new and merely requests that the resulting records be ordered in

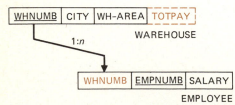

FIGURE 7.9 It can be convenient to imagine a summary field TOTPAY in WARE-HOUSE records. It does not exist, but for retrieval purposes we may imagine that data can be placed in it. In this case, TOTPAY in a WAREHOUSE record receives the sum of the SALARY values in its child EMPLOYEE records. (Note that if TOTPAY were a real field, then we could not update the SALARY field in an EMPLOYEE record without also updating the parent WAREHOUSE record.)

ascending (ASC) WHNUMB order. Use of DESC specifies descending order.] The result of this retrieval is:

```
WH1   21,000
WH1   25,000
WH2   22,000
WH2   25,000
WH3   23,000
```

where we have in effect partitioned the records according to WHNUMB value. Our ultimate aim is the sum of the SALARY values in each partition. We could now feed this data to an auxiliary program that would sum the SALARY values for each WHNUMB value. Ideally we need what has been called a *partitioned sum function* PSUM, where PSUM (A, B) sums each set of B values for a given A value. Thus ideally we could use the SQL expression:

```
SELECT PSUM(WHNUMB, SALARY)
FROM EMPLOYEE
ORDER BY WHNUMB ASC
```

to have the SALARY values summed for each WHNUMB value. Unfortunately, such a partitioned sum function is not currently available with SQL, although it may be available in the future. As well as a partitioned sum function, we could have a partitioned average function PAVE, a partitioned count function PCOUNT, and partitioned maximum and minimum functions PMAX and PMIN.

Retrieval-26: Computations on child records for each parent
What is the largest salary at each warehouse?

```
SELECT WHNUMB, LARPAY
FROM WAREHOUSE
WHERE LARPAY = (SELECT MAX(SALARY)
               FROM EMPLOYEE
               WHERE (WHNUMB = WAREHOUSE.WHNUMB)
```

The expression has exactly the same structure as the previous one. This time, however, an auxiliary and imaginary WAREHOUSE field called LARPAY is assigned the maximum value of the SALARY field in a group of child EMPLOYEE records. Thus we retrieve:

```
WH1   25,000
WH2   25,000
WH3   23,000
```

Were a partitioned maximum function available, a much simpler expression would be possible:

```
SELECT PMAX(WHNUMB, SALARY)
FROM EMPLOYEE
ORDER BY WHNUMB ASC
```

Retrieval-27: Predicate computation with the AVE function

In what cities is there a warehouse whose employees have an average salary greater than $23,000?

```
SELECT UNIQUE CITY
FROM WAREHOUSE
WHERE 23000  <  (SELECT AVE (SALARY)
                 FROM EMPLOYEE
                 WHERE (WHNUMB = WAREHOUSE.WHNUMB))
```

Here we perform no computations on the data retrieved, but a computation is specified in an inner S-F-W-block, which specifies or "retrieves" the average salary for the child **EMPLOYEE** records for the **WAREHOUSE** record being considered for retrieval. The response is:

```
WH2
```

Retrieval-28: Predicate computation with the SUM function

Find the warehouses with a floor area greater than 30,000 units that have a payroll exceeding $46,000.

```
SELECT WHNUMB
FROM WAREHOUSE
WHERE (WH-AREA > 30000)
   AND  46000  <  (SELECT SUM (SALARY)
                   FROM EMPLOYEE
                   WHERE (WHNUMB = WAREHOUSE.WHNUMB)
```

The response is:

```
WH2
```

The structure of the expression is much the same as that of the previous expression.

Retrieval 29: Predicate computation with MAX function

Find the best paid employee or employees.

```
SELECT EMPNUMB
FROM EMPLOYEE
WHERE SALARY = (SELECT MAX (SALARY)
                FROM EMPLOYEE)
```

The response is:

```
E4
E7
```

Again this expression is not unlike the previous expressions, except that we are dealing only with one relation. It should also be clear that particularly this type of expression can be replaced by a sequence of retrievals:

1. Find the maximum salary:

```
SELECT MAX (SALARY)
FROM EMPLOYEE
```

The response is:

```
25,000
```

2. Find the employee or employees earning $25,000.

```
SELECT EMPNUMB
FROM EMPLOYEE
WHERE (SALARY = 25000)
```

The response is:

```
E4
E7
```

Retrieval- 30:More complex predicate computation with MAX function
In what cities do the best paid employees work?

```
SELECT CITY
FROM WAREHOUSE
WHERE WHNUMB IS IN (SELECT WHNUMB
                    FROM EMPLOYEE
                    WHERE SALARY = (SELECT MAX(SALARY)
                                    FROM EMPLOYEE))
```

The response is:

```
NEW YORK
DALLAS
```

The first inner S-F-W-block together with the following nested S-F-W-block is a specification of the warehouse numbers with the best paid employees. With the data base in Figure 7.8 this is the list:

```
WH2
WH1
```

The overall expression then specifies the retrieval of the CITY values from WAREHOUSE records whose WHNUMB values are in this list.

Updating the data base with SQL

Few users of a relational data base in a large organization can be expected to have permission to update the data base. We shall return to this topic in Chapter 13 on management of the data base environment; for the present, however, we shall examine the facilities that are available through System R SQL for updating the data base via a terminal.

There are three basic updating commands as we might expect, and these are DELETE (for deleting records or rows), INSERT (for storing new records or rows), and UPDATE (for updating one or more fields of a record). There are unfortunately subtle technical difficulties with the use of all the updating commands and some controversy about the use of the DELETE and UPDATE commands. We shall take the three commands separately.

The SQL INSERT command

Suppose we wanted to insert into the relation WAREHOUSE the new record:

```
WH9    DENVER  25,000
```

We could simply issue the INSERT command:

```
INSERT INTO WAREHOUSE:
   'WH9', 'DENVER', 25,000
```

and the record would be inserted into the relation WAREHOUSE at the conceptual level, a corresponding storage record would be inserted at the storage level, and appropriate changes would be made to the underlying pointer system and associated indexes. Thus it would appear that nothing could be simpler, and indeed this is so, provided that the external-level relation being updated is either:

1. Also a relation at the conceptual level
2. Or a relation derived from a conceptual-level relation and which retains the primary key field or fields of the conceptual-level relation, for example, the relation (VIEW2) defined by:

```
DEFINE VIEW VIEW2 (WHNUMB, CITY)
AS SELECT WHNUMB CITY FROM WAREHOUSE
```

When these two conditions are met, the system is able to identify and construct a unique underlying storage record from which a conceptual and external record can be abstracted as described in Chapter 4.

If these conditions are not met, then the insertion request will be rejected by System R. If we have an external relation (VIEW3) defined as:

```
DEFINE VIEW VIEW3 (CITY WH-AREA)
AS SELECT CITY, WH-AREA FROM WAREHOUSE
```

then referring to Figure 7.8 we would have a relation that violated both conditions above, since the primary key from the underlying conceptual file is absent. With such an external relation, the INSERTION command:

```
INSERT INTO VIEW3:
   BOSTON   50,000
```

would have to be rejected, since a unique underlying storage record could not be constructed.

While not very relevant here, with System R it is also possible to define quite sophisticated external relations that are derived not from one underlying conceptual-level relation but from many such relations. We shall discuss such external relations in Section 8.2. With these relations insertion of a new record would require construction of new storage records for more than one underlying storage file. Because of the difficulties associated with identifying the storage records to be constructed, System R does not permit updating operations of any kind with such external relations.

The SQL DELETE command

Suppose we wanted to delete the WAREHOUSE record with key value 'WH1'. We would normally first retrieve this record (as a check) and then issue the DELETE command. The retrieval command is:

```
SELECT *
FROM WAREHOUSE
WHERE (WHNUMB = 'WH1')
```

and the subsequent DELETE command is:

```
DELETE WAREHOUSE
WHERE (WHNUMB = 'WH1')
```

The retrieval and DELETE commands are not in any way connected by the system, and had the DELETE command been issued separately, this would have been sufficient, although the risk of deleting the wrong record would have been greater.

An important feature of the DELETE command is that it contains an SQL predicate, which permits all records that satisfy the predicate to be deleted. Suppose that all warehouses with a floor area greater than 30,000 units are being closed down, so that the corresponding records in WAREHOUSE are to be deleted. We could issue:

```
DELETE WAREHOUSE
WHERE (WH-AREA > 30000)
```

and this would result in the deletion of the records:

```
WH1 DALLAS   37,000
WH2 NEW YORK 50,000
```

However, there is considerable controversy over this predicated deletion facility, for there are many who believe that it is too dangerous. It would indeed seem that the more prudent way of going about the above deletion would first involve finding the records for the warehouses being closed down, and then issuing a DELETE command for these specific records:

```
SELECT *
FROM WAREHOUSE
WHERE (WH-AREA > 30000)
```

The response is:

```
WH1 DALLAS    37,000
WH2 NEW YORK  50,000
```

We now issue the **DELETE** command:

```
DELETE WAREHOUSE
WHERE (WHNUMB IS IN ('WH1', 'WH2'))
```

We should also note the case where no predicate accompanies the **DELETE** clause:

```
DELETE WAREHOUSE
```

This would cause every record in the **WAREHOUSE** relation to be deleted.

We recall that with the **INSERT** command the system is easily able to construct the appropriate storage record if the external record being inserted contains the primary key field of the underlying conceptual-level relation, and that in other cases the update will be rejected. We have the same basic situation with the **DELETE** command. In order for the system to be able to delete the proper underlying storage record, there must be enough information in the external record being deleted to permit the proper storage record to be identified. This will be the case if the external record being deleted contains the primary key of the underlying conceptual record. As with the case of application of the SQL **INSERTION** command, when the external record being deleted does not contain the primary key field, the **DELETE** command will be rejected by System R.

The SQL UPDATE command

Let us suppose that employee 'E3' has had his salary increased to $24,000. To update the **EMPLOYEE** relation, we could proceed as follows. We first retrieve the record to be updated:

```
SELECT *
FROM EMPLOYEE
WHERE (EMPNUMB = 'E3')
```

with the response:

```
WH1  E3  21,000
```

We then issue the **UPDATE** command:

```
UPDATE EMPLOYEE
SET SALARY = 24000
WHERE (EMPNUMB = 'E3')
```

We might finally want to check that the data base had been correctly updated and issue the retrieval command above once more. If we did, the result would now be:

```
WH1  E3  24,000
```

If the user wanted to dispense with the checking (always a temptation that should be resisted, in the author's opinion), the **UPDATE** command above could be issued alone with the same result.

Readers should notice the structure of the **UPDATE** command. The **UPDATE** clause in the first line informs the system about which (external) relation is to be updated. The **SET** clause specifies what fields are to be updated and how. Finally, the SQL predicate following **WHERE** specifies the conditions to be fulfilled before a record is selected for updating. In the example above we had an SQL predicate that ensured that just one record would be updated, namely, the **EMPLOYEE** record with the key field value 'E3'. As an example where many records could be selected for updating, let us take the case where we wanted to give everyone earning under $25,000 a raise of $2000. We could issue the SQL **UPDATE** command:

```
UPDATE EMPLOYEE
SET SALARY = SALARY + 2000
WHERE (SALARY < 25000)
```

A more conservative method, however, would involve first retrieving the records for those employees who were to be rewarded:

```
SELECT *
FROM EMPLOYEE
WHERE (SALARY < 25000)
```

giving:

```
WH2   E1   22,000
WH1   E3   21,000
WH3   E6   23,000
```

When satisfied that this information is correct, perhaps by carrying out other checks, we could issue the **UPDATE** command for the records involved as follows:

```
UPDATE EMPLOYEE
SET SALARY = SALARY + 2000
WHERE (EMPNUMB IS IN ('E1', 'E3', 'E6'))
```

Following this, the retrieval command could be issued again, to ensure that the data base has been updated properly.

We can see that the SQL predicated **UPDATE** command is powerful, perhaps two powerful, for it is not difficult in SQL to construct incorrect predicates, especially when update conditions are complex. This is true even for experts in SQL. There is thus a strong argument for restricting terminal users to a version of SQL that permitted only simple predicates in **DELETE** and **UPDATE** commands. These predicates could allow selection of records on the basis of primary key field specifications only.

A different but related difficulty with the SQL **UPDATE** command has to do with updating an external relation that does not contain the primary key field of the conceptual-level relation from which it is derived, or with updating an external relation that is derived from more than one conceptual-level relation.

We had this problem with the **INSERTION** and **DELETE** commands as well, and as with these commands, for an **UPDATE** command to be carried out on a relation derived from a single underlying conceptual-level relation, the conceptual-level primary key must be present in the external relation; otherwise it will clearly be impossible for the system to uniquely identify the correct underlying storage record to be updated, causing the system to reject the **UPDATE** command.

SUMMARY

1. Relational data bases are defined by means of storage, conceptual, and external schemas. The conceptual schema requires only the definitions of the relations. No definitions of relationships are needed, in contrast with CODASYL, which requires the definition of owner-coupled sets in the conceptual schema. In the relational approach relationships are inferred from connection field values, and child connection fields must be included in child relations. In principle, relational storage schemas are no different from storage schemas with other approaches, and contain the usual collection of inversions, linked lists, and other pointer systems. IBM's System R is the best known example of a comprehensive relational data base system.

2. SQL is the most common data base manipulation language used with emerging and prototype relational systems, and is the language of System R. It has a version for use with terminals, and another version for embedding in host languages such as COBOL and PL/1. Essentially an SQL expression consists of an imperative followed by a predicate. In retrieval expressions, the imperative states what type of data is required, while the predicate expresses a condition that generally has the effect of narrowing the range of data values that can be retrieved. The predicate is a compound logical expression that is either **TRUE** or **FALSE**, and only data for which the predicate is **TRUE** is retrieved. Simple requests are easy to express with SQL. More complex requests require both a proficiency in logic and a familiarity with mathematical sets.

QUESTIONS

1. Define the System R conceptual schema for the data base consisting of the relations **SUPPLIER** and **PUR-ORDER** from Figure 7.8.
2. Explain the concept of a domain using the data base defined in Question 1.
3. Assuming that a new record (**WH7 NEW YORK 50,000**) is added to the relation **WAREHOUSE** in Figure 7.1, show the contents of an external relation **EXT-WAR** that contains only the **CITY** and **WH-AREA** fields from **WAREHOUSE**.

   The following retrieval requests are based on the data base in Figures 7.7 and 7.8. Both the SQL expression and the result of carrying out the retrieval should be given for each question.
4. Find the names of suppliers in Texas.
5. Find the orders issued to supplier 'S6'.

6. What employees issued orders to supplier 'S4' before 15th June, 1984?
7. What orders were issued to supplier 'S6' by employee 'E6'?
8. What employees have issued orders to supplier 'S3'? (Note that only one SELECT-FROM-WHERE-block and one relation are required here.)
9. Find the employee numbers and warehouse numbers for employees who have issued orders to supplier 'S3'. (Now two SELECT-FROM-WHERE-blocks and two relations are needed.)
10. What employees have issued no orders to supplier 'S3'? (This can be handled with only one relation, but it is easier to express with two.)
11. What employees that work in warehouse 'WH1' have issued no orders to supplier 'S3'?
12. What suppliers have no orders?
13. What employees have issued all but one of their orders before 1st May, 1984?
14. What Texas suppliers deal with both 'E1' and 'E3'?
15. What suppliers have never dealt with employee 'E6'?
16. What suppliers with orders have never dealt with employee 'E6'?
17. What are the names of suppliers that have received orders from 'E6', but have never received orders from employee 'E7'?
18. What employees have issued orders only to Texas and California companies?
19. Find the salary of each employee that has dealings with the supplier Robotek.
20. Find the names of suppliers that have no dealings with employees who earn under $22,000.
21. Find the names of suppliers with orders who have no dealings with employees earning under $22,000.
22. In what cities are there warehouses that have employees that have issued orders to supplier 'S4'?
23. What are the supplier numbers of suppliers that are supplying employees who make more than $24,000?
24. What are the supplier numbers of suppliers who are supplying warehouses that have a floor area in excess of 30,000 square feet?
25. What are the employee numbers of employees who work in New York and have issued orders to supplier 'S6'?
26. What are the employee numbers of employees who work in Chicago and have issued orders only to supplier 'S6'?
27. Find the order numbers for orders that are issued to suppliers in Texas by employees who make more than $23,000.

The following are computational retrievals.

28. How many warehouses are there?
29. What warehouse has the largest floor area?
30. What is the largest warehouse in New York?
31. What is the average size of a warehouse?
32. What is the average size of those warehouses that have issued orders to supplier 'S4'?

33. How many suppliers are there? How does the relation used affect the result?
34. Find the number of suppliers in each state or province?
35. Find the number of employees in each warehouse who earn more than $22,000.
36. In what cities are there warehouses whose payroll exceeds $44,000?
37. What are the names of suppliers who have more than two orders?
38. In what cities are there warehouses at which the average salary exceeds $22,000?
39. Find the supplier numbers for suppliers who deal with the smallest warehouse.
40. Find the employees who earn less than average at their warehouses.

The following questions involve alterations to the data base in Figures 7.7 and 7.8.

41. Insert a new **SUPPLIER** record (**S9 INFOGON ARIZONA**).
42. Delete all suppliers that are located in Texas. (What should we do about orders in the **PUR-ORDER** relation that are issued to these suppliers? See Chapter 8)
43. Delete all warehouses located in New York. (What about deletions of child records and so on? See Chapter 8)
44. Delete all orders issued by employees that work in New York warehouses.
45. Increase the size of all New York warehouses by 10,000 square feet.
46. Increase by 10,000 square feet the size of all warehouses that deal with supplier 'S6'.
47. Add $1000 to the salaries of employees who work in New York.
48. Add $1000 to the salaries of employees who work in Chicago and who have dealings with supplier 'S6'.
49. Add $1000 to the salaries of employees who deal with California companies.
50. Increase by $500 the salaries of those employees who are under the average for all employees.

ADDITIONAL PERSPECTIVE
COBOL BATCH USE OF SQL WITH SYSTEM R

As we saw in Chapter 4, while it is convenient to be able to use a query language such as SQL to access a data base from a terminal directly, a great deal of routine data base manipulation is carried out by the execution of higher language programs. Such programs are executed either at regular intervals as with batch processing or as needed in on-line systems. Within such programs are special commands that permit either retrieval of records from the data base or update of data in the data base. We had some detailed examples of this with COBOL and CODASYL data base commands in Chapter 6. We say that the data base manipulation language commands are *embedded* in the *host* higher language such as COBOL.

In the case of System R and most relational systems either on the market or being developed, it is a version of SQL that is embedded in the host language. It has not been easy to embed SQL in higher languages such as COBOL and PL/1. The SQL that is used is very close to that used at a terminal, but the differences are of a technical nature and are caused mainly by the fact that COBOL (and PL/1) are oriented toward dealing with records one at a time, while SQL can retrieve (and even update) many records at a time. The solution that is used with System R SQL is quite technical, and we give the essentials of it in this supplement for the sake of completeness.

(Readers are reminded that System R had not been released by IBM at the time this book went to press. Although the material in this supplement was based on the most current information available, the author cannot guarantee that it will accurately reflect how SQL is embedded in COBOL in a release of System R. Although major differences appear unlikely, minor differences are always a possibility.)

Overview of the SQL/COBOL interface in System R

Since SQL deals with many external records at a time and COBOL is oriented toward dealing with one (storage) record at a time, two solutions are:

1. A User Work Area (that is, a data area accessible to both the applications program and the data base system) that permits or can contain more than one external record of the same type. This is illustrated in Figure 7.10 for the case where the application program is dealing with an external-level relation that is the same as the **WAREHOUSE** conceptual-level relation from Figure 7.8. A UWA structure for external records would be equivalent to a COBOL record array specified with the **OCCURS** clause. Elements of the array, that is, **WAREHOUSE** external records, would be available for COBOL program manipulation one at a time in any required order. At the same time the execution of an SQL command for retrieval of **WAREHOUSE** external records would place the retrieved records in the UWA array. Similarly, SQL update commands could take data from the array for updating the data base as specified in the commands. This appears to be the simplest method of designing the interface as far as the user of the data base system is concerned. Unfortunately this solution is difficult to implement, and a simpler alternative from the point of view of the System R architects was chosen.

2. The solution used with System R is a special buffer entirely under the control of the data base system, as illustrated in Figure 7.11. This buffer cannot be accessed directly by the COBOL program. Because it is under the control of System R, its structure is flexible, and it can hold any relation that can be defined in an SQL retrieval expression. To make a record available to the COBOL program, the COBOL program must issue a request to System R for a specific record from this buffer. In order that requests for specific records be possible, a special *curser variable* is used to keep track of a program's position within the buffer. The UWA is now simply a collection of variables corresponding to the fields of the relations defined in the external schema. When System R delivers a record

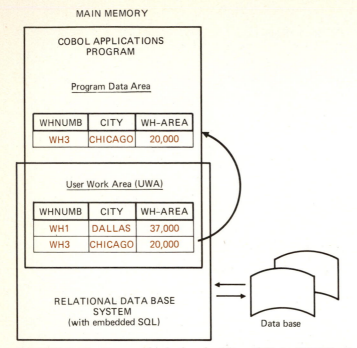

FIGURE 7.10 One method of embedding SQL in COBOL. For each relation that could be retrieved there is a UWA structure that is the equivalent of a COBOL record array declared with the OCCURS clause. The relational data base system can place many records at a time in the UWA, or it can take data out of the UWA for updating the data base. The COBOL program has access to the UWA too and can take a record from the UWA and place it in a program data area for further processing (and vice versa).

from the special buffer, it merely places the field values from that record in the corresponding UWA variables as illustrated in Figure 7.11.

In order for the reader to gain insight into the kind of detail necessary for embedding an SQL retrieval in COBOL with System R, we shall first outline a System R COBOL program that carries out a retrieval, and which is consistent with the method described in solution 2 above. We conclude with a COBOL SQL program to load a data base and a COBOL updating program.

An SQL/COBOL retrieval program with System R

Let us suppose that we wish to retrieve all data on warehouses under 40,000 units in area. At a terminal we would simply issue the SQL command:

```
SELECT *
FROM WAREHOUSE
WHERE (WH-AREA < 40,000)
```

However, let us suppose that we want a COBOL program to retrieve this information and print it out. We would proceed as follows (readers should also refer to

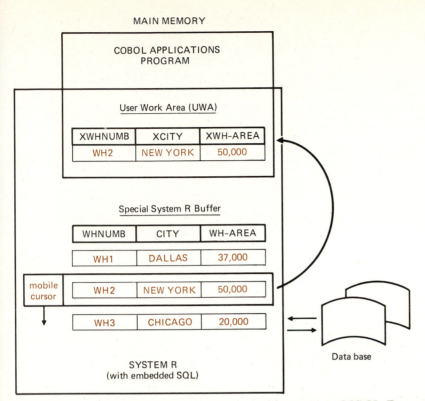

MAIN MEMORY

FIGURE 7.11 The System R method of embedding SQL in COBOL. For each field value that could be retrieved from an external record, there is a UWA variable, declared in the COBOL program with a name different from that used in the data base definition (we have used XWHNUMB for WHNUMB, and so on). In the COBOL program there is a LET command, requesting that System R set up a special buffer that can hold a relation to be retrieved by a SQL command. This buffer is not accessible by the COBOL program, but by means of a cursor variable the program can request that System R deliver a record in the special buffer to the UWA. Thus System R retains a retrieved relation and delivers records from it to the program one at a time.

Figures 2.3 and 2.4 for an overview of the structure of a COBOL program):

```
DATA DIVISION.
WORKING-STORAGE SECTION.
$77 XWHNUMB    PIC X(5).
$77 XCITY      PIC X(20).
$77 XWH-AREA   PIC 9(6).
```

*Comment: This is the User Work Area. Specification of data names or
*variables must have a $ sign prefix. While the same names can be used as in
*the external data base definition, these names are the names of data quanti-
*ties in the UWA and not the data base, and System R will distinguish
*between them. So it is better to use different but perhaps similar names.

```
$SYR.
```

*Comment: SYR is a special structure variable used by System R. One of the
*components of SYR is a variable called SYR-CODE. This variable plays
*much the same role as DB-STATUS in CODASYL. Following each CALL
*to System R, a return code is placed in SYR-CODE to indicate whether
*System R has been able to carry out the command normally, or whether
*something has gone wrong.

```
77  TARGET-FL-AREA   PIC 9(6)  DISPLAY.
```

*Comment: Auxiliary variable for holding the target floor area. In this case it
*will be 40,000 as in the SQL expression above.

```
$LET CURS BE (SELECT WHNUMB, CITY, WH-AREA
             INTO XWHNUMB, XCITY, XWH-AREA
             WHERE (WH-AREA < TARGET-FL-AREA)
```

*Comment: Here we have defined a cursor variable arbitrarily named CURS.
*This cursor variable can point to any record in the relation specified by the
*SELECT expression. The relation specified in the SELECT expression will
*be placed in the special buffer illustrated in Figure 7.11. However, the
*SELECT expression is not executed at this point, but only when a request is
*made to System R for a record from the special buffer. This is done in the
*PROCEDURE DIVISION.

```
PROCEDURE DIVISION.
 INPUT-DATA.
      ACCEPT TARGET-FL-AREA.
```

*Comment: Assume that the variable TARGET-FL-AREA now holds 40,000.

```
ACCESS-DATA-BASE.
    $BEGIN TRANSACTION.
```

*Comment. This is a command to System R and readies the data base for
*processing. This is always the first data base command. The last data base
*command in the program must be $END TRANSACTION. If a program ends
*without a $END TRANSACTION command being executed, all changes to
*the data base since the $BEGIN TRANSACTION command was executed
*are cancelled. See the transaction concept in Chapter 6.

```
        $OPEN CURS.
```

*Comment: The cursor variable CURS is activated and ready for use. At the
*same time the SELECT expression following the specification of CURS in
*the WORKING-STORAGE SECTION is executed, and the retrieved relation
*is placed in the special buffer that is also shown in Figure 7.11.

```
RETRIEVAL-LOOP.
    $FETCH CURS.
```

*Comment: The first time this is executed the first record in the special
*System R buffer is placed in the UWA variables. Thus it functions almost
*like a COBOL **READ** command.

```
        IF SYR-CODE = "O.K." THEN
            DISPLAY XWHNUMB, XCITY, XWH-AREA
```

*Comment: The record transferred to the UWA via **CURS** by System R is
*printed out.

```
        GO TO RETRIEVAL-LOOP
```

*Comment: The next execution of **$FETCH CURS** will cause the next re
*cord in the special System R buffer to be transferred to the UWA variables.
*As we scan through the special buffer, we will eventually reach the end of
*it as indicated by the **SYR-CODE** value.

```
        ELSE IF SYR-CODE NOT = 'END OF RELATION'
                DISPLAY "PROBLEM WITH SYSTEM R CURSOR,
                PROCESSING STOPPED" STOP RUN.
    $CLOSE CURS.
```

*Comment: Cursor is now deactivated, and the special System R buffer is
*emptied. However, if we now wanted the **WAREHOUSE** records for **WH-**
***REA** values less than 30,000, it is only necessary to place the 30,000 in
***TARGET-FL-AREA** and activate the cursor variable **CURS** once more. This
*time the special System R buffer will be filled with **WAREHOUSE** records
*with **WH-AREA** value less than 30,000. As was illustrated above, these can
*be placed in the UWA one by one using the **$FETCH CURS** command.

```
    $END TRANSACTION.
    STOP RUN.
```

It is evident that the specification of all variables that System R has access to
(the UWA variables, for example), the specification of the special buffer (see
Figure 7.11), and the System R commands (such as **$OPEN CURS**) are all
prefixed by a $ sign. This is necessary because the actual COBOL statements that
would be required to interface with System R are much more complex than those
given above. Before the COBOL program is submitted to the COBOL compiler for
translation, it is first processed by the System R precompiler. The precompiler
processing causes every statement beginning with a $ sign to be replaced with
the correct (but much more complex) coding for interfacing with System R. This
is illustrated in Figure 7.12.

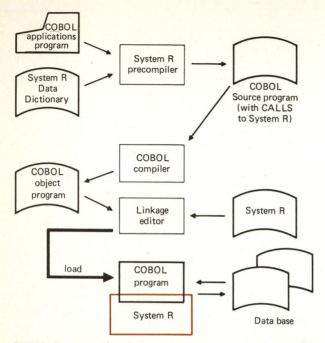

FIGURE 7.12 The steps in preparing a COBOL program for execution, when the program interfaces with System R. The original COBOL program (entered either at a terminal or via a card-reader) contains statements prefixed by a $ sign. The precompiler replaces these statements with a more complex COBOL code required for correct interfacing with System R; it uses the data dictionary to do this since field and relation names are involved. When the resulting source program has been compiled or translated by the COBOL compiler, the system linkage editor joins it with System R (which functions as a subprogram of the application program).

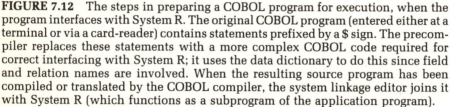

An SQL/COBOL loading program with System R
So far in our discussions of relational data base manipulation, we have assumed the existence of a relational data base. It is now appropriate to give an example of how a relational data base could be initially loaded or populated. Normally COBOL (or PL/1) loading programs would be used for this purpose, since the amount of data in a typical commercial data base would preclude loading records one at a time at a terminal via SQL **INSERT** expressions. Instead the records for a typical relation would be available as a COBOL sequential file on disk or tape (see Chapter 2), for example, the sequential file **ZWAREHOUSE** from which the relation **WAREHOUSE** could be loaded. **ZWAREHOUSE** records are read one by one using the COBOL **READ** statement. As each record is read, it is placed in the data base using the SQL **INSERT** command. Thus the loading operation is little more than a copying operation (Figure 7.13).

In the following example, we shall outline the essential details of loading the relation **WAREHOUSE** from the sequential file **ZWAREHOUSE** using embedded SQL. Note that when we read a **ZWAREHOUSE** record, it is placed in a program data area structure called **ZWAREHOUSEREC**; it is then transferred to the UWA

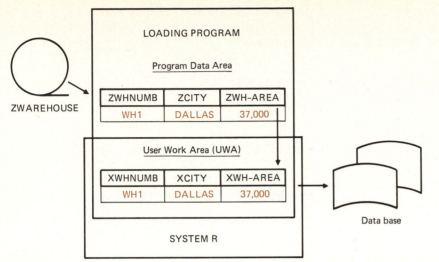

FIGURE 7.13 Loading the WAREHOUSE relation from a sequential file ZWARE-HOUSE. A record from ZWAREHOUSE is first read into the program data area, then moved to the UWA, and then placed in the storage version of the relation WARE-HOUSE by means of an SQL INSERT command.

(specified with $ sign prefixes) and then to the **WAREHOUSE** relation via the SQL **INSERT** command.

```
            DATA DIVISION.
            FILE SECTION.
            FD ZWAREHOUSE

            ...
            WORKING-STORAGE SECTION.
            01  ZWAREHOUSEREC
                02  ZWHNUMB   PIC X(5).
                02  ZCITY     PIC X(20).
                02  ZWH-NUMB  PIC 9(6).
```

*Comment: Specification of UWA follows.

```
            $77 XWHNUMB  PIC X(5).
            $77 XCITY    PIC X(20).
            $77 XWH-AREA PIC 9(6).
            $SYR.


            PROCEDURE DIVISION.
            STARTUP.
                OPEN INPUT ZWAREHOUSE.
            MAINLOOP.
                READ ZWAREHOUSE INTO ZWAREHOUSEREC
                        AT END CLOSE ZWAREHOUSE, STOP RUN.
```

*Comment: Now move the data in ZWAREHOUSEREC to the UWA vari-
*ables. Actually we could have read a record from ZWAREHOUSE directly
*into the UWA, but we do it this way to clearly lay out the steps.

```
        MOVE ZWHNUMB TO XWHNUMB.
        MOVE ZCITY TO XCITY.
        MOVE ZWH-AREA TO XWH-AREA.
        $BEGIN TRANSACTION.
        $INSERT INTO WAREHOUSE (WHNUMB, CITY, WH-AREA)
              $XWHNUMB, $XCITY, $WH-AREA
        IF SYR-CODE NOT = 'O.K.' THEN
                DISPLAY "PROBLEM WITH SYSTEM R
                STORAGE OPERATION, PROGRAM STOPPED"
                DISPLAY "KEY OF PROBLEM RECORD WAS: ",
                ZWHNUMB, STOP RUN.
        $END TRANSACTION.
```

*Comment: We have defined a System R transaction as the insertion of one
*record into the storage version of the relation WAREHOUSE. Alternatively,
*we could have placed the $BEGIN and $END outside the loop MAINLOOP,
*in which case the complete loading of WAREHOUSE would have been a
*transaction; this would mean that if a record could not be stored for some
*reason, so that execution stopped, we would have a cancellation of all
*records stored in WAREHOUSE up to that point.

```
        GO TO MAINLOOP.
```

The other relations in the data base could be loaded in a similar manner. Of course it should be remembered that in practice a loading program would be more complex than is the case with the excerpt above. Extensive checking of the data being placed in the data base would be carried out, the data might well be taken from several source files, and routines would be incorporated to cover all the possibilities for things going wrong. The above excerpt gives only the essentials of how the SQL INSERT commands are embedded in a COBOL program.

An SQL/COBOL updating program with System R
For the sake of completeness we now give a short COBOL excerpt to show how the SQL DELETE and UPDATE commands are embedded in a COBOL program. Our simple program will do two things:

1. Delete all EMPLOYEE records for which the salary is greater than $24,000.
2. Give all employees earning less than $23,000 (which we read in) a raise of $500 (which we also read in).

```
DATA DIVISION.
WORKING-STORAGE SECTION.
$77 RAISE PIC 9(6).
$77 TARGET-SALARY PIC 9(6).
$SYR.
PROCEDURE DIVISION.
DELETE-PARAGRAPH.
    $BEGIN TRANSACTION.
    $DELETE EMPLOYEE
     WHERE (SALARY > 24000).
    IF SYR-CODE NOT = 'O.K.' THEN
            DISPLAY "SYSTEM R ERROR DURING DELETION"
            STOP RUN.
    $END TRANSACTION.
UPDATE-PARAGRAPH.
    $BEGIN TRANSACTION.
    ACCEPT RAISE.
```

*Comment: Assume 500 read in.

```
    ACCEPT TARAGET-SALARY.
```

*Comment: Assume 23,000 read in.

```
    $UPDATE EMPLOYEE
    SET SALARY = SALARY + $RAISE
    WHERE (SALARY < $TARGET-SALARY).
    IF SYR-CODE  NOT = 'O.K.' THEN
        DISPLAY "SYSTEM R UPDATING CANCELLED".
    $END TRANSACTION.
    STOP RUN.
```

Note that in practice it would be more conservative to first retrieve the records to be deleted and print them out, before the actual deletion. Similarly, it would be a good idea to retrieve and print the records being updated, both before and after updating.

Summary of rules for the use of the $ sign with embedded System R SQL
Some readers will probably be confused as to exactly where a $ sign is needed with embedded SQL. The following rules may help:

1. The names specified in either view (external schema) definitions or base table (conceptual schema) definitions cannot be used in ordinary COBOL statements, only within SQL statements.
2. The specification of the UWA variables in a COBOL program must be preceded by a $ sign.
3. When a UWA variable is used as an ordinary COBOL variable in a COBOL statement, no $ sign is required.

4. When a UWA variable is used within an SQL expression, a $ sign is required.
5. When names specified in view or base table definitions are used within an SQL expression, no $ signs are used.
6. A $ sign must precede all requests to System R.
7. Specification of the control structure variable SYR is preceded by a $ sign, but when SYR-CODE is used in a COBOL statement, no $ sign is required.

These $ sign rules, as well as the need for a special buffer and cursor variable with SQL retrievals, are unfortunate since they add a layer of detail to an otherwise elegant system. It probably means that business managers and personal computer users who have access to System R data bases may tend to restrict their efforts to the use of the System R query version of SQL, already described.

Incidently, the same $ sign rules apply to embedded SQL in PL/1 with System R (Refs. 2 and 5). Readers should note that IBM may well make changes to reduce the inconvenience of these $ sign rules before System R is released.

QUESTIONS

For each of the following questions, give the essentials of a COBOL program with embedded SQL. The questions apply to the data base in Figures 7.7 and 7.8.

52. Find names of suppliers in state X who have dealings with employee Y. The values of X and Y should be read in by the program.
53. Find the salaries of employees who have issued no orders to supplier X. The value of X should be read in by the program.
54. Find the warehouse numbers of warehouses in city X that have employees that earn more than $22,000. The value of X should be read in by the program.
55. Delete all suppliers located in Texas.
56. Update the data base to reflect the move of all Texas suppliers to Arizona.

REFERENCES

1. Alter, S. L., 1980. *Decision Support Systems*, Addison-Wesley, Reading, Mass.
2. Bradley, J., 1982. *File and Data Base Techniques*. Holt, Rinehart & Winston, New York.
3. Chamberlin, D. D., and R. F. Boyce, 1974. "SEQUEL, a Structured English Query Language." *Proc. ACM SIGMOD Workshop on Data Description, Access, and Control*, 249–264.[1]

---

[1]Originally SQL was called SEQUEL.

4. Chamberlin, D. D. and others, 1981. "Support for Repetitive Transactions and AD HOC Queries in System R," *ACM Trans. on Database Systems,* 6(1):70–94.

5. Date, C. J., 1981. *Introduction to Data Base Systems.* Addison-Wesley, Reading, Mass.

6. King, W. F., 1980. "Relational Data Base Systems: Where We Stand Today," IFIP Congress 1980. North Holland, New York, 369–381.

Query-by-Example and Other Relational Features

We shall continue our study of the relational approach in this chapter. First we shall study a novel relational terminal language known as Query-By-Example (QBE), which is likely to become very important for the casual use of a relational data base in business (Refs. 3, 4, and 5). Then we shall examine two more advanced relational topics, namely, *derived user views*, or *derived external relations*, and *integrity constraints*. Derived external relations are constructed from more than one relation from the conceptual data base and can drastically simplify the retrieval of information; integrity constraints are used to prevent incorrect data from creeping into a data base.

8.1 LEARNING QUERY-BY-EXAMPLE (QBE)

The relational query language Query-By-Example is a novel and unique language. It is unique for two reasons:

1. It is unusually easy to learn, an hour's practice at a terminal being sufficient for acquisition of a good working knowledge.
2. A user does not usually have to construct a query language expression (with all the possibilities for doing it incorrectly). Instead it is necessary only to make a few brief specifications in a table that the system constructs on the terminal screen.

The language is in fact only suitable for use at a terminal, and it is unlikely that an embedded version will ever be implemented. Currently QBE is available from IBM as a stand-alone system (Ref. 3). It is not part of System R, but it is possible to use it to query relations that have been copied from IMS data bases. (IMS is an older hierarchical data base system from IBM that is still very widely used, and is described in Chapter 9.) In the future we can expect that it will be available for use with System R data bases, and other data bases as well. Its great ease of use, especially with simpler retrieval requests, is likely to ensure that it will become a favorite with the busy executive with a portable terminal. Currently QBE runs under the operating system VM/CMS (see Chapter 1).

Simple retrievals with a single relation

The best way to describe the use of QBE is by demonstrating a sample session. We shall use the data base in Figures 7.7 and 7.8, shown again in Figures 8.1 and 8.2. When a session is initiated at a terminal, the user is presented with an empty table:

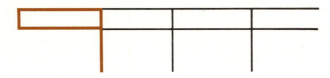

The name of the game is to have the system fill in most of the empty spaces in answer to a request for information, and to get the system to do this, the user must fill in a few spaces too. Learning to use QBE then consists of learning what to put into the spaces in order to have required information inserted into the table.

We notice the thicker box in color at the top left of the table. This always contains the name of the relation we are trying to extract information about, and it is here we type our first entry. (This box is neither thick nor colored in practice; it is this way in this book for expositional purposes.)

Suppose we know nothing about the data base in Figure 8.1 except that it has

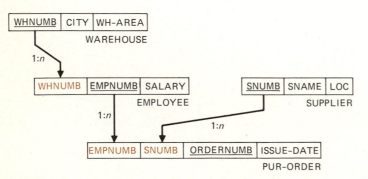

FIGURE 8.1 The external relational data base from Figure 7.7. Sample contents are shown in Figure 8.2.

WHNUMB	CITY	WH-AREA
WH1	DALLAS	37,000
WH2	NEW YORK	50,000
WH3	CHICAGO	20,000
WH5	DENVER	13,000

WAREHOUSE

WHNUMB	EMPNUMB	SALARY
WH2	E1	22,000
WH1	E3	21,000
WH2	E4	25,000
WH3	E6	23,000
WH1	E7	25,000

EMPLOYEE

SNUMB	SNAME	LOC
S3	TRONOTON	CALIFORNIA
S4	ROBOTEK	TEXAS
S6	MIKREL	ONTARIO
S7	RAYTEX	TEXAS

SUPPLIER

EMPNUMB	SNUMB	ORDERNUMB	ISSUE-DATE
E3	S7	OR67	84/06/23
E1	S4	OR73	84/07/28
E7	S4	OR76	84/05/25
E6	S6	OR77	84/06/19
E3	S4	OR79	84/06/23
E1	S6	OR80	84/07/29
E3	S6	OR90	85/06/22
E3	S3	OR91	85/07/13

PUR-ORDER

FIGURE 8.2 Contents of the external data base in Figure 8.1. The contents are the same as those in Figure 7.8.

a relation called **EMPLOYEE**. We can find out what fields are in the relation merely by typing:

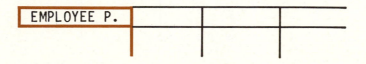

where **P.** stands for **PRINT**. The system responds with a list of all the fields in **EMPLOYEE**. (Note that the computer prints in color here, and the user in black.)

EMPLOYEE	WHNUMB	EMPNUMB	SALARY

However, if the user does not have authorization for an external data base that includes the **SALARY** field, the **SALARY** field will not be printed. We are now in a position to retrieve information from the **EMPLOYEE** relation.

Retrieval-1: Single column
In what warehouses do employees work?
   We simply ask for the **WHNUMB** column to be printed as follows:

EMPLOYEE	WHNUMB	EMPNUMB	SALARY
	P.		

and the response is:

EMPLOYEE	WHNUMB	EMPNUMB	SALARY
	WH2		
	WH1		
	WH3		

and referring to Figure 8.1, we see that duplicates have been removed. If we do not want them removed, we would have requested instead:

EMPLOYEE	WHNUMB	EMPNUMB	SALARY
	P.ALL		

with the result:

EMPLOYEE	WHNUMB	EMPNUMB	SALARY
	WH2		
	WH1		
	WH2		
	WH3		
	WH1		

   We notice also that when we just used **P.**, the **WHNUMB** values were printed in the order in which they occurred in the **WAREHOUSE** relation with duplicates removed. Had we wanted the values in ascending order (**AO**) or descending order (DO), we would have printed P.AO. or P.DO., respectively:

EMPLOYEE	WHNUMB	EMPNUMB	SALARY
	P.AO.		

which results in:

EMPLOYEE	WHNUMB	EMPNUMB	SALARY
	WH1		
	WH2		
	WH3		

Retrieval-2: Complete relation
Retrieve all data about employees in the **EMPLOYEE** *relation.*
We could enter either:

EMPLOYEE	WHNUMB	EMPNUMB	SALARY
P.			

or, more explicitly:

EMPLOYEE	WHNUMB	EMPNUMB	SALARY
	P.	P.	P.

which results in:

EMPLOYEE	WHNUMB	EMPNUMB	SALARY
	WH2	E1	22,000
	WH1	E3	21,000
	WH2	E4	25,000
	WH3	E6	23,000
	WH1	E7	25,000

which is the way it is stored in the **EMPLOYEE** relation. Had we wanted the data in ascending **WHNUMB** order, we would have entered:

EMPLOYEE	WHNUMB	EMPNUMB	SALARY
	P.AO.	P.	P.

and this would cause the system to sort the **EMPLOYEE** relation in ascending **WHNUMB** order prior to printing. However, had we wanted the relation sorted in ascending **WHNUMB** order as primary sort key, and in descending **SALARY** order as secondary sort key, we would have entered:

EMPLOYEE	WHNUMB	EMPNUMB	SALARY
	P.AO.(1).	P.	P.DO(2).

with the response:

EMPLOYEE	WHNUMB	EMPNUMB	SALARY
	WH1	E7	25,000
	WH1	E3	21,000
	WH2	E4	25,000
	WH2	E1	22,000
	WH3	E6	23,000

It is thus clear that QBE can be used for generating reports.

Retrieval-3: Simple conditional retrieval
Find the employee numbers of employees who earn less than $25,000.
    We insert both the column required and the retrieval condition into the table on the screen:

EMPLOYEE	WHNUMB	EMPNUMB	SALARY
		P.	< 25000

with the response:

EMPLOYEE	WHNUMB	EMPNUMB	SALARY
		E1	
		E3	
		E6	

    The **EMPNUMB** values printed are from those records for which the **SALARY** field satisfies the condition (**SALARY** < 25000).

Retrieval-4: Two retrieval conditions
Find the employee numbers of employees who work in warehouse 'WH2' and earn more than $22,000.
    Note that the retrieval condition is (**WHNUMB** = 'WH2') and (**SALARY** >

22000). We enter

EMPLOYEE	WHNUMB	EMPNUMB	SALARY
	WH2	P.	>22000

giving the response:

EMPLOYEE	WHNUMB	EMPNUMB	SALARY
		E4	

We could also have obtained the salaries of employees satisfying the above conditions, that is, the column for which a condition is also specified. This is illustrated in the next retrieval.

Retrieval-5: Retrieval of a field for which a condition is specified
Find the employee numbers and salaries for employees earning less than $25,000.
We must place both **P.** and < 25000 under the **SALARY** field:

EMPLOYEE	WHNUMB	EMPNUMB	SALARY
		P.	P. $<$ 22000

This gives the result:

EMPLOYEE	WHNUMB	EMPNUMB	SALARY
		E1	22,000
		E3	21,000
		E6	23,000

Retrieval-6: AND-condition
Find the employees that earn more than $21,000 and less than $25,000.
Here we want to pick out each **EMPLOYEE** record for which

$$(SALARY > 21000) \quad AND \quad (SALARY < 25000)$$

We enter:

EMPLOYEE	WHNUMB	EMPNUMB	SALARY
		P.	$>$ 21000 $<$ 25000

and the response is:

EMPLOYEE	WHNUMB	EMPNUMB	SALARY
		E4	

Here the **AND** is said to be implicit, since it is not stated on the screen; note also that the **AND** used in Retrieval-4 was also implicit. The rule for connecting conditions together by an **AND** is simple:

> Whenever we have more than one condition and either of the following, then **AND** is assumed:
>
> 1. A single **PRINT** for a record or a field from a record
> 2. **PRINT** entries in multiple columns for multiple fields from a record

We see that in both Retrieval-4 and Retrieval-6 we are dealing with case 1. The next retrieval illustrates case 2.

Retrieval-7: AND-condition with multiple field retrieval

Find the employee numbers and salaries for employees who work in warehouse 'WH2' and earn more than $22,000.

Except for the additional requirement that we retrieve the **SALARY** values for each record that satisfies the conditions, the retrieval is the same as Retrieval-4. We enter:

EMPLOYEE	WHNUMB	EMPNUMB	SALARY
	WH2	P.	P. > 22000

with the response:

EMPLOYEE	WHNUMB	EMPNUMB	SALARY
		E4	25000

Specifying two conditions connected by logical-**OR** is quite subtle, as the following retrievals illustrate.

Retrieval-8: OR-condition with a single field retrieval

Find the employee numbers for employees who either work in warehouse 'WH2' or earn more than $22,000.

This request can be considered as two retrievals connected by **AND**:

1. Retrieve the employee numbers of employees who work in warehouse 'WH2'.

AND

2. Retrieve the employee numbers of employees who earn more than $22,000.

Clearly, if the system can carry out both these requests together, then the resulting **EMPNUMB** values satisfy Retrieval-8. We must therefore specify the two retrievals together, and we specify them on separate lines:

EMPLOYEE	WHNUMB	EMPNUMB	SALARY
	WH2	P.	
		P.	> 22000

The system in this case will automatically eliminate duplicates, and the result is:

EMPLOYEE	WHNUMB	EMPNUMB	SALARY
		E1	
		E4	
		E6	

PRINT requests on separate lines are considered to be connected by **AND**.

Retrieval-9: OR-condition

Find the employees who either earn more than $24,000 or less than $22,000.

We handle the **OR**-condition in much the same way as in the previous case. The request can be regarded as the combination of two requests:

1. Find the employees who earn more than $24,000.

AND

2. Find the employees who earn less than $22,000.

We enter two separate requests, therefore:

EMPLOYEE	WHNUMB	EMPNUMB	SALARY
		P.	> 24000
		P.	< 22000

and the system responds:

EMPLOYEE	WHNUMB	EMPNUMB	SALARY
		E3	
		E4	
		E7	

Every system has strong points and weak points, and the need with QBE to juggle elementary conditions connected by an **OR**, such as:

(SALARY   24,000) OR (SALARY   22,000)

must surely rank as a classic weakness. We must not forget that the retrievals so far are all elementary. When **OR** is involved with more complex retrievals, we use a *condition box*, to be explained later.

Retrieval-10: Use of negation

Find the employee numbers and salaries for employees who do not work at warehouse 'WH2'.

   We enter:

EMPLOYEE	WHNUMB	EMPNUMB	SALARY
	⌐ WHZ	P.	P.

and the response is:

EMPLOYEE	WHNUMB	EMPNUMB	SALARY
		E3	21,000
		E6	23,000
		E7	25,000

Here we use the symbol ⌐ for **NOT**.

Queries that use examples

With all of the above retrieval requests we could have incorporated a QBE *example*, although they were all so simple that an example was not necessary. It is from the specification of such examples that Query-by-Example gets its name.

   To understand the example concept, let us consider Retrieval-3 once more, which asked for the employee numbers of employees that earned less than $25,000. We could rephrase this as:

   Find the **EMPNUMB** values such as 'E6' where the **SALARY** value is less than $25,000.

We can only do this, of course, if we know that 'E6' satisfies the retrieval condition. But let us suppose that we know. We could then enter:

EMPLOYEE	WHNUMB	EMPNUMB	SALARY
		P.E6	<25000

Here P.E6 means "print EMPNUMB values such as 'E6', for example." In order to clearly specify that 'E6' is merely an example, it must be underlined. If we do not know any value of EMPNUMB that satisfies the condition, any EMPNUMB value would do, and we could just as well use P.E7 instead. However, we can go even further with the use of an example. If we do not know any EMPNUMB values that could be used as an example, we can make an example up, and *anything at all will do*. Thus we could enter:

EMPLOYEE	WHNUMB	EMPNUMB	SALARY
		P.EX	<25000

Here **EX** is an example. It must be underlined and is the most important type of QBE example.

We can apply this to all the retrievals so far, but Retrieval-6 and Retrieval-9 are worth examining more closely. With Retrieval-6 we wanted the employees that earn more than $21,000 *and* less than $25,000. We could have coded instead:

EMPLOYEE	WHNUMB	EMPNUMB	SALARY
		P.EX	>21000
		EX	<25000

This should be interpreted as:

> Print each **EMPNUMB** value such as **EX**, where the **SALARY** value for **EX** is greater than $21,000 and the **SALARY** value for **EX** is less than $25,000.

We have to be careful here, as can be seen from Retrieval-9 using an example. We recall that Retrieval-9 involved an implicit **OR**-condition, requesting those employees that either earn more than $24,000 *or* less than $22,000. With this retrieval we could have entered:

EMPLOYEE	WHNUMB	EMPNUMB	SALARY
		P.EX	>24000
		P.EY	<22000

This should be interpreted as:

> **1.** Print each **EMPNUMB** value such as **EX** where the **SALARY** value for **EX** is more than $24,000.

AND

> **2.** Print each **EMPNUMB** value such as **EY** where the **SALARY** value for **EY** is less than $22,000.

Here we have two separate retrieval commands with separate examples. As mentioned earlier, **OR** cannot be explicitly expressed in the table, and an expression involving logical-**OR** is replaced by two separate retrieval requests. Separate lines imply logical-**AND**.

Retrievals with more than one relation

As we saw in our study of SQL, many retrieval requests involve data from more than one relation. Such queries can be handled in QBE by giving examples of the key of a parent record and connection field of a child record. The technique is best learned by studying some examples. Our examples will mainly involve the relations WAREHOUSE and EMPLOYEE (see Figures 8.1 and 8.2).

In order to enter requests involving two relations, the user must first obtain two empty tables on the terminal screen. With the relations WAREHOUSE and EMPLOYEE, we would use:

WAREHOUSE	WHNUMB	CITY	WH-AREA

EMPLOYEE	WHNUMB	EMPNUMB	SALARY

Retrieval-11: Two relations, quantifier EXISTS equivalent
In what cities is there (or does there exist) at least one employee making $25,000?
We enter:

WAREHOUSE	WHNUMB	CITY	WH-AREA
	WX	P.	

EMPLOYEE	WHNUMB	EMPNUMB	SALARY
	WX		25000

We may explain this entry with the request:

> Print the CITY value from each WAREHOUSE record where, for example, the WHNUMB value is WX and where there is an EMPLOYEE record also with the (identical) WHNUMB value WX and with the SALARY value equal to $25,000.

Thus we are using the sample connection field value WX to logically link a parent WAREHOUSE record to a child EMPLOYEE record for which the SALARY value is $25,000; this is the basic method used with all retrievals involving two relations. It is useful to compare the above entries with the corresponding

SQL and (for readers who have studied SQL/N) SQL/N expressions:

1. SQL

```
SELECT CITY
FROM WAREHOUSE
WHERE  EXISTS (SELECT *
                FROM EMPLOYEE
                WHERE (SALARY = 25000)
                  AND (WAREHOUSE.WHNUMB = WHNUMB))
```

In this expression we have also linked a parent **WAREHOUSE** record to a child **EMPLOYEE**; this is done following **AND** in the last line of the expression.

2. SQL/N

```
SELECT CITY
FROM EACH WAREHOUSE OWNER RECORD
WHERE (THERE IS AT LEAST 1 EMPLOYEE MEMBER RECORD
        WHERE (SALARY = 25000)
```

In this expression there is no need to specify a specific link between parent and child records; we merely specify parent (owner) and child (member) records.

We see that the method of specifying the link between parent and child in QBE is quite unique, since it depends on giving an example of the link.

Retrieval-12: Two relations, quantifier NOT EXISTS equivalent
Find the city location of each warehouse whose employees (if there are any employees) all earn more than $21,000.
We enter:

WAREHOUSE	WHNUMB	CITY	WH-AREA
	WX	P.	

EMPLOYEE	WHNUMB	EMPNUMB	SALARY
¬	WX		< = 21000

This can be interpreted as:

Print the **CITY** value from each **WAREHOUSE** record where, for example, the **WHNUMB** value is WX and there does not exist an **EMPLOYEE** record with the identical **WHNUMB** value WX for which the **SALARY** field value is less than or equal to $21,000.

The significant point in this retrieval is the use of '⌐' or **NOT** in the **EMPLOYEE** table. It must appear under the name of the table and specifies 'there does not exist an **EMPLOYEE** record . . .', or simply ⌐EXISTS **EMPLOYEE RECORD**. . . . In the previous retrieval the space under **EMPLOYEE** in the table was empty, and as we would expect this specifies 'there exists an **EMPLOYEE** record . . .'.

The system response is:

WAREHOUSE	WHNUMB	CITY	WH-AREA
		NEW YORK	
		CHICAGO	
		DENVER	

We notice that the city of Denver is retrieved even though the warehouse 'WH5' has no employees. We had this difficulty with SQL earlier (see Retrieval-10 and Figure 7.6), although in this case the result is correct since we specifically asked for warehouses whose employees, if there were any employees, all earned more than $21,000. However, suppose the retrieval request had been:

Find the city location of each warehouse with one or more employees who all earn more than $21,000.

Here we are interested in a **WAREHOUSE** record only if it has some child employee records. This has to be spelled out in our QBE entries:

WAREHOUSE	WHNUMB	CITY	WH-AREA
	WX	P.	

EMPLOYEE	WHNUMB	EMPNUMB	WH-AREA
	WX		
⌐	WX		< = 21,000

This can be interpreted as:

Print the **CITY** value from each **WAREHOUSE** record where, for example, the **WHNUMB** value is WX and there is an **EMPLOYEE** with the identical **WHNUMB** value WX, *and* there is not (or there does not exist) an **EMPLOYEE** record with an identical **WHNUMB** value WX for which the **SALARY** field value is less than or equal to $21,000.

Note the use of the implicit logical-**AND** in the above entries. The two lines of the **EMPLOYEE** entries are connected by logical-**AND**. The response would be:

WAREHOUSE	WHNUMB	CITY	WH-AREA
	NEW YORK		
	CHICAGO		

This time Denver is excluded because we have specified in the **EMPLOYEE** table that for a parent there must be at least one child record in the **EMPLOYEE** relation.

Retrieval-13: Two relations, find child record given parent properties
Find the salaries of all employees in New York.
   We enter:

WAREHOUSE	WHNUMB	CITY	WH-AREA
	EX	NEW YORK	

EMPLOYEE	WHNUMB	EMPNUMB	SALARY
	EX		P.

This can be interpreted as:

   Print the **SALARY** value from each **EMPLOYEE** record where, for example, the **WHNUMB** value is WX and there is a **WAREHOUSE** record with an identical **WHNUMB** value WX for which the **CITY** value is 'NEW YORK'.

Thus we are interested in retrieving the **SALARY** value from each child **EMPLOYEE** record for which the **CITY** value in the parent **WAREHOUSE** record is 'NEW YORK'.
   The response would be:

EMPLOYEE	WHNUMB	EMPNUMB	SALARY
			22,000
			25,000

Complex retrievals with a single relation

It is possible to have complex retrieval requests with single quite simple relations. Such requests cannot be expected to be common, but for the sake of completeness we shall include a few examples. Typically we have to link different records from a single relation using field value examples.

Retrieval-14: Two linked records
Find the employee numbers for employees making the same salary as employee 'E4'.

We enter:

EMPLOYEE	WHNUMB	EMPNUMB	SALARY
		P.	SX
		E4	$\overline{\text{SX}}$

This can be interpreted as:

Print the EMPNUMB value from each EMPLOYEE record where, for example, the SALARY value is SX and there is an EMPLOYEE record with the identical SALARY value SX and the EMPNUMB value 'E4'.

In more ordinary English this becomes: Print the employee number from each record with a SALARY value that is the same as the SALARY value in the record with EMPNUMB value 'E4'. The response would be:

EMPLOYEE	WHNUMB	EMPNUMB	SALARY
		E4	
		E7	

We notice that 'E4' is retrieved by the system. This retrieval could have been specified quite differently, however. As is frequently the case with complex retrievals, a breakdown into two simpler retrievals is possible. We could first find the salary being earned by employee 'E4' as follows:

EMPLOYEE	WHNUMB	EMPNUMB	SALARY
		E4	P.

and this gives the SALARY value 25,000 in response. We can then find the employee numbers for employees earning $25,000:

EMPLOYEE	WHNUMB	EMPNUMB	SALARY
		P.	25000

and this gives the same response as our more complex request earlier.

Retrieval-15: Two linked records

Find each warehouse that has at least one employee earning a salary paid to an employee at warehouse 'WH2' as well.

We enter:

EMPLOYEE	WHNUMB	EMPNUMB	SALARY
	P.		SX
	WH2		SX

This may be interpreted as:

> Print the WHNUMB value from each EMPLOYEE record where, for example, the SALARY value is 'SX' and there is an EMPLOYEE record with the same SALARY value 'SX' and a WHNUMB value 'WH2'.

The response would be:

EMPLOYEE	WHNUMB	EMPNUMB	SALARY
	WH1		

Retrieval-16: Use of a condition box

Find the employee numbers for employees who make either more than $24,000 or less than $22,000 and who work at either warehouse 'WH1' or 'WH2'.

Because of the fairly complex retrieval conditions, it is difficult in QBE to construct suitable entries for the table. The solution is to use what is called a *condition box*, which is a special supplementary table to hold complex retrieval conditions. We would enter:

EMPLOYEE	WHNUMB	EMPNUMB	SALARY
	WX	P.	SX

CONDITIONS
SX = (>24000 / <22000)
WX = (WH1 /WH2)

This can be interpreted as:

> Print the EMPNUMB value from each record with, for example, a WHNUMB value WX and a SALARY value SX, where SX is either greater than 24,000 or less than 22,000 and where WX is equal to either 'WH1' or 'WH2'.

Note that each line of the condition box is a logical expression that is either true or false. Separate lines are considered to be connected by logical **AND**. The response of the system is:

EMPLOYEE	WHNUMB	EMPNUMB	SALARY
		E3	
		E4	
		E7	

Note that a condition box would have been useful with Retrieval-9, where we wanted the employees who either earned more than $24,000 or less than $22,000. We could have entered instead:

EMPLOYEE	WHNUMB	EMPNUMB	SALARY
		P.	SX

CONDITIONS
SX = (> 24000 / < 22000)

Computational retrievals

As was the case with SQL, we have two types of retrieval that require computations in addition to extraction of data from the data base. We recall that these two types were:

1. *Target computational retrievals.* With this type of retrieval, data is first retrieved and then this data is used to compute the desired result, such as the average salary at a certain warehouse.
2. *Predicate computational retrievals.* Here data is retrieved depending on the result of computations on other data, such as retrieval of the employee numbers of the employees who make more than the average salary.

Again, as with SQL, in order to specify the necessary computations, we make use of the functions **SUM**, **AVG** (for average), **MAX**, **MIN**, and **CNT** (for counting). In practice we specify:

```
CNT.ALL.     or     CNT.UNQ.ALL.
SUM.ALL.     or     SUM.UNQ.ALL.
AVG.ALL.     or     AVG.UNQ.ALL.
MAX.ALL.
MIN.ALL.
```

When **UNQ.** (corresponding to **UNIQUE** in SQL) is specified, duplicates are eliminated before application of the function; otherwise duplicates are included. The keyword **ALL.** is always used. We now look at some retrievals, beginning with target computational retrievals.

Retrieval-17: Use of CNT

Find the total number of warehouses.

This information appears to be in either the **WAREHOUSE** relation or the **EMPLOYEE** relation. With the **WAREHOUSE** relation we would enter:

WAREHOUSE	WHNUMB	CITY	WH-AREA
	P.CNT.ALL.		

This would retrieve the **WHNUMB** values:

```
'WH1'
'WH2'
'WH3'
'WH5'
```

assuming that we are dealing with the version of **WAREHOUSE** in Figure 8.2. The system then counts the number of values, giving 4 as the result. Had we used the **EMPLOYEE** relation, we would have to remove duplicate **WHNUMB** values (see Figure 8.2). We would have entered:

EMPLOYEE	WHNUMB	EMPNUMB	SALARY
	P.CNT.UNQ.ALL.		

This would retrieve the **WHNUMB** values:

```
'WH1'
'WH2'
'WH3'
```

and a count of these would give 3 as the result, so that there is a discrepancy between the result using the relation **WAREHOUSE** and the result using the relation **EMPLOYEE**. Referring to Figure 8.2, it is not difficult to discover the cause of the discrepancy. All warehouses are not listed in **EMPLOYEE** since there is a warehouse ('WH5') that has as yet no employees. The problem can hardly be blamed on QBE; the discrepancy would have been the same had we used SQL, or any other retrieval language. Even two different CODASYL programs, one using **EMPLOYEE** and the other using **WAREHOUSE**, would have shown the same discrepancy. The problem lies in the data base itself.

That such discrepancies can arise with the retrieval of data from a data base is a cause for concern, for we can expect that retrieval of accurate information from a data base will be a matter of life or death on occasion, when we are dealing with such crucial areas as medicine, search and rescue, and even military operations. Areas such as selection of business strategies, while less important, can also be seriously affected by the wrong retrieval of information from a data base. What can be done to prevent such wrong retrieval of information?

One possibility is the use of even more sophisticated systems that would actually warn a user of the possibility of error. For example, a user who used the relation **EMPLOYEE** for Retrieval-17 should be warned that there are **WHNUMB** values in **WAREHOUSE** that are not in **EMPLOYEE**, and vice versa. Such systems will not become available overnight, and anyway it is difficult to envisage one that could cover every contingency. The onus would therefore appear to rest with the user to prevent error. From this it would follow that in matters of life or death, or of great strategic significance, we cannot rely on information retrieved from a data base by a casual user, unless the fact of its correct retrieval is certified by an expert in the structure of the data base and use of the query language involved.

That is not to say that casual users should not use data bases, or even that in critical areas they are likely to obtain incorrect information. Management should simply be aware that there is a distinct possibility that the casual user will obtain incorrect information. And Murphy's laws tell us that where it can happen, sooner or later it will happen, and in a way calculated to do the most damage.

Retrieval-18: Use of SUM
Find the payroll for warehouse 'WH2'.

Here we use the **EMPLOYEE** relation:

EMPLOYEE	WHNUMB	EMPNUMB	SALARY
	WH2		P.SUM.ALL

giving the result $47,000 (see Figure 8.2). The **SALARY** values for records with the **WHNUMB** value 'WH2' are first retrieved and then summed.

Retrieval-19: Use of equivalent of the partitioned AVE function
For each warehouse find the warehouse number and the average salary paid.

Here we wish to group the **EMPLOYEE** records according to **WHNUMB** value, and for each such group retrieve the **WHNUMB** value and the average of the **SALARY** values. The reader will recall that with SQL Retrieval-25, we had a similar problem, and we briefly discussed the use of partitioned **SUM**, **AVE**, and other functions. We solve the problem in QBE by using **G.** to specify a grouping:

EMPLOYEE	WHNUMB	EMPNUMB	SALARY
	P.G.WX		P.AVE.ALL

This may be interpreted as:

> For each group of **EMPLOYEE** records with, for example, the **WHNUMB** value WX, print the **WHNUMB** value and the average **SALARY** value for the group.

The response would be:

EMPLOYEE	WHNUMB	EMPNUMB	SALARY
	WH1		23,000
	WH2		23,500
	WH3		23,000

using the data in Figure 8.2.

We note we have not fallen into the same trap as we did with Retrieval-15. The salary for warehouse 'WH5' is null, since this warehouse has no employees. However, we did not retrieve any information about 'WH5', and this is correct. We wanted the average salary at each warehouse, and there are *no* salaries at warehouse 'WH5'.

Retrieval-20: Predicate computation

Find the employee numbers for employees who earn less than the average.

Here the system must compute the average salary value from the **EMPLOYEE** relation, before a **SALARY** value in an **EMPLOYEE** record can be compared with the average. We cannot place the retrieval condition that **SALARY** is less than **AVERAGE** in the **EMPLOYEE** table on the screen. We use a supplementary condition box on the screen instead:

EMPLOYEE	WHNUMB	EMPNUMB	SALARY
			SY
		P.	SX

CONDITIONS
SX < AVE.ALL.SY

We can interpret this as:

> For each **EMPLOYEE** record, print the **EMPNUMB** value where the **SALARY** value, for example, is SX and there is a record with, for example, the **SALARY** value SY, provided that SX is less than the average of all possible SY values.

While retrievals that require a condition box are sometimes difficult to construct, they can often be avoided. For example, we could break the above retrieval down into two simpler retrievals. First find the average salary:

EMPLOYEE	WHNUMB	EMPNUMB	SALARY
			P.AVG.ALL.

and this gives us the value $23,200. We next find the employees earning less than $23,200:

EMPLOYEE	WHNUMB	EMPNUMB	SALARY
		P.	23200

with the response:

EMPLOYEE	WHNUMB	EMPNUMB	SALARY
		E1	
		E3	
		E6	

which is the same as the response generated by the specification above using the condition box.

Updating via QBE

It is convenient to use QBE for updating the data base. We begin with some examples that use the update command (U.), and then look at record deletion (D.) and insertion commands (I.).

Updating a single record

Suppose we want to change the salary for employee 'E5' to $23,000. We would enter:

EMPLOYEE	WHNUMB	EMPNUMB	SALARY
		E5	U.23000

Alternatively, we could use:

EMPLOYEE	WHNUMB	EMPNUMB	SALARY
U.		E5	23000

A record to be updated must be uniquely identified, and this is done by entering a key field value, such as the EMPNUMB value 'E5'.

Updating multiple records

Suppose we want to give everyone earning less than $25,000 a $1000 raise. We could enter:

EMPLOYEE	WHNUMB	EMPNUMB	SALARY
		EX	< 25000
U.		EX	SX + 1000

We can interpret this as:

Update the record with, for example, the key value EX and SALARY value, for example, SX so that the SALARY value becomes SX + 1000, where the key value EX is that of a record where the SALARY value is less than 25,000.

However, as mentioned in the coverage of SQL, multiple record update is a risky affair, since it is easy to make a mistake in specifying the conditions for selecting records for update. A more cautious approach would involve first retrieving the records to be updated:

EMPLOYEE	WHNUMB	EMPNUMB	SALARY
P.			< 25000

with the response:

EMPLOYEE	WHNUMB	EMPNUMB	SALARY
	WH2	E1	22,000
	WH1	E3	21,000
	WH3	E6	23,000

When we are satisfied that these are the records to be updated, and that none are missing from the retrieved list, we could issue the update command:

EMPLOYEE	WHNUMB	EMPNUMB	SALARY
U.		EX	SX + 1000

CONDITIONS
EX = (E1 /E3 /E6)

We would then retrieve the updated records to ensure that the updating had been carried out correctly.

As a second example of updating multiple records, suppose that we want to give everyone working in warehouse 'WH2' a 10 percent increase in salary. We could enter:

EMPLOYEE	WHNUMB	EMPNUMB	SALARY
U.	WH2	EX $\overline{\text{EX}}$	SX $\overline{\text{SX}}$*1.10

and this could be interpreted as

> For each **EMPLOYEE** record where the **WHNUMB** value is 'WH2' and the **EMPNUMB** value is EX, for example, and the **SALARY** value is SX, for example, multiply **SX** by 1.10.

As with the previous update we could proceed more cautiously by first retrieving the employee numbers of all those working in warehouse 'WH2' and then updating the retrieved records.

Deleting a single record

Suppose we want to delete the record for employee 'E4'; we would enter:

EMPLOYEE	WHNUMB	EMPNUMB	SALARY
D.		E4	

As with the update (U.) command, the delete command must have a uniquely identified record as its object.

Deleting multiple records

In general, we specify the deletion of multiple records in exactly the same way as we would specify the retrieval of multiple records, except that the **P.** under the relation name is replaced by **D**. As a first example suppose we want to delete all the records for employees who work at warehouse 'WH2'; we would enter:

EMPLOYEE	WHNUMB	EMPNUMB	SALARY
D.	WH2		

We may imagine that the system first retrieves all the records for which the **WHNUMB** value is WH2, and then deletes them. As with updating, a more cautious approach may be advisable, where we first retrieve the records, examine them, and only then delete them.

As another example, if we wanted to delete all the records in the **EMPLOYEE** relation, we would enter:

EMPLOYEE	WHNUMB	EMPNUMB	SALARY
D.			

and of course if we changed the D. to P., all the records in **EMPLOYEE** would be retrieved.

Storing a new record
Let us suppose that we wish to add the record:

WH10   E12   24,500

to the **EMPLOYEE** relation. We would enter:

EMPLOYEE	WHNUMB	EMPNUMB	SALARY
I.	WH10	E12	24500

Following insertion of the record, caution would indicate that we should retrieve it from the data base again as a check.

8.2 DERIVED EXTERNAL RELATIONS AND INTEGRITY CONSTRAINTS

We have three important features of the relational approach yet to discuss. Two of these will be discussed here, while the third, which involves the principles behind the design of relational conceptual schemas, will be dealt with in Chapter 9. (We have already dealt with the design of conceptual schemas involving conceptual files that are relations in Chapters 5 and 6 and at the beginning of Chapter 7. However, while this coverage is sufficient for an introduction to the subject, it has not dealt with the implications of what have come to be known as *functional dependencies*, which have to do with the maintenance of the long-term health of a data base. While this subject of functional dependence, and its implications for conceptual data base design, was largely developed within the relational approach, it is recognized today that it is important for all approaches to data base management, and for this reason it is dealt with separately in Chapter 9 and not as a part of the relational approach, as is the case with some other texts (for example, Ref. 1).

The two topics we discuss here are *derived external relations* and *integrity constraints*. While they are relevant to the relational approach in general, we shall discuss them in the context of IBM's System R, which is an excellent example of their application.

Derived relations

In the relational approach, the subschema or external schema consists of a definition of relations as we saw in Section 7.1. In System R, as would be the case in general, a relation defined in the external schema can be either the same as a conceptual-level relation (which is what we have assumed in our examples so far), or it may be derived from a relation by selecting only desired fields from a conceptual-level relation. For example, if a user needed to know only about employee numbers and in what warehouse an employee worked, then it would be sufficient to define an external relation or view such as VIEW12 (see Figure 8.3) as follows:

```
DEFINE VIEW  VIEW12 (EMPNUMB, WHNUMB)
AS SELECT EMPNUMB, WHNUMB
    FROM EMPLOYEE
```

We notice that a simple SQL expression is used in the definition of the external relation VIEW12, and this leads us to consider the possibility of defining an external relation with a more complex SQL expression. In System R such SQL expressions are used with the definition of external relations that are derived from more than one underlying conceptual relation. Such definitions can be very useful, especially to users who are not very expert in the use of query languages such as SQL.

For example, let us suppose that a manager in the personnel department continually had to deal with employee information that involved the employee number (EMPNUMB field), the employee salary (SALARY field), and the city in which the employee worked (the CITY field from the WAREHOUSE relation). Clearly, in retrieving information from the data base, the personnel manager or his or her assistant would have to be able to construct SQL expressions involving the two relations EMPLOYEE and WAREHOUSE which stand in a child-to-parent relationship to one another. As the reader may well have experienced by now, such SQL expressions are not all that easy to learn to construct. At best, it takes some time to learn the technique, and that may be more time than many busy managers have available.

Fortunately there is an alternative. System R, and relational systems in

EMPNUMB	WHNUMB
E1	WH2
E3	WH1
E4	WH2
E6	WH3
E7	WH1

VIEW12

FIGURE 8.3 A simple external relation, or *view* as it is called in System R. VIEW12 is derived from the conceptual-level relation EMPLOYEE from the data base in Figure 8.2.

EMPNUMB	SALARY	CITY
E1	22,000	NEW YORK
E3	21,000	DALLAS
E4	25,000	NEW YORK
E6	23,000	CHICAGO
E7	25,000	DALLAS

EMPSALCITY

FIGURE 8.4 An external relation or view that is derived from two distinct conceptual-level relations, namely, the EMPLOYEE and WAREHOUSE relations. In the definition of such an external relation we use the same SQL expression that would be needed to retrieve the relation from the underlying conceptual-level relations. Such derived relations can be very useful for information retrieval purposes since SQL expressions for retrieving data from a single relation are usually much simpler than expressions needed with retrieval from multiple relations.

general, would allow us to define an external relation with just the required fields EMPNUMB, SALARY, and CITY. With this external relation, illustrated in Figure 8.4 and called EMPSALCITY, most SQL expressions for extracting data would be quite simple. Of course a more complex SQL expression might be needed initially to define the derived relation, but this could be done by systems personnel at the data base administration department. In the case of EMPSALCITY the definition is not difficult:

```
DEFINE  VIEW EMPSALCITY (EMPNUMB, SALARY, CITY)
AS SELECT (EMPNUMB, SALARY, CITY)
   FROM EMPLOYEE, WAREHOUSE
WHERE (EMPLOYEE.WHNUMB = WAREHOUSE.WHNUMB)
```

As a demonstration that retrieval of information with this relation is easier than with EMPLOYEE and WAREHOUSE, we shall examine some retrievals.

Retrieval-1: Simple predicate
In what cities is there at least one employee earning more than $22,000?
Using the relation EMPSALCITY, we need only code:

```
SELECT CITY
FROM EMPSALCITY
WHERE  SALARY > 22000
```

However, with the EMPLOYEE and WAREHOUSE relations we would have to take into account the relationship between them. We could code:

```
SELECT CITY
FROM WAREHOUSE
WHERE WHNUMB IS IN (SELECT WHNUMB
                     FROM EMPLOYEE
                     WHERE SALARY > 22,000)
```

While this expression is clearly more complex than the one using the relation **EMPSALCITY**, it is clearly not all that much more difficult. However, there are cases where the difference is very great, as is illustrated by the next retrieval.

Retrieval-2: Complex predicate
Find the salaries of employees who work in the same city as employee 'E4'.
    With the relation **EMPSALCITY** we would code:

```
SELECT SALARY
FROM EMPSALCITY
WHERE CITY = (SELECT CITY
                  FROM EMPSALCITY
                  WHERE EMPNUMB = 'E4')
```

The SQL expression using the relations **WAREHOUSE** and **EMPLOYEE** would be:

```
SELECT SALARY
FROM EMPLOYEE
WHERE WHNUMB IS IN (SELECT WHNUMB
               FROM WAREHOUSE
               WHERE CITY = (SELECT CITY
                             FROM WAREHOUSE
                             WHERE WHNUMB IS IN (SELECT WHNUMB
                                                 FROM EMPLOYEE
                                                 WHERE EMPNUMB = 'E4')))
```

This expression is clearly much more complex than the expression involving the view **EMPSALCITY**. In the last two S-F-W-blocks we retrieve the city in which employee 'E4' works. The remaining part of the expression (the first six lines) retrieves the salaries of employees who work in this city.

However, it may be argued that a view derived from multiple conceptual-level relations is unnecessary, and that the nonexpert can manage quite well without it. For example, while the retrieval expression above is much more difficult to construct than the one using the view **EMPSALCITY**, there is nothing to prevent the casual user from tackling the retrieval in smaller steps, using the original relations **WAREHOUSE** and **EMPLOYEE**. With the retrieval request above we could first retrieve the city in which employee 'E4' works. This is straightforward, and the expression is the same in structure as the last two S-F-W-blocks above. Referring to the data in Figure 7.8, the result would be New York. We can then find the salaries of all employees in New York.

Updating views derived from multiple relations
While in theory it is possible to construct rules for updating views derived from conceptual-level relations or base tables (as they are called in System R), such rules would tend to be complex, since they would be aimed at identifying cases where the underlying conceptual-level relations or base views could be unique-

ly identified. With System R the problem was solved by prohibiting the update of views derived from more than one underlying conceptual-level relation. Such views are thus used only for facilitating information retrieval.

Derived relations and the CODASYL approach

As pointed out in Chapter 5, the conceptual files of the CODASYL approach do not have to be relations. However, in our general coverage of data base conceptual-level structures in Chapter 5, we used only relations, and similarly with the CODASYL material in Chapter 6. Indeed, since relations are simpler than any other kind of conceptual file, and since relations are permitted with the CODASYL approach, we can expect that many CODASYL conceptual data bases will consist of relations.

The question that naturally follows is whether external files derived from more than one conceptual file should or could be allowed with the CODASYL approach, especially if the CODASYL conceptual data base is constructed from relations. The answer appears to be that such CODASYL-derived external files both could and should be allowed for the benefit of the user who prefers to extract data from only one external file at a time. However, at the time of writing, as far as the author is aware, no such facility has been provided for either in the CODASYL specifications or by a vender of a CODASYL data base system. A language such as SQL/N could be used to define such useful external files.

Integrity constraints

Integrity constraints are part of the definition of conceptual-level relations and, as the name suggests, are a specification of what updates may not be performed on a relation or group of relations. Integrity has to do with maintaining the internal accuracy of a data base. A simple example of a lack of integrity is a relation in which the same fact is stored differently in two different places; in the relation in Figure 5.5 (**PART-WAREHOUSE**) it is possible to have the warehouse 'WH1' described in one record as being in Dallas, and in another record as being in some other city. Of course the possibility of this type of lack of integrity can be reduced or even eliminated by a data base design that requires a single fact to be stored only once, as is the case with the data base in Figure 7.8.

However, other types of inaccuracy can creep into a data base. For example, we could have an accidental entry of an employee's height as 99 feet, or number of children as 77. It is by means of integrity constraints that such inaccuracies can be prevented. With the relational approach, very sophisticated integrity constraints are possible.

Following Date (Ref. 1) we can distinguish three main types of integrity constraints, namely, key constraints, connection or referential constraints, and general constraints. We shall examine these briefly in turn.

Key constraints

This constraint ensures that each record of a conceptual-level relation is unique, and is implied by the specification of a primary key. Thus we cannot insert into the data base a new record with the same primary key value as an existing record, nor can we update an existing primary key to the value null. With System R, we specify that a primary key cannot have a null value by specifying **NONULL**, as was described at the beginning of this chapter. (However, to specify that a field or field combination must always have a unique value in System R, we must use a storage data base specification of a primary index; it is only in this way that a primary key can be specified in System R.)

Connection or referential constraints

This type of constraint ensures that there is a parent record for each child record. In practice this means that we cannot delete (or update) a parent connection field value as long as there is a child connection field with that value. This is a very reasonable restriction. For example, in the data base in Figure 7.8, it would be quite unreasonable to allow the **WAREHOUSE** record with the **WHNUMB** primary key value 'WH1' to be deleted, while there are still **EMPLOYEE** records with **WHNUMB** child connection field value 'WH1'. With System R there is no automatic provision of a connection restraint for a relationship between two relations, and it is up to the designer of the data base to incorporate needed restraints. This is done by means of **ASSERT** commands (described below) usually at the time the relations involved are defined.

We note that with the CODASYL approach the specification of an owner-coupled set can be made to approximate the referential or connection restraint of the relational approach; that is, by means of the owner-coupled set specification, we can ensure that there will be a parent (or owner) for each child (or member) record.

General constraints

We can divide general constraints into two types, namely, static constraints and dynamic restraints.

> *Static constraints.*   Here we are dealing with constraints on the properties of the data in the relations at any given instant. For example, if minimum wage laws prevented anyone having a salary less than $10,000, then we could not have a **SALARY** value in **EMPLOYEE** less than $10,000.
>
> *Dynamic constraints.*   Here we are dealing with constraints on the properties of the data in the data base at any instant as compared with some time in the past. For example, suppose that the government decided that the only way to reduce the rate of price inflation was by imposing a ceiling of 6 percent on salary increases; then a **SALARY** value at any instant would be not more than 6 percent higher than the **SALARY** value of a year ago. This of course would be a very difficult constraint to arrange as it would require the storage of historical data. A simpler but similar constraint might prohibit salary increases of more than 6 percent.

We recall that an SQL expression really consists of an imperative followed by an often complex condition after the word **WHERE**, and that this condition, which can be either true or false, is known as a predicate. We can use such predicates to specify properties of the data base that must hold true in the face of updates. In System R an **ASSERT** command is used to specify that an SQL predicate must hold true, and thus to specify a constraint.

The System R ASSERT command for constraint specification

The System R **ASSERT** command has two forms. When asserting a constraint on the properties of a single relation, we use:

ASSERT *assertion-name* **ON** *base-table-name: SQL-predicate*

If the constraint deals with the properties of two or more relations, as does a connection or referential constraint, for example, we use the form:

ASSERT *assertion-name: SQL-predicate*

We shall look at a few examples of constraints, beginning with a constraint on the relation **EMPLOYEE**:

```
ASSERT CONSTRAINT-1 ON EMPLOYEE: 1000 < =  SELECT MIN(SALARY)
                                            FROM EMPLOYEE
```

This constraint specification requires that the minimum **SALARY** value in the **EMPLOYEE** relation be greater than or equal to $10,000.

As another example let us suppose that nobody is allowed to earn more than employee 'E4'. We would need the following restraint specification:

```
ASSERT CONSTRAINT-2 ON EMPLOYEE: (SELECT MAX(SALARY)
                                  FROM EMPLOYEE)
                                 < =
                                 (SELECT SALARY
                                 FROM EMPLOYEE
                                 WHERE EMPNUMB = 'E4')
```

Each time a **SALARY** value in **EMPLOYEE** was involved in an update, the system would check for the validity of the above predicate. An update that caused the predicate to be violated would be rejected.

As an example of a constraint on the properties of two relations, let us suppose that all the warehouses in Chicago could have no more than a total of 20 employees. We use the constraint:

```
ASSERT CONSTRAINT-3 : 20 > = (SELECT COUNT(*)
                             FROM EMPLOYEE
                             WHERE WHNUMB IS IN (SELECT WHNUMB
                                                 FROM WAREHOUSE
                                                 WHERE CITY = 'CHICAGO'))
```

The previous three constraints were static; as an example of the specification of a dynamic constraint, let us suppose that nobody can get a salary increase in excess of $1000. We would use the constraint:

```
ASSERT CONSTRAINT-4:  1000 > = (SELECT MAX(NEW.SALARY - OLD.SALARY)
                               FROM EMPLOYEE
```

In this constraint we have used the SQL keywords **OLD** and **NEW**.

As a final example, we could consider the specification of the connection or referential constraint for the connection field **WHNUMB** in the relations **EMPLOYEE** and **WAREHOUSE**. We want to specify that every **EMPLOYEE** child record must have a parent. However, it is acceptable for a parent not to have a child. Thus the set of **WHNUMB** values from **WAREHOUSE** must contain the set of **WHNUMB** values from **EMPLOYEE**. Thus our constraint will be:

```
ASSERT CONSTRAINT-5:   (SELECT WHNUMB
                         FROM WAREHOUSE)
                        CONTAINS
                        (SELECT WHNUMB
                         FROM EMPLOYEE)
```

Thus an attempt to delete a **WAREHOUSE** record that has child **EMPLOYEE** records would invalidate the constraint specification, and would thus be rejected.

Integrity with concurrent processing

As with many other data base systems, the concept of a transaction is used with System R to prevent updating programs running concurrently from interfering with one another (see Chapter 6). A transaction is initiated in a program by a **BEGIN TRANSACTION** command. From this point until an **END TRANSACTION** command is issued, all retrievals and updates are considered part of a transaction. Examples of the practical use of these commands with COBOL are given in the supplement to Chapter 7. Updates made to the data base during a transaction are said to be *committed*, that is, made permanent, only *after* the **END TRANSACTION** command is issued.

When a **BEGIN TRANSACTION** command is issued, a user can define one of three levels of concurrency protection. *Level-3* gives the greatest protection and in effect gives the program exclusive control over the relations involved in the transaction. *Level-1* gives the least protection, and even allows one program to retrieve data updated by another program but not yet committed. *Level-2* prevents a program from retrieving uncommitted changes, but it does permit a second program to commit changes between successive retrievals within a first program's transaction. Thus a program running with level-2 protection could retrieve different data when the same **SELECT** command is issued on different occasions within a transaction.

Recovery

System R uses log files and periodic dumps to provide for recovery in the case of a system crash; as with other systems, special routines are available to reconstruct a current copy of the data base from the most recent dump or (*image copy*) and the updates in the log file. Additional details are given in Ref. 2.

8.3 COMPARISON OF THE CODASYL AND RELATIONAL APPROACHES

It is worth pausing to compare the CODASYL and relational approaches. We do so because there are strong indications that in the future these two approaches will dominate. The CODASYL approach probably will have a wide following because it will likely become an American National Standard and because CODASYL data base system recommendations are developed by the body that successfully developed the COBOL programming language. The relational approach can also be expected to have a wide following because it too will probably become an American National Standard, because it is the approach favored by IBM, and because it has a wide following among the theoreticians, especially academic theoreticians.

The conceptual data base

With both the relational and CODASYL approaches the conceptual data base is a collection of related conceptual files. With the relational approach a conceptual file must be a relation, while a CODASYL conceptual file may or may not be a relation, all according to the whim of the designer of the data base. However, since there is no reason for a CODASYL conceptual file not to be a relation, and since there are great advantages in terms of simplicity (many of which have yet to be explained; see Chapter 9) to the use of relations, we can expect that most future CODASYL data bases will consist of relations. Here at least, then, we can uncover no fundamental difference between the two approaches. Thus, if we consider the now familiar data base consisting of the WAREHOUSE and EM-PLOYEE conceptual files shown again in Figure 8.5, the important point is that the conceptual files could be from *either* a relational or a CODASYL data base.

However, while the structures specified in a relational conceptual schema are relations, and only relations, additional structures may be specified in a CODASYL conceptual schema, namely, owner-coupled sets, and a CODASYL data base may be looked upon as a collection of owner-coupled set occurrences.

WHNUMB	CITY	WH-AREA
WH1	DALLAS	37,000
WH2	NEW YORK	50,000
WH3	CHICAGO	20,000
WH5	DENVER	13,000

WAREHOUSE

WHNUMB	EMPNUMB	SALARY
WH2	E1	22,000
WH1	E3	21,000
WH2	E4	25,000
WH3	E6	23,000
WH1	E7	25,000

EMPLOYEE

FIGURE 8.5   The conceptual files WAREHOUSE and EMPLOYEE above are also relations so that they could be part of either a relational or CODASYL data base. If the data base were relational, however, we can only specify the one-to-many relationship between WAREHOUSE and EMPLOYEE conceptual records by equating WHNUMB connection field values.

Thus the CODASYL data base containing the conceptual files **WAREHOUSE** and **EMPLOYEE** may also have the structure shown in Figure 8.6. Here each parent **WAREHOUSE** record is grouped with its **EMPLOYEE** children. Since owner-coupled sets have names that are specified in the conceptual schema definition, they may be referred to in data base manipulation commands.

Here indeed is a fundamental difference between the two approaches. The grouping of a parent with its children is a natural one and is a fundamental structure of the English. Thus it is natural to refer to a warehouse's employees, a company's divisions, a division's products, a ship's crew members, an aircraft's weapons, and so on. When we refer to a **WAR-EMP** occurrence in the data base in Figures 8.5 and 8.6, we are simply referring to a certain warehouse's employees.

Nevertheless it must be understood that such a grouping of records as an owner-coupled set is not at all necessary. It is merely an intellectual convenience. With a relational data base we are always able to specify the child records of a given parent record by specifying those child records for which the child connection field value equals the key value of the parent. This is quite sufficient and no more is necessary. However, on occasion this spartan equivalent of an owner-coupled set occurrence specification can be quite awkward for those who are not very mathematically inclined.

The relational approach has its origins in the theory of mathematical sets and relations, a fundamental branch of mathematics. To many theoreticians the method of dealing with relationships in the relational approach is the ultimate in simplicity, and indeed it is when looked at from a mathematical viewpoint. To the mathematician, simplicity is what is necessary and sufficient, as is the method of specifying a relationship by equating connection field values. We are reminded of the American philosopher Thoreau. During his years at Walden Pond in Massachusetts in the last century, Thoreau spent his time recording the

WHNUMB	CITY	WH-AREA	WHNUMB	EMPNUMB	SALARY
WH1	DALLAS	37,000	WH1 WH1	E3 E7	21,000 25,000
WH2	NEW YORK	50,000	WH2 WH2	E1 E4	22,000 25,000
WH3	CHICAGO	20,000	WH3	E6	23,000
WH5	DENVER	13,000			

WAR-EMP

FIGURE 8.6 In a CODASYL data base containing WAREHOUSE AND EMPLOYEE records the records are grouped into conceptual files as shown in Figure 8.5 and also into the owner-coupled set occurrences of an owner-coupled set, called WAR-EMP. This second method of grouping the records is probably the one that would be used in any business report about warehouses and their employees.

struggle of his contemporaries to obtain what he considered to be the unnecessary conveniences of life. Few business users of relational data bases can be expected to have the background of a mathematician or the outlook of Thoreau, so that while from a theoretical viewpoint the relational approach is a model of simplicity, from a business viewpoint it lacks a great deal of human conveniences. This is certainly true of such relational languages as SQL, as we shall discuss in the following pages. However, we can expect that as the relational approach becomes more widely used in business, additional facilities will gradually be incorporated, and that these facilities will make the approach much more convenient for the business user.

Data base manipulation languages

As explained briefly in Chapter 5, there are two main types of data base manipulation languages, namely, *procedural* and *nonprocedural* languages. With a procedural language we use a sequence of commands to the data base system to retrieve data from a data base; each command typically selects a single record, as with CODASYL commands, and the sequence of selected records form a navigational pathway through the data base. Thus a procedural data base manipulation language is typically a language that deals with a single record at a time.

On the other hand, a nonprocedural language does not require a sequence of commands to retrieve data from a data base. We merely specify what data is required by specifying the types of fields required and the conditions under which they are required. SQL is an excellent example of a nonprocedural language. Nonprocedural languages were largely developed with the relational approach. Their great advantage over procedural languages is the saving in programmer effort. For example, a retrieval request that required about 10 lines of SQL could easily require 200 lines of COBOL with embedded CODASYL commands. Furthermore, we can expect that most managers in business will be in a position to acquire an elementary knowledge of either SQL or QBE, while it is unlikely that many will ever be in a position to write COBOL or PL/1 programs containing CODASYL commands.

Even if we compare the CODASYL commands (embedded in a COBOL host program) with SQL embedded in a COBOL program (with those unpleasant $ sign details), it is still far easier with the embedded SQL. However, it can be argued that it is unfair to compare the CODASYL procedural language with the SQL nonprocedural language. Nonprocedural languages represent the latest in data processing technology and will be superior to procedural languages in general. It might be more appropriate to compare the CODASYL procedural language with a relational procedural language that deals with one record at a time. However, while such a language is possible, to the author's knowledge none have ever been implemented, and it seems unlikely that any ever will be.

An even more appropriate comparison might be between CODASYL nonprocedural languages and the relational nonprocedural languages such as SQL. CODASYL nonprocedural languages are a much more recent development than relational nonprocedural languages, and at the time of writing the CODASYL committee has yet to generate a proposal for a standard. There have been a number of languages developed in the past 5 years for nonprocedural manipulation of CODASYL data bases. For example, the nonprocedural SQL/N described in a supplement to Chapter 6 is a recent language that is an extension of IBM's SQL, and which can be used both with a CODASYL data base consisting of relations and with a conventional relational data base.

Earlier we pointed out that the lack of a simple specification of relationships in the relational approach makes relational languages somewhat inconvenient to use, and that the grouping of records in owner-coupled sets in the CODASYL approach is an intellectual convenience. SQL/N uses owner-coupled sets to specify retrievals, and the resulting convenience becomes apparent in common retrievals in which natural quantifiers or the equivalent are involved. We shall give just one example with SQL/N here that clearly brings out the convenience of owner-coupled sets as compared with the relational method of specifying a relationship in a retrieval expression. The retrieval request is:

Find the floor area of warehouses, all but one of whose employees earn more than $21,000.

A glance at the view of the data base in Figure 7.17 indicates that we want each **WAREHOUSE** record for which all the child records except one have a **SALARY** value greater than $21,000. The SQL/N expression closely mirrors the English expression:

```
SELECT WH-AREA
FROM EACH WAREHOUSE OWNER RECORD
WHERE (FOR ALL BUT ONE EMPLOYEE MEMBER RECORD
      (SALARY > 21000)
```

Alternatively, if all but one child **EMPLOYEE** records have to have a **SALARY** value greater than $21,000, that is the same as saying that only one or exactly one child record must have a **SALARY** value less than or equal to $21,000. We can find an SQL/N expression to mirror this English expression too, if we use the natural quantifier **FOR EXACTLY ONE** instead of **FOR ALL BUT ONE**:

```
SELECT WH-AREA
FROM EACH WAREHOUSE OWNER RECORD
WHERE (FOR EXACTLY ONE EMPLOYEE MEMBER RECORD
      (SALARY < = 21000)
```

With SQL the simplest expression is along the lines of the second SQL/N expression above. However, we must use a predicate computational retrieval expression that requires the use of something called a label variable:

```
SELECT WH-AREA
FROM WAREHOUSE, X
WHERE 1 = (SELECT COUNT (*)
           FROM EMPLOYEE
           WHERE WHNUMB = X.WHNUMB
           AND SALARY < = 21,000)
```

We can interpret this as follows:

> Select the **WH-AREA** field value from a **WAREHOUSE** record (that we shall henceforth refer to as X), provided a count of the **EMPLOYEE** records, for which the **WHNUMB** value is equal to the **WHNUMB** value in X, and for which the **SALARY** value is less than or equal to $21,000, gives the value 1.

To most who are not mathematicians the SQL expression is more complex, as would be the expression in the other relational languages that have been proposed. The source of the difficulty is clear. It lies with the need to express the one-to-many relationship between **WAREHOUSE** and **EMPLOYEE** by means of equating connections fields. Yet it may also be argued that from a mathematical viewpoint the SQL expression is simpler, for it requires fewer constructs than the SQL/N expressions. The SQL/N expressions require use of the **EMPLOYEE** and **WAREHOUSE** conceptual files and an owner-coupled set; the SQL expression requires only the **EMPLOYEE** and **WAREHOUSE** relations.

It would thus appear that there is a likelihood of CODASYL nonprocedural languages that are at least the equal of relational languages. But it must be remembered that there are currently a considerable number of implementations of SQL either available or in a late stage of development, and that the implementation of a nonprocedural data base language is a very large project. IBM's System R has taken some 8 years to develop, and System R SQL is probably the most powerful data base language currently available or likely to be available for some time. Thus it will be many years before a language as powerful and convenient as SQL/N could become available. However, data base technology does not stand still, and in the meantime we can expect to see new and improved versions of SQL. Unfortunately it is impossible to predict exactly how things will develop. We can be sure only that the technology will continue to advance.

SUMMARY

1. Query-By-Example (QBE) from IBM is an example of a relational query language that is eminently suitable for many types of retrieval of information from relational data bases by casual users. Retrieval expressions do not normally have to be constructed, and for simpler retrievals it is sufficient to make a few entries in the columns of a table displayed on a terminal. There is a table for each relation being dealt with. The entries the user places in the table are often examples of the kind of data that the user needs. More complex retrievals require the use of condition boxes which are essentially logical expressions. As with all query languages, complex queries can usually be handled by a sequence of simpler queries.

2. The relational approach permits external data bases that permit derived relations. A derived relation is an external-level relation or view that is derived from several relations (usually conceptual-level relations). A derived relation is typically specified using an SQL expression. It is easier to construct SQL expressions to retrieve data from such a derived relation than from the underlying relations from which it was derived. With System R updating cannot be carried out on such derived relations.

3. Relational data base systems permit powerful integrity constraints that are defined within the conceptual schema. These constraints are often in the form of SQL predicates that must always be true regardless of updates. Thus an update that violates a constraint will be rejected. Concurrently executing programs with System R are prevented from interfering with each other by required definitions of transactions within the programs. Recovery from failure is by means of logs and periodic dumps.

4. The essential difference between the CODASYL and relational approach is the use by CODASYL of owner-coupled sets. A less fundamental difference has been the historical tendency of CODASYL to rely on procedural manipulation of the data base, while relational languages are mainly nonprocedural. Nevertheless powerful nonprocedural languages (of which SQL/N is an example) can be based on the owner-coupled set concept, provided the data base is constructed from relations.

QUESTIONS

The following questions require the construction of suitable QBE tables to retrieve information from the data base in Figure 8.2.

1. Retrieve names and locations of suppliers.
2. Retrieve the salary and employee numbers of employees. The data should be ordered primarily in ascending salary order, and secondarily in ascending employee number.
3. Retrieve the names of suppliers located in California.
4. Retrieve the salary and employee numbers of employees who earn at least $22,000.
5. Retrieve the salary and employee numbers of employees who earn at least $22,000. The data should be ordered primarily in ascending salary order and secondarily in ascending employee number.
6. Retrieve the names of cities that have warehouses between 40,000 and 60,000 square feet in area.
7. Retrieve the names of suppliers that are located either in California or in Texas.
8. Retrieve the order numbers for orders that are either issued to supplier 'S4' or issued by employee 'E3'.
9. Retrieve the names of suppliers that are not located in California.
10. Find the names of suppliers that deal with employee 'E3'.
11. Find the states or provinces that have suppliers that do not deal with employee 'E3'.
12. Find the salaries of employees who have issued all orders before August 1984.
13. Find the issue date of orders for suppliers in Texas.
14. Find the issue date of all orders that are not for suppliers in Texas.
15. Find the names of suppliers that are located in the same state or province as Raytex.

16. Find the order numbers for orders that were either issued by employee 'E7' or 'E3' or were issued to supplier 'S6' or 'S4'. A condition box should be used, but readers might also want to try it without a condition box.
17. Find out how many suppliers there are.
18. Find out how many states and provinces must be dealt with when dealing with suppliers.
19. What is the total warehouse floor area?
20. What is the total payroll for all the warehouses?
21. What is the payroll at each warehouse?
22. What is the average salary at each warehouse?
23. What is the average floor area of warehouses in New York?
24. Find the names of cities in which there is a warehouse with less than the average floor area for all warehouses.
25. Find the employees who are paid the maximum salary.

The following questions require the construction of suitable tables to update the data base in Figure 8.2.

26. Update the data base to reflect the move of the supplier Raytex to Oregon.
27. Delete all suppliers in Texas.
28. Delete all orders issued by employee 'E3' to supplier 'S6'.
29. Increase the floor area of each New York warehouse by 10,000 square feet.
30. Increase by 10% the salaries of employees who deal with California suppliers. Use a sequence of retrieval and update operations.
31. Add the supplier record (S15 Siliton California).

The following questions deal with derived relations and integrity constraints with System R.

32. Create an external-level relation called SPO that gives all information about Texas suppliers and their orders.
33. Using the relation from Question 32, give an SQL expression for the names of Texas suppliers that deal with employee 'E7'.
34. Using the relation from Question 32, give an SQL expression for the names of Texas suppliers that do not deal with employee 'E7'.
35. Using the relation from Question 32, give an SQL expression for the employee numbers of employees who deal with California companies.
36. Using the relation from Question 32, give an SQL expression for the salaries of employees who deal with California suppliers.
37. Define an integrity constraint that prevents any supplier from being located in Hawaii.
38. Define an integrity constraint that prevents an employee in Denver from making more than $25,000.
39. Define an integrity constraint that requires that an employee must work in a warehouse in the WAREHOUSE relation.

40. Define an integrity constraint that requires that an order must be issued by some employee in the **EMPLOYEE** relation to some supplier in the **SUPPLIER** relation.

41. Explain how concurrently executing COBOL programs with embedded System R SQL are prevented from interfering with each other.

ADDITIONAL PERSPECTIVE
RELATIONAL ALGEBRA

Relational algebra is a highly original but important language developed by E. F. Codd (Ref. 1) at IBM. There are two reasons for its importance. First, it is widely used to specify operations used in data base design (although there are less technical ways of specifying these operations, as shown in Chapter 9). Second, the language is often used as a *target language*, that is, as the language into which higher language expressions, such as SQL expressions, are translated, in the first stage of compilation or translation of such expressions. The language allows us to specify different kinds of operations that may be carried out on relations. We may thus use it to construct a relational algebra program, which is a succession of statements, each of which specifies an operation to be carried out on relations. Thus the language might be considered to be procedural, although most writers would go only as far as stating that it is semiprocedural. The reason for this is that a relational algebra operation is very powerful, and will accomplish what would normally take many lines of code with procedural data base languages such as the CODASYL DML.

It was once thought that it would be commonly used for retrieval of information from data bases by casual users. This now seems unlikely, for experience has shown that relational algebra programs are quite difficult to construct, and even more difficult to read. Nevertheless, the basic operations that are permitted in relational algebra are individually not very difficult (with one notable exception). The advantage of studying it lies in the greater insight into the relational approach that a knowledge of it imparts. It is recommended only for readers who wish to perfect their knowledge of the relational approach, however. As far as the author is aware there are no significant commercial systems that permit users to query a relational data base by means of relational algebra.

There are two kinds of operations that are used in relational algebra. We may distinguish between *mathematical set operations*, which most readers are probably familiar with in other contexts, and certain *relational operations*, which are used only with relations. We look at them in turn.

The mathematic set operations in relational algebra

Let us suppose that we have two instances of the **WAREHOUSE** relation, namely, **WAREHOUSE-A** and **WAREHOUSE-B**, which have some records or tuples in common, as shown in Figure 8.7a. If we recall that the records or tuples of a

WHNUMB	CITY	WH-AREA
WH1	DALLAS	37,000
WH2	NEW YORK	50,000
WH3	CHICAGO	20,000

WAREHOUSE-A

WHNUMB	CITY	WH-AREA
WH2	NEW YORK	50,000
WH3	CHICAGO	20,000
WH7	CALGARY	18,000

WAREHOUSE-B

(a) Two instances of the relation WAREHOUSE.

WHNUMB	CITY	WH-AREA
WH1	DALLAS	37,000
WH2	NEW YORK	50,000
WH3	CHICAGO	20,000
WH7	CALGARY	18,000

WAREHOUSE-A
UNION
WAREHOUSE-B

WHNUMB	CITY	WH-AREA
WH2	NEW YORK	50,000
WH3	CHICAGO	20,000

WAREHOUSE-A
INTERSECTION
WAREHOUSE-B

WHNUMB	CITY	WH-AREA
WH1	DALLAS	37,000

WAREHOUSE-A
DIFFERENCE
WAREHOUSE-B

(b) The main mathematical set operations as applied to the relations in (a).

FIGURE 8.7 Mathematical set operations.

relation are unique, and so form a mathematical set of records, then the following operations are clearly possible.

1. *Set union operation*
   The operation WAREHOUSE-A UNION WAREHOUSE-B specifies the creation of a new relation (shown in Figure 8.7b) made up of all the unique records from WAREHOUSE-A and WAREHOUSE-B.
2. *Set intersection operation*
   The operation WAREHOUSE-A INTERSECTION WAREHOUSE-B specifies the creation of a new relation (shown in Figure 8.7b) made up of records that are common to both WAREHOUSE-A and WAREHOUSE-B.
3. *Set difference operation*
   The operation WAREHOUSE-A DIFFERENCE WAREHOUSE-B specifies the creation of a new relation (shown in Figure 8.7b) made up of records from WAREHOUSE-A that are not also in WAREHOUSE-B.

The relational operations

There are four basic relational operations: *selection*, *projection*, *natural join*, and *division*. We illustrate them both by means of diagrams and simple relational algebra programs.

The selection operation

This is the simplest operation, and involves creating a new relation by selecting certain records from a specified relation. Records are selected if they satisfy a logical condition involving the fields of the record. Thus if we want to create a new relation from the **EMPLOYEE** relation in Figure 8.8a, where the new relation is to be called **WELL-PAID**, and is to contain only records describing employees who make $25,000, we would code:

$$\text{WELL-PAID} = \text{SELECT(EMPLOYEE(SALARY = 25000))}$$

and this is an example of a one-line relational algebra program. The relation **WELL-PAID** is shown in Figure 8.8b. More complex conditions may be specified. For example, suppose we wanted a relation **EXTREME**, which would have records describing employees from **EMPLOYEE** who earned less than $22,000 or more than $24,000. We could have the one-line program:

$$\text{EXTREME} = \text{SELECT(EMPLOYEE((SALARY} > \text{24000) OR (SALARY} < \text{22000)))}$$

However we could generate **EXTREME** using a longer program with simpler steps that illustrate the use of the mathematical set union operation as well:

$$\text{RELATION-1} = \text{SELECT(EMPLOYEE(SALARY} > \text{24000))}$$
$$\text{RELATION-2} = \text{SELECT(EMPLOYEE(SALARY} < \text{22000))}$$
$$\text{EXTREME} = \text{RELATION-1 UNION RELATION-2}$$

First we form **RELATION-1** for employees earning more than $24,000, and then **RELATION-2** for employees earning less than $22,000. Then we use the **UNION** operation to combine these two relations into **EXTREME**.

This short program illustrates the essence of relational algebra. Each opera-

WHNUMB	EMPNUMB	SALARY
WH2	E1	22,000
WH1	E3	21,000
WH2	E4	25,000
WH3	E6	23,000
WH1	E7	25,000

EMPLOYEE

WHNUMB	EMPNUMB	SALARY
WH2	E4	25,000
WH1	E7	25,000

WELL-PAID

FIGURE 8.8 The relation WELL-PAID may be generated from the relation EMPLOYEE by a relational algebra selection operation that selects EMPLOYEE records with SALARY value equal to $25,000.

tion on the right of a statement involves one or more relations and forms a new relation which is the relation on the left. In a later statement an operation can act on a relation formed by an earlier operation. This RELATION-1 above is formed in the first operation, and then is itself used in the third operation to form the relation EXTREME.

The projection operation

This operation involves creating a new relation from a specified relation by the following process:

1. Select specified columns, thus forming a conceptual file that may contain duplicate records.
2. Eliminate duplicate records thus forming a relation.

As an example consider the projection of the relation WAREHOUSE (in Figure 8.9a) on the fields CITY and WH-AREA. The result of this projection is the new relation CITY-AREA, shown in Figure 8.9b, and specified by the relational algebra statement:

```
CITY-AREA = PROJECTION(WAREHOUSE(CITY, WH-AREA))
```

An arbitrary projection operation often does not appear to have too much meaning, but in this case we could argue that CITY-AREA contains records that tell us about what warehouse floor-areas occur in different cities (but not how many warehouses with a given area occur in a given city).

The projection operation is decidely useful, and is widely used in data base design, as will become evident from a study of Chapter 9. It is also useful in the following simple relational algebra program, which produces a relation containing the employee numbers of employees who earn more than $23,000:

```
RELATIONA = SELECTION(EMPLOYEE(SALARY > 23000))
RELATIONB = PROJECTION(RELATIONA(EMPNUMB))
```

WHNUMB	CITY	WH-AREA
WH1	DALLAS	37,000
WH2	NEW YORK	50,000
WH3	CHICAGO	20,000
WH4	NEW YORK	50,000
WH5	DENVER	13,000
WH6	CHICAGO	20,000

WAREHOUSE

CITY	WH-AREA
DALLAS	37,000
NEW YORK	50,000
CHICAGO	20,000
DENVER	13,000

CITY-AREA

FIGURE 8.9 Illustration of the projection operation. The relation CITY-AREA is the result of a projection of the relation WAREHOUSE on the fields CITY and WH-AREA. The columns CITY and WH-AREA are extracted from WAREHOUSE and duplicate records eliminated. If duplicates were not eliminated, the result would not be a relation.

The natural join operation

This operation is often used for joining or concatenating parent and child records. The process is controlled by what are called *join fields*, which in many cases are the connection fields we have already commonly encountered in dealing with relationships. Suppose that we produce a new relation WE from the two relations WAREHOUSE and EMPLOYEE shown in Figure 8.10a. The relation WE is formed by taking each EMPLOYEE relation and replacing the WHNUMB field by the WAREHOUSE record with the same WHNUMB value. This process is the *natural join* of WAREHOUSE and EMPLOYEE based on the join fields WHNUMB in WAREHOUSE and WHNUMB in EMPLOYEE. The relation WE is shown in Figure 8.10b. It is specified in the relational algebra statement:

$$\text{WE = WAREHOUSE(WHNUMB) JOIN EMPLOYEE(WHNUMB)}$$

In this statement each relation taking part in the natural join is followed by the join field involved. Notice that in order for a record from any one of the relations to take part in the natural join, its join field value must occur in the other relation. Thus the WAREHOUSE record with join field value 'WH5' does not take part,

WHNUMB	CITY	WH-AREA
WH1	DALLAS	37,000
WH2	NEW YORK	50,000
WH3	CHICAGO	20,000
WH5	DENVER	13,000

join
field　　　　　　WAREHOUSE

WHNUMB	EMPNUMB	SALARY
WH2	E1	22,000
WH1	E3	21,000
WH2	E4	25,000
WH3	E6	23,000
WH1	E7	25,000

join
field　　　　　　EMPLOYEE

(a) Two relations that take part in a natural join operation. Join fields and connections fields are often the same.

CITY	WH-AREA	WHNUMB	EMPNUMB	SALARY
NEW YORK	50,000	WH2	E1	22,000
DALLAS	37,000	WH1	E3	21,000
NEW YORK	50,000	WH2	E4	25,000
CHICAGO	20,000	WH3	E6	23,000
DALLAS	37,000	WH1	E7	25,000

WE

(b) The relation WE is the result of the natural join of the relations in (a) using the join fields shown. Note that not every record takes part in the natural join operation. The WAREHOUSE record with WHNUMB value 'WH5' cannot take part because there is no join field in EMPLOYEE with that value.

FIGURE 8.10 Illustration of the natural join operation.

because there is no record in EMPLOYEE with WHNUMB value 'WH5' (see Figure 8.10).

As an example of the use of the natural join and other relational algebra operations, suppose that we want the salaries of employees who work in New York (referring to the relations EMPLOYEE and WAREHOUSE in Figure 8.10*a*). We could use the following relational algebra program or procedure:

```
RELATION-1 = SELECTION(WAREHOUSE(CITY = 'NEW YORK'))
RELATION-2 = RELATION-1(WHNUMB) JOIN EMPLOYEE(WHNUMB)
RELATION-3 = PROJECTION(RELATION-2(SALARY))
```

The contents of the intermediate relations RELATION-1 and RELATION-2, as well as the final relation RELATION-3 are shown in Figure 8.11. Notice that the program would eliminate any duplicate salaries at New York warehouses.

The division operation

The division operation is the most difficult to grasp, and is normally used only in more complex retrievals. Involved in the operation are the *dividend* relation, the *divisor* relation, and the resulting or *quotient* relation. In the most common type of division operation the dividend relation has two fields, while the divisor has only one field. The dividend relation is always one that is in some way con-

WHNUMB	CITY	WH-AREA
WH2	NEW YORK	50,000

RELATION-1

WHNUMB	EMPNUMB	SALARY
WH2	E1	22,000
WH1	E3	21,000
WH2	E4	25,000
WH3	E6	23,000
WH1	E7	25,000

EMPLOYEE

CITY	WH-AREA	WHNUMB	EMPNUMB	SALARY
NEW YORK	50,000	WH2	E1	22,000
NEW YORK	50,000	WH2	E4	25,000

RELATION-2

SALARY
22,000
22,000

RELATION-3

FIGURE 8.11 Intermediate relations in the execution of a relational algebra program.

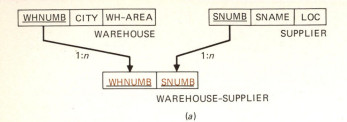

(a)

WHNUMB	SNUMB
WH1	S1
WH1	S2
WH1	S3
WH2	S3
WH3	S1
WH3	S2
WH5	S1
WH5	S2
WH5	S4
WH6	S2

WAREHOUSE-SUPPLIER

FIGURE 8.12 In the data base in (a) there is a many-to-many relationship between WAREHOUSE and SUPPLIER, since a warehouse deals with many suppliers and a supplier supplies many warehouses. The many-to-many relationship has been resolved into two one-to-many relationships involving the relation WAREHOUSE-SUPPLIER. In (b) we see that a record in WAREHOUSE-SUPPLIER indicates that a certain supplier supplies a certain warehouse, so that the many-to-many relationship between suppliers and warehouses is essentially described in the relation WAREHOUSE-SUPPLIER. It is such relations that participate in division operations as the dividend (see Figure 8.13).

nected with a many-to-many relationship, for example the one illustrated by the relation **WAREHOUSE-SUPPLIER** in Figure 8.12a. Here a warehouse deals with many suppliers and a supplier supplies many warehouses. The relation **WAREHOUSE-SUPPLIER** tells us exactly which warehouse deals with which supplier, as shown in Figure 8.12b.

Now let us suppose that we divide **WAREHOUSE-SUPPLIER** by a divisor relation **WAREHOUSE-NUMBERS** according to the relational algebra statement:

QUOT = WAREHOUSE-SUPPLIER ÷ WAREHOUSE-NUMBERS

To see how the division operation works, consider Figure 8.13. Here we have arranged the records of **WAREHOUSE-SUPPLIER** into groups. As far as possible a group contains the same WHNUMB values as the divisor relation **WARE-HOUSE-NUMBERS**, and all the records of the group have the same SNUMB

WHNUMB	SNUMB
WH1	S1
WH3	S1
WH5	S1
WH1	S2
WH3	S2
WH5	S2
WH2	S3
WH5	S4
WH6	S2
WH1	S3

WAREHOUSE-SUPPLIER
    (dividend)

WHNUMB

WH1
WH3
WH5

WAREHOUSE-NUMBERS
    (divisor)

÷

=

SNUMB

S1
S2

QUOT
(quotient)

FIGURE 8.13.   Illustration of the relational division operation. An SNUMB value from the dividend is placed in the quotient, whenever that SNUMB value appears in the records of the dividend along with every WHNUMB value in the divisor. Thus the quotient lists those suppliers listed in the dividend that supply at least those warehouses listed in the divisor.

value. The records of **WAREHOUSE-SUPPLIER** that cannot form such groups form a group of unordered records at the end. The resulting or quotient relation **QUOT** will contain each **SNUMB** value for which there is a group of **WARE-HOUSE-SUPPLIER** records with the **WHNUMB** values in the divisor relation **WAREHOUSE-NUMBERS**.

Despite initial appearances, the division operation has a definite meaning and utility. In the example above the operation has determined the supplier numbers for those suppliers that supply at least those warehouses listed in the divisor relation.

As an example of the use of the division operation in a relational algebra program, with reference to the data base in Figure 8.2, suppose that we want the salaries of employees who deal with suppliers 'S7', 'S4', and 'S6'. For convenience we shall assume that these supplier numbers are in the relation **DIVISOR**. We could code:

```
R1 = PROJECTION(PUR-ORDER(EMPNUMB,SNUMB))
R2 = R1 ÷ DIVISOR
R3 = R2(EMPNUMB) JOIN WAREHOUSE(EMPNUMB)
R4 = PROJECTION(R3(SALARY))
```

In support of our contention earlier that relational algebra programs are difficult to read, we leave it to the reader to decipher the program. All the operations used have already been explained.

QUESTIONS

For each of the following requests for information from the data base in Figure 8.2, a relational algebra procedure should be constructed.

42. Find the salaries of employees at warehouse 'WH2'.

43. Find the salaries of employees who work in New York.

44. Find the names of supplier who are located in California.

45. Find the names of suppliers who deal with employee 'E6'.

46. Find the cities with a warehouse whose employees all earn more than $21,000.

47. Find the salaries of employees who deal with all Texas suppliers.

48. Find the names of suppliers that deal with employees 'E1', 'E4', and 'E7'.

49. Find the states or provinces with suppliers that deal with no employees.

REFERENCES

1. Date, C. J., 1981. *Introduction to Database Systems.* Addison-Wesley, Reading, Mass.

2. Fernandez, E. B., R. C. Summers, and C. Wood, 1981. *Database Security and Integrity.* Addison-Wesley, Reading, Mass.

3. IBM. "Query-by-Example: Terminal User's Guide," IBM Form No. SH20–2078.

4. Martin, J., 1981. *An End-User's Guide to Data Base.* Prentice-Hall, Englewood Cliffs, N.J.

5. Zloof, M. M. 1977. "Design Aspects of the Query-by-Example Data Base Query Language." *IBM Sys. J.,* 16(4).

9

Conceptual Data Base Design

In Chapter 5 we covered the elements of data base structures, and the material in that chapter can also be taken as an elementary introduction to data base design. For example, we saw how a data base is composed of related conceptual files, how the conceptual structure needs to be designed to prevent unwary users falling into connection traps, and how many-to-many relationships can be decomposed into one-to-many relationships. Some readers will have noticed that we used only relations as conceptual files in the examples in Chapter 5, and also in the CODASYL data bases in Chapter 6. Our reasons for using relations were threefold:

1. A relation is the simplest kind of conceptual file.
2. There is widespread agreement among data base researchers that more complex conceptual files, that is, conceptual files that are not relations, are unnecessary.
3. Relations show wide variation in the level of complexity, and use of the simplest kinds of relations prevents many data base maintenance problems.

In the first part of this chapter we shall study how these simplest possible types of relations may be designed. In the second part we shall briefly study how *entity-relationship diagrams* can be used for designing conceptual data bases. In the chapter supplement we examine the structure of *recursive relationships*, since data bases that contain them are becoming more common.

353

It is only fair to point out to the reader that there have been intensive mathematical investigations into both the identification of relations that are *not* the simplest possible, and the subsequent *decomposition* of these relations into simpler relations. Investigators normally use mathematical tools based on relational algebra, which is described in the supplement to Chapter 8. In consequence a very large proportion of the literature on the subject is of a mathematical nature and not very accessible to the average business student. Nevertheless, by means of diagrams and examples it is possible to explain the essentials of the subject without using mathematics, and this is the approach we shall take. Readers will find that the material in the supplement to Chapter 8 will help, however, although it is not necesssary.

9.1 FUNCTIONAL DEPENDENCIES AND THE DESIGN OF CONCEPTUAL FILES

There are two basic steps in the design of a relation or relational conceptual file for use in a conceptual data base. We must:

1. Group together in as natural a manner as possible associated data elements that are already defined in the corporate data dictionary, and which are known to be needed by planned users of the data base. Such a grouping of data elements is a designer's *potential relation* or conceptual file.
2. Determine all the *functional dependencies* in each potential relation. If any dependencies are found to be undesirable, they should be removed, and this is done by decomposing the original potential relation into two or more relations that do not have the undesirable dependencies.

Construction of a corporate data dictionary for use (among other things) in data base design is discussed in Chapter 13. Assuming that a proper data dictionary is available, it is clear that the heart of the data base design process is the elimination of undesirable dependencies from a potential relation. Undesirable functional dependencies can make a data base difficult to maintain. Our first task, therefore, is to find out just what a functional dependency is and why some dependencies are undesirable. After that, as a design aid, we give a classification of relations and conceptual files. Relations without undesirable dependencies are the simplest possible.

The concept of functional dependence

The concept of functional dependence is not new and is the basic idea behind the concept of a function in elementary mathematics, something that has been understood for centuries. What is new is its application to relations. To begin, we shall take the simplest possible case of functional dependence, to give the reader an opportunity to acquire a thorough grasp of the basic idea.

Consider the relation COPPERPRICE in Figure 9.1. Each record of COPPERPRICE has two fields, namely, WEEK and PRICE, where price contains the price of copper (cents per pound) prevailing a number of weeks ago given by the value in WEEK; thus the price 2 weeks ago is 71.5¢, according to COPPER-

WEEK	PRICE
0	71.2
1	71.4
2	71.5
3	71.4
4	71.3
5	71.2
6	71.1
7	71.2
8	71.4
9	71.5
10	71.6
11	71.7
12	71.7
13	71.5
14	71.6
15	71.5

COPPERPRICE

FIGURE 9.1   The relation COPPERPRICE gives the price of copper (in cents per pound) over a 16-week period. Week 0 is the current week while, for example, week 2 is 2 weeks ago. The contents of COPPERPRICE can clearly be displayed as a graph (see Figure 9.2).

PRICE. The key field is clearly **WEEK**, since this holds a unique value. We note, for example, that the price is the same on four different weeks, namely, 71.5¢, so that **PRICE** is certainly not unique. We can display this relation **COPPERPRICE** as a graph (see Figure 9.2), placing the possible **PRICE** values along the Y axis and the **WEEK** values along the X axis. Now we can see more clearly that since **WEEK** values are unique, for a given **WEEK** value there is just one **PRICE** value,

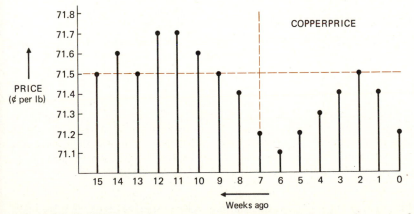

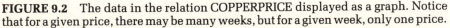

FIGURE 9.2   The data in the relation COPPERPRICE displayed as a graph. Notice that for a given price, there may be many weeks, but for a given week, only one price.

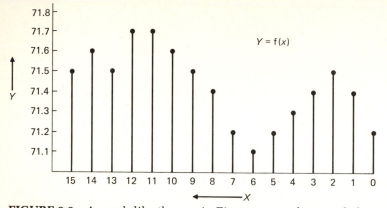

FIGURE 9.3 A graph like the one in Figure 9.2 can be regarded as a display of Y versus X for some function f, where $Y = f(X)$. X is always the independent or undetermined variable, while Y is the dependent or determined variable. Given a Y value, a unique corresponding X value is not determined, but given an X value there is determined a unique corresponding Y value. We say that Y is a function of X, or that Y is *functionally dependent* on X.

that is to say, the **WEEK** value determines the **PRICE** value; it is also clear that the **PRICE** value does not determine the **WEEK** value, since **PRICE** is not unique, there being many **WEEK** values for a single **PRICE** value.[1]

We can also say that **PRICE** *depends* on **WEEK**, or that **PRICE** is *functionally dependent* on **WEEK**, or that **PRICE** is a *function* of **WEEK**. This reminds us of the concept of a *function* in elementary mathematics, where $Y = f(X)$. Thus changing **PRICE** to Y and **WEEK** to X, we could have the graph in Figure 9.3. Clearly Y is here functionally dependent on X, an almost trivial conclusion. It is clearly also possible to display the data in the graph as a relation with the fields X (the key field) and Y (Figure 9.4). We can therefore also conclude that a functional dependency can be displayed as a relation, where the X values are the key field values.

We can see that the idea of functional dependence has its roots in the functions of elementary mathematics. However, traditionally such functions involve numerical quantities as does that in Figure 9.2. We shall now see that the concept of functional dependence may be applied equally well to relations with nonnumeric data.

---

[1]Note that the **PRICE** and **WEEK** axes strictly contain the data from the *domains* of **PRICE** and **WEEK**, where the domain of **PRICE** is the range of all possible **PRICE** values, of which the **PRICE** values in the column **PRICE** in Figure 9.1 are just a subset. The concept of the domain underlying a column in a relation was explained at the beginning of Chapter 7. It is not an altogether academic concept. The trader in copper futures who concentrates on the data in the **COPPERPRICE** relation might be inclined to forget that the domain for **PRICE** stretches from zero cents per pound to infinity; were he then to contract for future sale of copper at 71.5 cents per pound, with the spot price of copper subsequently going to the top of its domain (through the roof), he would in theory lose everything he owned.

X	Y
0	71.2
1	71.4
2	71.5
3	71.4
4	71.3
5	71.2
6	71.1
7	71.2
8	71.4
9	71.5
10	71.6
11	71.7
12	71.7
13	71.5
14	71.6
15	71.5

R

FIGURE 9.4 The function f, giving Y as a function of X, may be displayed as a relation R, where X is the key field.

Consider the relation **PLACE** in Figure 9.5. Each record describes a city in the United States. A **CITY** field contains a unique city name and serves as the key field; the **STATE** field has the name of the state containing the city and is clearly not unique, since more than one city in **PLACE** is in a state such as Texas. It is clear that if we are given a **CITY** value, the corresponding value of **STATE** is determined, since a city must be in some state. On the other hand, given a **STATE** value, the corresponding **CITY** value is not determined, since for one state there are many possible cities. We can thus see that the situation with the relation **PLACE** is the same as with the relation **COPPERPRICE**, so that **STATE** is functionally dependent on **CITY**, or **STATE** = f(**CITY**).

We can even display the functional dependency graphically in Figure 9.6.[1] **CITY** is the key field, and so we place **CITY** values along the X axis in ascending alphabetical order and **STATE** values along the Y axis in ascending alphabetical order. It is completely clear from the graph that there is one **STATE** value for a given **CITY** value and many **CITY** values for a given **STATE** value.

Functional dependency diagrams

We should by now have firmly grasped the fact that in a relation with the fields A and B, if A is functionally dependent on B, that is, if $A = f(B)$, then the functional

---

[1]Strictly, we should use **STATE** and **CITY** domains along the Y and X axes. The **STATE** domain would be all American states, and the **CITY** domain all American cities. However, the black circles would still represent the data in the relation **PLACE** in Figure 9.5.

CITY	STATE
ALBANY	NEW YORK
AUSTIN	TEXAS
BUFFALO	NEW YORK
DALLAS	TEXAS
FAIRBANKS	ALASKA
HOUSTON	TEXAS
JUNEAU	ALASKA
LOS ANGELES	CALIFORNIA
SACRAMENTO	CALIFORNIA
SAN ANTONIO	TEXAS
SAN FRANCISCO	CALIFORNIA
SEATTLE	WASHINGTON
SPOKANE	WASHINGTON

PLACE

FIGURE 9.5 In the relation PLACE a CITY value determines the STATE value, but the STATE value does not determine the CITY value. Thus STATE = f(CITY), or STATE is functionally dependent on CITY. Although the data involved is alphabetic, the functional dependency of STATE on CITY can still be displayed graphically (Figure 9.6).

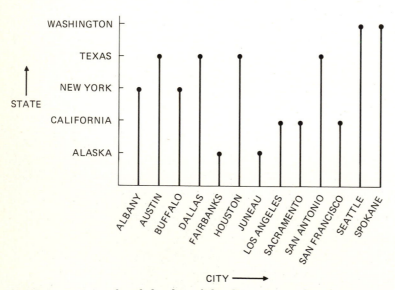

FIGURE 9.6 Graphical display of the data in the relation PLACE in Figure 9.5. Notice that for one STATE value there are many CITY values, while there is only one STATE value for a given CITY.

dependence can be displayed as a graph, with B values along the X axis and A values along the Y axis. However, this is a fairly awkward manner of displaying a functional dependency, especially if we are dealing with a large relation containing nonnumeric data. We need a more concise method, since later we shall have to deal with functional dependencies in relations with many fields and not just two as in the examples given so far. The solution is to use what are known as functional dependency diagrams. There are several types in use. They are all rather similar. We shall use a simple and explicit type that is closely related to the extended Bachman diagrams that we have been using to show the structure of conceptual and external data bases.

First let us take the STATE values from the relation PLACE by taking the complete STATE column in PLACE and removing duplicate values. As we have already seen, this process is called taking the *projection* of PLACE on the field STATE. It is equivalent to retrieving a relation from PLACE with the SQL command:

```
SELECT STATE
FROM PLACE
```

Let us give this *projection relation* with unique STATE values the name PROJ(STATE), since it is a projection on the field STATE, as shown in Figure 9.7. Each record in PROJ(STATE) is trivially simple, since there is only one field, the key field, in each record. Nevertheless, a glance at Figure 9.7 shows that there must be a 1:n relationship between the records of PROJ(STATE) and PLACE, since for a record in PROJ(STATE), such as 'TEXAS', there are many records in PLACE, such as the PLACE records describing cities in Texas. Clearly in this relationship, the child connection field is the STATE field in PLACE. In addition, for any record describing a city in PLACE, there can be just one record in PROJ(STATE), namely, the one describing the state containing the city.

Thus this one-to-many relationship between PROJ(STATE) and PLACE is just another consequence of the functional dependency of STATE on CITY. However, we have a diagrammatic technique for representing one-to-many relationships, namely, extended Bachman diagrams, so we can easily apply this technique to the relationship in Figure 9.7. The extended Bachman diagram or *functional dependency diagram* is shown in Figure 9.8.

We note that the box for the relation PROJ(STATE) is constructed by means of a colored dashed line. This is simply to signify that the relation PROJ(STATE) is completely imaginary and has no underlying storage file, as would the relation PLACE, since under normal circumstances PLACE would be part of a conceptual data base.

The diagram in Figure 9.8 is simply expressing the functional dependence of STATE on CITY. To determine functional dependency expressed by one of these diagrams, no matter how complex, we can always use the rule:

With any one-to-many relationship in a dependency diagram, the field depicted as the key field of the parent relation (for example, STATE in Figure

STATE		STATE	CITY
ALASKA		ALASKA	FAIRBANKS
		ALASKA	JUNEAU
CALIFORNIA		CALIFORNIA	LOS ANGELES
		CALIFORNIA	SACRAMENTO
		CALIFORNIA	SAN FRANCISCO
NEW YORK		NEW YORK	ALBANY
		NEW YORK	BUFFALO
TEXAS		TEXAS	DALLAS
		TEXAS	HOUSTON
		TEXAS	SAN ANTONIO
WASHINGTON		WASHINGTON	SEATTLE
		WASHINGTON	SPOKANE

PROJ(STATE)   PLACE records

FIGURE 9.7   On the left we have the relation formed by taking the unique STATE values from the relation PLACE in Figure 9.5. This process is called projection, and we name the new relation PROJ(STATE), meaning projection on STATE. At the same time we show the records from PLACE sorted in STATE order. It is clear that there is a one-to-many relationship between the relation PROJ(STATE) and the relation PLACE. This is another way of bringing out the functional dependence of STATE on CITY, that is, STATE = f(CITY).

9.8) is functionally dependent on the key field of the child relation (for example, CITY in Figure 9.8).

This rule will be useful with dependency diagrams for relations that have a lot of functional dependencies.

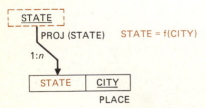

FIGURE 9.8   Functional dependency diagram. Since there is a one-to-many relationship between PROJ(STATE) and PLACE, it may be illustrated by means of an extended Bachman diagram. If we consider the projection relation PROJ(STATE) to be entirely imaginary, then the diagram depicts the functional dependency within the relation PLACE, with STATE functionally dependent on CITY.

Functional dependencies and the primary entity

There is another way of looking at functional dependencies. We can regard each record of a conceptual-level relation as describing some unique primary entity. For example, a record of the relation PLACE describes cities. In the case of the relation WAREHOUSE used in the previous chapter, a record described a warehouse. Such an entity described by a record of a relation is called the *primary entity*. Thus a city is the primary entity of the relation PLACE, and a warehouse is the primary entity of the relation WAREHOUSE. *The primary key field of a relation must therefore be the unique identifier of the primary entity.*

As we have seen with the relation PLACE in Figure 9.5, STATE is functionally dependent on CITY. But a CITY value is simply a unique identifier for a (primary) entity *city*, so that we could also say that a STATE value depends on the entity identified by the CITY value. Even more simply we can say that the STATE value *describes* the city entity identified by a CITY value, and this is something that the reader has probably known all along without the need of a concept like functional dependency.

So what is all the fuss about? Well, the entity city in the relation PLACE is the primary entity, and it will come as no surprise that a STATE value will describe a city entity; so would the value of every other field in this relation (if there were others). In other words, every field in a relation is functionally dependent on the primary key of the relation. The difficulty arises when a field is functionally dependent on a field that is not a key field, that is, when a field value describes an entity that is not the primary entity. As we shall see, such functional dependencies are undesirable for they can give rise to peculiar side effects when the data base is updated. The aim of the data base designer is simple relations in which each field of a relation is functionally dependent on the primary key field, and only on the primary key field. We shall now look in more detail at relations with more than one functional dependency.

Functional dependencies in relations with atomic keys

We saw that a functional dependency could involve fields that are either numeric or nonnumeric. However, from now on in our analysis of functional dependencies, we shall use mostly examples involving nonnumeric or character data. We do this merely for expositional purposes, since it will be easier for readers to remember nonnumeric data.

In this section we shall deal only with relations in which a single field serves as the primary key, that is, relations with *atomic primary keys*. Relations with *composite primary keys* are dealt with later in the chapter. We begin now with a relation with two functional dependencies. This relation is simply another version of the WAREHOUSE relation and is shown in Figure 9.9. We have replaced the numeric field WH-AREA (see Figure 8.2) with the nonnumeric field MINI which gives the name of the manufacturer of each warehouse's minicomputer (assuming that each warehouse is equipped with a minicomputer).

We can see from the WAREHOUSE relation that CITY value is determined by the WHNUMB value, but not vice versa, since for a given CITY value there are

WHNUMB	CITY	MINI
WH1	DALLAS	DIGITAL
WH2	NEW YORK	IBM
WH3	CHICAGO	DIGITAL
WH4	NEW YORK	UNIVAC
WH5	DENVER	IBM
WH6	DALLAS	DIGITAL
WH7	NEW YORK	DIGITAL
WH8	CHICAGO	IBM
WH9	DENVER	UNIVAC

WAREHOUSE

FIGURE 9.9 Another version of the relation WAREHOUSE, each record of which describes a warehouse. CITY gives the city in which the warehouse is located, and MINI gives the name of the manufacturer of the warehouse's minicomputer. (We may assume that each warehouse has its own minicomputer.)

many WHNUMB values, identifying many warehouses. We can make this more precise by taking the projection of WAREHOUSE on STATE as shown in Figure 9.10a. It is quite clear that for each CITY value in PROJ(CITY) there are many records in WAREHOUSE, that is, many warehouse entities. Thus we can be quite sure that CITY is functionally dependent on the primary key WHNUMB.

In a similar manner we can see that the MINI value is determined by the WHNUMB value, but not vice versa, since for a given MINI value there are many WHNUMB values. Again we can take a projection of WAREHOUSE on the field MINI, as shown in Figure 9.10b, and we can clearly see that there is a one-to-many relationship between PROJ(MINI) and WAREHOUSE. Thus there must be a functional dependency between MINI and WHNUMB.

The two functional dependencies in the relation WAREHOUSE are illustrated in the dependency diagram in Figure 9.11. Thus the relation WAREHOUSE is acceptably simple—the nonkey fields are functionally dependent on the key field, and there are no other functional dependencies. But how do we know that there are no other functional dependencies? And what harm would it do if there were? The first question can only be answered by examining every pair of fields in the relation for a possible dependency. The only possibilities remaining in the relation is that either CITY is functionally dependent on MINI or vice versa. But since a city does not determine which minicomputer manufacturer is used and vice versa, we can safely state that there are no other dependencies. To answer the second question, we must have an example of a dependency in which the key field is not involved, that is, an undesirable functional dependency.

A relation with an undesirable functional dependency

Let us now consider the functional dependencies in the relation WAREHOUSE-A in Figure 9.12. WAREHOUSE-A is the same as the relation WAREHOUSE in Figure 9.9, except that we have an additional field STATE and some additional

CITY
CHICAGO
DALLAS
DENVER
NEW YORK

PROJ(CITY)

CITY	WHNUMB	MINI
CHICAGO	WH3	DIGITAL
CHICAGO	WH8	IBM
DALLAS	WH1	DIGITAL
DALLAS	WH6	DIGITAL
DENVER	WH5	IBM
DENVER	WH9	UNIVAC
NEW YORK	WH2	IBM
NEW YORK	WH4	UNIVAC
NEW YORK	WH7	DIGITAL

WAREHOUSE records

(a) Use of the projection file PROJ(CITY) to illustrate the functional dependence of CITY on WHNUMB.

MINI
DIGITAL
IBM
UNIVAC

PROJ(MINI)

MINI	WHNUMB	CITY
DIGITAL	WH1	DALLAS
DIGITAL	WH3	CHICAGO
DIGITAL	WH6	DALLAS
DIGITAL	WH7	NEW YORK
IBM	WH2	NEW YORK
IBM	WH5	DENVER
IBM	WH8	CHICAGO
UNIVAC	WH4	NEW YORK
UNIVAC	WH9	DENVER

WAREHOUSE records

(b) Use of the projection relation PROJ(MINI) to illustrate the functional dependence of MINI on WHNUMB.

FIGURE 9.10   Illustration of the functional dependencies in the relation WAREHOUSE.

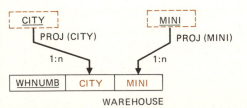

WAREHOUSE

FIGURE 9.11   Use of a functional dependency diagram to illustrate the functional dependencies in the relation WAREHOUSE. While the functional dependencies in WAREHOUSE are almost trivially simple, it is such simplicity that is desirable in the relations of a conceptual data base.

WHNUMB	CITY	STATE	MINI
WH1	DALLAS	TEXAS	DIGITAL
WH2	NEW YORK	NEW YORK	IBM
WH3	CHICAGO	ILLINOIS	DIGITAL
WH4	NEW YORK	NEW YORK	UNIVAC
WH5	DENVER	COLORADO	IBM
WH6	DALLAS	TEXAS	DIGITAL
WH7	NEW YORK	NEW YORK	DIGITAL
WH8	CHICAGO	ILLINOIS	IBM
WH9	DENVER	COLORADO	UNIVAC
WH10	HOUSTON	TEXAS	IBM
WH11	BUFFALO	NEW YORK	DIGITAL
WH12	PEORIA	ILLINOIS	UNIVAC
WH13	BUFFALO	NEW YORK	IBM

WAREHOUSE-A

FIGURE 9.12 A relation whose records describe warehouses. CITY and STATE give the city and state in which a warehouse is located, while MINI gives the manufacturer of a warehouse's minicomputer.

STATE
COLORADO
ILLINOIS
NEW YORK
TEXAS

STATE	WHNUMB	CITY	MINI
COLORADO	WH5	DENVER	IBM
COLORADO	WH9	DENVER	UNIVAC
ILLINOIS	WH3	CHICAGO	DIGITAL
ILLINOIS	WH8	CHICAGO	IBM
ILLINOIS	WH12	PEORIA	UNIVAC
NEW YORK	WH2	NEW YORK	IBM
NEW YORK	WH4	NEW YORK	UNIVAC
NEW YORK	WH7	NEW YORK	DIGITAL
NEW YORK	WH11	BUFFALO	DIGITAL
NEW YORK	WH13	BUFFALO	IBM
TEXAS	WH1	DALLAS	DIGITAL
TEXAS	WH6	DALLAS	DIGITAL
TEXAS	WH10	HOUSTON	IBM

PROJ(STATE)   WAREHOUSE-A records

FIGURE 9.13 The projection relation PROJ(STATE) illustrates the functional dependence of STATE on WAREHOUSE. For one STATE value there are many WHNUMB values, and for one WHNUMB value there is one STATE value, that is, the STATE value is determined.

records. It is clear that both CITY and MINI are still functionally dependent on WHNUMB, and we can construct the projection relations PROJ(CITY) and PROJ(MINI) which will be similar to those shown in Figure 9.10, and which will participate in one-to-many relationships with the relation WAREHOUSE.

As far as the field STATE is concerned, it is clear that the WHNUMB value determines the STATE value in a record but not vice versa. Thus we can expect that STATE is functionally dependent on WHNUMB, and the one-to-many relationship between PROJ(STATE) and WAREHOUSE-A is illustrated in Figure 9.13.

However, it is clear also that within a WAREHOUSE-A record, a CITY value determines the STATE value but not vice versa. In other words, for a given

STATE	STATE	CITY	CITY	WHNUMB	STATE	MINI
COLORADO	COLORADO	DENVER	DENVER	WH5	COLORADO	IBM
			DENVER	WH9	COLORADO	UNIVAC
ILLINOIS	ILLINOIS	CHICAGO	CHICAGO	WH3	ILLINOIS	DIGITAL
			CHICAGO	WH8	ILLINOIS	IBM
	ILLINOIS	PEORIA	PEORIA	WH12	ILLINOIS	UNIVAC
NEW YORK	NEW YORK	BUFFALO	BUFFALO	WH11	NEW YORK	DIGITAL
			BUFFALO	WH13	NEW YORK	IBM
	NEW YORK	NEW YORK	NEW YORK	WH2	NEW YORK	IBM
			NEW YORK	WH4	NEW YORK	UNIVAC
			NEW YORK	WH7	NEW YORK	DIGITAL
TEXAS	TEXAS	DALLAS	DALLAS	WH1	TEXAS	DIGITAL
			DALLAS	WH6	TEXAS	DIGITAL
PROJ(STATE)	TEXAS	HOUSTON	HOUSTON	WH10	TEXAS	IBM

| PROJ(STATE,CITY) records | WAREHOUSE-A records |

FIGURE 9.14 There is a one-to-many relationship between PROJ(STATE) and PROJ(STATE,CITY) which means that STATE is functionally dependent on CITY, since for a CITY value there is exactly one STATE value. There is also a one-to-many relationship between PROJ(STATE,CITY) and WAREHOUSE-A, which means that CITY is functionally dependent on WHNUMB, since the CITY values are unique in PROJ(STATE,CITY), and for one WHNUMB value there is exactly one CITY value. However there is also a one-to-many relationship between PROJ(STATE) and WAREHOUSE-A. This is clear both from the layout above and that in Figure 9.12, so that STATE is also functionally dependent on WHNUMB. All these dependencies are displayed in Figure 9.15.

STATE value there will be many CITY values, and for one CITY value just one STATE value. Thus if we take the projection of the relation WAREHOUSE-A on the two fields STATE and CITY, giving the relation PROJ(STATE, CITY), that is, the relation that would be retrieved by the SQL expression:

```
SELECT STATE CITY
FROM WAREHOUSE-A
```

then within this new relation, STATE will be functionally dependent on CITY. This should be clear from Figure 9.14. We see that PROJ(STATE), which incidently is both a projection on PROJ(STATE, CITY) and a projection on WAREHOUSE-A, is involved in a one-to-many relationship with PROJ(STATE, CITY). Since the STATE and CITY values in PROJ(STATE) and PROJ(STATE, CITY) are those in WAREHOUSE-A, it is clear that STATE is functionally dependent on CITY within WAREHOUSE-A, as well.

We can display these dependencies in the dependency diagram in Figure 9.15. We see that CITY, STATE, and MINI are all functionally dependent on WHNUMB. In addition, we see that STATE is functionally dependent on CITY, and CITY is not a key field in WAREHOUSE-A. This is undesirable, in this case for the following reasons:

1. *Inconsistent STATE values.* As the relation WAREHOUSE is constituted, there is nothing to prevent an inconsistent update or inconsistent insertion of a STATE value. For example, suppose a new record is inserted:

    ```
    WH15    BUFFALO    OHIO    IBM
    ```

    We now have the situation where in some records Buffalo is in New York, while in another it is in Ohio. The data base has become inconsistent. Because we are using a fairly trivial example for expositional purposes, most North Americans would spot the error at once. But if Mexican states were included, how many would know that Monterrey is not in Coahuila

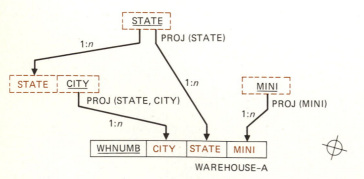

FIGURE 9.15 Dependency diagram for the relation WAREHOUSE-A in Figure 9.12. The dependency of STATE on CITY is undesirable as it can cause updating anomalies. The dependency can be removed by decomposing WAREHOUSE-A into two relations, as shown in Figure 9.16.

but in Nuevo Leon? In business, such an error could cause the loss of an important order, or a foul-up in delivery schedules. In medicine or perhaps military operations, an error permitted by a functional dependency of this type could even have fatal consequences.

2. *Impossibility of storing certain information.* It is clear that while a record in **WAREHOUSE-A** contains information about a warehouse, because of the functional dependence of **STATE** on **CITY**, it also contains information about a city, specifically what state a city is in. This might be looked upon as a kind of bonus. However, if it is important that the information about what state a city is in be available, sooner or later a need will arise for storing this information for a city that has (as yet) no warehouse. But if there is no warehouse, there can be no **WHNUMB** value, and thus no key field for the necessary record. Result: The information cannot be stored.

The solution to the first problem is to have information about what state a city is in stored only in one place, and the solution to the second difficulty is to have a separate place to store information about cities and states regardless of whether a city has a warehouse. We have both solutions if we construct a new data base to replace the **WAREHOUSE-A** relation by:

1. Eliminating the **STATE** field from **WAREHOUSE-A**, giving us a new relation which we shall call **WAREHOUSE** (we have had it already in Figure 9.9)
2. Setting up a new conceptual-level relation **PLACE** (with corresponding storage file), which is identical to **PROJ(STATE, CITY)**

This is illustrated in Figure 9.16. It is clear that the new data base consisting of **PLACE** and **WAREHOUSE** contains exactly the same information as the relation **WAREHOUSE-A** in Figure 9.15. There are still functional dependencies in this new data base as Figure 9.16 shows, but none of them are undesirable. In **PLACE**

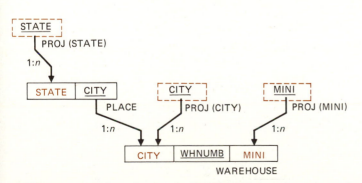

FIGURE 9.16 The relation WAREHOUSE-A is decomposed into two new relations, namely, PLACE [the same as PROJ(STATE, CITY) in Figure 9.14] and WAREHOUSE (see Figure 9.9). The is a one-to-many relationship between PLACE and WAREHOUSE. The simple dependencies for PLACE and WAREHOUSE are also shown.

the STATE field describes the primary entity, a *city*, and in WAREHOUSE the CITY and MINI fields describe the primary entity, a *warehouse*. There are thus no functional dependencies between nonkey fields.

Two undesirable functional dependencies in a single relation

The previous example of an undesirable functional dependency is one of the simplest possible. We can easily expand the example to include two undesirable functional dependencies, as shown in Figure 9.17. Here the relation WARE-HOUSE-B is the same as WAREHOUSE-A except that we have a new field AIRPORTS containing the number of airports that a city has. Some cities will have one airport, others two, a few three, and so on. Clearly, AIRPORTS is functionally dependent on CITY; given a CITY value, the AIRPORTS value is uniquely determined, but not vice versa, since if we have the number of airports a city has, that in general will not tell us what the city is. Thus there will be a one-to-many relationship between PROJ(AIRPORTS) and PROJ(STATE,AIR-PORTS,CITY), as shown in Figure 9.17. There must also be a one-to-many relationship between PROJ(AIRPORTS) and WAREHOUSE-B, since given a WHNUMB there will be a unique value for AIRPORTS, but not vice versa. This means that AIRPORTS is also functionally dependent on WHNUMB.

In addition, for the same reasons as with the relation WAREHOUSE-A in Figure 9.15, STATE is functionally dependent on both CITY and WHNUMB. Thus we have two undesirable dependencies, namely, the functional dependencies of both AIRPORTS and STATE on the nonkey field CITY. We have already discussed the difficulties that can arise in practice because of the dependence of STATE on CITY. Similar problems would be caused by the dependence of AIRPORTS on CITY. We have the danger of inconsistency, where a given CITY value in one record can have one AIRPORTS value and another AIRPORTS value in another record; furthermore, if we wished to record the number of airports for a city with no warehouse, it could not be done.

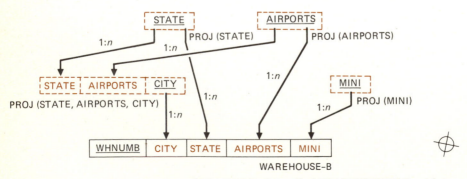

FIGURE 9.17 A new version of WAREHOUSE called WAREHOUSE-B with two undesirable dependencies. Both STATE and AIRPORTS are functionally dependent on CITY, which is not a key field in WAREHOUSE-B. These dependencies are illustrated by the one-to-many relationships between PROJ(STATE), PROJ(AIR-PORTS), and PROJ(STATE,AIRPORTS,CITY).

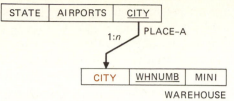

FIGURE 9.18 The undesirable dependencies in the relation WAREHOUSE in Figure 9.17 may be eliminated by constructing two new relations PLACE-A and WAREHOUSE. In PLACE-A, AIRPORTS and STATE are functionally dependent on CITY, while in WAREHOUSE we have both CITY and MINI functionally dependent on WHNUMB. PLACE-A is the same relation as PROJ(STATE,AIRPORTS,CITY), so that the dependency diagram in Figure 9.17 suggests the method of eliminating the undesirable dependencies (as was also the case in Figure 9.15).

The undesirable dependencies are eliminated in the data base in Figure 9.18. The relation **PLACE-A** describes cities, and the fields **AIRPORTS** and **STATE** give, respectively, the number of airports in a city and the state in which the city is located. The relation **WAREHOUSE** describes warehouses and is the same as the relation in Figure 9.9. Between **PLACE-A** and **WAREHOUSE** there is a one-to-many relation, and **CITY** in **WAREHOUSE** is the child connection field. There are no dependencies of a nonkey field on another nonkey field as was the case with **WAREHOUSE-B**. If desired, the reader could turn the extended Bachman diagram in Figure 9.18 into a dependency diagram, showing the functional dependencies for both **PLACE-A** and **WAREHOUSE** (see Figure 9.16).

The ideal relation with a single field (or atomic) key

The examples in the previous sections lead us to an inescapable conclusion. When we are dealing with a relation with a single field for a primary key (that is, an *atomic* primary key), the ideal is that all nonkey fields should be dependent on the key field and only on the key field. This ideal is illustrated in Figure 9.19. It may appear that this ideal is easy to attain in practice, by using the methods eliminating undesirable dependencies as described with the relations **WARE-HOUSE-A** and **WAREHOUSE-B**. This is usually only true when the number of fields in the relation being investigated is small. When the number is large, it is all too easy to overlook undesirable dependencies, and for this reason an independent check should always be made of the design of the relations (or concep-

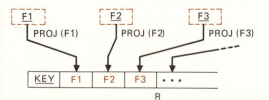

FIGURE 9.19 The ideal relation with a single field (KEY) for a key. Nonkey fields (F1, F2, ...) should be functionally dependent on the key field and only on the key field.

tual files) in a new data base. The designer may be good, but he or she is only human.

To appreciate the problem, let us suppose that a proposed relation is to have 10 fields, one of which is the key field. This means that we must examine the 9 dependencies of the nonkey fields on the key field. However, any *one* of the 9 nonkey fields could be dependent on any of the other 8 nonkey fields. Thus there are 9*8 possible additional dependencies that could give trouble. The designer must therefore investigate 9 + 9*8, or 81, possible dependencies. This is a lot of work. In general if there are *n* fields in an atomic-key relation (a relation with a single field key or atomic key), then there will be $(n-1)^2$ possible dependencies to check, and it is the fact that the number of investigations goes up with the square of the number of fields that is the core of the difficulty. [1] It is all too easy to neglect to investigate a certain possible dependency because one is sure that there is none, or simply because it is overlooked.

We can adapt Murphy's law to undesirable functional dependencies:

> An undesirable functional dependency may remain unnoticed for a long time, but sooner or later it will have an effect on the data base, and it will do so in a manner calculated to do the most damage to the business of users.

Use of the computer to detect undesirable dependencies

The computer can be enlisted in the task of detecting unwanted dependencies. For example, if it is suspected that there is a functional dependence of *F1* on *Fn* in a certain relation, the computer could generate the projection relation **PROJ**(*F1,Fn*). An analyst could then use this data to help confirm or deny the existence of the dependency.

It should be noted that if the *Fn* values in **PROJ**(*F1,Fn*) are not unique, then there can be no functional dependence of *F1* on *Fn*.[2] We could use the computer to determine that *Fn* is not unique in **PROJ**(*F1,Fn*) simply by writing a program to scan through the relation until it finds a duplicate *Fn* value. If no duplicate *Fn* values are found, however, that would not be proof that there *was* a functional dependence of *F1* on *Fn*, only that there might well be such a dependency. The analyst would still have to prove it from a knowledge of the type of data the fields *F1* and *Fn* contained.

Thus it is possible to have a computerized dependency checking system, which would check every pair of nonkey fields in a proposed atomic-key relation and print out a list of the cases where a dependency of *Fi* on *Fn* was a strong possibility, that is, cases where no duplicate *Fn* values were found in the projection file **PROJ**(*F1,Fn*). Of course, a precondition for such a computerized

---

[1] Actually there are even more than $(n-1)^2$ dependencies to check, since dependencies involving groups of fields or composites are possible. See the next section on functional dependencies in relations with composite keys.

[2] If there are duplicate *Fn* values, then an *Fn* value cannot determine an *F1* value, which it must if *Fi* = *f*(*Fn*).

checking of a proposed relation is the availability of the data (in machine-readable form) that the proposed relation is to contain.

Functional dependencies in relations with composite keys

In many relations the key field is made up of several fields, that is, the key is a composite. We can have much more elaborate dependencies in relations with composite keys because of the possibility of subkey fields being involved in undesirable dependencies. Readers who are mainly interested in a cursory coverage of the subject of functional dependencies could well skip this section, as no really new ideas are introduced.

We can have three types of undesirable functional dependency in a relation with a composite key:

1. *Dependence of a nonkey field on another nonkey field.* This is the type of dependency we have examined in previous sections in relations with atomic keys. There is no difference between such a dependency in an atomic-key relation and a composite-key relation, and we shall not give an example of it in the composite-key case.
2. *Dependence of a nonkey field on a subkey field.* This is a somewhat more complex type of dependency, and we give an example of it in the next section.
3. *Dependence of a subkey field on a nonkey field.* This is probably the most subtle type of functional dependency. It is not very common and was the last to be discovered. We give an example in a later section.

We shall therefore be dealing with dependencies that involve subkey fields in subsequent sections. We approach each type of dependency in the same manner as we approached the functional dependency of a nonkey field on another nonkey field in previous sections; that is, we first give an example of the dependency, we then show why it is undesirable, and finally we show how to eliminate it.

Dependence of a nonkey field on a subkey field

In Figure 9.20 we have a simple example of a composite-key relation called **INVENTORY-A**, which is a modification of the relation **INVENTORY** used earlier in Figures 5.12 and 5.13. The primary entity described by the relation is part type in a warehouse, so that we can determine, for example, that the quantity (**QTY**) of part type 'P2' in warehouse number 'WH3' is 550. However, the relation also has a field **CITY** that gives the city in which a warehouse with a given warehouse number (**WHNUMB**) is located.

We can see that **QTY** tells us something about part types in a warehouse, so that once we give the **WHNUMB** and **PTNUMB** values the **QTY** value is determined, but not vice versa, since for a **QTY** value such as 330 there are many possible inventories of part types in warehouses. Thus **QTY** is functionally dependent on the composite key **WHNUMB PTNUMB**.

WHNUMB	PTNUMB	QTY	CITY
WH1	P4	675	DALLAS
WH1	P7	250	DALLAS
WH2	P2	280	NEW YORK
WH2	P4	200	NEW YORK
WH2	P9	270	NEW YORK
WH3	P2	550	CHICAGO
WH3	P4	330	CHICAGO
WH4	P7	330	NEW YORK
WH4	P5	250	NEW YORK
WH6	P2	150	DALLAS
WH7	P6	550	NEW YORK
WH8	P4	330	CHICAGO
WH8	P7	500	CHICAGO

INVENTORY-A

FIGURE 9.20 A record of the relation INVENTORY-A (similar to INVENTORY in Figures 5.12 and 5.13) has a type of part in a warehouse as the primary entity. The warehouse number (WHNUMB) and part type number (PTNUMB) together form a composite key. The field QTY gives the quantity of a type of part at a warehouse, while CITY gives the CITY in which the warehouse is located.

The dependencies in which CITY participates are not quite so simple. It is clear that once we give a WHNUMB value the CITY value is determined, but not vice versa, since there are many warehouses in a single city. Thus there must be a one-to-many relationship between PROJ(CITY) and PROJ(CITY,WHNUMB), as shown in Figure 9.21. From all this it is clear the CITY is functionally dependent on WHNUMB, a subkey field in INVENTORY-A. It is also clear that for each record in PROJ(CITY,WHNUMB) there are many in INVENTORY-A, so that WHNUMB is functionally dependent on the composite key WHNUMB PTNUMB in INVEN-TORY-A, which is as it should be. We can further see from Figure 9.21 that for each PROJ(CITY) record there are many INVENTORY-A records, so that CITY is also functionally dependent on the composite key WHNUMB PTNUMB in IN-VENTORY-A.

These dependencies are shown in the dependency diagram in Figure 9.22. Also included for the sake of completeness is the dependency of PTNUMB on the composite key WHNUMB PTNUMB. Readers should verify this dependency by listing PROJ(PTNUMB) alongside INVENTORY-A records sorted on PTNUMB.

The unwanted dependency is clearly the dependency of CITY on the subkey field WHNUMB. It has many undesirable consequences for maintaining the relation INVENTORY-A. First, if we wish to store the information that a new warehouse (without any inventory as yet) is located in a certain city, we are unable to, until there is some inventory in the warehouse, since WHNUMB PTNUMB is the key field. Another problem arises if, for example, warehouse

CITY
CHICAGO
DALLAS
NEW YORK
PROJ(CITY)

CITY	WHNUMB
CHICAGO	WH3
CHICAGO	WH8
DALLAS	WH1
DALLAS	WH6
NEW YORK	WH2
NEW YORK	WH4
NEW YORK	WH7

PROJ(CITY,WHNUMB)
records

WHNUMB	PTNUMB	QTY	CITY
WH3	P2	550	CHICAGO
WH3	P4	330	CHICAGO
WH8	P4	330	CHICAGO
WH8	P7	500	CHICAGO
WH1	P4	675	DALLAS
WH1	P7	250	DALLAS
WH6	P2	150	DALLAS
WH2	P2	280	NEW YORK
WH2	P4	200	NEW YORK
WH2	P9	270	NEW YORK
WH4	P7	330	NEW YORK
WH4	P5	250	NEW YORK
WH7	P6	550	NEW YORK

INVENTORY-A records

FIGURE 9.21 The projection relations PROJ(CITY) and PROJ(CITY,WHNUMB) show that CITY is functionally dependent on WHNUMB, a subkey field in INVENTORY-A. At the same time CITY is functionally dependent on the INVENTORY-A composite key WHNUMB-PTNUMB, as is WHNUMB. All the functional dependencies in INVENTORY-A are displayed in Figure 9.22.

'WH3' is sold and a new warehouse in Milwaukee acquired that is also to be named 'WH3'. The CITY field in many records now has to be changed from 'CHICAGO' to 'MILWAUKEE'; during this updating process the CITY value for 'WH3' will not be consistent from one record to another, so that inconsistent information could in theory be retrieved by retrieval programs operating concurrently with the updating program (but note that this could not happen with a System R command to update all records with 'WHNUMB' value 'WH3' and CITY value 'CHICAGO'). And finally there is nothing to prevent the relation from becoming permanently inconsistent because of insertion of an incorrect record. For example, if the record

WH1 P3 250 CHICAGO

were accidently inserted, we would have warehouse 'WH1' supposedly in Chicago in one record and in Dallas in others.

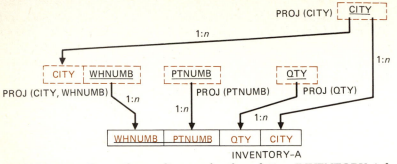

FIGURE 9.22 Dependency diagram for the relation INVENTORY-A from Figure 9.20.

As with previous dependency diagrams, the diagram in Figure 9.22 suggests the solution to these difficulties. We eliminate the offending dependency between **CITY** and **WHNUMB** by creating a new relation **WAREHOUSE-C** that is the same as **PROJ(CITY,WHNUMB)**. This is shown in Figure 9.23. At the same time we create a new version of **INVENTORY-A** called **INVENTORY**, simply by eliminating the **CITY** field, also shown in Figure 9.23. It is clear that there is a one-to-many relationship between **WAREHOUSE-C** and **INVENTORY** and that there are no undesirable dependencies.

Dependence of a subkey field on a nonkey field

Examples involving the dependency of a subkey field on either a single field or a composite field are usually quite complex, and while the example we shall use here is one of the simplest possible, it is nevertheless something of a brain-twister. The reader will probably also be surprised that so many functional dependencies could possibly occur within such an apparently simple relation.

Our example will involve employees at warehouses, specifically which employees are responsible for what part types. The meaning or *semantics* of the

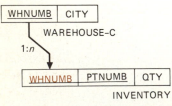

FIGURE 9.23 To remove the undesirable functional dependence of CITY on WHNUMB in the relation INVENTORY-A in Figure 9.22, we must replace INVENTORY-A with the two new relations WAREHOUSE-C and INVENTORY as shown above. In each of these relations the nonkey field is functionally dependent on the key, while in INVENTORY the subkey fields WHNUMB and PTNUMB are functionally dependent on the (composite) key. This decomposition of INVENTORY-A into WAREHOUSE-C and INVENTORY is suggested by the relation PROJ(CITY, WHNUMB) in Figure 9.22.

WH1			WH2		WH3	
E1	E2	E3	E4	E5	E6	E7
P1	P3	P2	P4	P6	P2	P4
P4	P6	P5	P3	P2	P3	
		P7	P1			

FIGURE 9.24 Some data about who does what at a warehouse. For example, at warehouse WH2 we have the employees E4 and E5. E4 looks after inventories of part types P1, P3, and P4, while E5 looks after inventories of part types P2 and P6. The following hold true: (a) A warehouse has many employees; (b) an employee works at just one warehouse; (c) at each warehouse a part type is looked after by just one employee. This data is also in the relation JURISDICTION in Figure 9.25.

data involved is very important, because it is from the meaning that the functional dependencies arise. Some examples of the data are shown in Figure 9.24; however it should be noted that this data is not arranged in the form of a relation. We shall do that presently. For now we must be clear on the meaning of the data, and this comes from the following semantic rules:

1. A warehouse has many employees.
2. An employee works at just one warehouse.
3. At each warehouse a part type is looked after by just one employee (but an employee can look after many part types).

Thus the rules are not unreasonable, and such rules could easily apply in practice to the warehouses of a large corporation. The data in Figure 9.24 is arranged to reflect these rules. For example, employees 'E4' and 'E5' work at warehouse 'WH2', and only at warehouse 'WH2'. Employee 'E4' looks after part types 'P4', 'P5', and 'P6', while employee 'E5' looks after part types 'P6' and 'P2'. Notice that according to rule 3, a part type, such as 'P4', can be looked after at warehouse 'WH2' by only one employee, such as 'E4'; 'P4' could not also be looked after by 'E5' at warehouse 'WH2'. Nevertheless, 'P4' can also be looked after at different warehouses, such as 'WH1' and 'WH3', but only by one employee at each warehouse.

The data in Figure 9.24 can be placed in a relation called JURISDICTION in Figure 9.25. Notice that the meaning or semantics of the data cannot be deduced from JURISDICTION without the semantic rules 1 to 3 above. Even with these semantic rules it is still difficult, and readers are advised to use the data as displayed in Figure 9.26 when examining the functional dependencies that occur.

Our first task is to decide on the primary key for JURISDICTION. It is clear that it has to be a composite key since there are duplicates in each column. We could use WHNUMB PTNUMB as the primary key, since a part type can be looked after at a warehouse by only one employee. If we chose this as our primary key, the relation JURISDICTION then tells us which employee looks after the inven-

WHNUMB	PTNUMB	EMPNUMB
WH1	P1	E1
WH1	P2	E3
WH1	P3	E2
WH1	P4	E1
WH1	P5	E3
WH1	P6	E2
WH1	P7	E3
WH2	P1	E4
WH2	P2	E5
WH2	P3	E4
WH2	P4	E4
WH2	P6	E5
WH3	P2	E6
WH3	P3	E6
WH3	P4	E7

JURISDICTION

FIGURE 9.25 The data from Figure 9.24 on who does what at a warehouse is arranged as records of the relation JURISDICTION. A record tells us what employee looks after the inventory of a part type at a warehouse. Thus WHNUMB PTNUMB is the primary key, and a part type at a warehouse is the primary entity. (Unfortunately the relation is more complex than it appears and there are two candidates for the primary key; we could also have PTNUMB EMPNUMB as the primary key, so that a · record tells us at what warehouse a type of part is looked after by an employee.)

tory of a part type at a warehouse. Thus a part type at a warehouse is the primary entity, as shown in Figure 9.25.

We must now examine every possible combination of fields in our search for functional dependencies. Guided by the fact that the key is WHNUMB PTNUMB, we can list the following:

1. **EMPNUMB** *functionally dependent on the key* **WHNUMB PTNUMB.**   For one part type at a warehouse there is one employee, and for a single employee there are many part types at a warehouse.
2. **PTNUMB** *functionally dependent on the key* **WHNUMB PTNUMB.** For one part type at a warehouse there is one part type, and for one part type there are many part-type-at-a-warehouse combinations (although all with the same **PTNUMB** value).
3. **WHNUMB** *functionally dependent on the key* **WHNUMB PTNUMB.** For one part type at a warehouse there is just one warehouse, and for one warehouse there are many part-type-at-a-warehouse combinations (although all with the same **WHNUMB** value).

Thus all the fields of **JURISDICTION** are functionally dependent on the primary key, which is as it should be. However, we also have:

4. **WHNUMB** *functionally dependent on* **EMPNUMB**. Looking at Figure 9.24, it is clear that for one **WHNUMB** value (such as 'WH2') there are many **EMPNUMB** values (such as 'E4' and 'E5'), while for one **EMPNUMB** value, such as 'E4', there can be but one **WHNUMB** value.

Now this is a case of a subkey field being functionally dependent on a nonkey field, the first that we have so far encountered. It is illustrated in the lower half of Figure 9.26, along with the three functional dependencies on the key **WHNUMB PTNUMB** (dependencies 1, 2, and 3). But it is clear that dependency 4 is undesirable. For example, if a new employee was assigned to a warehouse but had initially no part types to look after, a record could not be placed in **JURISDICTION** since we need a part type to form a key. Furthermore, there is nothing to prevent insertion of a new record such as

WH1 P3 E5

The **WHNUMB** value should clearly have been 'WH2', but following insertion of this record, the data base is inconsistent since according to one record 'E5' works at warehouse 'WH1', and according to two other records 'E5' works at warehouse 'WH2'.

The situation, however, is more complex than so far described, for we could have designated **PTNUMB EMPNUMB** as the primary key since at any warehouse a given part type can be looked after by only one employee. Thus **PTNUMB EMPNUMB** is another candidate for the primary key. The significance of this is that it is likely that the composite field **PTNUMB EMPNUMB** will take part in some functional dependencies, and these functional dependencies will be in force whether or not we chose **PTNUMB EMPNUMB** as the primary key. We therefore continue to assume that **WHNUMB PTNUMB** is the primary key, and list the dependencies involving **PTNUMB EMPNUMB**:

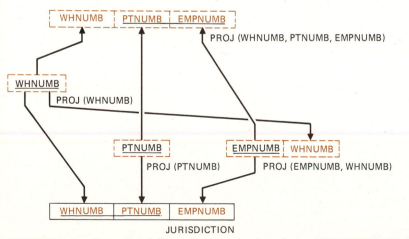

FIGURE 9.26 Functional dependencies for the relation JURISDICTION. The relation PROJ(WHNUMB,PTNUMB,EMPNUMB) is the same as JURISDICTION except for the primary key.

5. **WHNUMB** *functionally dependent on the composite field* **PTNUMB EMPNUMB.**

6. **PTNUMB** *functionally dependent on the composite field* **PTNUMB EMPNUMB.**

7. **EMPNUMB** *functionally dependent on the composite field* **PTNUMB EMPNUMB.**

All these dependencies are illustrated in Figure 9.26 by means of the projection relation **PROJ(WHNUMB,PTNUMB,EMPNUMB)** which is otherwise the same as **JURISDICTION** except that **PTNUMB EMPNUMB** forms the primary key. (Remember the rule for dependency diagrams given early in the chapter: With a one-to-many relationship in a dependency diagram, the field shown as the key field of a parent is functionally dependent on the key (atomic or composite) of its child relation.)

Note that dependencies 5 and 6 involve the dependence of a subkey field on a nonkey composite field, so that including dependency 4, we have altogether three dependencies involving the dependence of a subkey field on a nonkey.[1] It is clear that the relation **JURISDICTION** is far too complex and should be decomposed into simpler relations. The decomposition is shown in Figure 9.27 and consists of two relations **EMPLOYEE-A** and **GUARDIAN**. The contents of these relations are shown in Figure 9.28. It is clear that the fields of these new relations are dependent only on primary keys, and readers should satisfy themselves on this point by consulting Figures 9.24 and 9.28.

---

[1]If we had chosen **PTNUMB EMPNUMB** as the primary key instead of **WHNUMB PTNUMB**, the dependencies would still be the same. However, then we would have only two dependencies of a subkey field on a nonkey (dependencies 1 and 2).

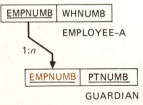

GUARDIAN

FIGURE 9.27 To eliminate undesirable dependencies, the relation JURISDICTION in Figure 9.25 is decomposed into the relations EMPLOYEE-A and GUARDIAN. The relation EMPLOYEE-A is suggested by the projection relation PROJ-(EMPNUMB,WHNUMB) in Figure 9.26 and simply describes an employee, giving the warehouse number where he or she works. Thus WHNUMB is functionally dependent on the key field EMPNUMB. GUARDIAN is the same as JURISDICTION with WHNUMB removed. The subkey fields of GUARDIAN are dependent only on the composite primary key. There is clearly a one-to-many relationship between EMPLOYEE-A and GUARDIAN (see Figure 9.28).

EMPNUMB	WHNUMB
E1	WH1
E2	WH1
E3	WH1
E4	WH2
E5	WH2
E6	WH3
E7	WH3

EMPNUMB	PTNUMB
E1	P1
E1	P4
E2	P3
E2	P6
E3	P2
E3	P5
E3	P7
E4	P1
E4	P3
E4	P4
E5	P2
E5	P6
E6	P2
E6	P3
E7	P4

EMPLOYEE-A   GUARDIAN

FIGURE 9.28   The one-to-many relationship between EMPLOYEE-A and GUARD-IAN.

9.2 CLASSIFICATION OF RELATIONS AND CONCEPTUAL FILES

For purposes of designing data bases, it is useful to have a classification of relations (and of all conceptual files) into those that should be used and those that are best avoided. We shall discuss two methods of classification: the *hierachical method* and the *normal form method*. We begin with the hierarchical method, as it reflects the manner in which we have discussed functional dependencies so far in this chapter.

The hierarchical classification

The hierarchical classification is shown in Figure 9.29. We take all conceptual files and divide them into those that are relations and those that are not. Those that are not (shown in color) should be avoided if at all possible. Of course if a relational data base system is being used, then conceptual files that are relations have to be used. With other data base systems such as CODASYL systems (Chapter 6), IMS (Chapter 10), or TOTAL, or ADABAS (Chapter 11), although

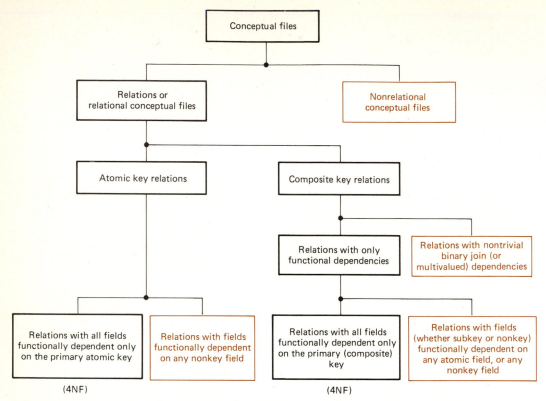

FIGURE 9.29 A hierarchical classification of conceptual files. Conceptual files and relations described in color are undesirable and should not be used if they can be avoided. The desirable atomic key and composite key relations (in black at the bottom of the hierarchy) are said to be in fourth normal form.

conceptual files that are not relations are allowed, relations should be used.

Relations are conveniently divided into those with atomic keys and those with composite keys, since composite-key relations allow many more dependencies than atomic-key relations.

Atomic-key relations

We have only two types of atomic-key relations, namely, those where every nonkey field is functionally dependent only on the primary key and those where a nonkey field can be functionally dependent on another nonkey field. This latter type (shown in color in the diagram) should be avoided because of undesirable updating effects, as described in Section 9.1.[1] Relations in which every

---

[1]Note that in the case of an atomic-key relation with a second candidate key field, the relation is strictly speaking undesirable, since we will have fields that are functionally dependent on the second candidate key field. However, there are no serious updating side effects with such a relation. An example is a relation with supplier number as the primary key, and supplier name as another candidate key.

nonkey field is functionally dependent on the primary key can also be called *fourth normal form* relations (or more accurately, atomic-key fourth normal form relations, since we can also have composite-key fourth normal form relations). The term *fourth normal form* comes from the normal form classification, to be described presently.

Composite-key relations

There are two distinct types of composite-key relations, those that contain only functional dependencies and those that also contain nontrivial *binary join* (or *multivalued*) dependencies. We have not so far discussed binary join dependencies. They are complex, and quite undesirable, but fortunately do not occur very often. A detailed analysis of binary join dependencies is beyond the scope of this book (see Ref. 4) although an example of such a dependency is given in the chapter supplement. Essentially, when a relation contains a *nontrivial* binary join dependency, insertion of a new record will require insertion of additional records to keep the relation consistent, and deletion of one record will require the deletion of additional records to keep the relation consistent. Readers will have noticed that a functional dependency involves a one-to-many relationship between fields of a relation; a binary join dependency involves a many-to-many relationship (of a special kind) between fields of a relation. Since the simplest case of a many-to-many relationship is a one-to-many relationship, the simplest case of a binary join dependency is actually a functional dependency or a *trivial* binary join dependency. It is the nontrivial kind involving nontrivial many-to-many relationships that cause all the trouble. *A composite key must have at least three subkey fields before a nontrivial binary join dependency is possible.*

Only relations that do not contain nontrivial binary join dependencies should be considered for use in a data base. Such relations may be further divided into those where every field is functionally dependent only on the composite primary key, and those for which this is not true. This later type (shown in color) is undesirable, for they permit a great many complex dependencies, some examples of which were given earlier. A composite-key relation in which all fields are functionally dependent on the composite primary key is also called a fourth normal form relation, provided of course that it does not contain a nontrivial binary join dependency.

The normal form (or historical) classification

The normal form (or historical) classification of conceptual files is shown in Figure 9.30. We start with the universe of all conceptual files and then select those conceptual files that are *normal form relations*. The relations selected are said to be in *first normal form* or in 1NF. They are a subset of the universe of all conceptual files. All the relations that we have dealt with so far are normal form relations. The term has a forboding air to it unfortunately. It was introduced to distinguish between relations in which each field contains just one item of data, or normal form relations, and relations in which a field can contain more than one item of data, or *unnormalized relations*. Only normal form relations, or

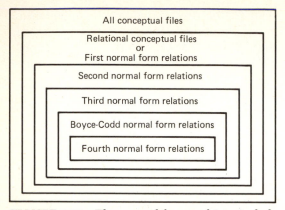

FIGURE 9.30 The normal form or historical classification of relations. As we go from first to fourth normal form, fewer and fewer dependencies are allowed. Fourth normal form relations are those that permit only functional dependencies on the key field (whether composite or atomic) and are thus semantically very simple. The classification may be regarded as historical, since during the 1970s, as each new dependency was discovered, a new and higher normal form was created to describe relations that did not contain the newly discovered dependency. The problem with this classification from a data base design point of view is that it does not distinguish between atomic key and composite key relations. The method by which we arrive at a higher normal form from a lower one is described in Figure 9.1.

normalized relations, are of interest in data base management, although an example of an unnormalized relation is given in the second supplement to this chapter. Thus a normal form relation, despite its forboding name, is just any old conceptual file with fixed length fixed format unique records, or in other words, the standard type of relation we have been dealing with all along.

Thus the first step in the classification process (see also Figure 9.31) is essentially to extract those conceptual files that are relations from the universe of all conceptual files, which is a very simple step. The next step is to select from the 1NF relations those relations where we do not have a nonkey field functionally dependent on a subkey field. These relations are said to be in *second normal form,* or 2NF. We note that a 1NF atomic-key relation is automatically in 2NF.

The next step is to select from the 2NF relations those relations in which no nonkey field is functionally dependent on another nonkey field. Such relations are said to be in *third normal form,* or 3NF, and we note that a 3NF relation can be either an atomic-key relation or a composite-key relation.

Next we select from the 3NF relations those relations in which there is no subkey field functionally dependent on any nonkey field whether composite or atomic. Such a relation is said to be in *Boyce-Codd normal form,* or BCNF. Note that a BCNF relation can have either atomic or composite primary keys and that an atomic-key 3NF relation is automatically a BCNF relation.

Finally we select from the BCNF relations those relations that have no nontrivial binary join (or multivalued) dependencies. These relations are said to

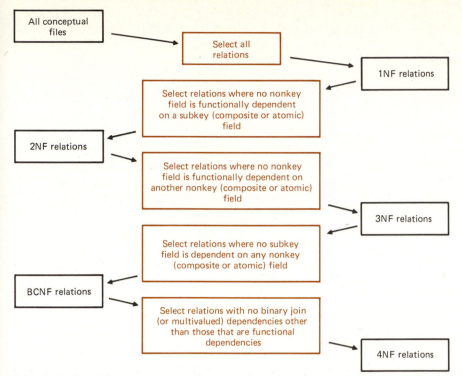

FIGURE 9.31 The method by which restrictions are placed on conceptual files until we arrive at a very restricted conceptual file, namely, the fourth normal form relation. The ideal conceptual file is a fourth normal form relation. Notice that it is not at all clear that a binary join dependency that is not a functional dependency can only occur in a composite key relation, or that a desirable atomic key relation according to Figure 9.29 is automatically in 4NF.

be in *fourth* normal form, or 4NF. We note that a 4NF relation can have either an atomic or composite primary key and that an atomic key 3NF or BCNF relation is automatically in 4NF. The method of step-by-step elimination until we come to 4NF relations is illustrated in Figure 9.31. Only 4NF relations should be used as conceptual files in data bases.

History of the normal form classification
The first significant work on the development of the relational approach was carried out by E. F. Codd of IBM during the early part of the 1970s, and in one of his early papers Codd outlined the concepts of 1st, 2nd, and 3rd normal forms, pointing out that 3NF relations were without undesirable dependencies that would cause updating difficulties. However, further research with composite-key relations indicated that this was not the case, since it was possible to have subkey fields functionally dependent on other fields. This was discovered by Codd and another researcher called Boyce, and BCNF was invented to describe relations that were in 3NF but did not have these undesirable subkey field

dependencies. Finally Fagin and others (Ref. 4) discovered binary join dependencies, and 4NF was conceived to describe relations without binary join dependencies and without undesirable functional dependencies. Recently (see Ref. 3) 5NF relations have been defined to eliminate a more subtle type of dependency (called a join dependency); however, the dependency involved is so contrived and uncommon that it is unlikely ever to occur in a practical data base design situation. We can safely forget about 5NF relations.

Disadvantages of the normal form classification

That the normal form classification has some disadvantages when used as a data base design tool is hardly surprising given its tortuous development as the result of a great deal of (very mathematical) research. Its main defect is that it does not classify relations into atomic-key relations, in which only limited dependencies are possible, and composite-key relations, in which many different dependencies are possible. Another problem is that it is difficult to remember the rules for placing relations in the various normal forms. We believe that the hierarchical classification in Figure 9.29 is easier to use when designing a data base. It should of course be remembered that it was possible to develop the hierarchical classification only after the completion of the basic and pioneering research on which the normal form classification is based.

9.3 ENTITY-RELATIONSHIP DIAGRAMS IN DATA BASE DESIGN

Throughout most of this book so far we have used extended Bachman diagrams to describe conceptual data bases. This diagrammatic technique is powerful and can be used with all the major approaches to data base management. However, there is another diagrammatic technique that can be used with most approaches to data base management, and which we shall discuss in this section. It is called the *entity-relationship* technique, and readers should be aware of it because it is sometimes used in the literature. An understanding of the technique will probably also give the reader a greater understanding of the nature of conceptual data bases; most of the concepts involved will be familiar to the reader and can also be applied to extended Bachman diagrams. However, before delving into entity relationships, a brief digression on the limitations of diagrammatic techniques in data base design is appropriate.

Limitations of diagrammatic techniques

As a method of specifying conceptual data bases, both extended Bachman and entity-relationship diagrams have an important limitation. They can give only a partial description of a conceptual data base. With a given data base management system, there will inevitably be conceptual schema definition details that either cannot be included in a conceptual data base diagram or can be included only with great difficulty. For example, with extended Bachman diagrams and a CODASYL data base system, it may be possible to add owner-coupled set connection and retention class specifications, but it is difficult to see how set selection specifications could be added in any useful way.

For this reason some authors believe that diagrams such as entity-relationship diagrams do not actually describe a conceptual data base in practice, for in practice a conceptual data base is specified by the conceptual schema definition language of some specific data base system. For this reason the data base described by an entity-relationship (or extended Bachman) diagram is sometimes referred to as the *enterprise data base*. In this book we largely ignore this hair-splitting distinction as stated earlier in Chapter 5.

Entity sets

The concept of an entity set is fundamental to entity-relationship diagrams. Although it is quite abstract, in practice an entity set turns out to be a conceptual file that is a relation. First we must define an *entity*. An entity is anything that a thinking being can sense or imagine to exist. (For the present, we can take a thinking being to be a human being.) Thus persons, offices, machine tools, computers, ball bearings, nails, and executive jets are all entities that our senses tell us exist. So are atoms, molecules, photons, viruses, protons, electrons, and mu-mesons, although these more elusive entities require the use of complex instruments before humans can sense them, this being the reason it took so long to discover them. Things that we can never sense, but only imagine to exist, such as ancient Roman gods and ghosts, are also entities.

We can now define an entity set. An entity set is a mathematical set of entities that have (1) similar properties, but (2) may be distinguished from one another. Thus we could have an entity set of persons, offices, machine tools, or executive jets, since persons have similar properties and are distinguishable, and so on. Even a collection of executive jets of the same make are distinguishable since they will have different identifying numbers, and probably different colors, owners, and interior designs. But what about an entity set of quarter inch ball bearings of the same make? Is that possible? Usually not, since these entities in general are not distinguishable from one another for most business purposes. However, under some circumstances an entity set would be possible; for example, if a group of quarter inch ball bearings of a certain type were undergoing reliability tests, microscopic examination of their surfaces could reveal distinct features that could be used to distinguish them for record-keeping purposes. Such distinct quarter inch ball bearings would form an entity set.

An entity has properties or *attributes*. For example, some attributes of an executive jet are its color, weight, cost, and identification number, and some one attribute or collection of attributes is the *key* and is used to identify an entity. For any given entity its attributes have *values*; thus the value of the cost attribute of a certain executive jet might be $3 million.

The collection of attribute values for a certain entity is a conceptual record or tuple, and the collection of tuples for the entities of an entity set is a relation. However, it is common to use the terms entity set and relation interchangeably, although strictly they are not quite the same. In simple terms the conceptual records of a relation describe the things in a collection of similar entities. Thus the records of the relation WAREHOUSE describe the warehouses in the entity set WAREHOUSE.

Entity sets and relations with indistinguishable entities

The difficulty mentioned earlier with an entity set of quarter inch ball bearings is a common one in data base design. For example, in the case of electronic parts such as transistors, a manufacturer typically manufactures thousands of the same type, all with the same type number. To have an entity set or relation for these transistors would not be possible for most business purposes since the transistors are not distinguishable, except during special tests. The same is true for most components such as nails, nuts, bolts, switches, springs, integrated circuits, and wheels. We must use entity sets of part *types*. That is why the relation **PART** that we introduced in Chapter 5 (see Figure 5.1) has records that describe part types and *not* individual parts.

Relationship sets

We can have a *relationship* between any number of entities, although typically there are just two entities. Thus if 'WH1' identifies a **WAREHOUSE** entity and 'E3' an **EMPLOYEE** entity, then the pair 'WH1 E1' is a relationship and the collection of all such pairs is a *relationship set*. Thus a relationship set is a relation. This is not quite the way we have been looking at things so far. However, the difference between this approach to relationships and that we have used so far with extended Bachman diagrams is really superficial. To make sure that the difference is clearly understood, we give some examples comparing the use of relationship sets in entity-relationship diagrams with relationships as depicted by extended Bachman diagrams. We take one-to-many relationships first and then many-to-many relationships.

One-to-many relationship sets

Consider the conceptual data base involving the relations **WAREHOUSE** and **EMPLOYEE** from Figure 7.1, the extended Bachman diagram for which is shown in Figure 9.32a. It is clear that we have a one-to-many relationship between the two relations, since there are many employees working at each warehouse. The entity-relationship diagram for this data base is shown in Figure 9.32b. The relations **WAREHOUSE** and **EMPLOYEE** are the same as in the extended Bachman diagram except that they are drawn differently. A relation name is placed in a box, and the attribute (or field) names are shown in trailing egg-shaped boxes.

A relationship set is shown as a diamond box and is usually given a name that is a composite of the names of the relations involved in the relationship. (This of course will not be the case if there are two relationships between a pair of relations.) The relationship set for the relationship between **WAREHOUSE** and **EMPLOYEE** is a relation. This must be continually borne in mind, for it is the key to understanding entity-relationship diagrams. This relation is shown in Figure 9.33. Each record in the relation relates a **WHNUMB** key value from **WARE-HOUSE** to an **EMPNUMB** key value from **EMPLOYEE**. In theory we do not have to have just the key values from the relations **WAREHOUSE** and **EMPLOYEE** in the relationship set **WAREHOUSE-EMPLOYEE**. Every complete **EMPLOYEE**

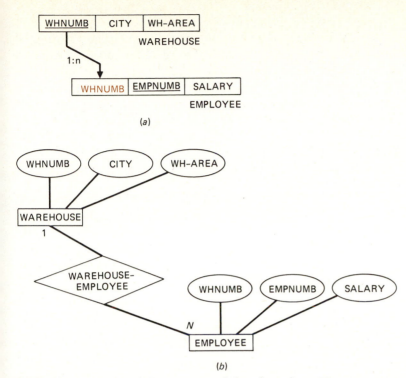

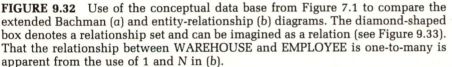

FIGURE 9.32 Use of the conceptual data base from Figure 7.1 to compare the extended Bachman (a) and entity-relationship (b) diagrams. The diamond-shaped box denotes a relationship set and can be imagined as a relation (see Figure 9.33). That the relationship between WAREHOUSE and EMPLOYEE is one-to-many is apparent from the use of 1 and N in (b).

record could be paired to its parent WAREHOUSE, so that in theory the fields or attributes of WAREHOUSE-EMPLOYEE could include WHNUMB, CITY, WH-AREA, EMPNUMB, and SALARY.

Readers may well wonder why the special relationship set is necessary, since after all the relationship is perfectly obvious from the connection field values. This is probably a valid objection, and together with the greater conciseness of extended Bachman diagrams, this is why we do not use entity-relationship diagrams in this book. Nevertheless, it must be admitted that the relationship set in Figures 9.32b and 9.33 does clearly bring out the nature of the relationship between WAREHOUSE and EMPLOYEE. Notice the use of the characters '1' and 'N' in the entity-relationship diagram to show that the relationship is one to many, or 1:N.

Many-to-many relationships
Consider the data base in Figure 5.1, for which the extended Bachman diagram is shown in Figure 9.34a. We have the relation WAREHOUSE describing ware-

```
WHNUMB  |  EMPNUMB
--------+--------
WH1     |  E3
WH1     |  E7
WH2     |  E1
WH2     |  E4
WH3     |  E6
```

WAREHOUSE-EMPLOYEE relation

FIGURE 9.33   Using the conceptual data base from Figure 7.1, the relationship set WAREHOUSE-EMPLOYEE from the entity-relationship diagram in Figure 9.32b has the records shown here. A relationship set from an entity-relationship diagram is a relation and will contain at least the keys identifying the entities involved in the relationship.

houses, the relation **PART** describing part types that are kept in the warehouses, and the relation **INVENTORY**, a record of which tells how many (**QTY** field) of a type of part are inventoried in a warehouse.

It is clear that we have a many-to-many relationship between **WAREHOUSE** and **PART** as described in Chapter 5. For each warehouse there are many types of part inventoried, and for each type of part there are many warehouses that stock it. This many-to-many relationship is actually contained within the relation **INVENTORY**, since from the child connection fields **WHNUMB** and **PTNUMB** we can tell what part type is inventoried at what warehouse.

The entity-relationship diagram (Figure 9.34b) is this time not all that different. Except for the differently shaped boxes, the depiction of the relations **WAREHOUSE** and **PART** is much the same as in the extended Bachman diagram. Since the relation **INVENTORY** contains the fundamental relationship between **WAREHOUSE** and **PART**, it is a relationship set and is shown as a diamond. Since the quantity of a type of part at a warehouse is a description of or attribute of a relationship between a warehouse and a part type, **QTY** is an attribute in the relationship set **INVENTORY**, as is shown in Figure 9.34b. To indicate that the relationship between **WAREHOUSE** and **PART** is many to many, or N:M, the characters 'N' and 'M' are placed beside the relation boxes in the diagram.

Dependency diagrams

It does not appear to be possible to extend entity-relationship diagrams to include functional dependencies, as can be easily done with extended Bachman diagrams. Since the determination of functional dependencies is an important phase of the data base design process, this would appear to be a fundamental drawback to the use of entity-relationship diagrams. However, those who favor entity-relationship diagrams usually compensate for this deficiency by employing a separate diagrammatic technique for dependencies. For other methods of illustrating dependencies, see Refs. 3 and 4. A good description of the entity-

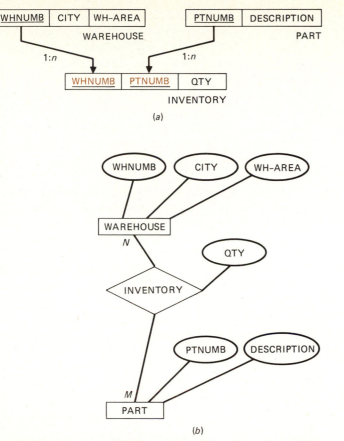

FIGURE 9.34 Use of the conceptual data base from Figure 5.1 to compare the extended Bachman (a) and entity-relationship (b) diagrams. The relationship set INVENTORY is depicted as a diamond-shaped box in (b) and has the attribute QTY. The relationship between WAREHOUSE and PART is many-to-many and is denoted by the use of N and M in the entity-relationship diagram. The relationship set INVENTORY in (b) is a relation that is identical to the relation INVENTORY in (a). See Figure 5.1 for the contents of the relation INVENTORY.

relationship method is given by P. P. S. Chen, the originator of the technique, in Ref. 2.

SUMMARY

1. The concept of functional dependency is important in data base design. A field Y is functionally dependent on a field X, that is $Y = f(X)$, if for an X value there is just one Y value, that is, X determines Y. Normally, also, for one Y value there will be many X values. Functional dependencies can be displayed by means of functional dependency diagrams.

2. In any relation all nonkey fields are functionally dependent on the primary key. If any field is functionally dependent on another field that is not the primary key, then that dependency is undesirable and leads to updating and insertion anomalies. The undesirable dependency can be eliminated by decomposing the relation into simpler relations.

3. Relationships may be classified into first, second, third, and Boyce-Codd normal form according to the type of functional dependencies they contain. Only Boyce-Codd normal form (BCNF) relations contain no undesirable functional dependencies. However, a BCNF relation may contain a binary join dependency, which is also undesirable because of insertion and deletion anomalies. A BCNF relation without a binary join dependency is said to be in fourth normal form (4NF), and for all practical purposes is the ideal relation or conceptual file for use in data bases. Binary join dependencies are covered in the second chapter supplement. Another method of classification of relations (the hierarchical method) employs both dependencies and the number of fields required for the primary key.

4. More than one type of diagrammatic method can be used in data base design. In addition to extended Bachman and similar diagrams, we can use entity-relationship diagrams. In this type of diagram a relationship is shown as a relation, and called a relationship set. In addition, the relations for the entities described by the data base are now called entity sets.

QUESTIONS

The following questions relate to functional dependencies
1. Give the functional dependencies and draw a functional dependency diagram for the relation **WAREHOUSE** in Figure 5.1.
2. Give the functional dependencies and draw a functional dependency diagram for the relation **INVENTORY** in Figure 5.1.
3. Give the functional dependencies and draw a functional dependency diagram for the relation **PART-WAREHOUSE** in Figure 5.5.
4. Decompose the relation **PART-WAREHOUSE** in Figure 5.5 so that the resulting relations are in 4NF.
5. In the relation **PARTICIPATION** we have the fields **MANAGER** (manager name), **PROJECT** (project name), **HOURS** (total hours spent on project), and **SALARY** (salary of a manager). A record in **PARTICIPATION** describes the total hours spent by a manager on a project, and gives the manager's salary. A manager's salary is fixed and he or she can work on many projects. In addition many managers will work on the same project!
   (a) What is the primary key for the relation?
   (b) Give some typical data for the relation.
   (c) Determine all the functional dependencies in the relation.
   (d) Draw a functional dependency diagram for the relation.

(e) Pinpoint the undesirable functional dependency.

(f) In which normal form is **PARTICIPATION**?

(g) Draw an extended Bachman diagram for the 4NF relations into which **PARTICIPATION** can be decomposed.

6. In the relation **EMPLOYEE** we have the field **EMPNUMB** (the employee number), **SALARY** (the employee's salary), **CHIEF** (the employee number of the employee's boss), and **TEL** (the employee's boss's telephone number). A record in **EMPLOYEE** gives information about an employee in an organization.

(a) Give some typical data for the relation.

(b) Give the primary key for the relation.

(c) Determine all the functional dependencies in the relation.

(d) Draw a functional dependency diagram for the relation.

(e) What is the undesirable functional dependency?

(f) In which normal form is **EMPLOYEE**?

(g) Draw an extended Bachman diagram for the 4NF relations into which **EMPLOYEE** can be decomposed.

7. A relation has three fields A, B, and C, where A is the primary key field. What normal form is the relation in if

(a) B is functionally dependent on A, while C is functionally dependent on B?

(b) C is functionally dependent on A, while B is functionally dependent on C?

8. A relation has four fields, A, B, C, and D, where A and B form a composite primary key. What normal form is the relation in if

(a) A, B, C, and D are each functionally dependent on AB?

(b) A, B, C, and D are each functionally dependent on AB, while D is functionally dependent on C?

(c) A, B, C, and D are each functionally dependent on AB, while D is functionally dependent on B?

(d) A, B, C, and D are functionally dependent on AB, while B is functionally dependent on C?

9. In what normal form is the relation **INVENTORY-A** in Figure 9.22?

10. In what normal form is the relation **JURISDICTION** in Figure 9.25?

The following questions relate to diagrammatic techniques.

11. Draw an entity-relationship diagram for the data base with the relations **SUPPLIER** and **PUR-ORDER** from Figure 8.2.

12. Draw an entity-relationship diagram for the data base with the relations **EMPLOYEE**, **PUR-ORDER**, and **SUPPLIER** from Figure 8.2. Use a many-to-many relationship set.

13. Repeat Question 12 using one-to-many relationship sets.

14. Draw two different entity-relationship diagrams for the data base in Figure 8.2.

ADDITIONAL PERSPECTIVE 1
RECURSIVE RELATIONSHIPS IN CORPORATE HOLDINGS
AND BILLS OF MATERIALS

Recursive relationships are frequently encountered in data base design. There are two main types of recursive relationships, namely, recursive one-to-many relationships and recursive many-to-many relationships. Despite the forbidding name, relationships of this type are quite common in business, and it is useful to examine them. Many data base systems are not equipped to handle them easily, and artificial data base structures are frequently used to compensate for the deficiencies of the data base system. The best business examples of recursive relationships appear in files describing corporate share holdings and bills of materials used in manufacturing, as we shall see.

Recursive one-to-many relationships

We first look at a single but very typical example of a recursive one-to-many relationship. Suppose that an investment firm needs to keep track of the wholly owned subsidiary companies of corporations for purposes of evaluation of investment alternatives. A wholly owned subsidiary is one whose common voting shares are wholly owned by some other corporation. Thus company A could be wholly owned by company B; company C could also be owned by company B, and company B could itself be wholly owned by company D, and so on. It is relationships of this nature that are involved in a recursive one-to-many relationship.

To make this example more realistic, let us suppose that the companies our investment firm is interested in are described in the conceptual file (or relation) COMPANY as shown in Figure 9.35. The fields are CNAME, the name of the company and the primary key field, the total number of authorized common shares (SHARES), the unconsolidated earning per share (E-S), and the name of the parent company (PARENT). Note that the unconsolidated earnings per share of a company are its earnings before the earnings of its subsidiaries are added. Thus if B is the only subsidiary of A, if B has no subsidiaries, if there are 100,000 outstanding common shares of both A and B, if the earnings per share of B are $2.00, and if the unconsolidated earnings per share of A are $1.00, then the consolidated earnings per share of A must be $3.00.

It is the CNAME and PARENT fields in COMPANY that determine the recursive one-to-many relationship. Looking at Figure 9.35, we see that some PARENT values are null, and this will happen in records describing companies that have no parent company, that is, companies that are not subsidiaries. The company 'ANTECK' has therefore no parent. However, we can see from Figure 9.36 that the companies 'EEWING', 'FLOWTEK', and 'GEOTHOR' all have 'ANTECK' as their parent, that is, one parent record has many child records. This is also shown in Figure 9.36. In addition, the company 'BETRON' has no parent but is clearly the parent of companies 'CANCORP' and 'DELTAK'; again for one

CNAME	E-S	SHARES	PARENT
ANTECK	0.35	2000	-
BETRON	1.50	3000	-
CANCORP	1.00	200	BETRON
DELTAK	2.00	1000	BETRON
EEWING	0.75	5000	ANTECK
FLOWTEK	2.20	1000	ANTECK
GEOTHOR	1.25	600	ANTECK
HORVEK	3.00	1000	EEWING
INFOGON	1.40	300	CANCORP
JETCORP	0.75	2500	DELTAK
KENROK	1.20	900	GEOTHOR
LANTHON	0.90	1000	FLOWTEK
MIDCO	2.50	500	FLOWTEK
NETCORP	0.50	1000	FLOWTEK

COMPANY

FIGURE 9.35 The conceptual file or relation COMPANY. The field CNAME holds a company name, E-S holds a company's unconsolidated earnings per share, and SHARES holds a company's total authorized common shares. In any record, the value of the PARENT field is the name of the company (if there is one) that wholly owns the company described by the record. Thus, for example, CANCORP and DELTAK are wholly owned by BETRON, which in turn is not owned by any other company. Thus there is a one-to-many relationship between the records of COMPANY. Since COMPANY is involved in a one-to-many relationship with itself, the relationship is said to be recursive. A value of SHARES is in thousands of shares.

parent record we have many child records, and this is further illustrated in Figure 9.36.

If we now take 'FLOWTEK', the subsidiary of 'ANTECK', we see from Figure 9.35 that it is the parent of 'LANTHON', 'MIDCO', and 'NETCORP'; again for one record we have many child records. In this manner we can deduce all the subsidiaries of both 'ANTECK' and 'BETRON' from the conceptual file in Figure

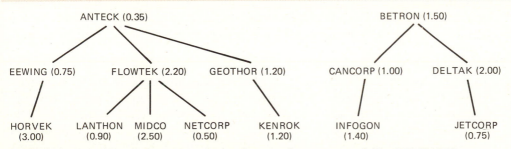

FIGURE 9.36 The parent-child relationships in the conceptual file COMPANY from Figure 9.35. Note that a recursive 1:n relationship within a conceptual file causes the records to be grouped into hierarchies. For convenience in later analysis the earnings per share are shown in parentheses.

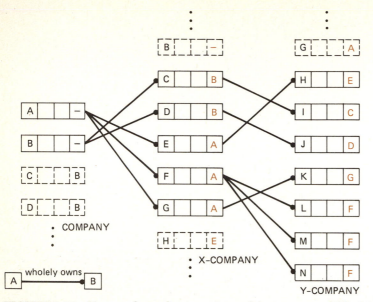

FIGURE 9.37 Here we have three versions of the conceptual file COMPANY, with company names abbreviated to their first letters (see Figure 9.35). The three versions are identical, but we have selected records from each version to show the one-to-many relationship between the records. The line between two records indicates that one company owns another, the circle indicates which one is owned. Clearly we can consider the recursive one-to-many relationship in COMPANY as giving rise to one-to-many relationships between versions of COMPANY as shown in Figure 9.35.

9.37, and these are shown in Figure 9.38 and, as might be expected, form the usual hierarchical organization of corporations with wholly owned subsidiaries.

It is clear that the records of **COMPANY** are involved in a one-to-many relationship, since in general for any one record describing a company *X*, there will be many records describing the subsidiaries of *X*. However, in all previous examples of a one-to-many relationship two conceptual files were involved, one of which contained the parent records and the other the child records. Here we have a one-to-many relationship with only one conceptual file. This is the hallmark of a recursive relationship—it occurs within a single conceptual file.

Records that are both parents and children

Another characteristic of a recursive one-to-many relationship is that some and often many records are both parent and child records in the relationship at the same time, something that cannot happen in a nonrecursive relationship. We can see this easily if we consider multiple versions of **COMPANY**, such as **COMPANY**, **X-COMPANY**, and **Y-COMPANY** as shown in Figure 9.37. We need as many versions as there are levels in the largest hierarchy in Figure 9.36. Of course all these versions except **COMPANY** are purely imaginary and are introduced only to lay bare the structure of a recursive one-to-many relationship.

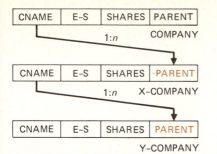

FIGURE 9.38 Extended Bachman diagram that displays the one-to-many relationships apparent in Figure 9.37. For any company described in a record in COMPANY, its immediate subsidiaries are the child records in X-COMPANY, and their immediate subsidiaries are the child records in Y-COMPANY. PARENT is clearly the child connection field in X-COMPANY and Y-COMPANY.

In the **COMPANY** file in Figure 9.37 we consider or select only those records describing companies that are not subsidiaries, in the **X-COMPANY** file we consider only those records describing immediate subsidiaries of companies considered in **COMPANY**, and in the **Y-COMPANY** file we consider only those records describing the immediate subsidiaries of the companies considered in **X-COMPANY**. From Figure 9.37 we can see that there is a one-to-many relationship between the selected records in **COMPANY** and the selected records in **X-COMPANY**, and a further one-to-many relationship between the selected records of **X-COMPANY** and the selected records of **Y-COMPANY**. In the first of these one-to-many relationships, the child connection field is **PARENT** in **X-COMPANY**, and in the second it is **PARENT** in **Y-COMPANY**, and both connection fields are shown in color in Figure 9.37.

We can easily see that a selected record from **X-COMPANY** is a child record in the one-to-many relationship between **COMPANY** and **X-COMPANY**; at the same time it is also a parent record in the one-to-many relationship between **X-COMPANY** and **Y-COMPANY**. Thus the selected records of **X-COMPANY** are both parents and children at the same time, a fact that makes it difficult to construct manipulation languages that can unambiguously handle recursive one-to-many relationships. We shall give a few examples of manipulation of these relationships, but first we must examine some methods for more simply describing recursive one-to-many relationships by means of diagrams.

Extended Bachman diagrams for recursive one-to-many relationships
One way of depicting a recursive one-to-many relationship without having to draw out the contents of the conceptual file involved is shown in Figure 9.38. Here we use the three versions of **COMPANY** that were used in Figure 9.37. The diagram simply reflects the one-to-many relationships that appear in Figure 9.37, and **PARENT** is the child connection field in both **X-COMPANY** and **Y-COMPANY**.

Now the number of versions of the **COMPANY** file required in both Figures 9.37 and 9.38 is $1 + n$ where n is the maximum number of subsidiary levels there

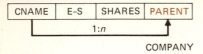

COMPANY

FIGURE 9.39 Extended Bachman diagram showing the recursive 1:n relationship in COMPANY. The field PARENT is the child connection field. Note that the arrow in an extended Bachman diagram is not a pointer and must end on the child connection field in any relationship, whether recursive or not.

can be below any company described in the file. In the file in Figure 9.37, n is clearly 2, so that we need three versions of COMPANY. However, in general we do not know how many subsidiary levels there are in a file such as COMPANY, so that perhaps we should place three dots underneath Y-COMPANY in Figure 9.38 to indicate that more versions may be needed for the general case. A more concise method is to use the extended Bachman diagram in Figure 9.39. Here we clearly indicate that the COMPANY conceptual file is involved in a one-to-many relationship with itself, and that the child connection field is PARENT.

The extended Bachman diagram also brings out the cyclic nature of a recursive one-to-many relationship (another name for a recursive one-to-many relationship is *cyclic relationship*). For example, any record in the file with primary key 'K1' has child records whose PARENT field values are all 'K1'; any of these child records, for example, one with primary key 'K17', has in turn child records whose PARENT field values are all 'K17', and so on in cyclic fashion. Note the way the arrow is drawn in this diagram. In all Bachman diagrams the arrow starts at the parent *file* and ends at the child file. However in a recursive one-to-many relationship a conceptual file has records that are both parent and child, so that does not tell us how to draw the arrow. But in an extended Bachman diagram the arrow starts at the primary key field of the parent file and ends on the child connection field of the child file, and in Figure 9.39 the arrow does just that, notwithstanding the fact that the parent and child files are one and the same.

Recursive one-to-many relationships at the storage level

Many students have difficulty with recursive relationships (especially many-to-many recursive relationships), and the author's experience is that these difficulties usually are caused by an inability to place recursive relationships in perspective. The best way to gain a better perspective is to examine how the conceptual file COMPANY and its recursive relationship could be implemented at the storage level. There are many ways of implementing COMPANY at the storage level, and a typical implementation is shown in Figure 9.40. Here we use both parent-to-first-child pointers (P-C-POINTER field) and next-child pointers (N-C-POINTER field).

Thus if we need to retrieve the subsidiaries of the parent company 'ANTECK', the system can access the parent company by direct access using the value 'ANTECK' as the primary key. The records describing the immediate subsidiaries of 'ANTECK' will in general be scattered all over the storage file

P–C–POINTER	CNAME	E–S	SHARES	PARENT	N–C–POINTER
EEWING	ANTECK	0.35	2000	—	--
CANCORP	BETRON	1.50	3000	—	--
INFOGON	CANCORP	1.00	200	BETRON	DELTAK
JETCORP	DELTAK	2.00	1000	BETRON	--
HORVEK	EEWING	0.75	5000	ANTECK	FLOWTEK
LANTHON	FLOWTEK	2.20	1000	ANTECK	GEOTHOR
KENROK	GEOTHOR	1.25	600	ANTECK	--
—	HORVEK	3.00	1000	EEWING	--
--	INFOGON	1.40	300	CANCORP	—
--	JETCORP	0.75	2500	DELTAK	—
--	KENROK	1.20	900	GEOTHOR	—
--	LANTHON	0.90	1000	FLOWTEK	MIDCO
--	MIDCO	2.50	500	FLOWTEK	NETCORP
--	NETCORP	0.50	1000	FLOWTEK	—

FIGURE 9.40 A storage version of the conceptual file COMPANY from Figure 9.35 with parent-to-first-child pointers (P-C-POINTER field) and next-child pointers (N-C-POINTER field). There are other ways of implementing the recursive relationship as well. The pointer arrows have been added for the corporate hierarchy with the company ANTECK (see Figure 9.36) at the head. Note that the records of the file in Figure 9.35 were selected in such a way that child records lie adjacent. This was done to enable the reader to more easily perceive the relationships in the file. In practice child records of a given parent would be scattered throughout the file and would need a pointer system like that shown above to permit direct access given the parent key.

(although not in Figure 9.40, where they are grouped close together to enable readers to more easily see the relationships in the file). The parent-to-child pointer field in the record for 'ANTECK' has the primary key of the record describing the first subsidiary, and on accessing the file with this key value ('EEWING') we have the record describing the subsidiary company 'EEWING'. This record has a next-child pointer to the next subsidiary of 'ANTECK' and the pointer field value is 'FLOWTEK'. Accessing the storage file with 'FLOWTEK' as primary key gives the record describing the subsidiary 'FLOWTEK', and so on. To find the subsidiaries of these subsidiaries, we start with the first-child pointers in the records describing the subsidiaries 'EEWING', 'FLOWTEK', and 'GEOTH-OR' (see also Figure 9.36), in the same way as we started with the first-child pointer in the record that described 'ANTECK'.

To find the parent record for a record such as that with the key 'FLOWTEK', the key of the parent record is the **PARENT** field value 'ANTECK'. Thus the system is able to obtain by direct access both the children of any record and its parent record. An alternative method of implementing the conceptual file **COMPANY** and its recursive relationship would involve the use of an inversion or secondary index based on the connection field **PARENT**. Readers should construct this inversion as an exercise.

Manipulation of recursive one-to-many relationships
We end this discussion of recursive one-to-many relationships with a brief look at how they may be manipulated in practice. However, it should be understood

that at the time of writing many data base systems in commercial use do not explicitly provide for recursive one-to-many relationships. Relational systems provide for them to a considerable extent almost automatically because relationships are not explicitly defined in the conceptual schema definition. Thus with System R we would merely have to define the relation **COMPANY** as shown in Figure 9.35; manipulation of the recursive relationship would then be carried out in SQL by equating parent and child connection field values (that is, **CNAME** and **PARENT** values). Nevertheless, there are some aspects of a recursive one-to-many relationship that SQL cannot handle, as we shall see.

The latest CODASYL specifications provide for the specification of recursive one-to-many relationships in the conceptual schema definition. This is done by specifying a recursive owner-coupled set, that is, an owner-coupled set in which the parent and child conceptual files are the same. With the recursive relationship in the conceptual file **COMPANY** we could specify an owner-coupled set **SUBSID**, defined as follows:

```
SET NAME IS SUBSID
OWNER IS COMPANY
ORDER IS PERMANENT CONNECTION IS LAST
MEMBER IS COMPANY
CONNECTION IS MANUAL RETENTION IS OPTIONAL
SET SELECTION IS THRU SUBSID OWNER
    IDENTIFIED BY KEY CNAME
    EQUAL TO PARENT IN EMPLOYEE.
```

We would have to use **RETENTION IS OPTIONAL** with the conceptual file **COMPANY**, since it is possible for a company that is a subsidiary to become independent or be sold to another parent company. Thus a record that is a member in a set occurrence should be able to give up membership in that set occurrence and either not be a member of any set occurrence or become a member of some other set occurrence.

As explained earlier, a record in a recursive one-to-many relationship can be both a parent and a child record. Similarily, a record in a recursive owner-coupled set is often both a member record in one set occurrence and an owner record in another occurrence. How this can happen is illustrated in Figure 9.41. This fact has given rise to some difficulties with those CODASDYL **FETCH** commands, for example the set-scan **FETCH** command, that depend on the identification of a set occurrence by means of the current record of set. For example, if we access the owner record with key 'FLOWTEK' by means of a simple direct access command such as the record key **FETCH** command (see Section 6.3), then that record becomes the current of the file **COMPANY** and the current record of the set **SUBSID**. But this current record of **SUBSID** no longer identifies a single **SUBSID** set occurrence. It identifies two set occurrences, the one with the record with key 'ANTECK' as owner and the one with the record with key 'FLOWTEK' as owner (see Figure 9.41). Thus the set scan **FETCH** command (for scanning the records of a set occurrence) has to be modified so that only one of the two set occurrences otherwise identified by the current record of set may be specified. For a detailed solution to this difficulty, see Ref. 1.

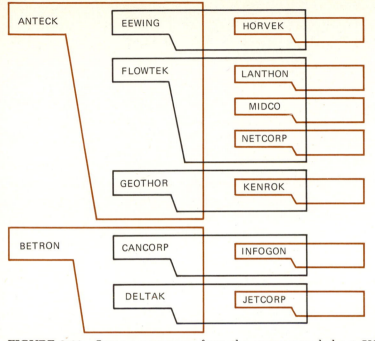

FIGURE 9.41   Some occurrences from the owner-coupled set SUBSID that embody the recursive one-to-many relationship in the conceptual file COMPANY in Figure 9.35. Note that every record is an owner record (even if only of an occurrence with no members, as is the case with record with key 'JETCORP'), and some records are both owner records and member records (for example, the record with key 'FLOWTEK'). Only the key fields of the records are shown.

At the time of writing many commercial data base systems (including CODASYL systems that have not implemented the lastest CODASYL specifications) do not explicitly provide for the specification and manipulation of recursive one-to-many relationships. In such cases the conceptual file containing the recursive relationship is often supplemented by an additional conceptual file, as illustrated in Figure 9.42 for the file COMPANY. The additional file LINK merely contains the key fields from COMPANY (actually it is the projection of COMPANY on CNAME), so that for each COMPANY record there is one LINK record. But for any LINK record there will also be many COMPANY records with PARENT values all equal to the key value of the LINK record. Thus there is also a one-to-many relationship between LINK and COMPANY. The one-to-one relationship between COMPANY and LINK can also be considered to be a one-to-many relationship, although of the simplest possible kind. Neither of these two relationships is recursive and can be handled by conventional methods. However, the additional file LINK complicates manipulation of the data base, and a facility for explicit definition and manipulation of recursive relationships is to be preferred. Note that with most commercial systems the recursive relationship would not be handled exactly as shown in Figure 9.42, but it would be dealt with along similar lines.

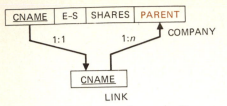

FIGURE 9.42 Use of an auxiliary conceptual file LINK to avoid a recursive one-to-many relationship. Between COMPANY and LINK the relationship is one-to-one (the trivial case of one-to-many), and between LINK and COMPANY it is one-to-many.

We conclude with some examples of how SQL and SQL/N would be used with the recursive relationship in COMPANY (Figure 9.35). With SQL we assume simply that the relation COMPANY has been defined in a relational conceptual schema along the lines explained in Chapter 7. With SQL/N we assume that in the conceptual schema there is a definition of COMPANY and the owner-coupled set embodying the relationship that is depicted in Figure 9.41.

Retrieval-1
Find out the names of companies whose immediate subsidiaries all make more than $0.80 per share.
The SQL expression is:

```
SELECT CNAME
FROM COMPANY
WHERE  CNAME IS NOT IN (SELECT PARENT
                        FROM COMPANY
                        WHERE (E-S < = 0.80))
```

This would retrieve the name 'EEWING', 'FLOWTEK', 'GEOTHOR', 'BETRON', and 'CANCORP' as we would expect (see Figures 9.36 and 9.35). However, it would also retrieve 'HORVEK', 'LANTHON', 'MIDCO', 'NETCORP', 'KENROK', 'INFOGON', and 'JETCORP', which we might not be prepared for. These would be retrieved because of the inevitable logic involved when we ask for companies that do not have a subsidiary making less than or equal to $0.80 per share. If a company has no subsidiaries, it will qualify! We had this problem before in Chapter 7.
The exactly equivalent SQL/N expression is:

```
SELECT  CNAME
FROM EACH  COMPANY OWNER RECORD
WHERE (FOR EACH IF ANY COMPANY MEMBER RECORD
                      (E-S > 0.80))
```

This expression will retrieve the same data as the SQL expression. This time the reason why 'HORVEK', 'LANTHON', and so on are retrieved is more obvious. Looking at Figure 9.41, we can see that, for example, the record with key 'HORVEK' is the owner of a set occurrence with no member records, and because of the use of the natural quantifier FOR EACH or FOR EACH IF ANY the predicate is true even if there are no members, and the record with key 'HORVEK' will be retrieved. If we wish not to retrieve records for companies with no subsidiaries at all, we need to specify this in our retrieval expressions; we might also be more specific in our retrieval request in English, as in the next request.

Retrieval-2
Find the name of each company that has one or more immediate subsidiaries, all of which earn more than $0.80 per share.
  The SQL expression is:

```
SELECT CNAME
FROM COMPANY
WHERE  CNAME IS IN (SELECT PARENT
                        FROM COMPANY)
    AND CNAME IS NOT IN (SELECT PARENT
                            FROM COMPANY
                            WHERE (E-S < = 0.80))
```

  This time we would just retrieve the name 'EEWING', 'FLOWTEK', 'BET-RON', and 'CANCORP' since in the first inner SELECT-FROM block we have specified that a record to be retrieved must have a child.
  The equivalent SQL/N expression is:

```
SELECT CNAME
FROM EACH COMPANY OWNER RECORD
WHERE (FOR ONE AND FOR ALL COMPANY MEMBER RECORDS
            (E-S > 0.80))
```

Here too we have stated that an owner record to be retrieved must have a member, for this is explicit in the natural quantifier FOR ONE AND FOR ALL.
  Let us now suppose that in the previous request we did not want to retrieve company names for companies that were themselves subsidiaries, that is, we want only independent companies. In that case our retrieval request would be as in Retrieval-3.

Retrieval-3
Find the name of each independent company with one or more immediate subsidiaries, all of which earn more than $0.80 per share.
  The SQL expression is:

```
SELECT CNAME
FROM COMPANY
WHERE ((PARENT = 'NULL') AND CNAME IS IN (SELECT PARENT
                                            FROM COMPANY))
    AND CNAME IS NOT IN (SELECT PARENT
                            FROM COMPANY
                            WHERE (E-S < = 0.80))
```

Here we merely specify in addition that a retrieved record must not have a parent. The result of the retrieval is just the company name 'BETRON'. The equivalent SQL/N expression is:

```
SELECT CNAME
FROM EACH COMPANY OWNER RECORD
WHERE ((PARENT = 'NULL')
    AND (FOR ONE AND FOR ALL COMPANY MEMBER RECORDS
            (E-S > 0.80)))
```

In all the retrievals so far we have been dealing with the immediate subsidiaries of a company. Suppose we need to deal with all the subsidiaries of a company. For example, suppose we wanted to retrieve a company such as 'ANTECK' in Figure 9.36, provided some condition was true for all its subsidiaries 'EEWING', 'FLOWTEK', 'GEOTHOR', 'HORVEK', 'LANTHON', 'MIDCO', 'NETCORP', and 'KENROK'. Retrieval-4 is of this type.

Retrieval-4

Find the name of each independent company with one or more subsidiaries, all of which earn more than $0.80 per share.

Note that this retrieval request is the same as that for Retrieval-3 except for the omission of the single word "immediate." This one word makes all the difference. Such is the expressive power of the English language; as every lawyer knows, a single word in a contract can be crucial.

Readers will be surprised to learn that the request cannot be expressed in SQL as it is presently constituted. The problem is that we do not know in general how many subsidiary levels are present in the relation such as COMPANY. (In the present case we do know, but that is only because we have all the information in a small version of the relation in front of us in Figure 9.35.). It is not possible to construct SQL expressions that can handle such requests because of the need to specify relationships by equating connection field values. In contrast, the request can easily be expressed in SQL/N. The expression is:

```
SELECT CNAME
FROM EACH  COMPANY OWNER RECORD
WHERE ((PARENT = 'NULL')
    AND (FOR ONE AND FOR ALL DESCENDENT COMPANY RECORDS
            (E-S > 0.80)))
```

We have only to change the word 'MEMBER' in the previous SQL/N expression to 'DESCENDENT'. Referring to Figure 9.41, this means that for a COMPANY (owner) record being considered for retrieval, the quantifier expression must hold true for its member records, their member records, and so on, all taken together. The SQL/N expression thus continues to mirror its English language counterpart. In the version of COMPANY in Figure 9.35, there are no records that satisfy the predicate in the above expression. However, if we change the 80¢ to 70¢, then the company name 'BETRON' would be retrieved. Note that in the converse example, 'OWNER' can be replaced by 'ASCENDENT'.

As a final example we consider a request that brings us into the realm of decision support systems.

Retrieval-5

What are the names and consolidated earnings per share of independent companies with one or more subsidiaries that all earn more than $0.70 per share?

To be able to carry out this request, the system would first have to retrieve the company names, earnings per share, and outstanding shares of each independent company satisfying the retrieval conditions, such as 'BETRON'. In addition, the earnings per share and number of outstanding shares of all the subsidiaries of these independent companies would have to be retrieved. From this data the consolidated earnings per share of the independent companies could be calculated as follows. If an independent company has (unconsolidated) earnings per share e and total outstanding shares s, and if its nth subsidiary has earnings per share e_n and total outstanding shares s_n, then the consolidated earnings per share of the independent company will be:

$$\frac{es + e_1s_1 + e_2s_2 + \cdots e_ne_n + \cdots}{s}$$

since we have to add up the total earnings of all the companies in a family and divide by the total shares for the independent parent company.

At the time of writing the author knows of no retrieval language that could manage this request, which can hardly be said to be complex. It is clearly a computational retrieval (Chapter 7) for which current tools do not permit expression of the necessary computations. If such a request were to occur frequently, then the only solution would be to construct a program that retrieved the necessary data and performed the necessary calculations. A suite of programs of this type would form a decision support system, if the programs were designed for interactive use at a terminal.

Recursive many-to-many relationships

There are two common examples in the business of recursive many-to-many relationships. One has to do with the interlocking ownership of joint stock companies, and the other with the positioning of components within subassemblies, and so on, in manufacturing. The examples are very similar, except for the possibility of greater complexity with the case of joint stock companies. We shall begin with a simple example of a recursive many-to-many relationship involving joint stock companies.

In Figure 9.43 we have two related conceptual files, COMPANY and INVEST. The file COMPANY is similar to that in Figure 9.35, except that there is no parent field. The records of COMPANY describe companies that this time are not generally 100 percent owned by some other company as was the case with the companies described by the records in Figure 9.35. Instead a company can be partly owned by one or more other companies that hold some of its shares, although in some cases (not occurring in Figure 9.43) a company could be 100 percent owned by another company. At the same time any company can own some shares in one or more other companies.

A record in the conceptual file INVEST in Figure 9.43 contains the number of shares (the POSSESSION field value) that one company (the PARENT field value) holds in another company (the SUBSIDIARY field value). Thus, for example, if we want to find out all about the companies DELTAK and JETCORP, we can begin by retrieving from the COMPANY file those records describing these companies. Subsequently, by accessing the INVEST record with composite key DELTAK JETCORP, we can find out how many shares of JETCORP are owned by DELTAK. (We ignore at this stage the possibility that at the same time JETCORP owns shares in DELTAK in a mutual back-scratching (quid pro quo) arrangement or, what is even more intricate, that JETCORP could own shares in a company X that in turn owns shares in DELTAK.)

If we want to determine which companies 'BETRON' partly (or wholely) owns, for example, we could access the COMPANY record with the key 'BETRON' and then retrieve the child records of this record in the file INVEST. The child INVEST records will be those with PARENT field value 'BETRON'. These child records will give us the names of the companies 'BETRON' owns (the names will be in the SUBSIDIARY field values), as well as the number of shares in each of them. To find out more about these companies that 'BETRON' owns, we could use the names from the SUBSIDIARY field values (in this case 'EEWING', 'FLOWTEK', and 'JETCORP', as is shown in Figure 9.43 to access the COMPANY file again.

Conversely, if we wish to find the companies that own shares in 'JETCORP', for example, we would first access the COMPANY file with the key 'JETCORP' and then obtain the child records in INVEST. However, this time the child records are those with SUBSIDIARY field value equal to 'JETCORP'. Taking the PARENT values from these child records and using them to access the COMPANY file again gives us descriptions of the records that own shares in 'JETCORP'.

Thus for any record in COMPANY describing company 'X' there are many records in COMPANY describing the companies that 'X' owns shares in; conversely, for any record in COMPANY describing company 'Y', there are many records in COMPANY describing the companies that own shares in 'Y'. The situation can more easily be understood if we imagine two versions of COMPANY, namely, L-COMPANY (on the left in Figure 9.44) and R-COMPANY (on the right in Figure 9.44); these two COMPANY versions are shown participating in an extended Bachman diagram with INVEST in Figure 9.44.

For any record in L-COMPANY describing company 'X', there will be many records in INVEST with child connection field value equal to 'X'; there will thus also be many records in R-COMPANY describing the companies that 'X' owns shares in. In a similar manner, for any record in R-COMPANY describing company 'Y', by means of the child connection field SUBSIDIARY in INVEST, there will be many records in COMPANY describing the companies that own shares in 'Y'. This means that there is a many-to-many relationship between L-COMPANY

CNAME	E-S	SHARES
ANTECK	0.35	2000
BETRON	1.50	3000
CANCORP	1.00	200
DELTAK	2.00	1000
EEWING	0.75	5000
FLOWTEK	2.20	1000
HORVEK	3.00	1000
INFOGON	1.40	300
JETCORP	0.75	2500
KENROK	1.20	900

COMPANY

PARENT	SUBSIDIARY	POSSESSION
ANTECK	DELTAK	100
ANTECK	EEWING	50
BETRON	EEWING	150
BETRON	FLOWTEK	75
BETRON	JETCORP	500
CANCORP	FLOWTEK	600
CANCORP	HORVEK	100
CANCORP	KENROK	70
DELTAK	JETCORP	1000
EEWING	INFOGON	30
FLOWTEK	HORVEK	60
FLOWTEK	JETCORP	100
FLOWTEK	KENROK	250

INVEST

FIGURE 9.43 The conceptual files COMPANY and INVEST. A COMPANY record contains the company name (CNAME), the earnings per share (E-S), and the outstanding shares (SHARES). An INVEST record gives the number of shares (POSSESSION) that one company (PARENT) holds in another company (SUBSIDIARY). A company such as 'FLOWTEK' can partly own several companies, and a company such as 'EEWING' can be partly owned by several companies. Thus COMPANY records must be taking part in a many-to-many relationship with themselves, that is, a recursive many-to-many relationship. SHARES and POSSESSION values are in 1000s of shares.

and R-COMPANY. As we saw in Chapter 5, a many-to-many relationship can consist of a pair of one-to-many relationships involving a third conceptual file; in this case the third conceptual file is INVEST, so that there is a one-to-many relationship between L-COMPANY and INVEST, and between R-COMPANY and INVEST.

However, since L-COMPANY and R-COMPANY in Figure 9.44 are really two identical versions of the same file COMPANY, so that if there is a many-to-many

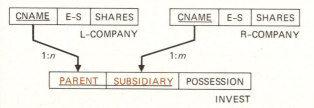

INVEST

FIGURE 9.44 An extended Bachman diagram for the data base in Figure 9.43. To illustrate the many-to-many relationship between COMPANY and itself, we have drawn two identical versions of COMPANY, one on the left (L-COMPANY) and one on the right (R-COMPANY). There is clearly a many-to-many relationship between L-COMPANY and R-COMPANY, and a record in INVEST gives how many shares a company from L-COMPANY has in a company from R-COMPANY.

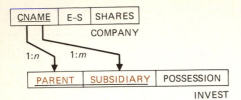

FIGURE 9.45 More concise version of the diagram in Figure 9.44. The conceptual file COMPANY is involved in a many-to-many relationship with itself, or a recursive many-to-many relationship. With the data in Figure 9.43, the recursive relationship contains three many-to-many subrelationships, as illustrated in Figure 9.46.

relationship between L-COMPANY and R-COMPANY, there must be a many-to-many relationship between COMPANY and itself, that is, a *recursive many-to-many relationship*.

This recursive relationship is illustrated in the extended Bachman diagram in Figure 9.45, in which we see that there are two different one-to-many relationships between COMPANY and INVEST. The one supported by the child connection field PARENT gives the names of the companies that are partly owned by the company described in the parent COMPANY record, while the one supported by the child connection field SUBSIDIARY gives the names of the companies that partly own the company described in the parent COMPANY record.

Subrelationships in a recursive many-to-many relationship

In our analysis of a recursive one-to-many relationship earlier, we saw that the recursion gave rise to a potentially large number of subrelationships. The same is true in the case of a recursive many-to-many relationship, although the subrelationships this time are many-to-many. To see how this comes about, consider the subrelationships in Figure 9.46. These subrelationships are those occurring in the data base in Figure 9.43. For the sake of brevity in Figure 9.46 we use only the first letter of the company names in Figure 9.43. In Figure 9.46, to indicate that company 'A' owns shares in company 'B', we connect the two by a line and place a circle on the end of the line at the box containing 'B'.

From Figure 9.43 we see that, for example, company 'BETRON' owns shares in 'EEWING', 'FLOWTEK' and 'JETCORP', and this is illustrated in Figure 9.46. However, from Figure 9.43 we can also see that 'EEWING' also has shares in 'INFOGON', while 'FLOWTEK' also has shares in 'HORVEK', 'JETCORP', and 'KENROK', and this is also shown in Figure 9.46. We see that in Figure 9.46 we have used three versions of COMPANY, and that out of these three versions we have selected three groups of records. These are:

1. Records describing companies that are not owned by any other company, that is, the records with keys 'A', 'B', and 'C'; we refer to these companies as *top* companies.
2. Records describing companies that do not own shares in other com-

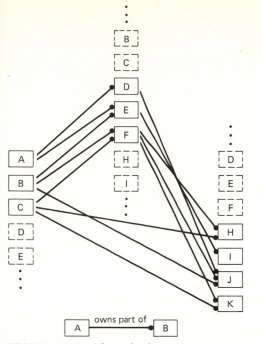

FIGURE 9.46 The subrelationships involved in the recursive relationship in the data base in Figures 9.43 and 9.45. Only the first letter of the keys of the records in COMPANY are shown. The companies are segregated into those with no subsidiaries ('H', 'I', 'J', and 'K'), those that are not themselves subsidiaries ('A', 'B', and 'C'), and the remainder ('D', 'E', and 'F') that are both subsidiaries and parents. Any pair of these groups is involved in a many-to-many relationship.

panies, that is, the records with keys 'H', 'I', 'J', and 'K'; we refer to these companies as *bottom* companies.

3. Records describing companies that are partly owned by top companies and that partly own bottom companies, that is, the records with keys 'D', 'E', and 'F'; we refer to these companies as *intermediate* companies.

Between any two of these groups of records there is a many-to-many relationship. For any top company there are many intermediate companies it has shares in, while for any intermediate company there are many top companies that own shares in it. Similarly, for any top company there are many bottom companies it owns shares in, while for any bottom company there are many top companies that own shares in it. Similarly, there is a many-to-many relationship between intermediate and bottom companies.

Each of the many-to-many subrelationships in Figures 9.43 and 9.46 may be decomposed into two one-to-many relationships, as can every many-to-many relationship (see Chapter 5). This is illustrated in Figure 9.47. We see that with each of the many-to-many subrelationships some of the records from **INVEST** are necessary for the two one-to-many relationships into which a many-to-many subrelationship may be decomposed.

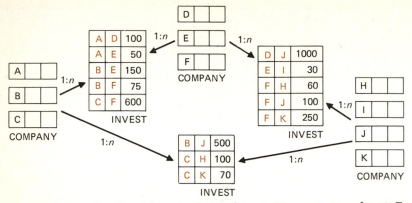

FIGURE 9.47 Details of the subrelationships in Figures 9.43 and 9.46. Each of the three many-to-many relationships in Figure 9.46 reduces to a pair of one-to-many relationships involving a group of records from the conceptual file INVEST (see Figure 9.43).

Number of subrelationships in a recursive many-to-many relationship

The number of subrelationships that can occur in a recursive many-to-many relationship depends on the number of levels of ownership or the number of record groups (such as those in Figure 9.46) that can be formed. In the simplest case we would have only two levels, namely, the top level for top companies that are not owned by any other companies and the bottom level for companies that do not own any other companies (but which are partly or wholly owned by top companies). In this simple case there will be a single relationship between top and bottom companies. In the next most simple case we have the three levels shown in Figure 9.46, giving us three subrelationships.

The next most simple case will involve four levels of ownership. There will be top companies and bottom companies as before. There will also be what we shall call *intermediate-A* companies that are owned partly by top companies, but which also own companies that in turn own bottom companies. We have therefore also *intermediate-B* companies that own bottom companies and are owned by intermediate-A companies. This situation is illustrated in Figure 9.48, although not in the detail of Figure 9.46 or Figure 9.47. The extended Bachman diagram in Figure 9.45 covers the general case of a recursive many-to-many relationship and is valid no matter how many ownership levels occur in COMPANY. There will be a many-to-many relationship between every pair from the four groups of companies in Figure 9.48, giving six many-to-many relationships altogether.

In the general case of n levels of ownership and thus n groups of companies, there will be $n(n-1)/2$ many-to-many subrelationships. The proof of this is simple. If there are n groups, any one group will have a many-to-many relationship with each of the other $n-1$ groups. This will be true for each of the n groups, giving $n(n-1)$ relationships altogether. But this deduction counts each relationship twice, so that the correct number of relationships is $n(n-1)/2$.

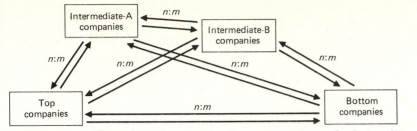

FIGURE 9.48   Shows how there can be six many-to-many subrelationships if there are four ownership levels in the COMPANY file.

Explosions and implosions

An *explosion* for a record in the **COMPANY** file that describes company 'X', for example, will give the records for companies partly owned by 'X', the records for companies owned by these companies, and so on down to the records for companies that do not own any further companies. Thus, referring to Figure 9.46 or Figure 9.47, the explosions for 'A' and 'B' are:

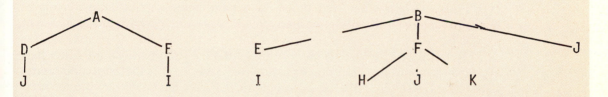

Similarly, we can have an *implosion* for a record in **COMPANY**. For a record in **COMPANY** that describes company 'Y', the implosion will give the records for companies that partly own 'Y', and the records for companies that partly own these companies, and so on. Thus the implosions for 'J' and 'H' in Figure 9.46 are:

Thus an explosion gives us all the companies a given company has either a direct or indirect interest in, while an implosion gives all the companies that have either a direct or indirect interest in a given company.

The bill-of-materials relationship

The recursive many-to-many relationship that occurs in a file describing companies that own shares in companies also occurs in a file describing part types or assemblies of part types that can contain part types. In the case of part types, the relationship is often called the bill-of-materials relationship.

The bill-of-materials relationship is depicted in the data base in Figure 9.49. The file **PART-TYPE** describes types of part which may contain other types of part also described in **PART-TYPE**. Thus the part types described might be more accurately called assemblies and subassemblies in many cases. The field **PART-CODE** gives unique identifiers of the part types, and we can assume these values are 'A', 'B', 'C', and so on. Since a part type can contain other part types, we can imagine that 'A' contains 'D' and 'E', and that 'B' contains 'E', 'F', and 'J', and so on. 'D' and 'E' could then contain other part types, and so on.

For convenience we could assume that Figure 9.46 also applies to the data base in Figure 9.49, so that the line between 'A' and 'B' should now be interpreted as 'A' contains 'B'. The details of which part type contains another part type are in the conceptual file **CONSTRUCTION**. A record in **CONSTRUCTION** gives the identifier of a part type (**OUTER** field value) that contains a part type (identified by the **INNER** field value) in a specified geometrical position (the **POSITION** field value). If the data in Figure 9.46 applies, then the part types are divided into three groups, those that are not contained within another part type, those that do not contain other part types, and those that both are contained within other part types and contain other part types. In general there can be many levels of containment just as there can be many levels of ownership with the data base in Figure 9.43.

From the data in the data base in Figure 9.49, a parts explosion for any part type may be obtained. Thus the explosion for part type 'B' is that shown in Figure 9.50 and is consistent with the data in Figure 9.46. We have arbitrarily given each type of part a unique shape to make the explosion more obvious. Such explosions are obviously of great importance in the manufacture of complex items, since they give precise descriptions of how the items are assembled. Parts implosions are also possible, as was the case with the data base in Figure 9.43, and give all the part types that contain a given type of part. Implosions are useful in the maintenance of complex items such as aircraft. For example, if a certain

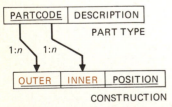

FIGURE 9.49 A conceptual data base showing how major part types (or assemblies) are constructed from minor part types (or subassemblies). A major part type will contain minor part types in fixed geometrical positions (POSITION field value). Thus a CONSTRUCTION record gives the position of a minor part type (INNER field value) in a major part type (OUTER field value). A minor part type can in turn contain further minor part types and so on. Thus the files shown here are analogous to the files COMPANY and INVEST in Figure 9.43, and PART-TYPE takes part in a recursive many-to-many relationship, often called the bill-of-materials relationship in this context.

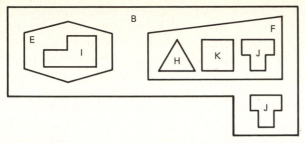

FIGURE 9.50 If we assume that the PARTCODE, OUTER, and INNER field values in Figure 9.49 appear (in abbreviated form) as do the CNAME, PARENT, and SUBSIDIARY values in Figure 9.43, the subrelationships of Figure 9.46 apply to the data base in Figure 9.49 as well. Thus an explosion of the part type B will have an appearance similar to that shown above. 'E', 'F', and 'J' are the immediate sub-assemblies in B; in turn 'E' contains an 'I' subassembly, while 'F' contains 'H', 'K', and 'J' subassemblies.

type of bolt is found to be defective, an implosion for that bolt will give all the subassemblies (in many types of aircraft) that contain that type of bolt. (This is an example of how lives could depend on the correct retrieval of information from a data base.)

Readers will notice a minor difference between the key fields in **INVEST** in Figure 9.45 and **CONSTRUCTION** in Figure 9.49. Since the composite **PARENT SUBSIDIARY** is the primary key in **INVEST**, we might expect by analogy that **OUTER INNER** will be the key in **CONSTRUCTION**. Nevertheless we must be careful, for the two data bases are not completely analogous, and there is an important difference that causes the keys in **INVEST** and **CONSTRUCTION** to differ. Referring to the explosion in Figure 9.50, we can see that a part type 'B' can contain a part type 'E'; similarly, we can see that a company 'B' can have shares in company 'E'. But it is possible for part type 'B' to contain two or more of 'E' part types within it in different geometrical positions. Thus within **CONSTRUCTION** we could have the records:

.
.
.

B	E	2,4
B	E	2,7
B	E	3,6

.
.
.

and these records are unique only because of the three different sets of geometrical coordinates for the position of the three parts of type 'E' within part type 'B'. In contrast, it is not possible for company 'B' to own common shares in company 'E' three times in the file **INVEST**. Company 'B' either owns shares in 'E' or it does not, and that is all. Thus **PARENT** and **SUBSIDIARY** values will uniquely identify a record in INVEST, but in general it takes OUTER, INNER, and POSITION values to uniquely identify a CONSTRUCTION record. Some readers may object that since no two objects in the universe can ever be in exactly the same position at the same time, then POSITION values must be unique and POSITION is the primary key. We leave readers to show why this argument is not applicable in this case.

As a footnote to this discussion, it is clear that if part type 'A' contains part type 'B', then it is physically impossible for 'B' to contain 'A'. Similarly, if part type 'A' contains 'F', and if 'F' contains 'B', then 'B' cannot contain 'A'. However, no such restriction applies in the case of companies. Thus if company 'A' has shares in company 'B', it is quite possible for 'B' to have shares in 'A' in a quid pro quo arrangement. We have not given any examples of this possibility, and a full discussion of its implications would take us beyond the scope of this book. We can mention that the possibility is implicit in the extended Bachman diagram in Figure 9.45, and that it leads to never-ending explosions and implosions.

Recursive many-to-many relationships at the storage level

It usually helps students of the subject to consider how a recursive many-to-many relationship is implemented at the storage level. There are many ways of implementing a data base containing a recursive relationship, and we have chosen the technique of parent-to-child and next-child pointers in Figure 9.51, which is the storage data base for the conceptual data base in Figure 9.43.

We need two separate pointer systems shown on the left and right of Figure 9.51. On the left we have parent-to-child pointers in the COMPANY file (the P-C-POINTERA field values) and next-child pointers in the INVEST file (the N-C-POINTERA field values). For any COMPANY record describing company 'X', the P-C-POINTERA value gives the address of the first-child INVEST record that names a company 'X' owns shares in; the N-C-POINTERA value in this first-child record gives the address of the next-child record naming a company 'X' has shares in. In Figure 9.51 we have chosen to use physical pointers, but for reasons of brevity only, since symbolic pointers in this case would involve the use of the composite keys in INVEST. The pointer system on the right is similar except that it connects a record in COMPANY, describing company 'Y', for example, to the child INVEST records that name (via the PARENT field values) the companies that own shares in 'X'.

In a few places we have supplemented the pointer field values with arrows, in particular those pointer fields involved in the generation of an explosion for the record with key 'ANTECK' and an implosion for the record with key 'HORVEK'.

Manipulation of recursive many-to-many relationships

As we saw earlier, many commerical data base systems do not explicitly provide for recursive one-to-many relationships. In contrast, with recursive many-to-many relationships, explicit provisions are to a large extent unnecessary, since the recursive many-to-many relationship can be dealt with by means of two

P-C-POINTERA	CNAME	E-S	SHARES	P-C-POINTERS
001	ANTECK	0.35	2000	–
003	BETRON	1.50	3000	–
006	CANCORP	1.00	200	–
009	DELTAK	2.00	1000	001
010	EEWING	0.75	5000	002
011	FLOWTEK	2.20	1000	004
–	HORVEK	3.00	1000	007
–	INFOGON	1.40	300	010
–	JETCORP	0.75	2500	005
–	KENROK	1.20	900	008

	N-C-POINTERA	PARENT	SUBSIDIARY	POSSESSION	N-C-POINTERS
001	002	ANTECK	DELTAK	100	–
002	–	ANTECK	EEWING	50	003
003	004	BETRON	EEWING	150	–
004	005	BETRON	FLOWTEK	75	006
005	–	BETRON	JETCORP	500	005
006	007	CANCORP	FLOWTEK	600	–
007	008	CANCORP	HORVEK	100	011
008	–	CANCORP	KENROK	70	013
009	–	DELTAK	JETCORP	1000	012
010	–	EEWING	INFOGON	30	–
011	012	FLOWTEK	HORVEK	60	–
012	013	FLOWTEK	JETCORP	100	–
013	–	FLOWTEK	KENROK	250	–

Record disk addresses

FIGURE 9.51 The storage version of the data base in Figure 9.43 with a parent-to-first-child and a child-to-next-child pointer system. The pointers are physical and give the disk addresses of the records pointed to; they could alternatively be symbolic. The arrows on the left trace the explosion for 'ANTECK', while those on the right trace the implosion for 'HORVEK'.

one-to-many relationships, such as those supported by the child connection fields in Figure 9.45 or Figure 9.49. Thus a great deal of manipulation of a recursive many-to-many relationship is possible with a commercial data base system that provides for normal one-to-many relationships, as most commercial systems do. Of course, data base programs that deal with recursive relationships are often complex, but usually the complexity is due to the complexity of the recursive relationship being manipulated.

If the data base in Figure 9.43 were being defined as a CODASYL data base, then the two one-to-many relationships between COMPANY and INVEST would be defined as owner-coupled sets, perhaps with the names shown in Figure 9.52, that is, PORTFOLIO and INVESTORS. Thus in a PORTFOLIO set occurrence, the company described in the owner record has shares in each of the companies described in the member records. In an INVESTORS set occurrence, the company described in the owner record is partly owned by the companies described in the member records.

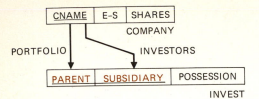

FIGURE 9.52 In a CODASYL conceptual schema definition of the data base in Figure 9.43, the two one-to-many relationships supported by the child connection fields PARENT and SUBSIDIARY would be defined as (nonrecursive) owner-coupled sets with such names as PORTFOLIO and INVESTORS. A PORTFOLIO set occurrence would describe the member companies the owner company has shares in; an INVESTORS set occurrence would describe the member companies that have shares in the owner company.

To determine the explosion for a company such as 'BETRON', we would use a CODASYL record-key FETCH (or FIND) command to retrieve the record for this company. Then we would use the set-scan FETCH command to retrieve the INVEST member records in the PORTFOLIO set occurrence with the 'BETRON' record as owner. These INVEST member records will give us the keys of the immediate subsidiaries of 'BETRON', namely, 'EEWING', 'FLOWTEK', and 'JET-CORP'. We then repeat the whole process to first find the immediate subsidiaries of 'EEWING', and then the other immediate subsidiaries, as is illustrated in Figure 9.53. A similar implosion procedure would be used to generate the implosion for a given COMPANY record, except that this time we would use the owner-coupled set INVESTORS.

Implementing the data base in Figure 9.43 as a relational data base would as usual require only the definition of the relations COMPANY and INVEST in the conceptual schema; no definition of any relationships would be needed, since any necessary relationships would be specified in relational data base manipulation commands, by equating parent and child connection fields. We conclude with some retrieval requests for information for the data base in Figure 9.45 using SQL; for comparison purposes we also give the corresponding SQL/N expressions using the set names from Figure 9.52.

Find the names of the companies that 'BETRON' has shares in, together with the number of shares owned for each subsidiary.

The SQL expression is:

```
SELECT SUBSIDIARY, POSSESSION
FROM INVEST
WHERE PARENT = 'BETRON'
```

The SQL/N expression is equally simple:

```
SELECT SUBSIDIARY, POSSESSION
FROM EACH INVEST RECORD
WHERE PARENT = 'BETRON'
```

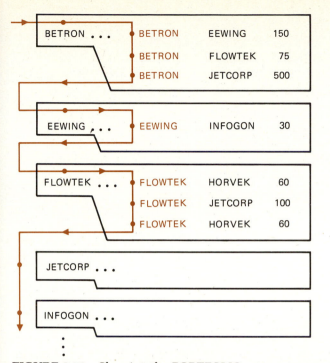

FIGURE 9.53 Showing the PORTFOLIO set occurrences from the CODASYL data base in Figure 9.52 that are involved in the generation of the explosion for*'BETRON'. The circles show the succession of CRUs generated by the explosion procedure.

Retrieval-6

For parent companies whose earnings per share is greater than $2.00, find their names and the names of all their immediate subsidiaries, together with the number of shares owned in each of these subsidiaries.

The SQL expression is:

```
SELECT *
FROM INVEST
WHERE PARENT IS IN (SELECT CNAME
                    FROM COMPANY
                    WHERE (E-S > 2.0))
```

In order for an **INVEST** record to be retrieved, its **PARENT** value must be the key of a **COMPANY** record for which the E-S value exceeds $2.00. Referring to Figure 9.43, the data retrieved would be:

```
FLOWTEK HORVEK   60
FLOWTEK JETCORP 100
FLOWTEK KENROK  250
```

The SQL/N expression would be:

```
SELECT PARENT, SUBSIDIARY, POSSESSION
FROM EACH MEMBER INVEST RECORD
WHERE (FOR THE ONE COMPANY OWNER RECORD IN PORTFOLIO
         (E-S > 2.0))
```

This SQL/N expression differs from every SQL/N expression presented so far, in that we specify the name of the owner-coupled set involved in a one-to-many relationship. In this case we have to specify the set **PORTFOLIO**. To omit it would make the expression ambiguous since for one **INVEST** member record there are two owner records, one in a **PORTFOLIO** set occurrence and the other in an **INVESTORS** set occurrence.

Retrieval-7

Find the name and earnings per share of each company that has at least one immediate subsidiary with more than 2 million outstanding shares.

The SQL expression is:

```
SELECT CNAME, E-S
FROM COMPANY
WHERE CNAME IS IN (SELECT PARENT
                   FROM INVEST
                   WHERE SUBSIDIARY IS IN (SELECT CNAME
                                           FROM COMPANY
                                           WHERE (SHARES > 2000)))
```

Here we take a parent **COMPANY** record and check if among its **INVEST** child records there is a record with a **SUBSIDIARY** value equal to the key of another **COMPANY** record for which the **SHARES** value is greater than 2 million. This expression would retrieve:

```
ANTECK    0.35
BETRON    1.50
FLOWTEK   2.20
```

The SQL/N expression will require the use of both **PORTFOLIO** and **INVESTORS** owner-coupled sets:

```
SELECT CNAME, E-S
FROM EACH COMPANY OWNER RECORD
WHERE (FOR AT LEAST 1 INVEST MEMBER RECORD IN PORTFOLIO
         (THERE IS EXACTLY 1 COMPANY OWNER RECORD IN INVESTORS
             WHERE (SHARES > 2000)))
```

Retrieval-8

Retrieve all information about the companies in the explosion of the company 'BETRON'.

Current SQL cannot express this request. Nevertheless, SQL/N allows for the owner-coupled set concept to be expanded to include the concepts of explosion and implosion, thus allowing expression of the request. The record being exploded may be referred to as an *explosion-owner*; the remaining records in the explosion are called the *explosion-members*. In SQL/N, instead of **COMPANY OWNER** in reference to an owner-coupled set occurrence, we can use **COMPANY EXPLOSION-OWNER**, and similarly we can use **COMPANY EXPLOSION-MEMBERS** for all the records in the explosion apart from the explosion-owner.

We also need a method of distinguishing between explosions and implosions in expressions. We know that in an explosion we start with a **COMPANY** record and then go to the child **INVEST** records using the **PARENT** child connection field, and then back to **COMPANY** parent records using **SUBSIDIARY** child connection fields, and so on. Thus we use the **PARENT** connection field first and then the **SUBSIDIARY** connection field. With an implosion the opposite is true, for we would take the **SUBSIDIARY** connection field first and then the **PARENT** connection field, and so on. Thus we could refer to an explosion "in the **PARENT:SUBSIDIARY** direction," or an implosion "in the **SUBSIDIARY:PARENT** direction." Thus in an SQL/N expression, we can replace a clause such as:

```
... COMPANY MEMBER RECORD IN PORTFOLIO ...
```

by

```
...COMPANY EXPLOSION-MEMBER RECORD IN PARENT:SUBSIDIARY EXPLOSION ...
```

to give an exact specification of the explosion required.

The SQL/N expression for Retrieval-8 is therefore:

```
SELECT CNAME, E-S, SHARES
FROM EACH EXPLOSION-MEMBER COMPANY RECORD
WHERE (FOR THE ONE EXPLOSION-OWNER COMPANY RECORD
       IN PARENT: SUBSIDIARY EXPLOSION
                    (CNAME = 'BETRON'))
```

Here we use the natural quantifier **FOR THE ONE** with the explosion parent record, since there can only be one of them. We could also have used **FOR EXACTLY 1**. The request cannot be expressed in SQL because we need to equate connection field values in all of the subrelationships involved but do not in general know how many levels of ownership must be so specified.

Retrieval-9

For each company in which 'BETRON' has either a direct or indirect interest, find the company name, the name of its immediate parent, and the number of shares the immediate parent holds.

We see that the information required is in the **INVEST** file. However, only the **COMPANY** records can be used in the specification of an explosion. The SQL/N expression is:

```
SELECT PARENT, SUBSIDIARY,POSSESSION
FROM EACH INVEST RECORD
WHERE (FOR THE ONE OWNER COMPANY RECORD IN INVESTORS
(THERE IS ONE EXPLOSION-OWNER COMPANY RECORD
     IN PARENT: SUBSIDIARY EXPLOSION
                WHERE (CNAME = 'BETRON'))
```

If a **SUBSIDIARY** field in an **INVEST** record is to contain the name of a company in the explosion of 'BETRON', then it must have the same value as the key field of a **COMPANY** record that takes part in the explosion.

The request cannot be expressed with current SQL because, as before, we do not know how many levels are involved. We must also remember that SQL/N is in a developmental stage, and remains to be implemented.

ADDITIONAL PERSPECTIVE 2
MULTIVALUED OR BINARY JOIN DEPENDENCIES

Because of peculiar insertion and deletion properties, relations that contain multivalued or binary join dependencies should be avoided in data base design. The problem with them is that insertion of one record usually requires insertion of additional records, and deletion of one record usually also requires deletion of additional records. We shall look at a typical example of a relation with a binary join dependency in this supplement, and illustrate both how the peculiar insertion and deletion properties arise, and how the binary join dependency can be eliminated.

Let us imagine that the marketing manager at a company that manufactures and sells personal computers is anxious to keep tabs on the activities of competitors in the business. We shall assume that in this business each computer company markets its models through its own computer shops. Thus our marketing manager could arrange the data for two of her competitors as shown in Figure 9.54. The arrangement reflects the semantic rules that are valid for this data:

1. A computer company makes many models, but a model or make is made by only one computer company.
2. A computer company has many computer stores, but a computer store belongs to only one computer company.
3. A computer company sells all of its models at all of its computer stores.

This is reflected in Figure 9.54, which has a large rectangle for each computer company. At the left of a rectangle are the models the company makes, and at the right are the computer stores (store name and city) that the company owns. Because of semantic rule (3) above, we can safely deduce that, for example, Busy Business Machines markets its model PC-2 at Joyland, New York, and that Pineapple Computers markets its Wiz-1 model at Datastore in San Francisco.

Incidentally, this very reasonable arrangement of the data in Figure 9.54 forms a relation, though not the kind of relation that can be used in relational data bases. It is an example of an *unnormalized relation*. Each rectangle in Figure 9.54 forms a tuple of the relation, but because a field value is not atomic, that is, because a field can have multiple values, such as 'PC-1' and 'PC-2', it is said to be unnormalized, as mentioned earlier in this chapter, and of little interest in relational data base design.

Computer make	Computer company	Computer store
PC-1 PC-2	BUSY BUSINESS MACHINES	JOYLAND, NEW YORK DATALAND, LOS ANGELES

WIZ-1 WIZ-2	PINEAPPLE COMPUTERS	INFOWORLD, CHICAGO DATASTORE, SAN FRANCISCO DATAJOY, TORONTO

FIGURE 9.54 The data above is kept by a marketing manager in a computer company and enables the manager to keep tabs on the activities of competitors such as the Busy Business Machines Corp., and Pineapple Computer Corp. To the left of each company are the computer models it markets, and to the right are company-owned computer stores in which it markets its computers. A computer company markets all of its computer models at each of its stores. The data above is actually laid out as an unnormalized relation. In Figure 9.55, the data is shown as a normalized relation, that is, as the type of relation used in relational data bases.

A relation with a binary join dependency

Eventually our marketing manager decides to construct a proper or normalized relation for her marketing data in Figure 9.54. She comes up with the relation **MARKET-CHANNEL**, as shown in Figure 9.55. There is nothing at all unreasonable about this relation, given the data in Figure 9.54, and the semantic rules behind it. Each record in the relation gives a computer manufacturer along with a computer model made by the manufacturer and a computer store at which the model is sold, and which belongs to the manufacturer. Thus, since, for example, the model PC-1 is sold at two stores, there have to be two records for the model, and similarly, since the model Wiz-1 is sold at three stores there have to be three records for it.

Unfortunately, the relation **MARKET-CHANNEL** contains a *binary join dependency*, and is highly undesirable for use in a relational (or any other) data base. Let us consider what must happen if, for example, Pineapple Computers brings out a new model, the Wiz-3 computer. According to semantic rule (3), this new computer must be marketed through all the Pineapple Computers stores. Thus we would have to insert the following records into **MARKET-CHANNEL**:

```
WIZ-3   PINEAPPLE COMPUTERS   DATAJOY TORONTO
WIZ-3   PINEAPPLE COMPUTERS   DATASTORE SANFRANCISCO
WIZ-3   PINEAPPLE COMPUTERS   INFOWORLD CHICAGO
```

Similarly, if Busy Business Machines opens a new store, because of semantic rule (3), we shall have to insert two new records.

COMPUTER-MAKE	COMPUTER-COMPANY	COMPUTER-STORE
PC-1	BUSY BUSINESS MACHINES	DATALAND LOS ANGELES
PC-1	BUSY BUSINESS MACHINES	JOYLAND NEW YORK
PC-2	BUSY BUSINESS MACHINES	DATALAND LOS ANGELES
PC-2	BUSY BUSINESS MACHINES	JOYLAND NEW YORK
WIZ-1	PINEAPPLE COMPUTERS	DATAJOY TORONTO
WIZ-1	PINEAPPLE COMPUTERS	DATASTORE SAN FRANCISCO
WIZ-1	PINEAPPLE COMPUTERS	INFOWORLD CHICAGO
WIZ-2	PINEAPPLE COMPUTERS	DATAJOY TORONTO
WIZ-2	PINEAPPLE COMPUTERS	DATASTORE SAN FRANCISCO
WIZ-2	PINEAPPLE COMPUTERS	INFOWORLD CHICAGO

MARKET-CHANNEL

FIGURE 9.55 A record from the relation MARKET-CHANNEL gives the manufacturer of a make of computer and the manufacturer's computer store at which it is sold. The relation contains the data from Figure 9.54, but has unusual properties, because of the requirement that a computer company market all of its computer models at all of its stores. This will mean that if Pineapple Computers brings out a new model (Wiz-3), it will be necessary to insert three new records in MARKET-CHANNEL in order to allow for the sale of the new model at all three of Pineapple Computer Corporation's stores. The relation is not in 4NF, and contains a nontrivial multivalued or binary join dependency.

We have the converse situation with deletions. Let us suppose that the Wiz-1 becomes obsolete and is withdrawn from the market. This means that it will not be sold any more at any of the company's stores. We must therefore delete the following three records:

```
WIZ-1   PINEAPPLE COMPUTERS   DATAJOY TORONTO
WIZ-1   PINEAPPLE COMPUTERS   DATASTORE SAN FRANCISCO
WIZ-1   PINEAPPLE COMPUTERS   INFOWORLD CHICAGO
```

The relation MARKET-CHANNEL is clearly undesirable, for sooner or later the wrong number of insertions or deletions will be carried out, and the relation will contain inconsistent data. The solution is to decompose it.

Elimination of the binary join dependency
The standard method of eliminating a binary join dependency is by decomposition of the offending relation into two of its projections, as shown in Figure 9.56.

COMPUTER-MAKE	COMPUTER-COMPANY
PC-1	BUSY BUSINESS MACHINES
PC-2	BUSY BUSINESS MACHINES
WIZ-1	PINEAPPLE COMPUTERS
WIZ-2	PINEAPPLE COMPUTERS

MODEL

COMPUTER-COMPANY	COMPUTER-STORE
BUSY BUSINESS MACHINES	JOYLAND NEW YORK
BUSY BUSINESS MACHINES	DATALAND LOS ANGELES
PINEAPPLE COMPUTERS	INFOWORLD CHICAGO
PINEAPPLE COMPUTERS	DATASTORE SAN FRANCISCO
PINEAPPLE COMPUTERS	DATAJOY TORONTO

STORE

FIGURE 9.56 The relation MODEL is formed from a projection of MARKET-CHANNEL on the fields COMPUTER-MAKE and COMPUTER-COMPANY, while the relation STORE is formed by a projection of MARKET-CHANNEL on COMPUTER-COMPANY and COMPUTER-STORE. These relations are free from the binary join dependency that occurs in MARKET-CHANNEL. The primary key fields are underlined.

The relation **MODEL** tells us about computer models and their manufacturers, while the relation **STORE** tells us about computer stores and their owners. We notice also that these two relations clearly contain the data in Figure 9.54.

Multiple all-to-all relationships

Thus by taking the two projections and forming the relations **MODEL** and **STORE** in Figure 9.56, we appear to have solved the problem. Well, this is not quite true. We have eliminated the binary join dependency, but we have another problem, and an examination of this problem will give us additional insight into the nature of binary join dependencies.

Our new problem is that there is nothing in the two relations **MODEL** and **STORE** to tell us that a model from manufacturer X is sold at all the stores belonging to X, or conversely that a store belonging to X sells all computers made by X. Thus for the data in Figure 9.54, and thus also for the data in Figure 9.56, we can have two possibilities: semantic rule (3) may apply, or it may not apply. Whether it applies or not, the relations **MODEL** and **STORE** will be the same. Thus the user must know whether or not the rule applies, and construct programs and expressions for information retrieval accordingly. If we assume that the rule does apply, then it will be up to the data base administrator to enforce programming standards that ensure that the rule is taken into account (see Chapter 13 for further details on data base administrator functions). But if Murphy's law is taken into account, sooner or later an important program will execute that does not take rule (3) into account, and wrong information will be retrieved.

Thus the core of our difficulties with the data in Figure 9.54 is rule (3), for this rule is stating a special kind of many-to-many relationship. Consider the models and stores for one computer manufacturer in Figure 9.54, such as Busy Business Machines. For this company, it is true that a model is sold not just at many stores but at all stores, and that a store sells not just many models, but all models. Thus for any computer company, there is not just a many-to-many relationship between the entities computer models and computer stores, but an *all-to-all* relationship, which is a special case of a many-to-many relationship. We recall that in Figure 8.2 we had a many-to-many relationship between **EMPLOYEE** and **SUPPLIER**. The relationship would be all-to-all if each employee dealt with all suppliers and each supplier dealt with all employees.

In Figure 9.54 for a given computer company, there is an all-to-all relationship just between the models and stores. But because we have a collection of computer companies, we in fact have a collection of all-to-all relationships, or multiple all-to-all relationships. Thus we can say that rule (3) is specifying multiple all-to-all relationships or that we have a binary-join dependency in any relation that contains multiple all-to-all relationships, as does the relation **MARKET-CHANNEL** in Figure 9.55.

Terminology

The term *multivalued dependency* was first introduced by Fagin (Ref. 4) but is an inappropriate one in the author's opinion. Since a computer company in

Figure 9.54 determines a set of computer models, a model can be said to have a multivalued (instead of functional) dependence on the computer company. Similarly, a computer store has a multivalued dependence on computer company. However, these dependencies are not in themselves enough to produce the insertion and deletion difficulties in the relation MARKET-CHANNEL. Rule (3) must apply if we are to have these difficulties.

The term binary-join dependency was introduced by Rissanen in a highly theoretical paper (Ref. 5). We can see why the term is much more appropriate by a closer examination of the relations MARKET-CHANNEL and its two projection relations, MODEL and STORE.

We can always generate the relation MARKET-CHANNEL by a natural join (see the supplement to Chapter 8) of MODEL and STORE on the join field COMPUTER-COMPANY. To confirm that this is so, the reader should try it as an exercise. (For each record in MODEL, simply concatenate to it all the records from STORE with the same COMPUTER-COMPANY value.) Now suppose that a new model Wiz-3 is brought to market; we shall need three new records in MARKET-CHANNEL, as we have already described, but only one new record in MODEL. Nevertheless, if we now take a natural join of the new version of MODEL and STORE, we will also generate the three new MARKET-CHANNEL records. Thus we come to the basic property of MARKET-CHANNEL that causes its peculiar insertion and deletion properties: the relation is at all times the natural (or binary) join of its two projections, MODEL and STORE. Hence the name binary-join dependency.

The term *multiple all-to-all relationship* was introduced by the author for expositional purposes. The term describes the special many-to-many relationships that give rise to binary join dependencies. For a method of displaying binary join dependencies by means of dependency diagrams, see Ref. 1.

QUESTIONS

The following retrievals have to do with the one-to-many recursive relationship in the relation COMPANY in Figure 9.35 (see also Figure 9.41). Retrieval requests should be formulated in SQL, and perhaps also in SQL/N.

15. What companies have no subsidiaries?
16. What companies have at least three subsidiaries?
17. What subsidiaries have parents that make more than $1 (of unconsolidated earnings) per share?
18. Find the earnings per share of companies that have at least one subsidiary earning more than $0.50 per share?
19. What companies earn more than Deltak?
20. What companies with no subsidiaries are owned by companies making more than $2.00 (of unconsolidated earnings) per share?
21. Find the ultimate parents (that is, at the top of the ownership hierarchy) of

companies earning more than $2.00 per share. (Cannot be handled with SQL. Use SQL/N.)

The following illustrate miscellaneous recursive one-to-many relationships.

22. The relation **EMPLOYEE** has the fields **EMPNUMB** (employee number), **SALARY** (employee's salary), **CHIEF** (employee number of employee's immediate supervisor). The relation describes all the employees in an organization, which has a hierarchical structure.
    (a) Place some sample data in **EMPLOYEE** (about 12 records).
    (b) Draw a diagram like the one in Figure 9.37 to illustrate the recursive relationship.
    (c) The relation should contain a single hierarchy (see Figure 9.36). Why? Draw the hierarchy.
    (d) Assuming that the relation will be used in a CODASYL data base, draw the recursive owner-coupled set occurrences (see Figure 9.41).
23. A national association of racing horse owners has a relation **RACEHORSE** that keeps track of the pedigree of race horses. **RACEHORSE** has the fields **HORSENUMB** (a unique number that identifies a horse), **BIRTHDATE**, **MOTHER** (number identifying a horse's mother) **FATHER** (number identifying the horse's father).
    (a) Place some sample data in **RACEHORSE** (about 25 records).
    (b) Explain why the relation contains two recursive 1:n relationships.
    (c) Using two colors, draw a diagram like the one in Figure 9.37 to illustrate the recursive relationships.
    (d) Assuming that the relation will be used in a CODASYL data base, draw a diagram showing the owner-coupled set occurrences for the two owner-coupled sets involved.

The following retrievals concern the many-to-many recursive relationship in the relation **COMPANY** *in Figure 9.43. Retrieval requests should be formulated in SQL, and perhaps also in SQL/N.*

24. What are the names of companies that Betron has shares in?
25. What are the names of companies that own more than 100 thousand shares of Eewing Corp.?
26. Find the number of outstanding shares and the company names for companies that own shares in Jetcorp.
27. Find the names of companies that have no immediate subsidiaries in which they own more than 500 shares.
28. Find the companies whose immediate subsidiaries all have more than 1 million shares outstanding. (Data in Figure 9.43 is given in thousands of shares.)
29. Find the earnings per share of those companies that are partly owned by companies whose earnings per share (unconsolidated) exceed $1.00.

30. Generate implosions for companies with more than 900 thousand shares outstanding.

The following questions are concerned with binary-join dependencies.

31. In any industrial training course there are a number of assigned manuals, a number of participants, and one instructor. Each participant has a copy of each manual. Construct a relation **TRAINING** with the fields **PARTICIPANT**, **MANUAL**, and **INSTRUCTOR** to cover all courses given by an industrial organization. Explain why the relation contains a binary-join dependency. Devise a decomposition to eliminate it.
32. A large manufacturing organization has many production lines. On each line there are a number of foreman and telephones. On a line each foreman can be reached via any of the phones. Construct the relation **PRODUCTION** with fields **FOREMAN, LINE, TELEPHONE**. Explain why the relation has a binary join dependency, and how to eliminate it.

REFERENCES

1. Bradley, J., 1982. *File & Data Base Techniques*. Holt, Rinehart and Winston, New York.
2. Chen, P. P. S. "The Entity-Relationship Model—Towards a Unified View of Data," *ACM Trans. on Database Systems*, 1(1):9–36.
3. Date, C. J., 1981. *An Introduction to Database Systems*. Addison-Wesley, Reading, Mass.
4. Fagin, R., 1977. "A New Normal Form for Relational Data Bases," *ACM Trans. on Database Systems*, 2(3):262–79.
5. Rissanen, J., 1978. "Theory of Relations for Data Bases," *Lecture Notes in Computer Science*, 64:536–61.[1]

---

[1]This reference is given for the sake of completeness only, and is not recommended reading for business students.

10

The Hierarchical Approach to Data Base Systems

As we saw in Chapter 5, a conceptual data base can have either a network structure or a hierarchical structure. Within a network a file can have more than one parent file, whereas within a hierarchy a file can have only one parent file. The network structure is the general case and, as we have seen, can be handled easily by both CODASYL and relational data base systems. A hierarchy is a special case of a network, so that CODASYL and relational systems can also handle conceptual data bases with a hierarchical structure. On the other hand, there are data base systems such as IBM's Information Management System (IMS) and MRI's System 2000 (Refs. 4 and 5) that are limited to the management of data bases with either a hierarchical structure or a *near hierarchical* structure.

A data base with a near hierarchical structure is one where most conceptual files have only one parent, but a few have more than one parent. Thus a data base with a near hierarchical structure is essentially a network. Unfortunately the manner in which hierarchical systems handle such networks is extremely complex. We shall therefore relegate the management of near hierarchical data bases to the chapter supplement and concentrate on a study of how straight hierarchical data bases are managed.

The most widely used hierarchical data base system is IBM's IMS. Unfortunately the design of the basic system dates from the late 1960s. Still, since its introduction, a stream of new features have been added, and the system is supported by significant peripheral packages such as the teleprocessing monitor CICS, to be described in Chapter 12. As a result the system is one of the most widely used data base systems with large IBM installations. Nevertheless, by any standard the system is old, and the complexity of the way it handles near hierarchical data bases bears witness to this.

A few years ago it was widely thought that IMS would be replaced by the new System R. It now appears that this is not going to happen and that IMS will continue to be heavily supported by IBM. Readers may find this paradoxical. If IBM has gone to great expense to develop System R with SQL, a system that is clearly both powerful and user-friendly, why would it not make sense to replace IMS with System R when it is eventually released? The answer involves the peculiar economics of computer systems in general and data base systems in particular. Widely used computer systems have economics similar to urban freeway systems—once in place they cannot easily be replaced. The reason why is obvious with urban freeway systems. With a data base system, after a period of wide use, billions of dollars worth of useful application programs come to be based on them, and these application programs would all have to be changed were the underlying system to be replaced. The owners of these application programs naturally balk at the cost of modifying all their programs. Thus, once a data base system has come into wide use, it cannot be replaced. The only possibility is the introduction of new versions of the system that are upward compatible with older versions, or add-on systems that provide facilities not previously available. IMS is just such a system.

Thus, although its basic design is old, IMS will probably remain in wide use, and we can expect the periodic issue of upgrades and add-on systems. An important add-on system was recently announced by IBM, namely, SQL/DS, a system that permits management to use SQL, the language of System R, to query an IMS data base. It is therefore clear that IMS is of fundamental importance, and we shall devote this chapter to a study of it. We begin with the definition of an IMS data base with a natural hierarchical structure. We shall then see how this data base is manipulated by the procedural DL/1 data manipulation language. In the chapter supplement we show how near hierarchical data bases are handled. In Chapter 12 we return to IMS for a look at its communications features.

10.1 DEFINITION OF A CONCEPTUAL HIERARCHICAL DATA BASE

With IMS the equivalent of the conceptual and storage schemas are specified together. This is left over from the early days of data base management when no distinction was made between the conceptual and storage data base. Fortunately with IMS it is possible to distinguish clearly between those parts of the definition that define the conceptual data base, and those parts that define the storage data base. Thus we can continue to deal with storage, conceptual, and external data bases with IMS, as with the CODASYL and relational approaches. We can also use extended Bachman diagrams.

A hierarchical data base in the banking industry

To illustrate the principles involved in the definition of a conceptual IMS data base with a hierarchical structure, we shall use an example from the banking industry. In Figure 10.1 is an illustration of a data base for a bank with a considerable number of branches. Naturally the data base is much oversimplified, but it does show how a data base with a hierarchical structure could be used for the important data in a bank. Each record in **BRANCH** describes a branch of the bank. A record in **TELLER** describes a teller at the bank, and a record in **CUSTOMER** describes a customer of the bank. For one branch there are many tellers, and for one branch many customers. A record in **ACCOUNT** describes a customer's savings account, while a record in **LOAN** describes a loan taken out by a customer. A customer can have several savings accounts, and several loans. Finally a record in **TRANSACTION** describes a transaction (deposit or withdrawal of funds) involving an account. For any account there can be many transac-

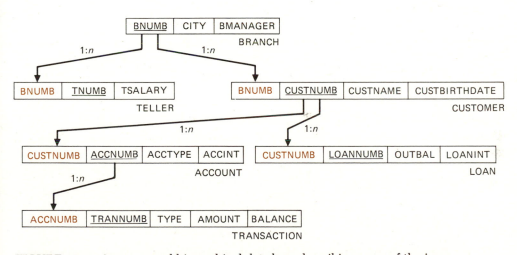

FIGURE 10.1 A conceptual hierarchical data base describing some of the important data at a bank with many branches, each of which is described in a BRANCH record, with the branch number (BNUMB) as the key. Each branch has many tellers and many customers. All the tellers with the bank are described in TELLER, and all customers in CUSTOMER. TNUMB (the teller number) and CUSTNUMB (the customer number) uniquely identify the tellers and customers, respectively, and serve as key fields. A customer has several accounts (ACCOUNT file) and loans (LOAN file), with the account numbers (ACCNUMB) and loan numbers (LOAN-NUMB) as keys, respectively. Finally for each account there will be many transactions (either deposit or withdrawals as given in TYPE field), each described in a TRANSACTION record in which the transaction number (TRANNUMB) is the key; TYPE informs whether it is a deposit or withdrawal, AMOUNT is the sum involved, and BALANCE is the balance of funds in the account. Because each file has one parent, the data base has a hierarchical structure. Note that we assume that a customer banks at only one branch.

tions. It is clear that each record (apart from BRANCH records) has only one parent record, so that the conceptual data base forms a hierarchy.

Later on we shall have to deal with the field values in this data base, so that we need a description of the kind of data in each field:

BRANCH *file.* BNUMB is the number of a branch, CITY is the city containing a branch, and BMANAGER is the name of the manager of a branch.

TELLER *file.* BNUMB gives the branch number of the branch in which a teller works, TNUMB gives a teller's employee number, and TSALARY gives a teller's annual salary.

CUSTOMER *file.* BNUMB gives the branch number of the branch where a customer has an account, CUSTNAME gives a customer's name, and CUST-BIRTHDATE a customer's birthdate. Note that for the purpose of the example, we assume that a customer deals with just one branch, so that CUST-NUMB is the primary key.

ACCOUNT *file.* CUSTNUMB gives the number of the customer owning the account, ACCNUMB gives the number of the account, ACCTYPE gives the type of the account (there are typically different types of savings account at a bank, paying different rates of interest), and ACCINT gives the annual rate of interest paid.

LOAN *file.* CUSTNUMB gives the number of the customer who has taken out a loan, LOANNUMB gives the number of the loan, OUTBAL gives the outstanding balance of the loan, and LOANINT gives the annual rate of interest on the loan.

TRANSACTION *file.* ACCNUMB gives the number of the account involved in a transaction, TRANNUMB gives the number of the transaction, TYPE gives the type of transaction (often deposit or withdrawal), AMOUNT gives the sum of money involved in the transaction, and BALANCE gives the balance of funds in the account at the end of the transaction.

Hierarchy types and occurrences

While it is correct to state that the data base in Figure 10.1 has a hierarchical structure, it is not strictly correct to state that it forms a hierarchy. Strictly speaking, we should state that it forms a *hierarchy type* as explained earlier in Chapter 4. This is necessary because a hierarchy type in turn consists of a number (often very large) of *hierarchy occurrences* or *data trees.* To be clear about this, consider Figures 10.2 and 10.3. Figure 10.2 shows the individual parent-child relationships for the records from the data base in Figure 10.1, which in turn are shown in full in Figure 10.3. For reasons of brevity just the key fields from the records in Figure 10.3 are shown in Figure 10.2.

We see that an individual BRANCH record, such as the one with key 'B1', is the parent of a group of TELLER records, and also the parent of a group of CUSTOMER records. Any one of these CUSTOMER records is the parent of a group of LOAN records and the parent of a group of ACCOUNT records. Any one of these ACCOUNT records is the parent of a group of TRANSACTION records.

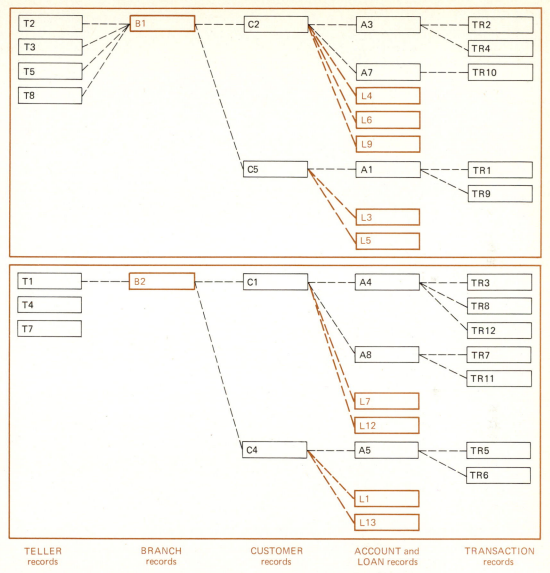

FIGURE 10.2 Occurrences of the hierarchy type in the data base in Figure 10.1 using the keys from the records in Figure 10.3. Due to space limitations we show two hierarchy occurrences; in practice there would be many, one for each BRANCH record (or segment). Branch records are called root records (or segments) with IMS. In the storage data base there is one storage record (with an internal hierarchical structure) for each hierarchy occurrence.

The complete group of descendant records of a given **BRANCH** record, such as the one with key 'B1', is a hierarchy occurrence or data tree. The record at the top of the tree, that is, a **BRANCH** record in this case, is called a *root record*, and the conceptual file of such records is called the *root file*. The complete set of

BNUMB	CITY	BMANAGER
B1	SAN JOSE	WRIGHT
B2	OAKLAND	QUICKLEY

BRANCH

BNUMB	TNUMB	TSALARY
B2	T1	15,000
B1	T2	14,500
B1	T3	16,000
B2	T4	15,500
B1	T5	16,500
B2	T7	16,000
B1	T8	15,000

TELLER

BNUMB	CUSTNUMB	CUSTNAME	CUSTBIRTHDATE
B2	C1	SMITH	19450915
B1	C2	GREEN	19380723
B2	C4	BROWN	19150327
B1	C5	JONES	19610415

CUSTOMER

CUSTNUMB	ACCNUMB	ACCTYPE	ACCINT
C5	A1	SAVINGS-A	10.0
C2	A3	SAVINGS-A	10.0
C1	A4	SAVINGS-A	10.0
C4	A5	SAVINGS-B	12.5
C2	A7	SAVINGS-B	12.5
C1	A8	SAVINGS-A	10.0

ACCOUNT

FIGURE 10.3

CUSTNUMB	LOANNUMB	OUTBAL	LOANINT
C4	L1	5,762	14.5
C5	L3	1,782	15.5
C2	L4	12,890	14.75
C5	L5	5,782	15.5
C2	L6	708	14.5
C1	L7	2,896	16.0
C2	L9	9,482	16.0
C1	L12	13,674	14.75
C4	L13	5,986	15.5

LOAN

ACCNUMB	TRANNUMB	TYPE	AMOUNT	BALANCE
A1	TR1	DEPOS	1000	3764
A3	TR2	WITHDRAW	500	3264
A4	TR3	WITHDRAW	300	1760
A3	TR4	DEPOS	200	1960
A5	TR5	WITHDRAW	1200	3800
A5	TR6	DEPOS	500	4300
A8	TR7	DEPOS	350	4650
A4	TR8	WITHDRAW	1000	2500
A1	TR9	DEPOS	600	3100
A7	TR10	DEPOS	200	500
A8	TR11	DEPOS	1300	1300
A4	TR12	WITHDRAW	200	1100

TRANSACTION

FIGURE 10.3 An example of the contents of the conceptual files in the conceptual data base in Figure 10.1. Connection fields are shown in color, and primary keys are underlined. The primary key for the file TRANSACTION is TRANNUMB, which gives the number of the transaction. Ascending TRANNUMB sequence is the sequence of execution of transactions in time. In the file ACCOUNT (describing savings accounts) the field ACCINT (interest payable on the account balance) is functionally dependent on the field ACCTYPE (savings account type), since the interest payable is determined by the type of account and not the number of the account (ACCNUMB, the primary key). The undesirable functional dependency could be eliminated by the decomposition in Figure 10.4, but this would mean a network data base, so that instead the dependency would often be tolerated.

hierarchy occurrences is the hierarchy type. It is clear that *the number of hierarchy occurrences in a hierarchy type is equal to the number of records in the root file*; in Figures 10.2 and 10.3 this number is two. In practice the number is usually a lot larger than that.

It should be remembered that hierarchy types and occurrences are conceptual-level structures, and that a hierarchy type consists of both hierarchy occurrences and conceptual files. We notice that the conceptual files in the hierarchy type in Figure 10.1 are all relations, and that the data base could in fact be a relational data base with a hierarchical structure. It is possible for the conceptual files of a hierarchy type not to be relations, but it is good design practice to ensure that they are all relations. As we have seen, one reason for using relations is that the data base is simpler and easier to maintain, but another reason of growing importance is that the use of relations makes it easier to have an add-on system that will make it possible to use SQL or QBE to manipulate a data base that was originally designed for use with a hierarchical data base system such as IMS.

Unwanted dependencies in a hierarchical data base

In Chapter 9 we saw that a data base is most easily maintained if its relations have no undesirable dependencies, that is, if its relations are in fourth normal form. The same applies to the relations used to construct a hierarchy type, but unfortunately the method used to eliminate an undesirable dependency from a relation will usually destroy the hierarchy type by turning the structure into a limited network or near hierarchy. An example of this is incorporated into the hierarchy type in Figure 10.1.

Consider the conceptual file ACCOUNT carefully. We saw that ACCINT contains the interest payable annually on the account. But the interest payable on a bank account depends normally on the type of account and not on an individual account number, so that ACCINT is functionally dependent on ACCTYPE. Thus if the bank were to change the interest payable on accounts of the type 'SAVINGS-B', then all the records with this type of account would have to be updated, and while it was being done the data base might be inconsistent. Furthermore, it would be possible for an updating error to cause two different customers with the same account type to receive different rates of interest over a given period. Lastly, if there was a type of account that no customers had opened, then the information about this type of account could not be kept in the conceptual file ACCOUNT because there would be no key for the record. Clearly this dependency is undesirable and should be eliminated.

It could in theory be eliminated by decomposing the old ACCOUNT file into two new files as shown in Figure 10.4. The field ACCINT is eliminated from the old ACCOUNT file to produce the new version of ACCOUNT. At the same time we generate a new file called ACCOUNT-DESCRIPTION to give the rate of interest at each type of account. For each type of account there will be many accounts owned by customers, so that there is a one-to-many relationship between ACCOUNT-DESCRIPTIONS and the new ACCOUNT file. If we now replace the old ACCOUNT file in Figure 10.1 with these two files in Figure 10.4, we have a problem. A record in the new ACCOUNT file will have two parents, one in

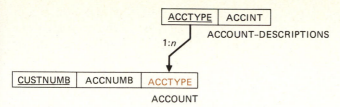

FIGURE 10.4 Shows how the single conceptual file ACCOUNT in Figures 10.1 and 10.3 can be replaced by a new file ACCOUNT-DESCRIPTIONS and a new version of ACCOUNT with the field ACCTYPE removed. In this way the functional dependency of ACCINT on ACCNUMB could be removed from the version of ACCOUNT in Figure 10.1.

ACCOUNT-DESCRIPTIONS and one in CUSTOMER, so that the new version of the data base no longer has a hierarchical structure, but a (limited) network or only near hierarchical structure instead. As mentioned at the beginning of this chapter, a hierarchical data base system such as IMS is designed primarily to handle conceptual data bases with a pure hierarchical structure, but the system can also handle near hierarchical data bases. The methods used with near hierarchies are quite complex and are best left until the reader has a good knowledge of how straight hierarchies are handled. For this reason we shall tolerate the undesirable dependency in the conceptual file ACCOUNT and thus define a schema for the data base in Figure 10.1 without any modification to eliminate that dependency.

Hierarchical sequence and associated concepts

Referring to the hierarchy occurrences in Figure 10.2, let us suppose that the schemas for this data base have been defined with IMS, and that we ask IMS for the first-child record of the parent BRANCH record with key 'B1'. Now a BRANCH record typically has both child TELLER records and child CUSTOMER records, and it is therefore necessary to define in the data base description which of the two types of child records comes first. This done by assigning a *hierarchical sequence code*, or *number*, to each type of conceptual record, as is illustrated in Figure 10.5. If we require the child records on the left of the hierarchy in a diagram to come before the child records on the right, then we can assign the sequence codes (1, 2, 3, . . .) to the conceptual files, the code value increasing as we go down the hierarchy and as we go from left to right in the hierarchy. Top to bottom, left to right assigment of the sequence codes is standard with IMS.

We recall that in the CODASYL approach the conceptual member records of an owner-coupled set occurrence were ordered, and that the order could be determined by the value of some field within the records, referred to as the set sort key. Similarly, in a hierarchy occurrence, the child records (of a given type, such as CUSTOMER records) of a parent record are also ordered in accordance with the value of a certain field, called the *sequence field*. In the hierarchy occurrences in Figure 10.2, the sequence fields were chosen to be the same as the

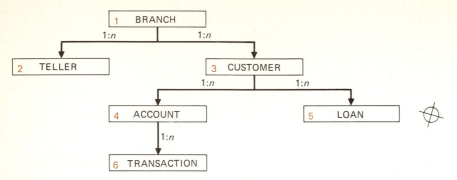

FIGURE 10.5 Each conceptual file in a hierarchy type must have a hierarchical sequence number or code, as shown above. If we are retrieving the child records of a given customer record, ACCOUNT child records will be retrieved first and the LOAN child records last. TELLER records also come before ACCOUNT records when the retrieval of the records is in hierarchical sequence (see Figure 10.6).

primary keys in Figure 10.3. With IMS this is normal practice. It is possible to have other fields with nonunique values as sequence fields, but this can lead to severe complications and is best avoided.

If we use the hierarchical sequence code to decide which type of child record comes first, and the sequence field value to decide the order of child records of a given type, it is possible to place all the records in a hierarchy type in what is called *hierarchical sequence*. This concept is important with IMS, because records are often retrieved in hierarchical sequence. In Figure 10.6, the records from Figures 10.2 and 10.3 are shown (top to bottom) in hierarchical sequence. To understand how the sequence is generated, compare closely with the records in the hierarchy occurrences in Figure 10.2.

We take the first **BRANCH** record as the first record, that is, the record with key 'B1'. Since **TELLER** records have a higher hierarchical sequence code than **CUSTOMER** records, the child **TELLER** records come next, that is, the **TELLER** records with sequence field values 'T2', 'T3', 'T5', and 'T8' in ascending sequence field order. Then comes the first-child **CUSTOMER** record with the lowest sequence field value, that is, the record with key value 'C2'. The next record is the first **ACCOUNT** child record of this **CUSTOMER** record, since **ACCOUNT** records have a higher sequence code than **LOAN** records. The next record is the first-child **TRANSACTION** record of this **ACCOUNT** record, and so on. If X is the current record in the sequence, the next record is the first child of X, if there is one; otherwise it is the next child of the parent of X, if there is one; otherwise it is the next child of the parent of the parent of X; and so on.

When all the records belonging to a given conceptual file are retrieved from a hierarchy type, they are retrieved in hierarchical sequence order, that is, the order in which they appear in Figure 10.6, or in Figure 10.2 (top to bottom), and not in primary key order as in Figure 10.3. For the sake of completeness, all the records from the conceptual files **TELLER**, **CUSTOMER**, and **ACCOUNT** are shown in Figure 10.7 in hierarchical sequence order.

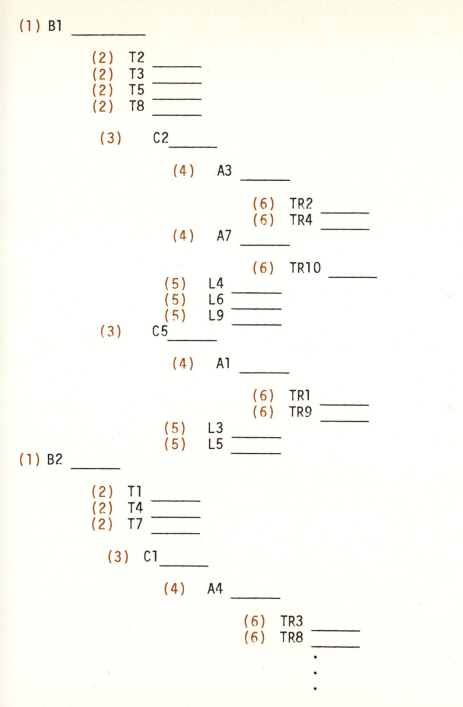

FIGURE 10.6 Shows the records from the data base in Figures 10.1 and 10.2 in hierarchical sequence order (top to bottom of page). Compare with the order in Figure 10.2. Hierarchical sequence codes (Figure 10.5) are given in parentheses.

T2	_____	C2	_____	A3	_____
T3	_____	C5	_____	A7	_____
T5	_____	C1	_____	A1	_____
T8	_____	C4	_____	A4	_____
T1	_____			A8	_____
T4	_____	CUSTOMER		A5	_____
T7	_____				

TELLER   CUSTOMER   ACCOUNT

FIGURE 10.7 Shows the order of records in some selected conceptual files from the data base in Figures 10.1 and 10.2, when the records from each of these files are retrieved in hierarchical sequence order. This order can also be seen in Figure 10.2, and it should be clear that it is not the same as the ascending primary key order shown in Figure 10.3. Records can be obtained from an IMS data base in primary key order only if a secondary index for the primary key is specified in the storage part of the IMS data base description (DBD).

Hierarchical sequence keys and fully concatenated keys

Two types of keys are important with IMS. These are the hierarchical sequence keys and the fully concatenated keys. They are fairly similar and are easily confused.

Hierarchical sequence keys. Every record in a hierarchy type has a hierarchical sequence key. It is formed by taking the sequence field value of the record and adding to it on the left the record's hierarchical sequence code; on

```
1 B1                                    B1
1 B1 2 T2                               B1 T2
1 B1 2 T3                               B1 T3
1 B1 2 T5                               B1 T5
1 B1 2 T8                               B1 T8
1 B1 3 C2                               B1 C2
1 B1 3 C2 4 A3                          B1 C2 A3
1 B1 3 C2 4 A3 6 TR2                    B1 C2 A3 TR2
1 B1 3 C2 4 A3 6 TR4                    B1 C2 A3 TR4
1 B1 3 C2 4 A7                          B1 C2 A7
              .                                    .
              .                                    .
              .                                    .
             (a)                                  (b)
```

FIGURE 10.8 The hierarchical sequence keys (a) and the fully concatenated keys (b) of the first few records from the data base in Figures 10.1 and 10.2 ordered in the hierarchical sequence order shown in Figure 10.6. In practice there are no blanks within the keys. Note that the keys in (b) are not in ascending fully concatenated key order since, for example, the fully concatenated key 'B1 C2' would come before 'B1 T2' if they were.

the left again is added the sequence key of the record's parent, and on the left again the sequence code of the record's parent, and so on with this record's parent. The hierarchical sequence keys for the first few records in Figure 10.6 are shown in Figure 10.8a. Sequence codes are shown in color, and blanks are inserted for the convenience of the reader. In practice there are no blanks. Notice that if we want to be concise about the hierarchical sequence of the records in Figure 10.6, we can state that they are arranged in order of ascending hierarchical sequence keys. Hierarchical sequence keys are used internally by IMS.

Fully concatenated keys.   Every record has a fully concatenated key and is the same as the hierarchical sequence key with the sequence codes removed, as can be seen from the fully concatenated keys for the first few records from Figure 10.6 as shown in Figure 10.8b. Notice that the keys in Figure 10.8b are not in ascending fully concatenated key sequence; the record with sequence field 'C2' comes after the record with sequence field 'T2' in hierarchical sequence, but the fully concatenated key 'B1 C2' comes before 'B1 T2' in ascending fully concatenated key sequence.

Primary keys

The concept of the primary key of a conceptual record is little used in practice in IMS, although the sequence field of the root file can be taken as the same as a primary key. The records of the root file will always be available in primary key order. It we wish to be able to directly access a record of a nonroot file, on the basis of a certain field value (typically the primary key value), then a special secondary index must be specified for that field in the internal part of the IMS data base description or definition.

IMS segments

The term conceptual record is actually not used with IMS. Instead the term *segment* is used. This has its origins in the way the storage data base for a conceptual hierarchy type is constructed. All the records in a single hierarchy occurrence can be placed in a single storage record, so that each record becomes a segment of this huge storage record. We shall look at the IMS storage data base later. (An example is shown later in Figure 10.10.)

Specifying the conceptual part of the IMS data base description (DBD)

As mentioned earlier, the specification of the conceptual and storage IMS data bases is specified in a single schema called the *data base description* (DBD). The DBD has distinct conceptual and internal or storage parts, and we take them in turn and specify the data base in Figures 10.1 and 10.2. However, before we do so, a note on some relevant IMS terminology is appropriate.

The hierarchy type defined by the conceptual part of the data base description is often referred to as the *physical data base,* or PDB. This as about as confusing as one can get, since a hierarchy type is a conceptual-level structure; however, the terminology was introduced long before the ANSI/SPARC 1975 report (see Chapter 4), and it seems that we are stuck with it. A hierarchy occurrence in turn is referred to as a physical data base record (PDBR). The truth of the matter is that IMS, strictly speaking, does not have a conceptual data base level and the data base description (DBD) defines a storage data base. In an effort to have as up-to-date a coverage of the subject as possible, however, we shall continue to regard the DBD as having a storage part and a conceptual part.

In Figure 10.9, we have a specification of the conceptual part of a DBD for the hierarchy type in Figure 10.1. The DBD is assigned the name **SAVELOAN** in this case, as given in the first line. The remainder of this part of the DBD consists of

```
01   DBD          NAME=SAVELOAN
02   SEGM         NAME=BRANCH,BYTES=44
03   FIELD        NAME=(BNUMB,SEQ),BYTES=4,START=1
04   FIELD        NAME=CITY,BYTES=20,START=5
05   FIELD        NAME=BMANAGER,BYTES=20,START=25
06   SEGM         NAME=TELLER,PARENT=BRANCH,BYTES=14
07   FIELD        NAME=(TNUMB,SEQ),BYTES=4,START=1
08   FIELD        NAME=BNUMB,BYTES=4,START=5
09   FIELD        NAME=TSALARY,BYTES=6,START=9
10   SEGM         NAME=CUSTOMER,PARENT=BRANCH,BYTES=37
11   FIELD        NAME=(CUSTNUMB,SEQ),BYTES=4,START=1
12   FIELD        NAME=BNUMB,BYTES=4,START=5
13   FIELD        NAME=CUSTNAME,BYTES=20,START=9
14   FIELD        NAME=CUSTBIDA,BYTES=8,START=29
15   SEGM         NAME=ACCOUNT,PARENT=CUSTOMER,BYTES=23
16   FIELD        NAME=(ACCNUMB,SEQ),BYTES=4,START=1
17   FIELD        NAME=CUSTNUMB,BYTES=4,START=5
18   FIELD        NAME=ACCTYPE,BYTES=10,START=9
19   FIELD        NAME=ACCINT,BYTES=4,START=19
20   SEGM         NAME=LOAN,PARENT=CUSTOMER,BYTES=21
21   FIELD        NAME=(LOANNUMB,SEQ),BYTES=4,START=1
22   FIELD        NAME=CUSTNUMB,BYTES=4,START=5
23   FIELD        NAME=OUTBAL,BYTES=8,START=9
24   FIELD        NAME=LOANINT,BYTES=4,START=17
25   SEGM         NAME=TRANSACT,PARENT=ACCOUNT,BYTES=36
26   FIELD        NAME=(TRANNUMB,SEQ),BYTES=10,START=1
27   FIELD        NAME=ACCNUMB,BYTES=4,START=11
28   FIELD        NAME=TYPE,BYTES=1,START=15
29   FIELD        NAME=AMOUNT,BYTES=6,START=16
30   FIELD        NAME=BALANCE,BYTES=8,START=24
```

FIGURE 10.9   The conceptual part of the data base description (DBD) for the data base in Figure 10.1. The storage part is very detailed and is not given. While child connection fields are included above, in many existing IMS data bases they are absent. However, omission means that the data base cannot be considered as a relational data base.

segment specifications, where each segment specification is followed immediately by its field specifications. A segment specification begins with the word **SEGM** and must contain the name of parent segment of the segment being specified, given after the **PARENT** specification.

A few detailed rules must be observed in generating a DBD. On any line, following the word **NAME**, there must be no blanks. A sequence field is specified by inserting **SEQ** after a field name, and the specification must be the first after the segment (**SEGM**) specification. With each field specification we must give the length of the field in bytes, and its position relative to the start of the segment (**START** specification). In addition, IMS names must not exceed eight characters. We note that there is no explicit specification of the hierarchical sequence code mentioned earlier. This is implicit in the order of the segment specifications in the DBD. Thus since the segment **ACCOUNT** is the fourth specified in Figure 10.9, its hierarchical sequence code is 4.

Notice that we have not specified a primary key for each of the conceptual files, as is common with other data base systems. As mentioned earlier, this is also possible in IMS, but it can only be done by means of an advanced feature known as IMS secondary indexing, which is discussed briefly in Section 10.4.

10.2 THE IMS STORAGE DATA BASE

With CODASYL and relational data bases, it is possible to acquire a satisfactory grasp of the essentials of the approaches without delving too deeply into the nature and method of specifying the storage or internal data bases. In addition, since this book has a deliberate business orientation, detailed descriptions of the CODASYL and relational internal data base technicalities would add little, especially when the basic principles of the necessary pointer systems are described in Chapter 3. Unfortunately, in the case of IMS, it is not possible to have a good understanding of the essentials of the system without a study of the different ways in which the storage data base can be constructed. IMS storage structures are unique, there are many variations, and they have a significant impact on the way a data base may be processed. Nevertheless, on first reading, readers are advised either to skip over the details of the IMS storage file organizations, or to briefly use the diagrams to learn the basic ideas. Some of the IMS storage organizations are extraordinarily complex.

We shall not show how IMS storage data bases are specified. (We recall that this specification is in the internal part of the data base description, following the conceptual part.) Instead we shall illustrate the possible internal structures using diagrams. For details of IMS storage data base specifications, see Refs. 1, 4, and 6.

Types of IMS storage data base organizations

It is convenient to distinguish between two main types of IMS storage organizations:

1. Storage organizations where the segments (conceptual records) from a single hierarchy occurrence (see Figure 10.2) are *physically contiguous* within the storage medium in a storage record.
2. Storage organizations where the segments from a single hierarchy occurrence are *physically distributed* in the storage medium and connected together by a pointer system.

The storage organizations with physically contiguous segments are constructed with:

1. HSAM: Hierarchical sequential access method
2. HISAM: Hierarchical indexed-sequential access method

and the storage organizations with physically distributed segments are constructed with:

3. HDAM: Hierarchical direct access method
4. HIDAM: Hierarchical indexed direct access method

While HSAM, HISAM, HDAM, and HIDAM are acronyms for the data base access methods (see Chapter 1 for a review of the concept of a file access method) or software subsystems used in constructing storage data bases, the acronyms are also widely used to describe the resulting storage structures. Thus an HSAM storage data base is one that was constructed using HSAM, and so on.

HSAM and HISAM: Storage organizations with contiguous segments

In both HSAM and HISAM organizations, one or more storage records are used to hold the segments of a hierarchy occurrence (physical data base record). In both cases the segments within a storage record are arranged contiguously in hierarchical sequence, with the hierarchical sequence code attached to enable segments to be retrieved. However, there are important differences between HSAM and HISAM organizations:

HSAM organization

To load the data base, the segments of a hierarchy type (for example, the one in Figure 10.2) are written out one by one in hierarchical sequence in fixed-length storage records (Figure 10.10). Typically it will happen that more than one storage record is needed to store all the segments in a hierarchy occurrence. A segment cannot span from one storage record to the next, and there will usually be unused space at the end of each storage record. At the end of a hierarchy occurrence, the root segment of the next hierarchy occurrence follows immediately, so that a root segment will not usually come first in a storage record.

Once created, an HSAM data base can be opened only for input, that is, it can only be read, and all segments, whether root segments or dependent segments, are accessible only in hierarchical sequence. The data base can be updated in the same way as a sequential tape file (Chapter 2); segments are read in hierarchical sequence and then written out again (with updated and inserted segments) in a

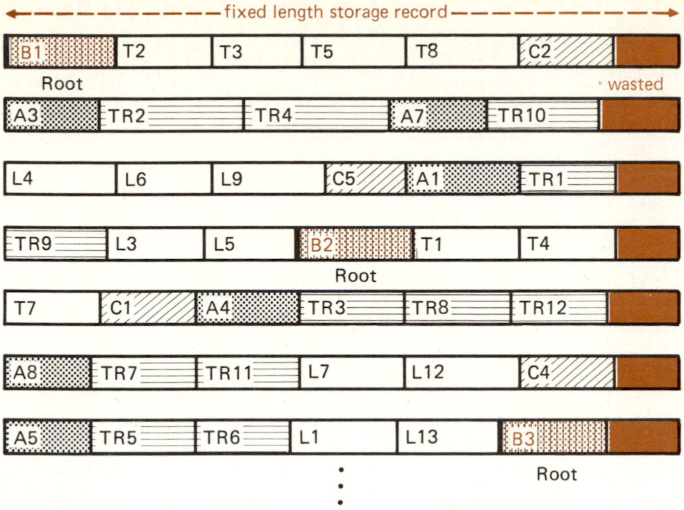

FIGURE 10.10 Storage records for an HSAM data base. An HSAM storage file consists of fixed length records arranged sequentially on tape or disk. These storage records are also blocked, as is usual with sequential files, but that is not shown above. The segments from the hierarchy type, for example that in Figure 10.2, are placed in the storage records in hierarchical sequence (see Figure 10.6). A segment cannot span a storage record, so that usually some space is wasted at the end of a storage record. When the last segment of a hierarchy *occurrence* is stored (for example, the segment with sequence field value 'L5' above), it is followed immediately by the root segment of the next hierarachy occurrence. Thus the root segments are stored in ascending root sequence field order, but they do not usually come first within a storage record. The hierarchical sequence code is attached to each segment to enable the system to extract segments from the storage records.

new HSAM data base. Thus we can have grandfather, father, and son HSAM storage data bases!

HISAM organization

This consists of an index (to root segments), a prime indexed-sequential storage file containing root segments (often followed by some subsidiary segments in hierarchical sequence) arranged in ascending root sequence field order, and a direct access overflow file (or dataset). The underlying indexed-sequential file can be either an ISAM or VSAM file (see Chapter 2). We consider the ISAM version first using the illustration in Figure 10.11.

The records in the ISAM file are fixed length and contain a pointer at either end; the ISAM record size is usually chosen to accommodate all but the longest hierarchy occurrences. When the file is loaded, the segments are presented in hierarchical sequence as was the case with HSAM. A root segment is placed at the beginning of an ISAM record followed by as many *dependent* or subsidiary segments as the record can hold. As with HSAM a segment cannot span a record, and there will usually be unused space at the end of each ISAM record. If there is not enough space in a single ISAM record for all the dependent segments of a

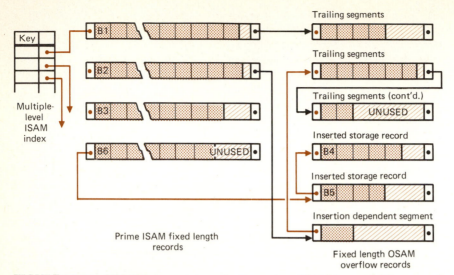

FIGURE 10.11 HISAM storage organization when ISAM is used. The records of the ISAM file are fixed length, and the first segment in a record is always a root segment. There is an ISAM multiple-level index to the root segments using the root segment sequence field as the key. In an ISAM record the segments following the root segment are in hierarchical sequence. A segment cannot span a record, and there is usually unused space at the end of an ISAM record. If the ISAM record is too small to hold all the segments that are dependent on the root segment, the trailing or overflow segments are placed in an overflow direct access file called an OSAM file. The OSAM file also holds inserted records, and segments pushed off an ISAM record because of segment insertions.

single root segment, the remaining or "trailing" segments are placed in an overflow file. This overflow file (or OSAM file, where OSAM is the acronym for overflow sequential access method) also contains fixed length storage records. If there are too many trailing segments from an ISAM record to fit into an OSAM record, the excess segments are placed in a second OSAM record, and so on. Because segments cannot span OSAM records either, there will be unused space at the end of each OSAM record too. An ISAM record is connected to its trailing segments by a pointer chain (Figure 10.11). Root segments may be retrieved in sequential order, or directly on presentation of the root sequence field; once a root segment is retrieved, the dependent segments may be retrieved in hierarchical sequence.

A segment is deleted by placing a deletion code at the beginning of a segment. The dependent segments of a deleted segment are automatically considered deleted. However, space freed by a deletion cannot be reused to accommodate other segment insertions. Two types of insertions are possible, which complicates the situation. Insertion of a new hierarchy occurrence (in the simplest case this means insertion of a root segment) takes place in the OSAM file, and a pointer system is used to maintain the root segments in sequential order (Figure 10.11). Insertion of a dependent segment is accomplished in an

ISAM record by pushing other segments to the right so that the inserted segment can be placed contiguously in hierarchical sequence. If pushing segments to the right causes one or more segments to be pushed off the storage record, affected segments are placed in the OSAM file in a separate record as shown in Figure 10.11; pointers are used to maintain the segments in hierarchical order. It is thus sometimes not quite true to state that segments are physically contiguous with HISAM organization.

When the indexed-sequential file is a VSAM file, the essential difference is that the overflow file is less complex. The overflow file used with the VSAM primary file is an entry-sequenced dataset (ESDS). (This is one of three types of dataset that can be managed by the VSAM package and essentially contains fixed length records in the order in which they are entered.) Since a VSAM indexed file can handle record insertions without recourse to an overflow area (Chapter 2), insertion of a new hierarchy occurrence takes place in the primary VSAM file and not in the ESDS overflow area. Figure 10.12 shows the situation had the ISAM file in Figure 10.11 been a VSAM field; the only essential difference is that the inserted hierarchy occurrences with root sequence field values 'B4' and 'B5' are now in the VSAM indexed-sequential file. Because of fewer overflow chains, it is clear that performance will be better with HISAM/VSAM than with HISAM/ISAM. Note also that with HISAM/VSAM space freed by segment deletions can often be reused.

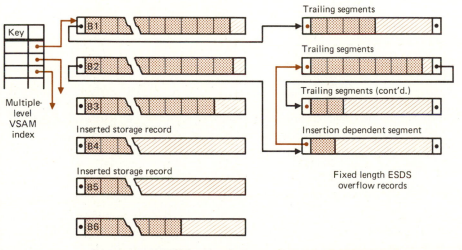

FIGURE 10.12 HISAM storage organization when VSAM is used. The records in the prime VSAM file are fixed length, and the first segment in a record is always a root segment, followed by the dependent segments for that root segment. A segment cannot span a record, and there is usually unused space at the end of a VSAM record. Overflow or trailer segments for a given root segment are placed in the overflow file, which can also hold segments pushed off a VSAM record because of segment insertions. Inserted records are placed in the prime VSAM file, and not in the overflow file.

HDAM and HIDAM: Storage organizations with distributed segments

With both HDAM and HIDAM there is direct access to root segments, by applying a hashing routine (see Chapter 2) to the root sequence field in the case of HDAM, and by simply presenting the root sequence field (which is used to search an index) in the case of HIDAM. The subsidiary segments need not be physically near to their parent root segments and may be distributed throughout the storage space. In order for them to be retrievable, they are connected to their parent root segments by means of a pointer system. Two types of pointer system may be used. One possibility is *hierarchical pointers*, as shown in Figure 10.13

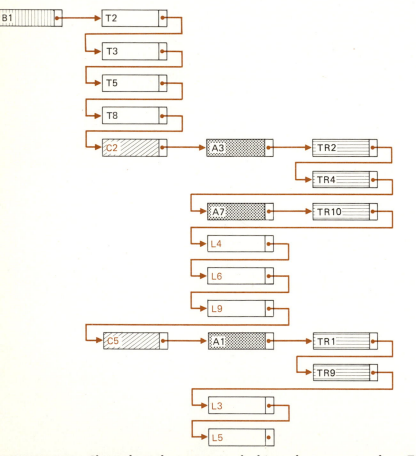

FIGURE 10.13 Shows how the segments of a hierarchy occurrence from Figure 10.2 may be connected together by hierarchical pointers. If we follow the pointers, we encounter the segments (conceptual records) in hierarchical sequence (as shown in Figure 10.6). Alternatively, we may use child/twin pointers as shown in Figure 10.14. If the storage records corresponding to the hierarchy occurrences (as in Figure 10.10) are organized as a sequential file (HSAM organization), such pointer systems are unnecessary, since insertion of new segments is not allowed with direct access storage files (HDAM). They are necessary with some direct access storage files (HDAM and HIDAM) to allow for insertion.

for a hierarchy type from Figure 10.2. Here the subsidiary records are simply connected in hierarchical sequence. Thus, referring to Figure 10.1, if we want **CUSTOMER** segments for a given branch, the **TELLER** segments must be read first, and remembering that the segments are distributed throughout the storage space, a lot of separate disk accesses will be involved. Alternatively, we can use *child/twin pointers* as shown in Figure 10.14. Twin pointers are used to connect all children of a given type that have the same parent, that is, "twin" segments are connected. At the same time the first child of a parent is connected to its parent. This means that it is possible, given the root segment, to descend the hierarchy occurrence to a given type of conceptual record (or segment) with only a few accesses.

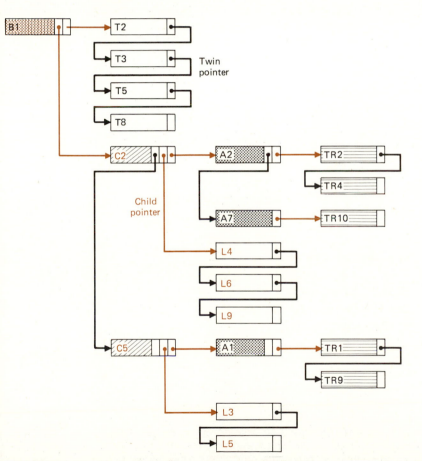

FIGURE 10.14   Shows how the segments of a hierarchy occurrence from Figure 10.2 may be connected together by child/twin pointers. A child pointer (in color) connects a parent segment to its first child (in ascending sequence field order), while a twin pointer (black) connects a child record of parent X to the next child of parent X (in ascending sequence field order). Referring to Figure 10.2, if a parent has two types of child record (as do BRANCH and CUSTOMER segments), there are two child pointers, one to the each first type of child segment.

Apart from having subsidiary or dependent segments distributed throughout the available storage space, HDAM and HISAM organizations are very different.

HDAM organization

With HDAM there is a prime storage dataset (shown in Figure 10.15) and an overflow dataset (not shown in Figure 10.15), consisting in both cases of fixed length records. (If the VSAM software package is used, both the prime and overflow files are ESDS areas; otherwise they are OSAM files of the kind used with HISAM.) In the prime area the records have relative addresses going from 1 to N, where N is specified by the data base designer before the file is created. The main way in which the file is loaded is illustrated in Figure 10.15. The root segments are loaded first, and each root segment is loaded into a record with an address generated by applying a hashing routine (see Chapter 2 for a discussion of hashing) to the root sequence field. A storage record can hold many root segments, so that we have a case of a hash file with address capacity greater than one, which means that very few root segments will overflow from their home addresses. The chained progressive overflow technique (see Chapter 2) is used to manage any such overflow root segments. Figure 10.15 has one short chain for the overflow record 'B3'. As was pointed out in Chapter 2, use of chained

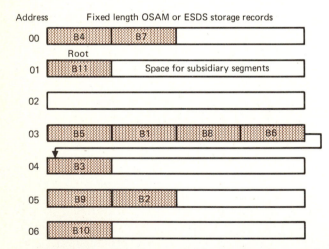

FIGURE 10.15 HDAM storage file organization consists essentially of a direct access file of fixed length records. The addresses of other records are relative and numbered zero to N, where N is specified by the data base designer. A hashing routine is used to generate a relative address for each root segment. Usually the root segments are loaded first, as shown above. A record can hold many root segments that have hashed to the same home address, and root segments overflowing from a home address are chained together in chained progressive overflow. Subsidiary segments are loaded later (not shown), each as close as possible to the address of the parent root segment. Subsidiary segments are connected to their parents by means of either the hierarchical pointer system (Figure 10.13) or the child/twin pointer system (Figure 10.14).

progressive overflow will significantly reduce the average search length for retrieval by direct access of (in this case) root segments.

When all the root segments have been loaded, the subsidiary or dependent segments can be added, preferably in hierarchical sequence. Subsidiary segments are simply placed in the remaining space in the storage records as close as possible to their root segments. Inevitably the subsidiary segments will be distributed over many storage records and are connected to one another and their root segments either by hierarchical pointers (Figure 10.13) or child/twin pointers (Figure 10.14). That such distribution will be necessary is clear from the typical situation in Figure 10.15 that results from loading the root segments first. However not all subsidiary segments will go into the prime area shown in Figure 10.15; a limit can be specified for the number of subsidiary segments of a root segment that can be loaded into the prime area, and subsidiary segments in excess of this are placed in records of the overflow area with the same pointer system as in the prime area. Also, should a new root segment be inserted for which there is no room in the prime area, it will be placed in the first available space in the separate overflow area, as the latest member of a progressive overflow chain.

An alternative method of loading the HDAM file involves loading the subsidiary segments of a root immediately after the root is loaded. This will ensure that a great many more subsidiary segments are on the same storage records as their root segments. This will make it faster to retrieve subsidiary segments, since fewer HDAM records will have to be retrieved because the subsidiaries will be spread over fewer records. Unfortunately, loading subsidiary segments immediately after a root has been loaded means that there will be less room in the HDAM record for subsequent root segments that hash to that HDAM record address, so that more of them will overflow and end up on progressive overflow chains. This will mean that the average search length for root segments will be higher than with the method of loading all the root segments first. Which loading method is chosen will depend on the way the data in the hierarchy type will be processed, a consideration that also applies to the choice of hierarchical or child/twin pointer systems for the subsidiary segments.

No matter how the segments are loaded, with proper design of the HDAM datasets, access to the data will be faster than with any other type of IMS storage structure, and HDAM is generally employed where speed of retrieval is vital. Updating is slowed down by deletions and insertions, however, because of the need to maintain the subsidiary hierarchical or child/twin pointer system and the root segment progressive overflow chains. Following a segment deletion the freed space may be reused, in contrast with HISAM/ISAM where it may not be reused.

HIDAM organization

Essentially a HIDAM storage data base consists of two data bases, namely, an HISAM data base (either HISAM/ISAM or HISAM/VSAM is possible) and a special form of the HSAM data base. The HISAM data base contains only root sequence fields (each one accompanied by a pointer) arranged as an indexed-sequential file, with new inserted root sequence fields overflowing into the usual overflow dataset as illustrated in Figure 10.16. Every root sequence field of a hierarchy type is stored in the HISAM data base (at the top in Figure 10.16), and we have direct access to each of these ISAM storage records via the ISAM multiple-level index.

The hierarchy occurrences of a hierarchy type are stored in another fixed-length record OSAM data base, and the root and subsidiary segments are initially loaded in exactly the same way as in an HSAM data base (Figure 10.10) with

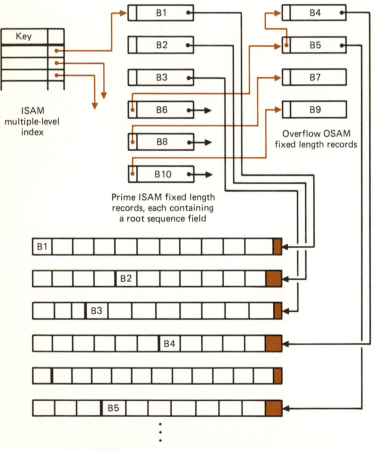

FIGURE 10.16 HIDAM organization using ISAM. Essentially there are two data bases. At the top is a HISAM/ISAM data base that contains only the sequence fields of root segments in the prime ISAM storage file (with later insertions in the overflow OSAM area at the top right). The usual multiple-level ISAM index is used for direct access to these root sequence fields in the ISAM dataset. Accompanying each root sequence field in the ISAM dataset is a pointer to the corresponding root segment in another OSAM dataset that contains all the root and subsidiary segments.

some unused space at the end of each storage record. The pointer accompanying a record containing a root sequence field in the HISAM/ISAM (or INDEX) data base points to the storage record in the HSAM-like data base that contains the root segment with the same root sequence field value. Thus to access a root segment, we present the root sequence field value; the system searches the ISAM index, to obtain the position of the ISAM (or OSAM) record with that sequence field value, and then follows the pointer (Figure 10.16) to the storage record with the root segment in the HSAM-like OSAM dataset.

When the root and subsidiary segments are initially loaded, they will be physically contiguous as with HSAM and as shown in Figure 10.16. However, segments have pointer fields attached, and these can be either hierarchical or child/twin pointers (not shown in Figure 10.16 to avoid clutter). All segments must be loaded initially in hierarchical sequence. When a segment is deleted, the hierarchical or child/twin pointer system is repaired, and the space freed. A new segment is inserted as close as possible to its root segment, to reduce the number of storage records that must be retrieved to obtain all the subsidiary segments of a given root. Unfortunately, if there are very many insertions and deletions, the segments belonging to a root segment can become widely scattered not only over the OSAM storage records but over a large number of disk cylinders, thus causing the expenditure of a larger number of time-consuming seeks (see Chapter 1) to retrieve them, and we can have the same problem with HDAM.

Referring again to the HIDAM data base in Figure 10.16, the use of ISAM for the indexed-sequential file of sequence fields means that we have to have an overflow file for inserted root sequence fields. If we use a VSAM indexed-sequential file instead, there is no need for the overflow area, since a VSAM indexed-sequential file handles insertions by the splitting of control intervals (see Chapter 2).

Summary of IMS storage data base properties

A summary of the essential characteristics of the different kinds of IMS storage data bases is shown in Figure 10.17. It is clear that the storage data bases can be quite complex and that it can at times be difficult to decide which one should be used in a given case. However, the storage data bases are often even more complex than described so far. As mentioned earlier, IMS can handle data bases that have a near hierarchical structure, that is, a limited hierarchical structure. It can do this because it is possible to specify an additional pointer system that connects segments of different storage data bases. These additional pointers are known as IMS *logical pointers*, and we return to this in the chapter supplement. The pointers used in the hierarchical and child/twin pointer systems in Figures 10.13 and 10.14 are known as IMS *physical pointers*.

Need for reorganization of IMS storage data bases

From the description of the three types of direct access IMS storage organizations (HISAM, HDAM, and HIDAM), we can see that a large number of insertions and

ORGANIZA-TION	LOADING	ROOT SEGMENT ACCESS	DEPENDENT SEGMENT ACCESS
HSAM	Hierarchical sequence	Storage records form sequential file. Root segments may be accessed sequentially in ascending root sequence field order.	Sequential access in hierarchical sequence (Figure 10.6)
HISAM	Hierarchical sequence	Storage records form indexed-sequential file. Root segments may be accessed either sequentially (in ascending root sequence field order) or directly.	Sequential access in hierarchical sequence

(a) IMS storage file organizations in which the segments of a storage record are physically contiguous (Figures 10.10 and 10.11).

ORGANIZA-TION	LOADING	ROOT SEGMENT ACCESS	DEPENDENT SEGMENT ACCESS
HDAM	Any order for roots, subsidiary segments in hierarchical sequence	Storage records form a hash file. Segments from a storage record distributed in storage medium. Direct access to root segments	If hierarchical pointers within storage records, sequential access in hierarchical sequence; if child/twin pointers, direct access
HIDAM	Hierarchical sequence	Storage records form indexed-sequential file. Segments from a storage record distributed in storage medium. Root segments may be accessed sequentially or directly.	If hierarchical pointers, sequential access in hierarchical sequence; if child/twin pointers, direct access

(b) IMS storage file organizations in which the segments of a storage are not generally physically contiguous but are connected by a pointer system (Figures 10.13 and 10.14).

FIGURE 10.17 IMS storage file organizations.

deletions will cause the storage data bases to become increasingly disorganized, with unused space and long pointer chains. In other words, with time entropy or disorder increases. The remedy is reorganization. The segments are read in hierarchical sequence and written out as an HSAM data base which will be used as a backup copy. The new direct access data base is then reloaded from the segments in the HSAM data base. Utility programs are also available for reorganizing storage data bases.

Storage data independence with IMS

IMS possesses a fair degree of storage data independence even though there is no formal distinction in the data base definition between the storage data base and the conceptual data base. We recall (see Chapter 4) that physical or storage data independence allows underlying storage structures to be changed without affecting the ability of application programs to execute.

It is possible to change an underlying IMS storage structure from one direct access structure to another with only minor effects on application programs, and in many cases no effect at all. Naturally we cannot switch from a direct access organization to the sequential HSAM organization in most cases, since updates cannot be made with HSAM storage data bases. Another lack of data independence arises when we switch from HISAM or HIDAM to HDAM: With HDAM storage data bases, we cannot process the root segments in ascending root sequence field order, as is possible with HISAM and HIDAM.

10.3 IMS EXTERNAL DATA BASES

An IMS external data base may be defined as any subset of the conceptual hierarchical data base that:

1. Contains the root conceptual file
2. Has a hierarchical structure
3. Has the same hierarchical sequence as the underlying conceptual data base

Some examples of external data bases derived from the conceptual data base in Figure 10.1 are shown in Figure 10.18. The simplest external data base that could be defined would contain only the **BRANCH** root conceptual file, while the most complex would be the full hierarchy type in Figure 10.1. A field that is in the underlying conceptual file cannot be omitted from an external data base. Thus the **TSALARY** field could not be omitted from the external data base in Figure 10.18a. The fields and conceptual files (segment types in IMS terminology) that are used in an external data base are said to be *sensitive*.

In IMS terminology an external data base is called a logical data base (LDB), and the logical data base definition (external schema specification) is given the name program communications block (PCB). (At this point we regret to have to point out that remembering the meaning of IMS acronyms is something of a problem for most people, and there are more important acronyms that we have not yet defined. They certainly do not help communication within an organization that has installed IMS. To help the reader, we have placed an IMS acronym dictionary at the end of the chapter. IMS acronyms are extensively employed in IMS literature and manuals.)

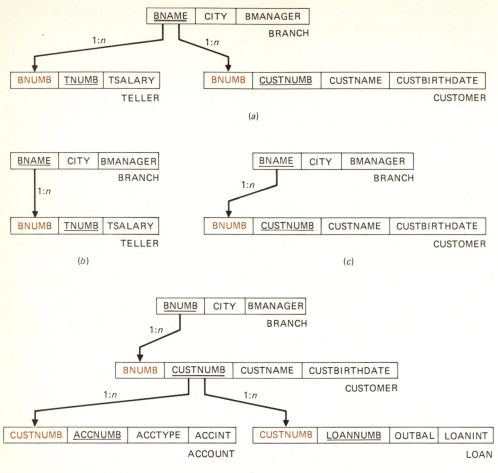

FIGURE 10.18 Some of the external hierarchical data bases that can be defined on the basis of the conceptual hierarchical data base in Figure 10.1. Any structure can be selected provided it forms a hierarchy, the structure contains the root conceptual file BRANCH, and no fields are omitted from any of the conceptual files used.

Defining a PCB

We first give a PCB for the external data base in Figure 10.18d, and after that we explain the features specified. The following PCB specification is typical:

```
1 PCB      TYPE=DB,DBDNAME=SAVELOAN,KEYLEN=12
2 SENSEG   NAME=BRANCH,PROCOPT=G
3 SENSEG   NAME=CUSTOMER,PARENT=BRANCH,PROCOPT=G
4 SENSEG   NAME=ACCOUNT,PARENT=CUSTOMER,PROCOPT=G
5 SENSEG   NAME=LOAN,PARENT=CUSTOMER,PROCOPT=G
```

The first line states that this is a data base PCB (the specification TYPE=DB). This is necessary, for there is another type of PCB that is described in Chapter 12 in connection with an IMS communications feature. Also on the first line is the name of the hierarchy-type specification (or DBD) for the underlying conceptual data base. Finally we have the **KEYLEN** specification, which gives the length in bytes of what is really an IMS equivalent of a currency indicator; we return to this in Section 10.4.

In each of the following lines we specify the sensitive segments (**SENSEG** specifications) that make up the external data base. In each **SENSEG** specification we have a **PROCOPT** or process option specification, which specifies how the external segment can be processed. For example, we can specify **G** (for "get") indicating retrieval only, or **I** (for "insert") indicating insertion only, or **D** (for "delete") indicating deletion only, or **R** (for "replace") indicating replacement or rewriting only. If processing will include retrieval, deletion, and insertion, we would specify **PROCOPT=GDI**. If we wish to leave out an intermediate level of a hierarchy type, we use the process option specification **K**. For example, if we did not want a special class of users to have access to the **CUSTOMER** segments in the external data base in Figure 10.18, but did want the users to have access to **ACCOUNT** and **LOAN** segments, then in the **SENSEG** specification for **CUS-TOMER** we would specify **PROCOPT=K**. Finally, when loading a data base, the sensitive segments will be all those in the underlying conceptual data base (for example, the one in Figure 10.1), and we would give each of these sensitive segments the specification **L** (for "load").

The IMS library

As we shall see, with IMS an application program can manipulate many data bases at the same time. Nevertheless, an application program can manipulate only one external schema derived from a given conceptual data base (defined in the DBD). To facilitate program manipulation of data bases, the necessary DBDs and PCBs are first placed in an IMS library, whence they are retrieved and placed in main memory prior to execution of the application program. As we saw in Chapter 4, the source versions of the schema definitions have to be translated into object versions for use by the data base system. With IMS, each source DBD is processed by a utility translation program (Figure 10.19a), and the resulting object DBD is placed in the IMS library. The source DBD is often entered on punched cards, but the use of terminals for DBD source entries is probably the more common today.

All the PCBs that define the external data bases that an application program will process are translated together in a single step and the resulting object PCBs placed in the IMS library. The collection of PCBs that define the external data bases for an application program are referred to as the *program specification block* (PSB) (Figure 10.19b). We return to the PSB again Section 10.4.

10.4 MANIPULATING AN IMS DATA BASE WITH DL/1

In this section we shall learn how to use Data Language/1, or DL/1, which is the sublanguage that is used for manipulating IMS data bases. DL/1 commands are

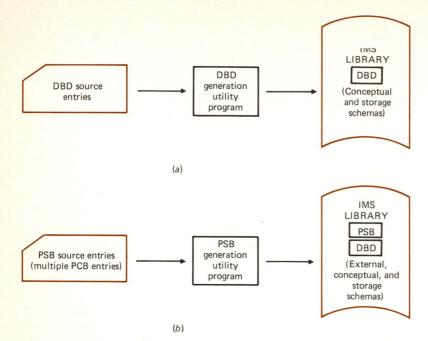

(a)

(b)

FIGURE 10.19 A user program can process many data bases: (a) Generating the object version of the DBD entries; (b) generating the object version of the PCB entries. (The object versions of each DBD (combined conceptual and storage schemas) are placed in an IMS library following processing of the manual or source DBD (see Figure 10.9). The PCBs for each of the external data bases to be processed by an application program are processed in a single step to generate the user's PSB, which is also placed in the IMS library.

embedded in a host language such as COBOL or PL/1, as was the case with CODASYL commands (see Chapter 6). As with CODASYL, a DL/1 command is really a **CALL** to a subprogram that manipulates the data base. This subprogram is called the DL/1 data base system, and not IMS. We shall examine the DL/1 commands in some detail in this section, but before we do so, we must look at the interface between the application program and the DL/1 data base system.

Communicating with the DL/1 data base system

The structures used for communication between an application program and Dl/1 (that is, the interface) are not at all difficult to understand. However, because of an elusive IMS terminology they often appear difficult. DL/1 is a procedural language, and for an application program to communicate with a procedural data base manipulation language, there has to be a loading/unloading area for data transmitted to and from the data base. There also has to be some registers into which the data base system will place messages about the success or failure of a data base command, and registers containing information about the current processing position in the data base (for example, the CODASYL

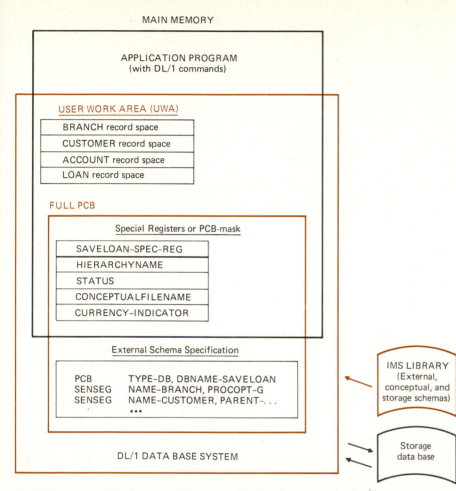

MAIN MEMORY

APPLICATION PROGRAM
(with DL/1 commands)

USER WORK AREA (UWA)

BRANCH record space
CUSTOMER record space
ACCOUNT record space
LOAN record space

FULL PCB

Special Registers or PCB-mask

SAVELOAN–SPEC–REG
HIERARCHYNAME
STATUS
CONCEPTUALFILENAME
CURRENCY–INDICATOR

External Schema Specification

PCB   TYPE-DB, DBNAME-SAVELOAN
SENSEG   NAME-BRANCH, PROCOPT-G
SENSEG   NAME-CUSTOMER, PARENT-...
            •••

DL/1 DATA BASE SYSTEM

IMS LIBRARY
(External,
conceptual, and
storage schemas)

Storage
data base

FIGURE 10.20 The basic architecture of IMS when a single data base is manipulated by an application program. The application program and the DL/1 data base
system each have access to the User Work Area (UWA, and not an IMS term) and the
special registers. Only DL/1 has access to the external schema specification or PCB.
The UWA has room for each type of segment transmitted to and from the data base,
and the special registers are passed information about the result of executing each
DL/1 command.

currency indicators). We have these structures with IMS, and in Figure 10.20 is
an overview of the interface between an application program and the DL/1
system when just one data base is being processed.

The user work area (UWA) or input area
The user work area must be declared by the user in the WORKING STORAGE
area of a COBOL program and consists of a record declaration for each of the
segment types (conceptual record types) in the external data base being proces-

sed. Thus if we are processing the external data base in Figure 10.18*d*, we would need the following declarations in COBOL for the UWA:

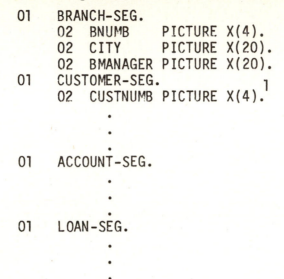

```
01   BRANCH-SEG.
     02   BNUMB     PICTURE X(4).
     02   CITY      PICTURE X(20).
     02   BMANAGER  PICTURE X(20).
01   CUSTOMER-SEG.
     02   CUSTNUMB  PICTURE X(4).¹
                   .
                   .
                   .
01   ACCOUNT-SEG.
                   .
                   .
                   .
01   LOAN-SEG.
                   .
                   .
                   .
```

The term user work area is not used in IMS manuals, the term *input area* often being used instead. Note, however, that the user work area is used for input of segments from the external data base, as well as for output of segments to the external data base.

It is clear that both the application program and the DL/1 system have access to the record areas defined in the UWA, and this is illustrated in Figure 10.20 which shows the UWA in a part of main memory in which the application program and the DL/1 system overlap. When a DL/1 command involves the retrieval or insertion of a segment, the name of the record area to receive or containing the segment must be included in the command. This is because there can be several UWAs, one for each external data base being processed, as we shall see later.

Special communications registers

A number of registers are used with DL/1 for communicating the status of DL/1 commands, a program's position in the data base and other information. Each register is a COBOL variable with a name that can be arbitrarily chosen by the COBOL programmer, and these registers are grouped together in the form of a COBOL group item with an arbitrary name that usually reflects the external data base involved. Thus we could declare the following special registers for processing the external data base in Figure 10.18*d*[2]:

---

[1]Sequence fields come first in a segment; see Figure 10.9.

[2]These declarations must be placed in the LINKAGE SECTION of the DATA DIVISION in COBOL.

```
01  BANKPCB.
    02 HIERARCHYNAME  PICTURE X(8).
    02 STATUS         PICTURE X(2).
    02 SEGMENTNAME    PICTURE X(8).
    02 CURRENCY-INDICATOR PICTURE X(12).
```

We have given only four special communications registers above. Actually there has to be eight, but the others are of marginal interest. The first entry (**BANKPCB**) is the name of the block or collection of special registers. This collection of registers is for processing a single external data base, and the system will place the name of the underlying conceptual data base specification (the DBD name '**SAVELOAN**' in this case) in the first register **HIERARCHYNAME**. We must declare a collection of special communications registers for each data base that is to be processed by the application program.

The register **STATUS** is the most important one for a user. Following each DL/1 command the system will place a two-character value in **STATUS** to indicate the success or failure of the command. A blank value means that everything went well, while, for example, the value "GE" means that the required segment was not found.

The register **SEGMENTNAME** contains the name of the last segment accessed by DL/1, while the register **CURRENCY-INDICATOR** contains the fully concatenated key of the last segment accessed. Examples of fully concatenated keys were given in Figure 10.8b earlier. Thus **CURRENCY-INDICATOR** maintains the position of the program with respect to the data base and is almost equivalent to the current of run-unit in CODASYL.

In Figure 10.20 we show the special registers within the application program, but also within the DL/1 system, since both the application program and the DL/1 system have access to them. However, the special registers are also shown as part of the "full PCB." With IMS the specification of the external schema is actually only a part of the program communications block, the remaining part being the special communications (block of) registers. The application program naturally has no need to access the external schema specifications, and so only a part of the full PCB, that is, the part containing the special communications registers, may be accessed by both the DL/1 system and the application program. Because they are part of a DL/1 system structure, the declaration of the special registers in the COBOL (or PL/1) program is called a *PCB-mask* in IMS manuals. To limit the use of acronyms, we shall normally use the term *special registers*.

The program specification block (PSB)

As mentioned earlier, an application program can process more than one external data base, provided the external data bases are all derived from different conceptual hierarchy types, or conceptual data bases. For each external data base there is a UWA, to hold segments from that external data base (Figure 10.21). There must also be a set of special registers for each external data base, so

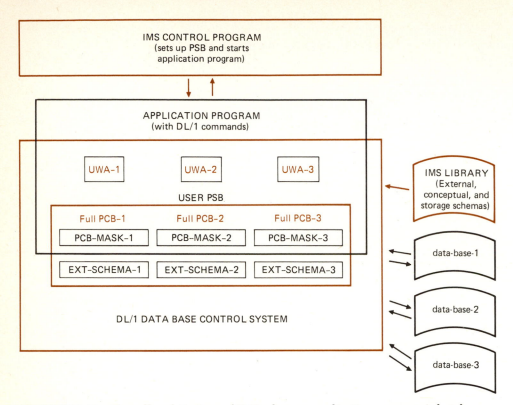

FIGURE 10.21   Overall architecture of IMS when an application program is batch processing three different data bases, each with its own schema specifications. For each data base, there must be a UWA (or input area) and a PCB. The collection of PCBs is called a user's Program Specification Block (or PSB). The DL/1 data base system carries out DL/1 commands issued by the application program, but there is also an IMS control program that sets ups the PSB and starts the execution of the application program.

that, for example, there can be a currency indicator to give the program's position in each data base. And naturally also there has to be an external schema for each data base. All this is illustrated in Figure 10.21. The complete collection of PCBs is called a *program specification block* (PSB) in IMS terminology. Even when there is only one PCB, this can still be called a PSB.

The IMS control program

Normally a data base system functions as a subprogram of an application program. This is still largely true in the case of IMS, but not completely. The DL/1 system functions as the subprogram and carries out DL/1 commands (DL/1 **CALL**s) issued by the application program. However, before the application program can execute, the special registers declared in the application program must be set up as part of the DL/1 system as well. There is an IMS control system that does this, and the application program executes as a subprogram of this control system (Figure 10.21). The IMS control system also loads the external schemas and starts the execution of the application program. Usually we can forget about the IMS control system. We mention it here for the sake of completeness, and because it often appears in IMS diagrams.

Batch processing with IMS

The diagram in Figure 10.21 applies to batch programming with IMS. Each batch processing job is distinct, and if there are two different application programs manipulating IMS data bases and executing concurrently, *there is no communication between them*. In Figure 10.22, application program **AP-1** is process-

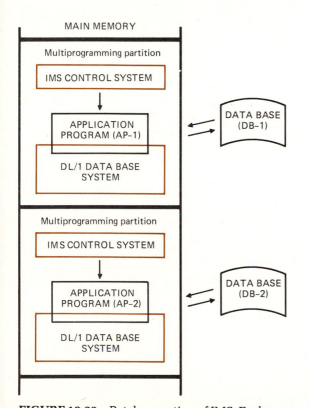

FIGURE 10.22 Batch operation of IMS. Each program processing an IMS data base executes in an independent operating system partition (see Figure 1.3), with independent copies of the IMS control system and DL/1 data base system. The data bases DB-1 and DB-2 should be different; if two programs are processing the same data base concurrently, there is nothing in batch operation to prevent the two programs interfering with each other's updating of the data base. Concurrency control is achieved only with on-line processing. Note that with commonly used virtual operating systems, each partition would be broken down into pages and paged in and out of main memory (Chapter 1).

ing data base **DB-1**, while **AP-2** is processing **DB-2**. **AP-1** operates in one partition or region (see Chapter 1) of the memory, while **AP-2** operates in another, and each has its own independent copy of the IMS control system and DL/1 system. Normally the two programs will be processing external data bases derived from different conceptual data bases. Were **DB-1** and **DB-2** based on the same conceptual data base, the two programs could interfere with each other's updating. We have proper concurrency control only under on-line processing with IMS, described in Chapter 12.

The DL/1 retrieval commands

There are three basic Dl/1 retrieval commands. These are:

1. The **GET FIRST**, or **GU**, command. (The command is actually the **GET UNIQUE** command but this is one of the many misnomers in IMS.) **GU** is followed by a condition or predicate. The system responds by scanning through the segments in hierarchical sequence until the segment that satisfies the condition is reached. While it would appear from the last statement that **GU** causes a sequential scan through the data base, this is not always so. For example, if the sequence field of a root segment is given as part of the condition, then the system will be able to directly access the root segment and continue the search from there.

2. The **GET NEXT**, or **GN**, command. This permits a scan of any segment type (and its subsidiaries) in hierarchical sequence, starting at the segment identified by the currency indicator. Typically we use **GU** to come directly to a type of segment, and then **GN** to continue the scan.

3. The **GET NEXT WITHIN PARENT**, or **GNP**, comand. This works like **GN**, except that the scan of a segment type is limited to those segments that are subsidiaries of a *current parent* segment. A current parent segment is one previously retrieved by a **GU** or **GN** command, but not a **GNP** command, as we shall see presently.

These features of the DL/1 command will be illustrated in the retrieval examples that follow shortly. A typical command has the structure:

```
GU (BANKPCB)    CUSTOMER-SEG
                     BRANCH (CITY = OAKLAND)
                     CUSTOMER (CUSTNAME = SMITH).
```

We want the system to retrieve the first **CUSTOMER** segment (in hierarchical sequence) that satisfies the conditions in the *segment search arguments* (SSAs). An SSA is a segment name that may be followed by a condition. Normally the segment named in the last SSA is the one that has to be retrieved. A parent segment always comes before a child segment in the list of SSAs. The retrieved segment is always placed in the UWA record structure specified (**CUSTOMER-SEG**), and the return status code, currency indicator value, and so on are placed in the special registers of the COBOL group item that is specified first in the command (BANKPCB).

Note that the DL/1 command structure given above does not include the detailed syntax. Actually the command is a CALL to DL/1 and can be quite detailed. In the examples that follow we ignore these details and give a streamlined version for the benefit of readers who want to see how the commands work. Later we shall give an example of the detailed syntax.

All our examples have to do with the external data base in Figure 10.18*d*, which is derived from the conceptual data base in Figures 10.1 and 10.3, as specified with IMS in Figure 10.9. We recall that a conceptual IMS data base is a hierarchy type, made up of a collection of hierarchy occurrences, each of which can approximate a storage record (at least with HISAM) in the storage data base. An external data base is a subhierarchy type, made up of subhierarchy occurrences. It is easy to deduce the shape of the external data base subhierarchy occurrences from the conceptual data base hierarchy occurrences in Figure 10.2. But for the convenience of the reader we give them in Figure 10.23. They should be examined carefully. Notice that the segments of the external data base are still in hierarchical sequence (for a review of the concept of hierarchical sequence, see Figures 10.6 and 10.7*a*), and not in ascending sequence field order (except for the BRANCH segments).

Retrieval-1. Root segment, sequential processing
Find the name of the manager of the first branch.

The necessary COBOL excerpt is:

```
GU (BANKPCB)  BRANCH-SEG
                BRANCH.
DISPLAY BMANAGER IN BRANCH-SEG.
```

Referring to Figure 10.23, the value output is 'WRIGHT'.

Unless we specify the sequence field value in a root SSA, GU will cause the external data base to be processed in hierarchical sequence. Thus the above GU command will cause BRANCH segments to be searched in hierarchical sequence; however, since there is no condition in the BRANCH SSA, the first BRANCH segment of the data base is retrieved.

Retrieval-2. Root segment, sequential processing
What is the name of the manager of the first Oakland branch?

```
GU (BANKPCB) BRANCH-SEG
                BRANCH (CITY = OAKLAND).
DISPLAY BMANAGER IN BRANCH-SEG.
```

The result is 'QUICKLEY'.

The system scans the BRANCH segments in hierarchical sequence until the first BRANCH segment satisfying the condition is reached.

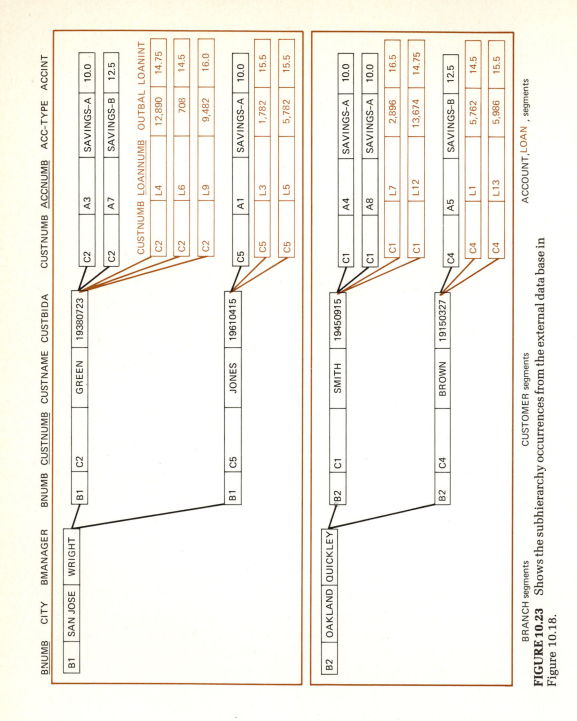

FIGURE 10.23 Shows the subhierarchy occurrences from the external data base in Figure 10.18.

Retrieval-3. Root segment, sequential processing
List the names of all branch managers.

```
        GU (BANKPCB) BRANCH-SEG
                          BRANCH.
        DISPLAY BMANAGER IN BRANCH-SEG.
   LOOP.
        GN (BANKPCB) BRANCH-SEG
                          BRANCH.
        IF STATUS = " "  THEN
                DISPLAY BMANAGER IN BRANCH-SEG
                GO TO LOOP
        ELSE STOP RUN.
```

The result is:

```
   WRIGHT
   QUICKLEY
```

We use **GU** to retrieve the first **BRANCH** segment as with retrieval-1. This gives us a position in the data base. With a **GN** command, we scan forward (in hierarchical sequence) from the *current segment*, that is, from the last segment retrieved and the one currently named in the special register **SEGMENTNAME**. Only the segments named in the **GN** command are scanned, and the scan goes all the way to the end of the data base. In the above case the remaining **BRANCH** segments will be scanned. Following each execution of a **GN** command (don't forget **GN** is within a loop), we check the return code in **STATUS**. Eventually 'GE' will appear in **STATUS**, indicating that there is no next segment, and the program will stop.

Retrieval-4. Root segment, direct access
What city is branch 'B2' in?

```
        GU (BANKPCB)  BRANCH-SEG
                      BRANCH (BNUMB = B2).
        DISPLAY CITY IN BRANCH-SEG.
```

The result of this is 'OAKLAND'.
Because we have given the sequence field value of the required root segment, the system can access the **BRANCH** segment for branch 'B2' directly provided the storage data base is not an HSAM data base, as illustrated in Figure 10.10. If it is an HSAM data base, then the access will involve a sequential scan of the segments.

Retrieval-5. CUSTOMER segment, sequential access
Find the name of the first customer that was born before 1930.

```
GU (BANKPCB) CUSTOMER-SEG
              BRANCH
              CUSTOMER·(CUSTBIDA < 19300101).
DISPLAY CUSTNAME IN CUSTOMER-SEG
```

The result is 'BROWN'.

The system scans through data base segments in hierarchical sequence until the **CUSTOMER** segment satisfying the SSA is reached. Remember that when there are several SSAs in a command, it is the segment specified in the last one that is retrieved.

Retrieval-6. CUSTOMER segment, direct access

Find the name of the first customer of branch 'B2', who was born before 1930.

```
GU (BANKPCB)  CUSTOMER-SEG
                  BRANCH (BNUMB = B2)
                  CUSTOMER (CUSTBIDA < 19300101).
DISPLAY CUSTNAME IN CUSTOMER-SEG.
```

Here the result is the same as before, but we have direct access to the correct **BRANCH** segment, followed by a sequential search of the subsidiary **CUSTOMER** segments of this branch. We have direct access to the **BRANCH** segment, because the sequence field value is specified.

Retrieval-7. CUSTOMER segment, sequential scan

Find the names of all bank customers born after 1940.

```
        GU (BANKPCB) BRANCH-SEG
                     BRANCH.
    LOOP.
        GN (BANKPCB) CUSTOMER-SEG
                CUSTOMER (CUSTBIDA  > 19401231)
        IF STATUS = "GE" THEN STOP RUN
        ELSE DISPLAY CUSTNAME IN CUSTOMER-SEG
            GO TO LOOP.
```

We retrieve:

```
JONES
SMITH
```

The **GU** command gives us a current position at the first **BRANCH** segment in the data base. We then use **GN** to search all the **CUSTOMER** segments *in the data base,* and *not* just the subsidiary segments of a parent.

Retrieval-8. LOAN segment, sequential scan

Find the customer numbers of customers who owe the bank more than $6000.

```
    GU (BANKPCB)  LOAN-SEG
                  BRANCH
                  CUSTOMER
                  LOAN (OUTBAL > 6000)
         DISPLAY CUSTNUMB IN LOAN-SEG.
LOOP.
         GN (BANKPCB) LOAN-SEG
                  LOAN (OUTBAL > 6000).
         IF STATUS = "GE" THEN STOP RUN
         ELSE DISPLAY CUSTNUMB IN LOAN-SEG
             GO TO LOOP.
```

We retrieve:

```
    C2
    C2
    C1
```

Duplicate 'C2' values are retrieved because customer 'C2' has two loans with outstanding balances greater than $6000. However, examining the data in Figure 10.23 carefully, we begin to see that something is wrong with this retrieval. We see, for example, that customer 'C5' has one debt of $5782 and another of $1782, so that this customer owes the bank more than $6000, but was not retrieved. The same is true for customer 'C4'. This is just one more example of how easy it is to retrieve incorrect or incomplete information from a data base. The COBOL and DL/1 above would be correct for the following request, however:

Find the customer numbers of customers that have one or more loans with an outstanding balance exceeding $6000.

We scan the segments sequentially with a **GU** command until we come to the first one with **OUTBAL** value greater than $6000; then we scan the remaining **CUSTOMER** segments using the **GN** command embedded in a COBOL loop.

To carry out the original request with IMS, we have two choices:

1. Retrieve the **CUSTNUMB** and **OUTBAL** values from all **LOAN** segments in the data base. This retrieved data then has to be further processed: For each **CUSTNUMB** value, **OUTBAL** values are summed and those **CUSTNUMB** values for which this sum exceeds $6000 are printed out.
2. Redesign the data base so that there is a summary field in each **CUSTOMER** segment. This summary field would contain the sum of the **OUTBAL** values in child **LOAN** segments. If this field is called **DEBT**, the original retrieval request could then be carried out with:

```
    GU (BANKPCB) CUSTOMER-SEG
                 BRANCH
                 CUSTOMER (DEBT > 6000).
```

and so on. Such summary values are common in data bases. However, there is a strong argument for not having them, since they introduce what may be called an *interfile dependency*. We cannot update the **OUTBAL** field of a **LOAN** conceptual record in this case without also updating the **DEBT** field of a parent **CUSTOMER** conceptual record. Remembering Murphy's law, sooner or later, an **OUTBAL** field will be updated without the **DEBT** field being updated, thus making the data base inconsistent (or causing a loss of integrity).

A third possible solution is to use an SQL enhancement with the data base as it stands in Figure 10.23 (provided the conceptual data base was originally designed as a relational data base, which it was). This is not currently possible with most versions of IMS, but it is with versions that run under the virtual IBM operating system for smaller configurations, namely, DOS/VSE. The enhancement is called SQL/DS. We shall look at the possibility of manipulating hierarchical data bases with SQL in more detail later. It is widely expected that in the not too distant future it will be possible to manipulate most IMS data bases using SQL. (This is a further demonstration of the fundamental importance of SQL, described in detail in Chapter 7.)

Retrieval-9. CUSTOMER segment, direct access
Find the customer numbers for customers at branch 'B2' who were born after 1940.

```
GU (BANKPCB) BRANCH-SEQ
                BRANCH (BNUMB = B2).
LOOP.
     GNP (BANKPCB) CUSTOMER-SEG
             CUSTOMER (CUSTBIDA >= 19410101).
     IF STATUS = "GE" THEN STOP RUN
     ELSE DISPLAY CUSTNUMB IN CUSTOMER-SEG
     GO TO LOOP.
```

The result is 'C1'.

We use the **GU** command to directly access the **BRANCH** segment with sequence field 'B2'. This establishes this **BRANCH** segment as the *current segment*, that is, the last segment retrieved. The **GNP** command causes the system to examine the next **CUSTOMER** segment that is a child of the previously retrieved **BRANCH** segment. Because of the **GNP** command, the **BRANCH** segment is given the status of *current parent* and retains this status each time the **GNP** command is executed. The **GNP** command can retrieve only segments that are children of this current parent. Each **CUSTOMER** segment retrieved by the **GNP** command becomes the current segment, but the **BRANCH** segment remains the current parent. A current parent can be created only by a **GU** or **GN** command. In addition, any ancestor segment can function as the current parent of a segment specified in a **GNP** command, as is illustrated in the next retrieval.

Retrieval-10. LOAN segment, direct access

Find the customer numbers for customers at branch 'B2' who have one or more loans with outstanding balances exceeding $5000.

```
        GU (BANKPCB) BRANCH-SEG
                    BRANCH (BNUMB = B2)
LOOP.
        GNP (BANKPCB) LOAN-SEG
                    LOAN (OUTBAL > 5000)
        IF STATUS = "GE" THEN STOP RUN
        ELSE DISPLAY CUSTNUMB IN LOAN-SEG
                GO TO LOOP.
```

The result is:

```
C1
C4
C4
```

The **GU** command causes direct access to the **BRANCH** segment, which becomes a parent segment when the **GNP** command is executed. The **GNP** commands within the loop cause the system to check all the **LOAN** segments that are ultimately subordinate to the parent **BRANCH** segment with branch number 'B2'.

Retrieval-11. Direct access, complex conditions

Find the loan number of the first loan at branch 'B2' that has an outstanding balance of more than $8000 and pays an interest rate in excess of 15 percent.

```
GU (BANKPCB) LOAN-SEG
            BRANCH (BNUMB = B2)
            CUSTOMER
            LOAN ((OUTBAL > 8000) AND (LOANINT > 15.0)).
```

The result is 'L9'.

Simple logical expressions can be connected by **AND** or **OR** and preceded by **NOT**.

Retrieval 12. Two-segment retrieval

Find the name of the first customer who was born before 1963 and who has a loan with an outstanding balance of more than $12,000; find also the interest on the loan.

```
GU (BANKPCB)  CUSTOMER-SEG LOAN-SEG
            BRANCH
            CUSTOMER*D (CUSTBIDA < 19630000)
            LOAN (OUTBAL > 12,000).
    DISPLAY CUSTNAME IN CUSTOMER-SEG, LOANINT IN LOAN-SEG.
```

The result is GREEN 14.75.

Here we need the LOANINT value from a LOAN segment and the CUSTNAME value from the CUSTOMER parent segment of this LOAN segment. Normally only the LOAN segment in the last SSA would be retrieved, but by inserting the *command code* 'D' after the specification of the parent CUSTOMER segment in the command, we also retrieve that segment. Had we in addition wanted the parent BRANCH segment, we would have specified BRANCH*D in the command.

Retrieval-13. Two types of child segment
Find the loan and account numbers of the customer with customer number 'C1'.

```
        GU (BANKPCB) CUSTOMER-SEG
                     BRANCH
                     CUSTOMER (CUSTNUMB = C1).
  LOOP1.
        GNP (BANKPCB) ACCOUNT-SEG
                      ACCOUNT.
        IF STATUS = " " THEN  DISPLAY  ACCNUMB IN ACCOUNT-SEG
                              GO TO LOOP1.
  LOOP2.
        GNP (BANKPCB) LOAN-SEG
                      LOAN.
        IF STATUS = " " THEN DISPLAY LOANNUMB IN LOAN-SEG
                             GO TO LOOP2
        ELSE STOP RUN.
```

The result is:

```
    A4
    A8
    L7
    L12
```

The initial GU command retrieves the CUSTOMER segment with customer number 'C1' (see Figure 10.23), and this segment becomes both the current segment and the current parent. The first set of GNP commands in LOOP1 retrieves all the ACCOUNT segments that are children of the current parent, while the second set of GNP commands in LOOP2 retrieves all the LOAN segments that are children of the current parent.

Effect of IMS secondary indexing
As the data base in Figure 10.1 was specified in Figure 10.9, direct access is possible only on presentation of a root sequence field value (that is, a BNUMB value) in an SSA. Thus in the previous request, a sequential search would be necessary until the CUSTOMER segment with CUSTNUMB value 'C1' is re-

trieved. However, a **CUSTNUMB** value is a sequence field in a **CUSTOMER** segment, and in the conceptual data base in Figure 10.1 it is a primary key field in the conceptual file **CUSTOMER**. It seems unreasonable that we do not have direct access on presentation of a **CUSTNUMB** value. Fortunately it is possible to have direct access on the basis of a field value other than a root sequence field value, if we construct an *IMS secondary index*, as mentioned earlier. An IMS secondary index is a variation on the theme of an inverted file, as discussed in Chapter 3. We take a brief look at the basic principle.

Let us suppose that we want direct access to the data base on the basis of the **CUSTNUMB** sequence field values in **CUSTOMER** segments (refer to Figure 10.23). We could construct a special inversion as follows:

CUSTNUMB	BNUMB
C1	B2
C2	B1
C4	B2
C5	B1

Here **CUSTNUMB** is the primary key field. If this inversion is implemented as a direct access file, then on presentation of a **CUSTNUMB** value we obtain the **BNUMB** value for the hierarchy occurrence containing that **CUSTNUMB** value. This hierarchy occurrence can then be directly accessed using the **BNUMB** root sequence field value.

Such an inversion can be specified with IMS and is implemented as the index portion of a HIDAM data base (see the top structures in Figure 10.16) except that VSAM is used and not ISAM. The full details of IMS secondary indexes are beyond the scope of this book. It is simply worth remembering that it is possible to have an IMS secondary index on any field and that, as usual, the existence of an inversion will slow down updating of the data base, because of the need to update the secondary index (see Chapter 3 for the cost of maintaining simple inversions).

COBOL DL/1 command syntax

The syntax of the DL/1 commands that we have been using was simplified to make it more readable. Actual DL/1 commands are COBOL **CALL**s to a subprogram called **CBLTDL**, and the **GU** command in Retrieval-13 would have the COBOL syntax:

```
CALL "CBLTDL1" USING "GU ", BANKPCB, CUSTOMER-SEG
"BRANCH", "CUSTOMER  (CUSTNUMB  =  B1)"
```

An irritating detail is that blanks usually have to be inserted in SSAs to maintain standard lengths. Blanks also have to be specified with command specifications such as "GUbb".

DL/1 updating commands

We give some typical examples of how to delete, alter, or insert segments.

Deletion

Customer 'C1' has left the country, having closed out her accounts and repaid all her loans. Delete the segment for this customer and all subsidiary segments. Referring to Figure 10.23, we proceed as follows:

```
GHU (BANKPCB) CUSTOMER-SEG
              BRANCH
              CUSTOMER (CUSTNUMB = C1).
DLET (BANKPCB)  CUSTOMER-SEG.
```

First we must retrieve and hold the required customer segment, and this is done with a **GET HOLD UNIQUE (GHU)** command, which is the same as a **GU** command except it permits subsequent deletion or alteration commands to be carried out for the segment held. (We also have **GHN** and **GHNP** versions of **GN** and **GNP**, respectively.) The **DLET** command then causes this segment and all its subsidiary **ACCOUNT** and **LOAN** segments to be deleted. At the same same the **TRANSACTION** segments that are children of the deleted **ACCOUNT** segments are also deleted. (Note, however, that a **DLET** command will be carried out only if all the subsidiary segments that need to be deleted are defined in the external schema.)

Alteration of segments

A segment in an IMS data base is modified by replacing the complete segment by means of a **REPLACE** or **REPL** command. The segment to be replaced is first read, then it is updated, and then rewritten back into the data base. Suppose that we want to update the outstanding balance of the loan with loan number 'L7' to $2500 (see Figure 10.23); we would proceed as follows:

```
GHU (BANKPCB)  LOAN-SEG
               BRANCH
               CUSTOMER
               LOAN (LOANNUMB = L7).
DISPLAY "OLD BALANCE: ",OUTBAL IN LOAN-SEG.
COMPUTE OUTBAL IN LOAN-SEG = OUTBAL IN LOAN-SEG - 386.
REPL (BANKPCB) LOAN-SEG.
```

The **REPLACE** command operates on the last segment read, that is, the current segment.

Insertion of segments

There are a number of different ways of inserting segments with DL/1, and it is best to consider them separately.

1. *Insertion of a root segment.*   We first place the segment to be inserted in the proper UWA record area. Then we can issue an **INSERT** or **INSRT** command. Assume that the new **BRANCH** segment to be inserted is:

```
B4   SACRAMENTO   BANKS
```

then we would code:

```
MOVE "B4" TO BNUMB IN BRANCH-SEG.
MOVE "SACRAMENTO" TO CITY IN BRANCH-SEG.
MOVE "BANKS" TO BMANAGER IN BRANCH-SEG.
INSRT (BANKPCB) BRANCH-SEG
                BRANCH*D.
```

The command code **D** has to be used when inserting a root segment.

2. *Inserting a root segment and subsidiary segments.*   Suppose that we wanted to insert a new **BRANCH** segment, together with a child **CUSTOMER** segment and a child **ACCOUNT** segment, where the three segments are available in the COBOL group items **NEW-BRANCH**, **NEW-CUSTOMER**, and **NEW-ACCOUNT**. They can all be entered with a single **INSRT** command, as follows:

```
MOVE NEW-BRANCH TO BRANCH-SEG.
MOVE NEW-CUSTOMER TO CUSTOMER-SEG.
MOVE NEW-ACCOUNT TO ACCOUNT-SEG.
INSRT (BANKPCB)  BRANCH-SEG, CUSTOMER-SEG, ACCOUNT-SEG
                 BRANCH*D
                 CUSTOMER
                 ACCOUNT.
```

We still need the command code **D** for the root segment insertion, and the segments must all be available in the UWA, as shown above.

3. *Insertion of a subsidiary segment.*   To insert a subsidiary segment, the ancestors of this segment all the way up to its root segment must be known. Now suppose we wanted to insert a new **LOAN** segment (available in the COBOL group item **NEW-LOAN**) for the customer 'C1' at branch 'B2'. We could do it either of two ways. One of these is as follows:

```
MOVE NEW-LOAN TO LOAN-SEG.
INSRT (BANKPCB) LOAN-SEG
                BRANCH (BNUMB = B2)
                CUSTOMER (CUSTNUMB = C1)
                LOAN.
```

When the command code **D** is not included, it is only the segment type specified in the last segment search argument of an **INSRT** command that is actually inserted. The new **LOAN** segment is placed in the data base such that hierarchical sequence is preserved. Alternatively, we could proceed in a different manner:

```
GU (BANKPCB) CUSTOMER-SEG
                BRANCH (BNUMB = B2)
                CUSTOMER (CUSTNUMB = C1).
MOVE NEW-LOAN TO LOAN-SEG.
INSRT (BANKPCB) LOAN-SEG
                LOAN.
```

First we retrieve the parent CUSTOMER segment of the LOAN segment to be inserted; this CUSTOMER segment becomes the current segment. We then issue the INSRT command with just the new LOAN segment, and this causes the inserted segment to be inserted as the child of the current segment.

The INSRT command is the one used to insert segments when the data base is being loaded initially, and we look at this next.

Loading an IMS data base

The method used to loan an IMS data base is dependent on the nature of the storage data base (see the description of IMS storage data bases given earlier in this chapter). One method is used with HSAM, HISAM, and HIDAM data bases and another with HDAM data bases, as we would expect.

Loading a HSAM, HISAM, or HIDAM data base

Here the segments of the storage data base must be available in hierarchical sequence, that is, in the order given in Figure 10.6 for the conceptual data base in Figure 10.1. Getting the segments in hierarchical sequence is not as simple a task as it might appear at first sight. A glance at Figure 10.2 will show, for example, that TRANSACTION segments are in fully concatenated key order. They are not in TRANNUMB sequence field order, nor are they in ACCNUMB parent sequence field order. In practice we could assume that each of the different types of segment is available as a tape file. Thus the tape file XBRANCH could hold the BRANCH segments, XTELLER the TELLER segments, and so on. An XBRANCH record is a BRANCH segment in the storage data base. Within each of these tape files the records must be in the hierarchical sequence of the corresponding segments in the completed data base (that is, as in Figures 10.2 and 10.23). An outline of the loading program for the data base in Figure 10.1 is shown on the next page. The method is a classic example of nesting of programming loops, or "wheels within wheels," and mirrors the hierarchical structure of a hierarchy occurrence. Readers who know a little COBOL should be able to complete the details of the COBOL loading program. However, for the details of where to place blanks in the COBOL CALL statements corresponding to DL/1 INSERT commands, it will be necessary to consult a manual (Ref. 4).

As mentioned earlier, the records of the tape files XBRANCH, XTELLER, and so on must be in hierarchical sequence. To get the parent XBRANCH records in the proper sequence is no problem, since hierarchical sequence here is the same as ascending BNUMB sequence. A sort on BNUMB is all that is required. With

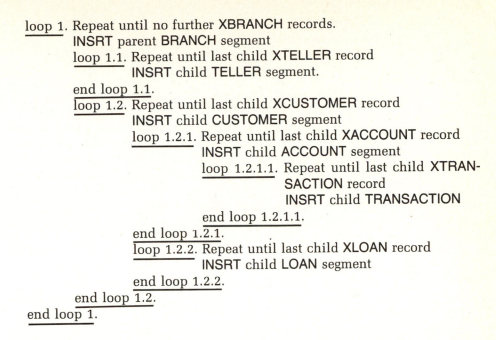

loop 1. Repeat until no further **XBRANCH** records.
      INSRT parent **BRANCH** segment
      loop 1.1. Repeat until last child **XTELLER** record
            INSRT child **TELLER** segment.
      end loop 1.1.
      loop 1.2. Repeat until last child **XCUSTOMER** record
            INSRT child **CUSTOMER** segment
            loop 1.2.1. Repeat until last child **XACCOUNT** record
                  INSRT child **ACCOUNT** segment
                  loop 1.2.1.1. Repeat until last child **XTRAN-SACTION** record
                        INSRT child **TRANSACTION**
                  end loop 1.2.1.1.
            end loop 1.2.1.
            loop 1.2.2. Repeat until last child **XLOAN** record
                  INSRT child **LOAN** segment
            end loop 1.2.2.
      end loop 1.2.
end loop 1.

XCUSTOMER records the required sequence is clearly primarily ascending **BNUMB** sequence and secondarily ascending **CUSTNUMB** sequence, so that a sort with the composite **BNUMB CUSTNUMB** as the sort key is needed.

As we go deeper into the hierarchy, the problems multiply. For example, with **XACCOUNT** records, the correct sequence is primarily **BNUMB** ascending sequence, secondarily ascending **CUSTNUMB** sequence, and last in order of priority, ascending **ACCNUMB** sequence. However, **XACCOUNT** records have no **BNUMB** field, so we have to temporarily attach one. This is done by sequential processing of both **XCUSTOMER** and **XACCOUNT** with both files previously sorted on their common **CUSTNUMB** field, giving a new version of **XACCOUNT** with the necessary **BNUMB, CUSTNUMB,** and **ACCNUMB** fields, which can then be sorted in the proper hierarchical sequence and the unwanted **BNUMB** field removed. We can arrange the **TRANSACTION** and **LOAN** records in hierarchical sequence in a similar manner. The **TRANSACTION** records are the most difficult, since they must be arranged primarily in ascending **BNUMB** order, then in ascending **CUSTNUMB** order, then in ascending **ACCNUMB** order, and last of all in ascending **TRANNUMB** order.

Loading an HDAM data base
In our description of HDAM earlier we discussed the merits of two different methods of loading an HDAM data base, and interested readers should refer back to this discussion. We recall that with an HDAM data base a root segment is placed in a storage address, according to the result of applying a hashing routine to the root sequence field. The loading program does not present the hash address to DL/1, however, and the **INSRT** command to load a root segment is the

same as with other storage data bases; it is the system that automatically applies the hashing routine.

We can summarize the two methods of loading an HDAM data base in the light of the data base in Figure 10.1:

1. *Root segments first.*   Just the root **BRANCH** segments are loaded in the first stage. This ensures that as few as possible are in the overflow area. Then, for each root segment the subsidiary segments are loaded in hierarchical sequence. Almost the same method is used in this second stage as with an HSAM data base; the only difference is that the root segments are not loaded.
2. *One hierarchical occurrence at a time.*   The method used is exactly the same as with an HSAM data base. This will result in more root segments in the overflow area than with the first method (see Figure 10.15).

Security from unauthorized access

With batch processing, security is enforced primarily by means of the external data base specification (the PCB). To access the data base a program must have a PCB, and naturally this can be obtained only with the permission of the data base administrator. The PCB will constrain the program to the manipulation of certain segments only. In addition, the type of manipulation permitted is specified in the PCB by means of the **PROCOPT** entries.

In Chapter 12 we briefly cover the essentials of on-line processing with the IMS data communications feature. This provides additional security. Normally an on-line program can be executed only if a password is specified by the user at a remote terminal. In addition, only certain programs can be run from any given terminal.

Interference due to concurrent processing

IMS programs can execute concurrently as on-line programs only when the data communications feature is installed. An on-line program can prevent other programs fron interfering with its manipulation of an IMS data base in two ways. First, a specification of 'E' for the **PROCOPT** entry for a segment type gives the program exclusive control over that segment type. The program will be allowed to execute only when no other programs are using that segment type, and once the program is running, no other programs that need the segment type will be allowed to run until the program is finished. Second, as indicated already, specification of a **GET HOLD** command, such as **GHU**, will prevent other programs from updating the segment retrieved, although they may retrieve it. The program is said to hold a *shared lock* on the segment. This system can lead to deadlock, where one program holds segment *A* and is waiting for *B*, whole another holds *B* and is waiting for *A*. There is a DL/1 command **ROLL** to permit a program to roll back any changes it has made to the data base whenever deadlock is detected, thus allowing the other program to proceed. For details see Refs. 3 and 4.

Recovery

IMS has a set of support routines to permit the maintenance of a system log of all updates to the data bases, for dumping the data base at regular intervals and for restoring it following system failure. Further details are given in Refs. 1 and 3.

10.5 HIGHER MANAGEMENT USE OF AN IMS DATA BASE WITH SQL

We have so far only studied the use of IMS for batch processing, which, it must be admitted, is still the most common way to process a data base. It is also possible to have on-line processing of an IMS data base, along the lines illustrated in Figure 4.16. Here many on-line programs are concurrently processing a single copy of the data base (compare with IMS batch processing as illustrated in Figure 10.22). Typically a teleprocessing monitor or a data base/data communications system supervises the execution of these different applications programs. We shall look at this type of on-line processing in greater detail in Chapter 12.

Referring again to Figure 4.16, it is also possible to have interactive processing of an IMS data base by means of a query processor. The query language that has been used in many installations so far is IBM's Generalized Information System (GIS). Unfortunately this query language is quite complex and designed mainly for use by programmers. It appears unlikely that it will ever be used by management and the casual user. Another problem with it is that it is not very powerful compared with a language like SQL (Chapter 7).

For some time in the recent past it was widely thought that IMS would be rendered obsolete by the advent of relational data base systems, particularly System R. Such a development now seems to be highly unlikely, for the reasons explained at the beginning of this chapter. Another reason for the longevity of IMS, not mentioned at the beginning of the chapter, is that the performance of IMS is exceptionally good. The reason why should now be apparent to most readers. Just after loading a hierarchy type it is possible to retrieve a complete hierarchy occurrence with only a few accesses, since a hierarchy occurrence, no matter how large, is stored where possible as a single storage record. In contrast, with CODASYL systems and with relational systems, each of the conceptual files in Figure 10.1 would probably (although not necessarily, depending on the implementation) have its own storage file, with all the storage files connected by a pointer system; thus retrieval of a complete hierarchy occurrence could involve hundreds of accesses.

It is now almost certain that the road forward will involve the use of SQL enhancements, for both batch and query processing for IMS data bases. Currently an enhancement called SQL/DS is available for IMS running under the DOS/VS operating system. It is therefore appropriate to consider the application of SQL to a typical hierarchical data base. We have already dealt with SQL in detail in Chapters 7 and 9, and so our coverage here will be limited to dealing with situations that are likely to be common with hierarchical data bases. However, first we must consider an IMS data base in the light of relational data base design principles.

Relational IMS data bases

Readers will notice that the conceptual data base in Figure 10.1 is a relational data base, although it is also a hierarchical data base. We were careful to use a relation for each conceptual file in this data base, and with the exception of the relation **ACCOUNT**, all the relations are in fourth normal form. In addition each child relation carries the key field of its parent relation, that is, a connection field or key. From our description of IMS and DL/1 in the previous sections it is clear that connection fields are not necessary and, it must be pointed out, are rarely used in IMS data bases. However, if we are to view the data base in Figure 10.1 as a relational data base to be manipulated by languages such as SQL or QBE, as well as DL/1, then the connection fields are best included. Nevertheless, it is likely that this will never be strictly necessary with IMS data bases, since it will always be possible for an enhancement such as SQL/DS to simulate the existence of the connection fields in user views of the data base. After all, the connection field value can always be obtained from the parent segment, although possibly at a cost of an additional disk access with HDAM and HIDAM.

On balance, however, we would recommend the conservative approach, namely, that future data bases be designed as relational data bases, complete with child connection keys. This should mean that the organization will be able to take advantage of any future enhancements that will allow casual manipulation of the data base with SQL and QBE (and perhaps in the more distant future with SQL/N, which turns out to be ideally suited to hierarchical data base manipulation).

SQL retrievals with an IMS data base

In the following retrieval examples we use the external data base in Figure 10.18d, whose contents are shown in Figure 10.23. We give mainly SQL examples that are impossible with a single DL/1 expression (in fact with many DL/1 expressions), and which typify the retrieval needs of the casual user.

Retrieval-14. Computational retrieval
Find the sum of the outstanding balances of all of the loans of customer 'C2'.

The SQL expression is almost trivial, but it involves the use of the **SUM** function:

```
SELECT SUM (OUTBAL)
FROM LOAN
WHERE (CUSTNUMB = 'C2')
```

We recall that in the DL/1 Retrieval-8 we were not able to generate a DL/1 expression for taking a sum of **OUTBAL** values; with that retrieval we also discussed the widespread practice of including a summary value in the parent segment, so that each **CUSTOMER** segment would carry an extra field **DEBT** containing the total of the **OUTBAL** values in its child **LOAN** records. We saw that the problem with this was that it was necessary to update the **DEBT** field every time we updated an **OUTBAL** field, a requirement that sooner or later would be forgotten, causing loss of integrity in the data base. It is clear that the availability of SQL makes such a summary field in **CUSTOMER** unnecessary.

Retrieval-15. Predicate computational retrieval
What managers have customers whose total loans exceed $20,000?
    The SQL expression is:

```
SELECT BMANAGER FROM
FROM BRANCH
WHERE BNUMB IS IN (SELECT BNUMB
                   FROM CUSTOMER
                   WHERE 20000 >(SELECT SUM (OUTBAL)
                                 FROM LOAN
                                 WHERE CUSTNUMB = CUSTOMER.CUSTNUMB))
```

The result of this is 'WRIGHT'.
    The expression is rather long, but at least the request can be expressed in SQL. Part of the trouble is that we must specify the complete descent down the hierarchy, even though we are not really interested in **CUSTOMER** conceptual records. A related expression is to be found in Retrieval-26 in Chapter 7.

Retrieval-16. Universal quantification
Who are the managers at branches where all loans have an outstanding balance in excess of $2000?
    The SQL expression is:

```
SELECT BMANAGER
FROM BRANCH
WHERE BNUMB IS NOT IN (SELECT BNUMB
                       FROM CUSTOMER
                       WHERE CUSTNUMB IS IN (SELECT CUSTNUMB
                                             FROM LOAN
                                             WHERE (OUTBAL <= 2000)))
```

The expression is really constructed according to the retrieval request:

Find the managers of branches where there is no customer that has a loan less than or equal to $2000.

Again we must descend the hierarchy even though we are not interested in **CUSTOMER** conceptual records.
    (With SQL/N we can avoid having to specify properties of **CUSTOMER** records, as was possible with the original English request.

```
SELECT BMANAGER
FROM EACH BRANCH RECORD
WHERE (FOR EACH DESCENDANT  LOAN RECORD
          (OUTBAL > 2000))
```

Thus the expression is very close to the English expression. The word **DESCEN-DANT** permits us to skip unnecessary levels in a hierarchically structured data base, a facility not available with SQL. A **LOAN** record is a **DESCENDANT** of a **BRANCH** record, if the **BRANCH** record is ultimately an ancestor of the **LOAN** record. In the simplest case, a **LOAN** record is a **MEMBER** (or **CHILD**) of a **BRANCH** record, if the **BRANCH** record is the parent of the **LOAN** record.)

The result of this retrieval would be 'QUICKLEY' with both expressions, when applied to the data base in Figure 10.23. Note that there is a slight flaw in the SQL expression. It is not quite complete and would retrieve the names of managers with no loans. This type of problem was discussed at length in Chapter 7, and interested readers should complete the SQL expression. [With the SQL/N expression, we can solve the problem by replacing **FOR EACH (IF ANY)** by **FOR ONE AND FOR ALL**.]

Retrieval-17. Ascending the hierarchy
What is the highest interest rate being paid on a savings account at branches in Oakland?

The SQL expression is:

```
SELECT MAX(ACCINT)
FROM ACCOUNT
WHERE CUSTNUMB IS IN (SELECT CUSTNUMB
                      FROM CUSTOMER
                      WHERE BNUMB IS IN (SELECT BNUMB
                                         FROM BRANCH
                                         WHERE (CITY = 'OAKLAND')
```

This time we have to ascend the hierarchy, with a specification of the intermediate **CUSTOMER** records even though we do not need them. Nevertheless, an expression is easy to construct with SQL, while with DL/1 it would not be possible. (As in the previous example, we can eliminate expression of unnecessary conceptual **CUSTOMER** records with SQL/N:

```
SELECT MAX(ACCINT)
FROM EACH ACCOUNT RECORD
WHERE (THERE IS ONE ASCENDANT BRANCH RECORD
                        (WHERE (CITY = 'OAKLAND')))
```

Here we use the specification **ASCENDANT** in the same way we used **DESCEN-DANT** in the previous retrieval.)

Note on use of SQL with a host programming language
In theory it would be possible to provide an enhancement that would allow SQL to be used with a COBOL or PL/1 host language to process an IMS data base that had a relational structure. The advantage would probably be improved programmer productivity, since a lot of involved programming could often be replaced by a single SQL expression. Currently there is no sign of such a development. It cannot be ruled out, however, and is an obvious next step for the developers of IMS.

SUMMARY

1. IMS is an older but widely used system from IBM. It was designed before the ANSI/SPARC three-level data base structure became widely accepted, although an IMS data base does conform to some degree to the ANSI/SPARC recommendations. Since its introduction many new features have been added.

2. We must distinguish between IMS data bases with a clear hierarchical structure and those with a near hierarchical structure, for the methods of handling them are quite different. The first type is covered in the body of the chapter and summarized here, while the other type is covered in the chapter supplement.

3. The conceptual and storage definitions are combined in a single schema (the DBD). An IMS conceptual data base is a hierarchy type, made up of hierarchy occurrences. There are many distinct ways of constructing the storage version of a hierarchy type. Within a hierarchy type, conceptual records (or segments) are stored and are available in hierarchical sequence order.

4. An IMS data base manipulation program communicates with the data base system via a user work area and a collection of registers called a PCB-mask. There is a separate user work area (UWA) and PCB-mask for each data base the program manipulates, for a program can manipulate more than one data base. The data manipulation language is a procedural language called DL/1. It is designed for manipulation of hierarchy occurrences, and permits the construction of commands involving multiple segments and quite complex retrieval conditions. Because many segments can be retrieved in a single disk access, IMS performs quite well.

5. Because of its wide use, it seems unlikely that IMS will be replaced in the foreseeable future, despite the development of System R. Instead it seems likely that enhancements will appear, which allow for the manipulation of IMS data bases with SQL.

QUESTIONS

1. Show the records from **LOAN** in Figure 10.3 in hierarchical sequence order.
2. Show the records from **TRANSACTION** in Figure 10.3 in hierarchical sequence.
3. Redraw Figure 10.6 if **TELLER** has the sequence code 3 and **CUSTOMER** the sequence code 2.
4. In Figures 5.21 and 5.22, assuming that **INVENTORY** has the sequence code 3 and **EMPLOYEE** the sequence code 2, give the records in hierarchical sequence.
5. Repeat Question 4 this time placing the records in fully concatenated key sequence.
6. Give the root segments for the IMS data base in Figure 5.22.
7. For the data base in Figure 5.21, give the conceptual part of the DBD.
8. Draw a HSAM data base for the hierarchy occurrences in Figure 5.22.
9. Draw a HISAM data base for the hierarchy occurrences in Figure 5.22. Use ISAM.

10. Repeat Question 9 using VSAM.
11. Draw a hierarchical pointer system for the segments in Figure 5.22.
12. Draw a child/twin pointer system for the segments in Figure 5.22.
13. Give three examples of external data bases derived from the data base in Figure 5.21.
14. Give a PCB for an external data base that is identical to the data base in Figure 5.21.

Questions 15–37 deal with the data base in Figure 10.1, which we assume has been defined as an IMS external data base. Use the PCB and UWA definitions given in the chapter, and construct appropriate COBOL DL/1 program excerpts.

15. Find the city in which the first branch is located.
16. Find the city in which the second and third branches are located.
17. Find the manager of the first branch in a city other than San José.
18. Find the names of all cities that have branches.
19. Find the date of birth of the first customer called Green.
20. Find the names of all customers born between 1940 and 1950.
21. Find the account number of the first savings account that pays more than 11% annual interest.
22. Find the account number of the first account in Oakland that pays more than 11%.
23. Find the account numbers of all the accounts in Oakland that pay more than 11%.
24. Find the outstanding balance for each of Brown's loans. Use the first Brown.
25. Find the outstanding balance for each of Brown's accounts. Use the first Brown.
26. Find all the salaries paid at Oakland. Assume that there are several branches in Oakland.
27. Find the total bank payroll in Oakland, assuming several branches in that city.
28. Find the customer name, account number, and outstanding balance for each customer of branch 'B1'.
29. For each branch, find the branch manager's name and the names of the customers at that branch.
30. Add the following **CUSTOMER** record or segment to the data base:

    (B2 C7 SMITH 19580421)

31. Add the following **LOAN** record to the data base:

    (C2 L2 15,000 13.0)

32. Add the following **TRANSACTION** record to the data base:

    (A7 TR15 DEPOS 300   ?)

33. Customer 'C2' pays off all loans. Update the data by deleting the appropriate LOAN records or segments.

34. Customer 'C2' pays back 100 dollars on loan 'L4'. Update the data base.
35. Customer 'C2' moves to Oakland taking all accounts and loans to the Oakland branch. Update the data base
36. Customer 'C2' closes all accounts, and pays off all loans. Update the data base.
37. Assuming that the data in **BRANCH TELLER**, and **CUSTOMER** in Figure 10.3 is available on the tape files **XBRANCH**, **XTELLER**, and **XCUSTOMER**. Write a COBOL program excerpt to load part of the data base, assuming that HISAM is being used. State how the data in the source files should be sorted, assuming that the hierarchy occurrences are loaded sequentially.

Use SQL with the following retrievals from the database in Figure 10.1.

38. What branches have no customers with an account whose balance is below $1,000?
39. What customers are being paid more than 11% on a loan in San José?
40. What are the total deposits at branches in Oakland?
41. How much money in total do customers at branch 'B1' owe the bank?
42. At what branches are there loans in excess of $12,000?

ADDITIONAL PERSPECTIVE
APPLYING IMS TO NETWORK STRUCTURED DATA BASES

So far we have dealt only with an IMS data base that has a hierarchical structure at the conceptual level. We mentioned at the beginning of this chapter that IMS could also handle the case where the conceptual data base (or more precisely the enterprise data base) has a limited network structure. By a limited network, we mean one where most conceptual files have one parent file each, but a few have more than one. This supplement deals with how such limited network data bases are handled in IMS. We begin with an example of a limited network.

A limited network data base in the banking industry

Our limited network data base is a modification of the banking data base that we have been dealing with all along, shown orginally in Figure 10.1 (with sample contents in Figure 10.3). An assumption in that design was that while a branch could have many customers, a customer could have only one branch. This assumption could not hold in practice, for it will frequently happen that a customer has accounts (and possibly even loans) from more than one branch. Thus in practice there will be a many-to-many relationship between branches and customers: A customer has accounts at many branches, while a branch has accounts belonging to many customers.

Another way of looking at this in the light of the original data base in Figure

10.1 would involve allowing for the fact that **CUSTNUMB** values in **CUSTOMER** segments were not unique (see also Figure 10.23), so that a **CUSTOMER** segment with **CUSTNUMB** value 'C1' could appear in several hierarchy occurrences; this is allowed in IMS, and there is no requirement that segments be unique, or that a unique sequence field be specified in the DBD (Figure 10.9). However, there are two problems with handling the many-to-many relationship between branches and customers in this way. First, it will cause a very large duplication of data if many customers deal at several branches, with a risk of inconsistent updates of **CUSTOMER** segments. Second, it will be difficult to retrieve information about the different branches a customer deals with. To find all the branches that customer 'C1' has accounts with would require a sequential search of all the **CUSTOMER** segments in the data base. Information of this type could be needed quite often; it is clear that a loan officer, considering a loan to a customer, would have more than a passing interest in the activities of that customer at other branches (also at other banks, but that is another story).

A better approach is to look at the data base in Figure 10.1 as a network, and a modified version is shown in Figure 10.24. To keep our analysis simple, we have omitted the conceptual files **LOAN** and **TRANSACTION**. Here we see clearly that a customer has many accounts, but possibly at different branches, while a branch has many accounts belonging to different customers. Thus the many-to-many relationship between **BRANCH** and **CUSTOMER** breaks down into two one-to-many relationships between **BRANCH** and **ACCOUNT** and between **CUSTOMER** and **ACCOUNT**. Notice that all the child connection fields are included, and that because this data base has a different structure from the one in Figure 10.1, the **CUSTOMER** and **ACCOUNT** conceptual files have been modified to allow for the connection fields.

Some sample records from the conceptual files in Figure 10.24 are shown in Figure 10.25. We have used just enough data in Figure 10.25 to make the example realistic. Notice that, for example, customer 'C1' has an account ('A4') at branch 'B2', and also an account ('A8') at branch 'B1'. Similarly, customer 'C2' has accounts at different branches.

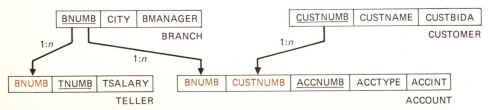

FIGURE 10.24 Modified version of the hierarchical data base in Figure 10.1. For simplicity we have not included the conceptual files LOAN and TRANSACTION. In the original hierarchical data base it was assumed that a customer would always have his or her savings accounts as a single branch. In this data base a customer can have many accounts at different branches, and a branch has many accounts belonging to different customers. Thus there is a many-to-many relationship between BRANCH and CUSTOMER determined by the distributions of savings accounts over branches and customers. We could have another many-to-many relationship between BRANCH and CUSTOMER determined by the distribution of loans over branches and customers, as is illustrated in Figure 10.26.

BNUMB	CITY	BMANAGER
B1	SAN JOSE	WRIGHT
B2	OAKLAND	QUICKLEY

BRANCH

CUSTNUMB	CUSTNAME	CUSTBIDA
C1	SMITH	19450915
C2	GREEN	19380723

CUSTOMER

BNUMB	TNUMB	TSALARY
B2	T1	15,000
B1	T2	14,500
B1	T3	16,000

TELLER

BNUMB	CUSTNUMB	ACCNUMB	ACCTYPE	ACCINT
B1	C2	A3	SAVINGS-A	10.0
B2	C1	A4	SAVINGS-A	10.0
B2	C2	A7	SAVINGS-B	12.5
B1	C1	A8	SAVINGS-B	12.5

ACCOUNT

FIGURE 10.25 Shows some records from the conceptual files in Figure 10.24.

A many-to-many relationship determined by loans at different branches
We have not considered another disturbing flaw in the data base in Figure 10.1. If a customer can have accounts at different branches, what is to prevent a customer having loans at different branches? Nothing really, unless the bank has a policy that prohibits such loans. Such a policy might be bad for business, but it would certainly simplify the data base. For the sake of completeness we show how the data base in Figure 10.1 can be modified to give the idealized network data base in Figure 10.26. This might be regarded as more than just a limited network. However, it can be handled in IMS by the techniques soon to be described. Nevertheless we shall illustrate these special IMS techniques using the simpler data base in Figure 10.24, with only one many-to-many relationship. With this data base we might assume that loans to a customer at multiple branches violates bank policy.

Note on enterprise data bases with IMS
Both conceptual data bases in Figures 10.24 and 10.26 are what we may call *enterprise* data bases, as explained at the start of Chapter 5. The corresponding conceptual data base with IMS is not a single data base at all, but a collection of

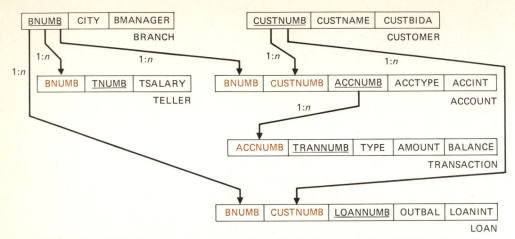

FIGURE 10.26 Modification of the data base in Figure 10.1 to allow for the possibility of a customer having both accounts at different branches and loans from different branches. This results in two many-to-many relationships between BRANCH and CUSTOMER. There is one many-to-many relationship because a branch has many accounts belonging to different customers, and because a customer has many accounts at different branches. There is another one because a branch has issued many loans to different customers, and because a customer has taken out loans at many different branches. Thus the data base becomes a network. It could be handled by the IMS logical data base techniques described in the following pages. However, we use the simpler network data base in Figure 10.24 to illustrate these techniques.

IMS hierarchical data bases. IMS can accommodate a network data base only if it is first split into a collection of smaller hierarchical data bases as we shall now see.

Decomposing networks into hierarchies

If we look closely at the network data base in Figure 10.24, we see that it could be split into two hierarchical data bases. This can be done in two ways:

1. One conceptual data base has BRANCH, TELLER, and ACCOUNT conceptual files, and the other just the CUSTOMER conceptual file.
2. One conceptual data base has BRANCH and TELLER conceptual files, and the other the CUSTOMER and ACCOUNT files.

Either way we get a pair of conceptual data bases, each with a hierarchical structure. Somewhat arbitrarily we choose the second pair to show how IMS can handle the original network data base. This second pair of data bases is shown in Figure 10.27, and using the data from Figure 10.25, the contents of the hierarchy occurrences for these hierarchical conceptual data bases are also shown.

For each of these data bases we would generate a distinct DBD (see Figure 10.9); we give the name BRANCHDB to the data base in Figure 10.27a and the name CUSTDB to the data base in Figure 10.27b. If we now simply load these two data bases, it would in theory be possible to process them as if they formed the

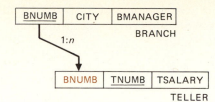

BRANCHDB conceptual data base

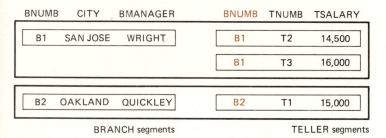

(a) IMS conceptual data base BRANCHDB (top), with storage hierarchy occurrences (bottom).

CUSTDB conceptual data base

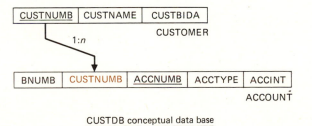

(b) IMS conceptual data base CUSTDB (top), with storage hierarchy occurrences (bottom).

FIGURE 10.27   Shows how the network data base in Figure 10.24 can be split into IMS hierarchical data bases BRANCHDB and CUSTDB.

single data base in Figure 10.24, but it would be awkward and often involve a lot of tedious programming. The programmer would always have to remember the structures of two data bases, and the navigation would involve jumping around between them. We give a few examples.

Suppose that we wanted to retrieve the names of the branch managers at the branches customer 'C1' deals with. We could start by accessing the CUSTDB data base, to get the first ACCOUNT segment:

```
GU CUSTOMER (CUSTNUMB = C1)
    ACCOUNT
```

Taking the BNUMB value out of the UWA (we have omitted the name of the block of special registers and the UWA structure from the command), we then retrieve the BRANCH segment from the BRANCHDB data base:

```
GU BRANCH (BNUMB = B2)
```

and referring to Figure 10.27, we see that the name of the branch manager in the UWA structure will be 'QUICKLEY'. We would then apply a GNP command to the CUSTDB data base, once more using the retrieved BNUMB value to access the BRANCHDB data base, and so on, until all child ACCOUNT segments of the CUSTOMER segment with CUSTNUMB value 'C1' have been processed. We notice that it is possible to get from the CUSTDB data base to the BRANCHDB data base only because the child BNUMB connection field from the ACCOUNT file in the original network data base is included in the ACCOUNT segments of the IMS CUSTDB. Often such child connection fields would not be included in IMS data bases since strictly they are unnecessary. The conclusion is that by means of a judicious inclusion of child connection fields, it is possible but inconvenient to process two IMS data bases to handle a many-to-many relationship in an idealized network data base.

Another example would involve the retrieval of accounts at the branch 'B1'. In the idealized network data base in Figure 10.24, the retrieval would involve obtaining the child ACCOUNT records of a BRANCH record. Unfortunately ACCOUNT is not a child of BRANCH in either the IMS CUSTDB or BRANCHDB data base. Thus the only solution is to scan all the ACCOUNT segments in the CUSTDB data base, picking out those with BNUMB value equal to 'B1'. Thus the processing of the many-to-many relationship between BRANCH and CUSTOMER in the idealized network data base is again possible by means of the split IMS data bases, but it is not very efficient in this case. Of course we could improve things if we were to construct an IMS secondary index for BNUMB in ACCOUNT in the IMS data base CUSTDB. This would avoid the need for a sequential scan to find all the ACCOUNT segments for a given branch.

However, there is another solution to these problems of processing a network data base by splitting it into hierarchical data bases, and that solution involves the construction of what are known as IMS logical data bases. This method is very widely used, is convenient for programmers, and is quite good as far as performance is concerned.

IMS LOGICAL DATA BASES

Let us suppose that when using the conceptual data base CUSTDB in Figure 10.27a, we frequently need the parent BRANCH record (in Figure 10.24). One way to achieve this is to have a new data base as shown in Figure 10.28a. This

CUSTNUMB	CUSTNAME	CUSTBIDA

CUSTOMER

1:*n*

BNUMB	CUSTNUMB	ACCNUMB	ACCTYPE	ACCINT	BNUMB	CITY	MANAGER

ACC-BRAN

(a) Secondary conceptual data base (IMS terminology: logical data base, second kind) formed by attaching the parent BRANCH record to each child ACCOUNT record in the CUSTDB data base in Figure 10.27*b*. The BRANCH records are not physically attached but are connected to the ACCOUNT records by a (logical) pointer system. We shall call this data base CUSTLDB. There is no storage CUSTLDB data base.

C1	SMITH	19450915						
			B2	C1	A4	SAVINGS-A	10.0	B2	OAKLAND	QUICKLEY
			B1	C1	A8	SAVINGS-B	12.5	B1	SAN JOSE	WRIGHT

C2	GREEN	19380723						
			B1	C2	A3	SAVINGS-A	10.0	B1	SAN JOSE	WRIGHT
			B2	C2	A7	SAVINGS-B	12.5	B2	OAKLAND	QUICKLEY

CUSTOMER segments   ACC-BRAN segments

(b) The hierarchy occurrences of the secondary data base CUSTLDB in (a). This should not be interpreted as the storage data base for CUSTLDB, since it does not have one. The CUSTLDB data base is simulated by using a pointer system to connect the storage data bases for BRANCHDB and CUSTDB, as illustrated in Figure 10.29.

FIGURE 10.28

new data base is much the same as the **CUSTDB** data base from Figure 10.27*b*, except that the **ACCOUNT** records have been replaced by **ACC-BRAN** records. An **ACC-BRAN** record is an **ACCOUNT** record joined or concatenated to its parent **BRANCH** record (in Figure 10.24). The hierarchy occurrences for this new data base are shown in Figure 10.28*a*. We call this data base **CUSTLDB**.

With this data base, finding the manager of a branch that customer 'C1' deals with now involves the use of only one data base. To find the first such manager, we simply issue the DL/1 command:

```
GU CUSTOMER (BNUMB = 'C1')
   ACC-BRAN
```

and the required **BMANAGER** value will be in the UWA. This is all very well, but some readers may object that now we have **BRANCH** segments in the IMS

BRANCHDB data base in Figure 10.27*a*, and again in our new **CUSTLDB** data base in Figure 10.28, a clear duplication of data and likely to lead to inconsistency in the data bases. This is not the case, however, because the new **CUSTLDB** is a special form of conceptual data base found only in IMS and called a *logical data base* (LDB). [Just to confuse matters, a normal external data base defined in IMS by a PCB (see end of Section 10.3) is also called a logical data base.]

What is special about an IMS logical data base of this type is that it is a conceptual data base that does not have an underlying storage data base as do more standard (physical, in IMS terminology) conceptual data bases such as **BRANCHDB** and **CUSTDB** in Figure 10.27. Instead a storage data base for the logical data base is simulated using a pointer system within the storage data bases underlying the conceptual data bases from which the logical data base is derived.

This is illustrated in Figure 10.29. The conventional way to represent the pointer system is to draw (conceptual-level) diagrams for the two conceptual data bases involved as we have done in Figure 10.29*a*, and include a pointer (shown in color in the diagram; remember that the extended Bachman arrow in black is not a pointer) to show how a child **ACCOUNT** record in **CUSTDB** is connected to the parent **BRANCH** record in **BRANCHDB**. While this method is widely used in the literature about IMS, it can be confusing, because it is also widely agreed that pointers have no place in conceptual-level data base diagrams. The alternative in Figure 10.29*b* shows how the two storage data bases are connected by pointers from each **CUSTDB ACCOUNT** segment to each **BRANCHDB BRANCH** segment. The data bases in Figure 10.29*b* should be regarded as storage data bases, even though we have omitted the details of how the segments are actually packed onto the disk (see Section 10.2). It is on the basis of the pointer system that IMS enables the user to imagine that there is a **CUSTLDB** data base.

External data bases derived from logical data bases

While the IMS logical data base **CUSTLDB** could easily be regarded as a user view of the combined **CUSTDB** and **BRANCHDB** data bases, and thus as an external data base, it is more accurate in practice to regard it just as a special IMS conceptual data base without its own storage data base. The main reason for doing so is that we can also specify external data bases (using PCB definitions) that are derived from this special logical data base. With the simple logical data base **CUSTLDB** in Figure 10.28, only two possible external data bases could be derived, and these are:

1. The hierarchical data base consisting of just **CUSTOMER** segments
2. The hierarchical data base that is the same as **CUSTLDB**

However, it is not quite true to assume that a logical data base, or external data bases derived from it, can be treated in the same way as conventional IMS conceptual and external data bases. There are difficulties with updating, as we shall see shortly.

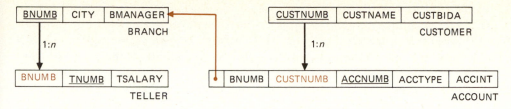

BRANCHDB conceptual data base · CUSTDB conceptual data base

(*a*) Conceptual-level diagram indicating how ACCOUNT records are connected to BRANCH records to form the imaginary ACC-BRAN records in the secondary (or logical) data base CUSTLDB in Figure 10.28. The details of the logical parent pointers used in the two storage data bases for BRANCHDB and CUSTDB are shown in (*b*), A BRANCH record is said to be a logical parent of an ACCOUNT record; an ACCOUNT record in turn is a logical child of BRANCH and a physical child of CUSTOMER.

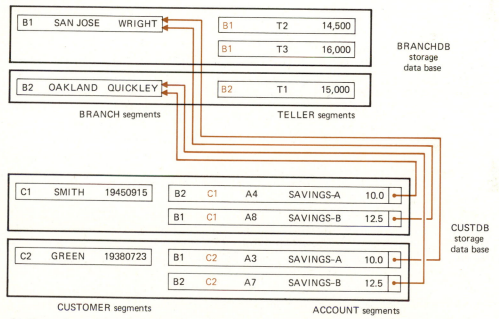

(*b*) Shows how the secondary conceptual data base CUSTLDB in Figure 10.28 may be simulated by means of logical parent pointers in the storage data bases for BRANCHDB and CUSTDB. There is no storage data base for CUSTLDB.

FIGURE 10.29

Terminology with IMS logical data bases

In Section 10.2 we covered a lot of the details of IMS storage data bases, much more than with any other system described in this book. We did this because of (1) the widespread use of IMS and (2) the impossibility of grasping the IMS logical data base concepts and terminology without a knowledge of IMS storage data bases.

The pointers used in the IMS storage data bases described in Section 10.2 are called *physical* pointers. Similarly, the child segments in standard IMS conceptual data bases (for example, those in Figure 10.27) are called *physical child* segments, and parent segments are called *physical parent* segments; in addition, segments of the same type with the same parent are called *physical twins*. For example, in Figure 10.27a, the TELLER segments with TNUMB values 'T2' and 'T3' are physical twins. Indeed a standard conceptual data base in IMS is called a *physical data base*, and a conceptual hierarchy occurrence is called a *physical data base record* (PDBR), as mentioned earlier.

In contrast, the pointers used to connect storage data bases to simulate a logical data base are called *logical pointers*, even though they are in storage data bases. In particular, the parent pointers in Figure 10.29b are called *logical parent* pointers. Furthermore, a BRANCH segment in BRANCHDB is a *logical parent* of an ACCOUNT segment in CUSTDB, while the ACCOUNT segment in turn is a *logical child* of the BRANCH segment.

Alternatives to the terms physical and logical are *primary* and *secondary*, respectively, which the author finds leads to a reduction in confusion. Thus the physical IMS conceptual data base is a primary conceptual data base with primary child and parent segments in the storage data base, and primary pointers. An IMS logical data base is then a secondary conceptual data base derived from primary data bases with secondary pointers in their storage data bases. As a result of this, some of the segments of the primary conceptual data bases are secondary children and parents as well.

Defining an IMS logical data base

In Section 10.2 we showed how to specify the conceptual part of a DBD, the combined conceptual and storage data base definition. The storage part of the DBD was not given since it involved considerable detail involving hierarchical access methods and pointers (hierarchical or child/twin). The definition of a logical or secondary data base involves similar details that are beyond the scope of this book. We shall merely give an outline. To specify the logical data base CUSTLDB in Figure 10.28, we need:

1. A DBD for the primary BRANCHDB data base (Figure 10.27a) that includes:
   (a) The usual conceptual part as in Figure 10.9
   (b) The storage part including a specification of the fact that BRANCH is a logical parent of ACCOUNT segments defined in the DBD for CUSTDB
2. A DBD for the primary CUSTDB data base (Figure 10.27b) that includes:
   (a) The usual conceptual part
   (b) The storage part including a specification of the logical parent pointer (see Figure 10.29b), as well as a specification that ACCOUNT segments are logical children of BRANCH segments defined in the DBD for BRANCHDB

3. A logical DBD for the **CUSTLDB** data base (Figure 10.28*a*) that specifies how the segments in the data base are derived from the physical or primary **BRANCHDB** and **CUSTDB** data bases

If **BRANCHDB** is the name of the DBD in (1), **CUSTDB** the name of the DBD in (2), and **CUSTLDB** the name of the logical DBD in (3), then the logical DBD **CUSTLDB** is defined approximately as follows:

```
DBD     NAME=CUSTLDB,ACCESS=LOGICAL
SEGM    NAME=CUSTOMER,SOURCE=((CUSTOMER,,CUSTDB))
SEGM    NAME=ACC-BRAN,PARENT=CUSTOMER,
        SOURCE=((ACCOUNT,,CUSTDB),(BRANCH,,BRANCHDB))
```

In the **CUSTOMER** segment definition we state that **CUSTOMER** segments are derived from **CUSTOMER** segments in the **CUSTDB** data base. In the **ACC-BRAN** definition (Figure 10.28*a*) we state that **CUSTOMER** in **CUSTLDB** is the parent segment, and that the **ACC-BRAN** segments are derived from **ACCOUNT** segments in the **CUSTDB** data base and **BRANCH** segments in the **BRANCHDB** data base. (The double commas indicate omitted parameters.)

Logical child and logical twin segments

Referring to the original idealized network data base in Figure 10.24 again, we see that the logical data base **CUSTLDB** enables a programmer to easily navigate from an **ACCOUNT** record to a **BRANCH** record, or in broader terms, from a **CUSTOMER** record to a **BRANCH** record via an **ACCOUNT** record. But supposing we want to navigate from a **BRANCH** record to a **CUSTOMER** record via an **ACCOUNT** record. We need a new logical data base to do that, as shown in Figure 10.30.

The new logical data base **BRAN-LDB** is derived from the two primary conceptual data bases **BRANCHDB** and **CUSTDB**. It contains a segment type **ACC-CUST** that is taken from the **CUSTDB** data base by concatenating **ACCOUNT** segments to their (physical) parent **CUSTOMER** segments. The pointer system in the storage **BRANCHDB** and **CUSTDB** data bases to accomplish this is shown in Figure 10.31. Each **BRANCH** segment in the **BRANCHDB** storage data base has a logical child pointer to its first logical child **ACCOUNT** segment (in hierarchical sequence). Each first logical child **ACCOUNT** segment has a logical twin pointer to the next logical twin **ACCOUNT** record with the same logical parent, and so on. At the same time each **ACCOUNT** segment in the **CUSTDB** storage data base has a physical pointer to its parent **CUSTOMER** segment to simulate the **ACC-CUST** segments of the logical **BRAN-LDB** data base.

Notice that in the **BRAN-LDB** logical data base in Figure 10.28*a*, the **BRANCH** segments are derived from the **BRANCHDB** primary data base, while the **ACC-CUST** segments are derived from the **CUSTDB** primary data base.

With the **BRAN-LDB** logical data base we can easily navigate from branches

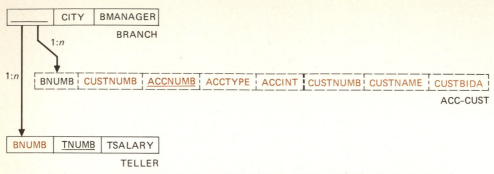

(a) A secondary (or logical) conceptual data base formed from the data bases BRANCHDB and CUSTDB in Figure 10.27. We shall call this logical data base BRAN-LDB. The ACC-CUST records do not physically exist in any storage data base, for BRAN-LDB has no storage data base. Instead, an ACC-CUST record is formed by joining an ACCOUNT record in CUSTDB to its parent CUSTOMER record; however, the join is not physical and is accomplished by means of a pointer system in the BRANCHDB and CUSTDB storage data bases (see Figure 10.31). Some hierarchy occurrences from the BRAN-LDB data base are shown in (b).

| BRANCH segments | TELLER, ACC-CUST segments |

(b) The hierarchy occurrences of the secondary or logical data base BRAN-LDB in (a). This should not be interpreted as the storage data base for BRAN-LDB, for there is none. BRAN-LDB is simulated by means of a pointer system in the storage versions of BRANCHDB and CUSTDB.

FIGURE 10.30

to customers. For example, if we wanted the names of customers at branch 'B1', to find the first one, we could issue:

```
GU BRANCH (BNUMB = B1)
   ACC-CUST
```

The first **ACC-CUST** segment would be placed in the UWA structure whence the **CUSTNAME** value could be obtained. Continuing with a loop containing **GNP** commands gives us the remaining names.

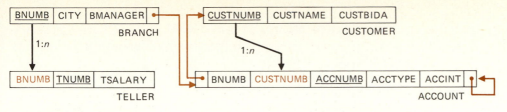

BRANCHDB conceptual data base   *CUSTDB conceptual data base*

(*a*) Conceptual-level diagram indicating how BRANCH records are connected to ACCOUNT records which are in turn connected to CUSTOMER records, in order to form the secondary or logical data base in Figure 10.30. The details of the pointer system are shown in (*b*). Here ACCOUNT is a logical child of BRANCH, and a BRANCH record is a logical parent of ACCOUNT. ACCOUNT records with the same logical parent are called logical (or secondary) twins.

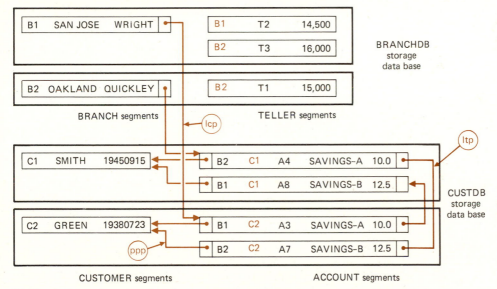

(*b*) Shows how the secondary conceptual data base BRAN-LDB in Figure 10.2 may be simulated by both logical child pointers (lcp), logical twin pointers (ltp), and physical parent pointers (ppp) in the storage data bases for BRANCHDB and CUSTDB. There is no storage data base for BRAN-LDB.

FIGURE 10.31

VIRTUAL PAIRING

We have now shown how the logical or secondary data bases **CUSTLDB** and **BRAN-LDB** may be constructed using logical or secondary pointers in the storage data bases for the primary or physical data bases **CUSTDB** and **BRANCHDB**. **CUSTLDB** enables the programmer to navigate from **CUSTOMER** segments to **BRANCH** segments, while **BRAN-LDB** enables the programmer to navigate from **BRANCH** to **CUSTOMER** segments. Thus, taken together these two logical data bases permit manipulation of the conceptual records involved in the many-to-many relationship between **BRANCH** and **CUSTOMER** in the idealized network data base in Figure 10.24, and from which the primary hierarchical data bases **BRANCHDB** and **CUSTDB** are derived.

Normally both logical data bases **BRAN-LDB** and **CUSTLDB** would be defined together. This means that the necessary pointer systems for both logical data bases have to be incorporated into the underlying storage data bases for the primary data bases **CUSTDB** and **BRANCHDB**, as is shown in Figure 10.32. The necessary definitions are:

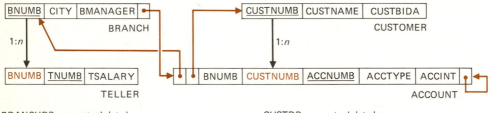

(a) Conventional representation of the logical pointer systems in virtual pairing. The actual pointers are shown in (b). The diagram is a combination of the diagrams in Figures 10.29a and 10.31a to support the logical data bases CUSTLDB and BRAN-LDB.

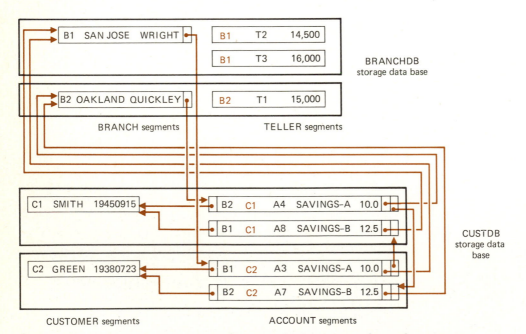

(b) The logical pointer systems in virtual pairing; the diagram combines the pointers

FIGURE 10.32 Virtual pairing. The conceptual file TELLER plays no part in the virtual pairing and could be omitted.

1. DBD for **CUSTDB** including logical pointer system
2. DBD for **BRANCHDB** including logical pointer system
3. A logical DBD for the logical data base **CUSTLDB**, showing the source of segments defined
4. A logical DBD for the logical data base **BRAN-LDB**, showing the source of the segments defined

With IMS, the definition of a pair of logical data bases in this way to handle a many-to-many relationship is known as virtual pairing. For specification details see Refs. 1 and 2.

Complexity in IMS data bases

A glance at the pointer system in Figure 10.32 indicates that the underlying physical data bases to support virtual pairing are complex. It should be remembered that the logical pointer system is in addition to the usual physical pointers to support storage HISAM, HDAM, or HIDAM. As a result IMS storage data bases are probably among the most complex, and readers should compare with the considerably less complex storage data base in Figure 5.26 for handling a CODASYL storage data base.

In defense of IMS complexity it can be argued that it is systems programmers that set up the necessary logical data bases, and that once these are set up, it is a relatively simple matter for programmers to write programs to manage the resulting hierarchical data bases. Another defense is that the use of storage data bases permits large numbers of segments in a single hierarchy occurrence to be retrieved in a single access, thus contributing to the high performance of IMS.

Updating a logical data base

While it is possible to use DL/1 to retrieve segments from a logical data base exactly as if it were a physical (or primary) data base, this is not the case for the use of the DL/1 updating commands **INSRT**, **DLET**, and **REPL**. The problem is the effect on the underlying physical data bases of operations carried out on logical segments that are constructed from two physical segments. An example is the logical **ACC-BRAN** segments in the logical **CUSTLDB** data base in Figure 10.28*a*. For example, if we delete an **ACC-BRAN** segment, with this data base we probably want to delete only the underlying **ACCOUNT** segment in the **CUSTDB** data base, and not the **BRANCH** segment in the **BRANCHDB** data base. However, with a different logical data base with the same structure, we might want to delete the equivalent of the **BRANCH** segment. Similarly, we could have a number of desirable outcomes to deletion of **CUSTOMER** segments in both the **CUSTDB** and **CUSTLDB** data bases, and so on. Also, more than one desired outcome is in theory possible with the DL/1 **INSRT** and **DLET** commands.

In order to ensure that an updating command has only one effect and that the effect is known in advance, an updating specification must be placed in the logical DBD following each segment specified. The full details of these specifications and their effects on processing are complex and beyond the scope of this book (see Ref. 2).

QUESTIONS

In the following questions, we assume the enterprise data base in Figure 10.24 with the data shown in Figure 10.25. In addition we assume the logical data bases **CUSTLDB** *in Figure 10.28 and* **BRAN-LDB** *in Figure 10.30. Assuming that the special registers for the data base* **CUSTLDB** *are in the structure* **CUSTPCB**, *while the registers for the data base* **BRAN-LDB** *are in the structure* **BRANPCB**, *construct COBOL DL/1 excerpts for the following retrievals.*

43. In what cities does customer 'C2' bank?
44. What customers bank at branches in Oakland?
45. At what branches is there at least one account that pays over 11%?
46. Find the data of birth of customers whose bank manager is called Quickley.
47. Find the names of the tellers at branches at which customer 'C2' has an account.

IMS ACRONYMS

The following acronyms appear in the order in which they are first mentioned in the text.

IMS	Information Management System, a hierarchical data base system from IBM.
CICS	Customer Information Control System, a teleprocessing monitor from IBM which interfaces to IMS. It is covered in Chapter 12.
DBD	Data Base Description, a combined IMS conceptual and storage schema.
PDB	Physical Data Base, a hierarchy type. (A hierarchy type is a collection of hierarchy occurrences, and both are conceptual-level structures.)
PDBR	Physical Data Base Record, a hierarchy occurrence.
HSAM	Hierarchical Sequential Access Method. Hierarchy occurrences can be stored on tape.
HISAM	Hierarchical Indexed Sequential Access Method. Hierarchy occurrences stored as ISAM or VSAM indexed-sequential files with special provision for overflow.
HDAM	Hierarchical Direct Access Method. Hierarchy occurrences stored as a hash file.
HIDAM	Hierarchical Indexed Direct Access Method. Root sequence fields of hierarchy occurrences stored as ISAM or VSAM indexed-sequential file with special provision for overflow. Each root sequence field is accompanied by a pointer to a direct access file containing the hierarchy occurrences.
ISAM	Indexed Sequential Access Method, covered in Chapter 2.
VSAM	Virtual Sequential Access Method, covered in Chapter 2. Used for constructing indexed-sequential files.
OSAM	Overflow Sequential Access Method. Used for storage overflow hierarchy occurrences and segments in IMS storage data bases.

ESDS   Entry Sequenced Dataset. Part of the VSAM package, used for storing overflow hierarchy occurrences and segments in IMS storage data bases.

LDB   Logical Data Base. First meaning: an external data base derived from a hierarchy type. Second meaning: a conceptual data base derived from one or more hierarchy types and used to simulate a network conceptual data base.

PCB   Program Communications Block. An external data base definition. A PCB-mask is a collection of special registers for communication between DL/1 and an application program.

PSB   Program Specification Block. The collection of PCBs for the external data bases manipulated by an application program.

DL/1   Data Language One. The IMS procedural data manipulation language.

GIS   Generalized Information System. A query language for use with IMS data bases.

REFERENCES

1. Cardenas. A. F., 1979. *Data Base Management Systems*. Allyn and Bacon, Boston, Mass.
2. Date, C. J., 1981. *An Introduction to Database Systems*. Addison-Wesley, Reading, Mass.
3. Fernandez, E. B., R. C. Summers, and C. Wood, 1981. *Database Security and Integrity*. Addison-Wesley, Reading, Mass.
4. IBM, *IMS/VS General Information Manual*. Form Number GH20–1260.
5. MRI, *System 2000 Reference Manual*. MRI System Corp., Austin, Texas.
6. Walsh, M. E., 1981. *Information Management Systems/Virtual Storage*. Reston, Reston, Va.

TOTAL and ADABAS

There are a considerable number of data base systems in commercial use that do not fit into the category of CODASYL, relational, or hierarchical system. In this chapter we select just two of these systems for a brief review. We shall look at a system called TOTAL and a system called ADABAS. Both systems are very versatile and can handle any network data base. We begin with TOTAL.

TOTAL is a very widely used system from Cincom Systems Inc. In some ways it can be regarded as a streamlined version of the CODASYL approach, although there are important differences. TOTAL is available for use with the commonly used mainframe and supermini operating systems. It is backed up by a wide variety of peripheral systems, such as the teleprocessing monitor EN-VIRON/1. For details of TOTAL, see Ref. 2. Overviews are given in Refs. 1 and 3.

11.1 TOTAL DATA BASE STRUCTURES

TOTAL dates from the late 1960s, and as a result no systematic distinction is made in the TOTAL literature between the storage and conceptual data bases. As we saw in Chapter 4, it was not until the mid-1970s that it became clear that distinct storage and conceptual data bases gavc rise to storage or physical data independence. Nevertheless, the basic structures allowed with TOTAL are quite restricted, and it turns out that it is quite easy to separate the conceptual from the storage data base, even if they are not specified separately in the schema or data base definition. We shall therefore discuss TOTAL in the light of distinct conceptual and storage structures, which is the widely accepted way of doing things today.

Basic concepts

Let us first consider the conceptual data base depicted in Figure 11.1, which describes the conceptual files **WAREHOUSE** and **EMPLOYEE** that are involved in a 1:n relationship. This simple data base was taken from the CODASYL data base in Figure 6.2. A CODASYL version is shown in Figure 11.1a and a TOTAL version in Figure 11.1b. The only difference appears to be that the **EMPLOYEE** box with TOTAL is hexagonal, while it is rectangular in a conventional extended Bachman diagram. Nevertheless, there is an additional difference in the illustration of the **EMPLOYEE** child or member file, for in the TOTAL case, **EMPNUMB** is not specified as a primary record key.

With TOTAL there is a strong distinction between parent and child files; indeed, a parent file is called a *master* file, while a child file is called a *detail* or *transaction* file. There is direct access only to a parent file on the basis of a primary key, or *control key* as it is called in TOTAL terminology. In contrast, child records are accessed according to the key of their parent record, and the relevant data manipulation language command is similar to the CODASYL set-scan **FETCH** command. Thus there is no control key for a child record. A further distinction between parent and child files is that a parent file cannot also be a child of some other file, nor can a child be a parent of some other file. This can cause some data base design problems, as we shall see.

Between a parent and a child file there is a 1:n relationship, and in TOTAL such a relationship is named as in CODASYL, because we are allowed more than

(a) CODASYL conceptual data base   (b) TOTAL conceptual data base

FIGURE 11.1 Comparison of CODASYL and TOTAL versions of a simple conceptual data base involving a parent and a child conceptual file. The named one-to-many relationship WAR-EMP in the TOTAL version is equivalent to the CODASYL owner-coupled set WAR-EMP. The major difference between the two approaches is the special status TOTAL imposes on a child file. A single child file can have many parent files, but it may not also be the parent of a further child file. Furthermore, a child file may not have a primary key, so that its records are directly accessible only via the parent records. A parent TOTAL file is called a master file, while a child file (denoted by a hexagon) is called a detail or transaction file. The relationship name WAR-EMP will actually be the name of the pointer field at the storage level used to connect the master and detail files (Figure 11.2). The data base is from Figure 6.2.

one relationship between two files. Thus in a TOTAL DML command, as with CODASYL, we can specify exactly which relationship we are referring to. CODASYL embodies a 1:n relationship in an owner-coupled set, although with TOTAL it is called a *linkage path*, a name that really should be used for describing a storage level structure.

An example of a TOTAL storage data base that could underlie the conceptual data base in Figure 11.1b is given in Figure 11.2. We see that each parent **WAREHOUSE** record is connected to its **EMPLOYEE** child records by means of a two-way linked list, implemented by a pair of backward and forward pointers in each record. Such a storage implementation of a relationship or owner-coupled set is permitted in CODASYL. However, CODASYL allows for considerable choice and there are other possibilities as well. In contrast, only the two-way linked list shown in Figure 11.2 is allowed with TOTAL. Thus we do not have to worry about the storage data independence consequences of changing the underlying pointer system linking parent and child records. It cannot be changed.

Notice that in Figure 11.2 the pair of pointer fields is given the name **WAR-EMP** in both the parent and the child file, and that this is the same name that was used with the relationship or linkage path in Figure 11.2. As we shall see, it is in this simple way that a relationship is specified in a TOTAL data base definition. It is merely necessary to give the name of the pair of backward and forward pointers in the data definition. This name is then used in DML commands to refer to that relationship.

In any TOTAL storage version of a master file, there has to be an additional pointer field called a *root pointer* field. The name of the pointer field is arbitrary and we have chosen **R** in Figure 11.2 for the root pointer field in the storage version of **WAREHOUSE**. This root field also contains a pair of forward and backward pointers for another linked list to handle progressive overflow chains. All TOTAL master files are stored as hash files in a relative address storage

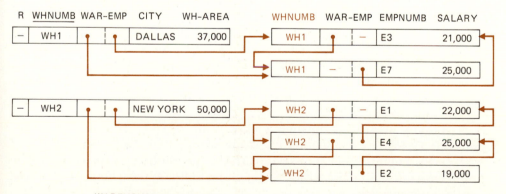

WAREHOUSE storage records   EMPLOYEE storage records

FIGURE 11.2   Shows the TOTAL storage files underlying the conceptual data base in Figure 11.1b. Each master record is connected to its detail records by means of a two-way linked list. A master file is a hash file, and the field R is for chaining overflow records.

space, just like the hash files described in Chapter 2. A propriety hashing routine is applied to the control key of the master file to generate the necessary disk addresses, and the overflow records are managed by chained progressive overflow. The overflow records belonging to a given home address are thus chained in a linked list that uses both forward and backward pointers, which are placed in the root pointer field. Since hashing with chained progressive overflow normally ensures a fairly low average search length (even if the distribution is worse than random), we would expect TOTAL to perform efficiently. And if its many users are to be believed, indeed it does. Note that the address capacity of TOTAL hash files can be greater than one (see Figure 2.29b).

The transaction records are also placed in a relative file, but there is no direct access to these records. These records are accessed by following the linked lists connecting parent and child records. A TOTAL storage data base is thus quite simple and effective.

Child files with multiple parents

Although a child or transaction file cannot itself be a parent, it may have more than one parent file, just as with a CODASYL data base. An example is given in Figure 11.3a, which shows the two 1:n relationships between EMPLOYEE and PUR-ORDER and between SUPPLIER and PUR-ORDER. The data base is taken from Figure 6.2, and we see that, as before, the only difference between the CODASYL and TOTAL data base at the conceptual level is that in the TOTAL case (Figure 11.3b) the ORDERNUMB field is not a primary key. Note that in the storage version of the PUR-ORDER file we have to have two distinct pointer pairs, one for the EMP-PUR relationship or linkage path, and the other for the SUP-PUR linkage path (Figure 11.3c).

Child file that is also a parent

We have seen that with more complex data bases a file B that is a child of file A can also commonly be a parent of another file C. We have this in the data base in Figure 6.2, from which we have taken the CODASYL data base in Figure 11.4a. If we want to construct a TOTAL version of this data base, we can proceed in either of two ways, both of which require the design of a new file involving a one-to-one (1:1) relationship.

The first alternative is shown in Figure 11.4b. WAREHOUSE is a master file and EMPLOYEE is a transaction file. Now strictly PUR-ORDER is a child of EMPLOYEE, but this is not allowed in TOTAL. The solution is to construct a new master with the unique EMPNUMB values from EMPLOYEE. There must then be a 1:n relationship between this new master, which we shall call EMPLOYEE-NUMBERS, and PUR-ORDER. PUR-ORDER can then be made a child of EMPLOYEE-NUMBERS, which is allowed (see Figure 11.4b), and the EMPNUMB field of EMPLOYEE-NUMBERS can be used as the control key. Since EMPLOYEE-NUMBERS contains the unique EMPNUMB values from EMPLOYEE, there is a 1:1 relationship between EMPLOYEE-NUMBERS and EMPLOYEE;

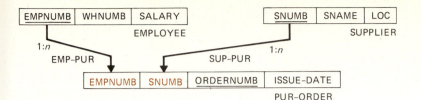

(a) CODASYL conceptual data base.

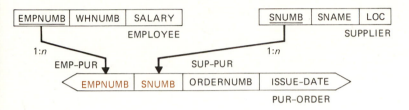

(b) TOTAL conceptual data base corresponding to (a). The PUR-ORDER detail file can be directly accessed only via either the EMPLOYEE or SUPPLIER master files.

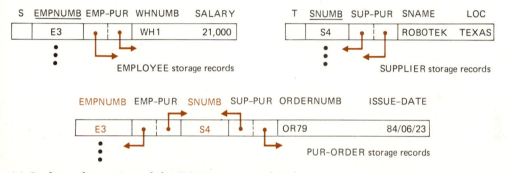

(c) Outline of structure of the TOTAL storage data base corresponding to (b).

FIGURE 11.3 Comparing TOTAL with CODASYL where a child file has two parent files. The data base is taken from Figures 5.25 and 6.2. The fields S and T in (c) are for the hash file overflow record chain pointers.

that is, for each **EMPLOYEE-NUMBERS** record there is one **EMPLOYEE** record. Since a 1:1 relationship is the simplest case of a 1:n relationship, we can have a relationship or linkage path for **EMPLOYEE-NUMBERS** and **EMPLOYEE**. This is called **E-N-E** in the diagram.

The other alternative is similar and is shown in Figure 11.4c. This time we make **EMPLOYEE** a master file with **PUR-ORDER** as a detail file. The problem is now the relationship between **WAREHOUSE**, which is also clearly a master, and **EMPLOYEE**, which cannot also be a transaction file. The problem is solved by introducing a new transaction file called **EMPLOYEE-NUMBERS**, containing the unique **EMPNUMB** values from **EMPLOYEE**. Because a transaction file must have a connection field, the **WHNUMB** value for each **EMPNUMB** value must also be included in **EMPLOYEE-NUMBERS**. As with the previous alternative, there will be a 1:1 relationship between **EMPLOYEE-NUMBERS** and **EMPLOYEE**.

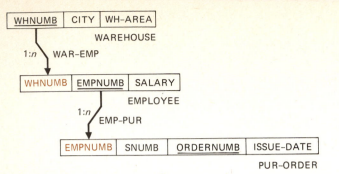

(a) A CODASYL conceptual data base in which the child (member) file EMPLOYEE is also a parent (owner) file. This is not allowed with TOTAL. Instead the data base must be modified as illustrated in (b) or (c).

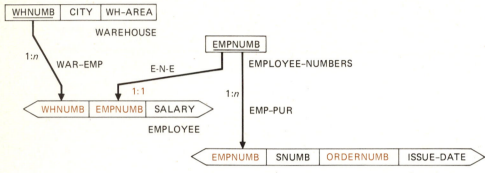

(b) A TOTAL conceptual data base corresponding to (a). A new master file EMPLOYEE-NUMBERS is introduced, and contains the unique EMPNUMB values from EMPLOYEE. Thus there will be a one-to-one relationship between EMPLOYEE-NUMBERS and the detail file EMPLOYEE. This is allowed because it is a special case of the standard one-to-many relationship.

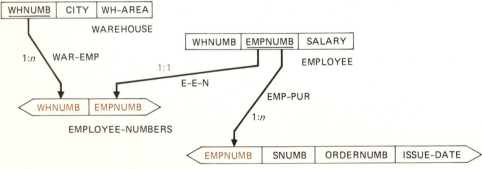

(c) Another TOTAL conceptual data base corresponding to (a). This time a new detail file EMPLOYEE-NUMBERS is introduced while EMPLOYEE is a master file and the parent of the detail file PUR-ORDER. The new detail file EMPLOYEE-NUMBERS contains the EMPNUMB values from EMPLOYEE; connection fields can never be omitted from TOTAL detail files, so that the WHNUMB field is required in EMPLOYEE-NUMBERS. There will be a one-to-one relationship between EMPLOYEE and EMPLOYEE-NUMBERS.

FIGURE 11.4 Shows how TOTAL deals with child files that are also parent files. The data base is taken from Figure 6.2.

We are now in a position to construct a TOTAL version of the complete conceptual data base from Figure 6.2, and this is shown in Figure 11.5. It is clear that the master files are parent files only, while the two transaction files are child files only, even if this requires the inclusion of the extra file **EMPLOYEE-NUMBERS**.

The external data base

There is no explicit external data base with TOTAL. Instead a number of smaller data bases are specified, which form a larger conceptual data base when taken together. For example, with the conceptual data base in Figure 11.5, if we are willing to do without the linkage path **E-N-E**, we could specify two separate data bases. One data base could contain the files **WAREHOUSE** and **EMPLOYEE**, while the other could contain the files **EMPLOYEE-NUMBERS**, **PUR-ORDER**, and **SUPPLIER**. Each of these smaller data bases could be defined separately for different groups of users and treated as external data bases.

TOTAL data base definition

The language used to define a TOTAL data base is best explained by an example, and in Figure 11.6 we show the essentials of the TOTAL data base definition for the data base in Figure 11.3. In each of the three boxes we have a definition of a storage file from Figure 11.3c, and the order of the fields shown in both Figure 11.3c and Figure 11.6 must be used. In the definition a master file is referred to as a *master dataset*, while the transaction file is called a *variable entry dataset*. This latter name is used because a transaction file can have variable length records, that is, it may contain more than one type of record. However, we cannot recommend use of variable length records, as this would mean that the child conceptual file was not a relation (see Chapter 9 for further discussion on the use of relations).

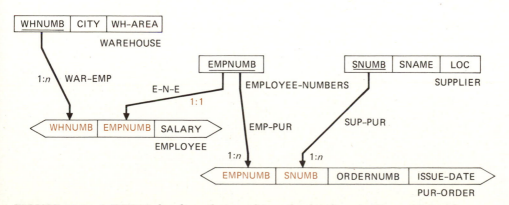

FIGURE 11.5 A TOTAL data base that combines the data base in Figure 11.3 with that in Figure 11.4b. It can also be taken as a TOTAL version of the data base in Figure 6.2.

```
BEGIN-DATA-BASE-GENERATION
DATA-BASE-NAME=FIGURE-11-3-EXAMPLE
        IOAREA=EMPLOYEE-SPACE          Specifies a user work area (UWA) that
        IOAREA=SUPPLIER-SPACE          can hold a record from each of the three
        IOAREA=PUR-ORDER-SPACE                       files in Figure 11.3b.
                 .
                 .
                 .
```

```
BEGIN-MASTER-DATA-SET                  We must specify the storage version of
   DATA-SET-NAME=EMPLOYEE              EMPLOYEE as shown in Figure 11.3c.
   IOAREA=EMPLOYEE-SPACE
            .
            .
            .
   MASTER-DATA:
      S=8                              Pointer field for chaining overflow records.
           EMPNUMB=5                   Control or primary key; 5 characters long.
      EMP-PUR=8                        Pointer connecting EMPLOYEE to PUR-ORDER.

           WHNUMB=5                    5-character field.
           SALARY=6
   END-DATA                           All EMPLOYEE storage fields now specified

   DEVICE=3380                         File will reside on IBM 3380 disk.
   TOTAL-TRACKS=500                    Details of physical storage file follow.
            .
            .
            .
END-MASTER-DATA-SET
```

```
BEGIN-MASTER-DATA-SET                  Specification of storage version of SUPPLIER
   DATA-SET-NAME=SUPPLIER
   IOAREA=SUPPLIER-SPACE
            .
            .
   MASTER-DATA:
      T=8                              Pointer field for chaining overflow records.
           SNUMB=5                     Control or primary key
      SUP-PUR=8                        Pointer connecting SUPPLIER to PUR-ORDER

           SNAME=20
           LOC=20
   END-DATA                           All SUPPLIER storage fileds now specified.

   DEVICE=3380                         Disk and physical storage file details.
            .
            .
            .
   END-MASTER-DATA-SET
```

FIGURE 11.6

508

```
BEGIN-VARIABLE-ENTRY-DATA-SET
    DATA-SET-NAME=PUR-ORDER
    IOAREA=PUR-ORDER-SPACE
        .
        .
        .
    BASE-DATA:
            EMPNUMB=5
        EMP-PUR=8
            SNUMB=5
        SUP-PUR=8
            ORDERNUMB=5
            ISSUE-DATE=8
    END-DATA

    DEVICE=3380
    .
    .
    .
 END-VARIABLE-ENTRY-DATA-SET:
```

Definition of transaction file

Definition of fields in storage PUR-ORDER records follows.
Pointers for two-way linked lists for EMP-PUR relationship.
Pointers for two way linked lists for SUP-PUR relationships.

Disk and storage file details.

```
END-DATA-BASE-GENERATION
```

FIGURE 11.6   Combined storage and conceptual schema for the TOTAL data base in Figure 11.3. The fields of each of the three storage files are specified. There is one type of file specification for master files and another for detail or transaction files. The relationships are specified by means of the pointers for the linked lists connecting the files, and the pointer field names EMP-PUR and SUP-PUR are used in data manipulation commands to refer to the relationships (see Figure 11.3). The 8-byte pointer field EMP-PUR will actually accommodate two 4-byte pointers, one for the forward pointer system and the other for the backward pointer system. (The indentation used above is for expositional purposes only.)

Notice that there is no explicit definition of any 1:n relationships as is the case with CODASYL. For example, to specify the linkage path EMP-PUR in Figure 11.3b, we simply specify pointer pairs with the name EMP-PUR in both the storage versions of **EMPLOYEE** and **PUR-ORDER** in Figure 11.6. These pointer pairs are always 8 bytes long.

At the begining of the data base definition in Figure 11.6, we specify the names of the COBOL structures that will hold records from the three datasets, and in each of the boxes we assign a COBOL structure to a dataset. In this way we have the equivalent of the CODASYL UWA, which is really an external data base definition feature. Thus we have parts of the storage, conceptual, and external data base all in one definition.

11.2 MANIPULATION OF A TOTAL DATA BASE

A TOTAL data base is manipulated in much the same way as a CODASYL data base, although TOTAL distinguishes clearly between commands that apply to the master files and commands that apply to transaction files. The general structure of a TOTAL DML command is shown in Figure 11.7. The master file command is a **CALL** to the data base system "**DATABAS**", and the normal parameters are a status variable for the return code, a function parameter indicating the function to be carried out, a dataset parameter to indicate which file is involved, a control-key parameter to identify the record, an element list parameter to indicate which fields of the record are involved, and the user-area parameter to indicate the UWA structure involved. If the command is for man-

```
CALL "DATBAS" USING

    FUNCTION,        The function to be carried out is contained as a value,
                     for example "READM" for "read a master record".
                     See Figure 11.8.

    STATUS,          If a command is executed correctly, TOTAL places the
                     code "****" here, otherwise other codes.

    DATASET,         The name of the dataset to be manipulated is contained
                     as a value, for example "EMPLOYEE".

    REFERENCE,       Following a command, TOTAL places a number here
                     to indicate the current position in the linkage path
                     (Internal Reference Point)

    LINKAGE-PATH,    The name of the linkage path to be manipulated is
                     placed here, for example "EMP-PUR" (see Figure 11.3b).

    CONTROL-KEY,     The primary key value is placed here, for example the
                     EMPNUMB value "E1".

    ELEMENT-LIST,    The names of the fields to be manipulated in a
                     record are concatenated (!) and placed here,
                     for example "WHNUMBSALARY".

    USER-AREA,       The name of the proper program structure to receive
                     a record is placed here as a value, for example
                     "EMPLOYEE-SPACE" for an EMPLOYEE storage record
                     (see Figure 11.6).

    "ENDP".          Indicates end of parameter list.
```

FIGURE 11.7 Structure of a TOTAL DML command. The parameters in black are all used in commands to manipulate a master file; if a transaction file is to be manipulated the parameters in color are used in addition. REFERENCE holds a quantity roughly equivalent to the CRU indicator with CODASYL.

Function	Effect
"READM"	Read a master record directly using the primary key (control key).
"RDNXT"	Read the next master record in record relative address order.
"ADD-M"	Add a record to a master file.
"DEL-M"	Delete a master record.
"WRITM"	Replace data in specified fields of master record.

(a) TOTAL functions for manipulating a master file.

Function	Effect
"RDNXT"	Read the next transaction record in record address order.
"READV"	Read the next transaction (variable) record in a chain. Current position in the chain, that is, the current internal reference point, must be given.
"READD"	Read a transaction record directly by presenting the internal reference point value.
"ADDVA"	Add a record to the transaction file, placing it in a chain or linked list <u>after</u> a record specified by an internal reference point value.
"ADDVB"	Add a record to the transaction file, placing it in a chain <u>before</u> a record specified by an internal reference point value.
"ADDVC"	Add a record to the transaction file placing at the end of a chain.
"DELVD"	Delete a transaction record directly, using its internal reference point value.
"WRITV"	Replace the data in specified fields of a transaction record, identified by its internal reference point value.

(b) TOTAL functions for manipulating a transaction file. Note that in all cases, which particular linked list or chain is involved is specified in a DML command by means of the control key value of the parent or master record.

FIGURE 11.8

ipulation of a transaction file, then we must also use a linkage path parameter to indicate which linkage path (owner-coupled set type equivalent) is involved, and a reference parameter to indicate the current position in the chain or linked list (owner-coupled set occurrence equivalent) being processed; in the case of a transaction record, the chain or linked list from the collection of chains making up the linkage path is identified by the master (parent) record, which is identified by the control-key value used in the control-key parameter.

The different functions that can be used are shown in Figure 11.8, and there is one set of functions for master files and another for transaction files. The functions for master files are quite straightforward. We can read a file directly (READM) on presentation of the control key, and sequentially in relative address order using the RDNXT function. (Remember that a master file is a hash file, and that in consequence the records are scattered over the available address space.) The other master file functions are for record insertion, deletion, and for updating fields.

The functions for transaction files are more complex, since manipulation of a chain is usually involved. An exception is the function RDNXT which permits a transaction file to be read sequentially in record address order. A transaction file is not a hash file, but the records nevertheless are often scattered in an unordered manner throughout the address space. Manipulation of a chain involves starting at the master record (see Figure 11.9) and reading the first transaction record (with 'OR73' value) followed by the next record in the chain ('OR80' value) and so on. We would use the function READV to read the records of the chain in this manner. Using the functions ADDVA, ADDVB, and ADDVC we can insert a new record into the transaction file in a specific position in the chain referenced in the linkage path and control key parameters. (How insertion is carried out when a transaction record occurs in two or more chains, as is the case with a PUR-ORDER record in Figure 11.3, is much more involved, and readers who are interested in the details should consult Ref. 2.) Finally we have functions for deletion and field updating.

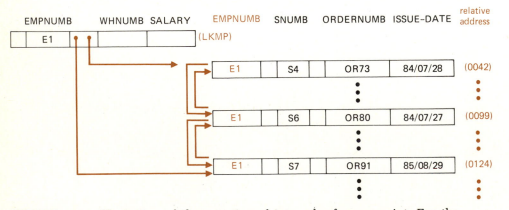

FIGURE 11.9 Illustration of the meaning of internal reference point. For the parent of a chain or linked list it is "LKMP". For a child it is its relative address as measured from the start of the transaction file. Thus a record from another chain could be at address 0055.

Example of reading a master file

We now give a specific example of reading a record with **EMPNUMB** key value 'E1' from the master file **EMPLOYEE** (see Figures 11.3, 11.6, and 11.8 for relevant details). We must first prepare all the parameters before issuing a **CALL** to 'DATABAS':

```
MOVE SPACES TO STATUS.
MOVE "E1" TO CONTROL-KEY.
MOVE "WHNUMBSALARY" TO ELEMENT-LIST.
MOVE SPACES TO USER-AREA.
```

*Now issue the **CALL** command with these parameter values.

```
CALL "DATBAS" USING
"READV", STATUS, "PUR-ORDER", REFERENCE, "EMP-PUR",
CONTROL-KEY, ELEMENT-LIST, USER-AREA, "ENDP".
```

*Check the value in **STATUS** first.

```
IF STATUS = "****" THEN DISPLAY WHNUMB IN EMPLOYEE-SPACE,
SALARY IN EMPLOYEE-SPACE
      ELSE GO TO ERROR-PARAGRAPH.
```

Apart from the syntax details, there is nothing difficult about this.

Example of chain traversal

In this example we shall read the **PUR-ORDER** child records that describe purchase orders issued by employee 'E1'. The records involved are shown in Figure 11.9. We shall suppose that we need to print out **SNUMB** and **ORDER-NUMB** field values. To start at the beginning of the chain we use the reference parameter value 'LKMP'. If we use the function **READV** to read the first **PUR-ORDER** record, TOTAL will place the relative address value 0042 in **REFERENCE**, and following reading the next **PUR-ORDER RECORD**, TOTAL places the relative address value 0099 in **REFERENCE**, and so on:

```
MOVE SPACES TO STATUS.
MOVE "LKMP" TO REFERENCE.
MOVE "E1" TO CONTROL-KEY.
MOVE "SNUMBORDERNUMB" TO ELEMENT-LIST.
LOOP. MOVE SPACES TO USER-AREA.
```

*Now issue a **CALL** command with these and other parameter values.

```
CALL "DATBAS" USING
    "READM", STATUS, "EMPLOYEE", CONTROL-KEY,
    ELEMENT-LIST, USER-AREA, "ENDP".
```

*We must check the **STATUS** value for a position at the end of the chain.

```
IF STATUS = "END OF CHAIN" THEN GO TO LAST-PARAGRAPH
      ELSE IF STATUS = "****" THEN
                DISPLAY SNUMB IN PUR-ORDER-SPACE,
                ORDERNUMB IN PUR-ORDER-SPACE
                GO TO LOOP
      ELSE GO TO ERROR-PARAGRAPH.
```

Notice that the **READV** function causes TOTAL to read the record following the record whose internal reference point is given in the **REFERENCE** parameter. Thus the value of **REFERENCE** closely corresponds to the CRU indicator value with CODASYL. The **REFERENCE**, **LINKAGE-PATH**, and **CONTROL-KEY** parameters are used with other transaction functions in much the same way as with the example above.

Concurrent processing, integrity, and security of data

TOTAL permits many different programs to manipulate the same data base concurrently, and to prevent update interference concurrency control commands may be used in an application program. There is a command **CNTRL/ RESERVE** that locks a file against use by any other program, and there is a less powerful command **CNTRL/SHARE** that prevents another program from updating the file, although it is allowed to read it. Finally there is a **CNTRL/RESERVE RECORD** command that locks a record against use by any other program.

Data security is enhanced by the provision of a TOTAL log file into which all data base updates are placed. The log file contains the state of the data before an update and after an update. There is a recovery utility that obtains a dump of the data base at regular intervals, and if at some later point the data base is damaged or incorrectly updated, the log file and the most recent dump are used by a recovery utility to restore the data base.

11.3 THE ADABAS DATA BASE SYSTEM

ADABAS is a widely used data base system from Software AG of North America. It is available for use with most of the widely used mainframe operating systems, and can interface to commonly used teleprocessing monitors, such as CICS (see Chapter 12). It is difficult to classify ADABAS. However if we restrict conceptual files to relations (no variable length records), then ADABAS lies somewhere between the relational approach and CODASYL. An overview of ADABAS is given in Ref. 3. Details are in Ref. 4. (Note that ADABAS is sometimes classified as an inverted file DBMS, because of its reliance on inverted files.)

The ADABAS conceptual schema

As with all other data bases described in this book we shall consider only the case where the conceptual data base is relational in structure, that is, each conceptual file is a relation. This introduces some very significant simplifications in the case of ADABAS that make the essentials of the system much easier to grasp. (Unfortunately, ADABAS permits repeating groups of fields and variable length conceptual records, that is, conceptual files that are not relations.)

Let us suppose that we want to implement the conceptual data base in Figure 11.10. This data base is taken from the data base in Figure 6.2 and has a one-to-many relationship between **SUPPLIER** and **PUR-ORDER**. Note that we show a primary and secondary key for both files. The secondary key **LOC** is in no way necessary and is there only to illustrate that ADABAS permits any field to be

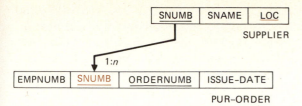

FIGURE 11.10 The conceptual files SUPPLIER and PUR-ORDER from the data base in Figure 6.1 are associated in a one-to-many relationship, as illustrated in Figure 11.11. This one-to-many relationship can be implemented directly in ADABAS. In contrast with TOTAL, a child field can be the parent of another child at a lower level. Also a child file can have many parents. Thus an ADABAS data base can form a network in the same way as a CODASYL or relational data base. Primary keys are underlined in black, secondary keys in color.

specified as a secondary key. The child connection field **SNUMB** is also specified as a secondary key, and this specification is necessary for the specification of the one-to-many relationship between **SUPPLIER** and **PUR-ORDER**. It is in this way that the relationship is specified and no other specification is needed.

We recall from the primitive data base in Chapter 3 that an inversion (or equivalent) on the child connection field permits all the child records of a parent to be accessed directly, given the key of the parent. This basic principle is incorporated into ADABAS data bases. As we shall see, the secondary key is always implemented at the storage level by means of an inversion of the connection field. With ADABAS all secondary keys are implemented by means of inverted files.

ADABAS has some special terminology that is used with primary and secondary keys and with connection fields. This terminology does not really distinguish between primary and secondary keys. At the storage level an inversion is also used for primary keys, although this is the trivial case of an inversion. A field that will be used to obtain direct access to a record is called a *descriptor* field in ADABAS terminology. A descriptor field may have unique values, as does the **SNUMB** field in **SUPPLIER**, or duplicate values as does the **LOC** field in **SUPPLIER**. When a conceptual file is defined in the equivalent of the conceptual schema, all the descriptor fields must be specified.

There are different types of descriptor fields, depending on their functions. With the data base in Figure 11.10, the fields **SNUMB** and **LOC** in **SUPPLIER**, and **SNUMB** and **ORDERNUMB** in **PUR-ORDER** would be specified as descriptor fields as follows: **SNUMB** and **LOC** in **SUPPLIER**, and **ORDERNUMB** in **PUR-ORDER** would be declared as *search* fields, since they would normally be used for retrieval of records on presentation of the search field value; in addition, **SNUMB** in **PUR-ORDER** would be declared as both a search field and a *coupling* field since it is used for connecting or coupling the two files. Thus we could have in a definition of the data base:

```
SUPPLIER    SNUMB (search),SNAME,LOC(search)
PUR-ORDER   EMPNUMB,SNUMB(search,coupling),ORDERNUMB(search),ISSUE-DATE
```

The above is merely intended to illustrate the ideas behind an ADABAS data base definition. Readers interested in the detailed syntax should consult Ref. 4. In practice the storage and conceptual schemas are combined in ADABAS, although they can be taken as separated for many purposes, especially if the data base design is relational. In addition, if a descriptor field X is declared as a sort field, it will be possible to process the file sequentially in ascending X value order.

User's view of an ADABAS data base

A user can view an ADABAS data base as made up of conceptual relational files that can form relationships. A one-to-many relationship can be viewed as shown in Figure 11.11. The relationship thus consists of a collection of occurrences, where each occurrence consists of a parent record and a number of child records. Thus an ADABAS data base can be viewed in much the same way as a CODASYL data base constructed with relations that all have connection fields.

A parent relation can have a child relation, and that child relation can also be the parent of other child relations. Furthermore a child relation can have many parent relations. Thus an ADABAS data base is a network data base, as are CODASYL and relational data bases. The data manipulation language permits the child records of a parent to be obtained, and the parent of a child record. Thus it might appear that ADABAS is as simple in appearance to the user as a relational data base. This is true only if the conceptual records are relations.

EMPNUMB	SNUMB	ORDERNUMB	ISSUE–DATE	SNUMB	SNAME	LOC
				S3	TRONOTON	CALIFORNIA
E1	S4	OR73	84/07/28	S4	ROBOTEK	TEXAS
E7	S4	OR76	84/05/25			
E3	S4	OR79	84/06/23			
E6	S6	OR77	84/06/19	S6	MIKREL	ONTARIO
E1	S6	OR80	84/07/29			
E3	S7	OR67	84/06/23	S7	RAYTEX	TEXAS

PUR–ORDER records   SUPPLIER records

FIGURE 11.11 With ADABAS a one-to-many relationship can be viewed as a collection of occurrences of parent records together with their child records, just like CODASYL owner-coupled set occurrences (see Figure 5.25). ADABAS data manipulation commands enable child records to be retrieved given the parent, and the parent record given the child. At the storage level the relationship is implemented by means of an inversion of PUR-ORDER on the connection field SNUMB (called a coupling field). The connection field must always be used.

While we shall not go into the details of it in this book, we must point out the following. With ADABAS a many-to-many relationship can easily be handled by resolving it into two one-to-many relationships, as can be done with CODASYL and relational approaches. (Note that this is not true for the peculiar many-to-many relationships found with binary join dependencies. See the second supplement to Chapter 9.) In addition, for reasons of performance, ADABAS permits a many-to-many relationship to be implemented by means of variable length record files. The method is not all that complicated but a data base in which this method is used cannot be considered relational. For details see Ref. 4.

The ADABAS storage data base

In this book we have tended to neglect the details of storage data bases, as long as they did not affect the manipulations of a user. In the case of ADABAS we are forced to examine the nature of the storage data base because of a special ADABAS storage concept that affects the data manipulation language. This is the concept of the *internal sequence number* or ISN.

To gain an understanding of the importance of the ISN concept with ADABAS we examine the storage version of the conceptual file **SUPPLIER** as illustrated in Figure 11.12. ADABAS storage records can be large and normally store many conceptual records. In Figure 11.12 we have arbitrarily shown a single storage record as containing two **SUPPLIER** conceptual records. When any conceptual record is stored in the data base ADABAS assigns a unique identifier to it, even if it already contains a unique primary key. This unique identifier is the internal sequence number, and in Figure 11.12, each supplier record is shown with its ISN value.

The storage records are stored in relative files. With a relative file, the underlying access method (Chapter 1) can retrieve a storage record given the relative address of the record. As we saw in Chapter 2, such storage files are commonly used for constructing hash files. They are also the storage files that TOTAL uses, but with ADABAS hashing is not used. Unless an application program has a conceptual record's ISN value, all direct access to a record is via indexes following presentation of a descriptor field value.

In Figure 11.12 we have illustrated the basic principle of direct access using ADABAS. Here we include an inversion of the file **SUPPLIER** on the descriptor field **LOC**. With ADABAS all inverted files are implemented as indexed-sequential files, with the associated index having up to three levels (see Chapter 2 for more on indexes). Now suppose that an application program needs to access the **SUPPLIER** file using the secondary **LOC** key value 'ONTARIO'. The program will issue a **FIND** command using this **LOC** value. ADABAS will then search the index for the inversion of **SUPPLIER** on **LOC** until it finds the inversion record with **LOC** value 'ONTARIO'. From this record the ISN for the required **SUPPLIER** record (with value 2) is retrieved and returned to the application.

The application now has the ISN value for the record it needs. Using this value it issues an appropriate command (a **READ** command) to retrieve the

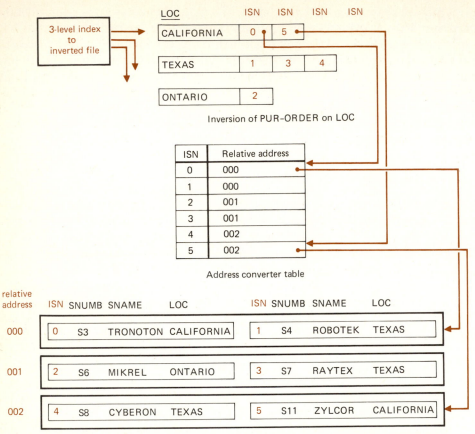

FIGURE 11.12 ADABAS storage version of the conceptual file SUPPLIER, showing an inversion on the field LOC. A storage file is a relative file whose records may be accessed on by means of the relative address. A storage record can hold multiple conceptual records. Associated with each record is a unique system identifier called an internal sequence number (ISN). An address converter table links a conceptual record's ISN to the relative address of the storage record containing it. The inverted file for LOC uses the ISN values as pointers. The inverted file is implemented as an indexed sequential file (primary key LOC) with up to three index levels (see Chapters 2 and 3).

required SUPPLIER conceptual record. ADABAS then checks for this ISN value in a table called an *address converter table*. This table matches all ISN values with the relative addresses of the storage records containing conceptual records (Figure 11.12). ADABAS then finds that 001 is the relative address of the storage record containing the conceptual SUPPLIER record with ISN value 2. It then accesses this storage record and returns the required SUPPLIER record to the program. Had we been interested in the primary key field SNUMB instead of the secondary key LOC, then we would have used the ADABAS "inversion" for the SNUMB field. Because the inversion records in this case would all be fixed length, they could simply be regarded as the lowest level of the index. Thus all direct access is by means of indexes with ADABAS, except when the application program already has the ISN value of the required record, as we have seen.

Utility of the ISN concept

The ISN concept with ADABAS frequently confuses students. However, there is really nothing difficult about it, as can be seen from Figure 11.12. The ISN is clearly a storage level concept, and some readers may object that it has no business being used in the DML, which is supposed to manipulate the conceptual data base. Nevertheless the ISN concept is useful for improving the efficiency of programs. For example, suppose we need to access the same record many different times during execution of a program. The first time it will be necessary for ADABAS to obtain the record's ISN value by searching the index, since the program will present a search field value. But from then on the program can use the ISN value, thus avoiding the need for time-consuming searches of the index and accesses to an inverted file. (A similar facility is available with CODASYL, and mentioned briefly in Chapter 6. With CODASYL the equivalent of an ISN is called a *data base key* and is the physical address of a storage record.)

11.4 THE ADABAS DATA MANIPULATION LANGUAGE

The syntax of the ADABAS DML is quite detailed (Ref. 4), and would be out of place in this description of the essentials of the system. We therefore merely list the main DML commands along with a description of their functions:

FIND *command* This command is used to obtain *all* the ISN values for records that satisfy conditions involving descriptor fields. Referring to Figure 11.12 we could retrieve the ISNs for those suppliers in California, or referring to Figure 11.11, we could retrieve the ISNs for the orders for supplier 'S4'.

READ RANDOM *command.* This command is used to retrieve specified field values given the ISN value for the record.

READ LOGICAL SEQUENTIAL *command.* This command can be used to process the conceptual (logical) records of a file sequentially. The sequential processing is in the order of a descriptor field defined as a sort field.

READ PHYSICAL SEQUENTIAL *command.* This permits the records of a file to be read in the order in which they appear in the storage records, that is, in the order in which they are physically stored.

READ DESCRIPTOR VALUE *command.* This command essentially processes an inverted file. For a specified descriptor field for a file, it gives the descriptor field values and the number of times they occur. Thus if we specify **LOC** in **SUPPLIER**, the first **READ** command would give 'CALIFORNIA' and 2, the next 'TEXAS' and 3, and so on (see Figure 11.12).

UPDATE *command.* This is used to modify field values.

ADD *command.* This is used to insert a new record. On insertion, ADABAS assigns an ISN value to the record.

DELETE *command.* Delete removes a conceptual record from a storage data base. The space vacated can be reused.

As an example of how we could use ADABAS to retrieve information from the data base, suppose we need the order numbers of orders issued to firms in Ontario. We could use the following procedure, assuming for simplicity that we know there is just one Ontario firm (see Figure 11.12).

Step 1. Use FIND for LOC value 'ONTARIO'. Assume ISN of record that satisfies this condition is placed in variable SUPPLIER-ISN.

Step 2. Use READ RANDOM command with value in SUPPLIER-ISN for retrieval of SNUMB value. Assume this SNUMB value is placed in variable CURRENT-SNUMB.

Step 3. Use FIND command with CURRENT-SNUMB value. Assume that the ISN values retrieved are placed in array ARRAY-ISN.

Step 4. Use READ RANDOM command to retrieve the ORDERNUMB field value from the next PUR-ORDER record whose ISN value is in ARRAY-ISN. If no ISN values are left in ARRAY-ISN, then stop.

Step 5. Print ORDERNUMB field value.

Step 6. Go to Step 4.

It is clear from this short procedure that the ISN concept is very important with ADABAS. The ADABAS DML can be used with such common host languages as COBOL, PL/1, and FORTRAN. A query language called NATURAL is also available and permits many basic retrievals. Records can be obtained from conceptual files on the basis of expressions involving descriptor fields. Child records can be obtained given the parent, and a parent given the child.

Concurrent processing

The transaction concept is used implicitly with ADABAS to prevent interference from other concurrent programs. Insertion of the word HOLD in a FIND or READ command signals the start of a transaction and intention to update a record. Let us suppose that program A issues a FIND HOLD command for record x. As soon as all other programs have finished with record x, program A is given exclusive control over x; that is, no other program can retrieve or update x. Program A retains exclusive control until it issues a MODIFY or DELETE command for that record x, thus signaling the end of the transaction.

ADABAS has a feature that permits a program to break out of deadlock. If program A holds record x and is waiting for y, while program B holds record y and is waiting for x, we have deadlock as we have seen earlier, and this type of deadlock can easily occur in most concurrent systems, including ADABAS systems. However if program A issues a FIND HOLD for y five times, it will be given control, and control taken from B. If we consider the analogy of the two trucks in Figure 6.17, it is as if the truck driver who shouts the longest can force the other truck to back up! The data base administrator must enforce the proper programming standards in all application programs for this to work (see Chapter 13).

Security facilities

In order to open an ADABAS data base and initiate processing, a password must be presented. In effect each user of the data base must have a password. Associated with each password in a *security table* is a list of the files and fields that the user can manipulate. This serves as an external schema definition. In the security table the type of manipulation that is allowed on each field (update or retrieval) for a given password is also listed.

Normally data in an ADABAS data base is compressed to save storage. For example, space can be saved by omitting blank characters and leading zeros, and substituting information about the numbers of such characters. However, in addition, ADABAS permits data to be *encrypted*, that is specially coded, so that a dump of the data base cannot be understood.

Recovery facilities

ADABAS provides facilities for regular dumps of the data base and the preservation of all updates in a log file. It also has facilities for automatically restoring the data base following system failure.

SUMMARY

1. TOTAL can be regarded as a streamlined version of CODASYL, although there is one fundamental feature that sets it apart: Conceptual files can be either master files which means that they can be parents of child files, or they can be transaction files, which means that they can be child files but not the parents of other children. Apart from this restriction, a master can be the parent of many transaction files, and a transaction file the child of many parents. In an enterprise schema, if a conceptual file X is both a parent and a child file, the corresponding TOTAL conceptual data base will contain an additional file in a one-to-one relationship. This permits TOTAL to handle any network data base.

2. TOTAL master files are stored as hash files, and overflow management is chained progressive using two-way chains. Address capacity greater than one is allowed. A parent master record is connected to its child transaction records by a two-way linked list. The name of the pointer field pair for these pointers is the same in both the parent and child files, and is used in DML commands to refer to a particular type of relationship. Transaction records are stored in a relative file and access is via the parent master records. The DML language permits a scan of the child records given the parent and retrieval of a parent given the child. It also permits direct access to a master record given the primary key value, and the sequential processing of master and transaction records in relative address order. Transaction records cannot be accessed directly on a primary key value.

3. In contrast with TOTAL, an ADABAS child file can also be a parent. Since a parent can have many children and a child many parents, ADABAS can handle any network, and except where a special ADABAS facility for many-to-many relationships is used, an ADABAS conceptual data base corresponds very closely to a data base as described by an extended BACHMAN diagram. ADABAS does not distinguish strongly between primary and secondary keys, all such fields being referred to as descriptor fields. A child connection field must be a descriptor field.

4. At the storage level, there are indexes for direct access to records on the basis of both primary and secondary keys. Indexed sequential inverted files are

used for secondary keys, a connection field being a secondary key. Each ADA-BAS conceptual record is given a unique identifier on storage, called an internal sequence code (ISN), and this is used in place of symbolic pointers at the storage level. The ISN value for a record can be used in a DML command. The DML permits the retrieval of all the ISNs for the child records given the parent, and the parent given the child. It also permits retrieval of any record given its ISN value. ADABAS also permits both direct and sequential processing of a conceptual file on the basis of a given descriptor field.

QUESTIONS

1. Explain the difference between TOTAL master and transaction files.
2. A corporate enterprise data base has a relation **DEPARTMENT**, describing departments, a relation **EMPLOYEES**, describing employees in the departments, and a relation **CHILDREN** describing the children (human) of employees. If an employee works in just one department, draw an extended Bachman diagram for the TOTAL master and transaction files needed.
3. Make a drawing of the storage files (including linkage paths but not the progressive overflow chains) for the TOTAL data base in Question 2.
4. Why do we give the same name to the linkage path pointer fields in both the TOTAL master and transaction files participating in a 1:n relationship?
5. Using the data base in Figure 11.3, write the core of a COBOL TOTAL program to retrieve the salaries of employees who have issued at least two orders (see Figure 5.25 for inspiration).
6. Using the data base in Figure 11.3, write the core of a COBOL TOTAL program to retrieve the salaries of employees who have issued orders to Texas suppliers.
7. Repeat Question 6 to retrieve the salaries of employees who have issued orders only to Texas suppliers.
8. Using the data base in Figure 11.3, write the core of a COBOL TOTAL program to find the orders issued by 'E3' to Texas suppliers.
9. Using the data base in Figure 11.1, write a COBOL TOTAL excerpt to add a new record to the data base. The new record is an **EMPLOYEE** record with fields (**WH2 E9 22,000**). The record should be added at the end of the appropriate linkage path chain.
10. Repeat Question 10, this time adding the new **EMPLOYEE** record as the second in the linkage path chain.
11. Explain the ADABAS concept of a descriptor field.
12. What is the essential difference between a network data base implemented as a TOTAL data base and as an ADABAS data base?
13. Explain the concept of the internal sequence number.
14. Why must a connection field be specified as a descriptor field with ADABAS?
15. Under what circumstances is a program likely to have to deal with ISN values?
16. Why is the ISN concept useful for improved performance with ADABAS?

17. Using the data base in Figure 6.2, give an ADABAS procedure for retrieving the records of employees who deal with Texas suppliers (for inspiration, see Figure 5.25).

18. Using the data base in Figure 6.2, give an ADABAS procedure to retrieve the salaries of all employees who deal with the supplier Robotek.

19. Using the data base Figure 6.2, write an efficient procedure for retrieving the total payroll for all warehouse employees.

20. Referring to the data base in Figure 6.2, suppose that warehouse 'WH2' is being closed down and its employees transferred to warehouse 'WH3'. Write an ADABAS procedure to update the data base.

21. Why would you expect that the ADABAS ISN concept would be much less necessary with TOTAL?

REFERENCES

1. Cardenas, A.F., 1979. *Data Base Management Systems.* Allyn and Bacon, Boston, Mass.
2. Cincom, *OS TOTAL Reference Manual.* Cincom Systems Inc., Cincinnati, Ohio.
3. Kroenke, D., 1979. *Database Processing.* Science Research Associates, Palo Alto, Calif.
4. Software AG. *ADABAS Reference Manual.* Software AG of North America, Reston, Va.

12

Data Base Teleprocessing

We have now completed a fairly detailed coverage of the three main approaches to data base management, as well as an outline of the less standard but widely used TOTAL and ADABAS data base systems. Generally, however, we have assumed that these systems were used either in a batch processing environment or in an interactive or time-sharing environment via a query language. In commerce there is another area in which data base systems are widely used, namely, the teleprocessing, or on-line, environment. So important has this area become that no book on data base management in business would be complete without some coverage of it. As we shall see, the main topic will be what are known as *data base/data base communications systems*, or *teleprocessing monitors*. We also need to include some elementary computer communications material.

12.1 ELEMENTARY (SINGLE-THREAD) ON-LINE SYSTEMS

We shall begin our study by looking at a simple on-line system, from which we can learn many of the basic principles needed for an understanding of the more sophisticated systems in use in commerce. However, before we develop this simple example, we need to look at the concept of interactive execution of programs from a terminal.

Interactive program execution

Most readers, especially if they work or study at institutions or colleges with a research or educational orientation, will probably have experienced interactive execution of programs with an interactive (or *time-sharing*) operating system. Examples of such operating systems are MULTICS, VM/CMS, and UNIX. They have all a great deal in common. Typically each user has the equivalent of his or her own memory partition (demand paged; see the end of Chapter 1), in which an editor, compiler, and application programs can all execute (and sometimes the application program can even be accompanied by an associated data base system). Users issue commands to the operating system for editor and compiler services via the terminal. They can also give a command for the execution of programs they have created.

When such a program runs at a terminal with an interactive operating system, COBOL **ACCEPT** and PL/1 **GET** statements will normally cause execution to stop, until required data for the **ACCEPT** or **GET** command is entered at the terminal. Similarly, COBOL **DISPLAY** and PL/1 **PUT** statements will cause output data to be printed on the screen. In this way the user interacts with the execution of the program, and execution is said to be interactive. Typically, at such an interactive computer installation, there can be hundreds of users at any given time, each with a small job that rarely involves processing large quantities of data on storage files. A prime characteristic and requirement of such systems is convenience of access to computer resources for fairly knowledgeable users, who typically want to use the editor (often as a word processor) or enter and run their own short programs.

Contrast this with the batch processing environment of such operating systems as OS/VS1, OS/MVS, DOS/VSE, or GCOS. Here we have a limited number of jobs being executed at any given time, and jobs often involve the processing of large quantities of data on many different storage files. It is the large amount of input/output associated with jobs that limits the rate at which jobs can be processed. Jobs wait for their turn to execute in a job queue. A user typically enters a job into the job queue either from a card reader or from a terminal, and the job must be accompanied by complex job control language statements, which specify the resources that are required during execution. The job may wait a long time in the job queue before execution, and a delay of the order of hours is common. When the job eventually does execute, if input data from the user is required to satisfy program COBOL **ACCEPT** or PL/1 **GET** statements, this data should have been submitted to the job queue along with the job. If the job is programmed to output data to the user via COBOL **DISPLAY** or PL/1 **PUT** statements, the output appears either on a line printer or in a special buffer for access via a terminal, in both cases some time after the job has finished executing.

That such batch operating systems are not suitable for use by large numbers of students at educational establishments is obvious. Nevertheless such systems are the most commonly used in business and commerce; for batch processing is still the most efficient method of processing large quantities of business data, regardless of whether this data resides in conventional storage files or in data bases.

Interactive execution with batch operating systems

However, there is also a need in commerce for interactive execution of programs, as many of the examples in this book have shown. With a batch operating system, when a job is executing, program input/output statements do not cause data to be read from or written onto a terminal, as we have seen. Still, there is no technical reason why a facility to permit this could not be incorporated into a batch operating system. Unfortunately such a facility could verge on the ridiculous, because of the long delay that can occur between submission of a job for execution and its subsequent execution. One can visualize a computer operator telephoning a user in the middle of the night to inform him that he could now interact with the job he had submitted that afternoon, since it was about to execute!

A much simpler and more sensible method of permitting interactive execution of programs with batch operating systems is available and fairly widely used. One or more of the memory partitions are simply reserved for execution of an interactive or time-sharing subsystem for terminal users. This subsystem can handle many users at different terminals concurrently. At a terminal a user can ask this subsystem to execute a program in much the same way as with an interactive operating system. The subsystem can permit the user's program to execute at once and interact with the user via the terminal. A limited number of interactive programs can thus execute in this way under the umbrella of the interactive subsystem, which appears as an unending job to the batch operating system. A well-known example of such an interactive or time-sharing subsystem is TSO (Time-Sharing Option) from IBM.

A simple on-line system

On-line processing is a special category of interactive processing. With on-line processing we typically have a large number of geographically distributed terminals that enable a large number of unsophisticated users to communicate with a limited number of prewritten programs. Users typically want to insert new data into a data base, update the data base, or retrieve data out of it. The prewritten programs are written to accept short instructions or *messages* from the users about the operations to be carried out on the data base. The situation is partly illustrated in Figure 12.1. At a given instant one group of users at terminals need the devices offered by one application program, another group by another program, and so on. The application programs can be taken as being associated with a data base system and a data base. In the simplest possible on-line system there would be just one application program, and it is this case we shall deal with in this introductory section.

An on-line system with a single application program is illustrated in Figure 12.2. At any instant there can be many remote terminal users who need the

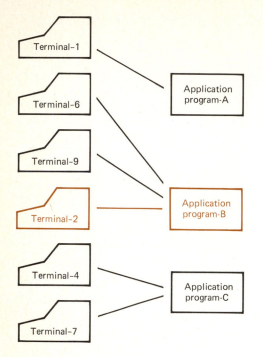

FIGURE 12.1 In a typical on-line system, at any instant, one or more terminals will need the services offered by an application program. In a simple (or single thread) system, only one application program (color in diagram) can execute at a time, and must completely process the message from a single terminal (color) before another terminal can be served, possibly by another application program.

services of the single application program, which manipulates a data base by means of a data base system. We notice that the system takes up two memory partitions. One partition contains a *terminal manager* that executes independently of the application program. At any instant there can be many terminals communicating with the terminal manager. This function of the terminal manager is the key to understanding on-line systems, and we must consider it carefully. The users at the terminals actually do not directly interact with the application program although they may think they do. They deal only with the terminal manager. The terminal manager continually polls the terminals, accepting the latest input (or incoming) message from one terminal, and displaying the latest output (or outgoing) message on another terminal. Thus many terminals are in concurrent operation and under the control of the terminal manager.

Messages received by the terminal manager are placed in an *input,* or *incoming, message queue* on disk. The application program has access to this message queue. When it has completed its most recent processing, it begins again and takes the next message from the message queue, which we can imagine is from terminal T3 in Figure 12.2. The message typically could be a command to retrieve some data from the data base. Having analyzed the message, the applica-

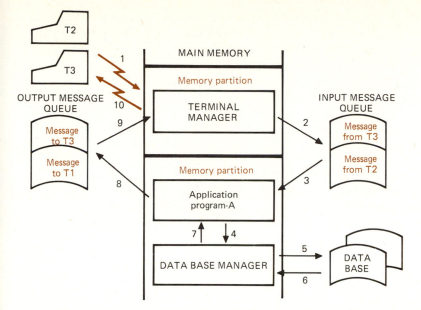

FIGURE 12.2   The basic principle behind teleprocessing with a single application program. A terminal manager executes independently of an application program in a separate memory partition or region. It polls terminals and places messages in an input message queue. The application program sequentially processes an input message and places a response in the output message queue. Some time later the terminal manager reads the output message and transmits it to the terminal.

tion program, or *message processing program* as it is often called, carries out the instructions in the message and calls in the data base system to retrieve the required data. While the data base system is doing this, the application program is stopped. No other message can be processed until processing of the current message is complete, although the terminal manager can operate concurrently as it continues to poll the terminals and maintain the message queues.

On receipt of the data from the data base system, the application program carries on and prepares a response for terminal T3 and places it in an *output,* or *outgoing, message queue.* It is then ready to process another message, in all probability from another terminal. While this is going on, the terminal manager sooner or later will retrieve the message for T3 from the output message queue and transmit it to the terminal. This is called *single thread* processing, because the time thread of processing a message is not interrupted by the processing of another message. Unfortunately single-thread processing can be very slow, so that users at terminals often experience considerable delays. If a message processing program has to make many data base or file accesses in order to process a message, then another user, whose message has been submitted but is not yet being processed, will have to wait a long time. In addition, if there are many terminals in use, then a message from a user may spend a long time in the message queue before it is processed.

Relationship with the operating system

The system in Figure 12.2. is a simple example of an on-line system that runs under a batch operating system. The terminal manager can be regarded as a batch job that never finishes, but which has access to a large number of terminals. The application program with associated data base system is another batch job that never finishes, but which continually accesses the incoming message queue looking for work. In other memory partitions, ordinary batch jobs will be running. Normally the partitions handling the on-line processing will have much higher priority than batch jobs; indeed the batch jobs are often called *background jobs* that can execute when the on-line partitions are not busy.

Multiple message processing programs

The simple on-line system described in Figure 12.2 could be improved upon by providing for the execution of any program from a *library of message processing programs*. Still referring to Figure 12.2, in this way when one user at terminal T3 was finished with program *A*, another user at terminal T1 could use program *C*. The terminal manager would load a new message processing program in response to a message. Only one program would be in main memory at any given time, however, and one message would have to be processed before another message could be dealt with (usually by another program). Thus processing would still be single thread, and users would often experience delays.

12.2 PACKET-SWITCHED COMMUNICATIONS SYSTEMS

If we examine once more the simple on-line system in Figure 12.2, we notice again that the terminal manager communicates with users at distant terminals, some of which may be thousands of miles away. The terminal manager can communicate at such distances only if the proper hardware and software is in place to exploit a communications network. It is not possible to understand on-line systems without a grasp of modern communications networks. Unfortunately the subject is vast, and many books are available on the subject. These books tend to be of an electrical engineering nature and cover the many different types of communications systems to a level of detail that surpasses the requirements of a student of business. In this section we shall cover only the essential principles behind what are known as *packet-switched computer communications systems*. This type of system is becoming widespread in the United States. It is covered by important standards recommendations, and is already the standard in many industrialized nations, including Canada.

Overview of communications in an on-line system

In Figure 12.3 we have drawn a more detailed picture of how the terminal manager in a simple on-line system communicates with remote users at terminals, and even with another remote computer. We recall (Chapter 1) that when an application program transmits a block of data to or from a disk, it does so by first calling up the services of a system subprogram or access method, which

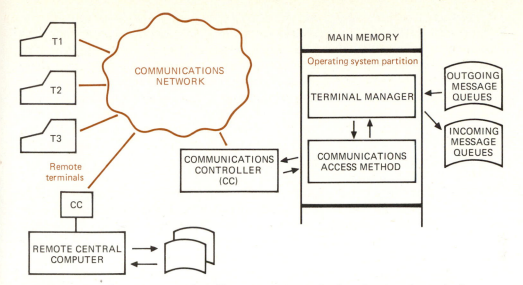

FIGURE 12.3   Shows in more detail how input (incoming) and output (outgoing) messages are handled by the terminal manager in Figure 12.2. When the terminal manager retrieves a message from the outgoing message queue, it passes it to the communications access method, which edits it and forwards it to the communications controller. The communications access method is also responsible for initially setting up the session with the remote terminal (which in a few cases will be a remote computer), and for checking that messages are transmitted without error. On receipt of the message from the access method, the communications controller splits the message into packets, chooses the first link of the route to the remote terminal, and transmits the packets one by one. The communications network chooses the remaining links of the route, and shunts the packets along by a store and forward process (Figure 12.5).

leads to a disk controller manipulating the disk. Similarly, to communicate with a remote terminal, the terminal manager calls up the services of a *communications access method*, which leads to manipulation of the communications network by a *communications controller*.

Suppose that the terminal manager has a message to transmit to a terminal. It first passes it to the access method, for editing. The access method then passes it to the communications controller, which breaks it up into *packets*, each at most 131 bytes, or characters, long (the length of a printed line on a video display terminal or printer). The communications controller then chooses the first leg of a route through the communications network and transmits the first packet. On receipt of an acknowledgment of the safe reception of this packet from a network computer, it transmits the next packet, and so on until all the packets have been sent. Eventually the packets are accumulated by another communications controller attached to the destination terminal. This controller assembles the packets into a message and displays it on the terminal. Usually a group or *cluster* of terminals is served by a single controller, which is known as a *cluster controller*.

The remote user does not have to be a person at a terminal and may be some application program in a remote computer. In such cases the communication is symmetrical. Received packets are assembled by the remote computer's communications controller and passed to its application program via the communications access method, terminal manager, and incoming message queue. When a terminal manager deals with remote computers as well as terminals, it is usually called a *communications manager*.

Packet switching principles

A variation of the packet switching technique was known and used long before the days of computers and is useful for grasping the basic principle involved. In Figure 12.4 we have a drawing of an old-fashioned manual message switching center, which we imagine to be located in an office in Chicago. In this office there are manually operated teletypewriters connected to similar teletypes in Denver, Toronto, New York, and Miami. One teletype in the Chicago office (teletype-1) is used for receiving messages from Denver, and the others are used for transmitting messages to Toronto, New York, and Miami. We imagine that each message carries a header giving its ultimate destination.

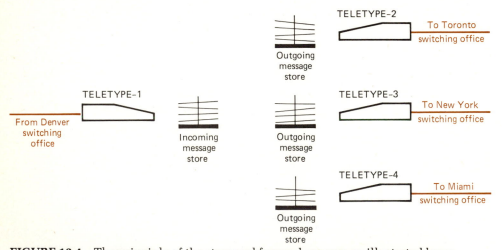

FIGURE 12.4 The principle of the store and forward process, as illustrated by an imaginary manual switching office in Chicago that uses old-fashioned teletypewriters. Teletype-1 receives only messages from Denver, but addressed to other destinations. These messages are stored in an incoming message store. The other teletypes are used for transmitting messages to other locations. The operator at each of these teletypes sends messages from an outgoing message store. The office manager personally examines each incoming message and, on the basis of the address at the head of the message, places it in the appropriate outgoing message store. Thus there can be a considerable delay between arrival of a message in Chicago and its subsequent transmission to the New York switching office, and perhaps another delay before transmission to Albany, the ultimate destination. The manual system can be replaced by a computer (Figure 12.5) but the principle is the same. Switching delays, however, are small fractions of a second with the computerized system.

Beside each machine is a store of messages (in a stack with a pin through the middle)—an incoming message store for the Denver line and outgoing message stores for each of the other lines. As messages are received from Denver, the teletype-1 operator places them in the incoming message store. At regular intervals, the office manager takes the messages from the incoming message store and distributes them among the outgoing message stores for the other three teletypes. For example, a message to Ottawa would go to the store for teletype-2, and a message for Albany to the store beside teletype-3, and so on. In this way the operators on teletypes to Toronto, New York, and Miami have a steady supply of messages to forward.

This is the *store and forward* principle in its simplest form. An incoming message is stored and then forwarded along the next leg of its journey when a transmission facility is available. Unfortunately this method of handling messages can be very slow, and it can take a message hours to pass through a manual switching office if there is a backlog. The next development was the computerized packet switching office.

Storing and forwarding by computer

In a packet switched store and forward system, each office contains at least one store and forward computer. (There are often as many as three such computers at a switching office of a widely used network, to improve reliability and to handle peak loads.) The store and forward computer has a communications controller attached to lines going to other switching offices, and usually also to other computers and terminals (Figure 12.5). The store and forward computer handles standard packets, and incoming packets are placed in an incoming packet store, as shown in Figure 12.5. When large volumes of packets are being handled, the packet store is on disk. However, speed is of the essence with a packet switching

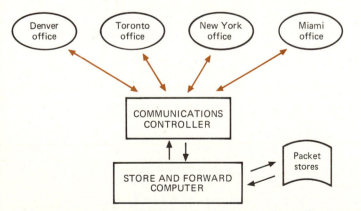

FIGURE 12.5 Store and forward packet switching office. An incoming packet is temporarily placed in a packet store on disk. Later the computer retrieves the packet and, on the basis of the address in the packet header, decides which office the message must be forwarded to. Notice that a packet switching office stores and forwards packets, not messages. A message is made up of packets, which are the basic units of transmission.

office, and the packet store can be in main memory. The next packet to be forwarded is retrieved from the packet store by the store and forward computer and passed to the communications controller, which decides its destination and transmits. As with a manual message switching office, there is a delay in moving a packet through a packet switching office, although normally this is only a fraction of a second.

Packet switched networks

A packet switched network consists of interconnected packet switching offices, to some of which other computers and terminals are attached, as shown in Figure 12.6. As can be seen from this simple network there is more than one pathway from one switching office to another. For example, a message from office-A to office-D could travel directly or via office-C or office-D, and often the packets of a single message will travel by different routes to get to a common destination. At each switching office on the journey, a communications controller decides which link to use next, depending on availability of resources. Thus if one switching office goes down, the others will shunt packets around the defective office.

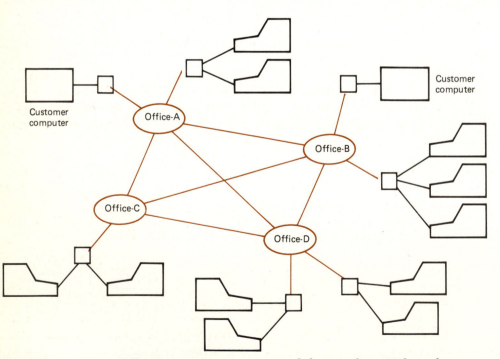

FIGURE 12.6 Many different customer computers and clusters of terminals can be connected to a packet-switched network. Terminals are often connected via a cluster controller.

Ownership of communications networks

Networks for computer communications can be either public or private. Many large corporations have their own private networks, which are constructed partly from leased lines and partly from equipment owned by the corporation. Some corporations have several networks for different tasks. Typically these networks began on a small scale; for example, one would handle manufacturing data for different plants, while another would be designed for sales information. These networks then just grew.

Most advanced nations now have a public packet switched communications system. The United States has several, and the best known are GT&E's TELENET, A.T.&T's Advanced Communications Service (ACS), and TYMNET. In Canada all major centers coast to coast are connected by DATAPAC, run by the Trans Canada Telephone System. Development of public packet switched networks is a relatively recent phenomenon, and it is expected that as their use intensifies, economies of scale will make it more economical for large businesses to make use of them. Many of the private networks use less expensive but older *circuit-switched* technology, which essentially is based on leased telephone lines switched by telephone central office equipment. A full discussion of circuit-switched networks would take us beyond the scope of this book (see Ref. 6).

The CCITT X.25 packet switching recommendation

The Consultative Committee on International Telegraphy and Telephony (CCITT), based in Geneva and a body of the International Telecommunications Union, has developed almost universally accepted standards recommendations for computer communications. One of the best known of these is recommendation X.25 which deals with packet switching, and it is on the basis of the X.25 recommendation that most public packet switching networks are built. Essentially the recommendation standardizes the format of packets and how such packets are to be handled by the network.

X.25 packets

An outline of the format of X.25 packets is shown in Figure 12.7. Each packet has 3 bytes (24 bits) of system information and up to 128 bytes or characters of text from the message. The system information includes the destination of the packet and the sequence number of a packet as sent. As the packet is shunted through the network, the destination is read by the communications controller (or equivalent) at each switching office and used to decide the next switching office it should be sent to. As we mentioned earlier, a message in an on-line system is broken up into packets by the communications controller. These packets will be transmitted initially in their natural order, with their initial sequence numbers included in the system information. It is possible for individual packets to take different routes, so that packets constituting a single message can easily arrive at their destination in the wrong sequence. Using the packet sequence numbers, the communications controller can reconstruct the message.

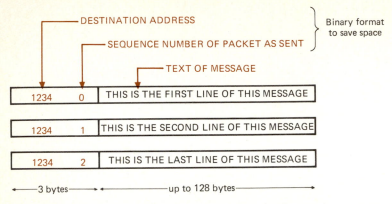

FIGURE 12.7 Outline of the structure of three packets making up a single message. Each of the packets has the same destination (coded address 1234). However, since they may each take a different route through the network to the destination (see Figure 12.6), they must be numbered in the sequence sent, so that if they arrive out of sequence, the complete message can be reconstructed. Additional system information in the packets is omitted above. The format of packets has been standardized by an important recommendation (called X.25) of the Consultative Committee on International Telegraphy and Telephony (CCITT).

Functions in network management

The functions that are carried out by software and hardware components in a packet switched network are listed in Figure 12.8. At the top we have a single high-level function (level-7) for sending a message, while at the bottom we have the lowest level functions of managing the features of the physical links. Many different kinds of physical links are possible, for example, a simple pair of telephone wires, a coaxial cable (of the kind used with cable television), microwave towers, glass fibers for transmission of visible light (*fiber optics link*), and even satellite links. Most of the details of these belong to electrical engineering.

When a message is to be sent, it must often be edited. This is a higher level function (level-6) that can be carried out by the communications access method (see Figure 12.9 or Figure 12.3). Another level-6 function involves compacting the data before transmission, to lower network charges. At a lower level (level-5) we have the job of setting up and terminating sessions with users. Typically the user first sends a message identifying himself, herself, or itself (if it is another computer), requiring a message in response from the central computer. This function can be carried out by the communications access method too. At an even lower level (level-4) we have the task of ensuring that each message sent is received and that it is not received twice. This will involve the transmission of short control messages. This function is also covered by the communications access method at the central computer.

With the remaining lower level functions, the X.25 recommendations apply. At level-3 a message is divided into the standard X.25 packets, which are transmitted one by one. At the next level (level-2) we have the control of the progress of a packet down each link. This involves standard *protocols*. When a

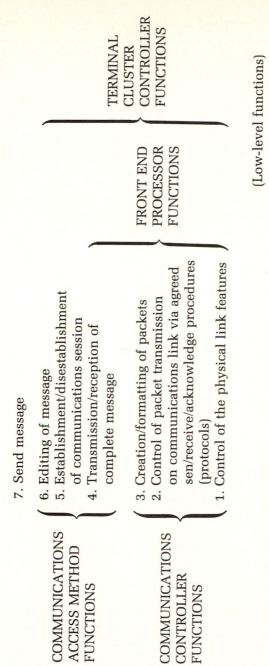

(High-level functions)

TERMINAL CLUSTER CONTROLLER FUNCTIONS

FRONT END PROCESSOR FUNCTIONS

(Low-level functions)

COMMUNICATIONS ACCESS METHOD FUNCTIONS

7. Send message
6. Editing of message
5. Establishment/disestablishment of communications session
4. Transmission/reception of complete message

COMMUNICATIONS CONTROLLER FUNCTIONS

3. Creation/formatting of packets
2. Control of packet transmission on communications link via agreed sen/receive/acknowledge procedures (protocols)
1. Control of the physical link features

FIGURE 12.8 Function that must be carried out to send a packet-switched message (see Figure 12.3). Replacement of the communications controller in Figure 12.3 by a front end processor would permit more functions to be offloaded from the main computer. The functions in color have been standardized by the CCITT X.25 recommendation.

switching office-A sends a packet to office-B, office-B must send an acknowledgment of receipt to office-A, and so on. The X.25 recommendation covers this link protocol, which is quite complex and designed to cover almost every circumstance that could occur. At the lowest level, level-1, the X.25 recommendation covers the functional characteristics of the physical links, as already mentioned. Typically, these last three X.25 functional layers are carried out by the communications controller in the case of a central computer, but they may also be carried out by a cluster controller, or what is often called a *front-end processor* (FEP). An FEP is simply a minicomputer that replaces the communications controller, and which can off-load some additional functions, usually level-4 functions, from the central computer. Figure 12.8 shows what functions can be carried out by communications controllers, front-end processors, and cluster controllers. However, the assignment of functions given in the figure should not be taken too literally, as a fair amount of variation is common in practice. The seven functional levels are defined by ISO, the International Standards Organization, while the bottom three are defined in detail for packet switching by the CCITT X.25 recommendation (see Ref. 6).

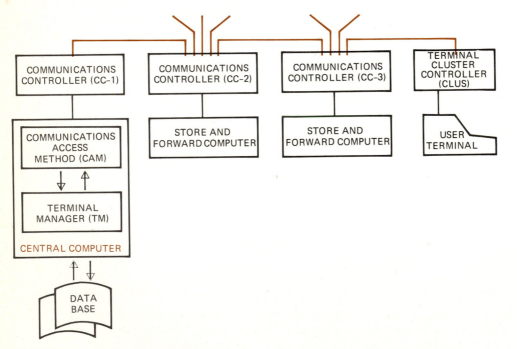

FIGURE 12.9 Typical communication between a central computer and a remote terminal over a path with three links. The functions that must be carried out to transmit a message from computer to terminal are listed in Figure 12.8. Using the pathway and abreviations shown above, an idea of how the functions shown in Figure 12.8 are distributed among the components above is illustrated in Figure 12.10.

Example of a three-link path through a network

The information in Figure 12.8 is rather abstract, and we can get a better idea of the functions involved in transmission of messages over a network by taking a specific example, as shown in Figures 12.9 and 12.10. Figure 12.9 shows part of a packet switched network where a central computer running an on-line system communicates with a remote terminal attached to a cluster controller. Now consider how the cluster controller, the store and forward computers, the central computer communications controller, and the communications access method of the central computer are all involved in the functions listed in Figure 12.8, particularly when the terminal manager sends a single message to the remote terminal. To simplify matters, we start with the level-4 function of ensuring transmission and reception of the complete message. The communications access method does this (Figure 12.10). This will involve creation and formatting of the necessary packets, and their reconstruction again at the remote cluster controller. These level-3 functions are shown in Figure 12.10. At the next lowest level we have a lot of packets (and some control packets) that must be transmitted, received, and acknowledged. All the communications controllers and cluster controllers have a lot of level-2 functions to carry out here (see Figure 12.10). For each physical act of sending, receiving, or acknowledging a packet on a link, different physical control functions must be carried out depending on the type of link (level-1 functions). This is also shown in Figure 12.10.

Thus we see that a single send message command results in the communications controllers and cluster controller carrying out a large number of coordinated and concurrent level-1 tasks that ensure the transmission of the message. This *cascade* effect of a message transmission command corresponds well to the

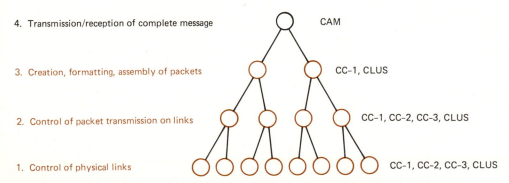

4. Transmission/reception of complete message — CAM

3. Creation, formatting, assembly of packets — CC–1, CLUS

2. Control of packet transmission on links — CC–1, CC–2, CC–3, CLUS

1. Control of physical links — CC–1, CC–2, CC–3, CLUS

FIGURE 12.10 Very much idealized distribution of communications functions over software and hardware components in Figure 12.9. For example, the transmission of a message (level 4) results in the control of many physical links (level-1 function) by different controllers at many different times during transmission of the individual packets that make up the message. However, the distribution is incomplete. If we consider the function of sending a message (level-7 function; see Figure 12.8), then because of the handshaking messages that must be sent to set up a session and to terminate a session, we would have a much taller and wider pyramid of operations.

effect of an executive order issued at a high level in a large corporation or in government. The order cascades downward, so that in the end large numbers of widely dispersed employees at low levels undertake concurrent, diverse, but coordinated tasks in compliance with the high-level order.

12.3 MULTIPLE-THREAD ON-LINE SYSTEMS: THE IMS DATA BASE/DATA COMMUNICATIONS SYSTEM AND CICS

Today, many on-line systems are *multiple thread*, that is, many messages are dealt with concurrently, which reduces delays experienced by terminal users. In order to have concurrent message processing we have to have concurrent processing by the programs that process the messages, and this is accomplished by assigning a memory partition (or sometimes a memory subpartition) to each message processing program. This makes matters a great deal more complicated, and we need additional software to manage the concurrent message processing programs.

We shall now look at two related ways in which a multiple-thread on-line data base system can be set up:

1. Using a data base/data communications (DB/DC) system or teleprocessing monitor that is available as a component of a data base management system
2. Using a generalized teleprocessing monitor that provides a wider variety of services and which usually can interface to a variety of data base systems

The basic principles behind DB/DC systems or teleprocessing monitors

The basic principle behind a DB/DC system with multiple-thread message processing is illustrated in Figure 12.11. As before, the terminal manager communicates with remote users at terminals or other computers. It places incoming messages in one queue and retrieves outgoing messages from another queue (usually on the same disk) for transmission to users. The messages in the incoming message queue do not all require processing by the same program. A transaction type code in each message identifies the message processing program to be used. Associated with the terminal manager (usually located in the same memory partition) is the *program scheduler* for scheduling the loading of message processing programs from a message processing program library (Figure 12.11).

More than one memory partition is available for running message processing programs, and when a message processing program has dealt with a message, its partition is available for use by some other program. The program scheduler then takes the next message from the incoming message queue, reads the transaction type code in the message, and loads the appropriate message processing program into the available partition. Sooner or later this partition is given control, and the message processing program executes and processes its message, placing an appropriate response in the outgoing message queue.

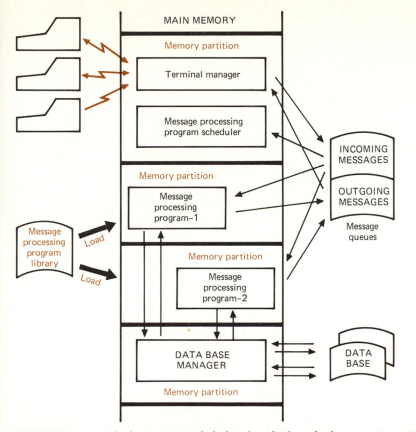

FIGURE 12.11 The basic principle behind multithread teleprocessing with multiple application (or message processing) programs. The diagram is an extension of Figure 12.2. The terminal manager independently polls remote terminals and maintains the resulting message queues, as before. However, this time there is a program scheduler that works closely with the terminal manager. To process a new incoming message, the scheduler loads a message processing program from a library into an independent memory partition. The message processing program calls up the services of the data base system, which runs independently in an independent partition. There can be many partitions running message programs concurrently and passing calls to the data base system. Thus the processing of incoming messages is interleaved, and there is parallel (multithread) processing of messages.

Need for data base concurrency control

At any given time there are several message processing programs in varying stages of execution. These programs can all call the same copy of the data base management system as needed, so that the data base system must be able to handle calls from concurrently executing programs. In order to process a message, a message processing program will typically make at least three calls: one to open or ready the data base, one for data base manipulation, and one to close the data base. It is important to understand that while the data base system processes one call completely before it processes another, the sequence of calls from the various message processing programs will be interleaved, and we could have a sequence like the following:

Call-1 from program-1
Call-1 from program-3
Call-2 from program-3
Call-2 from program-1
Call-3 from program-3

Thus as we saw in our studies of the CODASYL, relational, and hierarchical approaches, application programs must include a code to shield their manipulations of a data base from interference due to interleaved calls in an on-line environment.

Need for deadlock prevention and resolution

In an on-line system the interleaved sequence of calls to the data base system can cause two or more message processing programs to become deadlocked, as we saw earlier. Note that in an on-line system this will not necessarily bring the system down. Most likely the two message programs involved will simply stop executing, while other programs can continue unaffected. Nevertheless, it is clear that the message processing programs should include code to prevent deadlock, and that they must be able to roll back updates of the data base to resolve the deadlock where necessary.

Multiple-thread processing

Referring again to the idealized DB/DC system in Figure 12.11, it should be noted that the processing of messages by the message processing programs is interleaved in time. Processing a message can involve many data base calls (and perhaps even manipulation of nondata base files), and there will be many periods during which a message processing program cannot function because it is waiting for a response from the data base system. However, since the message processing programs are in memory partitions controlled by a multiprogramming operating system, there will usually be some message program that is able to execute. Thus the typical sequence is something like:

Start of message-1 processing
Continuation of message-4 processing
Continuation of message-2 processing
Continuation of message-1 processing
Continuation of message-2 processing

and so on. This interleaved processing of messages is called multiple-thread processing, since at any given instant there are many time threads of processing of messages. In a single-thread system, a message must be completely processed before the processing of a second message can begin.

The DB/DC system with IMS

Many data base managements have an associated data base/data communications system for use with on-line systems. It is not possible in a book of this sort to cover all of them, or even one of them in any significant detail. However, we shall give the reader an overview of the IMS DB/DC system, since this is one of the most widely used (Ref. 5).

Figure 12.12 shows how the different components of an IMS DB/DC on-line system are arranged. The first point to note is that the terminal manager (com-

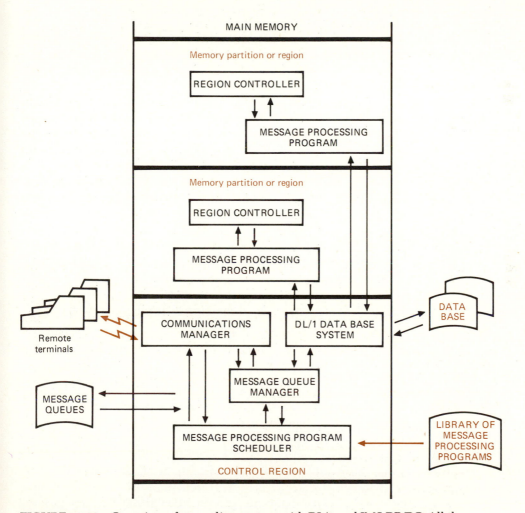

FIGURE 12.12 Overview of an on-line system with DL/1 and IMS DB/DC. All the system control modules are in a single memory partition (the control region). The data base system controls the data base, the communications manager controls the remote terminals, while the program scheduler controls execution of the message processing programs.

munications manager), program scheduler, and data base management system (in this case the DL/1 system as described in Chapter 10) are all placed in a single partition or region of the batch operating system. The message processing programs are distributed over the remaining operating system partitions allotted to the on-line system. The operation of the system is similar to that described for the more idealized system in Figure 12.11, although there are important differences.

The communications manager receives incoming messages and transmits outgoing messages, using a communications access method and the usual communications controller, or the equivalent, as already described. A received message is passed to a message queue manager for storage in a message queue, and a message to be transmitted is taken from the message queue by the queue manager and transferred to the communications manager for transmission to a remote terminal. So far only the message queue manager is new, but it has another function, as we shall see presently.

When a memory partition is released by the operating system, the program scheduler examines the next incoming message in the message queue and loads the correct message processing program, together with all necessary PCBs for interaction with the DL/1 data base system. There is a library of message processing programs and the usual IMS library containing PCBs.

When a message processing program is executing, it can read a message from the message queue and can place a message in the message queue for transmission to a terminal. However, it is the way in which this is done that is unique to IMS DB/DC. The message queue is treated by DL/1 as if it were a data base, admittedly a fairly simple data base. To retrieve a message from the message queue, the message processing program uses DL/1 GU and GN commands. Similarly, to insert a message into the queue, the application program issues a DL/1 INSRT command. We need to look at this in more detail, particularly the nature of the interface between a message processing or application program and DL/1.

The on-line interface to DL/1

In Figure 12.13 we have more detail of how a message processing program communicates with DL/1. Note that with Figure 12.13, for reasons of space limitations, we have drawn only one message processing program, and the drawing assumes that the message processing program is dealing with just one external IMS data base, which, we recall, is specified in a PCB. This means that we need a UWA or I/O area that can hold any of the different kinds of IMS segment that can be retrieved from the external data base, as we saw in more detail in Chapter 10. We must also have a PCB, which, in its object form, contains both the external data base specifications and the special registers for passing control information between the application program and the DL/1 system. This was also explained in Chapter 10. The PCB is actually located with the DL/1 system in the control region or partition, but because the application program has to have access to the special registers that are a part of the PCB, a *PCB-mask* is

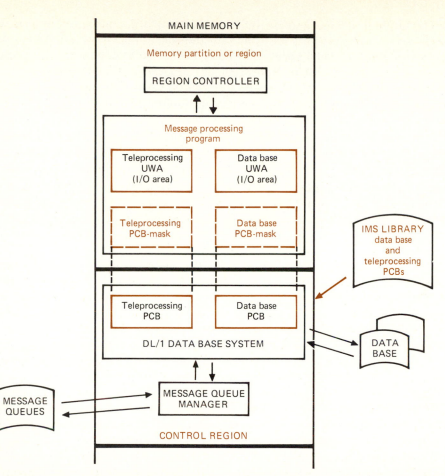

FIGURE 12.13 More detail from the interface in Figure 12.12 between message processing programs (only one shown) and the data base system. Instead of each message processing program independently accessing the message queue, it is the DL/1 data base system that does it, on receipt of a request from the message processing program. This requires the use of a teleprocessing I/O area and teleprocessing PCB for the terminal, much as for an external data base.

used in the application program and must be declared in the program along with the I/O area and other declarations.[1]

---

[1]This should not be interpreted as meaning that we have two distinct sets of special registers in an on-line system, namely, one set in the PCB-mask and another in the PCB proper, instead of just one set as in IMS batch diagrams in Chapter 10. Because of the distinct memory partitions involved, in Figure 12.13 we are forced to draw the PCB and PCB-mask separately. However, there is just one PCB held in the control region. The PCB-mask is declared in the application program with a pointer to the actual PCB, permitting the program to treat it *as if* it were the real PCB.

We mentioned that DL/1 treats the message queue for a message processing program as if it were a simple data base. This data base consists of a sequence of fixed length segments, each segment usually about the length of a line on the terminal. This is shown in Figure 12.14. A message consists of a group of segments. A message is identified by its transaction code at the beginning of the first segment of the message. The segments are read by an application program in chronological order, and when a message is read it is deleted from the queue.

It is by means of DL/1 commands that the application program reads the segments from this message queue data base. Thus, as with all DL/1 data bases, we need:

1. A UWA or I/O area to hold a message segment retrieved, or to be inserted
2. A teleprocessing (TP) PCB for the message-queue data base, and for the associated collection of special registers with which DL/1 will communicate with the application program about the message queue

Thus, as illustrated in Figure 12.13, in an on-line application program there must be both a teleprocessing UWA and a teleprocessing PCB-mask for the message queue that is treated like a DL/1 data base. In addition, the application program will have the normal UWA and PCB-mask for the organization's data base. In order to be able to process these two data bases, the DL/1 system must have access to the teleprocessing (or TP) PCB, as well as the normal PCB, and just before execution of the application program these are taken from the IMS library and loaded by the program scheduler (see Figure 12.12).

We saw in Chapter 10 that a normal PCB more or less corresponds to an external schema specification, which is first specified manually and then translated (Figure 10.18d) by a special utility and placed in the IMS library. A teleprocessing PCB must also be placed in the IMS library for later use by DL/1, but fortunately this is generated automatically when the normal PCB is being translated, and in most cases no manual TP PCB specification is needed. (An

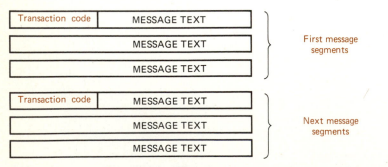

FIGURE 12.14 Shows how a TP message queue is a sequential data base with IMS segments of the same length that are grouped into messages. A DL/1 GU command is used to retrieve the first segment in the file, while the remaining segments of that message are retrieved by repeated GN commands. Retrieval of a message causes it to be removed from the queue, so that the next GU command retrieves the first segment of the next message.

initial manual TP PCB is needed only if a response to a message from one terminal is to go to a second terminal.)

Manipulating the message queue with DL/1

To retrieve a message, the application program then issues a GU command without any SSAs, as shown in Figure 12.15. The first segment of the message goes to the I/O area, and the program then checks to see if there are any more segments, by checking in the special register STATUS. If there are, a GN command is issued and repeated until all the segments of the message have been read by the program. As a result of processing the message, the program will probably carry out some manipulation of the organization's data base and construct a response in the form of segments in the TP user work area. Using DL/1 INSRT commands, the program places these segments in the message queue one by one. Thus we see that the message queue manager is available not only to the telecommunications manager but also to the DL/1 data base system as shown in Figure 12.12.

Formatting the messages for the user

Messages are entered at a terminal by a person who is normally not a computer expert. As an aid to the user, such messages normally contain a lot of redundant information, and the message received by the program is usually much more

```
      CALL "CBLTDL1" USING "GU ", TP-PCB, TP-IN-SEG.

      IF STATUS = "QD" THEN GO TO MESSAGE-PROCESS-PARAGRAPH.
    *That is, if no more segments in message
         .
         .
         .
MESSAGE-SEG-LOOP.

      CALL "CBLTDL1" USING "GN  ", TP-PCB, TP-IN-SEG.

      IF STATUS = "QD" THEN GO TO MESSAGE-PROCESS-PARAGRAPH.
         .
         .
         .
      GO TO MESSAGE-SEG-LOOP.
MESSAGE-PROCESS-PARAGRAPH.
    *Now program accesses the data base in response to message, and so on
```

FIGURE 12.15 Shows how COBOL DL/1 GU and GN commands are used to retrieve the segments of a message from the message queue. Each segment is initially placed in the UWA structure TP-IN-SEG. The teleprocessing PCB called TP-PCB must be declared in the program.

terse. Similarly, the message sent by the message processing program is a much condensed version of the one that is displayed on the terminal. A significant but detailed task in the design of an on-line system involves the specification of the correspondence of messages as seen by the message processing program and messages as seen by the user. With IMS DB/DC, these user and program message specifications are placed in a *message format library*, as shown in Figure 12.16. When a message is received by the communications manager, it is edited or formatted by a message formatting system, which is really a subsystem of the telecommunications manager. The message formatting system uses the specifications in the message format library to correctly format the incoming message. Following formatting the message is placed in a message queue. Similarly, an outgoing message is formatted to suit the display terminal and user.

Four kinds of format specifications are kept in the message format library:

1. Specification of incoming message as it appears to program, or *message input description* (MID)
2. Specification of incoming message as it appears at the terminal, or *device input format* (DIF)
3. Specification of outgoing message as it appears to program, or *message output description* (MOD)
4. Specification of outgoing message as it appears at the terminal, or *device output format* (DOF)

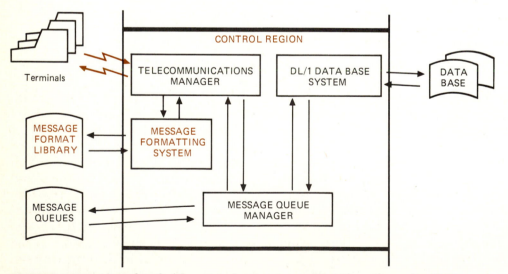

FIGURE 12.16 More detail of the control region (or partition) from the on-line IMS DB/DC system in Figure 12.12. The message received by a message processing program is normally quite different from the one entered at a terminal, and vice versa. A message formatting system is used for conversions between the message as seen by a message processing program and a message as it appears on a terminal. Required program and terminal message formats are stored in a message format library, and part of the job of setting up an on-line system involves designing these detailed formats to be placed in the format library.

The specification of these formats is a tedious and detailed task and must be done for each type of message and each class of terminal in the on-line system. This brings us to the concept of the logical terminal, or logical terminal message.

Logical terminal concept

In Chapters 1 and 2 we saw that the concept of physical and logical storage records was useful in distinguishing between records as they are seen by a conventional file processing COBOL or PL/1 program and records as they are physically formatted on a disk track. The application program deals with the logical storage records, and a hidden subsystem (access method and disk controller) deals with the formatted physical storage records; generally, except for calculations of how many records can fit on a track, we rarely worry about the physical records.

Similarly, it is mentally useful to think in terms of *logical* and *physical terminal messages*, or less accurately, *logical and physical terminals*. The message as seen by the program is the logical message and is generally fairly simple; the message as seen at the terminal is the physical message and is generally quite complex, since it must take the physical characteristics of the terminal (and user) into account. As we have seen, a subsystem that is transparent to the user looks after conversions between physical and logical messages. It is also convenient to think in terms of logical and physical terminals; just as with conventional disk files we could use the concept of physical and logical disks, instead of physical and logical storage files and records.

The teleprocessing monitor CICS

The idealized systems and the IMS DB/DC system described so far illustrate the basic principles behind teleprocessing with data bases. However, these basic systems can be improved upon, and at the time of writing, general purpose teleprocessing monitors such as IBM's Customer Information Control System (CICS) provide the ultimate in the management of on-line systems.

With a batch operating system, the basic aim is to keep the CPU busy. As we saw in Chapter 1, when an application program in an operating system partition requires a record from a disk, it temporarily suspends execution while the record is being fetched, and in the meantime a program in some other partition is given permission to execute. With an on-line system, the aim is different. Users at terminals require that the system respond quickly to their requests, that is, the users need to be kept busy. Thus the most important single measure of the efficiency of an on-line system is the *response time*, that is, the time between pressing the RETURN key on the terminal and the response of the system. Response times of less than 1 second are usually regarded as acceptable. Unfortunately, even with multiple thread processing, as the number of users logged onto an on-line system grows, more and more of the messages must wait in the incoming message queue because of limitations in the number of partitions available to message processing programs. This is usually a major system bottleneck, and it is here that general purpose teleprocessing monitors can improve the response time. The methods used are somewhat involved, but the basic ideas are not all that hard to grasp.

Overview of a CICS on-line system

In Figure 12.17 we have an overview of an on-line system controlled by IBM's CICS and using DL/1 as the data base manager. We shall restrict our coverage to CICS, both because it is probably the most widely used teleprocessing monitor and because it is fairly typical (Ref. 3). The first point to note is that CICS and the message processing programs use just one rather large memory partition provided by the operating system, instead of the large number used by IMS DB/DC.

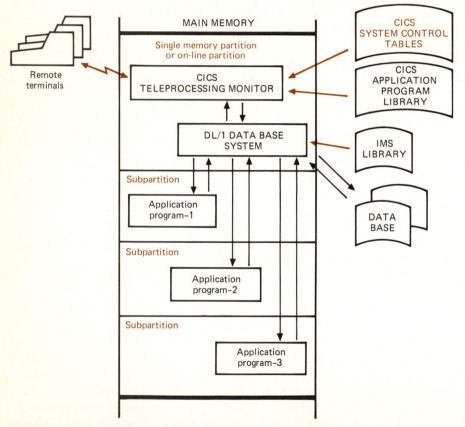

FIGURE 12.17 Overview of IBM's CICS general purpose teleprocessing monitor or DB/DC system. The teleprocessing monitor and the application or message processing programs run in a single batch memory partition, called an on-line or real-time partition. The application programs run in concurrent subpartitions controlled by CICS in order to increase speed of response to transactions arriving from terminals. For a particular on-line system, application programs, terminals, and transactions must be defined in CICS system control tables, which CICS uses to manage the system. CICS makes little use of message queues, creating a task instead to handle each incoming transaction as soon as it arrives (Figure 12.18).

The single CICS partition is known as an *on-line or real-time partition,* and within this partition we have a variable number of subpartitions, each containing an application program. Control of program execution in any of these subpartitions rests with CICS, and this in itself speeds things up since the overhead of the operating system is not involved when switching from one application program to another, as is the case with IMS DB/DC. However, this arrangment is used to increase the response time in another way as we shall see in a moment. For the present let us continue with our overview.

It is CICS that loads an application or message processing program in response to an incoming message or *transaction,* and the application program has to be available in a library, as shown in Figure 12.17. To set the system up, a major design task is the complete definition of each element to be used in the on-line system. The definitions are placed in *system control tables* for use by CICS in controlling a specific system. These system control tables are almost the on-line equivalent of data base definitions. The most important tables that must be defined are:

1. *Program control table (PCT).* This table defines transaction codes for each message processing program. A user at a terminal must enter the appropriate transaction code in order to have a transaction processed by a particular message processing program. Other aspects of transactions, such as priorities, are also defined in this table.
2. *Sign-on table (SNT).* The entries in this table provide security against unauthorized use of the system. The name of each user and his or her password is listed in the table.
3. *Processing program table (PPT).* This table contains a list of all the message processing programs that will be stored in the CICS library.
4. *Terminal control table (TCT).* This table lists all the terminal and communications lines that make up the on-line system.
5. *File control table (FCT).* This table identifies all datasets that will be accessed by message processing programs. Datasets can be conventional storage files, such as VSAM or ISAM files. They can also be IMS datasets, that is, storage hierarchy types, implemented with such hierarchical access methods as HISAM or HDAM (see Chapter 10).

The technical details of how to define these tables is beyond the scope of this book (see Ref. 4). We might point out, however, that each table consists of a collection of entries, for example, an entry for each dataset or message processing program. Each entry is similar in format to a JCL statement. Note that even a simple application involving a few message processing programs, a few datasets, and a few terminals, would require up to a hundred lines of code to define the tables. The tables are normally set up by system programmers and this is one of the major tasks in setting up an on-line system.

CICS programs
More specifications are required than those for the system control tables when a CICS on-line system is being set up. An important specification job involves the

creation of *mapsets* for the format of screens as they will appear to the user, and for corresponding data fields as they will appear to the message processing programs. Provision is made in a mapset definition for the use of a cursor on a terminal screen. In their object form the mapsets play a role similar to the role of the message format library with IMS DB/DC. They thus permit a message processing program to deal with certain data fields, leaving the details of formatting the screen to CICS, which carries out this task with the help of an appropriate mapset.

A COBOL or PL/1 message processing program communicates with the terminals and all datasets and data bases via CICS commands that are embedded in the program. Thus conventional COBOL **READ** and **WRITE** statements cannot be used. CICS input/output commands are used instead. Special CICS DL/1 commands are also used. There are many CICS commands and as a result CICS programming is a special skill, and one that is currently very much in demand. Details are beyond the scope of this book. See Ref. 2.

A single program with multiple concurrent tasks

We mentioned earlier that there is another way in which the use of subpartitions contribute to a low response time. The idea is ingenious, and readers should carefully consider the explanation embodied in Figure 12.18. The diagram shows just a single subpartition containing application program-1; we can assume other application programs in other subpartitions that are not shown. We recall from the beginning of Chapter 1 just exactly what execution of a program entails. Instructions stored in main memory are executed in sequence, and each instruction typically causes the CPU to alter the data in a separate data area. Some compilers generate what is called *reentrant code*, which separates each instruction from any explicit reference to exactly where data in the data area is located. This permits the application program to be used for several different concurrent executions each with a different data area.

This concept needs to be thought about, but we can understand it without descending to the machine language level of computing. Consider a small advertising office that has to deliver fliers to households in a city where we have 1st St., 2nd St., and so on. If each delivery person is to cover three streets, they could all be issued with the instructions:

Deliver to Xth St.
Deliver to $(X+1)$st St.
Deliver to $(X+2)$nd St.

If each delivery person is also given a value for X, then each one executes the same delivery program but processes a different set of streets. Similarly, in Figure 11.18 we have two separate executions of application program-1, each one applying to different data areas, that is, each one is processing a different message. Each of these executions is called a *task*, and there has to be a *task control area* set up by CICS for supervision of each task. Very roughly, this task control area is where the equivalent of the value for X in the delivery program analogy is held. It should be understood that two or more tasks using a single

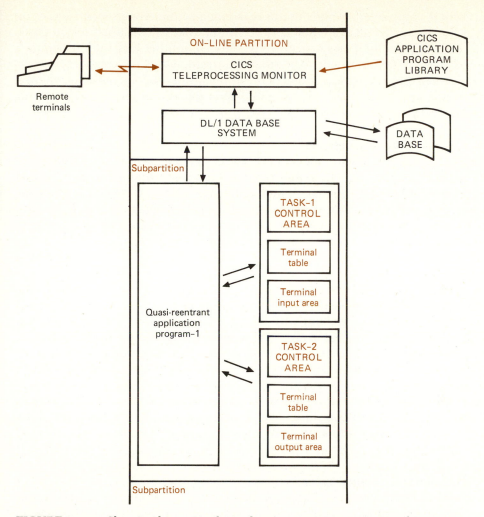

FIGURE 12.18 Showing how a single application program in a CICS subpartition can be used to concurrently process several different transactions. Program-1 above is dealing with two transactions in two separate tasks. Task-1 consists of an execution of program-1 to process a message or transaction in a terminal input area. Interleaved with this execution is another execution (task-2) for another transaction, which has reached the stage of preparing an outgoing message in the terminal output area. Data areas (such as the terminal input area with task-2) are reallocated when no longer needed.

application program can go on concurrently. For example, if task-1 execution of program-1 is temporarily stopped while waiting for a return from the data base system, task-2 execution of program-1 can resume from some point in the program where it left off earlier. Data to keep track of the last position of a task with respect to the application program is also kept in the task control area.

Not all compilers generate reentrant code. The IBM PL/1 compilers do, but the COBOL compiler does not. For this reason the application programs used for multiple tasks with CICS are not fully reentrant, that is, execution for one task with program-1 cannot be stopped anywhere and another task with program-1 started. The programs are said to be *quasi-reentrant,* which means that tasks can start and stop only at certain points in the application program, notably where a call to the data base system is made and thus where the task would have to temporarily stop anyway.

Elimination of message queues

The fact that CICS is able to concurrently process several messages with the same application program decreases the response time and for practical purposes eliminates the message queues. When a message arrives, CICS either loads an application program to process it at once, and we recall it can do this by setting up a new subpartition if necessary for the program to run in, or it creates a new task (with almost no increase in memory requirements) if the required application program is already processing. Either way, processing of the message begins at once.

Prevention of system overload

The absence of message queues with CICS has another practical effect. Since a message is generally processed almost as soon as it is submitted to the system by creation of a new task, it is clear that submission of too many messages will cause the creation of too many tasks. If there were two many tasks each task would execute slowly and in this way the response time would rise. To prevent this from happening, limits to the number of tasks that can be created are normally entered into the system control tables. When the system begins to approach its limits, it simply refuses to accept any more messages or transactions until the load decreases.

Conservation of memory space

Each task has a *terminal input area* for the incoming message, a *terminal output area* where the response is constructed, and a *terminal table* for information about the terminal involved. Notice that in Figure 11.18 we have shown a terminal input area only for task-1 and a terminal output area for task-2. This illustrates another way in which CICS conserves memory space and thus has more room for subpartitions for the different applications. When task-1 is in its beginning stages, it will have no need of space for an output area. Later, it will need space for an output message but will have no need for the input area. CICS allocates storage for these areas only as needed, and when no longer needed, the storage is either reallocated or made part of a reserve pool.

The main components of CICS

Now that we understand how CICS works and what it does, we shall end with a brief look at the various parts of CICS, which is really a collection of modules, many of which carry on functions of the kind discussed earlier with more elementary on-line systems. Referring to Figure 11.19, there is a *terminal mana-*

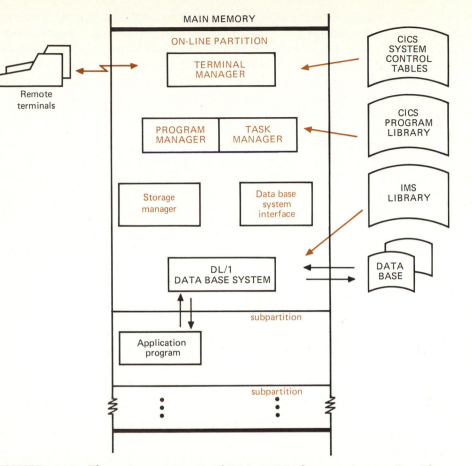

FIGURE 12.19 The main components of IBM's CICS teleprocessing monitor. The function of the terminal manager is as with the simpler systems already described, while the program manager schedules the loading of application programs. The task manager controls the execution of programs that often handle several tasks. The memory storage manager minimizes the amount of main memory required by the on-line partition. Storage and task managers are unique to general purpose teleprocessing monitors and greatly improve the response time of on-line systems.

ger to manage the terminals. The *program manager* corresponds to the program scheduler that we met earlier, and its job is to load application programs in response to incoming messages, creating new subpartitions where necessary. It is closely associated with the *task manager*, which is responsible for setting up multiple tasks that use the same application program. Since availability of memory is crucial for the operation of a CICS on-line system, there has to be a *storage manager* for minimizing the use of this resource. Then we have an *interface* to the data base system. CICS coordinates the use of the data base system to avoid update interference between different tasks, as well as to prevent and resolve deadlock, as was discussed earlier.

If the on-line system does not use a data base, but uses instead a collection of independent conventional files, then use of a teleprocessing monitor such as CICS is probably the only practical way to build the system. In such cases the (special) data base system interface is not needed, and a module called a file manager is used instead to coordinate the manipulation of the files by the various tasks. A decade ago, before the widespread use of teleprocessing monitors, many organizations attempted to construct all the software for their on-line system in house. Usually the difficulties of such endeavors were not appreciated, and many either ended in failure or proved to be unreasonably expensive. Today the cost of a teleprocessing monitor is shared among its many users.

SUMMARY

1. The simplest on-line systems are single-thread systems, in which a message processing program must complete processing of a message before processing of a new message can begin. Since messages originating at user terminals cannot usually be processed at once, they are temporarily stored in an incoming message queue by the terminal manager, which can execute concurrently with a message processing program. Outgoing messages originating from message processing programs are queued in an outgoing message queue and eventually directed to appropriate terminals by the terminal manager.

2. Terminals in an on-line system are frequently geographically remote from the central data base. Messages are transmitted between terminal and central computer either by setting up a temporary physical circuit connection similar to a long-distance telephone connection or by breaking the message up into packets and shunting them through a packet switching communications network. Packet switching networks are expected to become standard, and most systems are based on the CCITT X.25 recommendation. A great many software and hardware modules are involved in packet switching.

3. Single-thread on-line systems tend to be slow. By permitting concurrent execution of message processing programs, response time can be decreased. A special on-line management system called a teleprocessing monitor is required to manage such concurrent processing. Some teleprocessing monitors are designed to function only with a specific data base system. An example is IMS DB/DC for use with IMS. A more generalized system is CICS from IBM, which is very widely used, and which can be used to build an on-line system using either a data base or conventional files. Because the processing of messages from different terminals is interleaved, such on-line systems are known as multiple-thread systems.

QUESTIONS

1. Explain the difference between an interactive operating system, an interactive subsystem embedded in a batch operating system, and an on-line system.

2. Suppose that with the simple on-line system in Figure 12.2, the data base consists of a single indexed sequential file on an IBM 3350 disk. Assume also that the message queues are in relative files on IBM 3350 disks, where the application program is forwarded the address of the next message by the terminal manager, and vice versa. If it requires 10 direct accesses to the data base file to process a message, where each direct access requires two disk accesses to search the index, and if it takes 100 milliseconds to display a response on a local user's screen, what is the shortest possible response time? Use the disk data in Appendix 1.

3. Repeat Question 2 assuming that the data base is a single hash file with average search length 1.1.

4. Assuming that all messages are like the one described in Question 2, how many messages per minute could the system in Figure 12.2 handle approximately.

5. If we expand the system in Figure 12.2 to include a library of different message processing programs but permit only single thread operation, why will this not improve the response time?

6. What is the basic principle of a store and forward packet switching network?

7. Explain why message packets do not all need to take the same route to their common destination. Is this possible in a communications network based on temporary physical circuit connections similar to telephone connections?

8. What is a communications protocol?

9. Explain what the following do: (a) communications access method, (b) communications controller, (c) front-end processor, and (d) terminal cluster controller.

10. Explain to a lay person what the CCITT X.25 recommendation means for the future of computer communications.

11. With IMS DB/DC explain the difference between a teleprocessing PCB and a data base PCB.

12. With the IMS DB/DC how does a message processing program handle the formatting of terminal screens?

13. With IMS DB/DC how does a message processing program communicate with a remote terminal?

14. How is concurrent processing managed with IMS DB/DC?

15. How is an on-line system defined with CICS?

16. How are incoming and outgoing message queues avoided with CICS?

17. Explain the concept of a task with CICS.

18. What is a CICS mapset, and what is it used for?

19. In a message processing program run under CICS, why can we not use conventional COBOL or PL/1 READ/WRITE commands?

20. What are some of the major software tasks in setting up an on-line system?

21. How is system overload prevented in a CICS on-line system?

22. How does CICS conserve the use of main memory when many tasks are in operation?

23. Explain why construction of an on-line system without some kind of commercially available teleprocessing monitor is likely to fail?

24. If you were a data processing manager responsible for setting up an on-line system for many bank branches, give an account of some of the software you would consider acquiring and the kinds of computer specialists you would consider hiring.

25. Make up a newspaper advertisement to hire the people needed for the construction of the on-line system in Question 24. Compare your advertisement with a real one clipped from a newspaper or computer magazine.

ADDITIONAL PERSPECTIVE
DISTRIBUTED DATA BASES

In this book so far we have always assumed that we were dealing with one or more data bases in the same single central location. However, at the present time considerable efforts are being made to develop systems that will permit an organization's data bases to be distributed or dispersed geographically. There are powerful economic motivations behind these efforts:

1. *Cost of data transmission.* It is uneconomic to centrally store data in Chicago, for example, if that data concerns plant operations in San Francisco and is needed mostly by San Francisco users. Telecommunications costs would be much reduced if the data mostly used in San Francisco were stored locally, and if the data mostly needed in Chicago were also stored locally.

2. *Reduction in data processing bureaucracy.* Data processing was centralized originally because of the high cost of computers. With time, data processing centers have grown very complex. They are becoming increasingly difficult to manage well, and there are many who wonder if their costs do not exceed their benefits in many instances. The rise of data base management systems has unfortunately accelerated the trend toward centralization. The problem of bureaucracy in data processing appears to be a real one, and user complaints about the data processing bureaucrats, whose efforts often appear to make things worse, are becoming common. There is a trend toward reducing the power of the central computing bureaucracy by giving more data processing autonomy to local users. The belief is that it is much easier to control costs and measure local benefits with smaller local data processing departments that are the custodians of the locally needed data.

3. *Costs of computers have dropped significantly.* Minicomputers today are as powerful as the mainframes of a decade ago. And with the continual advances in microelectronics, it seems likely that before the 1980s are over, we shall have personal computers with the power of today's super minicomputers, such as Digital Equipment's VAX 11/780, but with much reduced initial cost.

For all these reasons it seems desirable to use data that is distributed geographically within an organization. We have seen that it is also desirable to store data in data bases where possible because of the advantages of data independence, lack of significant duplication of data, and the possibility of using powerful data base query languages such as SQL and QBE. Thus the next big development in data base management must be systems to enable an organization's data bases to be distributed to the best possible advantage.

In the past 5 years there has been considerable research and development effort in the field of distributed data bases. A noteworthy example is the distributed system SDD.1 from Computer Corporation of America, which we shall look at later. First we look at the basic concepts in distributed data bases.

The unit of distribution and relational fragments

When we talk of distributing the data of a business organization geographically, we must be careful as to the nature of the *unit of distribution*. For example, in a data base involving 10 relations, we might want to place 5 of them at one site or *node* where they are mostly used, and 5 relations at another site. In such a case the unit of distribution is the relation. However, research into distributed data bases has shown that such a large unit of distribution is far too coarse in many cases. Consider the case of a corporation with major business activities in two cities, namely, Seattle and Miami. This corporation has an **EMPLOYEE** conceptual file (in this case also a relation) as shown in Figure 12.20*a*. We can see that employees are located in either Miami or Seattle. Thus it would be reasonable to distribute records of this relation according to the **LOCATION** value. That part of the relation for which **LOCATION** has the value '**SEATTLE**' is shown in Figure 12.20*a*, and this *fragment* would be stored in Seattle while the other fragment for which the **LOCATION** value is '**MIAMI**' would be stored in Miami. If the distributed data base system allows a relation to be broken up or *fragmented* in this way, we can say that the unit of distribution is a *relational fragment*. Most authorities agree that relational fragments should be the unit of distribution.

The method used to generate the fragment in Figure 12.20*b* is called *horizontal partitioning*. We can also use *vertical partitioning*. For example, it might be that the only commonly used information in Seattle about Seattle employees is salary information. Thus we could further partition the fragment in Figure 12.20*b* into the fragment in Figure 12.20*c*. This new fragment is arrived at by selecting out appropriate columns.[1]

Most of the work on distributed data bases has involved relational data bases, and the processes used to define fragments are as a result relational algebra processes. Thus horizontal partitioning is the relational algebra *selection operation*, while vertical partitioning is the relational algebra *projection operation*, which we met briefly in Chapter 9. There is a description of relational

---

[1]Note that when columns are selected, it may happen that there are duplicate rows in the resulting fragment. If the fragment is to remain a relation, these duplicate rows must be eliminated.

EMPNUMB	LOCATION	SALARY	SKILL
E1	SEATTLE	20,000	PROGRAMMER
E3	MIAMI	25,000	ENGINEER
E4	MIAMI	26,000	MANAGER
E6	SEATTLE	23,000	SALESREP
E7	SEATTLE	24,000	ACCOUNTANT
E9	MIAMI	27,000	ENGINEER
E10	SEATTLE	18,000	SECRETARY

EMPLOYEE

(a) A relation that is distributed geographically into distributed fragments;

EMPNUMB	LOCATION	SALARY	SKILL
E1	SEATTLE	20,000	PROGRAMMER
E6	SEATTLE	23,000	SALESREP
E7	SEATTLE	24,000	ACCOUNTANT
E10	SEATTLE	18,000	SECRETARY

(b) horizontal fragmentation of the relation EMPLOYEE in (a);

EMPNUMB	SALARY
E1	20,000
E6	23,000
E7	24,000
E10	18,000

(c) further vertical fragmentation of the relation in (b).

FIGURE 12.20 Decomposition of a global relation into fragments for distribution. A fragment may be generated by either the horizontal or vertical fragmentation process, or by both processes. Fragments are distributed geographically, although the same fragment may be replicated at different sites.

algebra in an Additional Perspective on Chapter 7. However, readers need to be aware only of the concept of a fragment in order to grasp the essentials of distributed data bases. It should also be noted that the tendency to use relational data bases in the development of distributed data base systems is further evidence of the trend to relational data bases and of the need to design all data bases, whether or not they are to be managed by a relational system, as relational data bases.

Global and local data bases

We recall that a relation is a conceptual file of a restricted type, and that a conceptual file does not really exist but is abstracted from a storage file which does exist. The relation **EMPLOYEE** in Figure 12.20 is a relation, but if it is fragmented and distributed to different sites, it is clearly not a relation like any we have come across so far. The fragments of this relation will normally also be relations, and so they too are conceptual files abstracted from storage files. Thus the storage files underlying the fragments must also be physically distributed, and a collection of these storage files at a given site will be a *local storage data base.*

Abstracted from a local storage data base is a *local conceptual data base* (Figure 12.21), where a local conceptual data base will contain relations, some of which are fragments. Fragments from many different local conceptual data bases can be joined together to form a global relation or global conceptual file, such as **EMPLOYEE** in Figure 12.20. A collection of global relations is a *global conceptual data base.*

A distributed data base therefore contains but one global conceptual data base and is made up of a collection of global relations. Some of these global relations will be fragmented and the fragments distributed to different sites. Other global relations will simply be located at a single site without fragmentation.

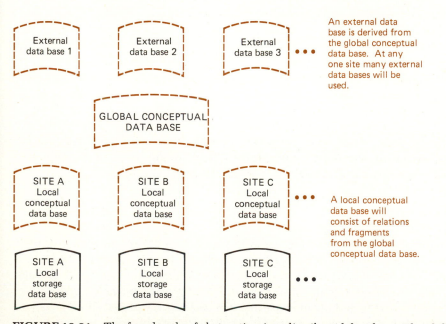

FIGURE 12.21   The four levels of abstraction in a distributed data base. The global conceptual data base encompasses all the data in the distributed data base, and external data bases are abstracted from it. The global conceptual data base is also a combination of all the local conceptual data bases at different sites. Each local conceptual data base is abstracted from a local storage data base. Only local storage data bases actually exist physically. The global conceptual data base can be *defined* at one central site, there can be replication of the definition at many sites, or the definition can be distributed by means of special directories.

A user of a distributed data base normally is not aware that the data is distributed and views the data base by means of his or her external data base. This external data base is abstracted from a conceptual data base as is usual, but this time it must be abstracted from the global conceptual data base, since the user will in all likelihood need to deal with data that is stored at other sites in the network. Typically at any given site there will be many different external data bases.

Thus a distributed data base is a four-level data base as is shown in Figure 12.21. However, it must be remembered that only the local storage data bases actually exist. A further point worth remembering is that a relation (or relational fragment) at one site may be duplicated or replicated at other sites without any effect on the global conceptual data base.

The reason for the four levels of abstraction with distributed data bases is the same as the reason for three levels with conventional data bases—data independence. If the proper management software is in place, with a distributed data base three types of data independence must be preserved:

1. *Physical or storage data independence.* It must be possible to alter the organization of the storage data base at any site without affecting the ability of a single application program to execute. Naturally the performance of application programs will be affected by changes of the organization to the local storage data bases.

2. *Logical or local conceptual data independence.* The addition or subtraction of fields making up a local relation must not affect the ability of an application program to execute, if the fields involved are not used by the program.

3. *Global data independence.* It must be possible to change the way in which the global conceptual data base is distributed without affecting the ability of an application program to run. Thus a program should be independent of a change of relation X from site A to site B, or of a new way of fragmenting and distributing a certain global relation.

The schemas for distributed data bases

There will be a schema or data base definition for each of the four levels of data base abstraction. Each user will need an external schema, and for accessing a local data base, there will be a need for a local conceptual and local storage schema. The distributed data base system will have to be able to obtain a definition of the entire global data base at any site. Thus the global schema can be either replicated at every site, or it could be itself distributed.

A further definition is needed with a distributed data base in order for it to be possible to determine at just which site or sites a given global relation is located. This definition is contained in what is sometimes called a *geographic location directory*, or just plain *location directory*. We can get a better idea of why the location directory is needed by examining a distributed data base system.

Elements of a distributed data base system

In Figure 12.22 we show the essential components *at a single site* in an idealized distributed data base system. The system has a four-level architecture, reflecting the four levels of abstraction in a distributed data base. The single application program can be assumed to be manipulating an external data base, whose external schema is available to the distributed data base system, as shown in the diagram. We can also assume that the external data base is ultimately based on storage data bases at different sites.

Suppose that the program requires data from the data base, and that the request is in the form of an SQL command involving many external relations. This request goes to a global data base manager, which deals with all matters involving the global data base, from which the external data base will have been abstracted. The global manager analyzes the request and determines which relations are needed to carry it out. From the data in the global conceptual schema and in the geographic location directory, the global manager can determine how the relations involved are associated and where they are located in the

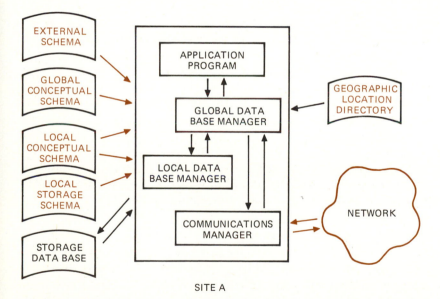

SITE A

FIGURE 12.22 Elements of a distributed data base system at a single site. An application program can manipulate the entire distributed data base or a part of it, which may also be distributed. The application program passes requests for data (or for updating) to the global DB manager, which makes use of the external schema and global conceptual schema to determine which global relations are involved. It then uses the geographic location directory to determine where the underlying local conceptual relations and fragments are related. It then sends instructions to the local data base managers at the sites involved to retrieve the required data. The global DB manager uses the communications manager to communicate with the other sites. All sites have the type of structures and systems shown above.

network. The global manager then constructs routines that will be sent to each of the sites involved and which will be executed by the local data base managers. Each of these routines is a sequence of data base commands, and normally the first thing a local data base manager must do is place the relations involved, or at least the parts of the relations involved, under lock, to prevent interference by other application programs. It is the global data base manager that generates the concurrency control strategy for a given request from an application program, and this adds to the complexity of the global manager.

Each local data base manager is really a conventional data base system that has no cognizance of the global aspect of things. The local data base manager carries out its instructions from the global manager much as would a conventional data base system. When the required data has been obtained by the local data base managers, it is then sent to the site whence the request first was issued, where the global manager will probably carry out further manipulation of this data. Finally, the global manager returns the result to the application program that issued the request.

A similar sequence takes place when the request issued by the application program is an updating request. As we saw with SQL in Chapter 7, a request can involve a retrieval part and an updating part. Here the global manager determines the retrieval and updating routines for each site and forwards them to the local data base managers. The update data is forwarded along with these routines. Concurrency control is important, and the appropriate parts of the affected local data bases must be all concurrently locked while the retrievals and updatings are taking place. The concurrency control aspects of a distributed data base system are among the most difficult. Many different methods have been proposed and investigated, and significant advances have taken place (see Ref. 1). When we state here that relevant parts of the distributed data base must be locked to ensure effective concurrency control, this should not be taken too literally. With some experimental systems, such as SDD.1, relevant portions of the local data bases are locked for only a fraction of the time required for carrying out an update or retrieval; this is accomplished by allowing each local data base manager to carry out a great deal of manipulation on copies of the affected data base portions that are held in special work spaces. The local data bases have to be locked only when data is being transferred to and from these work spaces. These work spaces thus provide the local data base managers with consistent sets of data that are free from interference by other applications.

SDD.1

Although distributed data base management is still in its infancy, some systems have been developed. The most significant system to date is probably Computer Corporation of America's System for Distributed Data Bases, or SDD.1. This system was developed in the late 1970s for the United States Department of Defense under contract from the Advanced Research Projects Agency (ARPA). Detailed descriptions may be found in Ref. 1.

The essentials of the system are illustrated in Figure 12.23 and are similar to that of the idealized system in Figure 12.22, although the details differ. Requests

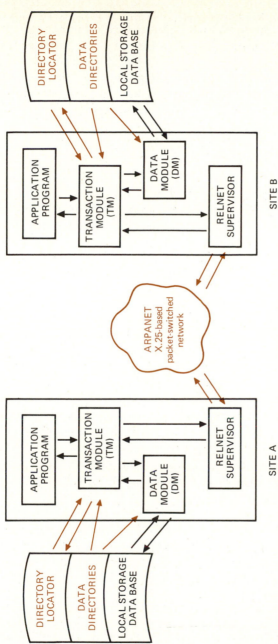

FIGURE 12.23 Essentials of SDD.1, a distributed data base management system from Computer Corporation of America. The transaction module (TM) is the global data base manager, while the data module (DM) is built around a relational data base system called Datacomputer and serves as the local data base system. Descriptions of local and global data bases, as well as a directory locator, are stored as relational data bases along with the user data bases at each site. The directory locator may be needed at a local site because the directory itself can be distributed. The directory locator thus enables the system to determine where a needed data directory is located in the network. The diagram above shows only two nodes of the network. The RELNET supervisor manages communications within the network.

SITE A

SITE B

DIRECTORY LOCATOR

DATA DIRECTORIES

LOCAL STORAGE DATA BASE

APPLICATION PROGRAM

TRANSACTION MODULE (TM)

DATA MODULE (DM)

RELNET SUPERVISOR

ARPANET X.25-based packet-switched network

from application programs (and terminal users) are passed to the *transaction monitor* (TM), which functions as the global data base manager. It is called a transaction monitor because each request for retrieval or update of data issued anywhere in the system by an application program or terminal user is called a *transaction*. Thus any SQL command is equivalent to an SDD.1 transaction. However, SQL is not used in the system; instead a language called Datalanguage is used, which is the language of a relational data base system called Datacomputer developed by Computer Corporation of America. However, the differences between this language and SQL are not important for understanding SDD.1, and readers can conveniently imagine that a transaction is an SQL command.

At each site there will also be at least one system called a data monitor (DM), which functions as a local data base manager. DM is based on Datacomputer and can manipulate a local relational data base. Each local data base can contain fragments of global relations; these fragments are generated by vertical or horizontal partitioning or both.

When DDD.1 was being planned in the mid-seventies, the ANSI/SPARC report recommending three-level data bases had yet to be issued (see Chapter 4), and SDD.1 does not appear to make use of a clean four-level structure, as illustrated in Figure 12.22. The equivalent of the four schema types and location directory are all present, however, and are contained in the site data directories. However, a data directory is structured like a relational data base and can also be distributed. To enable the TM to determine where a needed part of a data directory is located, a directory locator can be used at each site. As its name implies, the directory locator contains information about where fragments and relations of the data directory are stored in the system. The TM can then send a request to the local DMs to transmit the required data directory information. The RELNET (reliable network) supervisor at each site looks after data transmission at the request of the TM. The TM accepts all update and retrieval requests and generates routines for execution by the DMs at remote sites in much the same way as described for the idealized distributed system in the previous section. For details see Ref. 1.

The network

The network used by SDD.1 is ARPANET, which is a packet-switched network that grew up in the United States in the 1970s. Today it includes installations in Canada and Europe. This network is used differently from the commercial networks used by large corporations for on-line systems. Most of the users of ARPANET are universities and research establishments, and a user at one node on the net can have a program executed at another node. ARPANET is frequently used for experimenting with new communications systems, which probably explains why it was used with SDD.1. ARPANET conforms to the CCITT X.25 packet switching standards recommendation.

Universal distributed data base systems

Although it may well find significant use commercially, SDD.1 is a special purpose distributed data base system. The problem for most large organizations currently running one or more of the well-established commercial data base systems is that SDD.1 works only with the local data base manager Datacomputer. A large organization that has one data base system such as IMS operating in New York, another in Texas such IDMS, and another in California, would need a distributed system that could interface all of these existing systems. As was discussed in Chapter 10, once a particular data base system has become entrenched in an organization, for better or for worse, the organization is forced to continue with it because of the enormous cost of rewriting application programs if it were replaced. The days of *software revolutions* are long gone. Today's economics dictate *software evolution*, and what is needed is a distributed system that can work with any of today's established data base systems.

The solution to the problem appears to be along the lines shown in Figure 12.24. The diagram shows the major components at one site of a distributed system that has many different types of data base system in use for local data management. We recall that with SDD.1, and with other distributed systems as well, it is necessary for application programs to pass requests to the global data base manager, not to the local data base manager. Thus an IMS application program, for example, should be able to ask for data from an external data base specified in a PCB regardless of where the data is actually located in the network,

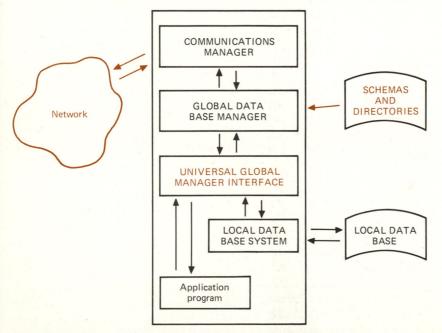

FIGURE 12.24   A site at a distributed data base system that can handle a variety of local data base systems. The global data base manager is the same at all sites, while the local data base system could be any of the established commercial data base systems. In a distributed system the local application programs and local data base manager must be able to interface with the global data manager, so that there is a need for an interface module, or universal global manager interface. The trend is toward development of distributed data base systems of this type.

requiring that application programs pass requests to the global data manager via a special IMS interface. At some other site a (CODASYL) IDMS system could be in operation with the same global manager, so that here too we would need a special interface. Ideally a universal interface would enable any widely used data base system and associated application programs to be attached to the standard global data base manager as shown in Figure 11.24. This interface is likely to be extraordinarily complex, if an application program at a site is to be able to view the distributed data base as an IMS, CODASYL, relational, or other type of data base, when in reality the distributed data base is a conglomerate of many different types of data base.

QUESTIONS

26. Give an explanation of the advantages to an organization of distributing its data bases.
27. Why do you think that distributed data base systems are currently not more commonly used?
28. Explain the concepts of the unit of distribution and relational fragment.
29. Explain the concept of the global data base.
30. Explain how an external data base in a distributed system can be ultimately based on storage relations and fragments that are physically distributed.
31. Explain the difference between a global and local data base manager.
32. Explain how global data independence is related to logical (or local conceptual) data independence.
33. Why is concurrency control a much more difficult problem with distributed data bases compared with conventional (local) data bases?
34. Why is a location directory or equivalent needed with a distributed data base system. Give an analogy using telephone directories for a large number of North American cities.
35. Give some arguments in favor of a distributed data base management system that has many different types of local data base systems such as IDMS, IMS, TOTAL, or ADABAS.

REFERENCES

1. Bernstein, P. A., D. W. Shipman, and J. B. Rothie, 1980. "Concurrency Control in a System for Distributed Data Bases (SDD-1)." *ACM Trans. on Data Base Sys.*, 5(1):18–51.
2. IBM, *CICS Application Program Reference Manual*. Form Number SC33–0077.
3. IBM, *CICS General Information Manual*. Form Number GC33–0066.
4. IBM, *CICS System Programmer's Reference Manual*. Form Number SC33–0069.
5. IBM, *IMS/VS General Information Manual*. Form Number GH20–1260
6. Martin James, 1981. *Computer Networks and Distributed Processing*. Prentice-Hall, Englewood Cliffs, N.J.

13

The Management of the Data Base Environment

Since the early 1970s, when data base management came into widespread commercial use, experience has shown that there are two essentials for the successful management of the data base environment. One of these is the creation of a group in the organization called a *data base administration group,* and the other is the provision and use of a more technical tool called a *data dictionary system.*

A data base administration group is essential for the resolution and prevention of the many conflicts that arise when shared data bases are used in an organization. The data dictionary system permits the data base administration group to create and maintain a corporate data dictionary, which permits standardization of data within the organization.

Since a data dictionary system is a tool of the data base administration group, it is better to look at data dictionary systems before we study the functions and organization of the data base administration group, often referred to simply as the data base administrator (DBA). In smaller organizations the data base administration group is often a single person.

13.1 DATA DICTIONARY SYSTEMS

In Chapter 4 we introduced the basic concept of a data dictionary and associated data dictionary system. In this chapter we continue with a more detailed coverage of data dictionary systems in the light of their fundamental role in the management of the data base environment. We begin with the evolution of the subject, as this is without doubt the easiest way to gain insight into data dictionary systems that are in use or under development.

Evolution of data dictionary systems

In the early days, a data dictionary system was a pencil and paper system, as is illustrated in Figure 13.1a. As a data base was being planned and developed, the DBA found it useful to write down descriptions of each field that was important to the organization and likely to be used by applications that would become data base applications. This manual list of fields or data elements underwent continual modification as data base design and development work proceeded. At the same time many different people needed to know the details about individual fields, for example, application programmers working on data base applications, data base designers, and even user groups for their own planning purposes. All these people found it useful to have a copy of at least a part of the manual field lists or data dictionary. But because the dictionary was under continual revision during the early stages of data base development, it proved difficult to have an up-to-date copy in the hands of each of those in the organization with a need to know. The solution was to use the computer.

This brings us to the next step in the development of data dictionary systems, as is illustrated in Figure 13.1b. The list of field descriptions that largely formed the manual data dictionary was placed on disk in a sequential file using the facilities of either an interactive operating system such as VM/CMS or an interactive subsystem such as TSO that was embedded in a batch operating system (see Chapter 12). Typically, the editor was then used to update and retrieve data from the data dictionary files. The immediate benefit was that everybody had access to an up-to-date data dictionary. While a single file data dictionary for listing field descriptions was common, people soon began to construct more elaborate data dictionaries, containing additional dictionary files such as a file for data base file descriptions. Thus we began to have the makings of the data dictionary data base.

To manage this more complex data dictionary, the independent data dictionary system appeared, as illustrated in Figure 13.1c. This gave the DBA a primitive command or query language with which to update and interrogate the data dictionary. The heart of the system was the data dictionary manager, which essentially was a primitive data base system. Common also was a report generator that could generate different types of data dictionary reports on the basis of instructions entered at a terminal. While this data dictionary was essentially a data base and the data dictionary manager was essentially a data base system, the whole system was essentially a *stand-alone system* and had nothing to do with the data base system that was used to manage the corporate data bases.

The next step was a partial integration of the data dictionary system and the data base management system. Systems of this type are commonly used, and a good example is IBM's Data Dictionary/Directory, which is illustrated in Figure

13.1d. The first point is that the data dictionary is stored as a collection of IMS (physical) data bases. Actually there are five simple data bases:

1. A data base that describes each (physical) IMS data base (we recall that with IMS each hierarchy type is implemented as a single IMS data base).
2. A data base that describes IMS segments or conceptual records.
3. A data base that describes IMS fields.
4. A data base for all the PCBs used with the IMS data bases.
5. A data base about applications.

The second point is that it is the DL/1 data base system that manages these IMS data dictionary data bases, although DL/1 merely carries out the commands issued by the equivalent of a data dictionary manager. Many different data dictionary modules interface with the DL/1 manager via the dictionary manager as shown in Figure 12.1d. There is a report generator for generating data dictionary reports and a query processor so that the dictionary can be interrogated from a terminal. Then there is a *source PSB generator*, which permits the automatic

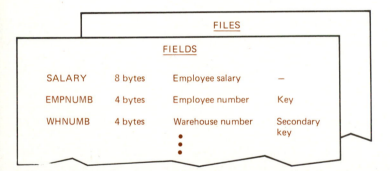

(a) Manual data dictionary system. A list of fields and tentative files are kept on paper and regularly updated as development proceeds. Up-to-date corporatewide copies cannot easily be made available.

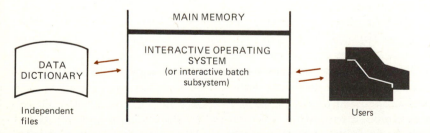

(b) Data dictionary stored on disk. A data dictionary of the type shown in (a) is simply stored as a set of independent files using the facilities of an interactive operating system such as VM/CMS or an interactive subsystem such as TSO embedded in a batch operating system. This permits concurrent access by corporatewide users.

FIGURE 13.1 Evolution of data dictionary systems

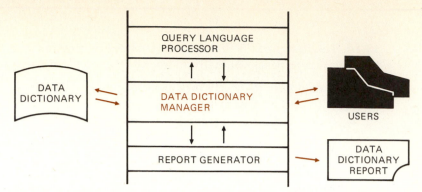

(c) DBMS independent data dictionary system. The former data dictionary files are now integrated and form a data base. Typically we have a dictionary manager that interfaces to a query processor and a report generator. Thus many users can access the data dictionary data base via the terminals, and reports can be made available to all working on the design of the enterprise and conceptual schemas and to many users of the data base. The system is completely independent of the data base system that manages the data base whose fields and files are listed in the dictionary. User and DBMS data are commonly stored in the dictionary.

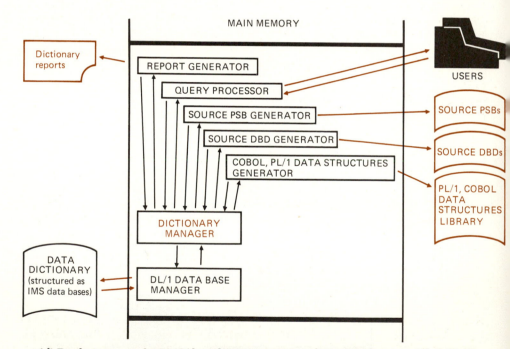

(d) Partly integrated DBMS/data dictionary system from IBM for use with IMS. The data dictionary is structured as a collection of IMS data bases and is managed indirectly by the dictionary manager via the DL/1 data base manager. In addition to being able to respond to queries about the dictionary and generate reports about it, there are subsystems for generating source PSBs and DBDs for use with the corporate IMS data bases. These source PSBs and DBDs must be translated in the usual way (see Figure 10.19) and placed in the IMS library for use in normal data base processing. There is no connection between use of DL/1 with the corporate data bases and with its use by the dictionary manager.

FIGURE 13.1   (continued)

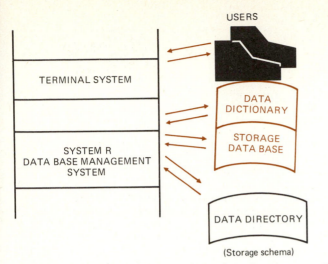

USERS

TERMINAL SYSTEM

DATA
DICTIONARY

STORAGE
DATA BASE

SYSTEM R
DATA BASE MANAGEMENT
SYSTEM

DATA DIRECTORY

(Storage schema)

(e) State of the art integration of the data dictionary and data base management systems in System R. The conceptual and external schemas or views used by System R to manipulate the corporate storage data base are stored in a data dictionary. The data dictionary has a relational structure and is stored as a relational data base. This means that it is possible for a user to both update the data dictionary from a terminal and to interrogate it using the System R query language SQL (see Chapter 8). The basic structure of the System R data dictionary is close to that shown for the conceptual files FILE and FIELD-IN-FILE in Figure 13.4. These conceptual data dictionary files contain information that the data base system must have access to. A user could extend the data dictionary by creating additional System R relations to give a structure along the lines shown in Figure 13.4.

FIGURE 13.1   (continued)

generation of source PSBs from the data in the dictionary. We recall that a PSB is the collection of PCBs, where a PCB is roughly equivalent to an external schema, and the PSB is used in an application program to permit manipulation of a number of external IMS data bases. Referring to Figure 10.19, this source PSB, even if generated by the data dictionary facility, must still be translated and placed in the proper IMS library before the relevant application program can run.

In a similar manner the data dictionary system can generate a source DBD (see Figure 10.9), which must then be translated before being placed in the IMS library. There is also a facility for generating COBOL and PL/1 data structures (UWAs) for use in application programs. For more on the IMS data dictionary system, see Ref. 8.

It is thus clear that there is a fairly high degree of integration between the data dictionary system and the IMS data base management system. Nevertheless, when an application is running and using the DL/1 system and one or more external IMS data bases, the data dictionary is not involved in any way, since the schemas or data base definitions used by DL/1 in running an application, and the data dictionary, are physically distinct. The next step is the full integration of the

FILENAME	CREATOR	NFIELDS

DB-FILES

1:*n*

FILENAME	FIELDNAME	TYPE	LENGTH

DB-FIELDS

FIGURE 13.2 The basic files in the System R data dictionary (but with different names). Each record in DB-FILES describes a file or base table in the System R data base: FILENAME gives the name of the System R file, CREATOR gives the name of the group that created it, and NFIELDS gives the number of fields in the file. Each record in DB-FIELDS describes a file in a System R file, so that if a field is used in three files there will be three records in DB-FIELDS: FIELDNAME gives the name of a System R field, FILENAME gives the name of a file it is used in, TYPE gives the type of field (numeric, alphanumeric, or other), and LENGTH gives the length of a field. Since a file has many fields, there will be a one-to-many relationship between DB-FILES and DB-FIELDS. (Diagram reproduced from the author's "File & Data Base Techniques," Holt, Rinehart & Winston, 1982.)

system that manages the data dictionary with the system that manages the corporate data bases.

Although it has not been released at the time of writing, IBM's System R is such a system and probably represents the state of the art in *fully integrated data dictionary systems*. It contains the data dictionary/directory facility described in the overview of data dictionaries in Chapter 4. An overview of System R in an interactive environment is shown in Figure 13.1e. The main point is that the data base system employs conceptual and external schemas that are a major component of the data dictionary. Thus we do not have a data dictionary that is distinct from the conceptual and external schemas as with less sophisticated systems, and the System R data base system manages two data bases, namely, the data dictionary data base and the corporate (storage) data base. This means that we can apply SQL to the retrieval of information about the data base, that is, information in the data dictionary. A minimum System R data dictionary has the basic structure shown in Figure 13.2 (although with different field and file names). The data in this dictionary may be accessed like a normal System R data base using SQL (Refs. 1 and 2). If we wanted to know what data base files (or base tables) a given field such as **EMPNUMB** was used in, we could issue the SQL request:

```
SELECT FILENAME
FROM DB-FILES
WHERE (FIELDNAME = 'EMPNUMB')
```

Outline of a comprehensive data dictionary

With a fully integrated data dictionary system like the one in System R, it is possible to extend the data dictionary as required to satisfy user, DBA, and auditor needs, as opposed to DBMS needs. An example of such an extended data dictionary is shown in Figure 13.3. There is a record in the dictionary file **DOMAIN** for every domain in the data base, and there will be a one-to-many relationship between **DOMAIN** and the records describing data base fields in the dictionary file **FIELD** (for the domain concept see Chapter 7). There will be a many-to-many relationship between the records of the dictionary file **FILE**, that describe data base files, and the records of **FIELD**, that describe data base fields, since a file has many fields and a field can occur in many files. (Notwithstanding the fact that one of the major aims of the data base approach is elimination of duplicate fields, in practice there is a controlled redundancy. For example, in a data base designed as a relational data base the existence of connection fields will ensure that certain fields occur in several data base files.) The many-to-many relationship between **FILE** and **FIELD** resolves into two one-to-many relationships involving the dictionary file **FIELD-IN-FILE**, each record of which gives information about a field in a file. The **STATUS** field in **FIELD-IN-FILE** is

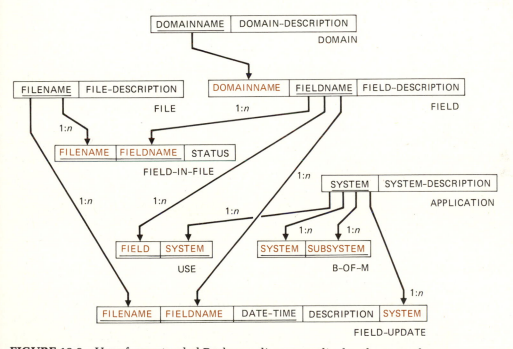

FIGURE 13.3 Use of an extended Bachman diagram to display the general structure of a data dictionary data base. Based on each domain (assuming that the data base being described is a relational data base) there will be many fields, so that there is a one-to-many relationship between DOMAIN and FIELD. Each data base file described in a FILE record has many fields that are described in FIELD records, and vice versa, so that there is a many-to-many relationship between the files FILE and FIELD. A field has a status that depends on what file it is in (see Figure 4.9a), so that we need STATUS in the file FIELD-IN-FILE. We need the file USE for the many-to-many relationship between a field in FIELD and application program or system in SYSTEM. Subsystems are structured as in a bill-of-materials file (B-OF-M). To provide for an audit trail for auditors we keep track of all updates by systems in FIELD-UPDATE.

used to keep track of different field functions. For example, in one file the field **EMPNUMB** (employee number) could be a secondary key and a connection field, while in another it could be a primary key.

It is useful to know what systems or applications fields are used in. Since a field can be used in many applications and an application uses many fields, there will be another many-to-many relationship between the records of **FIELD** and the records of **APPLICATION**, where an **APPLICATION** record describes an application program or system. The auxiliary dictionary file **USE** enables this many-to-many relationship to be resolved into the usual pair of one-to-many relationships.

In a Chapter 9 supplement we covered recursive many-to-many relationships and bills of materials, which deal with components within components. While readers have probably never thought about it, computer applications are designed today in the same modular way that hardware systems are designed, so that a software subsystem is used in many application systems, and an application system has many subsystems, and so on. Thus the application systems of a large organization form a bill of (software) materials, and the dictionary files **APPLICATION** and **B-OF-M** in Figure 13.3 reflect this. Readers who have studied the Chapter 9 supplement should take time to draw a diagram similar to that in Figure 9.46, to ensure that they understand the recursive relationship inherent in the two dictionary files **APPLICATION** and **B-OF-M**.

Finally we have the dictionary file **FIELD-UPDATE** that logs every update to the fields of the data base. Its primary purpose is to provide an audit trail for auditors. Each record in the dictionary file **FIELD-UPDATE** describes an update to a field in the organization's data bases. An update is uniquely identified by the field that is updated, the data base file in which the field resides, and the time when it happened. The data in the description field or fields should be sufficiently comprehensive to permit an auditor to trace the source of the update, that is, to follow an audit trail. We shall return to auditing and audit trails in a later section.

13.2 FUNCTIONS OF THE DBA

The data base administrator group, or DBA, interacts with many different individuals, groups, and systems and is responsible for many different functions. As a result the DBA plays a central role in an organization employing data base processing, as is illustrated in Figure 13.4. Nevertheless, as mentioned at the beginning of the chapter, the primary overall function of the DBA is the prevention and resolution of the inevitable conflicts caused by the pooling in common data bases of the operational data that was once the preserve of individual departments or groups—under the old regime of conventional file processing. However, this all important conflict resolution and prevention function cannot be easily defined and in fact resolves into a fairly large number of more explicit functions, that we shall examine individually in this section. Conflict resolution and prevention is normally one of the important results of the DBA accepting responsibility for each of these more explicit functions, which we now try to classify.

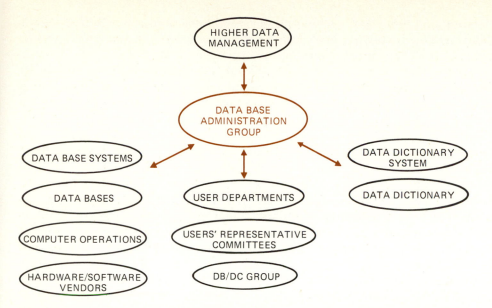

FIGURE 13.4   The data base administration group occupies a key position in an organization that uses the data base approach and interacts with many groups and systems. Apart from the interaction with upper management, the DBA activities can be classified into those that deal with data dictionaries (right), those that deal with the system software connected with data bases (left), and those that deal with users (middle). This classification is further refined in Figure 13.5. It may also be said that the overall function of the DBA is the prevention of conflicts, and the resolution of conflicts when they occur.

Classification of the functions of the DBA

There appear to be three useful ways in which the plethora of DBA functions can be classified:

1. Into administrative as opposed to technical functions
2. In accordance with the entities affected, that is, into data dictionary/data dictionary system functions, into user and applications–oriented functions, and into data base and data base system–oriented functions
3. Into functions that predominate in the earlier data base developmental stages, as opposed to those that dominate during the mature production or operational stages.

Classification (1) is useful because most business enterprises are organized in a hierarchical fashion, with administrative and managerical functions at the top and technical functions at the bottom. Classification (2) is useful because it groups the functions according to the interactions of the DBA, as has been illustrated in Figure 13.4. Classifications (1) and (2) are interrelated as is illustrated in Figure 13.5, which lists the many DBA functions in six categories.

Classification (3) is useful as a guide to adapting the organization of the DBA group to the evolving data base environment. Unfortunately, from an expositional standpoint, this classification into developmental and production–oriented DBA functions involves a great deal of overlap, since many DBA functions are common to both the initial planning and implementation stages and the mature production stage. We therefore make use only of classifications (1) and (2), as illustrated in Figure 13.5, in our discussions of the individual DBA functions.

Data dictionary–oriented administrative functions

The major administrative data dictionary functions are to a large extent independent of the kind of data dictionary system being used and are listed at the top left of Figure 13.5. We take them in turn.

Development of data element standards

Every data element or field used in a data base must have a format and meaning that every user is aware of and has agreed to. For example, it could be agreed that the field **SALARY** must be a positive seven-digit figure containing an employee's salary. When changing from file processing to data base processing, all data elements from file processing would have to be identified and used as the basis for constructing a new set of standard data elements. The names of all relations (or conceptual files) used must also be standardized.

This may not be as easy as it looks. For example, the components specification department may regard the field **PART-TYPE-NUMB** as containing the number of a type of component whose constituent parts never occur within the company. However, engineering may have a more relaxed view and prefer to consider a subassembly as a type of part, even if the subassembly is assembled from components within the organization. A conflict like this has the makings of a never-ending wrangle, especially if each side has a lot of programs, procedures, and documentation that would need to be changed if its view has to be modified. The DBA also needs skills in diplomacy.

Development of the data dictionary

The corporate data dictionary can be partly developed or documented as a result of efforts to standardize data elements. It cannot be completed, however, until the conceptual schema has been designed, for it is normal practice for the data dictionary to contain the name of the conceptual file or relation in which a data element occurs. The partly completed data dictionary should be placed on disk as early in the development stage as possible and managed by means of the data dictionary system, in order that those who need to know can have access to an up-to-date version.

Today it is commonly agreed that there should be a data dictionary for all fields and data items used in computer processing, whether or not these are used in a data base. Immediate benefits are elimination of many misunderstandings and easier processing of nondata base files to answer ad hoc queries. A later benefit is greater ease of conversion to data base processing. The disadvantage is the cost of changing existing programs and documentation, as well as the cost of obtaining agreement about the standards used.

	DATA DICTIONARY-ORIENTED	APPLICATIONS/USER-ORIENTED	DATA BASE SYSTEM/DATA BASE-ORIENTED
ADMINISTRATIVE FUNCTIONS	Develops data element standards Develops data dictionary Cooperates with auditors	Develops enterprise schemas Controls data redundancy Controls schema changes Analyzes costs/benefits of new applications Carries out data base systems analysis for data base applications Allocates ownership rights and duties Manages data base security systems Sets programming standards Cooperates with DB/DC group	Procures hardware and software for processing and storing data bases Designs procedures for recovery from system failure Sets performance standards
TECHNICAL FUNCTIONS	Constructs and maintains data dictionary Arranges for generation of data dictionary reports	Constructs and maintains conceptual and external schemas Develops user documentation Conducts user training activities Monitors programming standards	Constructs and maintains storage schemas Monitors system performance Loads and reorganizes data bases Tunes data bases Installs system enhancements Evaluates hardware and software

FIGURE 13.5 Classification of DBA functions. Functions can be classified as either administrative or technical, or as data dictionary–oriented, applications/user–oriented, and systems–oriented. The DBA group could be structured to fit either classification. Each of the six groups could be subdivided (but with considerable overlap) into those that predominate in the initial stages of development and those that predominate in a later mature production environment.

Cooperating with auditors

One major DBA function in this area involves assisting auditors in the pursuit of data base audit trails. Readers should be clear on what an audit trail is. It may be defined as a time sequence of events that affect a data item, and with computer systems we can distinguish two types of audit trail. First, there is the time sequence of data item updates, deletions, and insertions, that is, the *conventional* or *accounting audit trail,* which is essentially the type of audit trail that had its origins in manual accounting systems. The other type of audit trail is the *system audit trail,* which is unique to computer systems. This type of trail is a time sequence of all system events surrounding a data item or data items, such as the execution of an application program, that either gains access to the data or attempts to gain access, or even the recompilation of an application program (Ref. 6).

The information for the two types of audit trail is rarely in one place. If the data base management system logs all updates to the data base, as is usually the case, most of the information for the accounting audit trail will be available from the data base log files. Nevertheless, the log files may be maintained as part of the data dictionary. On the other hand, the information necessary to reconstruct the system audit trail will probably be partly in the data dictionary and partly in the operating system log files. Thus following audit trails can be a complex task in a data base environment, and external auditors especially will need the help of the DBA.

Another function of the DBA in this area involves helping the auditors to develop audit data control procedures, practices, and systems which ensure that data that is part of the audit trail is preserved. The DBA can help by a data dictionary design that captures audit data, as well as with the design of systems that lock this information in the dictionary.

Despite the DBA's close cooperation in the audit process, auditors should not involve the DBA any more than necessary and should try to be as independent as possible. Note that there will normally be two types of auditor for the DBA to deal with, namely, internal auditors employed by the organization and external auditors from an independent auditing firm, who carry out audits of the organization's books as required by law. For a more detailed account of auditing in data base and computer environments, see Refs. 3 and 6.

Applications and user–oriented DBA functions

There are a large number of functions in this category, as can be seen from Figure 13.5, and we deal with them in a reasonably meaningful order.

Development of the enterprise schema

We mentioned in Chapter 9 on data base design that there is a fine distinction between the enterprise schema and the conceptual schema. This distinction can be important in data base design in practice, because it is becoming more common for a data base to be designed without regard to the data base management system that is eventually used. This resulting conceptual design is the enterprise schema. When the data base system to be used is known, the conceptual schema can be generated on the basis of the enterprise schema design.

The enterprise schema design is probably one of the more important single functions of the DBA and is intimately connected with almost every other DBA function. It should be remembered that in all probability the business will have several data bases, so that more than one enterprise schema will need to be designed. It should also be remembered that the overall function of the DBA is the prevention and resolution of conflicts, for the effectiveness of the enterprise schema design will go a long way in determining the level of conflict among users of the data base.

Finally, it should be repeated that the enterprise schema should never be drawn up before:

1. An agreed data dictionary contains all the fields to be used in the design.
2. There is agreement about the use to which the data base will be put both currently and in the foreseeable future.
3. Clear directives have been made available from higher level management about the business objectives of the organization, in order to encourage a design that would help the attainment of these objectives.

Controlling redundancy of data in data bases

Redundancy can occur in an organization's data bases in a number of ways:

1. Use of parent and child connection fields in related conceptual files.
2. Functional dependencies in conceptual files.
3. Duplication of conceptual files or fields within separate data bases, for example, use of the same segment type in two different IMS data bases.
4. Multivalued (or binary join) dependencies in conceptual files—not very common but possible. See Additional Perspective 2 in Chapter 9.

Ideally there should be no redundancy. But we live in an imperfect world, and there is always a considerable amount of redundant data in an organization's data bases. If the data base is relational, it is impossible to avoid the redundancy due to the connection fields. If it is not relational, for example, an IMS or CODASYL data base, it is possible to omit the child connection fields and so eliminate the redundancy. However, we have never done so in any of the examples in this book, for the good reason that the trend is strongly in the direction of relational data bases, so that all data bases should be designed as if they were relational. Redundancy due to functional and multivalued dependencies can be eliminated by good initial design, but in practice unwanted dependencies are missed and the redundancy is designed in; the decomposition of relations to eliminate redundancy after the data base is in operation is a difficult task. Finally, a firm normally has a number of data bases between which there can be duplication of either conceptual files and fields. Nothing can be done about this, unless the data bases are one day integrated into a single corporate data base, an unlikely undertaking because of the cost. Another aspect to this type of redundancy in years to come will be the replication of data due to geographic distribution of data bases, as discussed briefly in Chapter 12.

It is the job of the DBA to ensure that the redundancies in the organization's data bases do not lead to inconsistency, that is, loss of data integrity. All programs that update the data base must be checked to ensure that allowance is made for the existence of redundant data, before they are placed in production. To take a trivial example, if the SALARY field is used in two data bases, then a program that updates the SALARY field must either update both of the occurrences, or its execution must be closely associated with the execution of a second update program that updates the second SALARY field occurrence.

Control of changes to schemas

As time goes on there will be pressure on the DBA to make changes to the schemas. Typically, user groups will want to change:

1. The performance of their applications
2. The structure or content of their external files

Before changes can be made to the storage data base to improve the performance of a particular user group, the effects of the change on the performance of the applications of other user groups must be determined, usually by experimentation, which is a technical DBA function. When the effects are known, prudence and consideration require that the DBA meet with all groups affected to obtain agreement about proposed changes. Often the changes would have such a drastic effect on other applications that modification of the storage data base is ruled out. In such cases all that can be done is a close examination of the application of the group that has the problem to determine if redesign of their data base programs would reduce the number of data base accesses and so improve the performance.

Normally, because of the existence of distinct conceptual and external schema specifications (leading to logical data independence), it is possible to insert new fields to satisfy the needs of a user group without another application being affected, provided we are dealing with a single data base. But supposing a SALARY field is inserted in data base-B when it already exists in data base-A, to take a simple example. The applications of other groups updating data base-A might now require modification to update data base-B as well, which these groups will certainly object to, and so on. The DBA must conduct the usual conciliation meetings to try to find a solution acceptable to all.

Cost/benefit analysis for new data base applications

Every new proposal for a data base application has significant costs attached to it, many of which can only be brought to light by careful investigation and analysis on the part of the DBA. There is the obvious cost of the work to develop the application and the more subtle costs of the affect the new application will have on the performance of existing applications. The new application may involve extending the existing data base, with a requirement for more disk space, and it may involve significant duplication of data already in other data bases—we have already mentioned something of the problems that it can cause. Then there is the likely need for additional terminals or other I/O hardware, and the cost of a place to put them, and so on.

It may or may not be the DBA's job to determine the benefits of a given new application, but the DBA must obtain them, if only for deciding the priority to be assigned to the application. If the costs exceed the benefits, the DBA may have to refuse the application, or if the DP department operates by directly charging user groups for its services, the DBA will have to communicate the costs and an explanation of them, leaving it up to the user group to decide whether to proceed. In any event, the DBA will be involved in a great deal of interface work with that particular user group on the subject of costs and benefits.

Development of new data base applications

The DBA often takes the initiative in the development of a new application once general agreement of the need for it has been arrived at. The DBA can direct the data base aspects of the work of the implementation personnel, giving valuable advice as to pitfalls (for example, connection traps) and advantageous procedures that are related to the particular application.

Allocation of ownership rights and duties

In legal terms ownership is defined as a collection of rights and duties, and in the Western democracies, most property is privately owned and some is publicly owned, that is, collectively owned. In the case of collective ownership, for example, the streets and parks of a city, we arrive at our rights through the democratic process, and many of us feel very strongly about such rights. Our duties are the less pleasant side of things, especially with regard to such duties as payment of property taxes, but necessary nonetheless, if the system of limited collective ownership is to have benefits that exceed its costs.

Within a large organization, no department or asset is ever owned by its employees in the legal sense. Yet in practice many employees have rights and duties relating to the organization's property that are respected and even enforced. (Indeed there are many economists who assert that for all practical purposes it is top management, that is, a specific group of employees, and not the shareholders, who are the owners of the large corporation.) Thus in the corporate sense, employees own company property, if not in the legal sense. This sense of ownership is important to employees, and to the organization, for people normally manage well what they feel they own.

This brings us to a fundamental question in the management of data bases: Who owns the data in a corporate data base? The legal owners are clearly the shareholders, but that will not help the DBA, for it is ownership in the corporate sense that must be determined. A data base is a pooled resource, so that it can be argued that it is collectively owned, but in the corporate sense—a difficult concept. This means that many groups in the organization will have rights and duties associated with a data base, but unlike the case of the city streets and parks where all citizens have much the same rights and duties, the rights and duties of the collective owners of a corporate data base will vary widely. Some groups may use the data base for only a few retrievals yearly, while others undertake retrievals and updates on a daily basis.

One thing is clear: Ownership cannot rest with the DBA, since most of the data in the data base will not be of any use to the DBA; nor will the DBA be in a position to update the data base since the required transactions will be available only to user groups. The DBA will be the *corporate custodian* of the data, just as a bank is the custodian of its depositors' money. With the corporate data base it must be the users who own the data. However, allocating rights and duties to each user is a DBA task and one that must be done in close consultation with the different groups. For each group, the fields it has the right to retrieve must be decided, as well as the fields a group has the rights or duties to update.

The distinction between updating rights and duties must be taken seriously by the DBA, and updating duties frequently must be rigorously enforced. For example, if a group needs to use field A in its daily activities and regularly acquires the data necessary for updating A, then we can say that the group has update rights to A. We need not regard this updating as a duty, for it is in the group's direct interest to see that the updating of A is correctly and promptly carried out, since it makes use of field A in its activities. But suppose that the group also regularly acquires the information necessary for updating field X, even though X is not a field that is ever used by the group. Carrying out updates to X promptly and correctly is then a duty for that group and one that the DBA must enforce, by means of penalties if necessary. In practice each group unfortunately will be quick to extract what it can from a collectively owned property and less inclined to put its fair share of effort into maintaining it. This is the great drawback to any collectively owned resource, and one that the DBA must be constantly on guard against. The policy of the DBA must always be to allocate no more rights than are necessary and as few duties as possible, that is, the maximum benefit to users at minimum cost.

Common problems for the DBA who attempts to allocate as many ownership rights as necessary are objections from user groups who do not want "their" data to be "broadcast" all over the company. This desire for privacy is a real one, and unnecessary dissemination of data via a shared data base can do great harm. Thus it is clear that the DBA has to consider every such objection carefully, and where the objection is found to be a valid one, attempt to conciliate the parties involved. In this area therefore, as in many others, the DBA spends a great deal of time preventing and resolving conflicts.

Administration of data base security
The problem of data base security is related to the problem of allocating ownership rights and duties and is concerned with prevention of unauthorized access to the data base. Data base security is a problem because no matter how good the security system is, it would appear that a determined intruder can always find a way to beat the system if enough time, effort, and ingenuity is expended. The DBA cannot be held responsible for all aspects of data base security, however, for the subject merges into the much wider area of computer

installation security. It is hardly the DBA's responsibility to prevent a thief armed with the latest countersurveillance equipment from tunneling his or her way into a computer room in the dead of night and making off with a disk pack containing the bill-of-materials data base for a secret prototype.

It is the DBA's job to administer the security system that is built into the data base system and to allow for periodic audits of the data base. As we have seen in our studies of data base systems, there are many ways in which unauthorized use can be severely discouraged, if not prevented. For example, a user group must have an external data base for the fields and records it needs access to, and this can be provided only by the DBA. In addition, with some systems, locks can be placed on fields, records, and conceptual and external files so that only an authorized user in possession of the keys can use them. Furthermore, different keys may be needed for different operations such as retrieval and updating. Typically, also, any attempt to access the data base by a person without the proper key would be recorded and perhaps displayed on a security terminal. Most systems also provide for backup files and log files, so that the data base can be reconstructed in case of damage. It is also the DBA's responsibility to work closely with auditors to allow for the existence of audit trails, as we have seen. Finally, the DBA must work closely with the computer installation security staff to provide specialist input on security matters affecting the organization's data bases.

Setting programming standards for prevention of deadlock and update interference

As we have seen in our studies of data base systems, a practical problem with the manipulation of data bases is the possibility of either update interference from other concurrently executing programs, or deadlock. Most data base systems provide facilities for use in application programs for preventing interference and deadlock. However, these provisions are of no avail if they are not used or used incorrectly. It is the job of the DBA to set programming standards for using these data base facilities in an optimum manner, and to ensure that all programs adhere to them.

Cooperation with the DB/DC administrator

To handle the many administrative and technical tasks involved in the communications aspect of on-line systems, many organizations rely on a *DB/DC administrator*. Since on-line systems are widely used for remote access to data bases, the DB/DC administrator is also involved in managing the data base environment. Depending on the extent of the use of on-line processing, the DB/DC administrator can range all the way from being a technical specialist to a full department of communications specialists and administrators. In this book we have skimmed only the surface of the subject of on-line systems and communications since our major topic is data base management. For this reason a full discussion of the functions of the DB/DC administrator would be out of place. Essentially the DB/DC administrator is responsible for the design and implementation of the communications part of the on-line system, for maintaining it, for the design and installation of extensions, and for the evaluation and installation of enhancements. Almost every one of these functions affects the data base, so that the DBA and DB/DC administrator must often work closely together.

Data base and data base system–oriented administrative functions

The DBA has important functions of an administrative nature in connection with procurement and maintenance of data base software and data bases. These functions are listed in the top right section in 13.2, and we discuss them individually.

Procuring hardware and software for processing and storing data bases

To have a data base, there must be a data base management system for processing the data base. There also has to be disk storage to put it in. Both the disk storage and the data base system have to be procured. It may even be necessary to acquire two different data base systems: For example, if one data base has a strong network structure, a CODASYL or relational data base system might be used, while for another hierarchically structured data base IMS could be used.

The task of procuring this hardware and software is often carried out at the administrative level by the DBA. It is a very time-consuming activity, as anyone who has ever tried it can readily testify. Outline procurement specifications must be prepared, vendors selected, vendor representatives dealt with, evaluation tests arranged and documented, products selected, higher levels of management convinced of courses of action, and maintenance contracts arranged. A whole chapter could be written on the subject without coming near to exhausting it.

Design of recovery procedures

With all systems, whether software or hardware, Murphy's law must never be forgotten. Things will go wrong, and they will go wrong at the worst possible time. There can be mechanical failures such as when a flying disk read/write head "crashes" and destroys a whole disk track. (So fine is the separation between the head and the track that an ordinary dust particle lying on a track can have an effect comparable to having a large boulder on a highway!) There can be data transmission failures causing an incorrect update to the data base, and ordinary human carelessness can result in destruction of extensive areas of the data base. Finally, there are the failures caused by breaches of the security system by intruders, especially by malicious intruders. As already discussed, prevention of these failures is the combined responsibility of the DBA and installation security personnel.

Since failures will occur, from a business point of view one of the most important functions of the DBA is the design and maintenance of systems for recovery of the data base. The reason why is not hard to see. Loss of essential business data such as an accounts receivable file, an accounts payable file, or customer savings accounts file could destroy a business. The main method used to ensure recovery is the regular dump of the data base contents and the logging of all updates to the data base between dumps. Software systems have to be in a place that can automatically reconstruct a data base from the dumps and the log file when needed.

Setting and ensuring system performance standards

We saw in Chapter 1 that access to a disk file is slow by CPU standards, direct access times of about 35 milliseconds being considered quite good. Since manipulation of a data base will require many disk accesses by the data base system as requested by many different application programs, the process cannot be other than a very slow one, and data base systems are notorious for their poor performance. It is a common experience that installation of a data base system causes a marked deterioration in the performance of all applications, whether or not they make use of the data base. Sometimes the only solution is a larger CPU or multiple CPUs with additional channels or input/output processors (see Chapter 1).

It is the job of the DBA to set performance standards that can realistically be met within the confines of the data base cost/benefit trade-off. These performance standards should then be used as a bench mark against which actual performance can be measured and corrective action taken as required. Performance measurement can be carried out in either of two ways:

1. Special test application programs can be run at intervals, during periods of low data base activity, medium activity, and very high or peak activity. With each execution of the test program the times for different kinds of retrieval and updating can be printed out. This data can also be stored in a *performance log file*, so that time sequences of update and retrieval times over longer periods can be kept for statistical analysis as required.

    We must be careful to distinguish between the CPU time for a data base operation and the elapsed time. Because of the switching between programs caused by the multiprogramming operating system or by a teleprocessing monitor such as CICS, the elapsed time will usually be considerably longer. A long elapsed time compared with CPU time indicates long delays between the periods when an application program is allowed to run—a sure sign the system is overloaded. The DBA must initiate corrective action in such a case, and possible solutions are tuning of the operating system and data base system, tuning of the teleprocessing monitor, rearrangement of application programs and operating system partition priorities, and combinations of additional CPU, main memory, channel and disk capacity. When the CPU time is a significant part of the elapsed time, the system is usually not overloaded, but the system overhead may be high, indicating that there is too much data base or teleprocessing monitor activity associated with each data base operation. Possible solutions will be tuning of the data base system by altering the pointers, indexes, and file organizations of the storage data base, or tuning the teleprocessing monitor.

2. Another method involves the insertion of special routines called *software performance monitors* into selected application programs. These

routines are often provided by the DBMS vendor or by software houses and will measure times for DBMS retrieval and update operations requested by user application programs, that is, in a real-life environment. The disadvantage is that the execution of the performance monitors slows down the application programs.

When action is taken to ensure performance standards, most commonly a change to the storage schema is involved. This frequently means that while the performance of some applications improves, that of others deteriorates, so that conciliation efforts are often needed with affected user groups, as mentioned earlier.

Technical DBA functions

Almost all the administrative DBA functions outlined involve technical functions of the kind listed in the lower half of Figure 13.5. The details of these functions are for the most part dependent on the specific data base, data base system, or data dictionary system in use. However, from the material on data base management already covered, readers should have a good idea of the technical complexities involved. Since this book has a business rather than a technical orientation, we shall not delve any deeper. Readers interested in these more technical matters should consult Refs. 1 and 2.

13.3 ORGANIZING THE DBA FUNCTIONS

It is clear from Section 13.2 on the DBA functions that in a complex organization no one person could possibly have either the time or the expertise necessary to do the job alone. Thus the DBA function must be organized. In this short section we shall first look at ways in which the data base administration group is internally organized. Later we shall take a wider perspective and examine how the DBA group can be positioned within the overall corporate organization.

Internal organization of the DBA group

We recall that in Section 13.2 it was mentioned that the DBA functions in Figure 13.5 could be further classified into those functions that predominated in the planning and developmental stages, and those that dominated in the mature production stage. It is to the task of internally organizing the DBA group that this classification can be applied, for the organization clearly will depend on which types of DBA functions predominate. Thus we can have a DBA group organization for planning and development and a different organization for the mature production stage. We take them in turn.

Organizing the DBA group for planning and development

A typical DBA group organization in a large company with a centralized data base (or data bases) is shown in Figure 13.6a. The organization reflects the need for a great deal of planning and development. We need at least four specialists

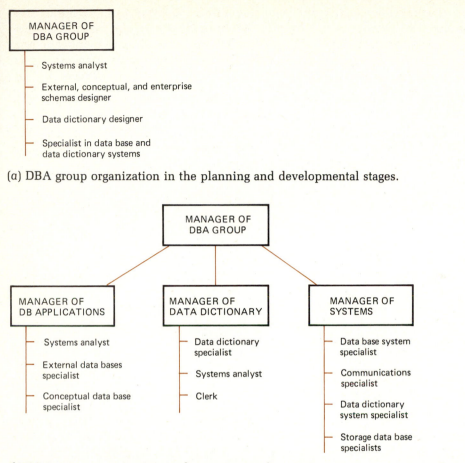

(a) DBA group organization in the planning and developmental stages.

(b) DBA group organization in the mature production stage.

FIGURE 13.6   Organization of the DBA group.

who work closely together. The systems analyst interfaces with user groups and provides information for the design of the enterprise schema and the data dictionary. On the basis of preliminary designs the systems software specialist evaluates data base management and data dictionary software and finally recommends specific systems. This permits construction of the data dictionary and conceptual schema by the dictionary and schema specialists, further development and analysis of applications by the systems analyst, and so on until the establishment of the firm's first data base environment is complete.

Organizing the DBA group for production

In the mature production stage, it can be expected that there will be several data bases with large numbers of applications serving many diverse user groups. This means a fairly large DBA function, much larger than in the initial planning and development stage, which typically involves only a fairly limited data base.

Conversion to the data base approach cannot be accomplished overnight, and while such conversions are common at the time of writing, not many organizations have reached the mature production stage with a significant number of data bases. For this reason the proper organization of the DBA group for this stage is less certain, although the organization shown in Figure 13.6b is probably reasonably typical.

In this organization there are three major DBA departments, which corresponds to the classification of functions shown in Figure 13.5. The data base applications department has systems analysts who develop and analyze applications, as well as the external and conceptual schema specialists necessary for interfacing these applications to the data base system. The data dictionary department has a dictionary specialist who interfaces with the systems analyst who deals with conflicts among user groups and standardization issues. A clerk is necessary for the large amount of clerical work associated with creation and maintenance of a corporate data dictionary. Finally, in the systems department are the specialists necessary for dealing with the DBMS, data dictionary, and storage schema. There may well also be a communications specialist who coordinates DBA activities with those of the communications group where a geographically distributed on-line system is in use.

Organizing the DBA function in a distributed data base environment
There is little practical experience in the distribution of the DBA function when the data base is distributed. The most commonly discussed organization is one in which there are divisional DBAs that are loosely controlled by a head office DBA. How this would work out in practice remains to be seen.

DBA position in the organization

The position of the DBA in the data processing organization is still something of a problem. Traditionally, data processing is organized along the lines shown in Figure 13.7a. The director of data processing supervises the activities of computer operations, which is a line department responsible for the scheduling and running of jobs. He or she also supervises two staff departments, namely, applications design and programming, and the systems department, which contains systems programmers who are expert in the operating system, compilers, and other systems software.

This basic structure is rarely altered when conversion to data processing takes place, and the DBA group is somehow fitted in. The problem is that the supervisory functions of the DBA group, together with its large number of interfaces, make it difficult for the DBA group to fit into the conventional hierarchical organization used in business. On the one hand the DBA must report to the director of data processing and on the other hand time interface with user departments, and have some control of the activities of the computer operations, applications, and systems departments. In addition, the director of data processing must remain responsible for the three conventional data processing departments. Thus the theoretical organization might be that shown in

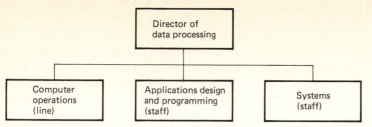

(a) Traditional organization of data processing.

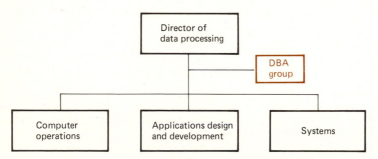

(b) Theoretical organization of data processing when data base management is involved. This organization violates organizational convention, which requires a hierarchical organization, never a network! Organizations (c) or (d) are used instead.

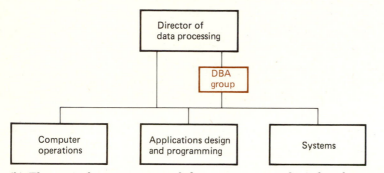

(c) Common position of the DBA group in the data processing organization.

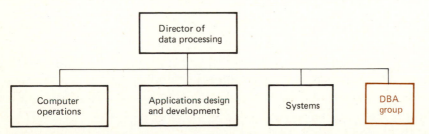

(d) Another common position of the DBA group. In this organization it does not look as if the DBA group has any control over the activities of the other data processing departments, although in practice it has. Thus this organization is really no different from that in (c).

FIGURE 13.7 The position of the DBA in the data processing organization.

Figure 13.7b, which is a network. In practice organization charts are restricted to hierarchies, and so the organization charts in Figure 13.7c and 13.7e are used instead. While the organization in Figure 13.7c gives the appearance of a higher level DBA group, in reality it is the same as that in Figure 13.7d. The influence and even power of the DBA group rests with its unique and essential functions, so that in the final analysis, its success depends on the people who staff it, and not on how it appears on an organization chart.

Support at the top

The DBA needs the co-operation of many diverse groups in an organization in order to be able to function. It is too much to expect that such co-operation will always be forthcoming, and there is increasing evidence that the DBA needs the support of top management in order to be able to function. For example if a user group in engineering refuses to co-operate in a situation where its co-operation is essential for the maintenance of the data base, there may be little the DBA can do about it. Only the top management in engineering would have the power to force co-operation, something engineering management in all likelihood would be unwilling to do unless it was fully committed to the data base approach.

A useful organizational device to ensure the commitment and subsequent support of top management throughout the company is a *data strategy group*. This group is made up of representatives of top management, and may even contain some important persons in the organization. It would meet on a regular basis, perhaps monthly, to formulate policy on computers and data bases, and would always attempt to obtain the broadest possible consensus and commitment. In this way the continuing support of top management for the maintenance of the corporate data bases can be assured.

The data strategist

Some authorities (Ref. 4) advocate the establishment of the post of *data strategist* to guide the activities of the data strategy group, since the members of the data strategy group would not generally be computer experts and would spend only a fraction of their time dealing with data strategy. We must be careful here, for this could well be the beginning of another branch of the corporate bureaucracy, with the data strategist in time evolving into yet another planning department—there is no limit to the amount of planning that can be carried out in an organization. For a detailed account of data base administration, see Ref. 7.

13.4 COST BENEFIT ANALYSIS OF DATA BASE MANAGEMENT

There are bandwagons in corporate affairs from time to time and at the time of writing the data base bandwagon is well under way. In practice it is the bandwagon argument that is frequently used to justify the conversion from conventional files to data bases. For an individual manager the argument can often go something like this. First, other companies of a similar nature have gone data base, and second, by not going data base the manager's company risks acquiring an old-fashioned image. Worse still, the manager also risks acquiring an old-fashioned image. This leads to another persuasive argument: If the company goes data base, this will permit the manager to acquire experience and skills in the data base area, which will be very useful when the time comes to find another job. Finally it is argued that by not going data base, ambitious staff members will move to companies where they can acquire data base skills.

Opposition to the bandwagon rarely comes from the computer people within an organization, for the introduction of data base management can only bring new growth and challenges as far as they are concerned. Enlightened opposition can come only from top management, advised presumably by a strategy group of the type mentioned in the previous chapter. In the absence of advice from a strategy group who have studied the business implications of employing computers and data bases, top management will often give in to the pressure, for they themselves will be affected by the bandwagon, and not wish to appear either backward or even ignorant of the "great advantages" of using data bases instead of conventional files.

While most readers will probably agree that this is hardly the right way to make a decision involving many millions of dollars in costs, in objective terms it is not all bad. For example if insurance company A is not using data base management while all the other insurance companies in town are and are prospering, then perhaps executives at A should be asked to justify why A is using conventional files, and not why they should move to data bases. Nevertheless, no two companies are the same, and the only proper method of justifying a shift from conventional files to data bases requires the conservative documentation of all advantages and disadvantages of the move to the company, both in the short and the long terms. Included must be the benefit costs involved in dollars and cents.

Advantages and disadvantages of data base processing

Clearly, for any given organization there will be specific advantages and disadvantages of using data bases, and the most we can do here is summarize some generalizations, all of which have already been mentioned earlier in the book in different places.

Advantages

1. Increased data independence makes it possible to add new types of data to the data base or change the way data is stored, without the need to rewrite existing programs. Thus maintenance costs for applications programs are greatly reduced.
2. Increased control of duplication of data means that storage space is saved, and that the risk of inconsistency in important data is much reduced. This means that management can expect much more reliable reports about the state of the company.

3. It is much cheaper to develop new applications involving complex relationships between different files. With conventional files such applications are very difficult to implement. Even if the data in the files can be taken to be consistent, the program has to include complex code to handle the relationships. The use of a data base system allows high level data base commands that can accomplish in a few lines of code what would take many lines without a data base system.

4. The advent of powerful query languages means that management is able to retrieve ad hoc information directly from the data base. A manager at a terminal can easily retrieve information from many different files dealing with many different aspects of a company's operations, he or she can do so in a few minutes using a language such as SQL, and can be confident that the information in the data base files is correct and current. For all practical purposes, retrieval of ad hoc information is impossible without a data base system.

5. Productive order prevails, and this often enables small problems to come to the attention of management before they become big problems.

Disadvantages

1. The cost of initial conversion to data base processing is high. Data base systems have to be acquired and installed, data bases have to be designed and loaded, and many new programs to do old jobs have to be written. Expensive training for existing staff is required, and additional staff will have to be hired. Outside consultants will probably also be needed.

2. Operating costs are much higher than with conventional file processing. A heavy processing overhead is associated with data base management systems, so that even the simple sequential processing of a data base file is much slower than before. Often a more powerful or additional CPU has to be acquired if a decent level of performance is to be maintained.

3. The success of the system may well be its own undoing. Because of the easier access to the data in the data bases, there will be more access to the data on the part of users. This will cause performance to slip, with resultant demands for increased capacity. It is difficult to determine if the increased access to the data base is really necessary.

4. When many different files are integrated into a single data base, a system failure involving one file can cause the whole data base to fail. Thus the organization can be much more vulnerable than before.

5. The pooling of the data of many user groups into common data bases can lead to many conflicts and the attitude among users that somebody else will look after the data.

6. The complexity of the management of the data base environment requires an expensive and sophisticated data administration group.

It is difficult to quantify the costs of these benefits in the absence of any specific case. However an industry perspective can help in the decision process, if we look at the relative importance of information in different types of business.

The importance of information spectrum

The importance of information in business varies over a wide spectrum. At one end of the spectrum we have industries whose business is information, such as insurance companies and commercial banks. With such companies that most powerful tools for managing data are almost a necessity, and so they will have data bases, data base administration groups, and probably even data strategists at a higher level, perhaps even at vice presidential level.

At the other end of the spectrum we have companies whose business concerns a single basic product sold to relatively few fixed corporate customers with long term contracts, and where information processing is minimal and commonly regarded by management as a necessary evil. An example is a coal mining company, that produces a single class of coal in a few grades which it sells to a limited number of utilities with long term contracts. Such a company has no need for sophisticated marketing, research, or even engineering divisions. The primary emphasis is on production with as little labor as possible. It is difficult to see what advantage the conversion to data base management could have for such a company. Even the classic argument of reduced maintenance costs because of data independence would probably not hold up. The company will have a relatively small number of computer applications, and files that are not likely to change much. We need not expect to find a vice president for data strategy here.

Somewhere in the middle of the spectrum we will find companies that manufacture many different types of products that are sold to many different customers in a market that is always changing. An example is a manufacturer of integrated circuits (electronic components). Typically such a company will have a considerable number of different production lines, each using a distinct technology. On any line a host of different types of integrated circuits are manufactured. Old components are soon replaced by new ones as the technology advances, and new production lines are set up as old ones are discarded. The marketing department is constantly analyzing sales patterns to detect trends, while engineering is constantly devising new integrated circuits and the research and development department is developing new production processes. Separate lines are used for final assembly of chips into packages (with connection pins) and there may be assembly lines as far away as Southeast Asia; marketing and warehousing will typically be throughout North America and Western Europe. Can such a company manage without the use of data bases? Probably it can, but in all likelihood it could do better with data base management. Its business is the production of integrated circuits, but information plays so large a part in marketing, market research, engineering, research and production, that it is difficult to see how it cannot make good use of the tools described in this book.

With our integrated circuit manufacturer, so too with many companies in the middle of the spectrum. They produce a wide assortment of goods and services, but in order to do so they make use of a great deal of information of a changing nature. Thus another method of attempting to decide whether or not to switch to data base management involves determining the importance of information to the company. If a cost benefit analysis on the basis of the advantages and disadvantages of data base management gives no clear-cut advantage either way, then a realization that information is very important to the company and is likely to become more important in the future may well be enough to tip the balance in favor of data bases.

Where only an agonizing or tentative decision to switch to data base management can be reached, the company would be well advised to proceed cautiously, and implement only a small data base with not more than five or six conceptual files (or one hierarchy type if IMS is used). The data base system could be rented for this project with an option to buy if it works out. The data base should consist of files where data independence can give immediate benefits, and the files should contain data that is frequently needed for generating reports for management. The experience gained with the resulting prototype data base environment should provide invaluable input for a final decision on a major shift to data base management.

SUMMARY

1. The successful management of the data base environment requires the use of a data dictionary, and the establishment of a data base administration group or DBA.
2. Data dictionary systems began with field lists on paper, evolved first to stand alone systems, and currently to systems that are integrated with the data base management system. IBM's System R is an example of a data base system with an integrated data dictionary system.
3. The DBA's overall function is the prevention and resolution of conflicts caused by the pooling of the data of many diverse user groups into shared data bases. This overall function resolves into a large number of explicit functions. These functions may be classified into administrative and technical functions. They may also be classified into functions that are oriented toward the data dictionary, functions that are oriented toward the user-groups, and functions that are oriented toward the data base.
4. Because of the large number of functions that the DBA must perform, there has to be a number of specialists in the DBA group. The DBA group will consist mostly of designers in the early stages of the use of corporate data bases. Later the group can be organized along functional lines. The DBA needs the support of higher management.
5. The decision to switch from conventional file processing to data base processing will normally hinge on an analysis of the costs and benefits involved in the light of the advantages and disadvantages of the data base approach. It can also help to determine the relative importance of information to the organization.

QUESTIONS

1. Why is a data dictionary important for the successful management of the data base environment?
2. Assuming that the data dictionary in Figure 13.3 is available, use SQL to

determine the dates on which the field 'X' was updated and a description of the systems that carried out the update.

3. Assuming that the data dictionary in Figure 13.3 is available, use SQL to obtain a description of all relations (conceptual files) updated by the system 'XSYS'.

4. Explain how you could use the IBM's Data Dictionary/Directory system to implement the data base in Figure 10.1.

5. Illustrate the subrelationships in the relations **APPLICATION** and **B-OF-M** in Figure 13.3. Readers should have studied the first supplement in Chapter 9 before attempting this question.

6. Using the information in Figure 13.5, give the administrative and technical functions of the DBA when an organization is in the process of setting up its first data bases.

7. Repeat Question 6 for the case when a significant number of data bases have been in use for a long time.

8. Give an original example of how it can be difficult to standardize a field that is to be described in a data dictionary.

9. Explain why it would be useful to have a data dictionary that contains all the fields used in the computer files of an organization. Why would this be an expensive task?

10. Distinguish between the accounting audit trail and the system audit trail. Do the concepts overlap? If so, in what way?

11. Using IMS as an example, explain the difference between the enterprise schema and the conceptual schema.

12. Suppose that an organization is using System R with several data bases. Each conceptual schema is equipped with integrity constraint specifications. Why should the DBA still need to check and control applications to prevent inconsistency?

13. Suppose that the data base in Figure 10.1 is implemented as an IMS HISAM data base, and that there is a user group X that regularly processes the segment **CUSTOMER** sequentially. Another user group succeeds in persuading the DBA to change the data base to a HDAM data base. Why might user group X strongly protest? If you were the DBA, what would you do in response?

14. Who do you think should set priorities for the development of new data base applications? Justify your answer.

15. Discuss the concept of data ownership in a corporate context.

16. Give an example of how data "published" in a corporate data base could damage the corporation.

17. Discuss the administration of data base security in the light of the Additional Perspective at the end of the chapter.

18. How can the DBA contribute to a lower frequency of deadlock and mutual interference by data base programs?

19. Explain why data base systems generally perform poorly. What can the DBA do to improve things?

20. What characteristics would you look for in the manager of the data base administration group?

ADDITIONAL PERSPECTIVE
HOW A DATA BASE CAN STORE MONEY

As we have seen in many parts of this book, data bases commonly hold data about money. However, what may not be clear to many readers is that in many instances a data base actually contains money. An explanation of how this can be the case is the purpose of this short additional perspective on the data base environment. Most of this explanation involves an examination of the nature of money, for it is only by understanding money that we can see how money can be stored in a data base. The whole subject of money has traditionally been veiled in mystery, and if we now add the complexity of data bases and data base management, then we risk making the subject of money even less comprehensible, to the detriment of those in business who must make rational decisions involving money. There is a need, therefore, for some simple but accurate explanations.

To clarify the principles involved, we shall use a narrative instead of the more conventional type of exposition used so far in this book. Our narrative concerns the early years of an imaginary island republic in the Pacific called Westhaven. The details of how the Republic of Westhaven came into existence do not really concern us, but in order to lend some credibility to our narrative, we may imagine that it was discovered by a band of adventurers from the major Pacific Rim countries just after it appeared out of the ocean as a result of geological action. It was originally claimed by most of the Pacific nations, but since it was never established just whose nationals had first set foot on the island, and since it appeared to have no strategic or economic value of significance, it was eventually agreed that the island should be allowed to join the community of nations as an independent republic.

Immediately after the independence festivities were over, the Westhaven president Mr. Bigger was engaged in conference with a consultant from a large New York bank. The problem was the usual one—the Westhaven government had only a small quantity of U.S. dollars in its treasury and was almost insolvent. In the rush for an independent republic, no thought had been given to the new nation's currency, or indeed if it should have a currency at all. Before independence, many different currencies from the Pacific nations were in use, although U.S. dollars were the most common. Mr. Bigger's reason for calling in the banking consultant was to find out how to go about arranging a sizable loan from an American bank. Because of the weak Westhaven economy and the high cost of such a loan, the consultant advised against such a course and instead recommended that the country set up its own currency.

The consultant explained that the government should found a new institution called a central bank, to be called the Westhaven Central Reserve Bank, with a staff of two and a printing press for printing the new currency. The new currency unit was the Westhaven dollar, equal in value to an American dollar, at least in the beginning. The bank staff was to consist of a chairperson and a clerk. Before leaving, the consultant warned about abuse of the right of the central bank to print money, as this would eventually lead to collapse of the currency and economic ruin, and recommended that the bank chairperson should be a financially responsible person with a tenured position.

The necessary legislation was quickly passed by the island's congress, and the president appointed a financial conservative called Mr. Meager as Chairperson of the Westhaven Central Reserve Bank. Next day Mr. Bigger went to see Mr. Meager about a loan of W$9000 for the government. The business was quickly transacted, but not before Mr. Meager gave Mr. Bigger a stern lecture on the evils of profligate government spending. The essentials of the transaction were as follows:

1. Mr. Bigger deposited a newly printed government bond with the central bank. This bond had a face value of W$9000, paid 3 percent annually, and was secured by government property.
2. The clerk gave Mr. Bigger W$9000 in newly printed banknotes and made the relevant entries in the bank's books.

The government used the W$9000 cash to meet its expenses, including payroll expenses, so that in a short time that new money was in circulation throughout the republic. To ensure that the new money was accepted by the population, in the legislation setting up the central bank it was stipulated that the new money was acceptable for the discharging of debts and for the payment of taxes to the government. In the course of time even more money was borrowed from the central bank by the government. However, because of the sound management of Mr. Meager, no more money was printed than was needed for the business activities of the country. The currency was a success, inflation was low, and so were interest rates.

We can learn something of the nature of money from the monetary history of Westhaven so far. First of all, *what may be used for money is simply whatever that government says can be used*. The Westhaven government through legislation declared that the new Westhaven dollar was to be considered money, and so it became money. Nevertheless, this dollar was only a rectangular piece of paper with an intricate pattern embedded in it. To this we can add the standard definitions of money:

1. It can be used as a medium of exchange.
2. It can be used as a store of value, although in times of inflation the wisdom of using it for this purpose is questionable.
3. It can be used to measure the value of items that can be exchanged.

Our Westhaven dollar easily satisfies these definitions. The government used it to pay its employees, who in turn used it to buy goods from merchants. The merchants were willing to accept the new money in return for their goods because they knew that the law of the land permitted them to use it to discharge debts and pay taxes. Thus it became widely used as a medium for exchanging goods and services. Because of the wise management of Mr. Meager, the population knew that the Westhaven dollar could be used next year as well as this year, and so it became a convenient store of value, for future use. Finally, because goods or property that had been sold could be compared with other goods and properties not currently for sale, it was possible to assign a value in Westhaven dollars to such entities. In this way the Westhaven dollar could be used as a measure of value.

The method used by the Westhaven government and the central bank to create money, or *increase the money supply*, if we want to put it technically, is the one used by most countries. Notice that the books of the central bank are balanced in this process. Neglecting its printing press, when the Westhaven Central Reserve Bank was founded, it had zero assets and zero liabilities. Following the creation of the first W$9000, its books showed:

ASSETS	LIABILITIES
9000	9000

The bank asset is the W$9000 government bond, while its liability is the W$9000 cash issued to the government. This cash is a liability to the bank, since one day the government could present the cash to the bank and demand its bond back. If the government were to do this, the books of the bank would show:

ASSETS	LIABILITIES
0	0

once again, and W$9000 would literally have been destroyed. This illustrates at once the great principle and the great mystery behind the management of the money supply. When the central bank buys bonds from the government (or from any other persons), money is created. When the central bank sells bonds to the government (or to any other persons), money is destroyed.

Many readers may feel somewhat uneasy about this apparent creation of money out of thin air, for our ordinary experience is that we have to work very hard for every dollar we have. However, it is untrue to state that the Westhaven Central Reserve Bank created the money out of thin air. It is more exact to state that it created it using a special type of paper and various inks. As we shall see, it can also be created on a disk track. The ability of the central bank to destroy money is an even harder concept to digest, for it is completely contrary to our everyday experience with money. How often have we heard: "The money must have gone somewhere; it can't just disappear." Well, it can.

There is another way in which money is commonly created in a modern society, and it is this type of money that is commonly stored in data bases. To find out about it, we continue with the monetary development of the Republic of Westhaven.

Following the successful issue of the new currency from the central bank, cash in the form of Westhaven dollar bills was freely circulating. Nobody used checks at this stage because there were no commercial banks. At this point one of the island's leading citizens, a Mr. Rich, decided to found a bank. He outlined his proposal to Mr. Meager at the central bank, who made recommendations to the president, who initiated legislation in the congress. The legislation provided for the creation of the First National Hamlet Bank with branches throughout the island. The bank's initial capital was to be W$1000, it would be allowed to borrow from the central bank, and it had to keep reserves at a figure that would be set by the central bank. Mr. Rich would have liked to have been able to print money just like the central bank, but the legislation specifically denied him the right to do this. However, he soon found out that he could create money in another way, connected with those "reserves" mentioned in the founding legislation.

The primary need of the citizens of Westhaven was for a safe place to deposit their money, and this Mr. Rich provided. Soon there were three depositors, a Mr. Green, a Mrs. Brown, and a Mr. Black who deposited W$2000, W$3000, and W$4000, respectively, for a total of W$9000. Each sum was placed in its own deposit box with a label indicating the owner. For the privilege of having their money in safe keeping the bank charged the depositors a fee, which they reluctantly paid.

Mr. Rich soon found that his business was not very profitable and called in a consultant from a New York bank. The consultant explained that the so-called First National Hamlet Bank was not operating as a modern bank should; rather it was operating as a depository. Thus if Mr. Black deposited a certain W$10 bill at the bank, he could be sure that he would get exactly that W$10 bill back later, and not some other bill. In the same way if a person deposits a coat at a checkroom, he or she expects to get the same coat on checking out and not some other coat.

Following his talk with the consultant, Mr. Rich began to operate his business as a modern bank. The deposits of his customers were placed in a single deposit box, and how much each person had deposited was recorded in the bank's books as follows:

ASSETS	Asset type	LIABILITIES	Depositor
10,000	Cash	—	
		2000	Mr. Green
		3000	Mrs. Brown
		4000	Mr. Black
10,000		9000	

We see that the bank's excess of assets over liabilities is W$1000, the firm's initial capital. The consultant had pointed out that on balance depositors never make use of all the money they have deposited, so that it was safe for the bank to lend some of it at interest. Interest could also be paid to the depositors to encourage them to keep their deposits in the bank, and perhaps even encourage further deposits. Anyway, a short time later the bank lends W$6000 to a Mrs. Quick, who uses the funds to pay a contractor, Mr. Builder. Mr. Builder now opens an account with the bank and deposits his W$6000. The bank's books now have the following entries:

ASSETS	Asset type	LIABILITIES	Depositor	Borrower
10,000	Cash			
		2000	Mr. Green	
		3000	Mrs. Brown	
		4000	Mr. Black	
6000	Loan	—		Mrs. Quick
		6000	Mr. Builder	
16,000		15,000		

Here we have the apparent magic of commercial banking: By the simple process of lending W$6000 in existing cash, a further W$6000 new money is created by the bank. This is clear from the fact that the bank is now liable to each of its four depositors for a total of W$15,000. Each of these four persons believes that the bank has the money he or she deposited. And so it has, but not in cash. The bank has only W$10,000 in cash, and were each of the depositors to come and attempt to withdraw his or her funds in cash, the bank could not pay. However, in practice such an attempt at mass withdrawal or "run" will normally not happen, since depositors place funds in the bank they are not currently using.

This creation of money by a commercial bank by the process of lending has been much discussed and widely misunderstood. Many bankers will even deny that they are capable of creating money, but there is no doubt at all that they can (see Ref. 5). The question that is of importance for data base adminstrators is where exactly this newly created money resides. Clearly, it is not in cash in the bank's deposit box or vault. Without going into a detailed analysis, we may perceive that the bank has created it by a process of time-sharing its cash assets: Depositors cannot all use the cash as the same time, but it is all right for them to use it at different times, which is what they will need to do in practice. Nevertheless we cannot argue from this that the depositors do not have all their money in the bank. The depositors believe their money is in the bank, the bank is legally liable to pay it back, the depositors know from experience that they can get it, and in addition, in most advanced countries deposits are insured (up to $100,000 in the United States). Thus we must accept that money has been created, and that it is not in cash. The only conclusion is that the funds reside in the bank's books in paper and ink. To see what this can lead to, let us return to the activities of the First National Hamlet Bank.

When Mr. Builder deposited the $6000 that had been loaned to Mrs. Quick, the bank noticed that it had the same cash assets (or "reserves") that it had before the loan, and so loaned some additional funds to another borrower. These funds too were eventually deposited by a new depositor. Additional funds were loaned, which came back in the form of new deposits, and so on, until one day the bank's position was as follows:

ASSETS	Asset type	LIABILITIES	Liability type
10,000	Cash reserves	—	
—		50,000	Total deposits
41,000	Loans and bonds	—	
51,000		50,000	

The bank's assets still exceed its liabilities by its W$1000 initial capitalization, and we have neglected the affect on its assets of interest paid to the bank. However, the process of making loans and accepting new deposits has caused deposits to grow to W$50,000, that is, five times the amount of cash reserves; in other words, the bank has created W$41,000.

By permitting further borrowing, the bank could create even more money, but the process is severely limited by the central bank, and in most advanced nations deposits are limited to around five times reserves. If the limit were 20 times, for example, that would mean that every W$20,000 in deposits was backed by only W$1000 in cash, which would make the risk of a run on the bank very real. In the United States it is the Federal Reserve System (the American central bank) that controls this all important reserve ratio.[1]

From this brief story of the First National Hamlet Bank, we can see that most (that is, about 80 percent) of the depositor's money is not cash and is simply entries on the bank's books. We assumed that the bank was the only commercial bank in Westhaven in order to come quickly to the heart of the matter. Had there been two banks, they would both have created money by the process of lending. However, the mechanism would have been more involved, although the result would have been the same. When bank-A loaned money to a borrower, typically the borrower would buy something with it as before. However, the new owner of the money might well deposit it in bank-B so that this alone would not increase bank-A's deposits. But if at the same time bank-B was lending money to another borrower who spent the funds which were then deposited in bank-A, then this would compensate for the deposit bank-A lost to bank-B, and vice versa. In this way the granting of loans by bank-A and bank-B causes the deposits of both banks to grow even though their reserves are not significantly changed. A full description of the mechanism when many banks are involved is beyond the scope of this book (see Ref. 5), although it is fundamentally similar to what we have already described. For the purpose of explaining the principles involved, we shall therefore continue with the assumption that Westhaven has only one (monopoly) commercial bank.

With the passage of time and sound management on the part of the government and the central and commercial banks, the economy of Westhaven prospered, and the branches of the First National Hamlet Bank multiplied. At the same time the use of checks for paying bills and for business transactions became the norm, and cash was used only for minor transactions. Thus when Mr. Green paid Mr. Black W$1000 by check, all that happened at the bank was an updating of the accounts of Mr. Green and Mr. Black: Green's account balance was reduced by W$1000 and Black's was increased by the same amount. Money had become numbers in ink on paper, and the circulation of money merely involved updating the numbers. And so a modern money system evolved in Westhaven.

Soon the sheer volume of paperwork involved began to cut into the bank's profits, and at the main branch a computer was installed to help. An army of specialists came with the computer. The systems that were designed in the beginning were simple and resulted in substantial savings. This lead to the usual

---

[1]The Federal Reserve (or "Fed") uses this to exert powerful control over the nation's supply of money. If the Fed creates $1 billion by buying bonds from the government, when the government places this money in circulation by paying its bills, it ends up in the commercial banks, which use it to create an additional $4 billion. Conversely, the sale of $1 billion worth of government bonds by the Fed eventually causes the supply of money to fall by $5 billion.

demand for more ambitious systems. But in time there was duplicate data in files used in different applications, development of new applications became slower and more costly, the bulk of the computer center's staff labored just to keep the old systems running, and complaints about errors multiplied.

A consultant was hired to help, and she recommended a switch to data bases and the establishment of a data base administration group. In time a number of data bases were constructed, and one of them contained data about customer accounts as shown in Figure 13.8. We show only part of the data base. In Figure 13.8a we have an extended Bachman diagram for the relations **ACCOUNT** and **TRANSACTION** that were used in Chapter 10, and in Figure 13.8b we show some data for several accounts and transactions related to these accounts. For any account there are typically many transactions, so that there is a one-to many relationship between **ACCOUNT** records and **TRANSACTION** records. For any account, each associated **TRANSACTION** record contains the account balance at the completion of the transaction. Thus the record for the latest transaction for an account contains the current balance for that account; for example, we can see from Figure 13.8a that account number 'A6' currently has a balance of W$7700.

The balance in account 'A6', like that of other deposit accounts, is simply one of the many deposits in the bank that came into existence because of the creation of money by the granting of loans by the bank. (For the United States, with its many commercial banks, the deposit would have come into existence because of loans by the aggregate of banks, that is, by the banking system.) The deposit is not backed by cash, for the total deposits in the bank will likely be some five times its reserves, and most likely those reserves will not be in cash, but in deposits of the First National Hamlet bank with the Central Reserve Bank of Westhaven; that is, the commercial bank has the right to have the central bank print money up to the amount of its deposits with the central bank. So where is the money in an account actually located? There can be only one inescapable conclusion: *It is in the data base, physically stored on a disk track.*

This has one serious consequence for the modern banking system: It makes it possible to rob a bank by accessing its data base and carrying out certain updating operations, the details of which are perhaps better left unwritten. Of course in the old days when money was stored in ink on the paper of the bank's books, it was possible to rob the bank by updating its books. However, this was very difficult to do, especially for nonemployees; even for employees it was difficult, for only a few had access to the books. Thus whenever it did happen, the number of suspects were few, and consequently the probability of early detection was high. The situation is completely different when the funds are stored in data bases. A determined and innovative computer criminal could in theory work from a remote terminal, break the data base security system, and transfer funds (electronically) out of the bank to another bank, and then by more legal means out of the country to some safe offshore haven. An auditor would undoubtedly detect the loss, and with the help of the DBA group, could determine exactly how it happened. But by that time the money would have flown, and for many in business the mechanism of its disappearance would be just as mystifying as the mechanism by which it was originally created.

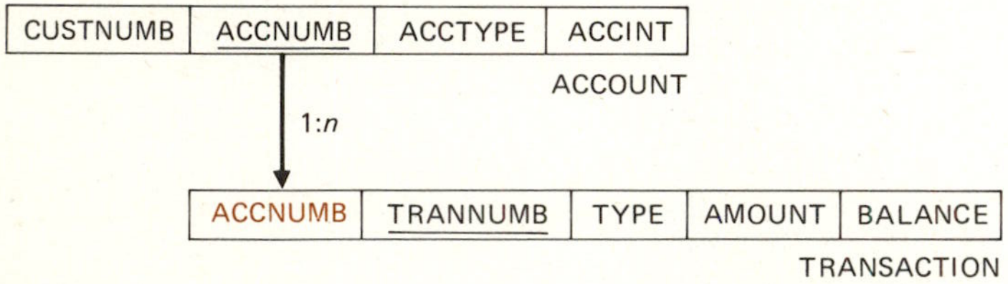

| CUSTNUMB | ACCNUMB | ACCTYPE | ACCINT |

ACCOUNT

1:n

| ACCNUMB | TRANNUMB | TYPE | AMOUNT | BALANCE |

TRANSACTION

(a) Two relations from a data base at the First National Hamlet Bank. For each account there are normally many transactions. A transaction can be a deposit or withdrawal transaction (TYPE field). AMOUNT is the amount of funds involved, and BALANCE is the account balance when the transaction has been completed. CUSTNUMB is the number of the customer holding an account, ACCNUMB gives the number of an account, ACCTYPE gives the type of account, and ACCINT gives the interest paid, if any.

CUSTNUMB	ACCNUMB	ACCTYPE	ACCINT
C10	A6	CHECKING	0
C13	A9	SAVINGS	10

ACCNUMB	TRANNUMB	TYPE	AMOUNT	BALANCE
A6	T11	DEP	1000	9000
A6	T15	DEP	700	9700
A6	T27	WITHD	2000	7700
A9	T13	WITHD	3000	6000
A9	T17	DEP	1000	7000

(b) Some data from the relations ACCOUNT (left) and TRANSACTION (right) from the data base in (a). The data base shows that customer 'C10' has W$7700 in account 'A6' at the bank. However, because the W$7700 does not exist in cash at the bank, the money is actually stored in the data base as magnetic alignments on a disk track.

FIGURE 13.8 A data base containing money as well as data.

REFERENCES

1. Bradley, J., 1982. *File & Data Base Techniques*. Holt, Rinehart & Winston, New York.
2. Date, C. J., 1981. *An Introduction to Database Systems*. Addison-Wesley, Reading, Mass.
3. Fernandez, E. B., R. C. Summers, C. Wood. *Data Base Security and Integrity*. Addison-Wesley, Reading, Mass.
4. Martin, J., 1981. *An End-User's Guide to Data Base*. Prentice-Hall, Englewood Cliffs, N.J.
5. Samuelson, P. A., 1979. *Economics*. McGraw-Hill, New York.
6. Weber, R., 1982. *EDP Auditing*. McGraw-Hill, New York.
7. Weldon, J., 1981. *Data Base Administration*. Plenum Press, New York.
8. Walsh, M. E., 1981. *Information Management Systems/Virtual Storage*. Reston, Reston, Va.

Appendix: IBM Disk Data

In this Appendix we give an explanation of the IBM disk data necessary for calculation of track capacities and access times. We use the IBM 3350 and IBM 3380 disks as examples. The IBM 3350 disk is one of the most widely used. The IBM 3380 disk is the successor of the IBM 3350. It was announced in 1980, but was not actually delivered in any quantity until early 1982. Because the increased data density on an IBM 3380 disk track requires the insertion of additional system data, calculations with the disk are more complex than with the IBM 3350. Note that a data subblock is the last subblock of a count-data or count-key data block, and holds the logical records.

THE IBM 3350 DISK

We distinguish between track capacity and timing calculations, although the parameters for both are given in Figure A1.1.

Track capacity calculations

If B is the size of the data subblock in bytes (or characters), and if the size of a primary record key is k bytes, the number of storage blocks (n) a track can hold is:

$$n = \left\lfloor \frac{S}{c + B} \right\rfloor \quad \textit{for count-data format,} \tag{1}$$

and

$$n = \left\lfloor \frac{S}{r + (k+B)} \right\rfloor \quad \textit{for count-key data format.} \tag{2}$$

Note that $\lfloor x \rfloor$ means the nearest integer below or equal to x, while $\lceil x \rceil$ means the nearest integer above or equal to x. Thus $\lfloor 1.5 \rfloor$ equals 1, but $\lfloor 2 \rfloor$ equals 2.

EXAMPLE 1.   *150 byte records have a blocking factor of 12. How many physical storage blocks can be on a track of an IBM 3350 disk in count data format? How many in a cylinder? How many records per cylinder?*

Size of the data subblock (B) is 150*12 or 1800 bytes. Using data in Figure A1.1 and the formula (1), we have:

$$n = \left\lfloor \frac{19,254}{185 + 1800} \right\rfloor = \lfloor 9.69 \rfloor = 9 \text{ blocks per track}$$

Number of blocks in a cylinder is 9*30, or 270 blocks.
Number of records in a cylinder is 270*12 or 3240.

	IBM 3350 (1976)	IBM 3380 (1980)
Tracks per cylinder	30	15
Cylinders per drive	555	1,770
Nominal track capacity (S) in bytes	19,254	47,968
Maximum (user-data) track capacity (bytes)	19,069	47,476
Maximum (user-data) cylinder capacity (bytes)	572,070	712,140
Maximum (user-data) drive capacity (bytes)	317,498,850	1,260,487,800
Count-data factor (c) in bytes	185	480
Count-key-data factor (r) in bytes	267	704
Nominal data transmission rate (s) in bytes/sec	1,198,000	3,000,000
Rotation time (P) in msecs	16.7	16.7
Average seek time (P) in msecs	25	16
Independent read/write actuators per drive	1	2

Figure A1.1   Parameters for the IBM 3350 and IBM 3380 disks. Reprinted from the author's File & Data Base Techniques, Holt, Rinehart & Winston, 1982.

EXAMPLE 2   *140-byte records have a blocking factor of 17 and a record key length of 9 bytes. How many blocks can be on a track of an IBM 3350 disk in count-key data format.*

Size of the data subblock is 140*17 + 9, or 2389 bytes.[1] Using the data in Figure A1.1. and formula (2), we have:

$$n = \left\lfloor \frac{19{,}254}{267 + (9+2389)} \right\rfloor = \lfloor 7.25 \rfloor = 7 \text{ blocks}$$

Track capacity table

For a fixed number of blocks per track in count-data format, for example, 5 blocks, the *maximum value* of B is that value which ensures that there is *almost* no wasted space at the end of the track. This value of B is 3665 bytes, since

$$n = \left\lfloor \frac{19254}{185 + 3665} \right\rfloor = \lfloor 5.001 \rfloor = 5 \text{ blocks}$$

On the other hand, the *minimum value* of B is that value that ensures that there is *almost* room for another full block. This value of B is 3025 bytes, since

$$n = \left\lfloor \frac{19{,}254}{185 + 3025} \right\rfloor = \lfloor 5.998 \rfloor = 5 \text{ blocks}$$

In fact if we reduce B by just one byte to 3024, then there *will* be room for an extra block. These maximum and minimum values are given in a table in Figure A1.2.

We can use this table to avoid calculations. For example if we want the number of blocks per track in count data format for B equal to 2300 bytes we look for the pair of maximum and minimum values this value of B lies between. We see that this is 2222 and 2565, so that the track can hold 7 blocks.

Similarly we can have maximum and minimum values of (k + B) in the case of count-key data format, as shown in Figure A1.2. If we want the number of blocks per track in count-key data format for B equal to 2000 and k equal to 13, we look for the pair of maximum and minimum values that (k + B) or 2013 lies between. We see that this is 1873 and 2139, so that the track can hold 8 blocks.

Timing calculations

On average, a transmitted data block B can be transmitted between buffer and disk in T milliseconds according to:

---

[1]For details of the principles behind the calculation of the data subblock length B, see the last section in this appendix.

$$T = \quad R/2 + 1000B/s \qquad \text{for sequential access (3)}$$

$$T = \quad R/2 + P + 1000B/s \qquad \text{for direct access (4)}$$

where R, P, and s are given in Figure A1.1.

Thus the time to transmit a 2000 bytes block by direct access is $(8.3 + 25 + 2000/1198)$ or 35 milliseconds.

THE IBM 3380 DISK

The parameters for track capacity and timing calculations are given in Figure A1.1.

Track capacity calculations

Track capacity calculations are similar to those for the IBM 3350. However, formulas (1) and (2) require modification to allow for two new factors:

TRACK CAPACITY—IBM 3350 DISK				
Count-data blocks Bytes in a data subblock (B)		**Count-key data blocks** Bytes in key and data subblock ($k + B$)		**Blocks per track (n)**
Min.	Max.	Min.	Max.	
9443	19069	9361	18987	1
6234	9442	6152	9360	2
4629	6233	4547	6151	3
3666	4628	3584	4546	4
3025	3665	2943	3583	5
2566	3024	2484	2942	6
2222	2565	2140	2483	7
1955	2221	1873	2139	8
1741	1954	1659	1872	9
1566	1740	1484	1658	10
1420	1565	1338	1483	11
1297	1419	1215	1337	12
1191	1296	1109	1214	13
.	.	.	.	.
.	.	.	.	.
.	.	.	.	.

Figure A1.2   Reprinted from the author's File & Date Base Techniques, Holt, Rinehart & Winston, 1982

(a) In both key and data subblocks an additional 12 bytes must be inserted for system purposes.

(b) Following addition of this 12 bytes, the resulting subblock is further padded to bring the length up to a multiple of 32 bytes.

We can use the following formula for the number of blocks on a track (n):

Count-data format

$$n = \left\lfloor \frac{S}{c + B'} \right\rfloor \tag{5a}$$

where $B' = 32((B+12)/32)$ (5b)

Count-key data format

$$n = \left\lfloor \frac{S}{r + (k'+B')} \right\rfloor \tag{6a}$$

where
$$k' = 32((k+12)/32) \tag{6b}$$

and where
$$B' = 32((B+12)/32) \tag{6c}$$

Note that the formulas for k' and B' are a lot simpler than they look. To get the B' value for a given B value we simply add on 12 bytes and pad up to the nearest multiple of 32. The same method can be used to obtain k'.

EXAMPLE 3   *150-byte records have a blocking factor of 12. How many blocks can be stored on a track of an IBM 3380 disk in count data format?*

Size of the data subblock (B) is 150*12 or 1800 bytes. Before applying formula (5b), B' must be calculated. B' is the nearest multiple of 32 above (1800 + 12). We can get the exact value for B' using formula (5b):

$B' = 32* 56.6 = 32 * 57 = 1824$ bytes

Applying formula (5a), and using the data in Figure A1.1:

$$n = \left\lfloor \frac{47,968}{480 + 1824} \right\rfloor = \lfloor 20.8 \rfloor = 20 \text{ blocks}$$

EXAMPLE 4.   *140-byte records have a blocking factor of 17 and a record key length of 9 bytes. How many blocks can be on a track of an IBM 3380 disk in count-key data format?*

Size of the data subblock (B) is 17*140 + 9 or 2389 bytes.[1] Before applying formula (6a) we must evaluate both B' and k'.

 B' is the nearest multiple of 32 above (2389+12). Using equation (6c):

$$B' = 32 * \lceil 75.03 \rceil = 32 * 76 = 2432$$

 k' is the nearest multiple of 32 above (9+12). We could use formula (6b) here but k' is clearly 32. (In fact, since k will almost always be between 1 and 20, k' will almost always be 32.)

 We can now apply formula (6a):

$$n = \left\lfloor \frac{47,968}{704 + 32 + 2432} \right\rfloor = \lfloor 15.1 \rfloor = 15 \text{ blocks}$$

Track capacity table

For a fixed number of blocks per track, there is a minimum and maximum value for B as shown in Figure A1.3. In the case of 5 blocks per track, with count data format the minimum B value is 7477 and the maximum 9076. If B is one byte less than this minimum, for example 7476, there will be 6 blocks; if B is one byte greater than the maximum, for example 9077, we will have only four blocks on the track.

 Returning to Example 3 for the IBM 3380 disk, we could have saved ourselves the calculation by using the table. Since B is 1800 bytes it lies between the minimum and maximum values 1781 and 1876, and so must result in 20 blocks per track.

 With count-key data format a different set of values is used, as shown in Figure A1.3. The data here is used differently from in Figure A1.2. We do not deal with maximum and minimum values of (k+B). Instead we deal only with the maximum and minimum values of B, provided the key length (k) is between 1 and 20 bytes, which it usually is. If the key length is outside this range and between 21 and 54 bytes, a new table will be required, which can easily be constructed by subtracting 32 from each entry in Figure A1.3. Such high k lengths will rarely occur.

 Returning to Example 4 for the IBM 3380 disk, we could use the table in Figure A1.3 instead. The data subblock (B) is 2389 bytes, and from the table we see that this lies between the minimum and maximum values 2293 and 2440. Thus the number of blocks per track is 15.

Timing calculations

Equations (3) and (4) apply to the IBM 3380 disk as well. There is a significant improvement in access time only with direct access, because of the lower seek time for this disk (see Figure A1.1).

---

[1]See last section in this appendix.

TRACK CAPACITY–IBM 3380 DISK (1980)

Count-data blocks		Count-key data blocks		Blocks per track (n)
Bytes in data subblock or transmitted data block (B)		Bytes in data subblock (B), assuming key length (k) between 1 and 20 bytes. (For k values between 21 and 54, subtract 32 from each table entry.)		
Min.	Max.	Min.	Max.	
23477	47476	23221	47220	1
15477	23476	15221	23220	2
11477	15476	11221	15220	3
9077	11476	8821	11220	4
7477	9076	7221	8820	5
6357	7476	6101	7220	6
5493	6356	5237	6100	7
4821	5492	4565	5236	8
4277	4820	4021	4564	9
3861	4276	3605	4020	10
3477	3860	3221	3604	11
3189	3476	2933	3220	12
2933	3188	2677	2932	13
2676	2932	2421	2676	14
2485	2676	2229	2420	15
2325	2484	2069	2228	16
2165	2324	1909	2068	17
2005	2164	1749	1908	18
1877	2004	1621	1748	19
1781	1876	1525	1620	20
1685	1780	1429	1524	21
1589	1684	1333	1428	22
1493	1588	1237	1332	23
1397	1492	1141	1236	24
1333	1396	1077	1140	25
.	.	.	.	.
.	.	.	.	.
.	.	.	.	.

Figure A1.3

CALCULATING SUBBLOCK (B) LENGTHS

In Chapter 1 Figure 1.14 shows the transmitted data block as being equal to the data subblock. This is an oversimplification, which is convenient for expositional purposes. However, on occasion it can lead to error. If we take all the possibilities in account, the ways in which logical storage records are formatted in a data subblock can be quite complex. A knowledge of the formatting possibilities is needed for calculation of the data subblock length B, which in turn is crucial for track capacity estimations. Here we look only at the common data subblock formats for fixed length logical storage records (Figure A1.4). For formats with variable length records, see the manuals. In the following, we use the notation:

b blocking factor, number of logical storage records per block

k length of a primary key in a logical storage record (bytes)

r length of a logical storage record in bytes

Count-data format

The transmitted data block equals the data subblock as shown in Figure 1.13. Thus $B = br$. If we have 60-byte logical storage records with a block factor of 10, B will be 500.

Count-key-data format, embedded keys

This is the simplest format for a data subblock in count-key data format. The data subblock is slightly larger than the transmitted data block, and $B = br + k$. This reflects the fact that the key of the last record in the block is concatenated to the beginning of the data subblock—as well as being placed in the key subblock. Thus if we have 100 byte records with a block factor of 20 and a key length of 7, the value for B will be 2007, and not 2000, which is what we would get if we assumed that the data subblock equalled the transmitted data block. The error is a small one, but it can be significant on occasion. We say that the keys are *embedded,* since a primary key is within each record, and its position must be specified in the JCL.

Count-key data format, nonembedded keys

This format is much more complex, and is designed to improve performance at the expense of track space. As shown in Figure A1.4, the primary key of a record is concatenated to the beginning of each logical storage record, even if the key also occurs within the record. In addition, the last key is concatenated to the beginning of the data subblock. The formula for B is now:

$$B = b(r+k) + k$$

With this format, if we have 100-byte records with a block factor of 20 and a key

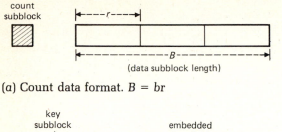

(a) Count data format. $B = br$

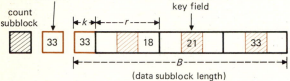

(b) Simplest case of count-key data format. Primary keys are embedded in records. $B = br + k$, since the last key is attached to the beginning of the data subblock.

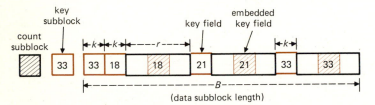

(c) More complex case of count-key data format. Primary keys are also attached to the beginning of each record. The last key is also attached to the beginning of the data subblock. Thus $B = b(r + k) + k$. Keys are said to be nonembedded. The nonembedded key at the beginning of each record is actually transmitted to the program.

FIGURE A1.4. Data subblock formats. All diagrams assume a blocking factor (b) of 3 with fixed length records.

length of 7, B would be 2147, and not 2000. The key of the last record is also stored in the key subblock.

Note that this case sabotages our specification of r as the logical storage record length. The access method actually transmits the nonembedded key to the program with the rest of the record, and the data structure used in the program must be designed to accept this additional key field. Thus in this case the logical storage record length is really $(r + k)$.

NOTE ON JCL SPECIFICATIONS

Generally, the value for B is not the same as the value used for **BLKSIZE** (blocksize) in DD statements—except in the simplest case. The rules for fixed length blocked records are summarized below:

	B (for track capacity calculations)	LRECL (for JCL)	BLKSIZE (for JCL)
Count data format	br	r	br
Count-key data format (embedded keys)	br + k	r	br
Count-key data format (nonembedded keys)	b(r + k) + k	r + k	b(r + k)

Glossary

Access method   An important and often very large subprogram provided by the operating system for arranging for the transmission of data to or from external storage. It responds to READ, WRITE, and other commands issued by the application program. It can move records between buffers and program data area, and can pass messages to the operating system requesting transmission of data blocks to and from external storage.

Attribute   A column of a relation when viewed as a table.

Average search length   The average number of disk accesses to retrieve a record from a file by direct access.

Backup file   A duplicate version of a master file kept in a safe place for purposes of security. Together with a log file it can be used to regenerate a master file.

Batch operating system   An operating system in which jobs are queued for execution; the jobs do not interact with users during execution.

Batch processing   A method of updating master files. Updates to a file are collected until either a sufficiently large batch is accumulated or a fixed period such as a day or week has passed. A batch updating program uses the accumulated updates to update the master file in a single processing run.

Blocking factor   The number of records in a data block.

Buffer   Normally the area of a program partition that holds exactly one block of data.

Chained progressive overflow management   Progressive overflow management, but where all records overflowing from a given home address are in a linked list, that is, connected by a chain of pointers.

Channel   The IBM term for an I/O processor.

Channel program   A program provided by the operating system for transmission of data between buffers and external storage. It can be executed only by the channel or I/O processor.

Child file   A conceptual file containing child records.

Child file   A file containing child records in a one-to-many relationship.

Child record   When one record from a file *A* is associated with one or more records from another file *B* in a one-to-many relationship, a record from *B* is a child record in that relationship.

CODASYL   An acronym for Conference on Data Systems Languages and the voluntary body that is responsible for recommending changes to COBOL. It is also the body that generated the CODASYL data base recommendations.

Conceptual file   An imaginary or abstract file formed by abstracting user-oriented fields (as opposed to file organization fields such as pointer fields) from one or more storage files.

Conceptual schema   A specification of all the conceptual files in a data base, and used by the data base (management) system for manipulation of the data base.

Concurrent execution   Only a portion of a program is executed before the operating or other control system switches to the execution of a portion of another program. Later the next portion of the first program is executed, following which execution control is switched elsewhere. We may also say that the execution of a collection of programs is interwoven or interleaved in time.

Connection fields   The fields used to pair parent and child records in a one-to-many relationship between conceptual files.

Connection trap   The assumption that a relationship exists between two files that are children of a third parent file, when in fact one does not.

Control interval   The indexed group of records in a VSAM file.

Cylinder   A collection of concentric disk tracks of the same radius. The number of cylinders in a disk pack thus equals the number of tracks.

Data base   A collection of files whose records cross reference one another. As with files we can have storage or internal data bases, conceptual data bases, and external data bases.

Data base administrator   The person or group of experts charged with the administration of all use of a data base or data bases.

Data base/data communications (DB/DC) system   Same as a teleprocessing monitor.

Data base description (or definition) language   A language used to define a data base. There are separate definition languages in many cases for the conceptual, external, and storage schemas.

Data base management system   The software system used for creating and maintaining a data base.

Data base manipulation language (DML)   The set of commands that may be used in an application program to manipulate a data base.

Data block   A group of records used both in the storage of data on external storage media, and in the transmission of data between external storage media and main memory buffer. It often has additional system data attached.

Data dictionary   In its minimum form it essentially is a list of all the fields in the conceptual and external schemas. It may also contain information about these fields that can be used by user groups but not by the data base system.

Data dictionary system   A software system used for creating and maintaining a data dictionary.

Data independence   A property of a file that permits changes to the storage file organization or number or type of fields in a record without affecting the ability of an application program using that file to execute.

Dataset   The IBM term for a physical storage file.

DD-statement   The JCL statement used to specify a storage file.

Deadlock   A state of affairs that prevents a program A from proceeding because it is waiting for data (often in a data base) that another program B currently has exclusive access to, while B is waiting for data that A currently has exclusive access to.

Disk controller   A unit that carries out I/O processor commands for controlling transmission of data to and from a disk.

Distributed data base   A data base in which files and fragments of files are geographically distributed among different sites.

Domain   A wide collection of field values for which the collection of field values of a given type in a relation are just a subset.

Enterprise schema   A minimum conceptual schema for a data base without the detailed specifications necessary for use by a specific data base management system.

External file   An imaginary file formed by abstracting a group of fields from a conceptual file.

External schema   A specification of that part of a conceptual data base that will be used by an application program.

Field   The smallest item of data that can be used to describe an entity.

File   A collection of records.

Functional dependency   The dependency of one field (Y) value in a conceptual file upon another field (X) value. Y is functionally dependent on X if the value of X always determines the value of Y. This means that for one Y value there can be many X values, but not vice versa.

Global data base   A data base abstracted from a collection of local data bases.

Global schema   A definition of a distributed data base without regard to where the individual parts of the data base (local data bases) are actually located.

Hash file   A file where the records are assigned disk addresses arrived at by hashing the primary keys, that is, by applying a standard routine to each key to calculate a disk address. When too many records are assigned by the hashing routine to a single address, special overflow management procedures are used to handle the excess records. Direct access is available to a disk address.

Hierarchical data base   A data base in which every record has at most one parent record.

Hierarchy occurrence A record from the root file of a hierarchy type together with its child records and the child records of these child records, and so on.

Hierarchy type A hierarchical conceptual data base. Each conceptual file has exactly one parent file, except for the root file at the top of the hierarchy, which has no parent.

Home address The address the hashing routine assigns to a record, regardless of whether there is room for the record.

Index A simple one-level index contains the entries for each of the indexed groups of records in an indexed sequential file. It provides for direct access since it is possible to search the index and obtain the address of the indexed group of records containing the record being sought. If a further index to the one-level index is constructed the pair is called a two-level index. Indexes with up to five levels are in use with commercial indexed sequential files such as ISAM and VSAM files.

Indexed groups of records The group of records in an indexed sequential file for which there is an entry in the index. An index entry contains the primary key of the last record in the group, and the disk address of the first record of the group.

Indexed sequential file A sequential file with an index for direct access on the basis of the primary key. Sequential access is also possible.

Integrity constraint A conceptual schema specification of a condition that must always hold true for the data base and which the data base system will enforce, thus limiting the possibility of integrity loss.

Integrity (data base) When the integrity of a data base is high, most data is correct and consistent from one part of the data base to another.

Interactive operating system A terminal oriented operating system in which each user can interact with his or her program that is executing concurrently with the programs of other users. Effectively each user is allocated a series of time slots.

Interactive processing The user at a terminal interacts directly with a program during its execution. When the program needs data it displays a request on the screen. The user responds by entering the required data.

Interblock gap On tape it is a relatively large space between adjacent physical storage blocks and the area in which the read/write head may stop relative to the tape. On disk it is a smaller gap between adjacent blocks.

Internal file The official ANSI/SPARC term for a storage file.

Inverted file A type of index used to provide direct access by means of a secondary key. For each secondary key value in a main file there is an inverted file record (variable length) containing the primary keys or addresses of all the records of the main file that contain that secondary key value.

I/O processor A small processor that transmits blocks of data to and from external storage.

ISAM Indexed sequential access method. An IBM access method used for constructing indexed sequential files in which inserted records may be kept in sequential order by means of chains or linked lists of records.

Job control language (JCL) The language used with batch IBM operating systems for specifying storage files and compilation and loading of application programs for execution. JCL statements are placed both before and after a program submitted for execution.

Journal file   Same as a log file.

Key   A single (or atomic) field or a group of fields (composite field) that may be used for identifying a record in a file.

Linked list   An ordered collection of storage records, in which each record in the list contains a pointer to the next record in the list. The records are normally not physically contiguous.

Local data base   The part of a distributed data base at a particular site.

Locate mode processing   A type of sequential file processing in which records are processed in the buffer.

Log file   A file that lists updates made to a master file. Together with a backup file it can be used to regenerate a master file.

Logical data independence   The type of data independence that permits insertion, removal, or alteration of a field type without affecting an application program's ability to execute.

Logical storage block   The collection of records in a data block.

Many-to-many relationship   A relationship in which any one record from a file A may be grouped or associated with one or more records from another file B, and vice versa.

Master file   A file containing important business data of lasting value, but which probably also require frequent updating. A common example is a file of customer information.

Member file   A term frequently used for *child file* when dealing with CODASYL data bases. Nevertheless it is not an official CODASYL term.

Member record   The term for a child record with CODASYL data bases.

Move mode processing   A type of file sequential file processing in which records are moved from buffer to program data area for manipulation.

Network data base   A data base in which at least one child record has more than one parent record.

Nonprocedural language   A language in which only the desired result needs to be specified and not the individual steps that must be carried out to achieve that result. The opposite extreme is a procedural language.

Normal form   The state of a conceptual file when each field (that is, atomic field) contains only a single data value. Conceptual files that are not in normal form are rarely if ever used in data processing.

One-to-many relationship   A relationship in which any one record from file A may be grouped or associated with one or more records from another file B. However, a record from B may be associated with only one record from A.

On-line processing   The opposite of batch processing. Each update is used to update a master file as soon as it becomes available. In order that any of a large number of updating programs be available immediately at any of a large number of terminals, special control systems are required.

On-line system   The complete set of control systems, application programs, and hardware necessary for on-line processing.

Operating system   The overall control program of a computer.

Owner-coupled set   A conceptual grouping of records used with CODA-SYL data bases. An owner-coupled set type is a collection of owner-coupled set occurrences. An owner-coupled set occurrence consists of a parent (owner) and associated child (member) records in a one-to-many relationship.

Owner file   A term frequently used for *parent file* when dealing with CODASYL data bases. It is not an official CODASYL term.

Owner record   The term for a parent record with CODASYL data bases.

Packet   The unit of data in data communications. It has a standardized format and length (up to 131 characters as recommended by committee X.25 of the Consultative Committee on International Telegraphy and Telephony (CCITT) based in Geneva). Messages are broken down into packets before transmission and reassembled at the destination. Packets of the same message may take different routes to the same destination.

Parent file   A conceptual file containing parent records in a one-to-many relationship.

Parent record   When a record from a file *A* is associated with one or more records from another file *B* in a one-to-many relationship, a record from *A* is a parent record in that relationship.

Partition (of memory)   A portion of main memory allocated by the operating system to an application program and associated routines and data structures. With virtual systems it will be divided into pages that are brought into main memory from external page storage as required for execution.

Performance tuning   Alteration of storage file structures to permit faster access.

Physical data independence   The type of data independence that permits changes to the storage file organization without affecting an application program's ability to execute. Also called storage data independence.

Physical pointer   A record field that contains the address of another record.

Physical storage block   A data block as it is stored on an external storage device.

Physical storage file   A file that physically resides in external storage. It is called a dataset in IBM terminology.

Pointer   A field in a record that contains the key or the address of another record, often in another file. A conceptual file by definition cannot contain pointers—only storage files can.

Primary key   A key that has unique values and which may be used by an application or system program to obtain direct access to a record.

Procedural language   A language in which the basic steps required for manipulation of data (perhaps in a data base) must be individually specified, as for example in a COBOL program. The opposite extreme is a nonprocedural language.

Program data area   The part of main memory allocated to the variables used by an application program, and thus containing the data manipulated by the program.

Progressive overflow management   A method of managing hash file overflow records. Essentially a record overflowing from an address is placed in the nearest address with an address value greater than the home address value.

Quantifier   A term or symbol that is used for specifying the number of elements of a specified type that must satisfy a specified condition.

Query language   A language used for specifying data to be retrieved from a data base or a file.

Record   A collection of contiguous fields or data items describing and identifying some entity that can be sensed or imagined by humans.

Recovery   The regeneration of a data base from backup and log files.

Recursive relationship   See the definition of relationship.

Relation   A restricted conceptual file, in which all records are unique and contain the same type and number of fields. It can also be defined as a mathematical set of tuples.

Relational data base   A data base in which the conceptual files are all relations.

Relational file   A conceptual file that is also a relation.

Relationship   The way in which records from one file (*A*) may be paired or grouped with records from another file (*B*). If *A* and *B* are the same file, the relationship is said to be recursive. One-to-many and many-to-many relationships are common in data bases.

Repeating group   A collection of field types that occurs many times within a record.

Root file   The file in a hierarchy type that has no parent.

Rotational delay   The time required following a seek for the required block to rotate to a position under a read/write head of a disk.

Secondary index   Same as an inverted file.

Security (data base)   The prevention of unauthorized access to a data base.

Seek time   The time taken for the read/write arm of a disk to move from one track to another.

Sequential file   A file in which the records are mostly arranged contiguously in external storage in ascending or descending primary key order. Records can only be accessed in sequential order.

Storage file   A file that may be manipulated by the READ, WRITE, and similar statements of such languages as COBOL and PL/1.

Storage schema (or internal schema)   A specification of all the storage files in a data base and used by the data base (management) system for manipulation of the data base.

Symbolic pointer   A record field that contains the key of another record.

Teleprocessing monitor   The basic software software system used to control an on-line system.

Time-sharing operating system   Same as interactive operating system.

Transmitted storage block   The data block as it appears in the buffer.

Tuple   A record in a conceptual file that is a relation. The term record is commonly used as well.

Unnormalized file   A file that is not in normal form.

Virtual operating system   An operating system in which the partitions reside on a fast disk or external page storage and which moves or *pages* small portions of partitions called pages into main memory for execution as required. This permits the execution of programs much larger than main memory.

VSAM Virtual sequential access method. An IBM access method for constructing indexed sequential files in which inserted records may be kept in sequential order by splitting indexed groups of records.

Index